LANDBRUG
Statistisk årbog

ΓΕΩΡΓΙΑ
Στατιστική επετηρίδα

AGRICULTURE
Statistical yearbook

AGRICULTURE
Annuaire statistique

LANDBOUW
Statistisch jaarboek

1988

8900003226

Denne publikation udgives også på følgende sprog:
Η παρούσα έκδοση υπάρχει επίσης στις γλώσσες:
This publication is also available in the following languages:
Cette publication est éditée aussi dans les versions suivantes:
Deze publikatie wordt eveneens in de volgende talen uitgegeven:

ES/DE/IT/PT: 92-825-7739-2

Bibliografiske data findes bagest i denne publikation
Βιβλιογραφικό σημείωμα δίδεται στο τέλος του βιβλίου
Cataloguing data can be found at the end of this publication
Une fiche bibliographique figure à la fin de l'ouvrage.
Bibliogafische data bevinden zich aan het einde van deze publikatie

Luxembourg: Office des publications officielles des Communautés européennes, 1988

ISBN 92-825-7738-4

Kat./cat.: CA-48-87-775-5E-C

Printed in Belgium

Forord

Denne årbog er en statistisk håndbog og indeholder de vigtigste oplysninger, som er offentliggjort i landbrugsstatistikkens specialhæfter om Landbrug, Skovbrug og Fiskeri.

Oplysningerne refererer til den seneste periode, for hvilken der foreligger bearbejdede data.

Oplysningerne er hentet fra nationale kilder; ved opstillingen er de tilpasset hinanden for at lette sammenligningen fra land til land. Det anbefales at bemærke indholdet af de metodologiske noter, da der trods væsentlige forbedringer i harmoniseringen af oplysningerne stadig kan forekomme uensartethed.

Bogen er suppleret med et indskudskort, som giver brugeren »yderligere oplysninger« om muligheden for at benytte databankerne og/eller de specialpublikationer, som Eurostat har til rådighed i 1987.

Bemærk: Foregående årbog: Landbrugsstatistisk Årbog 1986.

Indholdsfortegnelse

I. – LANDBRUG

I.A – Almindelig oversigt: Den almindelige oversigt opsummerer EF-landbrugets vigtigste data og placerer EF i verdenssammenhæng. Oplysningerne om lande uden for EF stammer fra FAO's årbog (tabel I.A.3, 4 og 5) og OECD's publikationer (tabel I.A.6).

I.A.7 – Bruttomerværdi i faktorpriser:

Bruttomerværdien i faktorpriser svarer i princippet ikke til branchesummen; afvigelsen skyldes tillagte banktjenester og statistiske justeringer.

I.A.9 – Levnedsmidler til dagspriser:

Herunder drikkevarer og tobaksvarer.

I.A.10 – Vægtning:

Vægtning af levnedsmiddelindustrien inkl. drikke- og tobaksvarer i industriproduktionsindekset.

I.A.11 til 15:

Forbundsrepublikken Tysklands samhandel med Den Tyske Demokratiske Republik og den sovjetiske sektor i Berlin er undtaget.

I.B. – Arealudnyttelse:

I mangel af årlige undersøgelser benytter Eurostat de oplysninger om afhøstede arealer, som er anslået af de landbrugsstatistiske kontorer i Grækenland, Spanien og Portugal.

I.C – Struktur:

Tabellerne I.C.1 til I.C.10 indeholder resultater fra fællesskabsundersøgelserne vedrørende landbrugsbedrifternes struktur 1966/67 til 1985; i disse tabeller kan der således kun anføres oplysninger for de år, i hvilke der har fundet undersøgelser sted. Tabellerne I.C.11-13 indeholder derimod oplysninger taget fra de årlige nationale undersøgelser.

Det skal bemærkes, at der i tabel I.C.11 kun indgår bedrifter, med et landbrugsmæssigt dyrket areal på mindst 1 ha. Derved opstår der forskelle i forhold til resultaterne af fællesskabsundersøgelser (f.eks. tabel I.C.4), hvori der også medtages bedrifter, som ganske vist har et landbrugsmæssigt dyrket areal på mindre end 1 ha, men som i et vist omfang producerer med salg for øje, eller hvis landbrugsproduktion overskrider bestemte naturlige grænser.

De vigtigste resultater af fællesskabsundersøgelserne vedrørende landbrugsbedrifternes struktur har Eurostat offentliggjort i en række publikationer, f.eks. bind I-VI vedrørende 1975 og bind I-IV vedrørende 1979/80 og tre bind i forbindelse med undersøgelsen i 1983. Der skal navnlig henvises til bind I i hver række, som indeholder en indledning, og som beskriver det metodologiske grundlag for disse undersøgelser. Bl.a. gives der definitioner på de

her anvendte begreber. Såfremt det juridiske grundlag for fællesskabsundersøgelserne ikke indgår som bilag i omtalte bind I, er de at finde i de relevante numre af *De Europæiske Fællesskabers Tidende.*

Tabellerne I.C.11-13 kræver nærmere forklaring.

– Tabel I.C.11

For visse landes vedkommende er der tale om ubetydelige afvigelser fra nogle af de angivne år eller tidsafsnit:

1900	Frankrig	–	1063
	Italien	=	1961
	Nederlandene	=	1959
	Belgien	=	1959
	Grækenland	=	1961
1967	Nederlandene	=	1966
	Irland	=	1965
1970	Grækenland	=	1971
1975	Grækenland	=	interpolation

– Tabel I.C.12

Det drejer sig primært om flerakslede traktorer, herunder larvefodstraktorer og redskabsbærere.

– Tabel I.C.13

Oplysningerne om forbrug af handelsgødning er primært baseret på gødningsstofindustriens leverancer til grossist- og detailleddet i løbet af et driftsår, og der er således ikke taget hensyn til lagerforskydninger hos mellemhandlere. Driftsåret er som regel perioden mellem 1. juli og 30. juni. For Frankrigs vedkommende ligger driftsåret med undtagelse af kvælstofenkeltgødning mellem 1. maj og 30. april samt for Det Forenede Kongeriges vedkommende mellem 1. juni og 31. maj. Kun for Grækenlands vedkommende gælder kalenderåret: 1979 for 1979/80 osv.

Ud over opdelingen efter de tre hovednæringsstofarter har man siden 1965/66 udarbejdet en statistik over opdelingen efter enkelt- og blandingsgødninger. Sidstnævnte indeholder både mekanisk og kemisk blandede næringsstoffer af flere næringsstofarter.

Definitioner af nogle mindre kendte begreber:

Standarddækningsbidrag (SDB)

»Standarddækningsbidraget« defineres som forskellen mellem den standardiserede pengeværdi af bruttoproduktionen og den standardiserede pengeværdi af bestemte specialomkostninger. Denne forskel bestemmes for de forskellige vegetabilske og animalske kendetegn (hhv. pr. ha og pr. dyr) på undersøgelsesområdeniveau og angives i europæiske valutaenheder (ECU). Ved multiplikation af det samlede areal hhv. antallet af dyr med de tilsvarende SDB og efterfølgende addition af disse produkter får man de samlede standarddækningsbidrag for den pågældende bedrift i ECU.

Økonomiske bedriftsstørrelser i ESE

De økonomiske bedriftsstørrelser defineres som det samlede standarddækningsbidrag for den pågældende bedrift for referencetidsrummet 1980 (gennemsnit af årene 1979-1981), angivet i europæiske størrelsesenheder (ESE). En ESE svarer til 1000 ECU.

Årsarbejdsenhed (ÅAE)

Den samlede årlige arbejdstid for de enkelte inden for landbruget beskæftigede personer bliver omregnet til såkaldte årsarbejdsenheder (ÅAE). En ÅAE er lig med det i de nationale lønoverenskomster fastlagte mindste antal timer pr. år. Såfremt antallet af timer ikke er fastlagt i disse overenskomster, sættes en ÅAE lig med 2 200 timer.

I.D og I.E – Statistikken over forsyningsbalancerne, kortere betegnelse »Bilan« (»balance«), som i de fleste tilfælde kun vedrører levnedsmidler, udgør i forbindelse med den fælles landbrugspolitik et af instrumenterne til oprettelse og forvaltning af de forskellige landbrugsmarkeder. De i disse balancer anførte forskellige oplysninger er uundværlige til vurdering af tendenserne og udviklingen på disse markeder. De resultater, som kan uddrages deraf, er et af de elementer, som de for landbrugspolitikken ansvarlige baserer deres afgørelser på.

De nationale forsyningsbalancer udarbejdes af medlemsstaterne på grundlag af fællesskabsbegreber, som er foreslået af Eurostat, nærmere betegnet Den Landbrugsstatistiske Komités ad hoc-arbejdsgruppe. Hos Eurostat kan fås en håndbog »Bilan« pr. produkt eller produktgruppe. Balancerne kan betragtes som et supplement af kvantitative oplysninger til landbrugsregnskaberne udtrykt i værdier, men underopdelt efter produkt.

I statistikken over forsyningsbalancerne er samhandelen med Den Tyske Demokratiske Republik og Østberlin indbefattet i Forbundsrepublikken Tysklands udenrigshandel.

Skema over forsyningsbalancerne

Dette standardskema kan tilpasses de enkelte balancer.
Ressourcer = anvendelig produktion + import.
Anvendelse = eksport + lagersvingninger + fødevareforbrug.

I.E – Animalsk produktion: De vigtigste oplysninger om kvægbestande, strukturen pr. størrelsesorden og produktionen af kød, mælk, mælkeprodukter og æg leveres af medlemsstaterne ved hjælp af undersøgelser og statistikker, der foretages i medfør af Fællesskabets retsakter, Rådets forordninger og direktiver samt Kommissionens direktiver og afgørelser.

I.F – Landbrugspriser og -prisindekser

a) *Landbrugspriser i absolutte værdier*

Landbrugsstatistikken i absolutte værdier skal gøre det muligt at sammenligne priser på så vidt muligt »ens« – dvs. nøje definerede – produkter i Fællesskabets forskellige medlemsstater. Definitionerne af produkter er dog i virkeligheden ikke fuldstændig identiske. Derfor udgiver Eurostat »kataloger over oplysninger om de landbrugsprisrækker, som er inddateret i Cronos«. En ny udgave af denne publikation er under udarbejdelse.

De af Eurostat registrerede landbrugspriser indeholder i princippet ingen moms. Kun den ikke-fradragsberettigede eller ikke-refunderbare moms, som er lagt på visse produktionsmidler, er inkluderet i de pågældende medlemsstaters priser. Det samme gælder andre afgifter eller støttebeløb, som er specifikke for visse produkter. Målet er at registrere de priser, som betinger landbrugernes indtjening.

For at landbrugspriserne udtrykt i national valuta kan sammenlignes mellem Fællesskabets medlemsstater, er de omregnet til ECU (Den Europæiske Valutaenhed).

b) *EF-indekser for landbrugspriser (output og input)*

EF-indekserne for landbrugspriser »EF-indekser for produktionspriser for landbrugsprodukter« og »EF-indekser for indkøbspriser for landbrugets produktionsmidler« udarbejdes efter Laspeyres' metode ved hjælp af bestemte vægtninger for basisåret (1980) og for en fast kurv af landbrugsprodukter (output-indekser) eller varer og tjenesteydelser (input-indekser). De månedlige prisindekser for frugt og grønsager bygger på variable vægtninger for basisårets tolv måneder. Året 1980 tjener ligeledes som referenceår.

EF-indekserne for landbrugspriser (output og input) er i alle Fællesskabets medlemsstater baseret på begrebet »den nationale landbrugsbedrift« og dækker derfor kun transaktionerne mellem landbrugsproduktionsenhederne og ikke-landbrugsproduktionsenhederne, herunder udenrigshandelen. Der er ikke taget hensyn til de direkte transaktioner mellem landbrugere, hverken i beregningen af vægtningerne eller i registreringen af produktionspriser og indkøbspriser.

Med hensyn til de forskellige poster, som de to prisindekser udgøres af, bør der dog tages hensyn til, at vægtningsskemaerne er tilpasset produktionsstrukturen (output og input) i hvert land, og at kurven af varer, som repræsenterer landbrugets salg og køb, varierer fra det ene land til det andet.

For at undgå indflydelse fra de varierende inflationsrater i Fællesskabet er EF-indekserne for landbrugspriser desuden beregnet i deflateret udgave. Deflateringen af disse nominelle prisindekser (output og input) foretages ved hjælp af indekset for forbrugerpriser.

I publikationen »Metodik for EF-indekserne for landbrugspriser (output og input)« findes yderligere enkeltheder vedrørende den metodik, der ligger til grund for EF-indekserne for landbrugspriser.

I.G – Landbrugsregnskaber:

Dataene refererer til afsnittet »Landbrugs- og jagtprodukter«. De opstilles ud fra begrebet »den nationale landbrugsbedrift«. For produktionens vedkommende er det begrebet »slutproduktion«, der svarer til dette begreb (se efterfølgende skema).

Forbrug af rå- og hjælpestoffer omfatter løbende forbrug af alle de goder (med undtagelse af faste kapitalgoder) og tjenesteydelser, som den nationale landbrugsbedrift har købt hos ikke-landbrugsenheder til benyttelse i landbrugsproduktionsprocessen.

Driftsstøttebeløb og produktionsafgifter udgør indkomstfordelingsoperationer, som er direkte forbundet med produktionsprocessen.

Afskrivningerne – dvs. forbruget af kapitalgoder – repræsenterer værdiforringelsen af de kapitalgoder, som anvendes I produktionsprocessen, som følge af normalt slid samt tab på grund af skader, der kan gøres til genstand for forsikring. De faste bruttoinvesteringer repræsenterer værdien af de varige goder, som den nationale landbrugsbedrift har erhvervet for egen regning til brug i mere end ét år i landbrugsproduktionsprocessen.

Landbrugets slutproduktion vurderes i princippet til prisen »fra bedrift«. Prisen »fra bedrift« er markedsprisen set fra producentens synspunkt.

Forbruget af rå- og hjælpestoffer og de faste bruttoinvesteringer vurderes til anskaffelsesprisen. Anskaffelsesprisen er markedsprisen set fra køberens synspunkt.

Dataene opstilles efter nettoregistreringssystemet for merværdiafgift (moms): de forskellige poster i slutproduktionen, forbruget af rå- og hjælpestoffer og de faste bruttoinvesteringer er ekskl. moms. Kun i det samlede beløb for rå- og hjælpestoffer er i givet fald inkluderet underkompensation for moms (= ikke-fradragsberettiget moms). Yderligere oplysninger kan findes i de forklarende bemærkninger og i Eurostats publikationer Tema 5, C-serien: *Økonomiske regnskaber – Landbrug, Skovbrug*.

Skematisk fremstilling af landbrugets slutproduktion

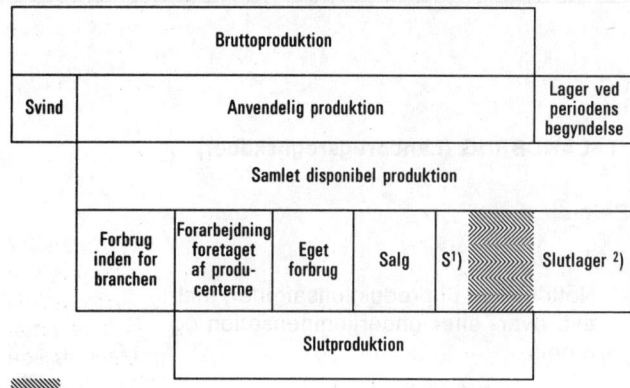

Lagerændringer

1) Byggeri for egen regning.
2) I ovenstående skema forudsættes det, at slutlageret er større end lageret ved periodens begyndelse.

Skematisk fremstilling af værditilvæksten og landbrugets indtjening

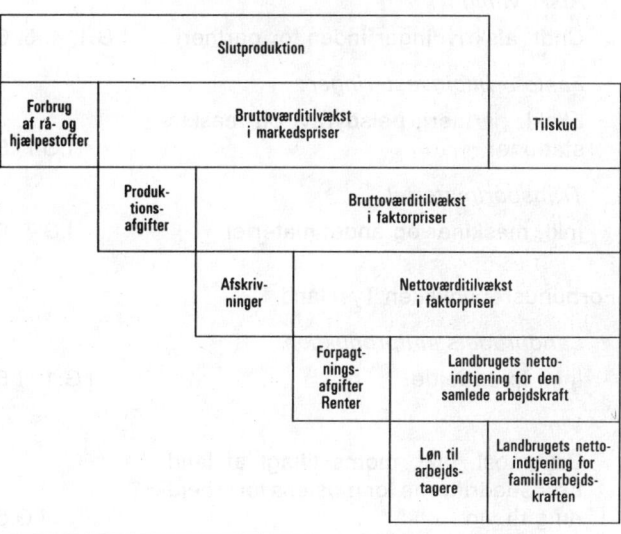

I. LANDBRUG (Landbrugsregnskaber)

Belgien

Tilskud:

Nettotilskud til produktionsafgifter, inkl. evt. over- eller underkompensation og moms   I.G.1, 4, 5, 6

Andre vegetabilske produkter.:

Inkl. salg foretaget af producenter, som kun sælger lejlighedsvis, ikke opdelt efter produkt   I.G.4, 5

Faste bruttoinvesteringer »I alt«:

Inkl. ikke-fradragsberettiget moms (detaljerede oplysninger ekskl. moms)   I.G.7, 8

Danmark

Afskrivninger:

Undt. afskrivninger inden for gartneri   I.G.1, 4, 5, 6

Faste bruttoinvesteringer:

Ekskl. gartneri, pelsdyravl og maskinstationer   I.G.7, 8

Transportmateriel:

Inkl. maskiner og andet materiel   I.G.7, 8

Forbundsrepublikken Tyskland

Landbrugets slutproduktion:

Inkl. lønarbejde   I.G.1 til 6

Vin:

Druemost, inkl. moms tillagt af landbrugsbedrifterne for mostens forarbejdning til vin   I.G.5

Avlsbygninger:

Inkl. andre bygninger og grundforbedring   I.G.7, 8

Frankrig

Landbrugets slutproduktion:

Inkl. lønarbejde   I.G.1 til 6

Faste bruttoinvesteringer »I alt«:

Inkl. ikke-fradragsberettiget moms (detaljerede oplysninger ekskl. moms)   I.G.7, 8

Italien

Vegetabilsk og animalsk slutproduktion:

Inkl. moms, men ekskl. andre produktionsafgifter   I.G.1 til 6

Landbrugets slutproduktion:

Inkl. moms og andre produktionsafgifter   I.G.1 til 6

Forbrug af rå- og hjælpestoffer:

Inkl. moms   I.G.1 til 6

Diverse:

Italien: andre produktionsafgifter end moms   I.G.4, 5

Faste bruttoinvesteringer:

Inkl. skovbrug og fiskeri   I.G.7, 8

Nyplantninger:

Inkl. avlsbygninger, andre bygninger og grundforbedring   I.G.7, 8

Maskiner og andet udstyr:

Inkl. andre faste bruttoinvesteringer   I.G.7, 8

Luxembourg

Avlsbygninger:

Inkl. andre bygninger, ekskl. grundforbedring   I.G.7, 8

Transportmateriel:

Inkl. maskiner og andet udstyr   I.G.7, 8

Nederlandene

Avlsbygninger:

Inkl. andre bygninger, ekskl. grundforbedring   I.G.7, 8

Det Forenede Kongerige

Landbrugets slutproduktion:

Inkl. lønarbejde   I.G.1 til 6

II. SKOVBRUG

II.A. Almindelig oversigt: Med hensyn til den egentlige metodik og mere specifikt bemærkningerne for hver enkelt medlemsstat henvises der til følgende to publikationer:

– *»Skovbrugsstatistik – metodik«,*
– *»Skovbrugsstatistik – tabeller«.*

Disse publikationer udgives af Eurostat på alle Fællesskabets sprog.

II.B. Skovbrugsregnskaber: se også bemærkninger til I.G. Dataene henfører til afsnittet »Tømmer«. De opstilles ud fra begrebet »den nationale skov« (analogt med begrebet »den nationale landbrugsbedrift« i landbrugsregnskaberne).

Skovbrugets slutproduktion vurderes til prisen »fra vejkant«.

Læseren henvises i øvrigt til de metodologiske noter til afsnittet I.G., som analogt også gælder her. Yderligere oplysninger kan findes i de forklarende bemærkninger og i Eurostats publikationer Tema 5, C-serien: »Økonomiske regnskaber – Landbrug, Skovbrug«.

Belgien

Tilskud:

Nettotilskud til produktionsafgifter, inkl.
evt. over- eller underkompensation og
moms   II.B.1

Forbundsrepublikken Tyskland

Referenceår:

Høstårene 1.10. - 30.9.   II.B.1

Slutproduktion:

Inkl. »Andre produkter«   II.B.1

Italien

Forbrug af rå- og hjælpestoffer:

Inkl. moms   II.B. I

Referenceår:

Høstårene 1.4. - 31.3.   II.B.1

Slutproduktion:

Inkl. »Andre produkter«   II.B.1

Luxembourg

Referenceår:

Høstårene 1.10. - 30.9.   II.B.1

Det Forenede Kongerige

Referenceår

Høstårene 1.4. - 31.3.   II.B.1

Referencedata:

Ekskl. Nordirland, for hvis vedkommende dataene er uden betydning og i øvrigt
ikke foreligger   II.B.1

III. FISKERI

III.2.3 – **Fangster:** Dataene vedrørende fangster indberettes af medlemsstaterne på spørgeskemaet efter Statlant-systemet, hvis anvendelse koordineres af FAO. Dataene gælder de nominelle fangster i ferskvand, brakvand og havvand af fisk, skaldyr, bløddyr og andre dyr og planter, som er slagtet, indsamlet, fanget, opdrættet eller dyrket til ethvert kommercielt, industrielt eller ernæringsmæssigt formål. Kvanta fanget ved lystfiskeri er ikke medregnet. Begrebet »nominelle fangster« refererer til tilførsler omregnet til levende vægt.

III.4 – **Fiskeriflåde:** Dataene er uddrag af det statistiske register over Fællesskabets fiskerfartøjer, men den nationale fortegnelse er ikke-eksisterende (ES + PO) eller ufuldstændig (f. eks. hvad angår lette fartøjer i DK, GR, IRL og UK); der er tilføjet data fra andre kilder.

Anvendte tegn og forkortelser

–	Nul
0	Mindre end det halve af den anvendte enhed
:	Oplysning foreligger ikke
S	Hemmelig oplysning
prov./p	Foreløbige tal
*	Skønsmæssigt angivet af Eurostat
n.d.a./a.d.a.	Ikke andetsteds anført
r	Nye eller korrigerede tal
M/Ø	Gennemsnit
MP/ØP	Vejet gennemsnit
%	Procent
% AT	Procentuel variation
AM	Gennemsnitlig årlig stigning
–I	Brud i sammenlignelighed
ECU	Europæisk valutaenhed
DM	Tyske mark
FF	Franske francs
LIT	Lire
HFL	Gylden
BFR	Belgiske francs
LFR	Luxembourgske francs
UKL	Pund sterling
IRL	Irske pund
DKR	Danske kroner
DR	Drachmer
ESC	Escudos
PTA	Pesetas
t	Metrisk ton

hl	Hektoliter
ha	Hektar
mio	Million
mm	Millimeter
°C	Celsiusgrader
m³(r)	Rummeter, tømmerækvivalent
AA/SAU	Udnyttet landbrugsareal
W/UGB	Storkreaturenhed
GRT/TJB	Bruttoregisterton
AWU/UTA	Årsarbejdsenhed (ÅAE)
SGM/MBS	Standarddækningsbidrag (SDB)
ESU/UDE	Europæisk størrelsesenhed (ESE)
EUR 10	EF-medlemsstaterne i alt, ekskl. Portugal og Spanien
EUR 12	EF-medlemsstaterne i alt
Eurostat	De Europæiske Fællesskabers Statistiske Kontor
EC/CE	De Europæiske Fællesskaber
DOM	Oversøiske departementer
B+L/ UEBL/BLEU	Belgisk-Luxembourgske Økonomiske Union
OECD/OCDE	Organisationen for Økonomisk Samarbejde og Udvikling
FAO	FN's Fødevare- og Landbrugsorganisation
IMF/FMI	Den Internationale Valutafond

Glosar: Glosaret indeholder de vigtigste termer anvendt i de tabeltekster, som ikke foreligger på alle ni fællesskabssprog.

Πρόλογος

Αυτός ο στατιστικός οδηγός αποτελεί μια σύνθεση των κυριότερων πληροφοριών που δημοσιεύονται στα ειδικά φυλλάδια των Γεωργικών Στατιστικών σχετικά με τη γεωργία, τη δασοκομία και την αλιεία.

Τα δεδομένα αναφέρονται στην πλέον πρόσφατη διαθέσιμη περίοδο.

Τα δεδομένα προέρχονται από τις αρμόδιες εθνικές υπηρεσίες· η παρουσίασή τους έχει εναρμονιστεί στα κοινοτικά πλαίσια, όσον αφορά τις έννοιες και τις αξίες (μετατροπή σε ECU), με σκοπό τη διευκόλυνση των προσεγγίσεων από χώρα σε χώρα. Για τις συγκρίσεις μεταξύ των χωρών συνιστάται η παραπομπή στις μεθοδολογικές σημειώσεις, δεδομένου ότι, παρ' όλες τις σημαντικές βελτιώσεις στην εναρμόνιση των δεδομένων, εξακολουθούν ακόμη να υφίστανται διαφορές.

Το παρόν έργο συμπληρώνεται από ένα ένθετο δελτίο το οποίο πληροφορεί το χρήστη ότι «για περισσότερες λεπτομέρειες» του παρέχεται η δυνατότητα αναζήτησης στοιχείων σε βάσεις δεδομένων και/ή στις ειδικές εκδόσεις που διατίθενται από την Eurostat το 1987.

Σημείωση: Προηγούμενη έκδοση: Γεωργία, Στατιστική επετηρίδα 1986.

Πίνακας περιεχομένων

GR

Μεθοδολογικές σημειώσεις

Ι. – ΓΕΩΡΓΙΑ

Ι.Α – Γενικό μέρος: Το γενικό μέρος συνοψίζει τα κυριότερα χαρακτηριστικά της γεωργίας στην ΕΚ και τοποθετεί την ΕΚ σε σχέση με τον κόσμο. Οι πληροφορίες εκτός ΕΚ έχουν ληφθεί από την επετηρίδα του FAO για τους πίνακες Ι.Α.3, 4 και 5 και από τις δημοσιεύσεις του ΟΟΣΑ για τον πίνακα Ι.Α.6.

Ι.Α.7 – Ακαθάριστη προστιθέμενη αξία στο κόστος συντελεστών παραγωγής:
Η ακαθάριστη προστιθέμενη αξία στο κόστος συντελεστών παραγωγής δεν αντιστοιχεί, καταρχήν, στο άθροισμα των κλάδων· η διαφορά οφείλεται σε δαπάνες τραπεζικών υπηρεσιών και σε στατιστικές διορθώσεις.

Ι.Α.9 – Είδη διατροφής σε τρέχουσες τιμές:
Περιλαμβάνονται τα ποτά και ο καπνός.

Ι.Α.10 – Σταθμίσεις:
Βάρος της βιομηχανίας ειδών διατροφής, ποτών και καπνού στο δείκτη βιομηχανικής παραγωγής.

Ι.Α.11 έως 15:
Δεν περιλαμβάνεται το εμπόριο της Ομοσπονδιακής Δημοκρατίας της Γερμανίας με τη Λαϊκή Δημοκρατία της Γερμανίας και το σοβιετικό τομέα του Βερολίνου.

Ι.Β – Χρήση γης: Ελλείψει ετήσιων απογραφών, η Eurostat χρησιμοποιεί τα κατ' εκτίμηση δεδομένα σχετικά με τις καλλιεργούμενες εκτάσεις που παρέχονται από τις γεωργικές στατιστικές υπηρεσίες της Ελλάδας, της Ισπανίας και της Πορτογαλίας.

Ι.Γ – Διάρθρωση:
Οι πίνακες Ι.Γ.1 ως Ι.Γ.10 περιέχουν στοιχεία, τα οποία περιλαμβάνουν τα αποτελέσματα κοινοτικών ερευνών σχετικά με τη διάρθρωση των γεωργικών εκμεταλλεύσεων από το 1966/67 έως το 1985 και κατά συνέπεια στους πίνακες αυτούς μπορούν να δοθούν στοιχεία μόνο για τα χρόνια κατά τα οποία διεξάχθηκαν έρευνες. Αντίθετα οι πίνακες Ι.Γ.11 ως Ι.Γ.13 περιλαμβάνουν στοιχεία που παρέχονται κάθε χρόνο από τις εθνικές έρευνες.

Ας σημειωθεί ότι στον πίνακα Ι.Γ.11 περιλαμβάνονται μόνο εκείνες οι εκμεταλλεύσεις οι οποίες διαθέτουν τουλάχιστον ένα εκτάριο εκμεταλλεύσιμης γεωργικής έκτασης (ΕΓΕ). Έτσι, δημιουργούνται διαφορές ως προς τα αποτελέσματα κοινοτικών ερευνών (π.χ. πίνακες Ι.Γ.4), στα οποία περιλαμβάνονται και εκείνες οι εκμεταλλεύσεις, οι οποίες διαθέτουν λιγότερο από ένα εκτάριο ΕΓΕ, αλλά η παραγωγή τους, μέχρις ενός ορίου, προορίζεται για πώληση ή των οποίων η γεωργική παραγωγή υπερβαίνει ορισμένα φυσικά όρια.

Τα σπουδαιότερα αποτελέσματα των κοινοτικών ερευνών σχετικά με τη διάρθρωση των γεωργικών εκμεταλλεύσεων έχουν δημοσιευτεί από την Eurostat σε μια σειρά τόμων, π.χ. τόμοι Ι έως IV για το 1975 και τόμοι Ι έως VI για το 1979/80 και τρεις τόμοι για την έρευνα του 1983. Συνιστάται ιδιαίτερα η εξέταση του τόμου Ι κάθε σειράς, ο οποίος περιέχει μια εισαγωγή και περιγράφει τις μεθοδολογικές αρχές αυτών των απογραφών. Εκεί αναφέρονται, μεταξύ άλλων, οι ορισμοί για τις έννοιες που χρησιμοποιούνται εδώ. Όταν δεν περιλαμβάνεται ως παράρτημα στον τόμο Ι, το νομικό πλαίσιο για τις κοινοτικές απογραφές υπάρχει στα σχετικά τεύχη της Επίσημης Εφημερίδας των Ευρωπαϊκών Κοινοτήτων.

Για τους πίνακες Ι.Γ.11 ως Ι.Γ.13 απαιτούνται ιδιαίτερες επεξηγήσεις.

– Πίνακας Ι.Γ.11

Ορισμένα από τα αναφερόμενα έτη ή χρονικά διαστήματα έχουν σε ορισμένες χώρες μια μικρή απόκλιση:

•	1960	Γαλλία	= 1963
		Ιταλία	= 1961
		Κάτω Χώρες	= 1959
		Βέλγιο	= 1959
		Ελλάδα	= 1961
•	1967	Κάτω Χώρες	= 1966
		Ιρλανδία	= 1965
•	1970	Ελλάδα	= 1971
•	1975	Ελλάδα	= στοιχεία εκ παρεμβολής

– Πίνακας Ι.Γ.12

Καταρχήν πρόκειται για πολυαξονικούς ελκυστήρες, συμπεριλαμβανομένων ερπυστριοφόρων ελκυστήρων και φορέων μηχανημάτων.

– Πίνακας Ι.Γ.13

Τα στοιχεία σχετικά με την κατανάλωση λιπασμάτων εμπορίου αναφέρονται καταρχήν σε παραδόσεις της βιομηχανίας λιπασμάτων στο αγροτικό εμπόριο κατά τη διάρκεια μιας περιόδου λίπανσης, χωρίς συνυπολογισμό των μεταβολών των αποθεμάτων στο εμπόριο. Ως περίοδος λίπανσης ισχύει κατά κανόνα το διάστημα μεταξύ 1ης Ιουλίου και 30ής Ιουνίου. Στη Γαλλία λαμβάνεται, με εξαίρεση τα μεμονωμένα αζωτούχα λιπάσματα, το διάστημα μεταξύ 1ης Μαΐου και 30ής Απριλίου, στο δε Ηνωμένο Βασίλειο μεταξύ 1ης Ιουνίου και 31ης Μαΐου. Μόνο για την Ελλάδα ισχύουν ημερολογιακά έτη: 1979 για το 1979/80, κλπ.

Εκτός από την κατάταξη κατά τα τρία κύρια είδη λιπασμάτων, από το 1965/66 υπάρχει μια στατιστική διαχωρισμού σε μονολιπάσματα και πολυλιπάσματα. Τα τελευταία περιλαμβάνουν τα είδη λιπασμάτων μηχανικής ανάμειξης αλλά και τα λιπάσματα χημικής σύζευξης.

Ορισμοί μερικών λιγότερο γνωστών εννοιών

Τυπικό ακαθάριστο κέρδος (ΤΑΚ)

Ως τυπικό ακαθάριστο κέρδος νοείται η διαφορά μεταξύ της σταθερής αξίας της ακαθάριστης παραγωγής και του σταθερού ποσού των ειδικών επιμεριζομένων δαπανών. Η διαφορά αυτή καθορίζεται για τους διάφορους κλάδους φυσικής και ζωικής παραγωγής (ανά εκτάριο ή ανά ζώο) σε κάθε περιοχή έρευνας και εκφράζεται σε ευρωπαϊκές νομισματικές μονάδες (ECU). Με πολλαπλασιασμό των εκτάσεων ή των αριθμών των ζώων με το αντίστοιχο ΤΑΚ και στη συνέχεια άθροιση αυτών των γινομένων λαμβάνουμε το συνολικό τυπικό ακαθάριστο κέρδος της υπό εξέταση εκμετάλλευσης σε ECU.

Οικονομικό μέγεθος εκμετάλλευσης σε ΕΜΜ

Το οικονομικό μέγεθος της εκμετάλλευσης προσδιορίζεται με βάση το συνολικό τυπικό ακαθάριστο κέρδος της, για την περίοδο αναφοράς 1980 (μέσος όρος των ετών 1979 έως 1981), και εκφράζεται σε ευρωπαϊκές μονάδες μεγέθους (EMM). Μία EMM ισοδυναμεί με 1 000 ECU.

Ανθρωποέτος (ΑΕ)

Ο συνολικός ετήσιος χρόνος εργασίας των απασχολουμένων στη γεωργία μετατρέπεται σε ανθρωποέτη (ΑΕ). Ως ένα ανθρωποέτος νοείται ο ελάχιστος αριθμός εργάσιμων ωρών ανά έτος που καθορίζεται στις εθνικές συμβάσεις εργασίας. Σε περίπτωση που ο αριθμός των ωρών δεν καθορίζεται σ' αυτές τις συμβάσεις, τότε ως βάση για τη μονάδα ΑΕ θεωρούνται οι 2 200 ώρες.

Ι.Δ και Ι.Ε – Η στατιστική των ισοζυγίων των προμηθειών που απλούστερα καλούνται «ισοζύγια», η οποία στις περισσότερες περιπτώσεις δεν αφορά παρά τα προϊόντα διατροφής, αποτελεί στα πλαίσια της κοινής αγροτικής πολιτικής ένα από τα όργανα καθιέρωσης και διαχείρισης των διαφόρων γεωργικών αγορών. Τα διάφορα δεδομένα που αναφέρονται σ' αυτά τα ισοζύγια είναι απαραίτητα για την αξιολόγηση του προσανατολισμού και της ανάπτυξης αυτών των αγορών. Τα αποτελέσματα που μπορούν να εξαχθούν αποτελούν ένα από τα στοιχεία στα οποία βασίζονται οι αποφάσεις των αρμοδίων για την αγροτική πολιτική.

Τα εθνικά ισοζύγια προμηθειών καταρτίζονται από τα κράτη μέλη με βάση τις κοινοτικές έννοιες που έχουν προταθεί από την Eurostat στα πλαίσια της ομάδας εργασίας ad hoc της Επιτροπής Γεωργικών Στατιστικών. Από την Eurostat διατίθεται ένα εγχειρίδιο «ισοζύγια» ανά προϊόν ή ανά ομάδα προϊόντων. Τα ισοζύγια μπορούν να θεωρηθούν ως το συμπλήρωμα, σε ποσοτικά δεδομένα, των λογαριασμών γεωργίας που εκφράζονται σε αξίες, με περαιτέρω υποδιαίρεση όμως κατά προϊόντα.

Στη στατιστική των ισοζυγίων προμηθειών, το εξωτερικό εμπόριο της Ομοσπονδιακής Δημοκρατίας της Γερμανίας περιλαμβάνει τις ανταλλαγές με τη Λαϊκή Δημοκρατία της Γερμανίας και το Ανατολικό Βερολίνο.

Σχηματική παράσταση του ισοζυγίου προμηθειών

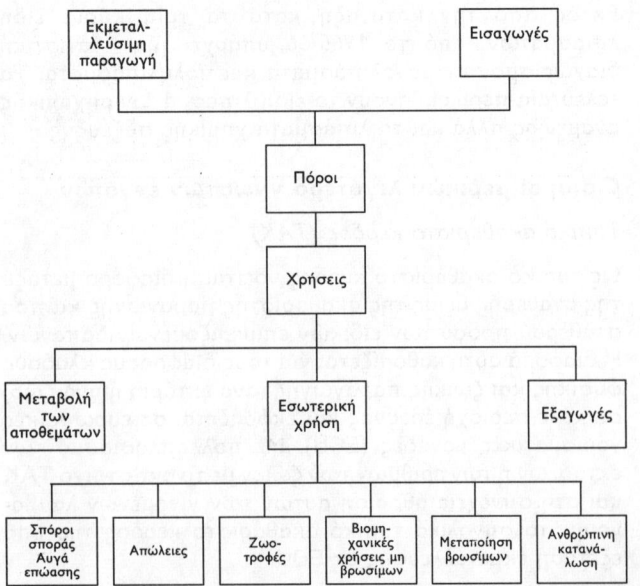

Αυτό το γενικό σχήμα μπορεί να προσαρμοστεί ανάλογα με το υπό εξέταση ισοζύγιο.
Πόροι = Χρησιμοποιήσιμη παραγωγή + Εισαγωγές
Χρήσεις = Εξαγωγές + Μεταβολή των αποθεμάτων + Εσωτερική χρήση

Ι.Ε – **Ζωική παραγωγή:** Ο βασικός όγκος των στοιχείων σχετικά με το ζωικό πληθυσμό, τη διάρθρωση των κτηνοτροφικών μονάδων κατά τάξεις μεγέθους και την παραγωγή κρέατος, γάλακτος και γαλακτοκομικών προϊόντων, καθώς και αυγών παρέχεται από τα κράτη μέλη στα πλαίσια ερευνών και στατιστικών που πραγματοποιούνται σε εφαρμογή κοινοτικών νομικών κειμένων, κανονισμών ή οδηγιών του Συμβουλίου και οδηγιών ή αποφάσεων της Επιτροπής.

Ι.Ζ – Τιμές και δείκτες τιμών γεωργικών προϊόντων

α) Τιμές γεωργικών προϊόντων σε απόλυτες τιμές

Η στατιστική των τιμών γεωργικών προϊόντων σε απόλυτες τιμές έχει ως σκοπό την παροχή δυνατότητας σύγκρισης τιμών προϊόντων κατά το δυνατό «ταυτόσημων» – δηλαδή ορισμένων με ακρίβεια – μεταξύ των κρατών μελών της Κοινότητας. Στην πραγματικότητα όμως, οι ορισμοί των προϊόντων δεν είναι πάντα εντελώς ταυτόσημοι. Αυτός είναι ο λόγος για τον οποίο η Eurostat δημοσιεύει τους «καταλόγους των χαρακτηριστικών σχετικά με τις σειρές των τιμών γεωργικών προϊόντων που βρίσκονται στην Cronos». Μια νέα έκδοση αυτής της δημοσίευσης είναι υπό προετοιμασία.

Οι τιμές γεωργικών προϊόντων που καταγράφονται από την Eurostat δεν περιέχουν καταρχήν κανένα φόρο επί της προστιθέμενης αξίας. Μόνο ο μη εκπεστέος ή μη επιστρεφόμενος ΦΠΑ που επιβαρύνει ορισμένα μέσα παραγωγής περιλαμβάνεται στις τιμές των αντίστοιχων κρατών μελών. Το ίδιο ισχύει και για άλλους εξειδικευμένους φόρους ή επιδοτήσεις ορισμένων προϊόντων. Ο σκοπός είναι η καταγραφή των τιμών που καθορίζουν τα εισοδήματα των γεωργών.

Για να υπάρξει δυνατότητα σύγκρισης των τιμών γεωργικών προϊόντων που εκφράζονται σε εθνικό νόμισμα μεταξύ κρατών μελών πραγματοποιείται μετατροπή τους σε ECU (ευρωπαϊκή νομισματική μονάδα).

β) Δείκτες ΕΚ των τιμών γεωργικών προϊόντων (εκροές και εισροές)

Οι δείκτες ΕΚ των τιμών γεωργικών προϊόντων «δείκτες ΕΚ των τιμών παραγωγής γεωργικών προϊόντων» και «δείκτες ΕΚ των τιμών αγοράς των μέσων γεωργικής παραγωγής» καθορίζονται σύμφωνα με τη μέθοδο του Laspeyres, μέσω συντελεστών στάθμισης που ορίζονται για το έτος βάσης (1980) και για συγκεκριμένο καλάθι γεωργικών προϊόντων (δείκτες εκροών) ή αγαθών και υπηρεσιών (δείκτες εισροών). Οι μηνιαίοι δείκτες τιμών νωπών φρούτων και λαχανικών βασίζονται σε μεταβλητές σταθμίσεις για τους 12 μήνες του έτους βάσης. Το 1980 λαμβάνεται επίσης ως έτος αναφοράς.

Οι δείκτες ΕΚ των τιμών γεωργικών προϊόντων (εκροές και εισροές) βασίζονται, σε όλα τα κράτη μέλη της Κοινότητας, στην έννοια του «εθνικού αγροκτήματος» και δεν καλύπτουν, κατά συνέπεια, παρά μόνο τις συναλλαγές μεταξύ των μονάδων γεωργικής παραγωγής και των μονάδων μη γεωργικής παραγωγής, συμπεριλαμβανομένου του εξωτερικού εμπορίου. Δεν λαμβάνονται υπόψη οι απευθείας συναλλαγές μεταξύ γεωργών ούτε στον υπολογισμό των σταθμίσεων, ούτε στην καταγραφή των τιμών παραγωγής ή των τιμών αγοράς.

Όσον αφορά τις διάφορες εγγραφές που συνθέτουν τους δύο δείκτες τιμών, θα πρέπει να λαμβάνεται υπόψη το γεγονός ότι τα συστήματα στάθμισης είναι προσαρμοσμένα στη διάρθρωση της παραγωγής (εκροές και εισροές) κάθε χώρας και ότι τα καλάθια των εμπορευμάτων που αντιπροσωπεύουν τις πωλήσεις και τις αγορές στη γεωργία διαφέρουν από χώρα σε χώρα.

Με σκοπό την εξάλειψη της επίδρασης των διαφορετικών δεικτών πληθωρισμού μέσα στην Κοινότητα, οι δείκτες τιμών γεωργικών προϊόντων της ΕΚ έχουν υπολογιστεί αποπληθωρισμένοι. Ο αποπληθωρισμός των δεικτών των ονομαστικών τιμών γεωργικών προϊόντων (εκροών και εισροών) γίνεται με τη βοήθεια του δείκτη τιμών κατανάλωσης.

Περισσότερες λεπτομέρειες σχετικά με τη μεθοδολογία υπολογισμού των δεικτών τιμών γεωργικών προϊόντων της ΕΚ υπάρχουν στην έκδοση «μεθοδολογία των δεικτών τιμών γεωργικών προϊόντων των ΕΚ (εκροές και εισροές)».

I.Η – Λογαριασμοί γεωργίας:

Τα στοιχεία αναφέρονται στον κλάδο «Γεωργικά προϊόντα και προϊόντα θήρας»˙ καταρτίζονται σύμφωνα με την έννοια του εθνικού αγροκτήματος. Σε επίπεδο παραγωγής, στην παραπάνω έννοια ανταποκρίνεται αυτή της τελικής παραγωγής (βλέπε παρακάτω σχήμα).

Οι ενδιάμεσες καταναλώσεις περιλαμβάνουν την τρέχουσα κατανάλωση όλων των αγαθών (με εξαίρεση τα αγαθά παγίου κεφαλαίου) και υπηρεσιών τα οποία έχουν αγοραστεί από μέρους του εθνικού αγροκτήματος από μη γεωργικές μονάδες για να χρησιμοποιηθούν στη γεωργική παραγωγική διαδικασία.

Οι επιδοτήσεις εκμετάλλευσης και οι φόροι που συνδέονται με την παραγωγή αντιπροσωπεύουν λειτουργίες κατανομής των εισοδημάτων που συνδέονται απευθείας με την παραγωγική διαδικασία.

Οι αποσβέσεις – δηλαδή η κατανάλωση παγίου κεφαλαίου – αντιπροσωπεύουν τη μείωση της αξίας του παγίου κεφαλαίου που χρησιμοποιείται στην παραγωγική διαδικασία λόγω συνήθους φθοράς και απώλειας εξαιτίας τυχαίων ασφαλίσιμων ζημιών. Οι ακαθάριστες επενδύσεις παγίου κεφαλαίου αντιπροσωπεύουν την αξία των διαρκών αγαθών τα οποία έχουν αποκτηθεί από το εθνικό αγρόκτημα για λογαριασμό του με σκοπό να χρησιμοποιηθούν κατά τη διάρκεια χρονικού διαστήματος μεγαλύτερου του ενός έτους στη γεωργική παραγωγική διαδικασία.

Καταρχήν, η τελική γεωργική παραγωγή αξιολογείται με τις τιμές «κατά την έξοδο από το αγρόκτημα». Η τιμή αυτή είναι η αγοραία τιμή από την πλευρά του παραγωγού.

Η ενδιάμεση κατανάλωση και οι ακαθάριστες επενδύσεις παγίου κεφαλαίου αξιολογούνται με βάση τις τιμές απόκτησης. Η τιμή απόκτησης είναι η αγοραία τιμή από την πλευρά του αγοραστή.

Τα δεδομένα καταρτίζονται σύμφωνα με το σύστημα καταγραφής του καθαρού φόρου προστιθέμενης αξίας (ΦΠΑ): οι διάφορες εγγραφές της τελικής παραγωγής, της ενδιάμεσης κατανάλωσης και των ακαθάριστων επενδύσεων παγίου κεφαλαίου δεν περιλαμβάνουν τον ΦΠΑ. Μόνο το σύνολο της ενδιάμεσης κατανάλωσης περιλαμβάνει, κατά περίπτωση, την υπο-αντιστάθμιση του ΦΠΑ (= μη εκπεστέος ΦΠΑ). Για περισσότερες διευκρινίσεις, ο αναγνώστης παραπέμπεται στις επεξηγηματικές σημειώσεις ή στις δημοσιεύσεις της Eurostat, Θέμα 5, Σειρά Γ: Οικονομικοί λογαριασμοί – γεωργία, δασοκομία.

Σχηματική παράσταση της τελικής γεωργικής παραγωγής

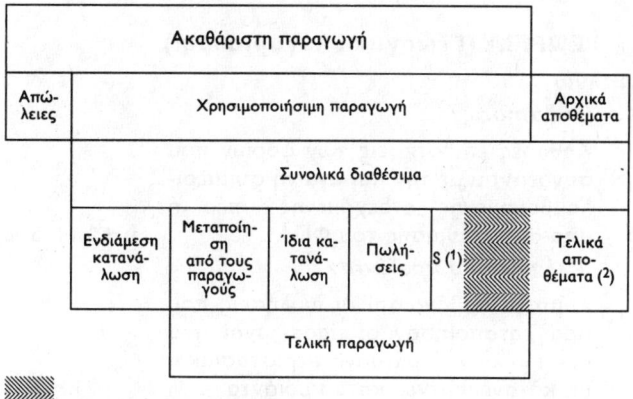

Μεταβολή των αποθεμάτων

(1) Δημιουργία για ιδίους σκοπούς.
(2) Στην παραπάνω σχηματική παράσταση προϋποτίθεται ότι τα τελικά αποθέματα είναι μεγαλύτερα από τα αρχικά.

Σχηματική παράσταση της προστιθέμενης αξίας και του γεωργικού εισοδήματος

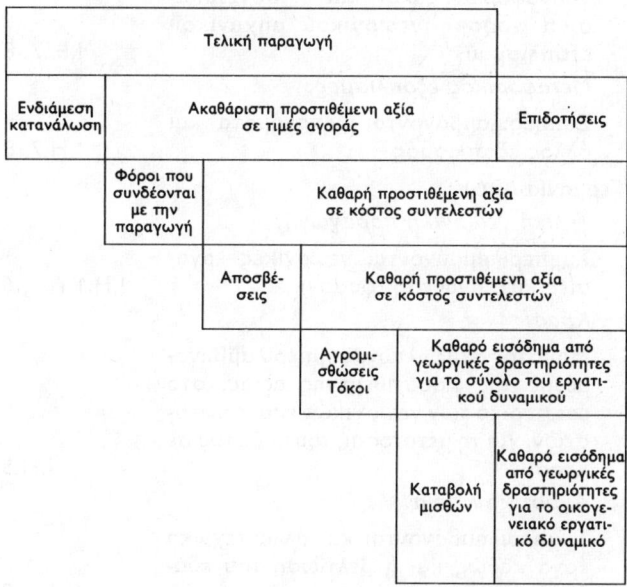

Επεξηγηματικές σημειώσεις κατά χώρα

I. ΓΕΩΡΓΙΑ (Γεωργικοί λογαριασμοί)

Βέλγιο

Επιδοτήσεις:

Καθαρές επιδοτήσεις των φόρων που συνδέονται με την παραγωγή συμπεριλαμβανομένης ενδεχόμενης υπέρ ή υπο-αντιστάθμισης του ΦΠΑ   I.H.1, 4, 5, 6

Άλλα φυτικά προϊόντα:

Συμπεριλαμβάνονται οι πωλήσεις που πραγματοποίησαν οι παραγωγοί που δεν πωλούν παρά μόνο περιστασιακά, μη κατανεμημένες κατά προϊόντα   I.H.4, 5

«Σύνολο» των ακαθάριστων επενδύσεων παγίου κεφαλαίου:

Συμπεριλαμβάνεται ο μη εκπεστέος ΦΠΑ (αναλυτικά στοιχεία χωρίς ΦΠΑ)   I.H.7, 8

Δανία

Αποσβέσεις:

Χωρίς τις αποσβέσεις της κηπουρικής   I.H.1, 4, 5, 6

Ακαθάριστες επενδύσεις παγίου κεφαλαίου:

Εξαιρούνται η κηπουρική, η εκτροφή γουνοφόρων ζώων και οι συνεταιρισμοί χρήσης γεωργικού μηχανικού εξοπλισμού   I.H.7, 8

Μεταφορικός εξοπλισμός:

Συμπεριλαμβάνονται μηχανήματα και άλλος εξοπλισμός   I.H.7, 8

Γερμανία (ΟΔ)

Τελική γεωργική παραγωγή:

Συμπεριλαμβάνονται γεωργικές εργασίες κατ' ανάθεση (φασόν)   I.H.1 έως 6

Κρασί:

Μούστος σταφυλιών, συμπεριλαμβανομένης της προστιθέμενης αξίας, στο εσωτερικό των γεωργικών εκμεταλλεύσεων, για τη μετατροπή του μούστου σε κρασί   I.H.5

Αγροτικά κτίρια:

Συμπεριλαμβάνονται και άλλα τεχνικά έργα καθώς και η βελτίωση του εδάφους   I.H.7, 8

Γαλλία

Τελική γεωργική παραγωγή:

Συμπεριλαμβάνονται οι γεωργικές εργασίες κατ' ανάθεση (φασόν)   I.H.1 έως 6

«Σύνολο» των ακαθάριστων επενδύσεων παγίου κεφαλαίου:

Συμπεριλαμβάνεται ο μη εκπεστέος ΦΠΑ (αναλυτικά δεδομένα χωρίς ΦΠΑ)

Ιταλία

Τελική φυτική και ζωική παραγωγή:

Συμπεριλαμβάνεται ο ΦΠΑ, αλλά εξαιρούνται οι άλλοι φόροι που συνδέονται με την παραγωγή   I.H.1 έως 6

Τελική γεωργική παραγωγή:

Συμπεριλαμβάνεται ο ΦΠΑ και οι άλλοι φόροι που συνδέονται με την παραγωγή   I.H.1 έως 6

Ενδιάμεση κατανάλωση:

Συμπεριλαμβάνεται ο ΦΠΑ   I.H.1 έως 6

Διάφορα:

Ιταλία: άλλοι φόροι, εκτός από τον ΦΠΑ, που συνδέονται με την παραγωγή   I.H.4, 5

Ακαθάριστες επενδύσεις παγίου κεφαλαίου:

Συμπεριλαμβάνονται η δασοκομία και η αλιεία   I.H.7, 8

Νέες φυτείες:

Συμπεριλαμβάνονται τα αγροτικά κτίρια, άλλα τεχνικά έργα και βελτίωση του εδάφους   I.H.7, 8

Μηχανήματα και άλλος εξοπλισμός:

Συμπεριλαμβάνονται και άλλα αγαθά ακαθάριστων επενδύσεων παγίου κεφαλαίου   I.H.7, 8

Λουξεμβούργο

Αγροτικά κτίρια:

Συμπεριλαμβάνονται και άλλα τεχνικά έργα, εξαιρείται όμως η βελτίωση του εδάφους   I.H.7, 8

Μεταφορικός εξοπλισμός:

Συμπεριλαμβάνονται τα μηχανήματα και λοιπός εξοπλισμός   I.H.7, 8

Κάτω Χώρες

Αγροτικά κτίρια:

Συμπεριλαμβάνονται και άλλα τεχνικά έργα, εξαιρείται όμως η βελτίωση του εδάφους   I.H.7, 8

Ηνωμένο Βασίλειο

Τελική γεωργική παραγωγή:

Συμπεριλαμβάνονται οι αγροτικές εργασίες κατ' ανάθεση (φασόν)   I.H.1 έως 6

II. ΔΑΣΟΚΟΜΙΑ:

II.Α – **Γενικό μέρος:** Για τη μεθοδολογία αυτή καθαυτή και ειδικότερα για ό,τι αφορά τις παρατηρήσεις για κάθε κράτος μέλος, ο αναγνώστης παραπέμπεται αντίστοιχα στις ακόλουθες δημοσιεύσεις:

- *«Δασικές στατιστικές – Μεθοδολογία»*
- *«Δασικές στατιστικές – Πίνακες»*

Αυτές οι δημοσιεύσεις εκδίδονται από την Eurostat σε όλες τις κοινοτικές γλώσσες.

II.Β – **Λογαριασμοί δασοκομίας:** βλέπε επίσης τις σημειώσεις στο I.H. Τα στοιχεία αναφέρονται στον κλάδο «ακατέργαστη ξυλεία». Καταρτίζονται σύμφωνα με την έννοια του «εθνικού δάσους» (κατ' αναλογία της έννοιας του «εθνικού αγροκτήματος» στους λογαριασμούς γεωργίας).

Η τελική δασική παραγωγή αξιολογείται σε τιμές «εκφορτωμένα παρά την οδό».

Εξάλλου, ο αναγνώστης παραπέμπεται στις μεθοδολογικές σημειώσεις του μέρους I.H οι οποίες εφαρμόζονται κατ' αναλογία. Περισσότερες διευκρινίσεις υπάρχουν στις επεξηγηματικές σημειώσεις ή τις δημοσιεύσεις της Eurostat, Θέμα 5, Σειρά Γ: Οικονομικοί λογαριασμοί – γεωργία, δασοκομία.

Βέλγιο

Επιδοτήσεις:

Καθαρές επιδοτήσεις των φόρων που συνδέονται με την παραγωγή, συμπεριλαμβανομένης της ενδεχόμενης υπερ- ή υπο-αντιστάθμισης του ΦΠΑ   II.B.1

Γερμανία (ΟΔ)

Έτος αναφοράς:

Καλλιεργητική περίοδος από 1.10 έως 30.9   II.B.1

Τελική παραγωγή:

Συμπεριλαμβάνονται τα «άλλα προϊόντα»   II.B.1

Ιταλία

Ενδιάμεση κατανάλωση:

Συμπεριλαμβάνεται ο ΦΠΑ   II.B.1

Έτος αναφοράς:

Καλλιεργητική περίοδος από 1.4 έως 31.3   II.B.1

Τελική παραγωγή:

Συμπεριλαμβάνονται τα «άλλα προϊόντα»   II.B.1

Λουξεμβούργο

Έτος αναφοράς:

Καλλιεργητική περίοδος από 1.10 έως 30.9   II.B.1

Ηνωμένο Βασίλειο

Έτος αναφοράς:

Καλλιεργητική περίοδος από 1.4 έως 31.3   II.B.1

Στοιχεία αναφοράς:

Χωρίς τη Βόρεια Ιρλανδία, για την οποία δεν είναι διαθέσιμα τα λιγότερο σημαντικά στοιχεία   II.B.1

III. ΑΛΙΕΙΑ

III.2.3 – **Αλιεύματα:** Τα δεδομένα για τα αλιεύματα παρέχονται από τα κράτη μέλη με βάση τα ερωτηματολόγια του συστήματος Statlant, η εκμετάλλευση του οποίου συντονίζεται από τη FAO. Τα δεδομένα βασίζονται στα ονομαστικά αλιεύματα σε γλυκά νερά, σε υφάλμυρα νερά, καθώς και στα θαλάσσια είδη των ψαριών, των οστρακοειδών, των μαλακίων και άλλων ζώων και φυτών τα οποία θανατώνονται, αλιεύονται, συλλαμβάνονται, συλλέγονται, εκτρέφονται ή καλλιεργούνται για κάθε εμπορικό, βιομηχανικό και επισιτιστικό σκοπό. Οι ποσότητες που συλλαμβάνονται από την ερασιτεχνική αλιεία εξαιρούνται. Η έννοια του ονομαστικού αλιεύματος αναφέρεται στις ποσότητες που εκφορτώνονται και που μετατρέπονται σε βάρος αλιεύματος.

III.4 – **Αλιευτικός στόλος:** Τα δεδομένα έχουν ληφθεί από το στατιστικό μητρώο των αλιευτικών πλοίων της Κοινότητας, το εθνικό μητρώο όμως δεν υπάρχει πάντα (Ε + Ρ) ή δεν είναι πλήρες (π.χ. για τα πλοία μικρής χωρητικότητας DK, GR, IRL και GB). Έχουν προστεθεί και δεδομένα από άλλες πηγές.

Χρησιμοποιούμενα σύμβολα και συντμήσεις

—	ουδέν
0	τιμή μικρότερη από το μισό της χρησιμο-ποιούμενης μονάδας
:	μη διαθέσιμα δεδομένα
S	απόρρητα δεδομένα
Prov./p	προσωρινά δεδομένα
*	εκτίμηση της Eurostat
μ.α.κ.	μη αλλού κατονομαζόμενα
R	νέο ή αναθεωρημένο στοιχείο
M/Ø	μέσος όρος
MP/MØ	σταθμισμένος μέσος όρος
%	ποσοστό
% AT	ποσοστό μεταβολής
AM	μέση ετήσια αύξηση
—Ι	ρήξη συγκρισιμότητας
ECU	ευρωπαϊκή νομισματική μονάδα
DM	γερμανικό μάρκο
FF	γαλλικό φράγκο
LIT	ιταλική λιρέτα
HFL	φιορίνι
BFR	βελγικό φράγκο
LFR	φράγκο Λουξεμβούργου
UKL	λίρα στερλίνα
IRL	λίρα Ιρλανδίας
DKR	δανική κορόνα
ΔΡΧ	δραχμή
ESC	εσκούδο
PTA	πεσέτα
T	μετρικός τόνος

HL	εκατόλιτρο
HA	εκτάριο
MIO	εκατομμύριο
MM	χιλιοστόμετρο
°C	βαθμός Κελσίου
m³ (r)	ισοδύναμο ακατέργαστης ξυλείας
AA/SAU	χρησιμοποιούμενη γεωργική έκταση
LU/UGB	μονάδα μεγάλων βοοειδών
GRT/TJB	τόνος ολικής χωρητικότητας (τόνος γκρος)
AWU/UTA	ανθρωποέτος
SGM/MBS	Τυπικό ακαθάριστο κέρδος (ΤΑΚ)
ESU/UDE	Μονάδα ευρωπαϊκού μεγέθους (ΜΕΜ)
EUR 10	σύνολο των κρατών μελών των ΕΚ χωρίς την Ισπανία και την Πορτογαλία
EUR 12	σύνολο των κρατών μελών των ΕΚ
Eurostat	Στατιστική Υπηρεσία των Ευρωπαϊκών Κοινοτήτων
EC/CE	Ευρωπαϊκές Κοινότητες
DOM	υπερπόντια γεωγραφικά διαμερίσματα
B + L/UEBL/ BLEU	Οικονομική Ένωση Βελγίου-Λουξεμ-βούργου
OECD/OCDE	Οργανισμός Οικονομικής Συνεργασίας και Ανάπτυξης (ΟΟΣΑ)
FAO	Οργανισμός Ηνωμένων Εθνών για τα Τρόφιμα και τη Γεωργία
IMF/FMI	Διεθνές Νομισματικό Ταμείο

Γλωσσάριο: Στο γλωσσάριο συγκεντρώνονται οι σημα-ντικότεροι όροι που χρησιμοποιούνται στο κύριο σώμα των πινάκων οι οποίοι δεν είναι διαθέσιμοι και στις εννέα γλώσσες της Κοινότητας.

Foreword

This yearbook is a statistical vade-mecum containing the most important data published in the specialized agricultural statistics booklets dealing with agriculture, forestry and fisheries.

The data relate to the last available period.

The data are taken from national sources; their presentation has been harmonized for Community purposes as regards concepts and values (conversion into ECU) in order to facilitate comparisons between countries, for which it is recommended to consult the methodological notes because, despite considerable improvements in the harmonization of data, some differences may still exist.

This volume contains an insert which tells the user who wants further information about facilities for consulting the data banks and/or specific publications available at Eurostat in 1987.

Note: previous publication: Agriculture — statistical yearbook 1986.

Table of contents

Methodological notes

I. – AGRICULTURE

I.A – General part:
the general part summarizes the main features of agriculture in the European Community and places the Community in a world context. The information on non-Community countries is taken from the FAO yearbook for Tables I.A.3, 4 and 5 and from OECD publications for Table I.A.6.

I.A.7 – Gross value-added at factor cost:

Gross value-added at factor cost does not, in principle, tally with the sum of the figures for the branches; the difference is due to imputed banking services and statistical adjustments.

I.A.9 – Foodstuffs at current prices:

Including beverages and tobacco.

I.A.10 – Weightings:

Weighting of the foodstuffs, beverages and tobacco industry in the index of industrial production.

I.A.11 to 15:

Trade of the Federal Republic of Germany with the German Democratic Republic and the Soviet sector of Berlin is not included.

I.B – Land use:
owing to the lack of annual surveys Eurostat uses the data on harvested areas estimated by the agricultural statistics departments in Greece, Spain and Portugal.

I.C – Structure:

Tables I.C.1 – I.C.10 contain data which represent the results of the Community surveys on the structure of agricultural holdings from 1966/67 to 1985; in these tables data can therefore be given only for the years in which surveys took place. Tables I.C.11 – I.C.13, on the other hand, contain data supplied on an annual basis by national surveys.

It should be noted that Table I.C.11 includes only holdings with at least 1 ha AA (agricultural area used). This leads to differences from results of Community surveys (e.g. Tables I.C.1 to 4), which covered in addition holdings with less than 1 ha AA but which produce to a certain extent for sale or whose agricultural production exceeds certain physical thresholds.

The most important results of the Community surveys on the structure of agricultural holdings have been published by Eurostat in a series of volumes, e.g. Vols I to VI for 1975 and Vols I to VI for 1979-80 and three volumes are also planned for the 1983 survey. Particular attention should be drawn to Vol. I in each series, which contains an introduction and describes the methodological principles of these surveys. It also contains the definitions of the concepts used in this volume. Where not set out in an annex to Vol. I, the underlying legislation for Community surveys can be found in the relevant *Official Journal of the European Communities*.

Tables I.C.5 – I.C.10 need special explanation.

– Table I.C.11

Some of the years or periods shown differ slightly for some countries:

- 1960 France = 1963
  Italy = 1961
  Netherlands = 1959
  Belgium = 1959
  Greece = 1961
- 1967 Netherlands = 1966
  Ireland = 1965
- 1970 Greece = 1971
- 1975 Greece = interpolation

– Table I.C.12

In principle, this table relates to multi-wheeled tractors, including caterpillar tractors and tool carriers.

– Table I.C.13

The data on consumption of commercial fertilizers relate in principle to deliveries by the fertilizer industry to agricultural dealers during a fertilizer year, not taking into account changes in stocks held by dealers. The fertilizer year is generally taken to be the period between 1 July and 30 June. For France it is between 1 May and 30 April (except in the case of straight nitrogenous fertilizers) and for the United Kingdom between 1 June and 31 May. Only for Greece is it the calendar year: 1979 for 1979/80, etc.

In addition to the breakdown according to the three main types of nutrient there have also been since 1965/66, when fully harmonized statistics for EUR 6 were introduced, statistics giving a division into straight and compound fertilizers. The latter include both mechanically mixed and chemically bound nutrients of several types.

Definitions of some less familiar concepts:

Standard gross margin (SGM)

The 'standard gross margin' is the difference between the standardized monetary value of gross production and the standardized monetary value of certain special costs. This difference is determined for the various crop and animal characteristics (per ha or per animal) at the level of the survey district and given in European currency units (ECU). By multiplying the areas or the number of animals by the corresponding SGM and then adding the products together, the total standard gross margin of the holding in question is obtained in ECU.

Economic size of holding in ESU

The economic size of holding is the total standard gross margin of the holding in question for the reference period 1980 (average of the years 1979 to 1981), given in European size units (ESU). One ESU is equal to 1 000 ECU.

Annual work unit (AWU)

The total annual working time of the persons employed in agriculture is converted into 'annual work units' (AWU). One AWU is taken to be the minimum number of hours per year laid down in the national collective agreements. If the number of hours is not laid down in these agreements, 2 200 hours are taken as the basis for one AWU.

I.D and I.E – The supply balance sheet statistics, referred to more simply as 'balance sheets', which in the majority of cases relate only to foodstuffs, constitute in the context of the common agricultural policy one of the instruments for the setting up and management of the various agricultural markets. The various data given in these balance sheets are essential for assessing the guidance and development of these markets. The results derived from them are one of the elements on which the agricultural policy-makers base their decisions.

The national supply balance sheets are drawn up by the Member States on the basis of Community concepts proposed by Eurostat in the *ad hoc* working party of the Agricultural Statistics Committee. A 'balance sheet' handbook is available at Eurostat for each product or group of products. The balance sheets can be regarded as the complement, in quantitative terms, to the agricultural accounts expressed in terms of value, but subdivided by product.

In the supply balance sheet statistics the external trade of the Federal Republic of Germany includes trade with the German Democratic Republic and East Berlin.

Schema for the supply balance sheets

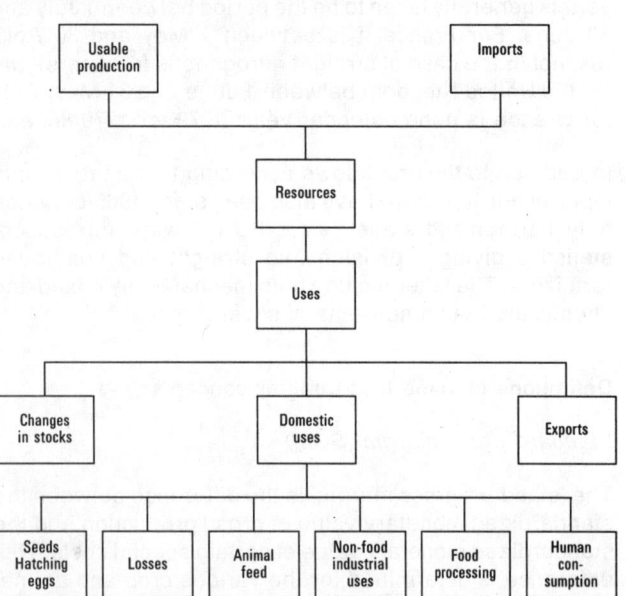

This general schema can be modified depending on the balance sheet under consideration.
Resources = Usable production + Imports
Uses = Exports + Changes in stocks + Domestic uses

I.E – Animal production: Most of the data on livestock numbers, the structure of livestock holdings by size class and production of meat, milk and milk products and eggs are supplied by the Member States as part of the surveys to be conducted and statistics to be compiled under Community legislation, i.e. Council Regulations or Directives and Commission Directives or Decisions.

I.F – Agricultural prices and price indices

(a) *Absolute agricultural prices*

The statistics on absolute agricultural prices are intended to permit comparisons of prices of, where possible, 'identical' – and therefore precisely defined – products between the Community Member States. In actual fact, however, the definitions of the products are not entirely identical. That is why Eurostat publishes 'catalogues of the characteristics of the agricultural price series stored in Cronos'. A new edition of this publication is currently being prepared.

The agricultural prices recorded by Eurostat do not, in principle, include any value-added tax. Only non-deductible or non-refundable VAT on certain means of production is included in the prices of the Member States concerned. The same applies to other taxes or subsidies specific to certain products. The aim is to record the prices which determine farmers' income.

In order to enable the agricultural prices expressed in national currency to be compared between Community Member States, they are converted into ECU (European currency units).

(b) *EC indices of agricultural prices (output and input)*

The EC indices of agricultural prices ('EC indices of producer prices of agricultural products' and 'EC indices of purchase prices of the means of agricultural production') are compiled according to the Laspeyres method, using weightings determined for the base year (1980) and a fixed basket of agricultural products (output indices) or goods and services (input indices). The indices of monthly prices of fresh fruit and vegetables are based on variable weightings for the 12 months of the base year. 1980 is also the reference year.

The EC indices of agricultural prices (output and input) are based, in all the Community Member States, on the concept of the 'national farm' and therefore cover only transactions between units of agricultural production and units of non-agricultural production, including external trade. Direct transactions between farmers are not taken into account either in calculating the weightings or in recording producer or purchase prices.

As regards the various items making up the two price indices, account must be taken, however, of the fact that the weighting schemes are adapted to the structure of production (output and input) in each country and that the baskets of goods representing the sales and purchases of agriculture vary from one country to another.

In order to eliminate the effect of the varying inflation rates recorded in the Community, the EC indices of agricultural prices have also been calculated in deflated form. The EC indices of nominal agricultural prices (output and input) are deflated by means of the consumer price index.

Further details of the methodology underlying the EC indices of agricultural prices are given in the publication *Methodology of the EC indices of agricultural prices (output and input)*.

I.G – Agricultural accounts:

The data relate to the branch 'Products of agriculture and hunting'. They are compiled in accordance with the concept of the national farm. In the case of production it is the concept of final production which corresponds to this concept (see diagram below).

Intermediate consumption comprises current consumption of all goods (except fixed capital goods) and services purchased by the national farm from non-agricultural units for use in the agricultural production process.

Operating subsidies and taxes linked to production represent income distribution transactions linked directly to the production process.

Depreciation – i.e. consumption of fixed capital – represents the depreciation of the fixed capital used in the production process as a result of normal wear and tear and loss following insurable accidental damage. Gross fixed capital formation represents the value of the durable goods acquired by the national farm for own account in order to be used for more than one year in the agricultural production process.

In principle, the final production of agriculture is valued at 'ex-farm' prices. From the producer's point of view the 'ex-farm' price is the market price.

Intermediate consumption and gross fixed capital formation are valued at purchase prices. From the purchaser's point of view the purchase price is the market price.

The data are compiled in accordance with the system of net recording of VAT: the various items making up final production, intermediate consumption and gross fixed capital formation do not include VAT. Only total intermediate consumption includes, where appropriate, under-compensation of VAT (= non-deductible VAT). For further details, see the explanatory notes or the Eurostat publications in Theme 5, Series C, particularly *Economic accounts – Agriculture, forestry, 1979-1984.*

Diagrammatic presentation of final agricultural production

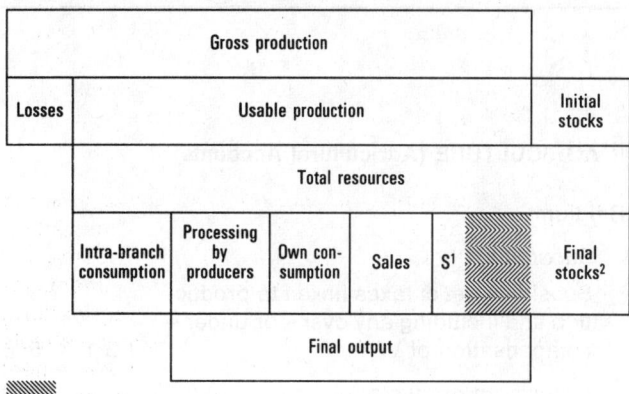

Change in stocks

[1] Own-account output of fixed capital goods.
[2] In the above diagram it is assumed that final stocks are greater than initial stocks.

Diagrammatic presentation of value-added and agricultural income

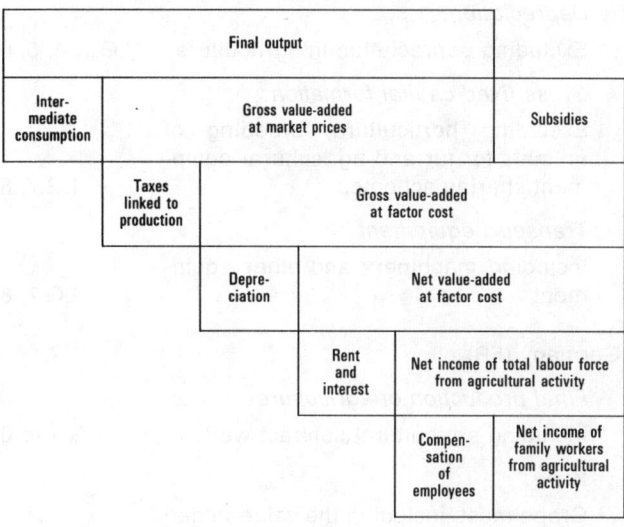

Explanatory notes by country

I. AGRICULTURE (Agricultural Accounts)

Belgium

Subsidies:

Subsidies net of taxes linked to production and including any over – or under – compensation of VAT   I.G.1, 4, 5, 6

Other crop products:

Including sales by producers who sell only occasionally, not broken down by product   I.G.4, 5

'Total' gross fixed capital formation:

Including non-deductible VAT (detailed data exclusive of VAT)   I.G.7, 8

Denmark

Depreciation:

Excluding depreciation in horticulture   I.G.1, 4, 5, 6

Gross fixed capital formation:

Excluding horticulture, breeding of animals for fur and agricultural equipment sharing schemes   I.G.7, 8

Transport equipment:

Including machinery and other equipment   I.G.7, 8

Germany (FR)

Final production of agriculture:

Including agricultural contract work   I.G.1 to 6

Wine:

Grape must, including the value-added within agricultural holdings, for processing must into wine   I.G.5

Farm buildings:

Including other structures and improvement of land   I.G.7, 8

France

Final production of agriculture:

Including agricultural contract work   I.G.1 to 6

'Total' gross fixed capital formation:

Including non-deductible VAT (detailed data exclusive of VAT)   I.G.7, 8

Italy

Final crop and animal production:

Including VAT but excluding other taxes linked to production   I.G.1 to 6

Final production of agriculture:

Including VAT and other taxes linked to production   I.G.1 to 6

Intermediate consumption:

Including VAT   I.G.1 to 6

Other:

Italy: taxes linked to production other than VAT   I.G.4, 5

Gross fixed capital formation:

Including forestry and fisheries   I.G.7, 8

New plantations:

Including farm buildings, other structures and improvement of land   I.G.7, 8

Machinery and other equipment:

Including other gross fixed capital formation goods   I.G.7, 8

Luxembourg

Farm buildings:

Including other structures except improvement of land   I.G.7, 8

Transport equipment:

Including machinery and other equipment   I.G.7, 8

Netherlands

Farm buildings:

Including other structures except improvement of land   I.G.7, 8

United Kingdom

Final production of agriculture:

Including agricultural contract work   I.G.1 to 6

II. FORESTRY

II.A. **General**: for the methodology as such and in particular for the data pertaining to the Member States, reference should be made to the following publications respectively:

– *Forestry statistics – Methodology,*
– *Forestry statistics – Tables.*

These publications are issued by Eurostat in all the Community languages.

II.B. **Forestry accounts**: see also the notes on I.G. The data relate to the branch 'Raw wood' and are compiled in accordance with the concept of 'national forest' (by analogy with the 'national farm' concept used in the agricultural accounts).

Final forestry production is valued at 'unloaded at side of road' prices.

The reader is also referred to the methodological notes in Part I.G., which are applicable by analogy. For further details see the explanatory notes or Eurostat publications in Theme 5, Series C, particularly *Economic accounts – Agriculture, forestry, 1979-1984.*

Belgium

Subsidies:

Subsidies net of taxes linked to production and including any over – or under – compensation of VAT II.B.1

Germany (FR)

Reference year:

Crop years from 1. 10 to 30. 9 .... II.B.1

Final production:

Including 'other products' II.B.1

Italy

Intermediate consumption:

Including VAT II.B.1

Reference year:

Crop years from 1. 4 to 31. 3 .... II.B.1

Final production:

Including 'other products' II.B.1

Luxembourg

Reference year:

Crop years from 1. 10 to 30. 9 .... II.B.1

United Kingdom

Reference year:

Crop years from 1. 4 to 31. 3 .... II.B.1

Reference data:

Excluding Northern Ireland, whose relatively insignificant data are not available II.B.1

III. **FISHERIES**

III.2.3 – **Catches:** the data on catches have been supplied by the Member States on the questionnaires used for the Statlant system, which is coordinated by the FAO. They relate to nominal catches in fresh water, and briny water and to the marine species of fish, crustaceans, molluscs and other animals and plants killed, taken, caught, collected, bred or cultivated for all commercial, industrial and food purposes. The quantities caught by sports fishermen are not included. The concept of nominal catches refers to landings converted into live weight.

III.4 – **Fishing fleet:** the data have been taken from the statistical register of fishing vessels in the Community, but in some cases the national register is lacking (E and P) or is incomplete (e.g. as regards low-tonnage vessels in DK, GR, IRL and UK); data from other sources have been added.

Abbreviations and symbols used

–	Nil
0	Data less than half the unit used
:	No data available
S	Confidential data
prov./p	Provisional data
*	Estimate made by Eurostat
n.d.a.	Not otherwise specified
r	New or revised data
M/Ø	Average
MP/ØP	Weighted average
%	Percentage
% AT	Percentage variation
AM	Average annual growth
–I	Break in comparability
ECU	European currency unit
BFR	Belgian franc
DKR	Danish crown
DM	German mark
DR	Greek drachma
ESC	Portuguese escudo
FF	French franc
HFL	Dutch guilder
IRL	Irish pound
LFR	Luxembourg franc
LIT	Italian lira
PTA	Spanish peseta
UKL	Pound sterling
t	Tonnes

hl	Hectolitre
ha	Hectare
Mio	Million
mm	Millimetre
°C	Degree Celsius
$m^3(r)$	Round cubic metre, raw wood equivalent
AA/SAU	Agricultural area used
W/UGB	Livestock unit
GRT/TJB	Gross registered tonnage
AWU/UTA	Annual work unit
SGM/MBS	Standard gross margin
ESU/UDE	European size unit
EUR 10	Total of the member countries of the EC excl. Spain and Portugal
EUR 12	Total of the member countries of the EC
Eurostat	Statistical Office of the European Communities
EC/CE	European Communities
DOM	Overseas 'Départements'
B + L/ UEBL/BLEU	Belgio-Luxembourg Economic Union
OECD/OCDE	Organization for Economic Cooperation and Development
FAO	Food and Agriculture Organization of the United Nations
IMF/FMI	International Monetary Fund

Glossary: the glossary contains the main terms used in the corpus of tables not available in the nine Community languages.

Préface

Cet ouvrage est un vade-mecum statistique dont le contenu représente la synthèse des principales informations qui sont publiées dans les brochures spécialisées de statistique agricole traitant de l'agriculture, de la sylviculture et de la pêche.

Les données se réfèrent à la période la plus récente disponible.

Elles proviennent de sources nationales, et leur présentation a été harmonisée dans le cadre communautaire pour les concepts et les valeurs (conversion en ECU) afin de faciliter les rapprochements de pays à pays. Pour les comparaisons entre pays, il est recommandé de consulter les notes méthodologiques car, malgré d'importantes améliorations dans l'harmonisation des données, des divergences peuvent subsister.

Cet ouvrage est complété par un signet encarté qui informe l'utilisateur « pour en savoir plus » sur la possibilité de consultation des banques de données et/ou des publications spécifiques disponibles à Eurostat en 1987.

Avertissement: ouvrage précédent = Agriculture, annuaire statistique 1986

FR

Table des matières

FR

Notes méthodologiques

I. – AGRICULTURE

I.A – Partie générale: la partie générale résume les principales caractéristiques de l'agriculture de la CE et situe la CE dans le monde. L'information extra-CE est extraite de l'annuaire de la FAO pour les tableaux I.A.3, 4 et 5, des publications de l'OCDE pour le tableau I.A.6.

I.A.7 – Valeur ajoutée brut au coût des facteurs:

la valeur ajoutée brute au coût des facteurs ne correspond pas, en principe, à la somme des branches; l'écart est dû à des services bancaires imputés et à des ajustements statistiques.

I.A.9 – Alimentation aux prix courants:

y compris les boissons et le tabac.

I.A.10 – Pondérations:

poids de l'industrie des denrées alimentaires, boissons et tabac, dans l'indice de la production industrielle.

I.A.11 à 15:

le commerce de la République fédérale d'Allemagne avec la République démocratique allemande et le secteur soviétique de Berlin est exclu.

I.B – Utilisation des terres: en l'absence d'enquêtes annuelles, Eurostat utilise les données des superficies récoltées estimées par les services statistiques agricoles de la Grèce, de l'Espagne et du Portugal.

I.C – Structure:

les tableaux I.C.1 à I.C.10 contiennent des données qui comportent les résultats des enquêtes communautaires de 1966-1967 à 1985 sur la structure des exploitations agricoles; ces tableaux ne peuvent donc présenter des données que pour les années au cours desquelles des enquêtes ont eu lieu. Les tableaux I.C.11 à I.C.13 par contre contiennent des données fournies chaque année par les enquêtes nationales.

Notons que le tableau I.C.11 ne couvre que les exploitations mettant en valeur au moins un hectare de SAU. Cela explique les différences par rapport aux résultats des enquêtes communautaires (par exemple tableaux I.C.4) qui recensent également les exploitations possédant certes moins de un hectare de SAU, mais qui produisent, dans une certaine mesure, pour la vente, ou dont l'unité de production dépasse certains seuils physiques.

Les principaux résultats des enquêtes communautaires sur la structure des exploitations agricoles ont été publiés par Eurostat dans une série de volumes: par exemple, volumes I à VI pour 1975 et volumes I à IV pour 1979-1980 et trois volumes pour l'enquête de 1983. Il convient, en particulier, de mentionner le volume I de chaque série qui présente une introduction et décrit les bases méthodologiques de ces enquêtes. On y trouve, entre autres, les définitions des concepts utilisés dans les enquêtes. Si elles ne figurent pas en annexe du volume I, les bases juridiques des enquêtes communautaires se trouvent dans le *Journal officiel des Communautés européennes*.

Les tableaux I.C.11 à I.C.13 nécessitent des commentaires particuliers.

– Tableau I.C.11

Certaines années ou périodes citées diffèrent légèrement pour certains pays membres:

- 1960 France   = 1963
  - Italie   = 1961
  - Pays-Bas   = 1959
  - Belgique   = 1959
  - Grèce   = 1961
- 1967 Pays-Bas   = 1966
  - Irlande   = 1965
- 1970 Grèce   = 1971
- 1975 Grèce   = interpolation

– Tableau I.C.12

En principe, il s'agit des tracteurs à plusieurs axes, y compris les tracteurs à chenilles et les porte-outils.

– Tableau I.C.13

En ce qui concerne la consommation d'engrais chimiques, il s'agit, en principe, de livraisons de l'industrie au secteur commercial pendant une campagne agricole, compte non tenu des variations de stocks. La campagne se situe en général entre le 1er juillet et le 30 juin. Pour la France, à l'exclusion des engrais azotés simples, la campagne se situe entre le 1er mai et le 30 avril, et pour le Royaume-Uni, entre le 1er juin et le 31 mai. Pour la Grèce uniquement, les données se réfèrent à l'année civile: 1979 à la place de 1979-1980, etc.

En plus de la répartition selon les trois catégories principales de fertilisants, il existe, à partir de 1965-1966, une statistique de la répartition entre engrais simples et engrais composés. Ces derniers comprennent soit les mélanges mécaniques, soit les compositions chimiques comprenant plusieurs fertilisants.

Définitions concernant quelques concepts moins connus

Marge brute standard (MBS)

La «marge brute standard» représente le solde entre la valeur standard de la production et le montant standard de certains coûts directs. Ce solde est déterminé au niveau de la circonscription d'enquête pour les différentes caractéristiques végétales et animales (par hectare ou par animal) et est exprimé en unités monétaires européennes (ECU). En multipliant les superficies ou le nombre des animaux par la MBS correspondante, puis en additionnant ces produits, on obtient la marge brute standard totale de l'exploitation concernée en ECU.

Dimension économique d'une exploitation (en UDE)

La dimension économique d'une exploitation correspond à la MBS totale de l'exploitation concernée pour la période de référence 1980 (moyenne des années 1979 à 1981), et est exprimée en unités de dimension européennes (UDE). Une UDE correspond à 1 000 ECU.

Unité - travail - année (UTA)

Le temps de travail annuel total des différentes personnes occupées dans l'agriculture est converti en unité-travail-année (UTA). Une UTA est égale au nombre d'heures minimales par an fixé dans les conventions collectives nationales. Si le nombre d'heures n'est pas indiqué dans ces conventions, le nombre de 2 200 heures est retenu pour une UTA.

I.D et I.E – **La statistique des bilans d'approvisionnement** dénommés plus simplement « bilan » qui, dans la majorité des cas, ne concerne que des produits alimentaires, constitue dans le cadre de la politique agricole commune l'un des instruments de mise en place et de gestion des divers marchés agricoles. Les différentes données figurant dans ces bilans sont indispensables pour apprécier l'orientation et le développement de ces marchés. Les résultats que l'on peut en tirer sont un des éléments sur lesquels se fondent les décisions des responsables de la politique agricole.

Les bilans d'approvisionnement nationaux sont élaborés par les États membres sur la base de concepts communautaires proposés par Eurostat dans le cadre du groupe de travail ad hoc du comité de statistique agricole. Un manuel « bilan » est disponible à Eurostat par produit ou groupe de produits. Les bilans peuvent être considérés comme le complément en données quantitatives des comptes de l'agriculture exprimés en valeur, mais subdivisés par produits.

Dans la statistique des bilans d'approvisionnement, le commerce extérieur de la République fédérale d'Allemagne comprend les échanges avec la République démocratique allemande et Berlin-Est.

Schéma des bilans d'approvisionnement

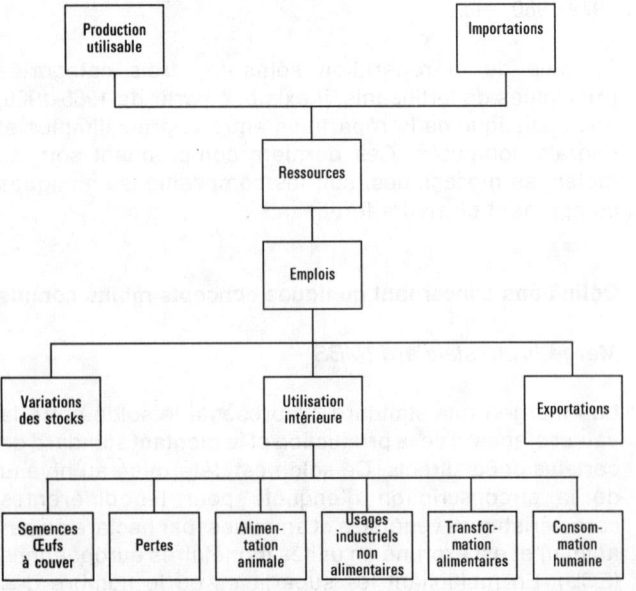

Ce schéma général peut être adapté selon les biens considérés
Ressources = Production utilisable + importations
Emplois = Exportations + variation des stocks + utilisation intérieure

I.E – **Production animale:** l'essentiel des données sur les effectifs d'animaux, sur la structure des élevages par classe de grandeur et les productions de viande, de lait et produits laitiers et d'œufs est fourni par les États membres dans le cadre des enquêtes et statistiques à réaliser en application de textes juridiques communautaires, règlements ou directives du Conseil et directives ou décisions de la Commission.

I.F – **Prix et indices des prix agricoles**

a) *Prix agricoles en valeur absolue*

La statistique des prix agricoles en valeur absolue doit permettre de faire des comparaisons de prix de produits si possible « identiques » – donc définis avec précision – entre les États membres de la Communauté. Les définitions des produits, en réalité, ne sont toutefois pas totalement identiques. C'est la raison pour laquelle Eurostat publie des « catalogues des caractéristiques des séries de prix agricoles mémorisées dans Cronos ». Une nouvelle édition de cette publication est en cours de préparation.

Les prix agricoles enregistrés par Eurostat ne contiennent en principe aucune taxe sur la valeur ajoutée. Seule la TVA non déductible ou non remboursable frappant certains moyens de production est incluse dans les prix des États membres concernés. La même chose vaut pour d'autres taxes ou subventions spécifiques à certains produits. L'objectif est d'enregistrer les prix qui déterminent le revenu des agriculteurs.

Pour que les prix agricoles exprimés en monnaie nationale puissent être comparés entre les États membres de la Communauté, ils sont convertis en ECU (unité monétaire européenne).

b) *Indices CE des prix agricoles (output et input)*

Les indices CE des prix agricoles (« indices CE des prix à la production des produits agricoles » et « indices CE des prix d'achat des moyens de production agricole ») sont établis selon la méthode de Laspeyres, au moyen de pondérations déterminées pour l'année de base (1980) et pour un panier fixe de produits agricoles (indices output) ou de biens et services (indices input). Les indices des prix mensuels des fruits et légumes frais reposent sur des pondérations variables pour les douze mois de l'année de base. L'année 1980 sert également d'année de référence.

Les indices CE des prix agricoles (output et input) reposent, dans tous les États membres de la Communauté, sur la notion de la « ferme nationale » et ils ne couvrent, par conséquent, que les transactions entre les unités de production agricole et les unités de production non agricole, y compris le commerce extérieur. Il n'est tenu compte des transactions directes entre agriculteurs ni dans le calcul des pondérations, ni dans l'enregistrement des prix à la production ou des prix d'achat.

En ce qui concerne les différents postes composant les deux indices de prix, il faut, toutefois, tenir compte du fait que les schémas de pondération sont adaptés à la structure de la production (output et input) de chaque pays et que les paniers de marchandises représentent les ventes et les achats de l'agriculture varient d'un pays à l'autre.

Afin d'éliminer l'influence des taux d'inflation variables enregistrés dans la Communauté, on a également calculé les indices CE des prix agricoles sous une forme déflatée. La déflation des indices CE des prix agricoles nominaux (output et input) s'effectue à l'aide de l'indice des prix à la consommation.

D'autres détails sur la méthodologie à la base des indices CE des prix agricoles figurent dans la publication *Méthodologie des indices CE des prix agricoles (output et input)*.

I.G – Comptes de l'agriculture:

les données se réfèrent à la branche «produits de l'agriculture et de la chasse». Elles sont établies suivant le concept de la ferme nationale. Au niveau de la production, c'est le concept de la production finale qui répond à cette notion (voir schéma ci-après).

Les consommations intermédiaires comprennent la consommation courante de tous les biens (à l'exception des biens de capital fixe) et services qui ont été achetés par la ferme nationale auprès des unités non agricoles pour être employés dans le processus de production agricole.

Les subventions d'exploitation et les impôts liés à la production représentent des opérations de répartition des revenus liées directement au processus de production.

Les amortissements – c'est-à-dire la consommation de capital fixe – représentent la dépréciation subie par le capital fixe employé dans le processus de production par suite d'usure normale et de perte à la suite de dommages accidentels assurables. La formation brute de capital fixe représente la valeur des biens durables acquis par la ferme nationale pour compte propre afin d'être utilisés pendant une durée supérieure à un an dans le processus de production agricole.

En principe, la production finale de l'agriculture est évaluée au prix «départ-ferme». Le prix «départ-ferme» est le prix du marché dans l'optique du producteur.

La consommation intermédiaire et la formation brute de capital fixe sont évaluées au prix d'acquisition. Le prix d'acquisition est le prix du marché dans l'optique de l'acheteur.

Les données sont établies d'après le système d'enregistrement net de la taxe sur la valeur ajoutée (TVA): les différents postes de la production finale, de la consommation intermédiaire et de la formation brute de capital fixe ne contiennent pas la TVA. Seul, le total de la consommation intermédiaire contient, le cas échéant, la sous-compensation de TVA (= TVA non déductible). Pour d'autres précisions, voir les notes explicatives ou les publications de l'Eurostat, thème 5, série C: *Comptes économiques – agriculture, sylviculture*.

Présentation schématique de la production agricole finale

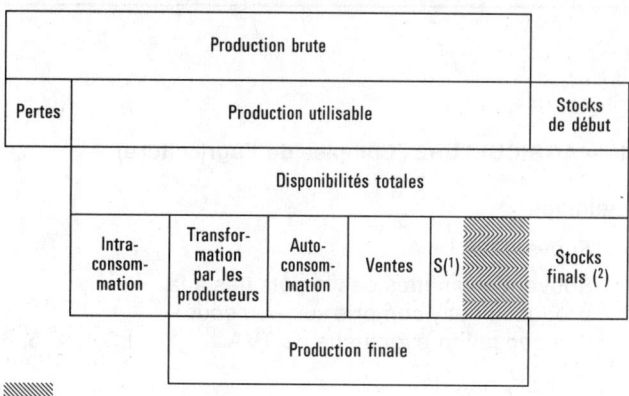

Variation des stocks

(1) Construction pour compte propre.
(2) Dans le schéma ci-dessus, il est supposé que les stocks finals sont plus grands que les stocks de début.

Présentation schématique de la valeur ajoutée et du revenu agricole

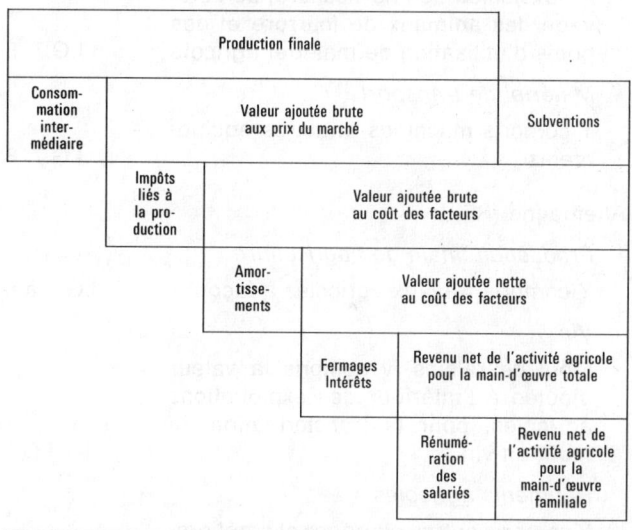

FR

Notes explicatives par pays

I — AGRICULTURE (Comptes de l'agriculture)

Belgique

Subventions

Subventions nettes des impôts liés à la production et y compris sur – ou sous – compensation éventuelle de TVA   I.G.1, 4, 5, 6

Autres produits végétaux

Y compris les ventes, effectuées par les producteurs qui ne vendent qu'occasionnellement, non réparties par produits   I.G.4, 5

Formation brute de capital fixe « total »

Y compris TVA non déductible (données détaillées hors TVA)   I.G.7, 8

Danemark

Amortissements

Sans amortissements de l'horticulture   I.G.1, 4, 5, 6

Formation brute de capital fixe

A l'exclusion de l'horticulture, de l'élevage des animaux de fourrure et des pools d'utilisation de matériel agricole   I.G.7, 8

Matériel de transport

Y compris machines et autres équipements   I.G.7, 8

Allemagne (RF)

Production finale de l'agriculture

Y compris travaux agricoles à façon   I.G.1 à 6

Vin

Moût de raisins, y compris la valeur ajoutée à l'intérieur des exploitations agricoles, pour la transformation de moût en vin   I.G.5

Bâtiments agricoles

Y compris autres ouvrages et améliorations des terres   I.G.7, 8

France

Production finale de l'agriculture

Y compris travaux agricoles à façon   I.G.1 à 6

Formation brute de capital fixe « total »

Y compris TVA non déductible (données détaillées hors TVA)   I.G.7, 8

Italie

Productions végétale et animale finales

Y compris TVA, mais à l'exclusion des autres impôts liés à la production   I.G.1 à 6

Production finale de l'agriculture

Y compris TVA et autres impôts liés à la production   I.G.1 à 6

Consommation intermédiaire

Y compris TVA   I.G.1 à 6

Divers

Italie : impôts liés à la production autres que TVA   I.G.4, 5

Formation brute de capital fixe

Y compris sylviculture et pêche   I.G.7, 8

Plantations nouvelles

Y compris bâtiments agricoles, autres ouvrages et améliorations des terres   I.G.7, 8

Machines et autres équipements

Y compris autres biens de formation brute de capital fixe   I.G.7, 8

Luxembourg

Bâtiments agricoles

Y compris autres ouvrages à l'exception de l'amélioration des terres   I.G.7, 8

Matériel de transport

Y compris machines et autres équipements   I.G.7, 8

Pays-Bas

Bâtiments agricoles

Y compris autres ouvrages à l'exception de l'amélioration des terres   I.G.7, 8

Royaume-Uni

Production finale de l'agriculture

Y compris travaux agricoles à façon   I.G.1 à 6

II — SYLVICULTURE

II.A – **Partie générale** : pour la méthodologie proprement dite et en ce qui concerne plus spécialement des observations propres aux États membres, il faut se référer respectivement aux publications suivantes :

- *Statistiques forestières – méthodologie,*
- *Statistiques forestières – tableaux.*

Ces publications sont éditées par Eurostat dans toutes les langues de la Communauté.

II.B – **Comptes de la sylviculture** : voir aussi notes sur I.G. Les données se réfèrent à la branche « bois brut ». Elles sont établies suivant le concept de « forêt nationale » (par analogie au concept de « ferme nationale » dans les comptes de l'agriculture).

La production finale sylvicole est évaluée au prix « débardé bordure route ».

Par ailleurs, le lecteur est renvoyé aux notes méthodologiques de la partie I.G qui sont applicables par analogie. Pour d'autres précisions, voir les notes explicatives ou les publications de l'Eurostat, thème 5, série C : *Comptes économiques – agriculture, sylviculture.*

Belgique

Subventions

Subventions nettes des impôts liés à la production et y compris sur – ou sous – compensation éventuelle de TVA ... II.B.1

Allemagne (RF)

Année de référence

Années campagne du 1er octobre au 30 septembre ... II.B.1

Production finale

Y compris « autres produits » ... II.B.1

Italie

Consommation intermédiaire

Y compris TVA ... II.B.1

Année de référence

Années campagne du 1er avril au 31 mars ... II.B.1

Production finale

Y compris « autres produits » ... II.B.1

Luxembourg

Année de référence

Années campagne du 1er octobre au 30 septembre ... II.B.1

Royaume-Uni

Année de référence

Années campagne du 1er avril au 31 mars ... II.B.1

Données de référence

Sans Irlande du Nord dont les données peu significatives ne sont pas disponibles ... II.B.1

III — PÊCHE

III.2.3 – **Captures:** les données sur les captures ont été fournies par les États membres sur les questionnaires du système Statlant dont l'exploitation est coordonnée par la FAO. Les données portent sur les captures nominales en eaux douces, en eaux saumâtres, ainsi que sur les espèces marines de poissons, de crustacés, de mollusques et autres animaux et plantes tués, pris, capturés, recueillis, élevés ou cultivés à toutes fins commerciales, industrielles et alimentaires. Les quantités capturées en pêche de loisir sont exclues. Le concept de captures nominales se réfère aux arrivages convertis en poids vif.

III.4 – **Flotte de pêche:** les données ont été extraites du registre statistique des navires de pêche de la Communauté, mais le registre national fait défaut (pour l'Espagne et le Portugal) ou est incomplet (par exemple pour les navires de faible tonnage du Danemark, de la Grèce, de l'Irlande et du Royaume-Uni); des données d'autres sources ont été ajoutées.

FR

Abréviations et signes employés

–	Néant
0	Donnée inférieure à la moitié de l'unité utilisée
:	Donnée non disponible
S	Donnée secrète
prov./p	Donnée provisoire
*	Estimation de l'Eurostat
n.d.a./a.d.a.	Non dénommé ailleurs
r	Donnée nouvelle ou révisée
M/Ø	Moyenne
MP/ØP	Moyenne pondérée
%	Pourcentage
% AT	Pourcentage de variation
AM	Accroissement moyen annuel
–I	Rupture dans la comparabilité
ECU	Unité monétaire européenne
BFR	Franc belge
DKR	Couronne danoise
DM	Mark allemand
DR	Drachme grecque
ESC	Escudo
FF	Franc français
HFL	Florin
IRL	Livre irlandaise
LIT	Lire italienne
LFR	Franc luxembourgeois
PTA	Peseta
UKL	Livre sterling
t	Tonne métrique

hl	Hectolitre
ha	Hectare
Mio	Million
mm	Millimètre
°C	Degré Celsius
$m^3(r)$	Mètre cube rond, bois brut équivalent
AA/SAU	Superficie agricole utilisée
W/UGB	Unité de gros bétail
GRT/TJB	Tonnage jauge brute
AWU/UTA	Unité de travail-année
SGM/MBS	Marge brute standard
ESU/UDE	Unité de dimension européenne
EUR 10	Ensemble des pays membres des CE, sauf l'Espagne et le Portugal
EUR 12	Ensemble des pays membres des CE
Eurostat	Office statistique des Communautés européennes
EC/CE	Communautés européennes
DOM	Départements d'outre-mer
B+L/ UEBL/BLEU	Union économique belgo-luxembourgeoise
OECD/OCDE	Organisation de coopération et de développement économiques
FAO	Food and Agriculture Organization of the United Nations
IMF/FMI	Fonds monétaire international

Glossaire: le glossaire rassemble les principaux termes utilisés dans le corps des tableaux non disponibles dans les neuf langues de la Communauté.

Voorwoord

In dit statistisch vademecum wordt een synthese gegeven van de belangrijkste informatie uit de gespecialiseerde brochures over de landbouwstatistiek, waarin de landbouw, de bosbouw en de visserij worden behandeld.

Het gaat hierbij om de meest recente informatie die beschikbaar is.

De gegevens zijn afkomstig uit nationale bronnen. De begrippen en de waarden (omgerekend in Ecu) zijn in communautair verband geharmoniseerd, ten einde vergelijkingen tussen de landen te vereenvoudigen. Toch wordt aanbevolen om voor deze vergelijkingen de toelichting op de methoden te raadplegen daar er ondanks belangrijke verbeteringen bij de harmonisatie van de gegevens verschillen blijven bestaan. ·

Dit werk omvat ook een los blad waarop de gebruiker die meer wenst te weten, op de hoogte wordt gebracht van de mogelijkheid de gegevensbanken en/of de in 1986 bij Eurostat beschikbare specifieke publikaties te raadplegen.

Opmerking: vorige publikatie: Landbouw, statistisch jaarboek 1986.

NL

Inhoud

NL

Toelichting op de methoden

I. – LANDBOUW

I.A – Het gedeelte „Algemeen": hierin wordt behalve een samenvatting van de belangrijkste kenmerken van de landbouw in de EG ook een beeld van de plaats van de EG in de wereld gegeven. De informatie over niet-EG-landen in de tabellen I.A.3, 4 en 5 is ontleend aan het jaarboek van de FAO en die in tabel I.A.6 aan publikaties van de OESO.

I.A.7 – Bruto toegevoegde waarde tegen factorkosten:

de bruto toegevoegde waarde tegen factorkosten komt in beginsel niet overeen met de som van de branches; het verschil is te wijten aan toegerekende bankdiensten en statistische correcties.

I.A.9 – Voeding tegen lopende prijzen:

met inbegrip van dranken en tabak.

I.A.10 – Wegingen:

gewicht van de voedingsmiddelen-, dranken- en tabaksindustrie in het indexcijfer van de industriële produktie.

I.A.11 – 15: zonder de handel van de Bondsrepubliek Duitsland met de Duitse Democratische Republiek en de Russische sector van Berlijn.

I.B – Bodemgebruik: wegens het ontbreken van jaarlijkse enquêtes maakt Eurostat gebruik van de door de landbouwstatistische diensten van Griekenland, Spanje en Portugal geschatte gegevens over het geoogste areaal.

I.C – Structuur:

De tabellen I.C.1 tot en met I.C.10 bevatten de resultaten van de gemeenschappelijke enquêtes naar de structuur van de landbouwbedrijven tussen 1966/67 en 1985; in deze tabellen kunnen derhalve alleen gegevens worden verstrekt voor jaren waarin enquêtes hebben plaatsgevonden. De tabellen I.C.11 tot en met I.C.13 bevatten daarentegen gegevens die jaarlijks worden ontleend aan de nationale enquêtes.

Opgemerkt zij dat in tabel I.C.11 alleen bedrijven zijn opgenomen met een OC van ten minste 1 hectare. Dientengevolge zijn er verschillen met de resultaten uit communautaire enquêtes (b.v. tabel I.C.4) waarin ook bedrijven werden geregistreerd met een OC van weliswaar minder dan 1 hectare, maar die in bepaalde mate voor de verkoop produceren of waarvan de produktie-eenheid boven bepaalde fysieke drempels ligt.

De belangrijkste resultaten van de communautaire enquêtes naar de structuur van de landbouwbedrijven zijn door Eurostat telkens in een reeks gepubliceerd, b.v. deel I t/m VI voor 1975, deel I t/m IV voor 1979/80 en drie delen voor de enquête van 1983. Met name dient te worden gewezen op deel I van iedere reeks, waarin een inleiding is opgenomen en de methodologische grondslagen van deze enquêtes worden beschreven. Zij bevatten o.a. de definities voor de hier gebruikte begrippen. Voor zover de

wettelijke grondslagen voor de communautaire enquêtes niet als bijlage bij deel I zijn opgenomen, zijn ze in de desbetreffende *Publikatiebladen van de Europese Gemeenschap* te vinden.

De tabellen I.C.11 tot en met I.C.13 behoeven een nadere toelichting.

– Tabellen I.C.11

Voor een aantal landen wijken de opgegeven jaren of tijdvakken enigszins af:

- 1960 Frankrijk = 1963
  - Italië = 1961
  - Nederland = 1959
  - België = 1959
  - Griekenland = 1961
- 1967 Nederland = 1966
  - Ierland = 1965
- 1970 Griekenland = 1971
- 1975 Griekenland = interpolatie

– Tabel I.C.12

In beginsel gaat het om vierwielige trekkers met inbegrip van rupstrekkers en werktuigtrekkers.

– Tabel I.C.13

Bij de gegevens over het verbruik van kunstmeststoffen gaat het in beginsel om leveringen van de kunstmestindustrie aan de handel in agrarische produkten tijdens een mestjaar, zonder rekening te houden met de voorraadmutatie bij de handel. Als mestjaar geldt in de regel de periode tussen 1 juli en 30 juni. Voor Frankrijk loopt het mestjaar, behalve voor enkelvoudige stikstofmeststoffen, van 1 mei t/m 30 april en voor het Verenigd Koninkrijk van 1 juni t/m 31 mei. Alleen voor Griekenland gelden kalenderjaren: 1979 voor 1979/80, enz.

Behalve de indeling in de drie hoofdmeststofsoorten bestaat er sedert 1965/66, een statistiek betreffende de indeling in enkelvoudige en samengestelde meststoffen. Samengestelde meststoffen bevatten zowel mechanisch gemengde als langs chemische weg bereide meststoffen van verschillende soorten.

Definitie van enige minder bekende begrippen:

Bruto standaardsaldo (BSS)

Het „bruto standaardsaldo" is het verschil tussen de standaardwaarde van de produktie en het standaardbedrag van bepaalde specifieke kosten. Dit saldo wordt in elke regio voor de verschillende gewassen en diersoorten (per ha, resp. per dier) bepaald en uitgedrukt in Europese valutaeenheden (Ecu). Door de arealen, resp. het aantal dieren met het desbetreffende BSS te vermenigvuldigen en deze produkten vervolgens bij elkaar op te tellen, verkrijgt men het totale bruto standaardsaldo van het desbetreffende bedrijf in Ecu.

Economische bedrijfsomvang in EGE

De economische bedrijfsomvang is het totale bruto standaardsaldo van het desbetreffende bedrijf voor de referentieperiode 1980 (een gemiddelde van de jaren 1979, 1980 en 1981), uitgedrukt in Europese grootte-eenheden (EGE). Een EGE is 1 000 Ecu.

Arbeidsjaareenheden (AJE)

De totale jaarlijkse arbeidstijd van de in de landbouw werkzame personen wordt omgerekend in zogenaamde arbeidsjaareenheden (AJE). Onder een AJE wordt verstaan het in de nationale collectieve arbeidsovereenkomsten vastgelegde minimum aantal arbeidsuren per jaar. Indien dit niet in dergelijke overeenkomsten is vastgelegd, wordt uitgegaan van een AJE van 2 200 uur.

I.D en I.E – De statistiek van de voorzieningsbalansen, of gewoon „balansen", die meestal alleen op voedingsmiddelen betrekking heeft, is in het gemeenschappelijk landbouwbeleid een van de instrumenten voor de totstandbrenging en het beheer van de verschillende landbouwmarkten. De cijfers in deze balansen zijn onontbeerlijk voor de beoordeling van de doelstellingen en de ontwikkeling van deze markten. Degenen die voor het landbouwbeleid verantwoordelijk zijn, baseren hun besluiten onder andere op informatie die aan de balansen kan worden ontleend.

De nationale voorzieningsbalansen worden door de Lid-Staten opgesteld aan de hand van de door Eurostat in het kader van de desbetreffende werkgroep van het Landbouwstatistisch Comité voorgestelde communautaire begrippen. Bij Eurostat is een handleiding „balansen" per produkt of groepprodukten beschikbaar. De balansen kunnen worden beschouwd als een kwantitatieve aanvulling op de in waarden uitgedrukte landbouwrekeningen, maar dan ingedeeld naar produkt.

In de statistiek van de voorzieningsbalansen omvat de buitenlandse handel van de Bondsrepubliek Duitsland de handel met de Duitse Democratische Republiek en Oost-Berlijn.

Schematische voorstelling der voorzieningsbalansen

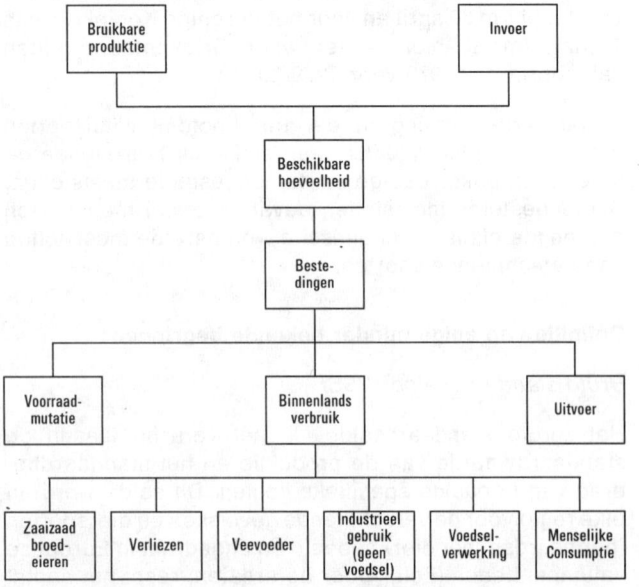

Deze algemene schematische voorstelling kan worden toegepast op de behandelde balansen.
Beschikbare hoeveelheid = Bruikbare produktie + Invoer
Gebruik = Uitvoer + Voorraadmutatie + Binnenlands verbruik

I.E – Dierlijke produktie: het grootste gedeelte van de gegevens over de veestapel, de structuur van de veehouderij naar grootteklasse en de produktie van vlees, melk en zuivelprodukten en eieren wordt door de Lid-Staten verstrekt in het kader van enquêtes en statistieken die uit hoofde van communautaire wetsteksten – verordeningen of richtlijnen van de Raad en richtlijnen of beschikkingen van de Commissie – moeten worden gehouden, resp. opgesteld.

I.F – „Prijzen en prijsindexcijfers"

a) Landbouwprijzen in absolute waarde

De statistiek van de landbouwprijzen in absolute waarde moet de mogelijkheid bieden vergelijkingen te maken van de prijzen van zo mogelijk „identieke" – en dus nauwkeurig gedefinieerde – produkten tussen de Lid-Staten van de Gemeenschap. In werkelijkheid zijn de definities van de produkten evenwel niet volkomen gelijk. Daarom publiceert Eurostat „catalogi van de kenmerken van de in Cronos opgeslagen reeksen landbouwprijzen". Een nieuwe editie van deze publikatie is in voorbereiding.

De door Eurostat geregistreerde landbouwprijzen omvatten in beginsel geen belasting over de toegevoegde waarde. Alleen de niet-aftrekbare of niet-terugvorderbare BTW op bepaalde produktiemiddelen is in de prijzen van de betrokken Lid-Staten begrepen. Dit geldt ook voor andere belastingen of subsidies die specifiek voor bepaalde produkten zijn. Het doel is de prijzen te registreren die het inkomen van de landbouwers bepalen.

Om ervoor te zorgen dat de in nationale valuta uitgedrukte landbouwprijzen in de Lid-Staten van de Gemeenschap onderling kunnen worden vergeleken, worden ze omgerekend in Ecu (Europese valuta-eenheid).

b) EG-indexcijfers van de landbouwprijzen (output en input)

De EG-indexcijfers van de landbouwprijzen „EG-indexcijfers van de producentenprijzen van landbouwprodukten" en de „EG-indexcijfers van de aankoopprijzen van landbouwproduktiemiddelen" zijn opgesteld volgens de methode van Laspeyres door middel van gewichten die zijn vastgesteld voor het basisjaar (1980) en een bepaald pakket landbouwprodukten (voor de output) of goederen en diensten (voor de input). Aan de maandelijkse prijsindexcijfers voor verse groente en fruit liggen variabele gewichten voor de twaalf maanden van het basisjaar ten grondslag. Ook in dit geval is 1980 het referentiejaar.

De EG-indexcijfers van de landbouwprijzen (output en input) berusten in alle Lid-Staten van de Gemeenschap op het begrip „nationaal bedrijf", zodat ze alleen op transacties tussen landbouwproduktie-eenheden en produktie-eenheden buiten de landbouw, met inbegrip van de buitenlandse handel, betrekking hebben. Er wordt geen rekening gehouden met rechtstreekse transacties tussen landbouwers, noch bij de berekening van de gewichten, noch bij de registratie van de produktie- of aankoopprijzen.

Wat de verschillende posten voor de samenstelling van de twee prijsindexcijfers betreft, dient evenwel rekening te worden gehouden met het feit dat de wegingsschema's zijn aangepast aan de produktiestructuur (output en input) van ieder land en dat de goederenpakketten die voor de verkopen en de aankopen van de landbouw zijn gekozen, van land tot land verschillen.

Om de invloed van de in de Gemeenschap geregistreerde uiteenlopende inflatiecijfers uit te sluiten zijn de EG-indexcijfers voor de landbouwprijzen ook in gedefleerde waarden berekend. De deflatie van de EG-indexcijfers van de nominale landbouwprijzen (output en input) geschiedt aan de hand van het prijsindexcijfer voor de gezinsconsumptie.

Andere aspecten van de methoden die aan de EG-indexcijfers van de landbouwprijzen ten grondslag liggen, zijn beschreven in „Methodology of EC Agricultural Price Indices (output and input)".

I.G – Landbouwrekeningen:

de gegevens hebben betrekking op de branche „Produkten van de landbouw en de jacht". Bij de opstelling ervan wordt uitgegaan van het begrip „nationaal bedrijf". Voor de produktie beantwoordt het begrip „finale produktie" hieraan (zie bovenstaand schema).

Exploitatiesubsidies en belastingen in verband met de produktie zijn transacties voor de verdeling van de inkomens, die rechtstreeks met het produktieproces zijn verbonden.

De afschrijvingen geven de waardevermindering weer die de bij het produktieproces gebruikte vaste activa ondergaan ten gevolge van normale slijtage en verlies ten gevolge van toevallige verzekerbare schade. De bruto-investeringen in vaste activa geven de waarde weer van de duurzame goederen die door het nationale bedrijf voor eigen rekening worden aangeschaft om gedurende langer dan één jaar in het landbouwproduktieproces te worden ingeschakeld.

In beginsel wordt de finale produktie van de landbouw gewaardeerd in prijzen „af-bedrijf". Deze prijs „af-bedrijf" is de marktprijs in de optiek van de producent.

Het intermediaire verbruik en de bruto-investeringen in vaste activa worden gewaardeerd in aankoopprijzen. De aankoopprijs is de marktprijs in de optiek van de koper.

De gegevens worden opgesteld volgens het stelsel van nettoregistratie van de belasting over de toegevoegde waarde (BTW): de verschillende posten van de finale produktie, het intermediaire verbruik en de bruto-investeringen in vaste activa zijn exclusief BTW. Enkel het totaal van het intermediaire verbruik omvat in voorkomend geval de ondercompensatie BTW (niet-aftrekbare BTW). Voor nadere informatie zij verwezen naar de toelichting of de publikaties van Eurostat, thema 5, reeks C: Economische rekeningen – Landbouw, bosbouw.

Schema van de finale landbouwproduktie

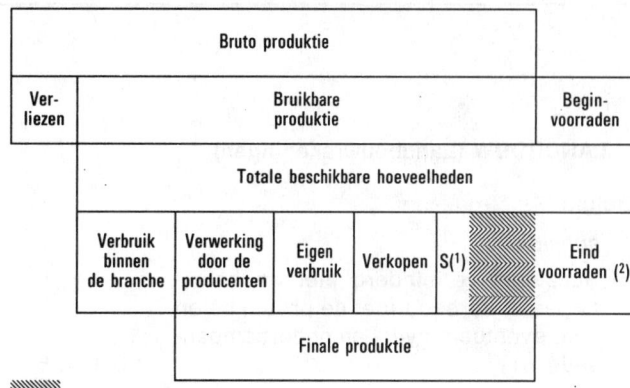

Voorraadmutatie

(¹) Bouw voor eigen rekening.
(²) In bovenstaand schema wordt ervan uitgegaan dat de eindvoorraden groter zijn dan de beginvoorraden.

Schema van de toegevoegde waarde en het landbouwinkomen

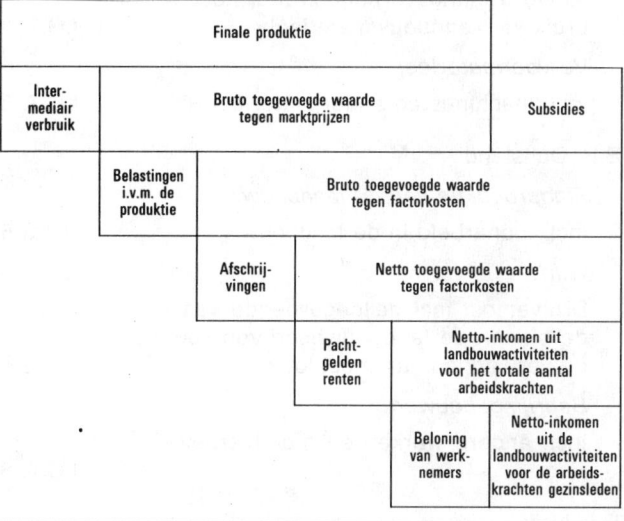

Toelichting per land

I. LANDBOUW (Landbouwrekeningen)

België

subsidies:

Subsidies verminderd met de belastingen in verband met de produktie en incl. eventuele over- en ondercompensatie BTW — I.G.1, 4, 5, 6

Overige plantaardige produkten:

incl. verkopen van producenten die slechts bij gelegenheid verkopen, niet ingedeeld naar produkt — I.G.4, 5

Bruto-investeringen in vaste activa „Totaal":

incl. niet-aftrekbare BTW (gedetailleerde gegevens excl. BTW) — I.G.7, 8

Denemarken

Afschrijvingen:

zonder afschrijvingen van de tuinbouw — I.G.1, 4, 5, 6

Bruto-investeringen in vaste activa:

excl. tuinbouw, fok van pelsdieren en samenwerkingsverbanden voor het gebruik van landbouwmaterieel — I.G.7, 8

Vervoermaterieel:

incl. machines en ander materieel — I.G.7, 8

B.R. Duitsland

Eindproduktie van de landbouw:

incl. loonarbeid in de landbouw — I.G.1 à 6

Wijn:

Druivemost, incl. de toegevoegde waarde binnen de landbouwbedrijven voor de verwerking van most tot wijn — I.G.5

Bedrijfsgebouwen:

incl. andere werken en grondverbetering — I.G.7, 8

Frankrijk

Eindproduktie van de landbouw:

incl. loonarbeid in de landbouw — I.G.1 à 6

Bruto-investeringen in vaste activa „Totaal":

incl. niet-aftrekbare BTW (gedetailleerde gegevens excl. BTW) — I.G.7, 8

Italië

Dierlijke en plantaardige eindproduktie:

incl. BTW, maar zonder andere belastingen in verband met de produktie — I.G.1 à 6

Eindproduktie van de landbouw:

incl. BTW en andere belastingen in verband met de produktie — I.G.1 à 6

Intermediair verbruik:

incl. BTW — I.G.1 à 6

Diversen:

Italië: belastingen in verband met de produktie met uitzondering van BTW — I.G.4, 5

Bruto-investeringen in vaste activa:

incl. bosbouw en visserij — I.G.7, 8

Nieuwe aanplantingen:

incl. bedrijfsgebouwen, andere werken en grondverbetering — I.G.7, 8

Machines en ander materieel:

incl. overige investeringsgoederen — I.G.7, 8

Luxemburg

Bedrijfsgebouwen:

incl. andere werken met uitzondering van grondverbetering — I.G.7, 8

Vervoermaterieel:

incl. machines en ander materieel — I.G.7, 8

Nederland

Bedrijfsgebouwen:

incl. andere werken met uitzondering van grondverbetering — I.G.7, 8

Verenigd Koninkrijk

Eindproduktie van de landbouw:

incl. loonarbeid in de landbouw — I.G.1 à 6

II. BOSBOUW

II.A. Algemeen overzicht: voor de methoden en met name voor de opmerkingen per Lid-Staat zij verwezen naar resp.

- „Bosstatistieken – Methoden"
- „Bosstatistieken – Tabellen".

Deze publikaties zijn door Eurostat in alle talen van de Gemeenschap gepubliceerd.

II.B. Bosbouwrekeningen: zie ook de toelichting op I.G. De gegevens hebben betrekking op de branche „Ruwhout". Bij de opstelling is uitgegaan van het begrip „nationaal bos" (naar analogie van het begrip „nationaal bedrijf" in de landbouwrekeningen).

De eindproduktie van de bosbouw is gewaardeerd in prijzen „uitgesleept, kant van de weg".

Verder zij de lezer verwezen naar de toelichting op de methoden in deel I.G., die naar analogie van toepassing zijn. Nadere informatie wordt gegeven in de toelichting of de publikaties van Eurostat, thema 5, reeks C: *Economische Rekeningen – Landbouw, Bosbouw.*

Belgïe

Subsidies:

subsidies verminderd met de belastingen, in verband met de produktie en incl. eventuele over - of ondercompensatie BTW.   II.B.1

BR Duitsland

Referentiejaar:

bosbouwjaar van 1. 10 t/m 30. 9   II.B.1

Eindproduktie: ·

incl. „overige produkten"   ·   II.B.1

Italïe

Intermediair verbruik:

incl. BTW   II.B.1

Referentiejaar:

bosbouwjaar van 1. 4 t/m 31. 3   II.B.1

Eindproduktie:

incl. „overige produkten"   II.B.1

Luxemburg

Referentiejaar:

bosbouwjaar van 1. 10 t/m 30. 9   II.B.1

Verenigd Koninkrijk

Referentiejaar:

Bosbouwjaar van 1. 4 t/m 31. 3   II.B.1

Referentiegegevens:

zonder Noord-Ierland waarvan de niet erg significante gegevens niet beschikbaar zijn   II.B.1

III. **VISSERIJ**

III.2.3 – **Vangsten:** de vangstgegevens zijn door de Lid-Staten verstrekt via vragenlijsten van het Statlant-stelsel, waarvan de verwerking door de FAO wordt gecoördineerd. De gegevens hebben betrekking op de nominale vangsten in zoet en brak water, alsmede op in zee levende soorten vissen, schaal-, schelp- en weekdieren en andere dieren en planten, gedood, gevangen, geplukt, gekweekt of gefokt voor alle commerciële, industriële of voedingsdoeleinden. De door de sportvisserij gevangen hoeveelheden worden buiten beschouwing gelaten. Het begrip nominale vangsten heeft betrekking op de aangevoerde hoeveelheden omgerekend in levend gewicht.

III.4 – **Vissersvloot:** de gegevens zijn ontleend aan het statistisch register van vissersvaartuigen van de Gemeenschap, maar soms ontbreekt het nationale register (E + P) of is het onvolledig (b.v. voor vaartuigen met een gering tonnenmaat in DK, GR. IRL en VK); de gegevens zijn aangevuld met informatie uit de andere bronnen.

NL

Tekens en afkortingen

–	Geen	hl	Hectoliter
0	Minder dan de helft van de gebruikte eenheid	ha	Hectare
		Mio	Miljoen
:	Geen gegevens beschikbaar	mm	Millimeter
S	Geheim	°C	Graad Celsius
prov./p	Voorlopig	m³(r)	Kubieke meter rondhout, ruwhoutequivalent
*	Schatting van Eurostat	AA/SAU	Oppervlakte cultuurgrond
n.d.a./a.d.a.	Elders genoemd noch elders onder begrepen	LU/UGB	Grootvee-eenheid
		GRT/TJB	Brutoregisterton
r	Nieuw of herzien cijfer	AWU/UTA	Arbeidsjaareenheid
M/Ø	Gemiddelde	SGM/MBS/	
MP/ØP	Gewogen gemiddelde	BSS	Bruto standaardsaldo
%	Percentage	ESU/UDE/	
% AT	Wijzigingspercentage	EGE	Europese Grootte-Eenheid
AM	Gemiddelde jaarlijkse toename	EUR 10	Alle Lid-Staten van de EG, behalve Spanje en Portugal
–I	Onderbreking in de vergelijkbaarheid	EUR 12	Alle Lid-Staten van de EG
ECU	Europese valuta-eenheid	Eurostat	Bureau voor de Statistiek van de Europese Gemeenschappen
BFR	Belgische frank		
DKR	Deense kroon	EC/CE	Europese Gemeenschappen
DM	Duitse mark	DOM	Overzeese departementen
DR	Drachme	B + L/	
ESC	Escudo	UEBL/BLEU	Belgisch-Luxemburgse Economische Unie
FF	Franse frank		
HFL	Gulden	OECD/OCDE/	
IRL	Iers pond	OESO	Organisatie voor Economische Samenwerking en Ontwikkeling
LIT	Lire		
LFR	Luxemburgse frank	FAO	Voedsel- en landbouworganisatie van de Verenigde Naties
PTA	Peseta		
UKL	Pond sterling	IMF/FMI	Internationaal Monetair Fonds
t	Metrieke ton		

Glossary

Glossaire

N° (CRONOS-ZPAI)

N°	Glosar over arealanvendelse	Γλωσσάριο χρήσης του εδάφους	Glossary of land use	Glossaire de l'utilisation des terres	Lijst van het bodemgebruik
0000	**SAMLET AREAL**	**ΣΥΝΟΛΙΚΗ ΕΚΤΑΣΗ**	**TOTAL AREA**	**SUPERFICIE TOTALE**	**TOTALE OPPERVLAKTE**
0009	Vand	Ύδατα	Water	Eaux	Water
0008	Landarealer	Έκταση της γης	Land area	Superficie des terres	Landoppervlakte
0007	Andre arealer, ikke andetsteds anført	Λοιπές εκτάσεις	Other area, not otherwise specified	Autre superficie, non dénommée ailleurs	Overige oppervlakte, nergens anders vermeld
0006	Skovbevokset areal	Δασικές εκτάσεις	Wooded area	Superficie boisée	Oppervlakte bos
0063	Skovareal	Δασική έκταση	Forest land	Superficie forestière	Bosgrond
0005	UDNYTTEDE LANDBRUGS-AREALER	ΧΡΗΣΙΜΟΠΟΙΟΥΜΕΝΗ ΓΕΩΡΓΙΚΗ ΓΗ	UTILIZED AGRICULTURAL AREA	SUPERFICIE AGRICOLE UTILISÉE	OPPERVLAKTE CULTUURGROND
0001	DYRKEDE AREALER	ΑΡΟΤΡΑΙΕΣ ΕΚΤΑΣΕΙΣ	ARABLE LAND	TERRES ARABLES	BOUWLAND
1050	**Korn i alt**	**Σύνολο δημητριακών**	**Total cereals**	**Céréales totales**	**Totaal granen**
1100	Hvede og spelt	Σιτάρι και όλυρα	Wheat and spelt	Blé et épeautre	Tarwe en spelt
1120	Blød hvede	Σιτάρι μαλακό	Common wheat	Blé tendre	Zachte tarwe
1123	Blød vinterhvede	Χειμερινό σιτάρι μαλακό	Common winter wheat	Blé tendre d'hiver	Zachte wintertarwe
1124	Blød vårhvede	Εαρινό σιτάρι μαλακό	Common spring wheat	Blé tendre de printemps	Zachte zomertarwe
1130	Hård hvede	Σιτάρι σκληρό	Durum wheat	Blé dur	Harde tarwe
1133	Hård vinterhvede	Χειμερινό σιτάρι σκληρό	Durum winter wheat	Blé dur d'hiver	Harde wintertarwe
1134	Hård vårhvede	Εαρινό σιτάρι σκληρό	Durum spring wheat	Blé dur de printemps	Harde zomertarwe
1150	Rug	Σίκαλη	Rye	Seigle	Rogge
1151	Vinterrug	Χειμερινή σίκαλη	Winter rye	Seigle d'hiver	Winterrogge
1152	Vårrug	Εαρινή σίκαλη	Spring rye	Seigle de printemps	Zomerrogge
1155	Vinterblandsæd	Σμιγός	Maslin	Méteil	Masteluin
1160	Byg	Κριθάρι	Barley	Orge	Gerst
1163	Vinterbyg	Χειμερινό κριθάρι	Winter barley	Orge d'hiver	Wintergerst
1164	Vårbyg	Εαρινό κριθάρι	Spring barley	Orge de printemps	Zomergerst
1180	Havre	Βρώμη	Oats	Avoine	Haver
1185	Blandsæd	Μείγματα θερινών δημητριακών	Mixed grains other than maslin	Mélanges de céréales d'été	Mengsels van zomergranen
1200	Majs	Σπόροι αραβοσίτου	Grain maize	Maïs grain	Korrelmaïs
1211	Milokron	Σόργο	Sorghum	Sorgho	Sorghum
1212	Triticale	Triticum (είδος σίτου)	Triticale	Triticale	Triticale
1219	Hirse, boghvede, kanariefrø, i.a.a.	Κεχρί, φαγόπυρο, φάλαρις (κέχρος ο μακρός)	Millet, buckwheat, canary seed, n.o.s.	Millet, sarrasin, alpiste, non dénommés ailleurs	Gierst, boekweit, kanariezaad, nergens anders vermeld
1250	**Ris**	**Ρύζι**	**Rice**	**Riz**	**Rijst**
1300	**Bælgsæd til modning**	**Ξηρά όσπρια**	**Dried pulses**	**Légumes secs**	**Droog geoogste peulvruchten**
1310	Ærter	Μπιζέλια	Peas	Pois	Erwten
1311	Andre ærter ekskl. foderærter	Ξηρά μπιζέλια εκτός κτηνοτροφικών μπιζελιών	Peas other than field peas	Pois secs autres que pois fourragers	Andere erwten dan voedererwten
1320	Foderærter	Κτηνοτροφικά μπιζέλια	Field peas	Pois fourragers	Voedererwten
1330	Bønner	Φασόλια, κουκιά και λάθηροι	Beans	Haricots, fèves et féveroles	Bonen
1331	Spisebønner	Ξηρά φασόλια	Kidney beans	Haricots secs	Bruine en witte bonen
1335	Hestebønner	Κουκιά και λάθηροι	Broad and field beans	Fèves et féveroles	Veldbonen
1338	Hestebønner, maj. og min. (fødevarer)	Κουκιά και λάθηροι (ανθρ. κατανάλωση)	Broad and field beans (human consumption)	Fèves et féveroles (cons. hum.)	Tuin- en veldbonen (menselijke consumptie)
1340	Anden bælgsæd	Λοιπά όσπρια	Other dried pulses	Autres légumes secs	Andere droog geoogste peulvruchten
1341	Linser	Φακές	Lentils	Lentilles	Linzen
1342	Vikker	Αρακάς	Vetches	Vesces	Wikken
1343	Lupiner	Λούπινα	Lupins	Lupins	Lupinen
1349	Anden bælgsæd, ikke andetsteds anført	Λοιπά ξηρά λαχανικά που δεν αναφέρονται αλλού	Other dried pulses, not otherwise specified	Autres légumes secs, non dénommés ailleurs	Andere droog geoogste peulvruchten, nergens anders vermeld
1350	**Rodfrugter**	**Φυτά με ριζώματα ή κονδύλους**	**Root crops**	**Plantes sarclées**	**Hakvruchten**
1360	Kartofler	Πατάτες	Potatoes	Pommes de terre	Aardappelen
1362	Tidlige kartofler	Πρώιμες πατάτες	Early potatoes	Pommes de terre hâtives	Vroege aardappelen
1363	Andre kartofler	Λοιπές πατάτες	Other potatoes	Autres pommes de terre	Andere aardappelen
1370	Sukkerroer	Ζαχαρότευτλα	Sugarbeets	Betteraves sucrières	Suikerbieten
1381	Runkelroer	Κτηνοτροφικά τεύτλα	Fodder beets	Betteraves fourragères	Voederbieten
1382	Andre rodfrugter	Λοιπά φυτά με ριζώματα ή κονδύλους	Other root crops	Autres plantes sarclées	Andere hakvruchten
1383	Foderkål	Κτηνοτροφικά λάχανα	Fodder kale	Choux fourragers	Voederkool
1384	Kålroer	Ράιβα (Ρουταμπάγα)	Swedes	Rutabagas	Koolrapen
1385	Gulerødder til foder	Κτηνοτροφικά καρότα	Carrots for stockfeeding	Carottes fourragères	Voederwortelen
1386	Turnips til foder	Κτηνοτροφικά γογγύλια	Turnips for stockfeeding	Navets fourragers	Stoppelknollen
1390	Andre rodfrugter, ikke andetsteds anført	Λοιπά φυτά με ριζώματα ή κονδύλους που δεν αναφέρονται αλλού	Other root crops, not otherwise specified	Autres plantes sarclées, non dénommées ailleurs	Andere hakvruchten, nergens anders vermeld
1400	**Industriplanter**	**Βιομηχανικά φυτά**	**Industrial crops**	**Plantes industrielles**	**Handelsgewassen**
1410	Olieholdige frø	Ελαιούχοι σπόροι	Oilseeds	Graines oléagineuses	Oliehoudende zaden
1420	Raps og rybs	Κράμβη ελαιώδης	Rape and turnip rape	Colza et navette	Koolzaad en raapzaad
1430	Raps	Κράμβη ελαιώδης	Rape	Colza	Koolzaad
1431	Vinterraps	Χειμερινή	Winter rape	Colza d'hiver	Winterkoolzaad
1432	Vårraps	Θερινή	Summer rape	Colza d'été	Zomerkoolzaad
1440	Rybs	Αγριογογγύλια	Turnip rape	Navette	Raapzaad
1450	Solsikkekerner	Ηλιόσπορος	Sunflower seeds	Graines de tournesol	Zonnebloempitten
1460	Oliehør	Ελαιώδες λινάρι	Oil flax	Lin oléagineux	Lijnzaad
1470	Sojabønner	Σπέρματα σόγιας	Soya beans	Graines de soja	Sojabonen
1480	Andre olieplanter	Λοιπά ελαιώδη φυτά από τα οποία:	Other oilseeds of which:	Autres plantes oléagineuses dont:	Andere oliehoudende gewassen waaronder:
1481	Sennepsfrø (:)	Σπόροι σινάπεως (:)	Mustard seed (:)	graines de moutarde (:)	Mosterdzaad (:)
1482	Valmuefrø (:)	Σπόροι μήκωνος (:)	Poppy seed (:)	graines d'œillette (:)	Blauwmaanzaad (:)
1485	Sesamfrø (:)	Σπόροι σησάμου (:)	Sesame seed (:)	graines de sésame (:)	Egyptisch oliezaad:
1490	Bomuldsfrø	Σπόροι βάμβακος	Cotton seed	graines de coton	Katoenzaad

Glosar over arealanvendelse	Γλωσσάριο χρήσης του εδάφους	Glossary of land use	Glossaire de l'utilisation des terres	Lijst van het bodemgebruik

Nº (CRONOS-ZPAI)

Nº	Danish	Greek	English	French	Dutch
1500	Tekstilplanter	Κλωστικά φυτά	Textile crops	Plantes textiles	Textielplanten
1520	Spindhør	Λινάρι	Flax	Lin	Vlas
1530	Hamp til spinding	Καννάβι	Hemp	Chanvre	Hennep
1540	Bomuld	Βαμβάκι	Cotton	Coton	Katoen
1545	Andre tekstilplanter	Λοιπά κλωστικά φυτά	Other textile crops	Autres plantes textiles	Andere textielplanten
1550	Tobak	Καπνός	Tobacco	Tabac	Tabak
1560	Humle	Λυκίσκος	Hops	Houblon	Hop
1570	Andre industriplanter	Λοιπά βιομηχανικά φυτά	Other industrial crops	Autres plantes industrielles	Andere handelsgewassen
1571	Cikorie	Κιχώριο (ραδίκι) για καφέ	Chicory	Chicorée à café	Chicorei
1580	Medicinalplanter, aroma- og krydderurter heraf:	Ιατρικά, αρωματικά και αρτυματικά φυτά από τα οποία:	Officinal herbs, aromatic plants, plants for seasoning of which:	Plantes médicinales, aromatiques et condimentaires dont:	Geneeskrachtige, aromatische en welriekende planten waaronder:
1582	Kommen	Κύμινο	caraway	le cumin	Karwij
1589	Andre industriplanter, ikke andetsteds anført	Λοιπά βιομηχανικά φυτά που δεν αναφέρονται αλλού	Other industrial crops, not otherwise specified	Autres plantes industrielles, non dénommées ailleurs	Andere handelsgewassen, nergens anders vermeld
1600	**Grønsager**	**Λαχανικά**	**Vegetables**	**Légumes**	**Groententeelt**
3001	**Blomster og prydplanter**	**Καλλωπιστικά φυτά και άνθη**	**Flowers and ornemental plants**	**Fleurs et plantes ornamentales**	**Bloemen- en siergewassenteelt**
2600	**Foder i alt**	**Σύνολο κτηνοτροφικών φυτών**	**Total fodder**	**Total fourrages**	**Totaal groenvoeder**
2610	Grovfoder i omdriften	Χλωρά κτηνοτροφικά φυτά από αροτραίες εκτάσεις	Green fodder from arable land	Fourrages verts des terres arables	Groenvoedergewassen
2611	Etårige grovfoderkulturer	Ετήσια χλωρά κτηνοτροφικά φυτά	Annual green fodder	Fourrages verts annuels	Eenjarige
2625	Fodermajs	Κτηνοτροφικός αραβόσιτος	Green maize	Maïs fourrage	Voedermaïs
2612	Andre etårige grovfoderkulturer	Λοιπά χλωρά ετήσια κτηνοτροφικά φυτά	Other annual green fodder	Autres fourrages verts annuels	Andere eenjarige groenvoedergewassen
2670	Flerårige grovfoderkulturer	Χλωρά πολυετή κτηνοτροφικά φυτά	Perennial green fodder	Fourrages verts pluriannuels	Meerjarige groenvoedergewassen
2671	Kløver og blandinger	Τριφύλλια και μείγματα	Clover and mixtures	Trèfles et mélanges	Klaver en mengsels
2672	Lucerne	Μηδική	Lucerne	Luzerne	Luzerne
2673	Andre bælgplanter	Λοιπά λαχανώδη	Other legumes	Autres légumineuses	Andere leguminosen
2680	Græsmark og græsgang i omdriften	Προσωρινοί λειμώνες και βοσκότοποι	Temporary grasses and grazings	Prairies et pâturages temporaires	Tijdelijk hooi- en weiland
2681	Græsmark i omdriften	Προσωρινοί λειμώνες	Temporary grasses	Prairies temporaires	Tijdelijk hooiland
2682	Græsgang i omdriften	Προσωρινοί βοσκότοποι	Temporary grazings	Pâturages temporaires	Tijdelijk weiland
0002	**VARIGE GRÆSEAREALER**	**ΕΚΤΑΣΕΙΣ ΜΟΝΙΜΩΣ ΚΑΛΥΜΜΕΝΕΣ ΜΕ ΧΟΡΤΟ**	**PERMANENT GRASSLAND**	**SUPERFICIES TOUJOURS COUVERTES D'HERBE**	**BLIJVEND GRASLAND**
2710	Græsmark uden for omdriften	Μόνιμοι λειμώνες	Permanent meadows	Prairies permanentes	Blijvend hooiland
2720	Græsgang uden for omdriften	Μόνιμοι βοσκότοποι	Permanent pastures	Pâturages permanents	Blijvend weiland
2721	– Værdifuld eller middelmådig	– Βοσκές	– Herbages	. – Herbages	– Goede en middelmatige weilanden
2722	– Lidet værdifuld	–'Άγριοι πτωχοί βοσκότοποι	– Rough grazings	– Parcours landes, alpages	– Arme weilanden
3310	**Frø til udsæd**	**Καλλιέργειες σποραπαραγωγής**	**Areas harvested for seed**	**Cultures de semence**	**Aanbouw van zaden**
2695	**Andre landbrugsafgrøder**	**Λοιπά προϊόντα αγρών**	**Other field products**	**Autres produits des champs**	**Overige akkerbouwprodukten**
2695	**Brak og grundforbedrings- planter**	**Αγραναπαύσεις και χλωρές λιπάνσεις**	**Fallow and green-manures**	**Jachères et engrais verts**	**Braakland en groenbemesting**
0003	**VARIGE KULTURER**	**ΜΟΝΙΜΕΣ ΦΥΤΕΙΕΣ**	**LAND UNDER PERMANENT CROPS**	**CULTURES PERMANENTES**	**BLIJVENDE GEWASSEN**
2040	Frugttræer	Οπωροφόρα δένδρα	Orchards	Arbres fruitiers	Fruitbomen
2060	Jordbær	Φράουλες	Strawberries	Fraises	Aardbeien
2270	Bær	Χαμοκέρασα, μούρα κλπ.	Soft fruit	Baies	Kleinfruit
2300	Citrusfrugter	Εσπεριδοειδή	Citrus fruit	Agrumes	Citrusvruchten
2410	Vindyrkning	Αμπέλια	Vineyards	Vignes	Wijngaarden
2450	Oliven	Ελαιόδενδρα	Olive growing	Oliveraies	Olijven
2810	Planteskoler	Φυτώρια	Hardy nursery stocks	Pépinières	Boomkwekerijen
2960	Vidjeplantning	Ιτεώνες	Osier-willows	Oseraies	Grienden
2980	Andre varige kulturer	Λοιπές μόνιμες φυτείες	Other land under permanent crops	Autres cultures permanentes	Overige blijvende gewassen
0004	**KØKKENHAVER**	**ΟΙΚΟΓΕΝΕΙΑΚΟΙ ΚΗΠΟΙ**	**KITCHEN GARDENS**	**JARDINS FAMILIAUX**	**TUINEN VOOR EIGEN GEBRUIK**
	(:) Oplysning foreligger ikke	(:) δεν παρέχονται στοιχεία	(:) no data available	(:) donnée non disponible	(:) Geen gegevens beschikbaar

Glosar over navne på grønsager	Γλωσσάριο ονομάτων λαχανικών	Glossary of vegetable names	Glossaire des noms de légumes	Lijst met namen van groenten

Nº (CRONOS-ZPAI)

Nº	Danish	Greek	English	French	Dutch
1600	**FRISKE GRØNSAGER**	**ΝΩΠΑ ΛΑΧΑΝΙΚΑ**	**FRESH VEGETABLES**	**LÉGUMES FRAIS**	**VERSE GROENTEN**
1610	**Spisekål**	**Φαγώσιμα λάχανα**	**All brassicas (excl. roots)**	**Choux potagers**	**Consumptiekool**
1620	Blomkål	Κουνουπίδια	Cauliflower	Choux-fleurs	Bloemkool
1631	Rosenkål	Λάχανα Βρυξελλών	Brussels sprouts	Choux de Bruxelles	Spruitkool
1635	Hvidkål	Λάχανο λευκό (ή πολυκέφαλο)	Cabbage	Choux blancs (ou cabus)	Witte kool
1655	Rødkål	Κόκκινο λάχανο	Red cabbage	Choux rouges	Roodkool
	Grønkål	Ουλοκράμβη	Curly kale	Choux frisés, choux verts	Boerenkool
	Savoykål	Λάχανο Σαβοΐας	Savoy	Choux de Savoie	Savooiekool
	Kinakål	Λάχανο Κίνας	Chinese cabbage	Choux de Chine, Petsai	Chinesekool
	Anden kål, ikke andetsteds anført	Λοιπά λάχανα	Brassicas, not otherwise specified	Autres choux, non dénommés ailleurs	Andere koolsoorten, nergens anders vermeld

Glosar over navne på grønsager	Γλωσσάριο ονομάτων λαχανικών	Glossary of vegetable names	Glossaire des noms de légumes	Lijst met namen van groenten

N° (CRONOS-ZPAI)

1660	Blad- og stængelgrønsager, ekskl. kål	Λοιπά φυλλώδη λαχανικά εκτός λαχάνων	Leafy or stalked vegetables excl. brassicas	Légumes feuillus et à tige sauf choux	Blad- en stengelgroenten anders dan kool
1670	Knoldselleri, bladselleri	Σέλινα	Celeriac and celery	Céleris-raves et céleris branche	Knolselderij en bleekselderij
1675	Porrer	Πράσσα	Leeks	Poireaux	Prei
1680	Salat	Μαρούλια	Lettuce	Laitues pommées	Sla
1685	Endivie	Ραδίκια	Endive	Chicorées frisées et scaroles	Andijvie
1690	Spinat	Σπανάκια	Spinach	Épinards	Spinazie
1700	Asparges	Σπαράγγια	Asparagus	Asperges	Asperges
1710	Cikorie	Αντίδια	Chicory	Chicorées (endives)	Chicorei
1720	Artiskokker	Αγκινάρες	Globe artichoke	Artichauts	Artisjokken
1725	Basilikum	Βασιλικός	Basil	Basilic	Bazielkruid
	Bladbede	Σέσκουλο	Chard, white beet	Bettes, poirées	Snijbiet
	Kardon	Αγριαγκινάρα	Cardoon	Cardons	Kardoen
	Kørvel	Χαιρέφυλλο (φραγκομαϊντανός)	Chervil	Cerfeuil	Kervel
	Karse	Κάρδαμο (λεπίδιο το εδώδιμο)	Garden cress	Cresson alénois	Tuinkers
	Brøndkarse	Νεροκάρδαμο (Σισύμβριο)	Watercress	Cresson de fontaine	Waterkers
	Estragon	Δρακόντιο (εστραγκόν)	Tarragon	Estragon	Dragon
	Fennikel	Φοινίκουλο το κοινό (Μάραθο)	Fennel	Fenouil	Venkel
	Vårsalat	Σμύριο	Corn-salad	Mâche	Veldsla
	Syre	Οξαλίδα	Sorrel	Oseille	Zuring
	Persille	Πετροσέλινο (μαϊντανός)	Parsley	Persil	Peterselie
	Løvetand	Αφάκη	Dandelion	Pissenlit	Molsla
	Portulak	Ανδράχνη	Purslane	Pourpier	Postelein
	Rabarber	Ρήο (ραβέντι)	Rhubarb	Rhubarbe	Rabarber
	Timian	Θύμος ο κοινός (θυμάρι)	Thyme	Thym	Tijm
	Andre blad- og stængelgrønsager, ikke andetsteds anført	Λοιπά φυλλώδη λαχανικά ή με στέλεχος που δεν αναφέρονται αλλού	Other leafy or stalked vegetables, not otherwise specified	Autres légumes feuillus et à tige, non dénommés ailleurs	Andere blad- en stengelgroenten, nergens anders vermeld

1740	Frugtgrønsager	Λαχανικά που καλλιεργούνται για τον καρπό	Vegetables cultivated for fruit	Légumes cultivés pour le fruit	Vruchtgroenten
1750	Tomater	Τομάτες	Tomatoes	Tomates	Tomaten
1761	Salatagurker (og asier)	Αγγούρια	Cucumbers	Concombres	Komkommers
1766					
1771	Drueagurker	Αγγουράκια	Gherkins	Cornichons	Augurken
1777	Meloner	Πεπόνια	Melons	Melons	Meloenen
1781	Vandmeloner	Καρπούζια	Watermelons	Pastèques	Watermeloenen
1785	Auberginer	Μελιτζάνες	Egg-plant	Aubergines	Aubergines
	Centnergræskar, mandelgræskar	Κολοκύθια, κολοκυθάκια, γλυκοκολοκύθες	Gourds, marrows, pumpkins	Courges, courgettes, citrouilles	Zucchini, reuzenkalebas
1790	Spansk peber, paprika	Πιπεριές κόκκινες	Red pepper, capsicum	Poivrons	Paprika
1799	Gombo	Ιβίσκος ο εδώδιμος (μπάμια)	Gombo, okra	Gombo	Gombo, Okra
	Andre frugtgrønsager, ikke andetsteds anført	Λοιπά λαχανικά που καλλιεργούνται για τον καρπό	Other veg. cultiv. for fruit, not otherwise specified	Autres lég. cultiv. pour le fruit, non dénommés ailleurs	Andere vruchtgroenten, nergens anders vermeld

1800	Rod- og knoldgrønsager	Φυτά με ριζώματα ή κονδύλους	Root and tuber vegetables	Racines, bulbes, tubercules	Wortelen en knollen
1810	Knudelkål, glaskålrabi	Γογγυλοκράμβες	Kohlrabi	Choux-raves	Koolrabi
1820	Majroer	Φαγώσιμα γογγύλια	Turnips	Navets potagers	Rapen (mei-, herfstknol)
1830	Karotter, gulerødder	Καρότα	Carrots	Carottes	Peen
1840	Hvidløg	Σκόρδα	Garlic	Ail	Knoflook
1851	Kepaløg	Κρεμμύδια	Onions	Oignons	Uien
1855	Skalotteløg	Ασκαλώνια	Shallots	Échalotes	Sjalotten
1860	Rødbeder	Εδώδιμα τεύτλα	Beetroot	Betteraves potagères	Kroten
1870	Havrerod og skorsonerrod	Τραγοπώγωνες	Salsify and scorzonera	Salsifis et scorsonères	Schorseneer en haverwortel
1877	Radiser	Ραφανίδες	Radish	Radis	Radijs
1884	Purløg	Κρόμμυο το σχοινόπρασο (πρασουλίδα)	Chives	Ciboulette, civette	Bieslook
	Kinesisk artiskok	Αγκινάρα Κίνας	Chinese artichoke	Crosnes	Andoorn
	Pastinak	Παστινάκη η εδώδιμος	Parsnip	Panais	Pastinaak
	Peberrod	Ράφανος (ρεπάνι)	Horse-radish	Raifort	Mierikswortel
	Sort ræddike	Ραφανίς η εδώδιμος (μαυρορὰπανο)	Black radish	Radis noirs	Ramenas
	Andre rod- og knoldgrønsager	Λοιπά φυτά με ριζώματα ή κονδύλους (Ρεπάνια κλπ.)	Other root and tuber vegetables	Autres racines, bulbes et tubercules	Andere wortelen en knollen

1885	Bælgfrugter	Λοβοφόρα λαχανικά	Pulses	Légumes à cosse	Peulvruchten
1890	Ærter i alt, uden bælge	Μπιζέλια αποφλοιωμένα	All peas, shelled weight	Petits pois, convertis en pois sans gousses	Doperwten omgerekend zonder peul
1901	Bønner	Χλωρά φασόλια	Beans, runner and French	Haricots verts	Snij- en sperziebonen
1905	Voksbønne	Φασίολος ο κοινός (φασόλια για αποφλοίωση)	Butter bean	Haricots à écosser	Dopboon
	Hestebønne	Φάβα	Broad bean	Fèves	Tuinboon
	Andre bælgfrugter, ikke andetsteds anført	Λοιπά λοβοφόρα λαχανικά	Other pulses, not otherwise specified	Autres légumes à cosse, non dénommés ailleurs	Andere peulvruchten, nergens anders vermeld

1910	Drevne champignons	Καλλιεργημένα μανιτάρια	Cultivated mushrooms	Champignons de culture	Champignons
1920	Sukkermajs	Γλυκό καλαμπόκι	Sweetcorn	Maïs doux	Zoete maïs
	Andre friske grønsager, ikke andetsteds anført	Λοιπά νωπά λαχανικά που δεν αναφέρονται αλλού	Other fresh vegetables, not otherwise specified	Autres légumes frais, non dénommés aileurs	Andere verse groenten, nergens anders vermeld

3718	VILDE PRODUKTER	ΣΥΓΚΟΜΙΖΟΜΕΝΑ ΑΓΡΙΑ ΠΡΟΪΟΝΤΑ	WILD PRODUCTS	PRODUITS DE CUEILLETTE	WILDGROEIENDE PRODUKTEN
	Mark- og skovchampignons	Αγριομανιτάρι	Field and forest mushrooms	Champignons des prés et forêts	Veld- en bospaddestoelen
	Trøfler	Τρούφα	Truffle	Truffes	Truffel
	Andre	Λοιπά	Other	Autres	Andere

2992	Friske grønsager (privatavl)	Νωπά λαχανικά (οικογενεια-κών κήπων)	Fresh vegetables (kitchen gardens)	Légumes frais (de jardins)	Verse groenten (tuin v. eigen gebruik)

Glosar over navne på frugter	Γλωσσάριο ονομάτων λαχανικών	Glossary of fruit names	Glossaire des noms de fruits	Lijst met namen van fruit
N° (CRONOS-ZPAI)				
FRISK FRUGT (2040 TIL 2059)	**ΝΩΠΑ ΦΡΟΥΤΑ (2040 έως 2259)**	**FRESH FRUIT (2040 to 2259)**	**FRUITS FRAIS (2040 à 2259)**	**VERS FRUIT (2040 TOT 2259)**
2008 Spisefrugt	Επιτραπέζια φρούτα	Dessert fruit	Fruits de table	Tafelfruit
2009 Spisefrugt (inkl. privatavl)	Επιτραπέζια φρούτα (περιλαμβανομένων και οικογενειακών κήπων)	Dessert fruit (incl. kitchen gardens)	Fruits de table (y compris jardins)	Tafelfruit (incl. tuin v. eigen gebruik)
2040 Frugttræer (ekskl. oliven og citrusfrugter)	Οπωροφόρα δένδρα (μη περιλαμβανομένων των ελαιοδένδρων και εσπεριδοειδών)	Fruit trees (excl. olives and citrus fruits)	Arbres fruitiers (sans olives et agrumes)	Fruitbomen (zonder olijven en citrusvruchten)
2090 Æbler	Μήλα	Apples	Pommes	Appelen
2110 heraf: Spiseæbler	από τα οποία: επιτραπέζια μήλα	comprising: dessert apples	dont: pommes de table	waarvan: tafelappelen
2095 Pærer	Αχλάδια	Pears	Poires	Peren
2130 heraf: Spisepærer	από τα οποία: επιτραπέζια αχλάδια	comprising dessert pears	dont: poires de table	waarvan: tafelperen
2170 Stenfrugter	**Πυρηνόκαρπα**	**Stone fruit**	**Fruits à noyau**	**Kernvruchten**
2180 Ferskner	Ροδάκινα	Peaches	Pêches	Perziken
2190 Abrikoser	Βερίκοκκα	Apricots	Abricots	Abrikozen
2200 Kirsebær	Κεράσια	Cherries	Cerises	Kersen
2210 Blommer (og reine-clauder, mirabeller, svedskeblommer)	Δαμάσκηνα	Plums (incl. mirabelle plums, greengages and damsons)	Prunes (y compris mirabelles, reines-claudes et quetsches)	Pruimen (incl. Reine-Clauden, mirabellen en kwetsen)
2221 Nektariner	Νεκταρίνια	Nectarines	Nectarines et brugnons	Nectarinen
2229 Slåen	Αγριόκορδμηλο (πρυύμνη η ακανθώδης)	Sloe	Prunelles	Sleepruim
Japansk mispel	Μούσμουλο Ιαπωνίας (Εριοβοτρύα η ιαπωνική)	Loquat, Japanese medlar	Nèfles du Japon, Bibaces	Japanse Mispel
Andre stenfrugter, ikke andetsteds anført	Άλλα πυρηνόκαρπα	Other stone fruit, not otherwise specified	Autres fruits à noyau, non dénommés ailleurs	Andere kernvruchten, nergens anders vermeld
2230 Nødder	**Καρποί με κέλυφος**	**Nuts**	**Fruits à coque**	**Schaalvruchten**
2231 Valnødder	Καρύδια	Walnuts	Noix	Walnoten
2232 Hasselnødder	Λεπτοκάρυδα (φουντούκια)	Hazelnuts	Noisettes	Hazelnoten
2233 Mandler	Αμύγδαλα	Almonds	Amandes	Amandelen
2236 Kastanier	Κάστανα	Chestnuts	Châtaignes	Kastanjes
2240 Pistace, grøn nød	Φιστίκι (Αιγίνης)	Pistachio nuts	Pistaches	Pistache
Andre nødder, ikke andetsteds anført	Λοιποί καρποί με κέλυφος	Other nuts, not otherwise specified	Autres fruits à coque, non dénommés ailleurs	Andere schaalvruchten, nergens anders vermeld
2250 Andre frugter af træer	**Άλλοι καρποί ξυλωδών φυτών**	**Other fruits of woody plants**	**Autres fruits de plantes ligneuses**	**Andere boomvruchten**
2251 Figen	Σύκα	Figs	Figues	Vijgen
2252 Kvæder	Κυδώνια	Quinces	Coings	Kweeën
2259 Banan	Μπανάνα	Banana	Bananes	Banaan
Ananas	Ανανάς	Pineapple	Ananas	Ananas
Advokatpære	Αβοκάντο (Περσέα η ηδύκαρπος)	Avocado	Avocats	Avocado
Mispel	Μούσμουλο (μεσπιλέα η γερμανική)	Medlar	Nèfles	Mispel
Daddel	Χουρμάς	Dates	Dattes	Dadel
Andre frugter af træer, ikke andetsteds anført	Καρποί ξυλωδών φυτών που δεν αναφέρονται αλλού	Other fruits of woody plants, not otherwise specified	Fruits de plantes ligneuses, non dénommés ailleurs	Andere boomvruchten, nergens anders vermeld
2260 JORDBÆR	**ΦΡΑΟΥΛΕΣ**	**STRAWBERRIES**	**FRAISES**	**AARDBEIEN**
2270 BÆR	**ΦΡΟΥΤΑ ΤΥΠΟΥ ΧΑΜΟΚΕΡΑΣΩΝ, ΜΟΥΡΩΝ κλπ.**	**SOFT FRUIT**	**BAIES**	**KLEINFRUIT**
2271 Ribs	Φραγκοστάφυλα, φραγκοστάφυλα μαύρα	Currants	Groseilles et cassis	Aalbessen
2278 Hindbær	Σμέουρα	Raspberries	Framboises	Frambozen
2281 Stikkelsbær	Λαγοκέρασα (Rives grossularia L.)	Gooseberries	Groseilles à maquereau	Stekelbessen
2290 Brombær	Βατόμουρο	Blackberry	Mûres	Braambes
Blåbær	Μύρτιλλο (βακκίνος ο μύρτιλλος)	Bilberry	Myrtilles	Blauwe bosbes
Kiwi	Ακτινίδιο	Chinese gooseberry	Kiwi	Kiwi
Granatæbler	Ρόδι	Pomegranate	Grenades	Granaatappel
Daddelblomme	Διόσπυρος (κάκι)	Persimmon	Kaki	Kaki
Indisk figen	Φραγκόσυκο	Prickly pear	Figues de Barbarie	Barbarijse vijg
Hyldebær	Καπνός ακτέας (κουφοξυλιά)	Elderberry	Sureaux	Vlierbes
Andre bær	Άλλα φρούτα τύπου χαμοκεράσων, μούρων κλπ.	Other soft fruit	Autres baies	Ander klein fruit
2300 CITRUSFRUGTER	**ΕΣΠΕΡΙΔΟΕΙΔΗ**	**CITRUS FRUITS**	**AGRUMES**	**CITRUSVRUCHTEN**
2310 Appelsiner	Πορτοκάλια	Oranges	Oranges	Sinaasappelen
2350 Mandariner	Μανταρίνια	Mandarins	Mandarines	Mandarijnen
2360 Clementiner	Κλημεντίνες	Clementines	Clémentines	Clementines
2370 Citroner	Λεμόνια	Lemons	Citrons	Citroenen
2380 Grapefrugter	Φράπες	Grapefruit	Pamplemousses	Pompelmoezen
2390 Bitter pomerans, Bitter orange, Bigarade	Νεράντζι	Bitter orange Seville orange	Bigarades	Bittere sinaasappel
Bergamot	Περγαμόντο	Bergamot	Bergamotes	Bergamot
Cedrat, Sukat	Κίτρο	Citron	Cédrats	Ceder
Andre citrusfrugter, ikke andetsteds anført	Άλλα εσπεριδοειδή που δεν αναφέρονται αλλού	Other citrus fruits, not otherwise specified	Autres agrumes, non dénommés ailleurs	Andere citrusvruchten, nergens anders vermeld
2410 DRUER	**ΣΤΑΦΥΛΙΑ**	**GRAPES**	**RAISINS**	**DRUIVEN**
2415 Friske druer (spiselig og rosiner)	Σταφύλια νωπά (για επιτραπέζια ή σταφίδες)	Fresh grapes (table and raisins)	Raisins frais (table et secs)	Verse druiven (tafel en rozijnen)
2416 Rosiner (frisk produkt)	Σταφίδες (σε αντίστοιχο βάρος νωπών)	Raisins (fresh weight)	Raisins secs (poids frais)	Rozijnen (vers gewicht)
2420 Spisedruer	Επετραπέζια σταφύλια	Table grapes	Raisins de table	Tafeldruiven
2440 Vindruer	Σταφύλια οινοποιίας	Wine grapes	Raisins de cuve	Wijndruiven

Glosar over navne på frugter	Γλωσσάριο ονομάτων λαχανικών	Glossary of fruit names	Glossaire des noms de fruits	Lijst met namen van fruit

N° (CRONOS-ZPAI)

2450 OLIVEN	**ΕΛΙΕΣ**	**OLIVES**	**OLIVES**	**OLIJVEN**
2460 heraf: Spiseoliven	Επιτραπέζιες ελιές	comprising: table olives	dont: olives de table	waarvan: tafelolijven
3719 VILDE PRODUKTER	**ΣΥΓΚΟΜΙΖΟΜΕΝΑ ΑΓΡΙΑ ΠΡΟΪΟΝΤΑ**	**WILD PRODUCTS**	**PRODUITS DE CUEILLETTE**	**WILDGROEIENDE PRODUKTEN**
2993 FRISK FRUGT (PRIVATAVL)	**ΝΩΠΑ ΦΡΟΥΤΑ (ΟΙΚΟΓΕ-ΝΕΙΑΚΩΝ ΚΗΠΩΝ)**	**FRESH FRUITS (KITCHEN GARDENS)**	**FRUITS FRAIS (DE JARDINS)**	**VERS FRUIT (TUIN V. EIGEN GEBRUIK)**

Glosar over navne på husdyrbestand	Γλωσσάριο ονομάτων Ζωικό κεφάλαιο	Glossary of livestock names	Glossaire des noms de cheptels	Lijst met namen van veestapel

N° (FSSRS)

J/01	Hovdyr	Ιπποειδή	Equidae	Équidés	Eenhoevige dieren
J/02	Hornkvæg under 1 år	Βοοειδή μικρότερα του ενός έτους	Bovine animals, under one year old	Bovins de moins de 1 an	Runderen jonger dan 1 jaar
J/02a	Hornkvæg under 1 år, handyr	Άρρενα	Bovine animals, under one year old, male	Bovins de moins de 1 an, mâles	Runderen jonger dan 1 jaar, mannelijke
J/02b	Hornkvæg under 1 år, hundyr	Θηλυκά	Bovine animals, under one year old, female	Bovins de moins de 1 an, femelles	Runderen jonger dan 1 jaar, vrouwelijke
J/03	Hornkvæg handyr 1 år, men under 2 år	Άρρενα βοοειδή από 1 έτους έως μικρότερα των 2 ετών	Male bovine animals, over 1 but under 2 years	Bovins mâles de 1 an à moins de 2 ans	Mannelijke runderen van 1 maar nog geen 2 jaar
J/04	Hornkvæg hundyr, 1 år, men under 2 år	Θηλυκά βοοειδή από 1 έτους έως μικρότερα των 2 ετών	Fem. bovine animals, over 1 but under 2 years	Bovins femelles de 1 an à moins de 2 ans	Vrouwelijke runderen van 1 maar nog geen 2 jaar
J/05	Hornkvæg handyr på 2 år og derover	Άρρενα βοοειδή 2 ετών και άνω	Male bovine animals, 2 years old and over	Bovins mâles de 2 ans et plus	Mannelijke runderen van 1 jaar en ouder
J/06	Kornkvæg hundyr på 2 år og derover	Δαμάλεις 2 ετών και άνω	Heifers, two years old and over	Génisses de 2 ans et plus	Vaarzen van 2 jaar en ouder
J/07	Malkekøer	Γαλακτοπαραγωγικές αγελάδες	Dairy cows	Vaches laitières	Melkkoeien
J/08	Andre Køer	Λοιπές αγελάδες	Other cows	Autres vaches	Overige koeien
J/09	Får (alle aldre)	Προβατοειδή (όλων των ηλικιών)	Sheep (all ages)	Ovins (tous âges)	Schapen (alle leeftijden)
J/09a	Moderfår	Προβατίνες	Ewes	Brebis	Ooien
J/09b	Andre får	Άλλα προβατοειδή	Other sheep	Autres ovins	Overige schapen
J/10	Geder (alle aldre)	Αιγοειδή (όλων των ηλικιών)	Goats (all ages)	Caprins (tous âges)	Geiten (alle leeftijden)
J/10a	Hungeder til avl	Από τα οποία, θηλυκά αναπαραγω-γής	Breeding females	Femelles reproductrices	Vrouwelijke voor voortplanting
J/10b	Andre geder	Λοιπά αιγοειδή	Other goats	Autres caprins	Overige geiten
J/11	Grise, hvis levende vægt er under 20 kg	Χοιρίδια ζώντος βάρους μικρότερου των 20 χιλιογράμμων	Piglets less than 20 kg live weight	Porcelets d'un poids vif de moins de 20 kg	Biggen met een levend gewicht < 20 kg
J/12	Avessoer på 50 kg og derover	Χοιρομητέρες αναπαραγωγής 50 χιλιογράμμων και άνω	Breeding sows weighing 50 kg and over	Truies reproductrices de 50 kg et plus	Fokzeugen van 50 kg en meer
J/13	Andre svin	Λοιποί χοίροι	Other pigs	Autres porcs	Andere varkens
J/14	Fedekyllinger	Κοτόπουλα κρεατοπαραγωγής	Broilers	Poulets de chair	Mesthoenders
J/15	Læggehøns	Ωοτόκες όρνιθες	Laying hens	Poules pondeuses	Leghennen
J/16	Andet fjerkæ	Λοιπά πουλερικά	Other poultry	Autres volailles	Overig pluimvee
J/17	Hunkaniner til avl	Κονικλομητέρες	Rabbits, breeding females	Lapines mères	Moederkonijnen
J/18	Bier	Μέλισσες	Bees	Abeilles	Bijen
J/19	Andre dyr	Άλλα ζώα	Other animals	Autres animaux	Andere beesten

BALANCEPOSTERNE	ΘΕΣΕΙΣ ΤΩΝ ΙΣΟΖΥΓΙΩΝ	ITEMS IN THE BALANCE SHEETS	POSTES DES BILANS	BALANSPOSTEN

N° (CRONOS-ZPAI)

	Forsyningsbalancer	Ισοζύγια προμηθειών	Supply balance sheets	Bilans d'approvisionnement	Voorzieningsbalansen
10	Officiel produktion	Επίσημη παραγωγή	Official production	Production officielle	Officiële produktie
12	Anvendelig produktion fra råstoffer	Χρησιμοποιήσιμη παραγωγή από πρώτες ύλες	Usable production from raw materials	Production utilisable à partir de matières premières	Bruikbare produktie uit grondstoffen
13	– indenlandsk produceret	– εγχώριες	– home produced	– indigènes	— binnenlandse
14	– importeret	– εισαγωγής	– imported	– importées	– ingevoerd
15	Salg fra erhvervsmæssige producenter	Πωλήσεις από παραγωγούς	Sales by professional producers	Ventes par les producteurs professionnels	Verkopen door professionele telers
20	Import	Εισαγωγές	Imports	Importations	Invoer
99	Ressourcer = Anvendelser	Πόροι = Χρήσεις	Resources = Uses	Ressources = Emplois	Beschikbare hoeveelheid = Gebruik
30	Eksport	Εξαγωγές	Exports	Exportations	Uitvoer
40	Slutlagre	Τελικά αποθέματα	Final stocks	Stocks finals	Eindvoorraden
42	Marked	εκ των οποίων στην αγορά	Market	Marché	Markt
45	Lagerændringer	Μεταβολή αποθεμάτων	Change in stocks	Variation de stocks	Voorraadmutatie
50	Indenlandsk anvendelse (i alt)	Συνολική εσωτερική κατανάλωση	Total domestic uses	Utilisation intérieure totale	Binnenlands verbruik totaal
51	Såsæd	Σπόροι	Seeds	Semences	Zaaizaad
53	Tab	Απώλειες	Losses	Pertes	Verliezen
55	Foderforbrug	Ζωοτροφές	Animal feed	Alimentation animale	Veevoeder
56	indenlandsk oprindelse	εκ των οποίων εσωτερικής προελεύσεως	domestic origin	origine indigène	binnenlandse oorsprong
57	på landbrugsbedriften (producentkonsum)	εκ των οποίων επί τόπου κατανάλωση	on the farm where grown	à la ferme (autoconsommation)	op de boerderij (zelfverbruik)
60	Industriel anvendelse	Βιομηχανικές χρήσεις	Industrial uses	Usages industriels	Industrieel gebruik
61	alkohol	Οινόπνευμα	alcohol	alcool	alkohol
62	øl	Μπύρα	beer	bière	bier
65	Forarbejdning	Μεταποίηση	Processing	Transformation	Verwerking
68	sleben ris	επεξεργασμένο ρύζι	milled rice	riz usiné	fabrieksrijst
66	sukker	ζάχαρη	sugar	sucré	suiker
80	Selvforsyningsgrad (%)	Αυτο-εφοδιασμός (%)	Self-sufficiency (%)	Auto-approvisionnement (%)	Zelfvoorziening (%)
	Fødevareforbrug	Ανθρώπινη κατανάλωση	Human consumption	Consommation humaine	Menselijk verbruik
71	– netto	– καθαρή	– nett	– nette	– netto
90	– kg/indb./år	– kg/κατά κεφαλή/έτος	– kg/head/year	– kg/tête/an	– kg/hoofd/jaar
90	– liter/indb./år	– λίτρα/κατά κεφαλή/έτος	– litre/head/year	– litres/tête/an	– liter/hoofd/jaar

Landbrugsregnskabet	Γεωργικοί λογαριασμοί	Agricultural accounts	Comptes de l'agriculture	Landbouwwerktuigen

No (CRONOS-COSA)

0000 Salgpris	Τιμή πώλησης	Sales price	Prix de vente	Verkoopprijs
1000 Vegetabilske produkter	Φυτικά προϊόντα	Crop products	Produits végétaux	Produkten van plantaardige oorsprong
4000 Animalske produkter	Ζωικά προϊόντα	Animal products	Produits animaux	Produkten van dierlijke oorsprong
0000 Landbrugets produktionsmidler	Μέσα Γεωργικής Παραγωγής	Means of agricultural production	Moyens de production agricole	Produktiemiddelen in de landbouw
0000 Nominalindeks	Ονομαστικοί δείκτες	Nominal indices	Indices nominaux	Nominale indices
0000 Deflationeret indeks	Αποπληθωρισμένοι δείκτες	Deflated indices	Indices déflatés	Gedefleerde indices
7500 Energi og smøremidler	Ενέργεια και λιπαντικά	Energy and lubricants	Énergie et lubrifiants	Energie en smeermiddelen
7600 Gødning og jordtilsætningsstoffer	Λιπάσματα και βελτιωτικά εδάφους	Fertilizers and soil improvers	Engrais et amendements	Meststoffen en grondverbeterings- middelen
7900 Midler til plantebeskyttelse og skadedyrsbekæmpelse	Προϊόντα προστασίας καλλιεργειών	Plant protection products	Produits de protection des cultures	Plantbeschermingsmiddelen
8010 Enkel gødning	Απλές ζωοτροφές	Straight feedingstuffs	Aliments simples	Enkelvoudige voeders
8210 Blandingsgødning	Σύνθετες ζωοτροφές	Compound feedingstuffs	Aliments composés	Mengvoeder
8410 Værktøj	Μηχανικός εξοπλισμός και μικρά εργαλεία	Material and small tools	Matériel et petit outillage	Materieel en klein gereedschap
8510 Vedligeholdelse og reparation	Συντήρηση και επισκευές	Maintenance and repair	Entretien et réparation	Onderhoud en reparaties
8730 Dyrlægebistand	Κτηνιατρικές υπηρεσίες	Veterinary services	Services vétérinaires	Veeartsenijkundige hulp
8790 Generelle udgifter	Γενικά έξοδα	General expenses	Frais généraux	Algemene uitgaven
9000 Investering	Επενδύσεις	Investments	Investissements	Investeringen
9300 Maskiner og anlæg	Μηχανήματα	Machines	Machines	Machines
9600 Bygninger	Έργα	Buildings	Ouvrages	Gebouwen

Skovbrug	Δασοκομία	Forestry	Sylviculture	Bosbouw

No (CRONOS-WOOD)

102 Douglasgran	Ψευδοτσούγκα	Douglas fir	Douglas	Douglasspar
Rødgran	Ερυθρελάτη	Spruces	Épicéas	Noorse sparren
Grantræer	Ελάτη	Firs	Sapins	Zilverdennen, abies-soorten
105 Nåletræer	Κωνοφόρα	Coniferous species	Conifères	Naaldbomen
106 Egetræer	Δρυς	Oaks	Chênes	Eiken
107 Bøgetræer	Οξυά	Beeches	Hêtres	Beuken
108 Popler	Λεύκες	Poplars	Peupliers	Populieren
109 Løvtræer	Πλατύφυλλα	Non-coniferous species	Feuillus	Loofbomen
112 Træarter	Είδη δένδρων	Tree species	Essences d'arbres	Boomsoorten
115 Statsskov	Δημόσια δάση	State forests	Forêts domaniales	Staatsbos
116 Offentlig skov	Δάση κοινής ιδιοκτησίας	Forests in public ownership	Forêts des collectivistes de droit public	Bos van publiekrechtelijke collectiviteiten
117 Privat skov	Ιδιωτικά δάση	Private forests	Forêts privées	Particuliere bossen
204 Samlet skovbevorkset areal	Συνολική δασωμένη επιφάνεια	Total wooded area	Superficie boisée totale	Totale beboste oppervlakte
215 Skovareal	Δασική έκταση	Forest area	Superficie forestière	Bosoppervlakte
216 Skovareal	Δασική έκταση	Forest land	Superficie forestière boisée	Bosgrond
217 Ubevoksset skovareal	Δασικές εκτάσεις χωρίς ξυλώδες κεφάλαιο	Unstocked forest land	Superficie forestière non boisée	Niet-bosgrond
218 Andre træbevoksede arealer	Άλλες δασωμένες επιφάνειες	Other wooded areas	Autres superficies boisées	Overige beboste oppervlakte
301 Indførsel	Εισαγωγές	Imports	Importations	Invoer
302 Udførsel	Εξαγωγές	Exports	Exportations	Uitvoer
307 Netto import	Καθαρές εισαγωγές	Net importation	Importations nettes	Netto import
308 Til rådighed	Διαθέσιμα	Available	Disponible	Beschikbaar
309 Selvforsyningsgrad	Ποσοστό αυτεπάρκειας	Degree of self-sufficiency	Degré d'auto-approvisionnement	Zelfvoorzieningsgraad
401 Produktion	Παραγωγή	Production	Production	Produktie

	FISKERI	ΑΛΙΕΙΑ	FISHERIES	PÊCHE	VISSERIJ

No Code CWP

PLE	Pleuronectes platessa	Rødspætte	Ευρωπαϊκοί πλάτακες	European plaice	Plie d'Europe	Schol
SOL	Soleo vulgaris	Tunge, søtunge	Κοινή γλώσσα	Common sole	Sole commune	Tong
COD	Gadus morhua	Torsk	Βακαλάος Ατλαντικού	Atlantic cod	Morue de l'Atlantique	Kabeljauw
HAD	Melanogrammus aeglefinus	Kuller, hvilling	Καλλαρίας	Haddock	Églefin	Schelvis
NOP	Trisopterus esmarkii	Sperling	Νορβηγικός βακαλάος	Norway pout	Tacaud norvégien	Kever
WHG	Merlangius merlangus	Hvilling	Γάδος	Whiting	Merlan	Wijting
POK	Pollachius virens	Sej	Μαύρος Γάδος	Saithe (Pollock)	Lieu noir	Koolvis
HKE	Merluccius merluccius	Kulmule	Μερλούκιοι	European hake	Merlu européen	Heek
SAN	Ammodytes spp	Tobis, sild	Σύκα	Sandeels	Lançon	Zandaal, Zandspiering
RED	Sebastes spp	Rødfisk	Σεβαστοί Ατλαντικού	Atlantic redfish	Sébastes de l'Atlantique	Roodbaars
HOM	Trachurus trachurus	Hestermakrel	Σαφρίδι Ατλαντικού	Atl. horse mackerel	Chinchard d'Europe	Horsmakreel
HER	Clupea harengus	Sild	Ρέγγα Ατλαντικού	Atlantic herring	Hareng de l'Atlantique	Haring
PIL	Sardina pilchardus	Lodsfisk, sardin	Ευρωπαϊκή σαρδέλα	Sardine (EUR pilchard)	Sardine d'Europe	Sardien
SPR	SpSprattus sprattus	Brisling	Παππαλίνα	Sprat	Sprat	Sprot
ANE	Engraulis encrasicolus	Ansjos	Ευρωπαϊκές αντζούγιες	European anchovy	Anchois d'Europe	Ansjovis
MAC	Scomber scombrus	Makrel	Σκόμβρος Ατλαντικού	Atlantic mackerel	Maquereau de l'Atlantique	Makreel

VALUES OF THE EUROPEAN CURRENCY UNIT

VALEUR DE L'UNITÉ MONÉTAIRE EUROPÉENNE

AVERAGE VALUE PER CALENDAR YEAR

VALEURS MOYENNES PAR ANNÉE CIVILE

ECU

		1977	1978	1979	1980	1981	1982	1983	1984	1985	1986
BLEU/ UEBL	100 ECU = ... BFR/LFR	4 088,26	4 006,11	4 016,51	4 059,79	4 129,46	4 471,15	4 543,80	4 544,20	4 491,36	4 379,78
	100 BFR/LFR = ... ECU	2,44603	2,49618	2,48972	2,46318	2,42162	2,23656	2,20080	2,20061	2,22650	2,28322
Danmark	100 ECU = ... DKR	685,567	701,945	720,911	782,736	792,255	815,687	813,188	814,647	801,876	793,565
	100 DKR = ... ECU	14,5865	14,2461	13,8713	12,7756	12,6221	12,2596	12,2973	12,2753	12,4708	12,6014
BR Deutschland	100 ECU = ... DM	264,831	255,607	251,087	252,421	251,390	237,599	227,052	223,811	222,632	212,819
	100 DM = ... ECU	37,7599	39,1225	39,8268	39,6163	39,7788	42,0877	44,0428	44,6806	44,9172	46,9883
Ellas	100 ECU = ... DR	4 203,53	4 678,29	5 077,38	5 932,28	6 162,41	6 534,18	7 808,83	8 834,03	10 573,90	13 742,46
	100 DR = ... ECU	2,37893	2,13753	1,96951	1,68569	1,62274	1,53041	1,28060	1,13199	0,94572	0,72767
España	100 ECU = ... PTA	8 684,71	9 742,94	9 196,65	9 970,17	10 267,56	10 755,76	12 750,26	12 656,93	12 916,45	13 745,63
	100 PTA = ... ECU	1,15145	1,02638	1,08735	1,00299	0,97394	0,92973	0,78430	0,79008	0,77421	0,72754
France	100 ECU = ... FF	560,607	573,983	582,945	586,895	603,992	643,117	677,078	687,165	679,502	679,976
	100 FF = ... ECU	17,8378	17,4221	17,1543	17,0388	16,5565	15,5492	14,7693	14,5525	14,7167	14,7064
Ireland	100 ECU = ... IRL	65,3701	66,3888	66,9482	67,5997	69,1021	68,9605	71,4956	72,5942	71,5170	73,3530
	100 IRL = ... ECU	152,975	150,627	149,369	147,929	144,713	145,010	139,869	137,752	139,827	136,327
Italia	100 ECU = ... LIT	100 678,5	108 021,6	113 849,8	118 920,5	126 318,0	132 377,9	134 992,4	138 138,1	144 798,7	146 187,4
	100 LIT = ... ECU	0,099326	0,092574	0,087835	0,084089	0,079165	0,075541	0,074078	0,072391	0,069061	0,068405
Nederland	100 ECU = ... HFL	280,010	275,409	274,864	276,027	277,510	261,390	253,720	252,334	251,101	240,089
	100 HFL = ... ECU	35,7130	36,3096	36,3816	36,2283	36,0347	38,2570	39,4135	39,6300	39,8246	41,5127
Portugal	100 ECU = ... ESC	4 359,07	5 586,07	6 704,17	6 955,21	6 849,47	7 800,66	9 868,86	11 568,01	13 025,15	14 708,84
	100 ESC = ... ECU	2,29407	1,79017	1,49161	1,43777	1,45997	1,28194	1,01329	0,86445	0,76775	0,67986
United Kingdom	100 ECU = ... UKL	65,3701	66,3910	64,6392	59,8488	55,3110	56,0454	58,7014	59,0626	58,8980	67,1540
	100 UKL = ... ECU	152,975	150,622	154,705	167,088	180,796	178,427	170,354	169,312	169,785	148,911
USA	100 ECU = ... USD	114,112	127,410	137,065	139,233	111,645	97,971	89,022	78,903	76,309	98,417
	100 USD = ... ECU	87,6332	78,4868	72,9581	71,8220	89,5696	102,0710	112,3318	126,7379	131,0461	101,6085

L

Graphs

Graphiques

Map No 1

Share of agricultural, forestry and fishery products in gross value-added at market prices.

Map No 2

Agricultural area by AWU (annual work unit).

Map No 3

Share of wooded area in total area.

Map No 4

Share of animal output in final agricultural output.

Map No 5

Share of milk in final agricultural output.

Map No 6

Share of cereals in final agricultural output.

Map No 7

Share of permanent crops in final agricultural output.

Map No 8

The main EC trade partners — agricultural products (SITC-O).

Carte nº 1

Part des produits de l'agriculture, de la sylviculture et de la pêche dans la valeur ajoutée brute aux prix du marché.

Carte nº 2

Superficie agricole utilisée par classe d'unité de travail-année (UTA).

Carte nº 3

Part des bois dans la superficie totale.

Carte nº 4

Part de la production animale dans la production finale de l'agriculture.

Carte nº 5

Part du lait dans la production finale de l'agriculture.

Carte nº 6

Part des céréales dans la production finale de l'agriculture.

Carte nº 7

Part des cultures permanentes dans la production finale de l'agriculture.

Carte nº 8

Les principaux partenaires commerciaux de la Communauté européenne (produits agricoles CTCI-O).

Share of agricultural, forestry and fishery products
in gross value added at market prices

Part des produits de l'agriculture, de la sylviculture et de la pêche
dans la valeur ajoutée brute aux prix du marché

1

– 1984 –

- < 2.5
2.5 ≦ – < 5
5 ≦ – < 7.5
7.5 ≦ – < 10
10 ≦

DK, GR : at factor cost / au coût des facteurs
GR, P : 1981
EUROSTAT-REGIO

Agricultural area by AWU (annual work unit)

2   Superficie agricole utilisée par classe d'unité de travail-année (U.T.A.)

– 1985 –

Legend:
- <10
- 10 ≤ – <15
- 15 ≤ – <20
- 20 ≤ – <25
- 25 ≤

0 70 140 210 280 350 km

P
0 20 40 60 80 100 km

E
0 50 100 150 200 250 km

Source : Community survey on the structure of agricultural holding

Source : Enquête communautaire sur la structure des exploitations agricoles
EUROSTAT-REGIO

Share of wooded area in total area

– 1984 –

Part des bois dans la superficie totale

	< 10
	10 ≤ – < 20
	20 ≤ – < 30
	30 ≤ – < 40
	40 ≤

0 70 140 210 280 350 km

P

0 20 40 60 80 100 km

0 50 100 150 200 250 km

E

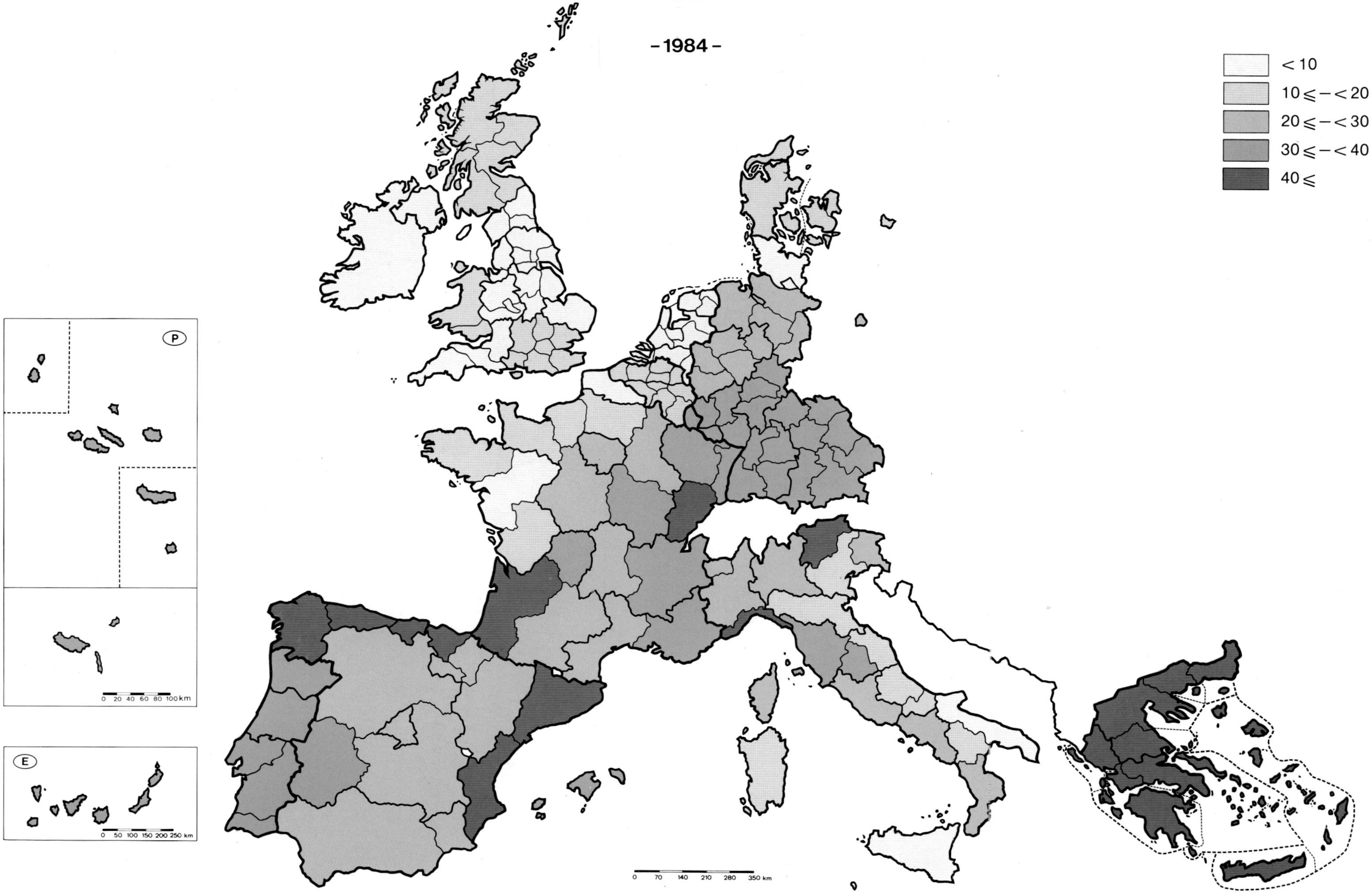

EUROSTAT-REGIO

LV

Share of animal output in final agricultural output

4 **Part de la production animale dans la production finale de l'agriculture**

– 1984 –

	< 25
	25 ≤ — < 50
	50 ≤ — < 75
	75 ≤

GR : 1982
EUROSTAT-REGIO

Share of milk in final agricultural output

Part du lait dans la production finale de l'agriculture

5

– 1984 –

	<10
	10 ≦ – <15
	15 ≦ – <20
	20 ≦ – <25
	25 ≦

0 70 140 210 280 350 km

P

0 20 40 60 80 100 km

E

0 50 100 150 200 250 km

GR : 1982
EUROSTAT-REGIO

Share of cereals in final agricultural output

Part des céréales dans la production finale de l'agriculture

6

– 1984 –

	<10
	10 ≦ – <15
	15 ≦ – <20
	20 ≦ – <25
	25 ≦

0 70 140 210 280 350 km

P

0 20 40 60 80 100 km

E

0 50 100 150 200 250 km

GR : 1982
EUROSTAT-REGIO

Share of permanent crops in final agricultural output

Part des cultures permanentes dans la production finale de l'agriculture

7

– 1984 –

< 5
5 ≤ – < 15
15 ≤ – < 25
25 ≤

0 70 140 210 280 350 km

P

0 20 40 60 80 100 km

E

0 50 100 150 200 250 km

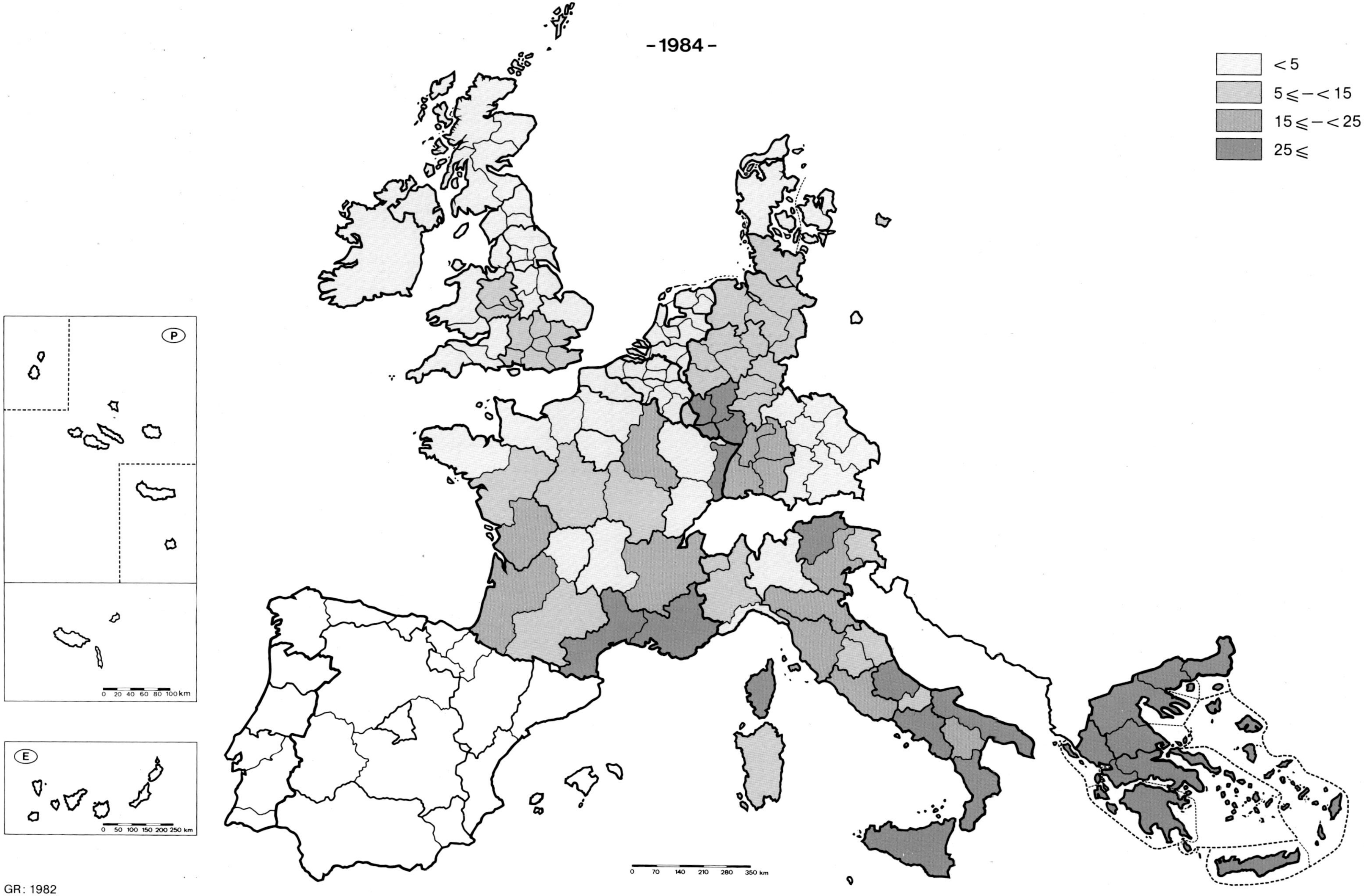

GR: 1982
EUROSTAT-REGIO

The main EC trade partners
agricultural products (SITC-O)

8

Les principaux partenaires commerciaux
de la Communauté Européenne
(produits agricoles CTCI-O)

IMPORT 1986
> 500 Mio ECU

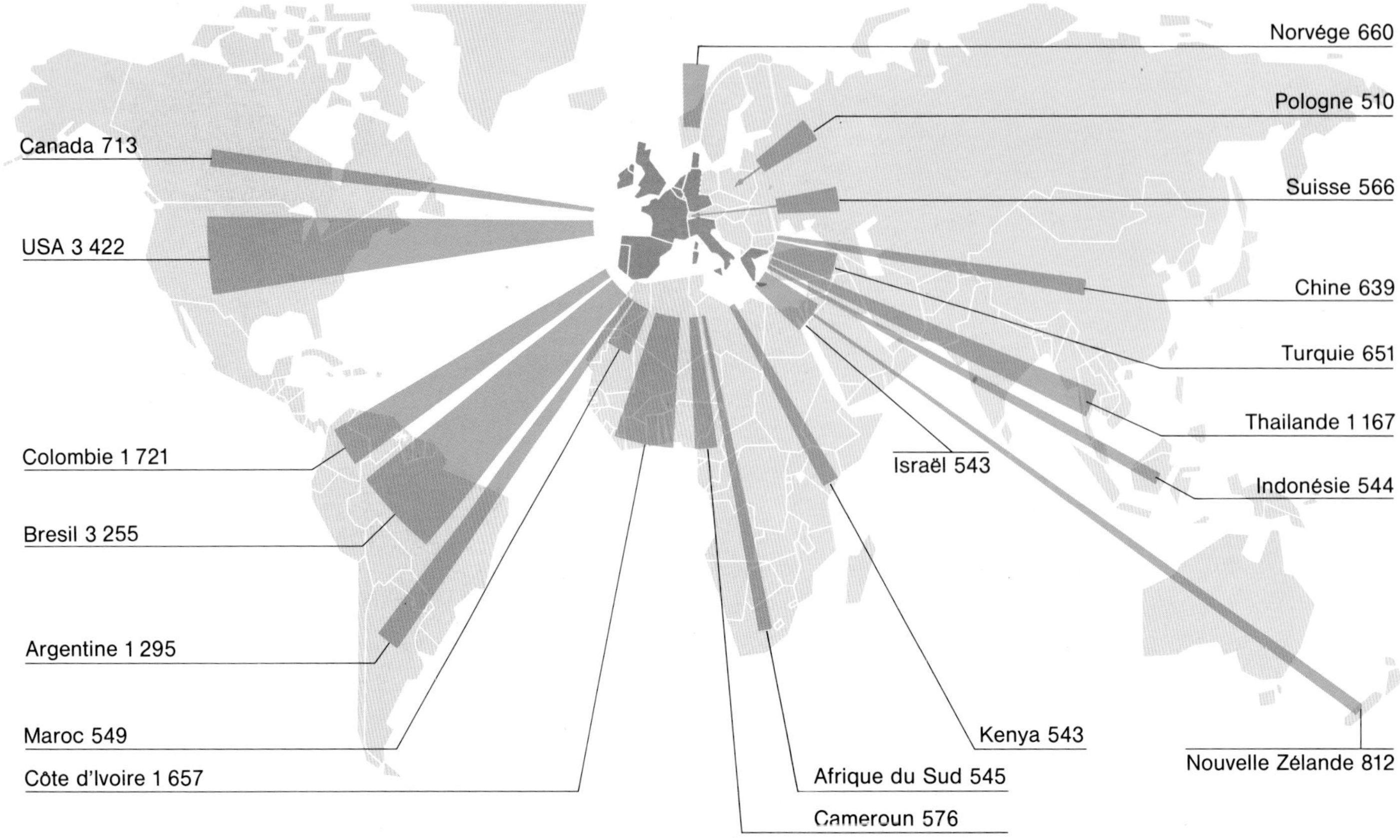

Norvège 660

Pologne 510

Suisse 566

Chine 639

Turquie 651

Thaïlande 1 167

Indonésie 544

Canada 713

USA 3 422

Colombie 1 721

Bresil 3 255

Argentine 1 295

Maroc 549

Côte d'Ivoire 1 657

Israël 543

Kenya 543

Afrique du Sud 545

Cameroun 576

Nouvelle Zélande 812

EXPORT 1986
> 200 Mio ECU

Norvège 381

Suède 734

Finlande 209

Suisse 1 380

Pologne 225

Autriche 746

URSS 1 081

Japon 997

Canada 426

USA 2 272

Iran 295

Emirats Arabes 212

Arabie Saoudite 1 140

Algérie 564

Egypte 651

Nigeria 275

Libye 411

EUROSTAT-COMEXT

LX

I

Agriculture

Agriculture

I A

General

Partie générale

Source / Source: EUROSTAT / DEUTSCHER WETTERDIENST, OFFENBACH AM MAIN

STATION	TEMPERATURE (C) / TEMPÉRATURE (C)						RAINFALL (MM) / PLUVIOMÉTRIE (MM)					
	DECADES (AV.) / DÉCADES (MOY.)				YEAR / ANNÉE		DECADES (TOT.) / DÉCADES (TOT.)				YEAR / ANNÉE	
	1 – 9	10 – 18	19 – 27	28 – 36	1986	AV / MOY	1 – 9	10 – 18	19 – 27	28 – 36	1986	AV / MOY
UNITED-KINGDOM												
1 Kinloss	2,7	6,3	3,6	6,9	4,9	5,3	121	140	26	128	415	508
2 Prestwick	2,7	9,5	12,1	7,9	8,1	8,4	210	212	289	470	1 181	1 160
3 Leuchars	2,5	8,8	12,6	7,0	7,7	7,2	112	180	280	171	743	606
4 Carlisle	2,8	10,0	12,6	7,9	8,3	8,6	170	202	167	338	877	1 043
5 Boulmer	2,7	8,6	12,4	7,4	7,8	7,4	135	174	206	149	664	621
6 Leeming	2,3	10,0	13,0	7,6	8,2	7,8	138	233	138	182	691	592
7 Valley	3,9	10,1	13,0	9,4	9,1	9,6	194	169	171	357	891	1 003
8 Blackpool	2,8	10,1	13,1	8,6	8,6	8,3	175	182	153	407	917	867
9 Manchester	2,7	10,5	13,2	8,0	8,6	9,2	162	202	142	509	1 015	1 333
10 Waddington	2,1	10,2	13,5	7,8	8,4	7,9	138	172	132	168	610	567
11 Shawbury	2,6	10,3	13,0	7,8	8,4	8,0	121	131	135	224	611	610
12 Dirmingham	2,1	10,0	10,5	0,1	0,5	0,9	140	170	100	247	729	1 245
13 Cardington	1,8	10,2	13,8	8,0	8,5	8,0	123	261	76	98	558	507
14 Honington	2,0	10,7	13,9	8,0	8,7	9,0	110	125	236	190	661	657
15 Lyneham	2,0	9,9	13,2	8,1	8,3	8,1	179	144	193	263	779	676
16 London/Heath.	3,2	11,7	15,3	9,3	9,9	9,7	158	132	138	196	624	955
17 Manston	2,6	10,6	14,8	8,8	9,2	8,7	127	108	144	179	558	490
18 Plymouth	4,8	10,6	13,8	10,3	9,9	9,5	272	241	222	377	1 112	951
19 Exeter	3,9	10,6	13,8	9,3	9,4	9,1	174	184	165	245	768	695
20 Bournemouth	3,0	10,5	13,8	8,8	9,0	8,7	196	153	170	315	834	773
21 Belfast/Alder	3,2	9,5	12,3	7,3	8,1	8,5	175	264	157	224	820	1 040
IRELAND												
22 Roches Point	5,0	9,5	13,0	9,2	9,2	9,9	178	256	232	334	1 000	1 478
23 Valentia	5,7	10,1	13,2	9,9	9,7	9,3	318	331	406	586	1 641	1 436
24 Kilkenny	3,9	9,9	12,9	7,8	8,6	8,3	143	196	191	287	817	805
25 Dublin	4,0	9,9	12,9	8,3	8,8	8,5	168	192	338	234	932	751
26 Clarremorris	3,4	9,4	12,1	7,5	8,1	7,9	294	327	259	517	1 397	1 126
27 Clones	3,2	9,5	12,2	7,3	8,0	7,9	200	221	206	367	994	898
DANMARK												
28 Alborg	− 2,3	9,8	13,2	5,7	6,6	6,4	108	89	148	152	497	578
29 Karup	− 2,0	10,6	13,5	6,3	7,1	6,6	180	118	169	302	769	757
30 Skrydstrup	− 1,9	10,2	13,3	6,2	6,9	6,7	150	110	176	463	899	819
31 København	− 1,6	10,4	14,3	6,3	7,3	7,8	74	181	263	339	857	182
NEDERLAND												
32 De Kooy	0,5	10,6	14,5	8,7	8,6	8,9	116	116	200	291	723	739
33 De Bilt	0,9	12,0	14,8	8,1	9,0	9,0	157	109	170	318	754	772
34 Eelde	− 0,2	11,0	13,7	7,0	7,9	8,3	174	164	153	330	821	745
35 Gilze-Rijen	1,3	12,3	15,1	8,5	9,3	9,5	174	142	139	268	723	686
36 Beek	0,7	12,3	15,0	8,1	9,0	9,1	185	158	135	231	709	746
BELGIQUE/BELGIË												
37 Uccle	1,5	12,4	15,1	8,2	9,3	9,6	266	189	203	298	956	802
38 St.-Hubert	− 1,7	9,5	12,7	5,5	6,5	6,2	311	304	287	280	1 182	1 120
LUXEMBOURG												
39 Luxembourg	− 0,5	11,5	14,6	6,0	7,9	8,1	255	237	269	333	1 094	821
FRANCE												
40 Abbeville	2,0	11,2	14,4	8,8	9,1	8,6	162	116	162	245	685	730
41 Lille	1,9	12,4	15,5	8,7	9,6	9,4	202	175	130	245	752	703
42 Caen	3,7	11,3	14,6	9,6	9,8	9,3	220	137	189	213	759	710
43 Rouen/Boos.	2,1	11,3	14,5	8,3	9,1	8,5	272	233	186	280	971	895
44 Saint-Quentin	1,5	11,8	14,7	8,0	9,0	8,3	207	149	136	204	696	662
45 Reims	1,3	12,3	15,5	8,2	9,3	8,5	153	157	148	291	749	653
46 Rostrenen	3,0	10,1	13,5	9,2	9,0	8,7	347	266	222	398	1 233	888
47 Rennes	3,9	11,8	15,2	9,8	10,2	9,7	222	191	176	175	764	659
48 Alençon	2,5	11,9	15,2	8,8	9,6	9,9	207	143	176	201	727	711
49 Paris-Le-Bour.	2,5	13,1	16,3	9,0	10,2	10,2	156	159	129	179	623	644
50 Nancy/Ess.	0,3	12,7	15,9	6,8	8,9	8,2	273	266	316	245	1 100	756
51 Nantes	4,5	13,0	16,7	10,4	11,1	11,3	295	146	148	269	858	770
52 Tours	2,7	12,6	16,4	9,0	10,2	10,5	195	125	111	212	643	700
53 Orléans	2,2	12,9	16,4	8,7	10,0	9,2	168	152	227	153	700	778
54 Bourges	3,0	13,1	17,4	8,6	10,5	10,6	198	208	188	162	756	627
55 Auxerre	1,9	13,1	16,8	8,2	10,0	10,1	161	259	218	168	806	694
56 Dijon	0,7	12,9	17,5	6,8	9,5	10,0	192	266	252	166	876	756
57 Luxeuil	− 0,1	12,9	16,5	6,3	8,9	8,3	392	400	284	459	1 535	1 266
58 Poitiers	3,7	12,8	17,1	9,0	10,7	9,7	231	178	100	148	657	672
59 Cognac	5,6	13,6	18,7	10,3	12,1	11,8	292	248	97	188	825	792
60 Limoges	3,4	12,0	17,2	8,6	10,3	10,2	273	255	164	262	954	1 073
61 Clermont-F.	3,5	13,0	18,0	8,8	10,8	10,3	79	250	189	57	575	644
62 Lyon	2,8	13,5	18,7	8,4	10,8	11,0	159	304	186	163	812	837
63 Bordeaux	6,1	13,6	18,9	10,2	12,2	11,2	301	209	179	231	920	914
64 Agen	5,8	14,3	19,4	9,7	12,3	10,9	229	150	111	122	612	646
65 Gourdon	5,2	13,7	18,9	9,4	11,8	10,5	211	235	126	209	781	803
66 Millau	3,6	13,4	19,5	8,8	11,3	9,5	207	153	106	147	613	639
67 Montélimar	5,2	15,7	21,7	10,1	13,2	11,4	188	330	87	157	762	828
68 St.-Auban	3,7	14,7	19,7	8,2	11,6	10,1	133	83	153	101	470	591
69 Mont-de-Marsan	6,8	14,2	19,6	10,2	12,7	11,3	360	236	115	218	929	918
70 Tarbes/Osson	5,9	12,8	18,2	9,7	11,7	10,6	378	191	117	284	970	1 099
71 Toulouse	6,1	14,5	20,3	10,5	12,9	12,3	177	125	85	110	497	707
72 Montpellier	7,1	16,4	22,1	11,8	14,4	13,6	289	82	88	258	717	676
73 Marignane	6,8	17,0	22,3	11,7	14,4	12,8	175	135	71	194	575	451
74 Nice	8,9	17,3	22,9	13,3	15,6	14,6	352	144	48	67	611	811
75 Perpignan	8,7	16,5	22,8	13,1	15,3	14,6	338	53	54	201	646	576
76 Ajaccio	8,9	16,6	22,2	13,2	15,2	13,2	569	141	84	131	925	648
ESPANA												
77 Oviedo	4,8	11,6	16,8	11,1	11,1	11,1	214	151	248	182	795	795
78 Santander	9,8	13,4	18,8	13,4	13,8	13,8	511	182	159	387	1 239	1 239
79 San Sebastian	8,5	12,5	17,6	12,3	12,7	12,7	505	421	263	385	1 574	1 574
80 Santiago	6,6	12,0	17,5	10,9	11,7	11,7	617	0	0	1	618	618

SOURCE: EUROSTAT, AGROMET DATA BANK

SOURCE: EUROSTAT, BANQUE DE DONNÉES AGROMET

| STATION | TEMPERATURE (C) / TEMPÉRATURE (C) | | | | | | RAINFALL (MM) / PLUVIOMÉTRIE (MM) | | | | | |
| | DECADES (AV.) / DÉCADES (MOY.) | | | | YEAR / ANNÉE | | DECADES (TOT.) / DÉCADES (TOT.) | | | | YEAR / ANNÉE | |
	1 – 9	10 – 18	19 – 27	28 – 36	1986	AV / MOY	1 – 9	10 – 18	19 – 27	28 – 36	1986	AV / MOY
ESPANA												
81 Leon	4,5	12,5	19,2	7,7	11,0	11,0	147	34	141	90	412	412
82 Burgos	3,7	12,5	19,2	7,5	10,7	10,7	0	5	4	8	17	17
83 Logrono	8,1	16,4	22,4	10,7	14,4	14,4	67	121	44	87	319	319
84 Valladolid	5,3	13,1	20,0	7,7	11,5	11,5	72	53	87	91	303	303
85 Zaragoza	9,0	17,8	23,7	11,0	15,4	15,4	26	169	63	71	329	329
86 Barcelona	9,0	16,1	22,7	12,6	15,1	15,1	205	103	182	193	683	683
87 Salamanca	5,2	12,9	19,6	7,7	11,4	11,4	88	30	115	63	296	296
88 Madrid	6,2	15,8	22,8	8,7	13,4	13,4	102	72	134	90	398	398
89 Calamocha	4,5	12,5	19,3	7,5	11,0	11,0	72	149	100	121	442	442
90 Tortosa	9,7	17,2	23,5	12,2	15,6	15,6	32	57	89	189	367	367
91 Caceres	8,8	16,8	24,0	12,1	15,4	15,4	134	35	76	84	329	329
92 Albacete	6,2	15,8	23,1	9,0	13,5	13,5	57	80	54	192	383	383
93 Valencia	11,1	18,3	24,5	14,0	17,0	17,0	33	68	121	369	591	591
94 Ciudad Real	7,0	16,6	24,0	9,8	14,3	14,3	131	108	30	110	379	379
95 Alicante	12,3	18,6	25,4	15,6	18,0	18,0	21	339	98	171	629	629
96 Sevilla	10,8	18,7	25,4	14,4	17,3	17,3	237	42	33	146	458	458
97 Cordoba	10,3	18,5	25,5	13,8	17,0	17,0	99	232	8	73	412	412
98 Granada	7,3	16,7	23,6	10,0	14,4	14,4	198	110	6	103	417	417
99 Murcia	11,6	18,1	24,8	15,0	17,3	17,3	37	23	83	242	385	385
100 Malaga	12,7	18,4	24,3	15,6	17,7	17,7	77	43	3	249	372	372
101 Almeria	12,7	19,1	25,2	16,5	18,4	18,4	63	13	20	63	159	159
PORTUGAL												
102 Coimbra	9,7	14,9	20,2	13,1	14,5	14,5	432	123	70	262	887	887
103 Faro	12,2	17,5	22,7	15,6	17,0	17,0	180	69	39	76	364	364
104 Beja	9,6	16,2	22,5	13,4	15,4	15,4	230	90	54	105	479	479
105 Vila Real	7,0	13,6	20,2	10,0	12,7	12,7	444	116	109	230	899	899
106 Portalegre	8,2	14,9	21,8	12,7	14,4	14,4	284	93	101	176	654	654
107 Bragança	5,7	13,1	20,3	8,9	12,0	12,0	208	68	118	137	531	531
108 Lisboa	7,7	15,9	21,3	14,3	14,8	14,8	201	77	76	258	612	612
BR DEUTSCHLAND												
109 Schlesswig	− 1,3	10,6	13,7	6,4	7,3	7,8	202	159	185	349	895	925
110 Hambourg	− 0,7	11,8	14,4	6,5	8,0	8,3	170	174	192	274	810	786
111 Bremen	− 0,4	11,8	14,5	6,8	8,2	7,7	143	107	184	211	645	653
112 Luechow	− 1,7	12,2	15,0	6,4	8,0	7,6	128	129	132	151	540	509
113 Osnabrueck	− 0,3	11,9	14,6	7,5	8,4	8,1	241	200	199	348	988	806
114 Braunschweig	− 1,1	12,1	15,1	7,0	8,3	8,5	144	170	188	211	713	611
115 Bocholt	0,7	12,2	14,9	7,7	8,9	8,3	166	213	161	296	836	718
116 Kassel	− 0,7	12,1	14,9	6,1	8,1	8,6	196	173	209	204	782	680
117 Köln	1,0	13,0	15,5	7,8	9,3	9,4	197	231	183	236	847	810
118 Giessen	− 0,1	13,0	15,6	6,2	8,7	8,0	163	136	166	207	672	693
119 Trier	0,2	12,4	15,3	6,8	8,7	8,0	186	177	167	208	738	766
120 Würzburg	− 0,4	13,2	15,7	6,1	8,6	8,8	143	190	206	208	747	600
121 Coburg	− 1,8	12,3	14,5	4,4	7,3	7,1	215	197	250	237	899	697
122 Mannheim	1,1	14,1	16,8	6,6	9,6	8,9	164	219	233	133	749	670
123 Stuttgart	− 0,6	12,8	15,7	5,5	8,3	8,4	118	320	270	151	859	709
124 Nürnberg	− 0,6	13,4	16,0	5,4	8,5	7,7	125	192	194	186	697	652
125 Regensburg	− 1,4	13,2	15,8	3,9	7,8	8,1	127	206	224	166	723	656
126 Freiburg	1,1	14,2	17,9	8,0	10,3	9,5	190	411	300	168	1 069	961
127 München	− 1,8	12,3	15,4	4,6	7,6	7,6	175	342	226	155	898	967
128 Passau	− 1,3	13,2	15,9	3,8	7,9	7,1	272	195	141	281	889	868
129 Konstanz	0,0	12,9	16,6	5,7	8,8	8,1	176	342	304	170	992	826
ITALIA												
130 Bolzano	2,7	16,5	20,6	4,9	11,2	10,1	54	233	195	57	539	861
131 Udine	3,2	17,3	21,0	8,4	12,5	12,3	210	406	433	231	1 280	1 260
132 Torino	2,7	16,2	20,7	7,9	11,9	10,5	207	457	220	113	997	796
133 Milano	3,6	17,2	21,6	8,0	12,6	11,9	277	163	104	85	629	1 022
134 Padova	3,7	18,1	22,0	7,7	12,9	12,3	269	172	58	53	552	850
135 Genova	7,9	18,0	23,5	13,8	15,8	13,8	281	248	125	158	812	930
136 Bologna	3,7	18,3	22,8	8,9	13,4	11,8	251	347	153	40	791	537
137 Pisa	7,1	16,7	22,2	10,9	14,2	13,7	276	245	188	226	935	852
138 Perugia	5,1	15,8	21,6	9,2	12,9	11,6	206	325	87	106	724	677
139 Falconara	6,0	17,3	22,1	10,6	14,0	13,7	304	147	140	120	711	803
140 Grosseto	7,8	17,0	22,9	11,9	14,9	13,4	324	289	89	79	781	757
141 Pescara	7,2	17,1	22,6	11,2	14,5	12,9	333	202	79	193	807	610
142 Roma	8,8	17,0	22,7	12,8	15,3	15,1	648	298	121	175	1 242	751
143 Amendola	8,2	18,4	23,8	11,8	15,5	14,9	220	92	101	116	529	519
144 Napoli	9,8	18,5	24,3	12,6	16,3	14,9	472	168	215	341	1 196	1 070
145 Capo Palinuro	10,0	17,8	23,8	13,7	16,3	14,2	434	94	43	233	804	859
146 Brindisi	10,5	19,1	24,5	14,3	17,1	15,0	284	39	84	201	608	487
147 Crotone	9,7	18,4	24,5	13,2	16,4	15,6	342	90	28	338	798	660
148 Messina	12,0	19,6	25,9	16,7	18,5	16,4	652	45	91	201	989	825
149 Trapani	12,2	18,6	24,8	15,7	17,8	17,2	205	32	21	201	459	470
150 Gela	11,7	18,2	24,6	16,5	17,8	16,7	465	18	28	169	680	552
151 Alghero	10,0	16,9	22,7	14,2	15,9	14,0	485	94	26	253	858	526
152 Cagliari	10,5	17,9	24,0	14,7	16,8	15,9	172	61	30	181	444	456
ELLAS												
153 Thessaloniki	38,5	18,6	23,7	9,4	22,6	14,5	183	136	63	78	460	524
154 Alexandroupolis	6,7	17,9	23,7	8,7	14,2	14,0	161	169	13	70	413	564
155 Larissa	7,1	18,6	24,1	9,0	14,7	14,6	114	70	23	227	434	414
156 Arta	10,9	19,7	24,5	13,6	17,2	16,6	214	53	23	179	469	989
157 Aliartos	11,2	20,6	26,3	12,5	17,7	17,2	78	33	25	244	380	573
158 Andravida	10,8	18,8	24,0	13,1	16,7	16,3	394	67	3	376	840	853
159 Kalamata	11,4	18,5	24,2	13,3	16,9	16,8	161	146	44	413	764	826
160 Heraklion	13,1	19,7	24,7	15,4	18,2	18,1	161	35	38	252	486	479

SOURCE: EUROSTAT, AGROMET DATA BANK

SOURCE: EUROSTAT, BANQUE DE DONNÉES AGROMET

YEAR ANNÉE	EUR 12	B	DK	D	GR	E	F	IRL	I	L	NL	P	UK

1000 HA

TOTAL AREA **SUPERFICIE TOTALE**

YEAR	EUR 12	B	DK	D	GR	E	F	IRL	I	L	NL	P	UK
1966	225 648	3 051	4 307	24 854	13 194	50 474	55 134	7 028	30 125	259	3 615	9 207	24 400
1976	225 558	3 054	4 307	24 862	13 199	50 471	54 909	7 028	30 126	259	3 695	9 207	24 411
1986	225 574	3 052	4 308	24 869	13 196	50 477	54 909	7 028	30 128	259	3 729	9 207	24 414

WATER **EAUX**

YEAR	EUR 12	B	DK	D	GR	E	F	IRL	I	L	NL	P	UK
1966	3 457	27	70	424	312	535	606	139	720	1	272	44	307
1976	3 547	27	70	456	312	534	624	139	718	1	314	44	308
1986	3 570	27	70	444	312	534	613	139	721	1	337	44	328

OTHER AREA **AUTRE SUPERFICIE N.D.A.**

YEAR	EUR 12	B	DK	D	GR	E	F	IRL	I	L	NL	P	UK
1966	35 501	770	745	3 421	1 327	8 939	8 073	784 *	3 778	40	795	1 333 *	3 085
1976	35 929	894	811	3 971	1 361	9 265	7 379	875	5 571	43	990	1 663 *	3 073
1986	39 562	996	922 *	5 065	1 388 *	10 219 *	8 258	886	5 865	48	1 075	1 663 *	3 177

WOODED AREA **SUPERFICIE BOISEE**

YEAR	EUR 12	B	DK	D	GR	E	F	IRL	I	L	NL	P	UK
1966	51 510	608	472	7 184	5 755	13 600	12 714	240 *	5 770	83	287	2 968 *	1 829
1976	53 319	613	493	7 165	5 755	13 000 *	14 567	304	6 022	83	304	2 968 *	2 045
1986	53 420	617	493	7 360	5 755	12 511	14 620	327	6 097	82	293 *	2 968 *	2 297

AGRICULTURE USED AREA **SUPERFICIE AGRICOLE UTILISÉE**

YEAR	EUR 12	B	DK	D	GR	E	F	IRL	I	L	NL	P	UK
1966	135 180	1 646	3 020	13 826	5 800 *	27 400 *	31 329	5 865 *	19 857	135	2 261	4 862	19 179
1976	132 763	1 519	2 933	13 270	5 771	27 672	32 339	5 710	17 815	131	2 086	4 532	18 985
1986	129 022	1 412 *	2 823	12 000	5 741 *	27 213 *	31 418	5 676	17 445	127	2 024 *	4 532 *	18 612

1986

EUR 12

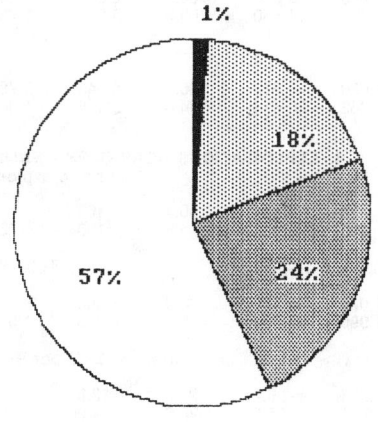

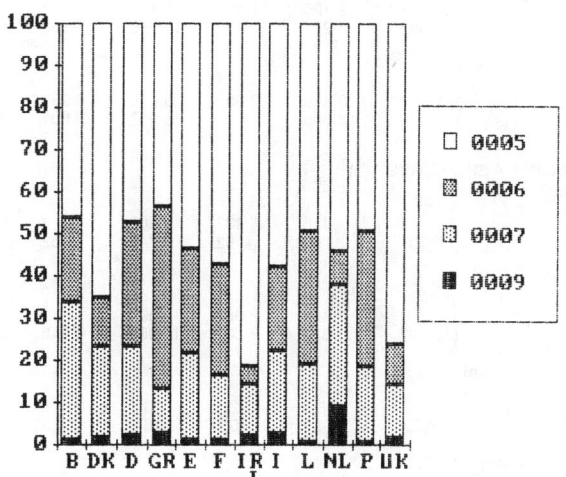

YEAR ANNÉE	EUR 12	B	DK	D	GR	E	F	IRL	I	L	NL	P	UK

1. AREA (1000 ha) / 1. SUPERFICIE (1000 ha)

Area (1) / Superficie (1)

	EUR 12	B	DK	D	GR	E	F	IRL	I	L	NL	P	UK
1966	225 648	3 051	4 307	24 854	13 194	50 474	55 134	7 028	30 125	259	3 615	9 207 *	24 400
1986	225 574	3 052	4 308	24 869	13 196	50 477	54 909	7 028	30 128	259	3 729	9 207	24 414

Agricultural used area, AA / Superficie agricole utilisée, SAU

	EUR 12	B	DK	D	GR	E	F	IRL	I	L	NL	P	UK
1966	135 180	1 646	3 020	13 826	5 800 *	27 400 *	31 329	5 865 *	19 857	135	2 261	4 862 *	19 179
1986	129 022	1 412	2 823	12 000	5 741	27 213	31 418	5 676 *	17 445	127	2 024	4 532	18 612

Arable area / Terres labourables

	EUR 12	B	DK	D	GR	E	F	IRL	I	L	NL	P	UK
1966	71 863	850	2 675	7 539	3 000 *	15 698	18 008	1 035	11 685	67	898	3 030 *	7 378
1986	67 783	734	2 592	7 244	2 925	15 651	17 735	1 062 *	9 061	56	876	2 906	6 942

2. POPULATION / 2. POPULATION

Population, yearly average (1000) / Population, moyenne annuelle (1000)

	EUR 12	B	DK	D	GR	E	F	IRL	I	L	NL	P	UK
1966	295 572	9 508	4 798	59 148	8 614	32 394	49 164	2 884	52 519	335	12 456	9 109	54 643
1986	322 699 *	9 860 *	5 116 *	61 020 *	9 960 *	38 616	55 392 *	3 537	57 260 *	368 *	14 570 *	10 210 *	56 790 *

Inhabitants/km² / Habitants/km²

	EUR 12	B	DK	D	GR	E	F	IRL	I	L	NL	P	UK
1966	131	312	111	238	65	64	89	41	174	129	345	99	224
1986	143	323	119	245	75	77	101	50	190	142	391	111	233

Inhabitants/ha AA / Habitants/ha SAU

	EUR 12	B	DK	D	GR	E	F	IRL	I	L	NL	P	UK
1966	2,2	5,8	1,6	4,3	1,5	1,6	1,6	0,5	2,6	2,5	5,5	1,9	2,8
1986	2,5	7,0	1,8	5,1	1,7	1,4	1,8	0,6	3,3	2,9	7,2	2,3	3,1

Inhabitants/ha arable area / Habitants/ha terres labourables

	EUR 12	B	DK	D	GR	E	F	IRL	I	L	NL	P	UK
1966	4,0	10,9	1,8	7,7	2,9	2,0	2,7	2,6	4,4	4,8	13,4	3,0	7,4
1986	4,8	13,4	2,0	8,4	3,4	2,5	3,1	3,3	6,3	6,6	16,6	3,5	8,2

3. CIVILIAN EMPLOYMENT BY SECTOR OF ACTIVITY (2) – (1000) / 3. EMPLOI CIVIL PAR SECTEUR D'ACTIVITÉ (2) – (1000)

Agriculture, forestry and fisheries / Agriculture, sylviculture et pêche

	EUR 12	B	DK	D	GR	E	F	IRL	I	L	NL	P	UK
1976	13 573 *	128	223	1 682	1 105 *	2 661	2 082	232	3 228	10,5	260	1 285	677
1986	10 108 *	103	:	1 345	1 026	1 742	1 536	168 *	2 242	6,5	248	890	619

Industry / Industrie

	EUR 12	B	DK	D	GR	E	F	IRL	I	L	NL	P	UK
1976	47 377 *	1 416	749	11 258	:	4 578	7 985	325	7 526	65,7	1 560	1 273	9 711
1986	40 589 *	1 058	:	10 333	1 012	3 466	6 567	301	6 823	54,2	1 375	1 386	7 529

Services / Services

	EUR 12	B	DK	D	GR	E	F	IRL	I	L	NL	P	UK
1976	60 470 *	2 125	1 420	12 115	:	5 076	10 947	493	8 858	80,4	2 823	1 231	14 096
1986	71 382 *	2 247	:	13 579	1 562	5 607	12 862	593	11 550	103,7	3 512	1 787	16 091

Total / Total

	EUR 12	B	DK	D	GR	E	F	IRL	I	L	NL	P	UK
1976	121 419 *	3 669	2 392	25 059	3 235 *	12 315	21 016	1 050	19 612	156,6	4 643	3 789	24 484
1986	122 078 *	3 608	:	25 257	3 601	10 814	20 965	1 062	20 614	164,4	5 135	4 063	24 239

4. FARM STRUCTURE – EEC SURVEY (3) / 4. EXPLOITATIONS AGRICOLES – ENQUÊTES CE (3)

Number of holdings (1000) / Nombre d'exploitations (1000)

	EUR 12	B	DK	D	GR	E	F	IRL	I	L	NL	P	UK
1975	:	138	132	908	:	:	1 315	228	2 664	6,4	163	:	281
1985	9 007	98	92	741	952	1 878	1 057	220	2 801	4,4	136	769	259

Total AA (1000 ha) / Total SAU (1000 ha)

	EUR 12	B	DK	D	GR	E	F	IRL	I	L	NL	P	UK
1975	:	1 468	2 966	12 399	:	:	29 464	5 077	16 486	136	2 086	:	16 469
1985	115 102	1 381	2 835	11 884	4 116	23 506	28 487	4 996	15 601	126	2 026	3 314	16 830

Average AA by holding (ha) / Moyenne SAU par exploitation (ha)

	EUR 12	B	DK	D	GR	E	F	IRL	I	L	NL	P	UK
1975	:	10,6	22,4	13,7	:	:	22,4	22,3	6,2	21,9	12,8	:	58,7
1985	12,8	14,1	30,7	16,0	4,3	12,9	27,0	22,7	5,6	28,6	14,9	4,3	65,1

Total labour force, in AWU (1000) / Total force de travail, en UTA (1000)

	EUR 12	B	DK	D	GR	E	F	IRL	I	L	NL	P	UK
1975	:	140	177	1 234	:	:	1 950	325	2 827	12,4	254	:	626
1985	9 421	107	122	918	931	1 432	1 569	276	2 126	7,2	234	1 156	543

Full time labour (%) / A temps plein (%)

	EUR 12	B	DK	D	GR	E	F	IRL	I	L	NL	P	UK
1975	:	70,3	65,4	52,5	:	:	54,0	57,4	31,3	78,4	59,9	:	71,5
1985	43,1	73,0	56,9	57,0	17,1	30,2	59,4	56,9	31,2	69,9	69,0	43,6	73,6

(1) Excluded DOM and territorial waters, CRONOS-ZPA1
(2) CRONOS-SOCI
(3) FSSRS data bank, PT (1979), ES (1982)

(1) Non compris les DOM et les territoires maritimes, CRONOS-ZPA1
(2) CRONOS-SOCI
(3) Banque de données FSSRS, PT (1979), ES (1982)

(× 1000)

YEAR ANNÉE	EUR 12 −Port.	EUR 10	B	DK	D	GR	E	F	IRL	I	L	NL	P	UK
TOTAL														**TOTAL**
1970			181,2		1 527			2 369		2 989,6		303,3		
1971			167,6		1 390			2 292		2 949,8		298,0		
1972			158,8		1 328			2 218		2 893,7		293,1		
1973			149,0	189,5	1 250	1 116		2 147		2 858,9	12,67	286,0		597,1
1974			143,3	176,3	1 198	1 092		2 078		2 845,7	12,21	281,0		574,0
1975		8 549	137,2	168,2	1 168	1 068		2 008	325	2 826,5	11,52	277,5		558,8
1976		8 390	130,5	162,9	1 139	1 045		1 965	314	2 786,5	10,83	273,7		563,0
1977		8 039	124,9	156,5	1 082	1 022		1 926	303	2 591,2	10,61	265,9		556,8
1978		7 862	120,8	150,5	1 059	999		1 895	305	2 506,6	10,07	259,9		555,4
1979	9 398	7 683	120,3	144,4	1 007	978	1 714,7	1 864	306	2 453,5	9,66	256,5	1 155,6	543,8
1980	9 127	7 548	115,6	137,6	987	956	1 579,8	1 834	310	2 414,0	9,16	254,3		529,2
1981	8 779	7 341	112,4	131,4	974	935	1 437,7	1 796	299	2 317,7	8,63	249,3		517,5
1982	8 513	7 129	110,2	126,7	951	924	1 384,7	1 762	288	2 197,5	8,28	248,0		513,1
1983	8 364	7 002	109,4	123,8	927	917	1 362,0	1 727	276	2 157,6	7,88	248,3		508,1
1984	8 075	6 807	108,7	120,3	912	918	1 267,1	1 692	276	2 025,5	7,48	246,7		500,8
1985	7 867	6 654	106,1	114,7	904	931	1 213,1	1 645	276	1 928,2	7,28	245,4		496,6
1986	7 664	6 514	104,8	111,4	890	921	1 150,4	1 603	276		7,03	241,7		485,8
1987											6,70			
FAMILY MEMBERS														**MEMBRES DE LA FAMILLE**
1970			166,9		1 383			1 992		2 394,8		253,7		
1971			156,3		1 241			1 934		2 361,7		247,8		
1972			148,4		1 184			1 878		2 306,6		244,3		
1973			139,0		1 122			1 824		2 279,3	12,07	237,5		343,2
1974			134,0		1 066			1 771		2 271,0	11,67	232,3		328,0
1975			129,1		1 045			1 716	292	2 262,5	11,00	228,9		322,7
1976			122,4		1 024			1 675	282	2 220,5	10,33	224,9		329,3
1977			117,2		971			1 639	272	2 070,9	10,09	217,1		324,6
1978			112,7		951			1 610	272	2 017,3	9,56	210,3		325,8
1979			112,9		895		1 317,6	1 581	272	1 982,8	9,13	207,0		319,3
1980			106,9	109,8	881		1 229,4	1 552	275	1 950,5	8,58	203,7		310,8
1981			104,1	105,0	860		1 120,3	1 524	264	1 897,8	8,03	198,8		306,3
1982			101,9	98,9	841		1 075,1	1 494	253	1 804,8	7,68	197,1		305,7
1983			100,7	95,8	820		1 051,9	1 466	242	1 795,1	7,27	197,6		304,0
1984			99,5	91,9	812		1 004,1	1 438	242	1 690,9	6,88	196,5		304,2
1985			99,1	86,7	791		937,0	1 400	242	1 613,5	6,70	193,7		303,4
1986			97,2	84,2	780		879,0	1 368	242		6,43	189,4		303,8
1987											6,15			
NON-FAMILY MEMBERS														**NON-MEMBRES DE LA FAMILLE**
1970			14,2		144			377		594,8		49,7		
1971			11,3		149			358		588,1		50,1		
1972			10,4		144			340		578,1		48,7		
1973			10,0		128			323		579,6	0,600	48,5		253,9
1974			9,41		132			307		574,7	0,535	48,7		245,9
1975			8.07		123			292	33	564,0	0,520	48,6		236,1
1976			8,10		115			290	32	566,1	0,500	48,8		233,7
1977			7,69		111			287	31	520,3	0,515	48,8		232,2
1978			7,07		108			285	33	489,3	0,510	49,6		229,6
1979			7,38		112		397,1	283	34	470,7	0,530	49,6		224,5
1980			6,94	27,8	106		350,4	278	35	463,5	0,575	50,6		218,4
1981			6,18	26,4	114		317,4	273	35	419,9	0,600	50,5		211,3
1982			6,48	27,8	110		309,6	268	34	392,7	0,595	50,9		207,5
1983			6,84	28,0	107		310,1	261	34	362,5	0,610	50,7		204,2
1984			7,20	28,5	100		263,0	254	34	334,6	0,600	50,2		196,7
1985			7,00	28,0	113		276,1	245	34	314,7	0,575	51,7		193,2
1986			7,60	27,2	110		271,4	235	34		0,599	52,3		183,0
1987											0,550			

Source: CE Survey and national date.

Source: Enquête CE et données nationales.

9

YEAR ANNÉE	WORLD MONDE	EUROPE		N. + C. AMERICA			S. AMERICA			ASIA		AFRICA	OCEA-NIA	USSR
		EUR 10	Rest	USA	Canada	Rest	Argent.	Brazil	Rest	China	Rest			
1. CATTLE (incl. buffaloes)												**1. BOVINS (y compris buffles)**		
1984	1 391,0	81,9	52,9	113,7	12,3	53,2	54,6	128,5	67,4	78,2	423,7	174,2	30,5	119,9
1985	1 399,7	80,7	51,8	109,7	11,7	54,2	54,0	127,3	69,0	82,3	429,7	176,7	31,3	121,4
1986	1 410,1	79,3	51,4	105,5	11,5	54,2	53,0	129,7	70,5	87,0	435,0	179,4	32,4	121,2
2. PIGS												**2. PORCINS**		
1984	795,0	79,3	100,1	56,7	10,8	26,8	3,8	32,3	14,9	312,7	63,0	11,0	4,9	78,7
1985	795,1	81,9	98,1	54,1	10,7	27,1	3,8	32,2	15,6	313,4	63,8	11,5	4,9	77,9
1986	822,5	83,8	95,4	52,3	10,7	28,1	4,0	33,0	16,5	338,1	65,9	12,0	5,0	77,8
3. SHEEP												**3. OVINS**		
1984	1 132,8	61,2	71,6	11,5	0,8	7,6	33,8	18,4	55,3	98,9	232,0	187,4	209,0	145,3
1985	1 131,9	61,8	73,5	10,4	0,7	9,0	29,4	18,4	57,6	95,2	224,4	191,0	217,6	142,9
1986	1 146,9	64,7	71,3	10,0	0,7	10,0	29,2	18,5	59,9	94,2	228,6	191,7	227,2	140,9
4. GOATS												**4. CAPRINS**		
1984	481,8	7,8	4,9	1,4	0,0	12,1	3,1	9,7	6,2	63,4	210,6	155,4	0,6	6,5
1985	484,7	8,0	5,4	1,6	0,0	12,5	3,1	9,5	6,3	63,4	208,8	159,0	0,9	6,3
1986	492,1	8,9	5,0	1,7	0,0	12,6	3,1	9,8	6,2	61,9	213,9	161,5	1,0	6,5
5. EQUIDAE												**5. ÉQUIDÉS**		
1984	119,0	1,8 *	4,7 *	10,5	0,4	15,6	3,3	8,3	8,5	24,8	16,3	18,1	0,6	6,0
1985	120,0	1,7 *	4,7 *	10,6	0,4	15,6	3,3	8,3	8,6	25,3	16,7	18,1	0,6	6,1
1986	121,0 *	1,7 *	4,6 *	10,6 *	0,4 *	15,6 *	3,3 *	8,3 *	8,7 *	25,8 *	17,2 *	18,1 *	0,6 *	6,1 *

YEAR ANNÉE	WORLD MONDE	EUROPE		N. + C. AMERICA			S. AMERICA			ASIA		AFRICA	OCEA-NIA	USSR
		EUR 10	Rest	USA	Canada	Rest	Argent.	Brazil	Rest	China	Rest			
1. BEEF AND VEAL (incl. buffalomeat)												**1. VIANDE DE BŒUF ET DE VEAU (y compris de buffle)**		
1984	46 913	7 507	3 580	10 928	997	1 504	2 548	2 161	1 849	380	3 240	3 182	1 792	7 244
1985	47 900	7 420	3 665	10 996	1 035	1 569	2 760	2 223	1 876	475	3 385	3 325	1 811	7 370
1986	48 620	7 529	3 621	11 300	1 020	1 653	2 800	1 900	1 893	558	3 477	3 390	1 859	7 620
2. PIGMEAT												**2. VIANDE DE PORC**		
1984	56 854	10 432	9 618	6 719	863	1 669	235	780	580	15 179	4 096	427	329	5 927
1985	59 149	10 549	9 586	6 716	900	1 540	240	770	598	17 337	4 283	435	342	5 853
1986	61 202	10 902	9 587	6 379	875	1 601	245	1 100	641	18 810	4 357	445	351	5 910
3. SHEEP AND GOAT MEAT												**3. VIANDE OVINS ET CAPRINS**		
1984	8 198	752	536	172	9	70	115	52	150	587	2 395	1 359	1 134	866
1985	8 319	769	531	162	9	73	110	52	152	594	2 399	1 395	1 246	827
1986	8 366	740 *	544 *	152	8	75	97	52	158	626	2 465	1 411	1 155	885
4. POULTRY MEAT												**4. VIANDE DE VOLAILLE**		
1984	29 826	4 331	3 014	7 469	565	955	381	1 416	813	1 757	4 604	1 484	350	2 686
1985	31 484	4 385	3 107	7 911	614	1 027	372	1 549	842	1 931	4 927	1 596	407	2 816
1986	33 085	4 492 *	3 166 *	8 398	634	1 114	382	1 639	901	2 075	5 151	1 657	430	3 045
5. ALL MEAT												**5. TOUTES VIANDES**		
1984	145 381	25 205	15 564	25 551	2 451	4 280	3 376	4 438	3 485	18 418	14 643	7 345	3 656	16 969
1985	150 559	25 256	15 775	26 085	2 576	4 289	3 579	4 619	3 551	20 877	15 311	7 656	3 855	17 131
1986	155 040	25 673 *	15 926 *	26 529	2 555	4 527	3 623	4 720	3 686	22 634	15 768	7 830	3 845	17 726

SOURCE: EUROSTAT (EUR10), FAO   SOURCE: EUROSTAT (EUR10), FAO

	1977	1978	1979	1980	1981	1982	1983	1984	1985	1986	
TOTAL WHEAT											**TOTAL BLÉ**
EC (1)	38 408	47 598	46 446	52 276	54 469	59 951	59 411	76 101	65 522 *	72 019 *	CE (1)
Canada	19 858	21 137	17 196	19 292	24 802	26 736	26 505	21 199	24 252	31 377	Canada
USA	55 671	48 323	58 081	64 800	75 806	75 251	65 858	70 618	65 999	56 794	États-Unis
Japan	236	367	541	583	587	742	695	741	874	876	Japon
USSR	92 161	120 936	90 296	98 182	81 100	84 300	77 519	68 633	78 078	92 306	URSS
World	387 290	451 187	428 508	446 312	455 730	482 688	494 263	516 932	505 739	535 379	Monde
BARLEY											*ORGE*
EC (1)	37 693	39 649	39 174	40 653	39 527	41 443	36 317	44 306	40 797 *	46 780	CE (1)
Canada	11 802	10 398	8 478	11 304	13 724	13 066	10 209	10 290	12 243	14 688	Canada
USA	9 314	9 901	8 343	7 863	10 309	11 233	11 080	13 046	12 876	13 292	États-Unis
Japan	206	326	406	385	383	390	379	396	378 *	344	Japon
USSR	52 687	62 118	47 956	43 450	36 100	43 000	49 780	41 848	46 540	53 889	URSS
World	160 258	179 939	158 214	160 117	152 300	164 258	161 936	171 826	176 133	181 858	Monde
GRAIN MAIZE											*MAÏS GRAIN*
EC (1)	15 510	16 352	17 394	16 413	18 721	19 896	19 956	20 407	22 008 *	25 972	CE (1)
Canada	4 249	4 480	5 276	5 733	6 673	6 513	5 933	7 024	7 472	5 912	Canada
USA	165 235	184 613	201 383	168 647	206 222	209 180	106 041	194 928	225 478	209 630	États-Unis
Japan	8	7	5	4	3	2	1	2	2	1 *	Japon
USSR	10 979	8 898	8 373	9 454	9 400	14 700	13 293	13 573	14 406	12 479	URSS
World	370 995	393 512	418 793	396 027	450 438	450 333	347 577	453 411	488 525	478 033	Monde
PADDY RICE											*RIZ PADDY*
EC (1)	715	984	1 138	993	941	1 117	1 145	1 139	1 287	1 913	CE (1)
Canada	–	–	–	–	–	–	–	–	–	–	Canada
USA	4 501	6 040	5 985	6 629	8 289	6 969	4 523	6 296	6 120	6 097	États-Unis
Japan	17 006	15 736	14 948	12 189	12 824	12 838	12 958	14 848	14 578	14 559	Japon
USSR	2 217	2 112	2 394	2 791	2 490	2 470	2 600	2 715	2 572	2 633	URSS
World	372 260	388 046	377 324	399 344	412 475	424 022	451 865	469 650	473 155	473 436	Monde
SOYA BEANS											*GRAINES DE SOJA*
EC (1)	3	5	22	18	20	31	89	155	343	915 *	CE (1)
Canada	580	516	657	690	607	848	735	944	1 048	958	Canada
USA	48 098	50 860	61 526	48 922	54 136	59 611	44 518	50 648	57 113	54 623	États-Unis
Japan	111	190	192	174	212	226	217	238	228	245	Japon
USSR	540	634	467	525	491	536	560	469	458	703	URSS
World	73 807	75 381	88 714	81 078	88 144	92 104	79 462	90 654	101 103	97 272	Monde
POTATOES											*POMMES DE TERRE*
EC (1)	38 789	37 855	35 023	32 775	33 679	34 146	28 617	34 610	35 879	39 639	CE (1)
Canada	2 525	2 513	2 752	2 478	2 647	2 781	2 556	2 798	3 030	2 850	Canada
USA	16 118	16 616	15 533	13 737	15 358	16 109	15 146	16 448	18 466	15 979	États-Unis
Japan	3 520	3 316	3 381	3 421	3 095	3 775	3 566	3 707	3 727	3 800 *	Japon
USSR	83 652	86 124	90 956	67 023	72 139	78 185	82 908	85 515	73 009	87 186	URSS
World	280 441	292 223	299 057	241 589	268 635	266 187	265 427	292 056	282 035	292 900	Monde
SUGAR (equiv. white sugar)											*SUCRE (équiv. sucre blanc)*
EC (1)	11 560	11 767	12 304	12 126	15 046	13 952	11 022	12 515 *	12 728 *	13 700 *	CE (1)
Canada	137	119	98	98	129	112	101	104	50	112	Canada
USA	4 834	4 925	4 656	4 905	5 192	4 841	4 698	4 934	5 035	5 419	États-Unis
Japan	592	653	692	740	716	849	742	859	850 *	856 *	Japon
USSR	8 119 *	8 280 *	7 084 *	6 578 *	5 704 *	6 808 *	8 059 *	7 990 *	7 599 *	7 958 *	URSS
World	82 486	83 131	81 309	77 450	85 812	94 499	89 593	91 932	91 052	92 922	Monde
WINE ('000 hl)											*VIN (1000 hl)*
EC (1)	128 288	138 337	177 171	158 471	140 064	171 935	168 243	147 662	142 752 *	209 300 *	CE (1)
Canada	380	520	440	450	450	460	530	610	501	581	Canada
USA	14 180	16 160	16 050	18 000	16 300	19 500	14 760	16 700	18 100	17 700	États-Unis
Japan	400	470	460	507	574	671	702	668	620	600	Japon
USSR	30 700	24 700	29 400	32 200	34 400	34 900	35 100	34 100	26 500	14 000	URSS
World	284 300	294 000	374 022	351 482	315 263	372 255	348 479	323 523	294 318	322 165	Monde

SOURCES: EC: EUROSTAT, others: FAO
(1) EC 9 up to 1980; EC 10 from 1981; EC 12 from 1986

SOURCES: CE: EUROSTAT, autres: FAO
(1) CE 9 jusqu'à 1980; CE 10 à partir de 1981; CE 12 à partir de 1986

	1976/77	1977/78	1978/79	1979/80	1980/81	1981/82	1982/83	1983/84	1984/85	1985/86	
TOTAL CEREALS (equiv. flour)											**TOTAL CÉRÉALES (équiv. farine)**
EC (1)	81	83	83	83	83	83	83	83	85	85	CE (1)
Canada	67	65	69	64	62	64	68	66	64	69	Canada
USA	66	59	63	65	59	63	58	64	62	65	États-Unis
Japan	34	34	34	34	34	34	34	33	33	33	Japon
USSR	180	176	178	177	174	171	173	174	173	171	URSS
TOTAL WHEAT (equiv. flour)											*TOTAL BLÉ (équiv. farine)*
EC (1)	74	75	75	76	76	75	71	71	73	73	CE (1)
Canada	62	60	64	59	56	58	61	59	58	63	Canada
USA	57	50	55	57	50	55	51	55	54	56	États-Unis
Japan	32	32	32	32	32	32	32	32	32	32	Japon
USSR	145	144	146	145	144	143	144	143	144	150	URSS
RICE (equiv. husked rice)											*RIZ (équiv. riz décortiqué)*
EC (1)	4	4	4	4	5	5	5	5	5	6	CE (1
Canada	3	3	3	3	3	3	4	4	4	4	Canada
USA	3	3	3	4	4	5	5	4	4	4	États-Unis
Japan	87	84	82	80	79	80	83	80	76	75	Japon
USSR	7	8	8	9	10	11	10	9	8	8	URSS
DRIED PULSES											*LÉGUMES SECS*
EC (1)	3	2	2	2	2	2	2	2	2	3	CE (1)
Canada	1	1	1	2	1	1	2	1	1	2	Canada
USA	3	3	2	3	3	3	3	3	3	3	États-Unis
Japan	4	3	3	3	3	3	3	3	3	3	Japon
USSR	4	4	3	3	3	3	3	3	3	3	URSSURSS
POTATOES											*POMMES DE TERRE*
EC (1)	71	77	78	77	76	75	76	74	75	81	CE (1)
Canada	67	71	75	77	71	65	67	77	61	68	Canada
USA	29	31	31	33	34	30	32	31	28	29	États-Unis
Japan	12	13	14	14	13	13	14	14	13	14	Japon
USSR	119	120	117	115	109	105	110	110	110	104	URSS
SUGAR (equiv. white sugar)											*SUCRE (équiv. sucre blanc)*
EC (1)	37	35	36	37	35	36	35	33	34	34	CE (1)
Canada	42	42	42	40	40	38	38	39	41	43	Canada
USA	40	40	39	41	38	36	34	33	31	30	États-Unis
Japan	25	26	25	25	23	22	22	21	21	21	Japon
USSR	42	42	43	42	44	44	45	44	44	42	URSS
VEGETABLES											*LÉGUMES*
EC (1)	92	104	102	104	105	103	108	108	110 *	120 *	CE (1)
Canada	72	70	74	78	77	76	79	79	82	84	Canada
USA	94	95	96	97	96	93	96	99	96	99	États-Unis
Japan	110	114	114	112	111	111	112	108	111	109	Japon
USSR (2)	68	68	68	68	68	68	68	68	68	102	URSS (2)
VEGETABLE FATS AND OILS											*GRAISSES ET HUILES VÉGÉTALES*
EC (1)	17	16	16	17	18	19	19	19	18 *	19 *	CE (1)
Canada	4	4	4	4	4	4	4	5	4	5	Canada
USA	10	10	9	10	10	11	11	11	11	11	États-Unis
Japan	9	9	9	10	10	11	11	11	11	12	Japon
USSR	:	:	:	:	:	:	:	:	:	10	URSS

SOURCES: EC: EUROSTAT, USSR: FAO, others: OECD
(1) EC 9 up to 1979/80; EC 10 from 1980/81; EC 12 from 1985/86
(2) Average 1964-1966 up to 1984/85

SOURCES: CE: EUROSTAT, URSS: FAO, autres OCDE
(1) CE 9 jusqu'à 1979/80; CE 10 à partir de 1980/81; CE 12 à partir de 1985/86
(2) Moyenne 1964-1966 jusqu'en 1984/85

GROSS VALUE ADDED AT FACTOR COST BY GROUPS OF ECONOMIC BRANCHES

VALEUR AJOUTÉE BRUTE AU COÛT DES FACTEURS PAR GROUPES DE BRANCHES ÉCONOMIQUES

MRD ECU

YEAR ANNÉE	EUR 12	EUR 10	B	DK	D	GR	E	F	IRL	I	L	NL	P	UK
AGRICULTURE, FORESTRY, FISHERIES													**AGRICULTURE, SYLVICULTURE, PÊCHE**	
1982	103,7	89,8	2,1	3,2	15,2	6,5	11,7	23,7	2,0	21,5	0,1	5,9	2,2	9,6
1983	104,4	91,2	2,4	3,1	13,9	5,9	11,1	23,1	2,2	25,2	0,1	6,2	2,1	9,1
1984	113,7	98,3	2,5	3,8	15,9	6,7	13,2	24,4	2,4	25,7	0,2	6,6	2,2	10,1
1985	114,9	98,7	2,5	3,7	17,3	6,7	13,7	24,9	2,3	25,3	0,2	6,5	2,5	9,3
INDUSTRY														**INDUSTRIE**
1982	923,2	850,0	26,5	13,5	249,6	10,3	64,5	191,7	6,1	130,3	1,3	45,3	8,7	175,4
1983	974,6	906,4	28,0	15,0	272,6	10,4	59,7	200,3	6,3	141,2	1,4	48,0	8,5	183,2
1984	1 043,8	968,7	29,7	16,1	286,9	11,1	66,2	213,3	6,8	155,9	1,6	51,6	8,9	195,7
1985	1 119,4	1 037,2	31,4	18,1	300,7	11,4	72,2	232,5	7,4	160,0	1,7	54,8	10,0	216,2
SERVICES														**SERVICES**
1982	1 441,3	1 323,5	53,6	33,2	366,1	18,6	105,3	310,5	9,7	192,8	2,3	82,7	12,5	254,0
1983	1 547,0	1 433,3	55,7	37,2	406,7	18,7	101,4	329,0	10,4	216,7	2,5	89,0	12,3	267,4
1984	1 679,1	1 547,6	60,2	40,5	433,8	20,2	118,6	357,1	11,4	245,4	2,8	92,2	12,9	284,0
1985	1 818,8	1 675,0	65,3	45,3	461,7	20,9	129,4	385,8	12,3	267,4	3,0	95,9	14,4	317,4
TOTAL														**TOTAL**
1982	2 468,3	2 263,4	82,2	49,9	630,9	35,4	181,5	525,9	17,8	344,6	3,7	134,0	23,4	439,0
1983	2 626,1	2 431,0	86,1	55,3	693,2	35,0	172,2	552,4	18,9	383,1	4,1	143,2	22,9	459,7
1984	2 836,6	2 614,5	92,4	60,4	736,6	38,0	198,1	594,8	20,6	427,0	4,5	150,4	24,0	489,8
1985	3 051,1	2 808,8	99,2	67,1	777,2	39,0	215,5	643,2	22,4	455,7	4,9	157,3	26,8	542,8

ECONOMIC BRANCHES AS A PERCENTAGE OF TOTAL GROSS VALUE ADDED AT FACTOR COST

BRANCHES ÉCONOMIQUES EN POURCENTAGE DU TOTAL DE LA VALEUR BRUTE AU COÛT DES FACTEURS

%

YEAR ANNÉE	EUR 12	EUR 10	B	DK	D	GR	E	F	IRL	I	L	NL	P	UK
AGRICULTURE, FORESTRY, FISHERIES													**AGRICULTURE, SYLVICULTURE, PÊCHE**	
1982	4,2	4,0	2,6	6,4	2,4	18,4	6,4	4,5	11,2	6,2	2,7	4,4	9,4	2,2
1983	4,0	3,8	2,8	5,6	2,0	16,9	6,4	4,2	11,6	6,6	2,4	4,3	9,2	2,0
1984	4,0	3,8	2,7	6,3	2,2	17,6	6,7	4,1	11,7	6,0	4,4	4,4	9,2	2,1
1985	3,8	3,5	2,5	5,5	2,2	17,2	6,4	3,9	10,3	5,6	4,1	4,1	9,3	1,7
INDUSTRY														**INDUSTRIE**
1982	37,4	37,6	32,2	27,1	39,6	29,1	35,5	36,5	34,3	37,8	35,1	33,8	37,2	40,0
1983	37,1	37,3	32,5	27,1	39,3	29,7	34,7	36,3	33,3	36,9	34,1	33,5	37,1	39,9
1984	36,8	37,1	32,1	26,7	38,9	29,2	33,4	35,9	33,0	36,5	35,6	34,3	37,1	40,0
1985	36,7	36,9	31,7	27,0	38,7	29,2	33,5	36,1	33,0	35,8	34,7	34,8	37,3	39,8
SERVICES														**SERVICES**
1982	58,4	58,5	65,2	66,5	58,0	52,5	58,0	59,0	54,5	55,9	62,2	61,7	53,4	57,9
1983	58,9	59,0	64,7	67,3	58,7	53,4	58,9	59,6	55,0	56,6	61,0	62,2	53,7	58,2
1984	59,2	59,2	65,2	67,1	58,9	53,2	59,9	60,0	55,3	57,5	62,2	61,3	53,8	58,0
1985	59,6	59,6	65,8	67,5	59,4	53,6	60,0	60,0	54,9	58,7	61,2	61,0	53,7	58,5
TOTAL														**TOTAL**
1982	100,0	100,0	100,0	100,0	100,0	100,0	100,0	100,0	100,0	100,0	100,0	100,0	100,0	100,0
1983	100,0	100,0	100,0	100,0	100,0	100,0	100,0	100,0	100,0	100,0	100,0	100,0	100,0	100,0
1984	100,0	100,0	100,0	100,0	100,0	100,0	100,0	100,0	100,0	100,0	100,0	100,0	100,0	100,0
1985	100,0	100,0	100,0	100,0	100,0	100,0	100,0	100,0	100,0	100,0	100,0	100,0	100,0	100,0

AGRICULTURE, FORESTRY, FISHERIES
AS A PERCENTAGE OF GROSS VALUE ADDED
AT FACTOR COST

AGRICULTURE, SYLVICULTURE, PÊCHE
EN POURCENTAGE DE LA VALEUR AJOUTEE BRUTE
AU COÛT DES FACTEURS

1985

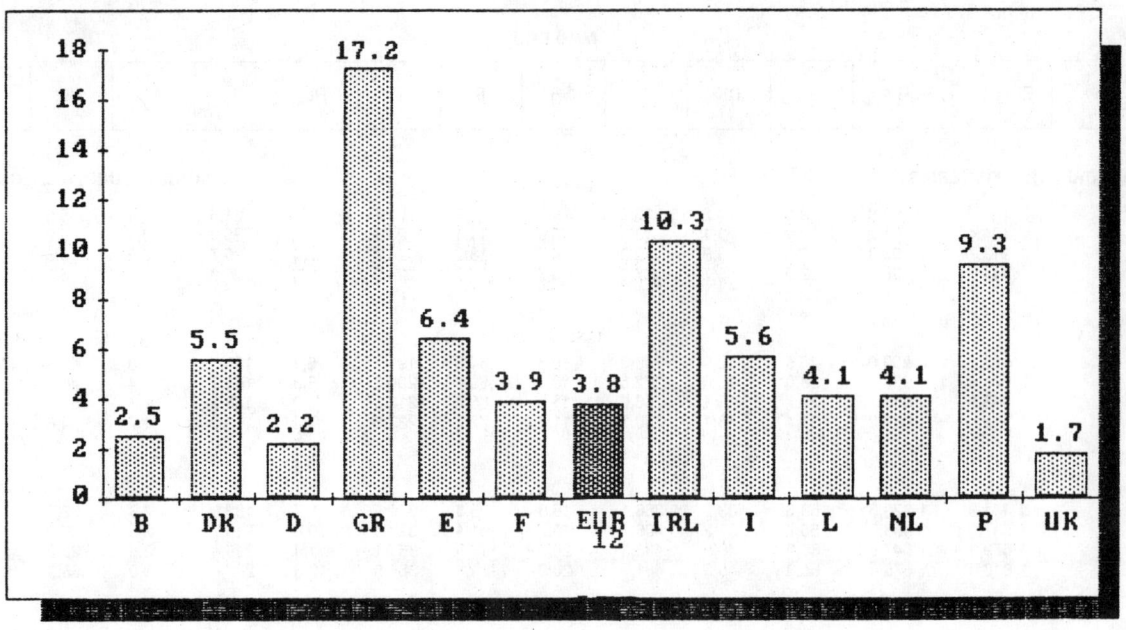

GROSS DOMESTIC PRODUCT AT MARKET PRICES

I A 8

PRODUIT INTÉRIEUR BRUT AU PRIX DU MARCHÉ

YEAR ANNÉE	EUR 12	EUR 10	B	DK	D	GR	E	F	IRL	I	L	NL	P	UK
TOTAL AT CURRENT PRICES					**MRD ECU**							**TOTAL AUX PRIX COURANTS**		
1982	2 682,7	2 477,0	86,7	56,9	672,5	39,1	181,9	554,6	19,3	411,8	3,6	141,1	23,8	491,3
1983	2 862,6	2 664,9	90,5	63,0	737,6	39,1	174,4	581,2	20,3	467,9	3,9	150,2	23,3	511,2
1984	3 084,8	2 861,9	96,9	68,7	783,8	42,7	198,5	623,3	22,2	521,7	4,4	157,9	24,4	540,3
1985	3 314,2	3 070,7	104,5	76,4	826,4	42,8	216,2	674,8	24,1	556,5	4,7	165,3	27,3	595,0
VOLUME INDEX NUMBERS					**1980 = 100**							**INDICES DE VOLUME**		
1982	100,7	100,6	100,3	102,1	99,5	99,5	101,0	102,3	104,8	101,4	100,5	97,9	106,2	99,8
1983	102,1	102,0	100,0	104,1	101,0	99,9	102,8	103,0	102,8	101,9	103,8	99,3	104,7	103,5
1984	104,5	104,6	101,7	107,7	103,8	102,7	104,7	104,6	107,1	105,5	109,4	101,6	101,8	105,8
1985	107,1	107,2	103,2	111,8	106,5	104,8	107,1	105,7	109,2	108,4	112,6	103,4	106,0	109,7
PER INHABITANT					**ECU**							**PAR HABITANT**		
1982	8 396	9 106	8 800	11 126	10 911	3 990	4 792	10 181	5 553	7 270	9 774	9 860	2 495	8 721
1983	8 943	9 782	9 181	12 320	12 009	3 968	4 568	10 619	5 804	8 232	10 682	10 454	2 450	9 068
1984	9 617	10 490	9 831	13 444	12 813	4 306	5 170	11 343	6 287	9 152	11 973	10 949	2 551	9 566
1985	10 307	11 235	10 605	14 945	13 543	4 286	5 602	12 231	6 815	9 738	12 884	11 409	2 831	10 509
PER CIVILIAN ACTIVE PERSON					**ECU**							**PAR PERSONNE ACTIVE CIVILE**		
1982	22 144	23 336	24 231	22 981	26 711	11 168	16 472	26 111	17 065	20 289	22 785	28 169	6 012	20 838
1983	23 747	25 283	25 551	25 200	29 750	11 048	15 872	27 457	18 288	22 993	24 841	30 252	5 629	21 962
1984	25 594	27 056	27 327	27 513	31 560	12 025	18 597	29 708	20 386	25 545	27 848	31 707	5 986	22 780
1985	27 347	28 815	29 223	29 890	33 051	11 925	20 460	32 287	22 693	27 136	29 375	32 565	6 729	24 649

FINAL CONSUMPTION OF HOUSEHOLDS

I A 9

CONSOMMATION FINALE DES MÉNAGES

YEAR ANNÉE	EUR 12	EUR 10	B	DK	D	GR	E	F	IRL	I	L	NL	P	UK
TOTAL AT CURRENT PRICES					**MRD ECU**							**TOTAL AUX PRIX COURANTS**		
1982	1 680,1	1 541,7	56,6	31,1	423,8	25,9	122,2	356,6	11,6	252,3	2,1	84,9	16,2	296,8
1983	1 789,3	1 657,3	58,9	34,1	464,8	25,8	116,1	374,4	12,1	284,8	2,3	90,6	15,9	309,5
1984	1 919,3	1 773,5	63,3	37,2	492,0	27,5	128,9	398,6	12,8	317,5	2,5	93,0	16,9	329,1
1985	2 058,0	1 900,7	68,1	41,4	514,3	28,1	139,2	435,2	13,7	340,0	2,6	97,5	18,1	359,4
VOLUME INDEX NUMBERS					**1980 = 100**							**INDICES DE VOLUME**		
1982	101,2	101,2	100,6	99,2	98,6	104,0	99,6	105,2	94,0	102,5	101,8	96,3	107,2	100,7
1983	102,5	102,7	99,0	101,1	100,1	105,0	99,9	106,2	92,4	102,7	102,6	97,2	103,6	104,7
1984	103,8	104,4	100,1	103,7	102,0	106,8	99,5	107,1	91,9	105,2	103,5	96,8	97,0	107,0
1985	106,4	107,0	101,6	108,2	103,9	109,8	101,3	109,6	93,4	108,2	106,0	98,4	99,9	110,7
PER INHABITANT					**ECU**							**PAR HABITANT**		
1982	5 284	5 697	5 741	6 124	6 961	2 650	3 219	6 571	3 339	4 474	5 858	5 930	1 705	5 268
1983	5 618	6 116	5 974	6 720	7 665	2 624	3 042	6 868	3 457	5 032	6 275	6 307	1 682	5 489
1984	6 014	6 536	6 419	7 338	8 146	2 777	3 358	7 283	3 613	5 595	6 733	6 450	1 777	5 827
1985	6 433	6 993	6 905	8 159	8 540	2 808	3 607	7 918	3 870	5 988	7 214	6 729	1 882	6 348
EXPENDITURE FOR FOOD					**%**							**DÉPENSES POUR L'ALIMENTATION**		
1982	22,5	21,8	21,4	25,4	18,4	44,0	29,0	21,3	44,0	27,0	23,8	19,8	38,9	20,2
1983	22,2	21,5	21,9	24,9	18,0	43,4	28,6	21,3	43,8	26,8	21,7	19,4	39,0	19,9
1984	21,9	21,3	22,0	25,0	17,6	43,3	28,9	21,4	44,5	25,7	20,0	19,5	39,1	19,5
1985	21,5	20,8	21,6	24,2	17,1	42,7	29,4	20,9	44,5	25,2	23,1	19,1	38,7	18,9

NOTE: FOR PORTUGAL FOOD EXPENDITURE INCLUDES DRINK AND TOBACCO

REMARQUE: POUR LE PORTUGAL LE TABAC ET LES BOISSONS SONT INCLUS DANS LES DÉPENSES POUR L'ALIMENTATION

1980 = 100

YEAR ANNÉE	EUR 12	EUR 10	B	DK	D	GR	E	F	IRL	I	L	NL	P	UK
TOTAL INDUSTRY														**INDUSTRIE TOTALE**
1983	97,8	97,4	99,1	106,0	95,9	101,9	100,5	98,2	111,4	92,5	100,3	97,0	106,8	101,9
1984	100,0	99,7	101,6	116,3	98,8	103,5	101,4	98,6	125,3	95,6	113,6	101,0	106,7	103,3
1985	103,3	103,1	104,1	121,2	104,4	107,0	103,4	99,4	128,1	96,9	121,4	105,0	118,3	108,1
1986	105,4	105,0	105,2	126,3	106,6	106,8	106,6	99,8	131,6	100,0	124,7	106,0	123,9	110,3
FOOD, DRINK, TOBACCO INDUSTRY												**INDUSTRIE DES ALIMENTS, BOISSONS, TABAC**		
1983	103,5	102,5	110,0	107,6	98,7	107,7	110,8	104,7	106,8	102,4	137,1	104,0	105,5	100,9
1984	104,4	103,7	112,3	111,5	100,3	114,3	111,7	105,4	110,1	101,4	130,1	108,0	98,3	101,9
1985	107,0	106,0	115,3	115,8	103,4	121,2	117,1	107,1	115,2	105,8	140,3	110,0	97,7	101,0
1986	108,6	107,6	116,1	120,6	104,6	114,2	116,1	107,7	119,0	109,8	148,2	113,0	113,0	102,4
FOOD INDUSTRY													**INDUSTRIE DES ALIMENTS**	
1983	103,9	103,4	112,9	110,9	99,3	108,4	106,0	109,5	101,3	101,3	108,5	104,0	105,4	103,7
1984	105,6	105,6	116,8	114,2	102,2	106,8	106,3	113,6	113,6	104,1	109,4	109,0	98,2	104,4
1985	107,5	107,0	121,6	119,7	105,6	111,9	107,9	118,7	118,7	103,2	108,8	110,0	107,4	103,9
1986	108,9	108,8	124,6	124,9	107,0	110,1	108,3	124,5	118,7	106,7	108,6	113,0	111,7	105,4
DRINK INDUSTRY													**INDUSTRIE DES BOISSONS**	
1983	102,3	100,8	103,5	96,0	99,9	105,7	110,9	101,1	103,4	108,4	148,4	101,0	105,3	97,1
1984	102,4	101,8	103,5	101,6	98,3	111,5	106,8	104,0	105,5	108,0	138,2	100,0	96,8	98,8
1985	106,3	104,8	101,4	102,2	99,0	125,4	115,7	105,5	110,2	125,1	152,6	101,0	105,1	99,5
1986	109,1	108,2	99,2	104,5	100,9	129,7	114,7	108,3	110,8	133,8	163,7	104,0	110,5	104,1
TOBACCO INDUSTRY													**INDUSTRIE DU TABAC**	
1983	100,8	96,9	107,8	102,7	96,4	115,3	135,5	85,3	84,2	112,5	...	117,0	119,2	90,4
1984	102,2	95,5	102,2	107,7	98,2	106,9	181,7	82,1	82,8	109,0	...	116,0	111,3	90,1
1985	103,1	96,4	105,2	109,4	102,5	118,5	176,4	92,0	88,5	107,4	...	128,0	129,3	82,6
1986	97,3	89,8	98,6	112,7	102,6	109,1	182,3	81,1	79,7	104,0	...	128,0	128,8	74,1

VALUES IN MIO ECU

VALEURS EN MIO ÉCU

SITC Rev. 2	List of products	import				export		Dénomination des produits	CTCI Rév. 2
		intra		extra		extra			
		1985	1986	1985	1986	1985	1986		
0-9	**TOTAL TRADE**	466 742	459 706	406 418	334 564	378 651	1 341 934	**COMMERCE TOTAL**	0-9
0	**Food and live animals chiefly for food**	50 182	52 179	35 058	32 483	22 823	18 824	**Produits alimentaires et animaux vivants**	0
00	Live animals chiefly for food	2 801	2 998	633	550	514	497	Animaux vivants dest. princip. à l'alimentation humaine	00
01	Meat and meat preparations	9 392	9 711	2 679	2 245	2 656	2 598	Viandes et préparations de viande	01
02	Dairy products and birds' eggs	7 737	8 103	697	696	3 736	2 982	Produits laitiers et œufs d'oiseaux	02
03	Fish, crustaceans and molluscs and preparations thereof	2 844	3 195	3 574	4 031	1 124	1 081	Poissons, crustacés, mollusques et préparations de poissons	03
04	Cereals and cereal preparations	7 441	8 022	1 535	1 535	5 890	3 926	Céréales et préparations à base de céréales	04
05	Vegetables and fruit	10 589	10 924	8 175	7 562	3 011	2 666	Légumes et fruits	05
06	Sugar, sugar preparations and honey	1 352	1 322	1 189	1 306	1 489	1 411	Sucres; préparations à base de sucre, et miel	06
07	Coffee, tea, cocoa, spices, and manufactures thereof	3 397	3 256	10 032	9 713	1 707	1 560	Café, thé, cacao, épices, et produits dérivés	07
08	Feeding stuff for animals (not including unmilled cereals)	2 911	2 892	4 727	4 543	1 306	997	Nourriture dest. aux animaux (à l'excl. des céréales non moulues)	08
09	Miscellaneous edible products and preparations	1 720	1 754	314	302	1 390	1 106	Produits et préparations alimentaires divers	09
1	**Beverages and tobacco**	7 113	7 136	2 780	2 317	6 394	5 857	**Boissons et tabacs**	1
11	Beverages	4 842	5 077	383	365	5 459	5 023	Boissons	11
12	Tobacco and tobacco manufactures	2 271	2 059	2 397	1 952	935	834	Tabacs bruts et fabriqués	12
2	**Crude materials, inedible, except fuels**	19 341	17 555	38 895	31 158	7 067	6 058	**Matières brutes non comestibles, carburants non compris**	2
21	Hides, skins and furskins, raw	1 622	1 422	2 026	1 598	667	601	Cuirs, peaux et pelleteries bruts	21
22	Seeds, oil and oleaginous fruit	1 300	1 359	5 135	3 558	42	30	Graines et fruits oléagineux	22
23	Crude rubber (including synthetic and reclaimed)	1 448	1 359	1 375	1 117	515	395	Caoutchouc brut (y compr. caoutchouc synthétique et régénéré)	23
24	Cork and wood	1 198	1 212	5 795	5 748	537	566	Liège et bois	24
25	Pulp and waste paper	1 078	1 030	4 325	3 890	241	200	Pâtes à papier et déchets de papier	25
26	Textile fibres (other than wool tops) and their wastes	2 608	2 277	5 842	4 085	1 469	1 193	Fibres textiles (excep. laines en rubans) et déchets n. transf.	26
27	Crude fertilizers + minerals (excl. coal, petrol + precious stones)	2 041	1 987	2 879	2 272	1 064	885	Engrais, minéraux, bruts (excl. charbon, pétrole, pierres préc.)	27
28	Metalliferous ores and metal scrap	4 875	3 450	9 947	7 434	1 224	852	Minerais métallifères et déchets de métaux	28
29	Crude animal and vegetable materials, n.e.s.	3 172	3 460	1 577	1 456	1 308	1 337	Matières brutes d'origine animale ou végétale, n.d.a.	29
3	**Mineral fuels, lubricats and related materials**	51 316	27 090	120 176	59 405	18 574	10 641	**Combustibles minéraux, lubrifiants et produits connexes**	3
32	Coal, coke and briquettes	2 305	1 868	6 250	4 623	648	413	Houilles, cokes et briquettes	32
33	Petroleum, petroleum products and related materials	42 074	21 402	103 820	49 221	16 858	9 480	Pétrole, produits dérivés du pétrole et produits connexes	33
34	Gas, natural and manufactured	6 361	3 328	9 483	4 919	606	263	Gaz naturel et gaz manufacturé	34
35	Electric current	581	491	632	642	464	485	Énergie électrique	35
4	**Animal and vegetable oils, fats and waxes**	3 205	2 292	2 745	1 465	1 865	1 174	**Huiles, graisses et cires d'origine animale ou végétale**	4
41	Animal oils and fats	402	251	553	295	75	56	Huiles et graisses d'origine animale	41
42	Fixed vegetable oils and fats	2 028	1 518	1 915	1 019	1 533	927	Huiles végétales fixes	42
43	Oils and fats, processed, and animal or vegetable waxes	775	523	277	151	257	190	Huiles et graisses élaborées; cires animales ou végétales	43
5	**Chemicals and related products, n.e.s.**	57 037	56 756	22 303	21 168	42 077	37 443	**Produits chimiques et produits connexes, n.d.a.**	5
51	Organic chemicals	15 963	14 339	6 473	5 715	8 933	7 416	Produits chimiques organiques	51
52	Inorganic chemicals	5 109	4 931	3 758	3 152	3 668	2 641	Produits chimiques inorganiques	52
53	Dyeing, tanning and colouring materials	2 984	3 431	980	1 092	3 271	3 242	Produits pour teinture et tannage et colorants	53
54	Medical and pharmaceutical products	4 849	5 133	2 965	3 107	6 894	6 813	Produits médicinaux et pharmaceutiques	54
55	Essential oils + perfume materials; toilet, polish + clean. preparat.	3 445	3 625	858	808	3 597	3 353	Huiles essent., produits pour parfumerie, toilette et entretien	55
56	Fertilizers, manufactured	2 217	1 984	1 279	1 248	1 160	719	Engrais manufacturés	56
57	Explosives and pyrotechnic products	132	155	73	72	116	83	Explosifs et articles de pyrotechnie	57
58	Artific. resins + plastic materials + cellulose esters and ethers	15 611	16 306	3 736	3 703	8 590	7 753	Mat. plast., artif., éthers, esters d.l. cellulose, résines artific.	58
59	Chemical materials and products, n.e.s.	6 727	6 851	2 181	2 271	5 849	5 422	Matières et produits chimiques, n.d.a.	59
6	**Manufactured goods classified chiefly by material**	85 330	87 603	48 372	47 899	71 833	61 774	**Art. manufact. classés princip. d'après la mat. première**	6
61	Leather, leather manufactures, n.e.s. and dressed furskins	2 468	2 507	1 798	1 756	1 810	1 656	Cuirs et peaux, prép. et ouvrages en cuir, n.d.a. pellet. apprêt.	61
62	Rubber manufactures, n.e.s.	4 416	4 857	1 322	1 415	3 248	2 995	Caoutchouc manufacturé, n.d.a.	62
63	Cork and wood manufactures (excluding furniture)	2 059	2 183	1 945	2 025	1 087	1 036	Ouvrages en liège et en bois (à l'exception des meubles)	63
64	Paper, paperboard, + art. of paper pulp, of paper or paperboard	9 087	9 616	7 979	8 367	3 955	3 609	Papiers, cartons, ouvrages en pâte cellul., en papier ou en carton	64
65	Textile yarn, fabrics, made-up articles, n.e.s., + related products	18 847	19 221	8 389	8 479	11 593	10 756	Fils, tissus, articles textiles façonnés, n.d.a., prod. connexes	65
66	Non-metallic mineral manufactures, n.e.s.	8 331	8 884	5 986	6 217	12 276	11 590	Articles minéraux non métalliques manufacturés, n.d.a.	66
67	Iron and steel	19 319	19 311	6 529	6 645	20 510	14 997	Fer et acier	67
68	Non-ferrous metals	10 143	9 463	9 892	8 330	5 805	4 931	Métaux non ferreux	68
69	Manufactures of metal, n.e.s.	10 658	11 562	4 531	4 666	11 395	10 029	Articles manufacturés en métal, n.d.a.	69
7	**Machinery and transport equipment**	31 314	143 758	76 545	78 860	138 631	133 595	**Machines et matériel de transport**	70
71	Power-generating machinery and equipment	8 140	8 757	7 467	7 180	12 180	11 328	Machines génératrices, moteurs et leur équipement	71
72	Machinery specialized for particular industries	13 058	14 209	6 963	8 134	21 915	21 967	Machines et appareils spécialisés pour les industries partic.	72
73	Metalworking machinery	2 619	3 202	2 017	2 457	4 890	5 361	Machines et appareils pour le travail des métaux	73
74	General indust. mach. + equipment, n.e.s., machine parts, n.e.s.	15 567	17 189	7 704	7 979	21 636	20 844	Mach. et app. industr., applic. gén., n.d.a., parties et pièces dét.	74
75	Office machines and automatic data-processing equipment	17 397	17 343	15 828	14 877	8 944	8 355	Mach. et app. bureau ou p. traitement automatique de l'information	75
76	Telecom. + sound reprod. + reprod. apparatus + equipment	5 968	7 149	8 571	9 373	6 531	6 238	App. et équipement de télécommunic., enregistr. reprod. du son	76
77	Electr. machinery, apparatus + appliances, n.e.s., + electr. parts	19 612	21 169	13 161	12 844	16 417	16 137	Mach. et app. électr., n.d.a., parties et pièces détachées électr.	77
78	Road vehicles (including air cushion vehicles)	43 363	49 626	10 932	13 281	35 416	34 393	Véhicules routiers (y compris les véhicules à coussin d'air)	78
79	Other transport equipment	5 594	5 113	4 905	5 058	8 939	7 107	Autre matériel de transport	79
8	**Miscellaneous manufactured articles**	47 894	52 976	35 469	37 761	47 346	45 091	**Articles manufacturés divers**	8
81	Sanitary, plumbing, heating + lighting fixtures + fittings, n.e.s.	1 460	1 670	379	418	1 148	1 029	App. sanitaire, appareillage de plomberie, chauffage, éclair. n.d.a.	81
82	Furniture and parts thereof	4 545	5 212	1 559	1 650	4 335	4 131	Meubles et leurs parties et pièces détachées	82
83	Travel goods, handbags and similar containers	572	619	713	813	800	851	Articles de voyage, sacs à main et contenants similaires	83
84	Articles of apparel and clothing accessories	12 507	14 071	10 687	11 996	8 183	8 236	Vêtements et accessoires du vêtement	84
85	Footwear	4 518	4 912	1 629	1 691	3 962	3 529	Chaussures	85
87	Professional, scientific + controlling instrum. + apparatus, n.e.s.	6 168	6 773	6 434	6 191	8 794	8 320	Instruments et app. profess., scientifiques et de contrôle, n.d.a.	87
88	Photogr. ap., equip. + suppl. + optic. goods; watches + clocks	4 304	4 380	4 626	4 890	4 195	3 834	App. et fournit. de photograph. et d'optique, n.d.a., montres	88
89	Miscellaneous manufactured articles, n.e.s.	13 821	15 339	9 441	10 114	15 850	15 083	Articles manufacturés divers, n.d.a.	89
9	**Goods not classified elsewhere in the SITC**	14 009	12 362	24 075	22 048	22 040	21 476	**Articles non classés ailleurs dans la CTCI**	9

VALUE IN MIO ECU   IMPORTATIONS

	1973	1974	1975	1976	1977	1978	1979	1980	1981	1982	1983	1984	1985	1986
WORLD	26 639	30 627	33 670	40 326	46 268	46 979	50 866	54 852	61 774	68 822	72 568	79 760	85 417	84 828
INTRA-EC	12 761	15 040	16 996	20 036	22 898	25 075	27 615	30 000	34 073	39 008	41 617	45 370	50 182	52 179
EXTRA-EC	13 879	15 587	16 674	20 290	23 369	21 904	23 231	24 763	27 606	29 688	30 767	34 213	35 058	32 247
Iceland	72	88	81	91	99	123	172	216	235	283	265	295	388	493
Faroe Isles	23	29	22	39	69	70	77	96	123	145	150	161	195	204
Norway	220	233	200	283	340	314	344	339	401	453	544	605	642	660
Sweden	112	115	106	126	122	133	148	175	197	233	234	289	330	260
Finland	23	26	20	55	74	49	51	44	43	53	68	118	79	67
Switzerland	139	157	176	454	238	262	271	297	343	411	423	441	512	566
Austria	113	106	118	146	152	172	198	207	237	306	300	322	428	382
Malta	4	3	2	5	5	4	4	3	2	2	2	5	4	2
Yugoslavia	237	145	152	229	245	248	258	260	254	316	415	400	445	417
Turkey	219	221	187	239	297	293	334	406	472	452	474	543	661	651
Soviet Union	56	67	75	81	87	75	78	74	82	89	88	123	140	123
German Dem. Rep.	62	77	118	117	45	95	58	48	86	43	17	38	48	62
Poland	360	310	248	329	351	349	373	377	294	336	393	488	571	510
Czechoslovakia	63	55	61	49	53	70	82	78	95	123	127	148	139	122
Hungary	271	242	243	242	286	313	329	336	359	404	431	480	518	432
Romania	177	166	182	169	114	114	111	97	92	80	76	96	96	94
Bulgaria	86	50	62	66	68	79	86	67	68	75	70	70	73	69
Morocco	317	278	285	335	331	348	383	413	387	406	436	434	558	549
Algeria	42	36	30	40	39	21	16	7	7	6	9	17	20	14
Tunisia	30	28	33	36	40	45	57	64	64	71	98	96	129	120
Egypt	47	38	23	76	66	45	55	64	62	63	58	81	59	59
Mauritania	5	6	5	6	7	9	5	22	46	48	30	38	42	43
Senegal	60	66	78	97	123	91	103	97	104	139	165	151	152	177
Siera Leone	7	6	8	7	22	19	28	35	36	17	44	32	44	39
Liberia	4	8	5	9	28	28	24	26	22	21	30	32	49	33
Ivory Coast	257	430	464	722	1 216	1 071	1 011	929	953	1 061	1 044	1 408	1 770	1 657
Ghana	104	184	179	220	392	370	281	282	201	292	165	226	256	191
Togo	21	33	27	40	60	46	49	49	55	47	33	47	47	78
Benin	19	13	7	7	11	5	12	21	8	11	18	37	65	50
Nigeria	116	104	106	222	359	369	282	231	193	193	275	283	306	210
Cameroon	129	234	216	263	393	451	441	458	393	421	429	622	598	576
Centr. Afric. Rep.	10	10	10	24	42	27	23	25	23	31	42	44	45	40
Gabon	5	8	6	6	10	12	16	17	21	20	21	25	25	26
Zaire	58	59	63	152	284	207	165	154	138	159	188	241	239	329
Rwanda	2	4	10	22	37	24	38	26	19	28	48	112	133	148
Burundi	3	7	14	18	30	20	20	27	21	40	61	74	103	108
Angola	100	106	72	52	18	40	22	15	19	40	25	33	27	28
Ethiopia	32	39	34	49	57	41	59	75	84	101	140	190	152	209
Kenya	112	120	116	207	467	342	300	328	305	347	416	618	596	543
Uganda	65	87	69	118	201	140	199	173	104	168	229	308	286	298
Tanzania	44	46	51	101	147	141	128	123	135	144	143	218	160	199
Madagascar	62	68	81	90	134	99	85	97	75	94	137	198	157	161
Reunion	42	38	54	76	94	87	92	90	77	55	49	82	61	115
Mauritius	58	93	185	161	163	176	175	244	199	254	252	277	240	237
Zimbabwe	3	0	—	—	—	—	0	13	14	28	41	92	84	81
Malawi	13	14	23	27	52	44	44	42	30	53	56	90	117	74
South Africa	400	482	566	533	469	531	587	610	584	675	547	535	586	545
Botswana	24	5	21	31	38	17	42	6	24	42	55	52	49	44
Swaziland	21	29	51	61	46	61	71	62	54	80	58	97	107	105
USA	2 744	3 506	4 154	4 697	3 986	3 859	4 106	5 163	6 307	5 986	5 750	5 295	4 329	3 422
Canada	556	835	806	858	761	730	743	884	1 072	1 060	1 051	971	930	713
Greenland	15	22	25	31	33	31	52	74	99	106	137	154	179	226
Mexico	54	76	113	143	176	150	180	183	157	162	140	137	122	226
Guatemala	57	83	141	130	205	148	153	150	157	168	136	137	137	159
Belize	4	10	20	14	19	20	20	21	28	27	23	33	26	29
Honduras	38	37	40	63	99	81	100	103	109	127	102	132	204	185
El Salvador	58	82	118	192	310	193	277	213	265	182	211	212	175	204
Nicaragua	31	37	51	66	136	104	89	73	73	83	95	107	116	136
Costa Rica	97	117	108	91	169	167	187	177	223	216	235	264	255	293
Panama	49	49	75	92	89	102	124	134	183	179	200	206	210	203
Cuba	71	191	328	155	152	94	127	139	158	132	111	125	133	133
S. Christ. Nev.	:	:	:	:	:	:	:	:	:	:	:	:	:	6
Haiti	12	13	13	28	40	37	36	56	36	47	60	58	69	73
Guadeloupe	55	53	67	73	75	85	66	68	74	78	64	93	89	108
Dominica	—	—	—	—	—	—	—	5	15	18	21	25	31	40
Martinique	41	53	67	82	86	94	62	39	76	94	99	111	120	140
Jamaica	63	47	83	67	71	75	63	58	79	81	59	86	95	88
St. Lucia	—	—	—	—	—	—	—	16	23	27	35	49	74	88
St. Vincent	—	—	—	—	—	—	—	12	17	19	23	24	37	32
Trinidad, Tobago	22	27	45	25	34	25	31	25	32	27	21	25	26	23
Colombia	204	263	299	435	633	738	802	957	835	1 041	1 082	1 272	1 274	1 721
Venezuela	8	14	12	15	28	23	23	23	16	13	25	37	27	35
Guyana	31	42	68	56	50	72	54	55	85	84	72	91	83	81
Surinam	16	21	24	27	26	36	43	42	54	61	82	64	76	62
Ecuador	70	109	110	120	189	171	163	156	127	134	126	152	250	223
Peru	61	57	55	60	61	55	67	52	55	87	54	80	96	127
Brazil	1 137	1 003	1 052	1 389	2 238	1 713	1 882	2 185	2 840	3 180	3 940	4 593	4 722	3 255
Chile	14	36	48	88	95	138	147	183	211	316	310	316	366	416
Paraguay	38	27	34	26	27	38	73	48	22	20	25	20	29	36
Uruguay	101	54	77	120	94	62	61	65	119	111	86	99	101	121
Argentina	1 209	1 287	812	1 163	1 456	1 336	1 406	973	1 121	1 280	1 506	1 571	1 641	1 295
Cyprus	58	50	49	100	117	74	93	109	117	136	126	146	152	137
Iran	34	33	27	27	44	38	56	35	29	24	22	28	39	77
Israel	178	195	224	273	300	325	380	370	467	493	520	590	686	543
Pakistan	31	28	24	28	37	44	48	48	75	73	71	65	100	75
India	189	177	184	314	416	245	379	360	359	414	437	571	355	394
Bangladesh	8	9	11	22	24	17	17	26	23	44	54	61	52	62
Sri Lanka	58	82	68	78	113	91	102	104	113	117	117	190	159	111
Thailand	112	182	208	353	434	539	533	612	846	1 111	915	1 081	1 284	1 167
Indonesia	115	152	174	255	361	343	423	381	363	319	353	454	517	544
Malaysia	34	59	63	80	111	116	137	148	159	178	201	282	326	244
Singapore	22	21	18	20	24	22	28	37	42	41	45	62	52	52
Philippines	45	54	98	102	114	112	123	161	196	196	216	223	175	192
China	127	140	173	184	151	187	238	238	335	343	340	392	426	458	639
South Korea	19	33	34	53	63	62	34	34	39	47	38	28	33	35
Japan	131	130	133	140	94	97	85	99	102	105	117	131	115	122
Taiwan	85	95	99	115	132	150	133	143	142	137	124	107	107	126
Hong Kong	7	10	8	11	12	13	12	13	15	16	15	18	18	18
Australia	450	279	237	314	305	162	217	216	223	285	239	227	253	278
Papua N. Guinea	16	28	34	41	118	98	120	118	75	79	91	130	163	157
New Zealand	480	406	433	472	506	572	593	621	776	877	792	853	869	812
Fiji	17	32	88	37	66	65	70	60	93	83	96	113	71	97
Not determined	12	47	67	32	18	15	9	10	4	34	27	12	7	6
Secret CTRS.	0	—	—	—	0	—	20	80	91	92	158	166	169	160

EXPORTATIONS

VALEUR EN MIO ÉCU

1973	1974	1975	1976	1977	1978	1979	1980	1981	1982	1983	1984	1985	1986	
17 652	21 379	24 027	28 272	31 511	34 172	38 421	44 155	54 059	57 189	60 239	68 475	71 946	70 510	MONDE
12 567	15 025	17 501	20 577	22 941	24 925	27 704	29 770	34 004	38 589	40 927	46 095	48 714	51 271	INTRA-CE
5 085	6 355	6 521	7 680	8 570	9 248	10 536	14 232	19 856	18 400	19 074	22 021	22 823	18 765	EXTRA-CE
13	16	15	21	23	22	23	28	30	33	37	39	43	39	Islande
116	144	159	176	188	178	188	232	270	249	268	290	341	381	Norvège
241	318	307	362	409	402	431	467	497	540	552	661	709	734	Suède
53	66	61	56	75	69	88	105	162	165	151	174	196	209	Finlande
525	602	621	916	677	748	805	889	1 036	1 116	1 203	1 284	1 394	1 380	Suisse
181	209	220	297	350	355	406	459	528	556	616	683	745	746	Autriche
14	15	18	23	30	34	49	61	66	59	58	68	77	84	Andorre
23	30	27	35	31	32	41	56	58	57	59	58	66	64	Malte
96	82	48	66	72	60	107	119	234	135	158	174	144	137	Yougoslavie
12	53	37	19	9	6	7	89	54	16	12	76	132	70	Turquie
191	183	187	297	285	201	412	1 093	1 774	1 357	1 755	1 595	1 742	1 081	Union Soviétique
52	49	52	58	55	93	94	141	347	126	184	147	121	71	R.d. allemande
98	105	119	170	104	230	285	539	712	441	318	374	315	225	Pologne
127	101	55	66	87	78	90	135	135	144	112	119	133	110	Tchécoslovaquie
72	70	40	40	90	72	76	78	87	84	97	93	77	77	Hongrie
40	40	25	69	57	45	87	154	378	107	30	32	52	121	Roumanie
15	37	31	38	29	33	47	33	46	39	60	50	149	66	Bulgarie
60	61	138	88	89	112	196	229	360	285	152	83	306	102	Maroc
95	175	288	173	273	319	365	549	732	968	991	962	966	564	Algérie
41	42	53	82	54	88	88	142	233	179	200	187	161	158	Tunisie
103	167	188	217	310	221	332	468	841	413	443	516	451	411	Libye
171	236	244	196	163	266	313	612	775	605	834	1 174	1 062	651	Égypte
11	5	12	13	16	26	48	43	67	103	44	75	167	65	Soudan
16	19	31	24	33	37	29	35	56	50	51	64	73	51	Mauritanie
15	15	9	9	7	13	8	13	28	38	29	52	63	38	Mali
9	17	9	8	12	15	12	15	23	22	17	24	34	26	Burkina-Faso
8	19	10	16	9	11	12	14	22	19	17	27	57	27	Niger
8	10	5	4	12	7	4	1	4	7	3	20	35	17	Tchad
2	4	10	7	10	12	8	14	12	14	19	23	21	15	Cap-Vert
49	40	37	45	45	45	59	59	76	77	87	92	89	71	Sénégal
2	5	3	5	6	9	9	12	14	16	19	25	26	28	Gambie
3	4	4	4	6	7	9	9	16	15	15	27	45	41	Guinée
7	9	9	12	15	17	17	22	22	22	27	25	25	18	Liberia
47	64	52	70	89	90	107	134	153	162	169	174	199	180	Côte-d'Ivoire
7	5	9	9	13	13	16	22	33	34	35	44	38	37	Togo
5	4	7	8	7	10	12	15	22	29	30	32	31	23	Benin
69	88	180	248	317	464	375	718	1 019	941	720	397	387	275	Nigeria
16	26	27	29	38	42	46	60	84	94	99	123	122	122	Cameroun
10	13	19	25	30	26	25	35	54	58	61	67	73	62	Gabon
8	11	15	18	19	22	23	29	42	47	47	54	53	39	Congo
47	61	37	55	43	50	40	28	40	50	62	99	125	101	Zaïre
22	27	16	29	67	50	39	89	112	104	121	204	190	89	Angola
3	11	15	12	18	22	34	17	42	56	56	84	162	107	Éthiopie
4	6	5	9	10	18	11	17	31	32	23	29	29	35	Djibouti
3	6	11	9	23	14	21	46	58	43	36	52	50	30	Somalie
13	16	11	20	13	14	10	18	32	18	12	53	33	49	Kenya
11	17	11	13	20	18	17	22	30	31	18	28	36	13	Tanzanie
10	10	13	9	15	19	14	19	27	37	48	48	49	26	Mozambique
26	38	43	40	46	55	67	81	89	99	112	126	117	120	Réunion
6	11	11	13	14	14	16	15	16	23	24	28	26	23	Maurice
32	65	53	33	30	29	38	50	90	91	108	118	93	87	Afr. du Sud
741	796	650	787	894	886	760	774	1 053	1 331	1 693	2 338	2 728	2 272	États-Unis
108	153	143	176	215	189	171	177	233	275	343	505	537	426	Canada
11	12	15	18	20	21	25	26	29	31	33	35	34	33	Groenland
22	46	7	15	28	30	37	87	105	74	95	76	62	48	Mexique
1	2	1	1	2	2	3	4	10	18	12	18	23	25	Nicaragua
18	61	59	45	18	31	38	98	93	201	104	110	88	29	Cuba
:	:	:	:	:	:	:	:	:	:	:	:	:	1	S. Christ. Nev.
25	28	37	41	48	49	56	68	73	86	94	104	109	112	Guadeloupe
24	27	34	40	46	50	57	66	76	88	94	105	110	114	Martinique
12	13	14	14	19	22	22	27	43	48	50	63	57	42	Trinidad, Tobago
42	40	73	76	131	113	97	153	287	219	130	201	169	73	Venezuela
6	6	8	9	11	12	13	16	19	23	26	31	34	34	Guyane Fr.
28	27	29	39	31	33	43	48	78	60	85	105	105	88	Chypre
54	67	57	58	101	90	99	117	174	193	185	221	155	130	Liban
33	63	40	79	80	108	142	199	182	163	182	223	218	184	Syrie
16	24	36	61	62	68	122	219	361	458	255	355	365	165	Iraq
28	55	135	146	216	233	241	552	757	425	489	546	397	295	Iran
48	79	44	73	74	67	85	92	154	145	142	172	158	199	Israël
16	23	26	47	40	53	91	111	129	144	120	182	148	134	Jordanie
53	79	119	206	318	353	459	665	967	1 019	1 104	1 695	1 286	1 140	Arabie Saoud.
38	47	48	81	81	84	97	129	179	197	194	239	222	180	Koweït
7	9	11	23	18	23	22	27	33	42	44	58	61	43	Bahrein
4	6	6	12	11	16	18	21	28	39	45	53	60	41	Qatar
17	27	35	97	78	78	94	129	174	208	217	251	253	212	Émirats arabes
4	8	11	18	21	23	23	27	37	46	64	80	89	69	Oman
16	12	15	35	58	85	82	117	137	174	170	247	250	139	Yemen du Nord
9	9	5	28	29	41	35	44	73	81	75	84	84	53	Yemen du Sud
19	24	55	30	29	43	51	40	70	59	68	80	63	101	Pakistan
15	39	181	84	68	63	76	76	185	126	15	135	244	91	Inde
38	37	78	34	88	51	57	54	75	113	62	120	85	75	Bangladesh
33	52	53	47	40	66	43	76	54	52	58	40	37	22	Sri Lanka
8	13	12	16	26	30	38	39	50	41	62	66	66	62	Thaïlande
18	38	24	22	31	23	21	14	30	34	54	32	36	32	Indonésie
15	27	16	21	28	38	43	47	51	50	62	61	58	50	Malaysia
18	29	31	27	33	33	39	47	65	77	98	110	100	78	Singapour
13	17	22	21	25	28	46	34	58	95	81	55	56	59	Philippines
1	26	1	1	2	27	26	19	114	151	220	30	84	53	Chine
4	3	3	4	4	15	9	7	37	15	16	30	25	48	Corée du Sud
187	226	237	295	328	394	548	436	684	553	647	842	951	997	Japon
4	6	5	8	16	27	33	36	42	46	55	63	80	76	T'ai-Wan
34	41	37	45	50	54	54	58	70	102	118	126	151	137	Hong-kong
45	77	64	73	84	89	87	83	104	145	153	218	228	175	Australie
6	9	7	7	8	7	7	7	11	13	21	30	25	22	Nouv. Zélande
9	11	11	11	12	13	14	16	21	23	28	35	35	38	Polynésie Fr.
3	5	2	1	7	13	17	15	23	38	34	43	64	62	Non déterminé
0	—	5	16	—	0	181	119	166	145	202	314	342	349	Secret

VALUE IN MIO ECU

List of products	SITC/CTCI	EUR 12	BL	DK	D	GR	E	F	IRL	I	NL	P	UK
Cereals and cereal preparations	04	1 535	110	16	135	10	167	170	4	279	110	249	285
Rice	042	254	46	0	16	0	6	35	0	38	34	20	58
Sugar beet, fresh, dried or powdered; sugar cane	054.82	0	0	0	0	0	0	0	0	0	0	0	0
Sugar and sugar preparations	06	1 308	22	44	147	1	42	206	18	69	87	44	628
Fruit and vegetables	05	7 580	418	106	2 050	30	200	1 341	41	549	1 338	86	1 421
Wine	112.1	122	5	4	56	0	0	14	1	0	2	0	39
Hops	054.84	24	3	0	16	0	0	0	0	0	0	0	4
Tobacco, unmanufactured and manufactured	12	1 961	124	91	587	15	197	116	23	125	306	15	361
Flax not spun, flax tow and waste (including pulled or garneted rags)	265.1	18	12	0	0	0	2	1	0	2	0	0	0
True hemp («Canabis sativa») not spun, tow and waste of true hemp (including pulled or garneted rags or ropes)	265.2	2	0	0	0	0	0	1	0	0	0	0	0
Oleaginous seeds and fruits	22	3 561	324	20	908	49	532	165	1	347	714	204	297
Animal and vegetable fats and oils	45F411.U	1 169	70	28	308	3	28	180	1	140	221	5	185
Animals of the bovine species	001.1	182	0	0	14	21	8	2	0	134	0	1	0
Swine	001.3	31	5	0	0	0	0	18	0	8	0	0	0
Live poultry (fowls, ducks, geese, turkeys and guinea fowls)	001.4	15	0	0	4	0	3	1	0	3	3	0	0
Dead poultry (fowls, ducks, geese, turkeys and guinea fowls) and edible offals thereof (except liver)	011.4	142	7	0	75	1	1	10	0	43	5	0	0
Milk and cream	022	47	0	1	4	0	30	2	2	0	3	1	2
Butter	023	205	0	0	0	0	0	1	0	1	0	1	202
Cheese and curd	024	425	43	3	68	3	14	53	0	180	9	6	46
Birds' eggs	025	19	1	1	8	1	0	2	0	3	3	0	0
Cork and wood, paper-making pulp	24ET25.U	9 719	413	372	2 280	211	405	1 277	72	1 880	726	94	1 990
Articles of cork and of wood (furniture excluded)	63	2 049	103	150	631	7	15	156	15	175	183	2	612
Paper and paperboard	64	9 071	446	620	2 472	102	201	1 002	123	661	832	41	2 572
Furniture and parts thereof	82	1 651	54	118	744	2	10	249	6	53	102	2	311
Fish and fish preparations, crustaceans and molluscs	03	4 032	123	523	400	69	372	873	4	596	105	177	789
Fish meal	08	4 543	269	333	965	6	243	701	75	415	1 005	70	462
Fish oils	411	295	28	3	82	0	41	15	0	8	69	5	44

SOURCE: EUROSTAT COMEXT

VALEURS EN MIO ÉCU

EUR 12	BL	DK	D	GR	E	F	IRL	I	NL	P	UK	Nº SITC/ CTCI	Libellé des produits
3 951	228	266	631	34	136	1 388	7	531	125	3	603	04	Céréales et produits à base de céréales
166	2	0	6	0	14	3	0	130	9	0	1	042	Riz
1	0	0	0	0	0	0	0	0	1	0	0	054.82	Betteraves à sucre, fraîches, séchées ou en poudre; cannes à sucre
1 525	252	118	320	5	92	406	8	25	165	2	132	06	Sucres et préparations à base de sucre
2 677	67	55	250	238	606	308	3	642	340	76	93	05	Fruits et légumes
1 953	1	5	159	10	178	1 137	0	383	1	60	20	112.1	Vin
62	0	0	60	0	0	1	0	0	0	0	0	054.84	Houblon
858	19	39	144	136	10	37	20	38	76	2	336	12	Tabacs bruts et manufacturés
61	41	0	0	0	0	19	0	0	0	0	1	265.1	Lin non filé, étoupes, déchets et effiloches
0	0	0	0	0	0	0	0	0	0	0	0	265.2	Chanvre non filé, étoupes, déchets et effiloches
30	1	1	9	1	0	2	0	2	11	1	2	22	Graines et fruits oléagineux
1 225	68	75	214	32	167	131	0	211	238	38	50	45F411	Graisses et huiles d'origine animale ou végétale
125	0	5	51	0	1	23	33	1	10	0	2	001.1	Animaux de l'espèce bovine y compris du genre buffle
4	1	1	0	0	0	1	0	0	1	0	1	001.3	Animaux de l'espèce porcine
115	13	2	20	0	4	16	0	3	47	0	10	001.4	Volaille vivante de basse-cour
338	15	39	8	0	3	254	0	3	12	0	5	011.4	Volaille morte de basse-cour et abats comestibles sauf foies
1 595	51	197	185	0	3	322	83	1	653	0	102	022	Lait et crème de lait
386	69	30	59	0	0	85	9	0	126	0	7	023	Beurre
881	3	214	124	12	3	264	2	98	130	10	21	024	Fromage et caillebotte
123	7	3	21	0	4	16	0	1	69	0	2	025	Œufs d'oiseaux
766	23	63	321	1	68	119	3	38	13	96	21	24ET25	Liège et bois, pâte à papier
1 039	24	107	381	13	62	124	1	160	24	94	48	63	Ouvrages en liège et en bois (meubles exclus)
3 620	119	108	1 460	29	154	578	9	370	277	22	494	64	Papiers et cartons
4 133	81	517	1 208	3	111	423	4	1 359	104	7	317	82	Meubles et pièces détachées
1 083	11	366	69	6	86	118	30	31	179	58	129	03	Poissons, crustacés et mollusques et préparations de poisson
1 017	100	99	365	29	18	77	1	87	176	4	63	08	Farines de poissons
56	2	12	13	0	4	3	0	3	9	1	9	411	Huiles de poissons

I B

Land use

Utilisation des terres

YEAR ANNÉE	EUR 12	EUR 10	B	DK	D	GR	E	F	IRL	I	L	NL	P	UK

1000 HA

0005 AGRICULTURE USED AREA / SUPERFICIE AGRICOLE UTILISEE

YEAR	EUR 12	EUR 10	B	DK	D	GR	E	F	IRL	I	L	NL	P	UK
1983	129 850 *	98 073 *	1 428	2 849 *	12 079 *	5 734 *	27 245	31 557	5 707 *	17 883	128	2 017 *	4 532 *	18 690
1984	129 531 *	97 769 *	1 424	2 868 *	12 044	5 741 *	27 230	31 492	5 705	17 665	128	2 025 *	4 532 *	18 676 *
1985	129 225 *	97 470 *	1 419	2 834	12 019	5 741 *	27 223 *	31 423	5 713	17 522	128	2 028 *	4 532 *	18 644 *
1986	128 994 *	97 250 *	1 412	2 823	12 000	5 741 *	27 213 *	31 389	5 676 *	17 445	128 *	2 024 *	4 532 *	18 612

0001 ARABLE LAND / TERRES ARABLES

YEAR	EUR 12	EUR 10	B	DK	D	GR	E	F	IRL	I	L	NL	P	UK
1983	67 590 *	49 093 *	740	2 600 *	7 226	2 920 *	15 591	17 410	1 083	9 319	55	833	2 906	6 907
1984	07 002 *	49 125 *	744	2 627 *	7 216	2 925 *	15 661	17 638	1 106	0 142	66	843	2 906	6 929
1985	67 779 *	49 223 *	742	2 601	7 233	2 913 *	15 651	17 649	1 099	9 068	55	860	2 906	7 001
1986	67 803 *	49 246 *	743	2 592	7 244	2 925 *	15 651 *	17 735	1 062 *	9 061	56 *	876	2 906	6 952

0002 PERMANENT GRASSLAND / SUPERFICIES TOUJOURS COUVERTES D'HERBE

YEAR	EUR 12	EUR 10	B	DK	D	GR	E	F	IRL	I	L	NL	P	UK
1983	49 791	42 385	653	236	4 630	1 789	6 645	12 535	4 622	5 002	71	1 143	761	11 704
1984	49 528	42 121	644	228	4 607	1 789	6 646	12 362	4 597	5 012	71	1 141	761	11 670
1985	49 153 *	41 746	640	221	4 566	1 789	6 646 *	12 200	4 612	4 954	71	1 127	761	11 567
1986	48 995 *	41 589	632	219	4 537	1 789	6 645 *	12 094	4 612	4 944	70	1 108	761	11 583

0003 LAND UNDER PERMANENT CROPS / CULTURES PERMANENTES

YEAR	EUR 12	EUR 10	B	DK	D	GR	E	F	IRL	I	L	NL	P	UK
1983	12 056 *	6 182 *	14	13	181 *	1 028 *	5 008	1 358	2 *	3 484	2	36	866 *	63
1984	11 914 *	6 115 *	14	12	182	1 036 *	4 933	1 339	2	3 431	2	36	865 *	61
1985	11 879 *	6 089 *	14	12	181	1 037 *	4 926 *	1 324	2	3 419	2	36	865 *	60 *
1986	11 798 *	6 016 *	14	12	181	1 040 *	4 917 *	1 311	2	3 359	2	35	865 *	61

0004 KITCHEN GARDENS / JARDINS FAMILIAUX

YEAR	EUR 12	EUR 10	B	DK	D	GR	E	F	IRL	I	L	NL	P	UK
1983	416 *	416 *	22	—	41	—	—	255	—	77	0	5 *	—	16
1984	417 *	417 *	22	—	40	—	—	254	—	80	0	5 *	—	16 *
1985	412 *	412 *	22	—	38	—	—	249	—	80	0	6 *	—	16
1986	411 *	411 *	22	—	38	—	—	250	—	81	0	5 *	—	16

EUR 12

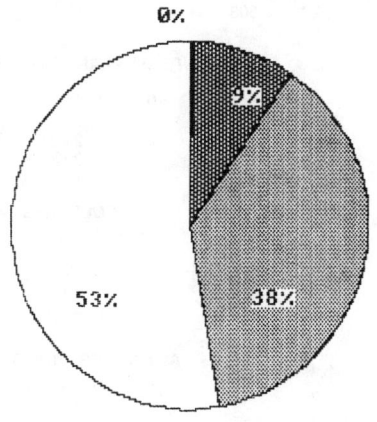

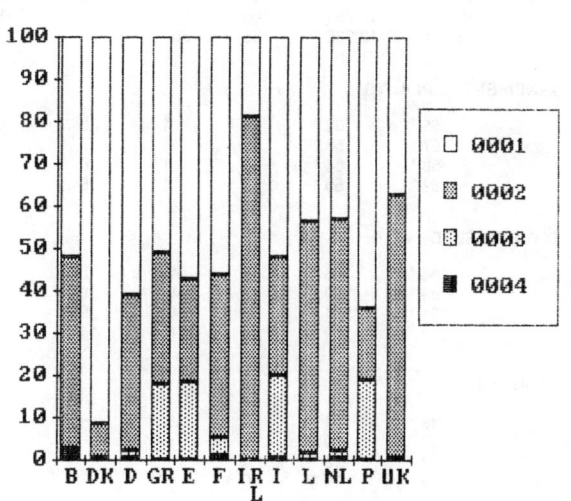

SOURCE: CRONOS-ZPA1 DATA BANK, AGRICULTURAL PRODUCTS

SOURCE: BANQUE DE DONNEES CRONOS-ZPA1, PRODUITS AGRICOLES

YEAR ANNÉE	EUR 12	EUR 10	B	DK	D	GR	E	F	IRL	I	L	NL	P	UK

1000 HA

CEREALS (EXC.RICE) / **CEREALES (EXC.RIZ)**

Year	EUR 12	EUR 10	B	DK	D	GR	E	F	IRL	I	L	NL	P	UK
1983	35 789 *	27 360 *	373 *	1 698	5 044 *	1 556	7 392	9 382	395	4 713	31	206	1 037	3 961 *
1984	36 056 *	27 587 *	361 *	1 669	4 941 *	1 518	7 511	9 715	406	4 709	35	198	958	4 036 *
1985	35 668 *	27 222 *	345	1 612	4 884	1 460 *	7 517	9 701	400	4 586	35	184	930	4 015 *
1986	35 403 *	26 839 *	350	1 588	4 812	1 446 *	7 592 *	9 487	380	4 549	34	170	973 *	4 024 *

RICE (PADDY) / **RIZ (PADDY)**

Year	EUR 12	EUR 10	B	DK	D	GR	E	F	IRL	I	L	NL	P	UK
1983	272	204	—	—	—	14	41	7	—	183	—	—	26	—
1984	308	205	—	—	—	15	73	9	—	180	—	—	30	—
1985	317	213	—	—	—	17	75	11	—	184	—	—	30	—
1986	328	218	—	—	—	18	79	12	—	188	—	—	31	—

DRIED PULSES / **LEGUMES SECS**

Year	EUR 12	EUR 10	B	DK	D	GR	E	F	IRL	I	L	NL	P	UK
1983	1 281 *	560 *	1	22 *	13	56	434	204	1	171	0	12	287	80
1984	1 323 *	632 *	1	57 *	16	50	425	232	1	171	0	16	266 *	88
1985	1 461 *	799 *	1	127 *	34	42	411	254	2 *	176	0	25	250 *	137
1986	1 654 *	966 *	3	140 *	69	43	417 *	354	2 *	174	0	32	270 *	150

ROOT CROPS / **PLANTES SARCLEES**

Year	EUR 12	EUR 10	B	DK	D	GR	E	F	IRL	I	L	NL	P	UK
1983	4 297 *	3 456	167	234	743	102	701	961	89	366	1	289	141 *	504
1984	4 295 *	3 480 *	177	237	741	88 *	677	968	97	370	1	292	138 *	508
1985	4 184 *	3 426 *	182	228	731	97 *	616	902	93	381	1	302	141 *	508
1986	4 054 *	3 325 *	175	221	700	98 *	588 *	828	90 *	419	1	307	141 *	486

INDUSTRIAL CROPS / **PLANTES INDUSTRIELLES**

Year	EUR 12	EUR 10	B	DK	D	GR	E	F	IRL	I	L	NL	P	UK
1983	3 247 *	2 151 *	14	166	255	290	1 072	1 008	3	164 *	1	21	24 *	228
1984	3 588 *	2 386 *	17	196 *	278	352	1 160	1 058	5 *	184	1	22	42 *	274
1985	3 891 *	2 695 *	16	220	289 *	389 *	1 152	1 249 *	4 *	208 *	1	19	44 *	301
1986	4 200 *	3 053 *	13	232 *	333 *	417 *	1 104 *	1 431 *	2 *	309 *	1	13	44 *	303

VEGETABLES / **LEGUMES**

Year	EUR 12	EUR 10	B	DK	D	GR	E	F	IRL	I	L	NL	P	UK
1983	1 635 *	1 092	26	13	41	152	454	249	3	409	0	61	89 *	135
1984	1 690 *	1 118	26	18	40	153	478	253	3	427	0	63	94 *	135
1985	1 691 *	1 125 *	30	18	45	151 *	472	250	3 *	415	0	69	94 *	144
1986	1 679 *	1 125 *	32	18 *	56	140 *	460 *	250 *	3 *	411	0	68	94 *	147

GREEN FODDER FROM ARABLE LAND / **FOURRAGES VERTS DES TERRES ARABLES**

Year	EUR 12	EUR 10	B	DK	D	GR	E	F	IRL	I	L	NL	P	UK
1983	14 170 *	12 549 *	147	400	1 104	327 *	1 151	5 214	587 *	2 685	16	198	:	1 871
1984	13 842 *	12 226 *	155	387	1 175	212 *	1 146	5 079	593 *	2 584	18	206	:	1 816
1985	13 871 *	12 291 *	160	357	1 224	241 *	1 110	5 020	596 *	2 637	18	218	:	1 820 *
1986	13 874 *	12 285 *	163	351	1 255	220 *	1 118 *	5 095	592 *	2 603	19	237 *	:	1 751

FLOWERS AND ORNEMENTAL PLANTS / **FLEURS ET PLANTES ORNEMENTALES**

Year	EUR 12	EUR 10	B	DK	D	GR	E	F	IRL	I	L	NL	P	UK
1983	55 *	52 *	1	1	8	:	:	7	0	7	0	19	0 *	7
1984	57 *	53 *	1	1	7	:	:	7	0	9	0	20	0 *	7
1985	58 *	54 *	1	1 *	8	:	:	7	0	8	0	21	0 *	7
1986	59 *	55 *	1	1 *	8	:	:	6	0	8	0	22	0 *	7

AREAS HARVESTED FOR SEED / **CULTURES DE SEMENCES**

Year	EUR 12	EUR 10	B	DK	D	GR	E	F	IRL	I	L	NL	P	UK
1983	186 *	186 *	2	45	8	:	:	55	1 *	32	—	20	0 *	16
1984	189 *	189 *	2	47	9	:	:	60	1 *	25 *	—	20	0 *	16
1985	184 *	184 *	2	47	9	:	:	66	1 *	15	—	18	0 *	19
1986	179 *	179 *	2	44	11	:	:	61 *	1 *	13	—	21	0 *	18

OTHER FIELD PRODUCTS / **AUTRES PRODUITS DES CHAMPS**

Year	EUR 12	EUR 10	B	DK	D	GR	E	F	IRL	I	L	NL	P	UK
1983	49 *	11 *	0	— *	—	:	:	—	2	—	—	—	38	7
1984	47 *	9 *	0	— *	—	:	:	—	3	—	—	—	38	5
1985	51 *	13 *	0	— *	—	:	:	—	3	—	—	—	38	9
1986	58 *	20 *	0	— *	—	:	:	—	3	—	—	—	38 *	16

YEAR ANNÉE	EUR 12	EUR 10	B	DK	D	GR	E	F	IRL	I	L	NL	P	UK

1000 HA

FALLOW AND GREEN-MANURES — **JACHERES ET ENGRAIS VERTS**

YEAR ANNÉE	EUR 12	EUR 10	B	DK	D	GR	E	F	IRL	I	L	NL	P	UK
1983	7 171	1 332	8	17	10	:	4 744	322	—	366	6	7	1 095	97
1984	6 699	1 031	3	3	7	:	4 573	163	—	338	0	4	1 095	42
1985	6 862 *	1 167	5	3	8	:	4 600 *	201	—	424	0	6	1 095	41
1986	6 833 *	1 138	4	3	9	:	4 600 *	219	—	376	0	7	1 095 *	48

COMMON WHEAT AND SPELT — **BLE TENDRE ET EPEAUTRE**

YEAR ANNÉE	EUR 12	EUR 10	B	DK	D	GR	E	F	IRL	I	L	NL	P	UK
1983	13 635 *	10 886	197	242	1 654	682	2 431	4 713	59	1 489	6	148	317 *	1 695
1984	10 079 *	11 255	100	332	1 029	553	2 154	4 970	77	1 410	8	145	270 *	1 939
1985	12 814 *	10 642 *	188	340	1 609	469	1 911	4 632	78	1 295	7	128	262	1 896 *
1986	12 892	10 628	189	353	1 623	426	1 990	4 604	76	1 245	7	116	274	1 987

DURUM WHEAT — **BLE DUR**

YEAR ANNÉE	EUR 12	EUR 10	B	DK	D	GR	E	F	IRL	I	L	NL	P	UK
1983	2 304 *	2 115 *	—	—	1	302	172	112	—	1 700	—	—	17 *	—
1984	2 398 *	2 224 *	—	—	6	314	151	131	—	1 773	—	—	23 *	—
1985	2 480 *	2 325 *	—	—	15	406	133	165	—	1 732	—	—	23	6
1986	2 731 *	2 602 *	—	1	25	478	105	261	—	1 827	—	—	24	10

RYE — **SEIGLE**

YEAR ANNÉE	EUR 12	EUR 10	B	DK	D	GR	E	F	IRL	I	L	NL	P	UK
1983	1 011	661	6	77	445	7	217	101	—	11	1	7	133	7
1984	1 061	700	7	122	439	10	231	100	—	9	1	6	130	6
1985	1 011	677	5	127	426	10	211	87	—	9	1	5	123	8
1986	998 *	652	4	121	414	13	223	80	—	8	1	4	123 *	7

BARLEY — **ORGE**

YEAR ANNÉE	EUR 12	EUR 10	B	DK	D	GR	E	F	IRL	I	L	NL	P	UK
1983	12 686	8 867	139	1 347	2 035	329	3 735	2 143	313	364	16	37	83	2 143
1984	12 639	8 533	136	1 181	2 006	365	4 023	2 108	304	406	16	34	84	1 978
1985	12 814	8 483	118	1 104	1 949	310	4 246	2 256	298	426	17	39	86	1 965
1986	12 647	8 226	128	1 088	1 947	266	4 334	2 097	283	440	18	42	87	1 916

OATS AND MIXED GRAIN — **AVOINE ET MELANGES DE CEREALES D'ETE**

YEAR ANNÉE	EUR 12	EUR 10	B	DK	D	GR	E	F	IRL	I	L	NL	P	UK
1983	2 378	1 733	26	32	729	43	454	546	23	196	8	14	191	116
1984	2 328	1 655	24	34	669	43	479	554	25	171	10	13	194	113
1985	2 364	1 715	24	41	692	43	459	547	23	181	10	12	190	141
1986	1 992	1 414	16	25	605	43	384	407	21	177	8	7	194	104

GRAIN MAIZE — **MAIS GRAIN**

YEAR ANNÉE	EUR 12	EUR 10	B	DK	D	GR	E	F	IRL	I	L	NL	P	UK
1983	3 625 *	2 976 *	5	—	169	192	354	1 685	—	924	—	0	295	— *
1984	3 774 *	3 077 *	8	—	182	231	440	1 743	—	913	—	0	257	— *
1985	3 995 *	3 223 *	7	—	181	221	526	1 891	—	923	—	0	246	— *
1986	3 925 *	3 129	7	—	187	218	525	1 884	—	833	—	0	271 *	—

RICE (PADDY) — **RIZ (PADDY)**

YEAR ANNÉE	EUR 12	EUR 10	B	DK	D	GR	E	F	IRL	I	L	NL	P	UK
1983	272	204	—	—	—	14	41	7	—	183	—	—	26	—
1984	308	205	—	—	—	15	73	9	—	180	—	—	30	—
1985	317	213	—	—	—	17	75	11	—	184	—	—	30	—
1986	328	218	—	—	—	18	79	12	—	188	—	—	31	—

DRIED PULSES — **LEGUMES SECS**

YEAR ANNÉE	EUR 12	EUR 10	B	DK	D	GR	E	F	IRL	I	L	NL	P	UK
1983	1 281 *	560 *	1	22 *	13	56	434	204	1	171	0	12	287	80
1984	1 323 *	632 *	1	57 *	16	50	425	232	1	171	0	16	266 *	88
1985	1 461 *	799 *	1	127 *	34	42	411	254	2 *	176	0	25	250 *	137
1986	1 654 *	966 *	3	140 *	69	43	417 *	354	2 *	174	0	32	270 *	150

PEAS OTHER THAN FIELDPEAS — **POIS SECS AUTRES QUE POIS FOURRAGERS**

YEAR ANNÉE	EUR 12	EUR 10	B	DK	D	GR	E	F	IRL	I	L	NL	P	UK
1983	176 *	56 *	1	0	—	8	92	10	0 *	11	0	8	29	18
1984	172 *	53 *	0	—	1 *	5	93	10	0 *	10	— *	11	26	14
1985	186 *	69 *	1	0	1 *	5	91	16	0 *	11 *	0	20	26	15
1986	191 *	77 *	2	0	2 *	5	90	19	0 *	11 *	0	22	24 *	15 *

SOURCE: CRONOS-ZPA1 DATA BANK, AGRICULTURAL PRODUCTS

SOURCE: BANQUE DE DONNEES CRONOS-ZPA1, PRODUITS AGRICOLES

1000 HA

YEAR ANNÉE	EUR 12	EUR 10	B	DK	D	GR	E	F	IRL	I	L	NL	P	UK
FIELDPEAS													**POIS FOURRAGERS**	
1983	147	144	:	21 *	—	0	3	115	—	—	:	—	:	29
1984	174 *	171 *	:	53 *	5 *	0	3	123	—	—	:	—	:	42
1985	271 *	267 *	:	123 *	14 *	0	4	175	—	— *	:	—	:	78
1986	387 *	382 *	:	135	33 *	0	5	273	—	— *	:	—	:	76 *
BEANS													**HARICOTS,FEVES,FEVEROLES**	
1983	712 *	291 *	1	— *	6	30	163	68	—	149	0	4	259	34
1984	718 *	311 *	1	— *	9 *	28	167	85	—	150	0	5	240 *	32
1985	682 *	302 *	1	— *	16 *	27	155	53	—	155	0	6	225 *	45
1986	732 *	331 *	1	— *	30 *	26	155	53	—	152	0	9	246 *	60
OTHER DRIED.PULSES													**AUTRES LEGUMES SECS**	
1983	229 *	53 *	0	1 *	7	17	176	12	—	16	0	—	:	—
1984	205 *	44 *	0	4 *	1 *	16	161	12	—	10	0	—	:	—
1985	198 *	37 *	0	4 *	3 *	10	161	9	—	10	— *	—	:	—
1986	208 *	41 *	0	5 *	4 *	11	167 *	10 *	—	10	— *	—	:	—
POTATOES													**POMMES DE TERRE**	
1983	1 550	1 079	43	30	224	64	340	204	34	121	1	163	132	195
1984	1 552	1 076	44	31	219	59	348	205	36	121	1	161	129	198
1985	1 546	1 083	49	30	220	56	331	211	33	122	1	169	132	191
1986	1 461	1 041	48	31	210	56	289	201	31	120	1	167	131	178
SUGAR BEET													**BETTERAVES SUCRIERES**	
1983	1 943	1 693	109	72	393	38	249	490	36	232	0	123	1	199
1984	1 958	1 737	117	74	405	29	220	526	35	224	0	129	1	199
1985	1 908	1 727	118	73	403	41	180	491	33	232	0	131	1	205
1986	1 913	1 717	113	70	390	42	195	449	37	273	0	138	1	205
FODDER BEET													**BETTERAVES FOURRAGERES**	
1983	435	417	15	121	120	0	17	136	6	13	0	2	:	5
1984	431 *	414 *	15	124	111	0 *	17	132	6	15	0	2	:	8
1985	403 *	387 *	15	120	102	0 *	17	116	6	14	0	2	:	12
1986	379 *	363 *	14	117	94	0 *	16 *	105	7	12	0	2	:	13
OTHER ROOT CROPS													**AUTRES PLANTES SARCLEES**	
1983	375	281	1	10	6	0	94	132	14	13	0	0	:	105
1984	339	247	1	8	6	0	93	106	14	10	—	0	:	102
1985	311 *	223 *	1	5	6	0 *	88	85	14 *	13	0	0	:	99
1986	286 *	198 *	0	0	6	0 *	88 *	74	13	14 *	0	0	:	91
INDUSTRIAL CROPS													**PLANTES INDUSTRIELLES**	
1983	3 247 *	2 151 *	14	166	255	290	1 072	1 008	3	164 *	1	21	24 *	228
1984	3 588 *	2 386 *	17	196 *	278	352	1 160	1 058	5 *	184	1	22	42 *	274
1985	3 891 *	2 695 *	16	220	289 *	389 *	1 152	1 249 *	4 *	208 *	1	19	44 *	301
1986	4 200 *	3 053 *	13	232 *	333 *	417 *	1 104 *	1 431 *	2 *	309 *	1	13	44 *	303
OILSEEDS													**PLANTES OLEAGINEUSES**	
1983	2 866 *	1 844	4	165	232	193	1 001	916	3	92	1	16	22 *	222
1984	3 206 *	2 065	5	195	254	255	1 101	960	4	108	1	16	40 *	269
1985	3 479 *	2 351	2	219	266	285	1 087	1 140	4	127	1	11	41 *	296
1986	3 813 *	2 729 *	3	230 *	308	313 *	1 043 *	1 335	2	232	1	6	41 *	299
RAPE AND TURNIP RAPE													**COLZA ET NAVETTE**	
1983	1 120	1 107	4	162	232	—	13	470	3	0	1	13	—	222
1984	1 181	1 173	5	191	254	—	8	433	4	2	1	13	—	269
1985	1 286	1 276	2	218	266	—	10	474	4	6	1	10	—	296
1986	1 250 *	1 245 *	3	227	308	—	5	386 *	2	14	1	6	—	299

SOURCE: CRONOS-ZPA1 DATA BANK, AGRICULTURAL PRODUCTS

SOURCE: BANQUE DE DONNEES CRONOS-ZPA1, PRODUITS AGRICOLES

eurostat

AGRICULTURE, SYLVICULTURE ET PÊCHE

POUR EN SAVOIR PLUS, VOIR... PROGRAMME 1987

( ) banque de données   • publication

Série	Titre	Périodicité

Thème 1 — Statistiques générales   couverture bleu nuit

	(Cronos – ICG)* Statistiques générales	
	(REGIO) Statistiques régionales	
	• Eurostat Revue	A
	• Statistiques de base	A
	• Régions – Annuaire statistique	A

Thème 5 — Agriculture, forêts et pêche   couverture verte

Ⓐ Annuaire	• AGRICULTURE – Annuaire statistique	A
➡ **Agriculture**	(Cronos – ZPA1) Productions	
	(Cronos – COSA) Comptes	
	(Cronos – PRAG) Prix et indices de prix	
	(Cronos – RICA) Comptabilité des exploitations	
	(FSSRS) Structure des exploitations	
Ⓑ Conjoncture	• PRODUCTION VÉGÉTALE	T
	• PRODUCTION ANIMALE	T
	• PRIX AGRICOLES – Publications ou microfiches	T
	• INDICE DES PRIX AGRICOLES (output et input)	S
Ⓒ Comptes, enquêtes	• BILANS FOURRAGERS	n.p.
et statistiques	• PRIX AGRICOLES : 1977-1986	A
	• COMPTES ÉCONOMIQUES – Agriculture, sylviculture	A
	• ENQUÊTE SUR LA STRUCTURE DES EXPLOITATIONS	
	AGRICOLES 1985 – Principaux résultats	n.p.
	— Résultats graphiques – Microfiches	
	• ENQUÊTE 1985, arbres fruitiers	n.p.
	• LA VIGNE DANS LA CE, 1985	n.p.
Ⓓ Études et analyses	• REVENU AGRICOLE – Analyses du revenu sectoriel –	
	1986	A
	• LE VERGER EUROPÉEN – 1986	n.p.
Ⓔ Méthodes	• MÉTHODOLOGIE DES INDICES CE DES PRIX	
	AGRICOLES (output et input)	n.p.
	• CATALOGUE DES CARACTÉRISTIQUES DES SÉRIES	
	DE PRIX AGRICOLES STOCKÉES DANS CRONOS	
	(nouveau)	n.p.
	• ENQUÊTES SUR LA STRUCTURE DES EXPLOITATIONS	
	AGRICOLES – Introduction et bases méthodologiques	n.p.
	• MANUEL DES COMPTES ÉCONOMIQUES AGRICOLES	
	ET FORESTIERS	n.p.
Ⓕ Statistiques rapides	• THÈME VARIABLE – environ 20 notes	n.p.
➡ **Forêts**	(Cronos – WOOD)	
Ⓒ Comptes, enquêtes	• STATISTIQUE FORESTIÈRE – TABLEAUX 1980-1984	n.p.
et statistiques	• COMPTES ÉCONOMIQUES – Agriculture, sylviculture	A
Ⓔ Méthodes	• STATISTIQUE FORESTIÈRE – Méthodologie	n.p.
➡ **Pêche**	(Cronos – FISH)	
Ⓒ Comptes, enquêtes	• STATISTIQUE DE LA PÊCHE	A
et statistiques		

A = annuelle   S = semestrielle   T = trimestrielle   n.p. = non périodique
* Indicateurs CE prix agricoles et productions sur réseaux nationaux par Serveurs et Minitel (Ovide)

eurostat

AGRICULTURE, FORESTRY AND FISHERIES

FOR FURTHER DETAILS, SEE... 1987 PROGRAMME

( ) data bank   ● publication

Series	Titles	Frequency

Theme 1 — General statistics

midnight
blue covers

(Cronos – ICG)* General statistics
(REGIO)   Regional statistics
● Eurostat review   A
● Basic statistics   A
● Regions – Statistical yearbook   A

Theme 5 — Agriculture, forestry and fisheries

green covers

Ⓐ Yearbook   ● AGRICULTURE – Statistical yearbook   A

➡ Agriculture
(Cronos – ZPA1)   Production
(Cronos – COSA)   Accounts
(Cronos – PRAG)   Prices and price indices
(Cronos – RICA)   Accountancy of agricultural holdings
(FSSRS)   Structure of agricultural holdings

Ⓑ Short-term trends
● CROP PRODUCTION   Q
● ANIMAL PRODUCTION   Q
● AGRICULTURAL PRICES – Publication and microfiche   Q
● EC AGRICULTURAL PRICE INDICES (output and input)   HY

Ⓒ Accounts, surveys
and statistics
● FEED BALANCE SHEET   A
● AGRICULTURAL PRICES: 1977-1986   A
● ECONOMIC ACCOUNTS – Agriculture, forestry   A
● SURVEY ON THE STRUCTURE OF AGRICULTURAL
HOLDINGS 1985 — Results – graphs - microfiche   n.p.
● SURVEY 1985, fruit trees   n.p.
● VINES IN THE EC, 1985   n.p.

Ⓓ Studies and
analyses
● AGRICULTURAL INCOME – Sectoral income index
analysis 1986   n.p.
● THE EUROPEAN ORCHARD – 1986   n.p.

Ⓔ Methods
● METHODOLOGY OF EC AGRICULTURAL PRICE
INDICES (Output-input)   n.p.
● CATALOGUE OF THE CHARACTERISTICS OF AGRICUL-
TURAL PRICE SERIES STORED IN CRONOS (new)   n.p.
● SURVEYS ON THE STRUCTURE OF AGRICULTURAL
HOLDINGS – Introduction and methodological base   n.p.
● MANUAL ON ECONOMIC ACCOUNTS FOR AGRICUL-
TURE AND FORESTRY (new)   n.p.

Ⓕ Rapid reports   ● CHANGEABLE THEME – approx. 20 notes   n.p.

➡ Forestry   (Cronos – WOOD)

Ⓒ Accounts, surveys
and statistics
● FORESTRY STATISTICS – tables 1980-84   n.p.
● ECONOMIC ACCOUNTS – Agriculture, Forestry   A

Ⓔ Methods   ● FORESTRY STATISTICS – methodology   n.p.

➡ Fisheries   (Cronos – FISH)

Ⓒ Accounts, surveys
and statistics
● FISHERIES STATISTICS   A

A = annually   HY = half yearly   Q = quarterly   n.p. = non-periodic
* EC prices and production indicators with national network by Servors et Minitel (Ovide).

1000 HA

YEAR ANNÉE	EUR 12	EUR 10	B	DK	D	GR	E	F	IRL	I	L	NL	P	UK
SUNFLOWER SEEDS													**GRAINES DE TOURNESOL**	
1983	1 464	517	–	–	–	13	926	431	–	72	–	–	21	–
1984	1 674	629	–	–	–	43	1 007	504	–	82	–	–	38	–
1985	1 801	773	–	–	–	50	989	639	–	84	–	–	40	–
1986	2 046	1 070	–	–	–	79	936	901	–	90	–	–	40	–
SOYABEANS													**GRAINES DE SOJA**	
1983	34	33	–	–	–	–	1	13	–	19	–	–	–	–
1984	48	45	–	–	–	0	3	22	–	23	–	–	–	–
1985	66	64	–	–	–	0	2	27	–	36	–	–	–	–
1986	178 *	175 *	–	–	–	0 *	3 *	47	–	128	–	–	–	–
OTHER OILSEEDS													**AUTRES PLANTES OLEAGINEUSES**	
1983	247	186	0	3	–	180	60	1	–	0	–	2	1	–
1984	302	218	0	3	–	211	82	0	–	0	–	2	2	–
1985	325	238	0	0	–	235	86	0	–	1	–	1	2	–
1986	338 *	238 *	0	3 *	–	234	99 *	0 *	–	0	–	0	1	–
TEXTILE CROPS													**PLANTES TEXTILES**	
1983	272	232	7	–	–	174	40	47	–	1	–	3	:	–
1984	337	277	10	–	–	207	60	55	–	1	–	4	:	–
1985	376 *	312 *	11	–	–	231	64	65 *	–	1	–	4	:	–
1986	371 *	294 *	8	–	–	230	77 *	53 *	–	0 *	–	3	:	–
TOBACCO													**TABAC**	
1983	203 *	179 *	0	–	3	91	22	14	–	70 *	–	–	1	–
1984	207	184	1	–	3	92	22	14	–	74	–	–	1	–
1985	221	195	1	–	3	98	25	15	–	79	–	–	2	–
1986	215	191	1	–	3	97	22	15	–	75	–	–	2	–
HOPS													**HOUBLON**	
1983	29 *	27	1	–	20	– *	2	1	0	–	–	–	:	6
1984	28 *	26	1	–	19	– *	2	1	0	–	–	–	:	5
1985	28 *	26	1	–	19	0 *	2	1	0	–	–	–	:	5
1986	27 *	25	1	–	20	0 *	2	1	0	–	–	–	:	4
OTHER INDUSTRIAL CROPS													**AUTRES PLANTES INDUSTRIELLES**	
1983	90 *	43 *	1	1	1	5	47	30	–	2 *	0	2	:	–
1984	76 *	41 *	1	1 *	1	5	35	28	– *	2	0	2	:	–
1985	82 *	43 *	1	1	1 *	6 *	39	28	– *	1 *	0	3	:	–
1986	80 *	44 *	1	2 *	3 *	7 *	36 *	28	– *	1 *	0	3	:	–
GREEN FODDER FROM ARABLE LAND													**FOURRAGES VERTS DE TERRES ARABLES**	
1983	14 170 *	12 549 *	147	400	1 104	327 *	1 151	5 214	587 *	2 685	16	198	:	1 871
1984	13 842 *	12 226 *	155	387	1 175	212 *	1 146	5 079	593 *	2 584	18	206	:	1 816
1985	13 871 *	12 291 *	160	357	1 224	241 *	1 110	5 020	596 *	2 637	18	218	:	1 820 *
1986	13 874 *	12 285 *	163	351	1 255	220 *	1 118 *	5 095	592 *	2 603	19	237 *	:	1 751
ANNUAL GREEN FODDER													**FOURRAGES VERTS ANNUELS**	
1983	4 419 *	3 902 *	109	80	813	173 *	518	1 657	1 *	862	7	157	:	40
1984	4 283 *	3 761 *	118	73	874	65 *	522	1 609	1 *	806	9	166	:	37
1985	4 417 *	3 915 *	129	75	937	66 *	502	1 648	1 *	832	10	177	:	40
1986	4 647 *	4 140 *	132	83	953	66 *	507 *	1 802	1 *	853	10	196	:	43
GREEN MAIZE													**MAIS FOURRAGE**	
1983	2 917 *	2 815 *	101	16	807	3	102	1 409	1 *	300 *	5	157	:	15
1984	2 962 *	2 856 *	108	21	869	3	106	1 405	1 *	260	6	166	:	16
1985	3 146 *	3 040 *	119	20	932	4 *	107	1 462	1 *	300 *	7	177	:	20
1986	3 348 *	3 241 *	120	25	947	4 *	107	1 619	1 *	300 *	7	196	:	23

YEAR ANNÉE	EUR 12	EUR 10	B	DK	D	GR	E	F	IRL	I	L	NL	P	UK

1000 HA

OTHER ANNUAL GREEN FODDER   **AUTRES FOURRAGES VERTS ANNUELS**

1983	1 502 *	1 086 *	9	64	6	170 *	416	248	— *	562 *	2	1	:	25
1984	1 320 *	904 *	10	53	5	62 *	416	203	— *	546	3	0	:	22
1985	1 269 *	874 *	11	54	6	62 *	395	186	— *	532 *	3	0	:	20
1986	1 298 *	898 *	12	58	7	62 *	400 *	183	— *	553 *	3	0	:	20

PERENNIAL GREEN FODDER   **FOURRAGES VERTS PLURIANNUELS**

1983	9 282	8 648	37	320	291	154	634	3 556	586	1 823	9	41	:	1 832
1984	9 090	8 466	37	314	301	147	624	3 470	592	1 778	9	40	:	1 779
1985	8 986 *	8 377 *	31	282	287	176	609	3 372	595	1 805	9	41	:	1 780 *
1986	8 757 *	8 146 *	32	268	301	154	611 *	3 293	591 *	1 750	9	40 *	:	1 708

CLOVER AND MIXTURES   **TREFLES ET MELANGES**

1983	625	:	2	:	160	:	15	112	—	335	1	0	:	:
1984	:	:	1	:	158	:	14	104	—	:	0	0	:	:
1985	:	:	1	:	153	:	14	97	—	:	0	0	:	:
1986	:	:	2	:	157	:	14 *	95	—	:	0	0	:	:

LUCERNE   **LUZERNE**

1983	2 135 *	1 808 *	1	3	29	154	327	567	—	1 050 *	0	2	:	—
1984	2 092	1 771	1	4	30	147	321	548	—	1 039	0	3	:	—
1985	:	:	1	4	28	176	308	514	—	:	0	3	:	0 *
1986	:	:	1	5	27	154	312	496	—	:	0	3	:	0

TEMPORARY GRASSES AND GRAZINGS   **PRAIRIES ET PATURAGES TEMPORAIRES**

1983	6 214 *	5 979 *	34	317	102	—	—	2 824	586	238 *	8	38	—	1 832
1984	6 119	5 885	34	311	113	—	—	2 762	592	249	8	37	—	1 779
1985	:	:	28	278	105	—	—	2 707	595	:	8	38	—	1 780
1986	:	:	29	264	117	—	—	2 652	591 *	:	9	37 *	—	1 708

PERMANENT GRASSLAND   **SUPERFICIES TOUJOURS COUVERTES D'HERBE**

1983	49 791	42 385	653	236	4 630	1 789	6 645	12 535	4 622	5 002	71	1 143	761	11 704
1984	49 528	42 121	644	228	4 607	1 789	6 646	12 362	4 597	5 012	71	1 141	761	11 670
1985	49 153 *	41 746	640	221	4 566	1 789	6 646 *	12 200	4 612	4 954	71	1 127	761	11 567
1986	48 995 *	41 589	632	219	4 537	1 789	6 645 *	12 094	4 612	4 944	70	1 108	761	11 583

PERMANENT MEADOWS   **PRAIRIES PERMANENTES**

1983	:	:	237	:	3 418	:	1 452	3 893	935	1 094	32	:	33 *	:
1984	:	:	238	:	3 404	:	1 440	3 825	937	1 085	28	:	33 *	:
1985	:	:	242	:	2 389	:	1 450 *	3 767	948	1 090	29	:	33 *	:
1986	:	:	246	:	2 370	:	1 450 *	3 800 *	940 *	1 088	28	:	33 *	:

PERMANENT PASTURES   **PATURAGES PERMANENTS**

1983	:	:	416	:	1 212	1 789	5 193	8 642	3 687	3 909	39	:	728 *	:
1984	:	:	406	:	1 203	1 789	5 206	8 538	3 660	3 927	42	:	728 *	:
1985	:	:	399	:	2 177	1 789	5 196 *	8 433	3 664	3 864	42	:	728 *	:
1986	:	:	386	:	2 167	1 789	5 195 *	8 294 *	3 672 *	3 856	42	:	728 *	:

LAND UNDER PERMANENT CROPS   **CULTURES PERMANENTES**

1983	12 056 *	6 182 *	14	13	181 *	1 028 *	5 008	1 358	2 *	3 484	2	36	866 *	63
1984	11 914 *	6 115 *	14	12	182	1 036 *	4 933	1 339	2	3 431	2	36	865 *	61
1985	11 879 *	6 089 *	14	12	181	1 037 *	4 926 *	1 324	2	3 419	2	36	865 *	60 *
1986	11 798 *	6 016 *	14	12	181	1 040 *	4 917 *	1 311	2	3 359	2	35	865 *	61

APPLE AND PEAR TREES   **POMMIERS ET POIRIERS**

1983	484 *	351 *	8	5	28	26	98	92	1	136	0	21	35	33 *
1984	479 *	350 *	9	5	28	26	96	91	1	136	0	21	34	33 *
1985	472 *	347 *	9	4	28	26 *	94	91	1	135	0	21	31	32 *
1986	468 *	344 *	9	4	28	26 *	93 *	91 *	1	135	0	20	31 *	31 *

YEAR ANNÉE	EUR 12	EUR 10	B	DK	D	GR	E	F	IRL	I	L	NL	P	UK
						1000 HA								
STONE FRUIT TREES													**FRUITS A NOYAU**	
1983	432 *	310 *	2	2	14	44 *	107	87	0	154	0	2	16	5
1984	443 *	314 *	2	2 *	14	46	113	88	0	156	0	2	16	4
1985	453 *	318 *	2	2	14	47 *	118	87	0	160	0	2	17	4
1986	457 *	320 *	2	2 *	14	48 *	121 *	88 *	0	161	0	1	17 *	4
NUT TREES													**FRUITS A COQUE**	
1983	1 329	624	0	—	0	60	607	27	—	537	—	—	98	—
1984	1 320	621	0	—	0	60	600	27	—	534	—	—	99	—
1985	1 331 *	620 *	0	—	0	60 *	612	27	—	533	—	—	99	—
1986	1 333 *	620 *	0	—	0	60 *	615 *	27 *	—	533 *	—	—	99 *	—
OTHER FRUIT TREES													**AUTRES ARBRES FRUITIERS**	
1983	170 *	36 *	0	—	6	11	43	1	1 *	14	—	—	91	3
1984	169 *	35 *	0	—	5	11	42	1	1 *	15	—	—	91	2
1985	166 *	35 *	0	—	5	10 *	40	1	1	15	—	—	91	2
1986	164 *	33 *	0	—	5	10 *	40 *	1 *	1	14	—	—	91 *	2
STRAWBERRIES													**FRAISES**	
1983	46	39	1	1	6	1	6	9	0	11	0	2	1	7
1984	46 *	38	1	1	7	1	7	9	0	10	0	2	1 *	7
1985	48 *	39	1	1	7	0	9	9	0	11	0	2	1 *	7
1986	49 *	38 *	1	1	7	0	10	9 *	0	11	0	2	1 *	7
SOFT FRUIT													**BAIES**	
1983	43	31	0	1	2	0	10	5	0	13	0	1	1	10
1984	46 *	34 *	0	1 *	2	0	10	5	0	15	0	1	1	9
1985	50 *	37 *	0	1	2	0 *	11	6	0	18	0	1	2	9
1986	54 *	40 *	0	1	2	0 *	12 *	7 *	0	21 *	0	1	2 *	8
CITRUS FRUIT													**AGRUMES**	
1983	501 *	236 *	—	—	—	50 *	236	2	—	183	—	—	29	—
1984	512 *	237 *	—	—	—	50 *	245	2	—	185	—	—	30	—
1985	520 *	237 *	—	—	—	51 *	252	2	—	184	—	—	30	—
1986	525 *	238 *	—	—	—	52 *	257 *	2 *	—	184	—	—	30 *	—
VINEYARDS													**VIGNES**	
1983	4 480 *	2 513	0	—	100	178	1 697	1 095	—	1 138	1	0	270	0 *
1984	4 387 *	2 483 *	0	—	101	175	1 633	1 076	—	1 129	1	0 *	270	0
1985	4 303 *	2 439 *	0	—	101	171 *	1 593	1 063	—	1 103	1	0 *	270	0 *
1986	4 263 *	2 418 *	0	—	101	170 *	1 574 *	1 049	—	1 097	1	0 *	270	0 *
OLIVES													**OLIVES**	
1983	4 323	1 916	—	—	—	643	2 090	19	—	1 254	—	—	317	—
1984	4 316	1 924	—	—	—	651	2 076	18	—	1 254	—	—	317	—
1985	4 283 *	1 880 *	—	—	—	655 *	2 087	17	—	1 207	—	—	317	—
1986	4 228 *	1 822 *	—	—	—	658 *	2 090 *	17	—	1 147	—	—	317	—
HARDY NURSERY STOCKS													**PEPINIERES**	
1983	78 *	76 *	3	3	20	1 *	:	20	0	18	0	6	2	5
1984	78 *	76 *	3	3	19	1 *	:	19	0	19	0	6 *	2	6
1985	78 *	77 *	3	4	19 *	1 *	:	19	0	18	0	7	2	6
1986	79 *	78 *	3	4 *	19 *	1 *	:	19	0	19	0	7	2 *	6
OSIER-WILLOWS													**OSERAIES**	
1983	20 *	18 *	0	—	4	8 *	2	1	—	0 *	0	4	:	—
1984	19 *	17 *	0	—	4	8 *	2	1	—	0	0	4	:	—
1985	19 *	17 *	0	—	4	8 *	2	1	—	0 *	0	4 *	:	—
1986	19 *	17 *	0	—	4	7 *	2 *	1	—	0	0	4 *	:	—

I c

Structure

Structure

YEAR ANNÉE	EUR 12	EUR 10	B	DK	D	EL	ES	F	IRL	I	L	NL	P	UK
TOTAL NUMBER OF HOLDINGS (in 1000)													**NOMBRE TOTAL D'EXPLOITATIONS (en 1000)**	
1966/67	:	:	214,8	:	1 246,0	991,5		1 708,0	:	2 980,5	8,61	247,0	:	:
1970/71	:	7 684,7	184,0	146,0	1 074,6	1 046,3		1 587,6	:	2 849,9	7,61	184,6	:	326,7
1975	:	:	138,1	132,3	907,9	:	:	1 315,1	228,0	2 664,2	6,21	162,6	:	280,6
1977	:	6 602,8	126,5	127,8	851,6	957,0	:	1 249,2	225,0	2 634,1	5,75	154,6	:	271,2
1979/80	:	6 820,3	115,1	122,7	849,9	998,9	:	1 255,3	223,5	2 832,4	5,17	148,7	769,4	268,6
1983	:	6 515,7	102,6	98,7	767,6	958,7	1 818,2	1 129,6	221,1	2 832,4	4,56	138,5	:	261,9
1985	:	6 359,3	97,8	92,4	740,5	951,6	:	1 056,9	220,2	2 801,1	4,41	135,9	:	258,5
TOTAL AA (in 1000 ha)													**SAU TOTALE (en 1000 ha)**	
1966/67	:	:	1 593,1	:	12 768,2	:	:	30 115,2	:	17 928,3	133,95	2 232,5	:	:
1970/71	:	92 566,2	1 540,3	2 965,5	12 651,1	3 565,1		29 940,0	:	17 178,8	135,14	2 142,6	:	17 710,5
1975	:	:	1 467,5	2 966,0	12 398,6	:	:	29 463,6	5 076,6	16 485,5	136,07	2 086,3	:	16 469,0
1977	:	90 193,8	1 448,7	2 927,5	12 214,5	3 372,6	:	29 305,8	5 067,8	16 517,5	132,36	2 060,3	:	17 146,7
1979/80	:	89 283,0	1 421,0	2 920,3	12 212,3	3 549,8	23 506,0	29 277,7	5 048,5	15 587,8	130,06	2 037,1	3 314,0	17 098,4
1983	:	88 474,8	1 392,8	2 846,5	11 922,6	3 907,7	:	28 759,6	5 036,6	15 857,8	127,42	2 010,2	:	16 883,6
1985	:	88 241,3	1 381,2	2 834,6	11 844,0	4 116,3	:	28 486,8	4 995,6	15 600,7	126,09	2 026,2	:	16 829,8
TOTAL SGM (in 1000 ESU)													**MBS TOTALE (en 1000 UDE)**	
1975	:	:	1 296,1	1 635,5	7 461,4	:	:	12 605,4	931,5	8 411,1	63,50	2 899,3	:	4 297,9
1979/80	:	78 755,5	2 104,7	2 668,6	11 631,9	3 818,0	:	21 224,7	1 613,9	17 169,1	97,68	9 850,5	5 850,5	8 576,4
1983	:	74 695,9	2 104,2	2 567,6	11 556,4	3 312,7	10 710,4	21 569,3	1 606,0	17 169,1	91,63	5 995,6	:	8 723,4
1985	:	86 942,1	2 326,5	2 854,9	12 818,9	4 405,3	:	24 086,4	1 910,6	22 052,5	82,3	5 953,8	:	10 450,9
TOTAL LABOUR FORCE (in 1000 AWU)													**MAIN-D'ŒUVRE TOTALE (en 1000 UTA)**	
1966/67	:	:	271,2	:	2 329,9	:	:	3 032,3	:	4 127,2	17,04	341,7	:	:
1970/71	:	:	188,6	:	1 611,0	:	:	2 368,8	:	2 989,9	12,27	289,7	:	:
1975	:	:	139,6	176,7	1 233,6	:	:	1 949,7	324,7	2 826,5	12,37	253,7	:	625,7
1977	:	:	:	:	:	:	:	:	:	:	:	:	:	:
1979/80	:	7 324,0	123,9	171,6	1 050,9	828,1	:	1 847,5	310,3	2 157,6	9,05	242,2	1 156,6	582,8
1983	:	7 020,7	111,8	140,3	945,9	917,5	1 432,5	1 658,2	276,1	2 157,6	7,75	243,4	:	562,1
1985	:	6 833,3	106,9	122,4	917,9	931,2	:	1 568,8	275,8	2 125,7	7 23	234,4	:	543,0
Distribution of the holdings by Member State (in %)													**Répartition des exploitations par État membre (en %)**	
1970/71	:	100,0	2,4	1,9	14,0	13,6		20,7	:	37,1	0,10	2,4	:	4,3
1975	:	:	2,4	2,3	15,6	:	:	22,5	3,9	45,6	0,10	2,8	:	4,8
1977	:	100,0	1,9	1,9	12,9	14,5	:	18,9	3,4	39,9	0,09	2,3	:	4,1
1979/80	:	100,0	1,7	1,8	12,5	14,6	:	18,4	3,3	41,5	0,08	2,2	:	3,9
1983	:	100,0	1,6	1,5	11,8	14,7	:	17,3	3,4	43,5	0,07	2,1	:	4,0
1985	:	100,0	1,5	1,5	11,6	15,0	:	16,6	:	44,0	0,07	2,1	:	4,1
Distribution of the AA by Member State (in %)													**Répartition de la SAU par État membre (en %)**	
1970/71	:	100,0	1,7	3,2	13,7	3,9		32,4	:	18,6	0,15	2,3	:	19,1
1975	:	:	1,7	3,4	14,3	:	:	34,0	5,9	19,0	0,16	2,4	:	19,0
1977	:	100,0	1,6	3,2	13,5	3,7	:	32,5	5,6	18,3	0,15	2,3	:	19,0
1979/80	:	100,0	1,6	3,3	13,6	4,0	:	32,7	5,6	17,7	0,15	2,3	:	19,1
1983	:	100,0	1,6	3,2	13,4	4,4	:	32,4	5,7	17,9	0,14	2,3	:	19,0
1985	:	100,0	1,6	3,2	13,4	4,7	:	32,3	5,7	17,7	0,14	2,3	:	19,1
Distribution of the SGM by Member State (in %)													**Répartition de la MBS par État membre (en %)**	
1975	:	:	3,3	4,1	18,8	:	:	31,8	2,6	21,2	0,16	7,3	:	10,9
1977	:	:	:	:	:	:	:	:	:	:	:	:	:	:
1979/80	:	:	3,0	3,8	16,6	:	:	30,3	2,3	24,5	0,14	8,4	:	10,9
1983	:	100,0	2,8	3,4	15,5	4,4	:	28,9	2,6	23,0	0,12	8,0	:	11,7
1985	:	100,0	2,7	3,3	14,7	5,1	:	27,7	2,2	25,4	0,09	6,8	:	12,0
Distribution of the AWU by Member State (in %)													**Répartition de la main-d'œuvre par État-membre (en %)**	
1975	:	:	1,9	2,3	16,4	:	:	25,8	4,3	37,5	0,16	3,4	:	8,3
1977	:	:	:	:	:	:	:	:	:	:	:	:	:	:
1979/80	:	100,0	1,7	2,3	14,3	11,3	:	25,2	4,2	29,5	0,12	3,3	:	8,0
1983	:	100,0	1,6	2,0	13,5	13,1	:	23,6	3,9	30,7	0,11	3,5	:	8,0
1985	:	100,0	1,6	1,8	13,4	13,6	:	23,0	4,0	31,1	0,10	3,4	:	7,9

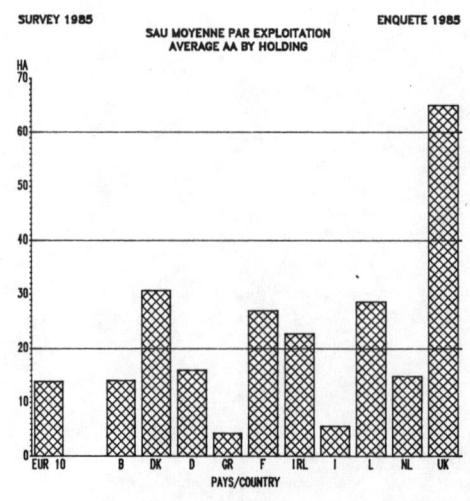

SURVEY 1985 — SAU MOYENNE PAR EXPLOITATION / AVERAGE AA BY HOLDING — ENQUETE 1985

PAYS/COUNTRY

EC SURVEY ON THE STRUCTURE OF AGRICULTURAL HOLDINGS

IC 2

ENQUÊTE CE SUR LA STRUCTURE DES EXPLOITATIONS AGRICOLES

1966/67 TO 1985

1966/67 À 1985

DATA IN 1000　　　　　　　　　　　　　　　　　　　　　　　　　　**DONNÉES EN 1000**

YEAR ANNÉE	EUR 12	EUR 10	B	DK	D	EL	ES	F	IRL	I	L	NL	P	UK

LEGAL PERSONALITY AND MANAGEMENT OF THE HOLDING — **PERSONNALITÉ JURIDIQUE ET GESTION DE L'EXPLOITATION**

Holdings under the responsibility of a natural person — Exploitations sous la responsabilité d'une personne physique

YEAR ANNÉE	EUR 12	EUR 10	B	DK	D	EL	ES	F	IRL	I	L	NL	P	UK
1966/67	:	:	213,6	:	1 240,4	:	:	1 705,8	:	2 962,5	8,61	244,8	:	:
1970/71	:	:	182,7	146,0	1 060,6	:	:	1 576,0	:	2 825,8	7,61	178,1	:	271,5
1975	:	:	136,9	132,1	904,0	:	:	1 303,3	227,3	2 646,7	6,20	160,6	:	266,5
1977	:	:	126,5	127,7	848,3	:	:	1 240,9	224,2	2 617,4	5,39	150,8	:	221,7
1979/80	:	6 736,3	114,4	122,5	845,2	998,0	:	1 214,1	222,7	2 816,3	5,12	146,4	765,2	251,6
1983	:	6 421,3	101,9	98,4	764,0	958,3	1 793,1	1 080,4	219,9	2 816,3	4,52	136,0	:	241,6
1985	:	6 265,7	97,1	92,1	737,4	951,2	:	1 003,8	219,1	2 786,4	4,38	133,6	:	240,6

Holdings where the holder is also the manager — Exploitations dont l'exploitant est aussi chef d'exploitation

YEAR ANNÉE	EUR 12	EUR 10	B	DK	D	EL	ES	F	IRL	I	L	NL	P	UK
1966/67	:	:	213,1	:	1 158,5	:	:	1 663,4	:	2 768,3	8,58	241,2	:	:
1970/71	:	:	182,4	:	1 030,3	:	:	1 567,4	:	:	7,23	177,5	:	:
1975	:	:	136,1	130,0	877,6	:	:	1 296,8	218,6	2 602,3	6,20	160,0	:	260,7
1977	:	:	:	:	:	:	:	:	:	:	:	:	:	:
1979/80	:	6 633,2	114,0	120,6	828,4	998,0	:	1 210,1	214,4	2 760,0	4,83	145,5	:	237,4
1983	:	6 315,7	101,2	96,8	750,0	957,3	1 793,1	1 075,0	214,3	2 760,0	4,21	134,9	:	222,0
1985	:	6 180,7	96,9	90,5	722,6	950,8	:	998,3	212,7	2 753,7	4,10	131,8	:	219,3

Holdings where the holder has another gainful activity — Exploitations dont l'exploitant exerce une autre activité

YEAR ANNÉE	EUR 12	EUR 10	B	DK	D	EL	ES	F	IRL	I	L	NL	P	UK
1966/67	:	:	74,0	:	445,9	:	:	323,2	:	887,7	1,18	62,4	:	:
1970/71	:	:	72,9	:	472,4	:	:	346,7	:	969,9	1,19	31,2	:	:
1975	:	:	32,2	27,0	378,1	:	:	257,7	:	772,3	1,42	30,0	:	60,2
1977	:	:	:	:	:	:	:	:	:	:	:	:	:	:
1979/80	:	:	37,1	24,0	361,6	:	:	461,4	48,9	818,5	1,06	30,4	336,0	:
1983	:	2 061,5	32,9	32,9	323,1	378,2	1 047,4	349,0	53,3	811,1	0,80	26,0	:	54,2
1985	:	1 923,4	30,8	28,8	311,1	325,5	:	324,2	70,3	725,3	0,82	27,1	:	79,5

Holdings with accounting — Exploitations avec comptabilité

YEAR ANNÉE	EUR 12	EUR 10	B	DK	D	EL	ES	F	IRL	I	L	NL	P	UK
1966/67	:	:	:	:	:	:	:	:	:	:	:	:	:	:
1970/71	:	:	12,7	:	84,2	:	:	:	:	231,8	0,58	172,5	:	:
1975	:	:	11,1	92,1	79,8	:	:	:	:	215,7	0,66	159,8	:	233,1
1977	:	:	:	:	:	:	:	:	:	:	:	:	:	:
1979/80	:	:	15,1	:	91,1	11,2	:	469,0	64,6	359,1	0,87	148,7	4,1	228,5
1983	:	:	:	:	:	:	:	:	:	:	:	:	:	:
1985	:	:	:	:	:	:	:	:	:	:	:	:	:	:

EC SURVEY ON THE STRUCTURE OF AGRICULTURAL HOLDINGS

IC 3

ENQUÊTE CE SUR LA STRUCTURE DES EXPLOITATIONS AGRICOLES

1966/67 TO 1985

1966/67 À 1985

DATA IN 1000　　　　　　　　　　　　　　　　　　　　　　　　　　**DONNÉES EN 1000**

MODES OF TENURE — **MODES DE FAIRE-VALOIR**

AA owner-farmed — SAU en faire-valoir direct

YEAR ANNÉE	EUR 12	EUR 10	B	DK	D	EL	ES	F	IRL	I	L	NL	P	UK
1966/67	:	:	466,8	:	9 847,3	:	:	15 671,1	:	12 542,9	86,45	1 140,9	:	:
1970/71	:	:	439,9	2 616,5	8 963,6	:	:	16 437,6	:	12 453,6	81,76	1 112,1	:	10 159,3
1975	:	:	398,4	2 548,0	8 745,9	:	:	15 260,6	4 897,4	12 798,7	79,63	1 161,9	:	9 335,5
1977	:	58 628,8	405,5	2 501,5	8 519,2	2 800,6	:	15 352,0	4 881,8	13 028,2	75,31	1 184,7	:	9 880,0
1979/80	:	:	391,4	2 478,1	8 495,9	:	:	14 657,4	4 760,8	12 536,0	78,10	1 208,6	:	:
1983	:	56 159,5	420,9	2 365,6	7 961,7	3 221,0	16 679,6	13 916,2	4 698,0	12 536,0	72,10	1 226,6	:	9 741,4
1985	:	56 025,1	423,2	2 323,7	7 802,7	3 174,0	:	13 516,1	4 799,7	12 218,1	65,82	1 282,6	:	10 419,2

AA tenant-farmed, other modes of tenure — SAU en fermage et autres modes

YEAR ANNÉE	EUR 12	EUR 10	B	DK	D	EL	ES	F	IRL	I	L	NL	P	UK
1966/67	:	:	1 126,3	:	2 830,9	:	:	14 444,0	:	5 385,4	47,50	1 091,6	:	:
1970/71	:	:	1 100,4	349,0	3 687,5	:	:	15 289,3	:	4 725,3	53,38	1 030,5	:	7 551,3
1975	:	:	1 069,1	418,0	3 652,7	:	:	14 203,0	179,3	3 686,8	56,43	924,4	:	7 133,6
1977	:	31 639,9	1 043,2	426,0	3 688,1	654,3	:	13 953,8	186,0	3 489,3	57,05	875,6	:	7 266,5
1979/80	:	:	1 029,4	442,2	3 716,7	:	:	14 618,5	163,2	3 291,9	54,40	828,6	:	:
1983	:	32 514,1	971,4	490,0	3 960,9	1 395,2	6 826,4	14 837,4	183,5	3 291,9	55,20	783,6	:	6 545,0
1985	:	32 409,1	957,7	510,9	4 081,4	1 139,1	:	14 970,7	190,1	3 347,7	60,21	743,6	:	6 407,7

EC SURVEY ON THE STRUCTURE
OF AGRICULTURAL HOLDINGS

IC 4

ENQUÊTE CE SUR LA STRUCTURE
DES EXPLOITATIONS AGRICOLES

1966/67 TO 1985

1966/67 À 1985

DATA IN 1000   DONNÉES EN 1000

YEAR ANNÉE	EUR 12	EUR 10	B	DK	D	EL	ES	F	IRL	I	L	NL	P	UK
NUMBER OF HOLDINGS BY SIZE CLASSES OF HOLDINGS													**NOMBRE D'EXPLOITATIONS PAR CLASSES DE GRANDEURS**	
Less than 1 ha														Moins d'un ha
1975	:	:	34,2	2,1	36,7	:	:	113,0	:	519,6	0,4	18,7	:	9,6
1979/80		1 362,3	22,8	3,0	42,5	247,0	:	114,0	0,1	906,3	0,5	16,7	419,9	9,4
1983		1 338,0	17,5	1,1	37,2	250,0	294,2	95,1		906,3	0,4	15,0	:	15,4
1985		1 321,7	15,6	1,1	36,6	245,3	:	82,4	0,1	909,3	0,4	15,0		16,0
From 1 to less than 2 ha														De 1 à moins de 2 ha
1975	:	:	11,5	3,6	106,6	:	:	94,6	9,3	673,7	0,3	12,5	:	9,1
1979/80		1 063,6	9,9	3,4	102,5	207,9	:	86,7	8,3	623,5	0,3	11,3	151,7	9,8
1983		1 004,2	8,7	0,5	86,8	181,2	367,2	74,0	8,9	623,5	0,2	10,8	:	9,6
1985		986,9	8,5	0,4	83,4	191,5	:	65,9	10,0	607,0	0,2	10,9		9,2
From 2 to less than 5 ha														De 2 à moins de 5 ha
1975	:	:	18,9	11,9	175,6	:	:	154,2	25,1	793,9	1,0	23,3	:	23,3
1979/80		1 431,3	16,1	10,2	156,8	333,5	:	151,9	25,6	688,8	0,6	20,6	120,8	27,4
1983		1 338,4	14,8	1,8	135,3	302,9	482,2	128,2	25,3	688,8	0,5	18,7	:	22,1
1985		1 289,0	14,4	1,4	127,5	300,2	:	114,8	25,2	665,9	0,5	18,4		20,7
From 5 to less than 10 ha														De 5 à moins de 10 ha
1975	:	:	23,1	25,4	174,2	:	:	183,2	37,7	373,7	0,5	30,7	:	31,6
1979/80		923,9	18,8	21,6	153,0	149,9	:	162,9	35,4	322,3	0,5	27,1	43,9	32,5
1983		866,5	16,3	17,3	135,7	149,0	274,2	137,0	33,9	322,3	0,4	24,3	:	30,3
1985		826,2	15,2	15,4	128,2	138,8	:	122,2	34,7	318,1	0,4	22,9		30,2
From 10 to less than 20 ha														De 10 à moins de 20 ha
1975	:	:	28,3	36,8	209,8	:	:	272,7	70,6	179,2	1,2	44,0	:	45,6
1979/80		847,7	24,8	32,1	186,4	46,6	:	243,9	67,7	166,8	0,7	38,6	18,3	40,1
1983		782,7	22,2	26,9	165,4	53,5	183,1	208,9	65,7	166,8	0,6	34,3	:	38,6
1985		751,0	20,8	24,1	157,4	53,1	:	193,2	63,8	168,1	0,5	32,2		37,7
From 20 to less than 30 ha														De 20 à moins de 30 ha
1975	:	:	11,5	23,1	108,2	:	:	184,1	35,8	50,9	1,0	19,3	:	35,6
1979/80		452,9	11,4	21,3	103,9	8,5	:	172,3	36,3	50,2	0,7	18,9	5,0	29,3
1983		429,0	11,1	18,9	97,3	10,7	70,1	157,5	36,7	50,2	0,5	18,5	:	27,5
1985		416,6	10,8	17,3	93,8	12,0	:	149,0	36,9	51,1	0,5	18,4		26,8
From 30 to less than 50 ha														De 30 à moins de 50 ha
1975	:	:	7,2	19,3	70,4	:	:	174,6	29,8	35,7	1,4	10,9	:	42,9
1979/80		400,0	7,6	19,6	74,6	3,9	:	175,7	30,3	36,6	1,1	11,8	3,7	38,7
1983		401,2	8,0	19,1	75,4	7,6	62,7	172,6	30,8	36,6	1,0	12,8	:	37,4
1985		400,3	8,1	10,0	76,4	6,2	:	168,4	29,9	41,6	0,9	13,5		36,7
From 50 to less than 100 ha														De 50 à moins de 100 ha
1975	:	:	2,9	8,2	22,5	:	:	106,6	15,9	23,6	0,5	2,9	:	45,6
1979/80		241,2	3,2	9,4	26,0	1,4	:	114,3	16,0	23,3	0,7	3,4	2,7	43,6
1983		253,8	3,5	10,6	29,7	2,8	49,1	120,2	16,1	23,3	0,9	3,8	:	42,9
1985		263,6	3,6	11,3	32,2	3,3	:	122,9	15,9	26,6	0,9	4,1		42,7
From 100 ha and more														100 ha et plus
1975	:	:	0,5	1,9	3,8	:	:	32,3	3,7	13,9	—	0,4	:	37,3
1979/80		97,4	0,6	2,1	4,3	0,3	:	33,6	3,7	14,7	—	0,4	3,5	37,8
1983		101,8	0,6	2,5	4,8	1,0	35,3	36,2	3,6	14,7	0,1	0,4	:	38,0
1985		103,9	0,7	2,8	5,1	1,3	:	37,9	3,7	13,4	0,1	0,5		38,4
TOTAL														**TOTAL**
1975	:	:	138,1	132,3	907,9	:	:	1 315,1	228,0	2 664,2	6,2	162,6	:	280,6
1979/80		6 820,3	115,1	122,7	849,9	998,9	:	1 255,3	223,5	2 832,4	5,2	148,7	769,4	268,6
1983		6 515,7	102,6	98,7	767,6	958,7	1 818,2	1 129,6	221,1	2 832,4	4,6	138,5	:	261,9
1985		6 359,1	97,8	92,4	740,5	951,6	:	1 056,9	220,2	2 801,1	4,4	135,9	:	258,5

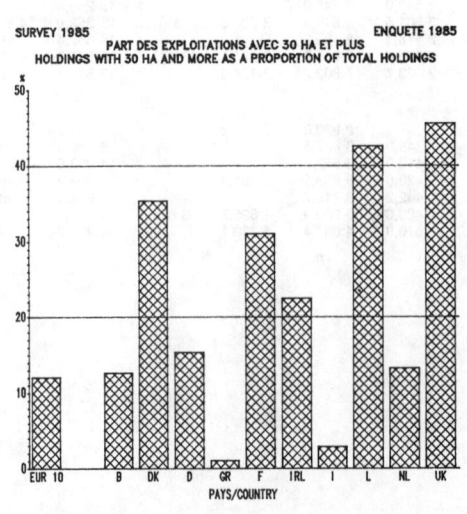

SURVEY 1985   ENQUETE 1985
PART DES EXPLOITATIONS AVEC 30 HA ET PLUS
HOLDINGS WITH 30 HA AND MORE AS A PROPORTION OF TOTAL HOLDINGS

DATA IN 1000 — DONNÉES EN 1000

AA BY SIZE CLASSES OF HOLDINGS — SAU PAR CLASSES DE GRANDEURS

YEAR / ANNÉE	EUR 12	EUR 10	B	DK	D	EL	ES	F	IRL	I	L	NL	P	UK
Less than 1 ha														Moins d'un ha
1975	:	:	16,0	1,0	18,9	:	:	57,9	:	297,7	0,2	8,4	:	4,1
1979/80	:	675,0	11,3	1,0	21,8	120,5	:	55,9	:	452,8	0,2	7,4	199,0	4,2
1983	:	655,3	8,5	0,4	18,8	118,0	129,8	46,1	:	452,8	0,2	6,8	:	3,7
1985	:	647,9	7,5	0,3	18,8	118,2	:	40,6	:	452,2	0,2	6,7	:	3,4
From 1 to less than 2 ha														De 1 à moins de 2 ha
1975	:	:	16,1	5,0	151,3	:	:	132,3	13,4	937,1	0,5	17,6	:	13,1
1979/80	:	1 485,0	13,7	4,8	144,1	289,5	:	122,1	11,7	869,0	0,5	15,8	210,7	13,8
1983	:	1 403,9	12,2	0,7	123,5	251,9	499,7	105,0	12,7	869,0	0,3	15,0	:	13,5
1985	:	1 360,6	11,8	0,5	117,5	265,6	:	93,3	14,0	829,6	0,3	15,1	:	12,9
From 2 to less than 5 ha														De 2 à moins de 5 ha
1975	:	:	63,0	10,1	690,0	:	:	515,1	86,8	2 476,5	3,4	78,1	:	81,9
1979/80	:	4 568,7	53,3	34,3	522,4	1 052,5	:	501,3	86,3	2 153,5	2,0	69,0	370,9	94,2
1983	:	4 264,9	49,0	6,4	452,4	957,1	1 507,3	424,2	84,8	2 153,5	1,8	62,8	:	72,8
1985	:	4 099,0	47,5	5,2	425,9	948,3	:	377,9	85,6	2 077,6	1,7	61,4	:	67,9
From 5 to less than 10 ha														De 5 à moins de 10 ha
1975	:	:	169,3	187,2	1 268,6	:	:	1 342,9	284,9	2 570,1	3,7	226,2	:	230,8
1979/80	:	6 534,9	137,8	157,7	1 113,6	1 004,2	:	1 189,5	264,9	2 229,4	3,8	199,3	300,7	234,9
1983	:	6 133,7	119,3	127,1	990,6	1 005,6	1 894,7	1 001,7	256,0	2 229,3	3,0	178,0	:	223,2
1985	:	5 824,1	111,1	113,1	932,3	931,7	:	895,2	260,5	2 187,5	2,9	167,8	:	222,1
From 10 to less than 20 ha														De 10 à moins de 20 ha
1975	:	:	404,4	532,1	3 042,1	:	:	3 989,6	1 019,0	2 436,7	16,5	630,9	:	672,4
1979/80	:	12 115,9	357,6	465,7	2 708,1	609,0	:	3 570,3	977,7	2 278,9	10,1	555,5	247,6	582,9
1983	:	11 182,0	320,8	391,2	2 409,2	699,7	2 522,9	3 070,4	948,9	2 278,9	9,0	495,2	:	558,7
1985	:	10 713,2	302,8	349,6	2 291,6	702,0	:	2 836,9	923,9	2 287,3	7,7	465,6	:	545,8
From 20 to less than 30 ha														De 20 à moins de 30 ha
1975	:	:	278,7	565,5	2 627,3	:	:	4 517,8	873,5	1 221,6	25,1	463,7	:	880,4
1979/80	:	11 045,8	275,9	521,6	2 535,6	199,2	:	4 221,9	886,4	1 210,0	16,4	456,0	119,9	722,9
1983	:	10 478,7	268,0	462,4	2 381,5	254,3	1 684,7	3 867,8	894,2	1 209,9	12,6	448,6	:	679,3
1985	:	10 173,0	263,2	423,7	2 298,3	282,5	:	3 665,9	898,3	1 221,4	11,3	447,3	:	661,1
From 30 to less than 50 ha														De 30 à moins de 50 ha
1975	:	:	267,2	726,7	2 631,4	:	:	6 682,3	1 131,6	1 337,8	53,3	404,9	:	1 676,8
1979/80	:	15 234,9	287,2	741,0	2 802,4	141,7	:	6 732,3	1 151,2	1 384,8	45,5	438,6	141,6	1 510,4
1983	:	15 296,4	301,0	725,4	2 853,4	277,3	2 385,5	6 605,3	1 173,2	1 384,8	39,6	477,5	:	1 459,1
1985	:	15 283,1	307,4	709,7	2 892,3	225,3	:	6 473,2	1 139,1	1 563,1	35,4	504,6	:	1 433,1
From 50 to less than 100 ha														De 50 à moins de 100 ha
1975	:	:	188,9	539,6	1 456,2	:	:	7 169,1	1 055,0	1 604,3	31,3	182,0	:	3 200,3
1979/80	:	16 261,8	209,0	612,7	1 675,6	87,7	:	7 692,0	1 061,0	1 591,2	46,5	215,8	188,9	3 070,4
1983	:	17 124,3	227,9	702,2	1 922,6	177,7	3 359,3	8 095,3	1 080,1	1 591,2	54,2	242,6	:	3 030,5
1985	:	17 786,8	239,8	752,3	2 094,0	207,7	:	8 298,6	1 064,2	1 791,3	58,8	262,8	:	3 017,2
From 100 ha and more														100 ha et plus
1975	:	:	63,9	368,7	613,8	:	:	5 056,6	612,4	3 603,6	2,1	74,5	:	9 709,2
1979/80	:	21 631,0	75,3	381,5	688,8	45,7	:	5 192,4	609,2	3 688,4	5,2	79,7	1 534,7	10 864,7
1983	:	22 205,8	86,1	430,7	770,5	166,1	9 522,1	5 543,9	586,7	3 688,4	6,7	83,7	:	10 843,0
1985	:	22 393,7	90,1	480,2	813,3	435,0	:	5 805,2	610,0	3 190,6	7,8	94,9	:	10 866,4
TOTAL														**TOTAL**
1975	:	:	1 467,5	2 966,0	12 398,6	:	:	29 463,6	5 076,6	16 485,5	136,1	2 086,3	:	16 469,0
1979/80	:	89 553,0	1 421,0	2 920,3	12 212,3	3 549,8	:	29 277,7	5 048,5	15 857,8	130,1	2 037,1	3 314,0	17 098,4
1983	:	88 745,0	1 392,8	2 846,5	11 922,6	3 907,7	23 506,0	28 759,6	5 036,6	15 857,8	127,4	2 010,2	:	16 883,6
1985	:	88 281,3	1 381,2	2 834,6	11 884,0	4 116,3	:	28 486,8	4 995,6	15 600,7	126,1	2 026,2	:	16 829,8

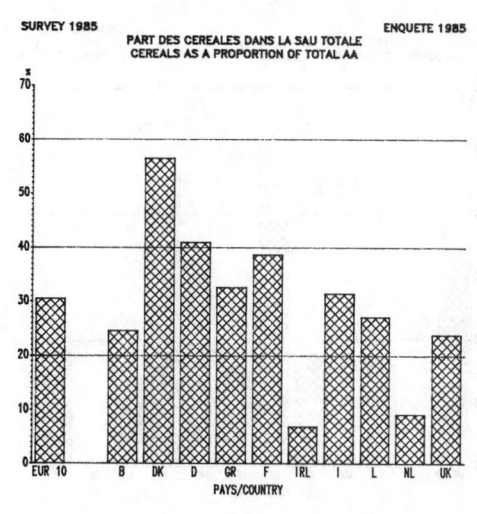

SURVEY 1985 — ENQUETE 1985

CEREALS AS A PROPORTION OF TOTAL AA — PART DES CEREALES DANS LA SAU TOTALE

PAYS/COUNTRY

DATA IN 1000   DONNÉES EN 1000

YEAR ANNÉE	EUR 12	EUR 10	B	DK	D	EL	ES	F	IRL	I	L	NL	P	UK
DISTRIBUTION OF HOLDINGS BY SIZE CLASSES OF ESU												**RÉPARTITION DES EXPLOITATIONS PAR CLASSE D'UDE**		
Less than 2 ESU														**Moins de 2 UDE**
1975	:	:	40,3	14,4	246,2	:	:	345,7	93,2	1 752,8	1,17	8,2	:	55,8
1979/80	:	2 990,2	22,2	9,6	172,5	473,4	:	246,9	61,9	1 969,2	0,48	0,7	585,6	34,0
1983	:	2 353,2	18,1	0,6	147,4	482,1	873,2	210,4	60,5	1 405,2	0,38	1,1	:	27,4
1985	:	2 138,6	15,7	0,4	128,9	424,0	:	157,9	72,5	1 291,0	0,62	—	:	47,6
From 2 to less than 4 ESU														**De 2 à moins de 4 UDE**
1975	:	:	16,2	17,4	155,9	:	:	177,5	53,4	454,8	0,79	16,7	:	39,3
1979/80	:	949,2	9,6	11,3	114,6	213,0	:	133,5	42,7	389,1	0,50	7,8	135,3	27,1
1983	:	1 039,1	8,6	7,6	98,7	200,0	353,7	108,0	41,0	544,7	0,44	7,0	:	23,1
1985	:	982,8	8,2	5,5	92,7	183,1	:	100,6	38,2	529,0	0,44	5,3	:	19,8
From 4 to less than 6 ESU														**De 4 à moins de 6 UDE**
1975	:	:	12,3	15,4	104,5	:	:	143,4	26,7	173,7	0,69	12,5	:	27,3
1979/80	:	518,5	7,1	10,0	80,6	117,9	:	94,1	25,8	157,0	0,41	8,4	43,8	17,2
1983	:	576,5	6,0	8,6	69,2	108,9	179,5	79,7	23,8	256,1	0,34	8,0	:	15,9
1985	:	549,6	5,7	7,5	63,9	109,1	:	73,0	23,2	250,0	0,30	1,9	:	15,0
From 6 to less than 8 ESU														**De 6 à moins de 8 UDE**
1975	:	:	10,5	13,3	80,1	:	:	127,8	15,3	87,0	0,48	10,7	:	20,9
1979/80	:	345,4	5,9	8,3	61,9	66,9	:	80,5	17,0	84,7	0,29	7,2	20,0	12,7
1983	:	378,4	4,9	7,3	55,2	62,0	110,3	65,8	16,6	148,2	0,25	6,5	:	11,6
1985	:	378,7	4,5	6,3	50,6	70,6	:	59,0	16,2	153,0	0,23	6,8	:	11,5
From 8 to less than 12 ESU														**De 8 à moins de 12 UDE**
1975	:	:	18,2	21,8	118,7	:	:	194,8	16,0	81,1	0,86	20,3	:	30,3
1979/80	:	459,6	10,4	13,9	93,3	64,9	:	138,6	22,0	86,0	0,48	11,2	17,7	18,8
1983	:	485,8	8,7	12,0	81,5	58,4	124,4	116,6	19,9	161,1	0,40	10,0	:	17,2
1985	:	501,3	7,7 .	10,2	75,1	77,6	:	104,0	20,8	178,0	0,38	10,5	:	17,0
From 12 to less than 16 ESU														**De 12 à moins de 16 UDE**
1975	:	:	13,6	16,9	78,4	:	:	117,2	6,9	39,0	0,77	19,7	:	22,0
1979/80	:	316,9	9,6	11,7	71,8	25,7	:	117,8	13,4	41,9	0,45	9,3	7,4	15,2
1983	:	320,9	7,9	9,5	63,7	21,9	61,6	97,3	12,8	85,9	0,36	7,8	:	13,7
1985	:	322,5	6,8	8,2	57,3	37,7	:	85,7	13,0	92,6	0,32	8,1	:	12,8
From 16 to less than 40 ESU														**De 16 à moins de 40 UDE**
1975	:	:	23,2	29,0	110,7	:	:	172,4	7,0	54,9	1,41	63,3	:	50,3
1979/80	:	835,2	37,3	40,7	206,7	25,7	:	328,7	23,1	64,8	1,96	47,6	11,1	58,6
1983	:	867,7	33,4	34,2	193,9	18,5	86,4	318,7	23,3	152,8	1,69	37,9	:	53,3
1985	:	919,1	30,3	31,0	193,0	42,4	:	317,1	28,6	186,6	1,58	38,1	:	50,4
From 40 to less than 100 ESU														**De 40 à moins de 100 UDE**
1975	:	:	2,8	3,4	11,5	:	:	30,6	0,5	14,8	0,05	10,1	:	18,0
1979/80	:	285,5	11,3	15,7	44,3	2,1	:	96,6	3,4	17,5	0,53	49,0	3,4	45,1
1983	:	343,1	13,2	17,0	53,2	1,1	21,3	110,0	3,8	47,3	0,59	50,7	:	46,2
1985	:	420,6	16,8	20,0	72,6	3,5	:	135,3	6,1	66,8	0,50	50,0	:	49,0
100 ESU and over														**100 UDE et plus**
1975	:	:	0,2	0,5	1,8	:	:	4,9	0,1	3,8	0,00	0,6	:	5,1
1979/80	:	54,9	1,0	1,7	4,2	0,3	:	16,7	0,3	4,9	0,01	7,7	1,4	18,1
1983	:	70,8	1,2	2,0	4,6	0,1	8,0	18,7	0,3	14,2	0,01	9,6	:	20,1
1985	:	96,1	1,8	3,3	6,4	3,6	:	24,0	0,5	21,5	0,01	9,2	:	25,8
TOTAL														**TOTAL**
1975	:	:	137,3	132,1	907,8	:	:	1 314,3	219,1	2 661,9	6,22	162,1	:	269,0
1979/80	:	6 755,3	114,4	122,9	849,9	989,9	:	1 253,4	209,6	2 815,1	5,11	148,9	825,7	246,8
1983	:	6 435,5	102,0	98,8	767,4	953,0	1 818,4	1 125,2	202,0	2 815,5	4,46	138,6	:	228,5
1985	:	6 309,4	97,5	92,4	740,5	951,6	:	1 056,6	219,1	2 768,5	4,38	129,9	:	248,9

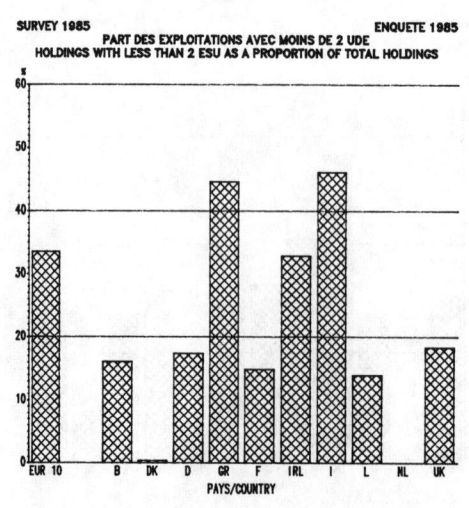

SURVEY 1985   ENQUETE 1985
PART DES EXPLOITATIONS AVEC MOINS DE 2 UDE
HOLDINGS WITH LESS THAN 2 ESU AS A PROPORTION OF TOTAL HOLDINGS

PAYS/COUNTRY

DATA IN 1000

DONNÉES EN 1000

YEAR ANNÉE	EUR 12	EUR 10	B	DK	D	EL	ES	F	IRL	I	L	NL	P	UK

DISTRIBUTION OF THE SGM BY CLASSES OF HOLDING — **RÉPARTITION DE LA MBS PAR CLASSE D'UDE**

Less than 2 ESU — **Moins de 2 UDE**

YEAR	EUR 12	EUR 10	B	DK	D	EL	ES	F	IRL	I	L	NL	P	UK
1975	:	:	30,7	16,5	243,3	:	:	301,5	94,3	1 452,3	1,39	12,1	:	56,1
1979/80	:	2 215,9	19,9	10,6	173,9	407,7	:	232,8	66,8	1 267,4	0,63	1,1	488,5	35,1
1983	:	2 124,5	16,4	0,9	151,7	400,7	760,0	192,3	64,9	1 267,4	0,52	1,6	:	28,1
1985	:	1 904,1	15,3	0,6	135,6	350,3	:	174,3	59,0	1 157,8	0,61	0,1	:	10,5

From 2 to less than 4 ESU — **De 2 à moins de 4 UDE**

YEAR	EUR 12	EUR 10	B	DK	D	EL	ES	F	IRL	I	L	NL	P	UK
1975	:	:	47,6	52,0	454,0	:	:	522,1	152,8	1 278,2	2,25	49,0	:	115,0
1979/80	:	3 185,6	28,1	33,9	335,7	615,9	:	392,1	123,8	1 551,4	1,47	24,2	376,3	79,0
1983	:	2 991,1	25,2	24,2	288,6	576,8	1 009,4	315,2	118,9	1 551,4	1,30	21,8	:	67,7
1985	:	2 822,6	24,0	17,9	270,0	531,0	:	292,9	110,9	1 509,6	1,29	17,3	:	47,7

From 4 to less than 6 ESU — **De 4 à moins de 6 UDE**

YEAR	EUR 12	EUR 10	B	DK	D	EL	ES	F	IRL	I	L	NL	P	UK
1975	:	:	61,0	77,2	518,6	:	:	712,7	130,9	846,3	3,47	62,2	:	131,9
1979/80	:	3 040,0	35,3	49,5	399,1	579,0	:	467,3	127,5	1 253,9	2,00	41,7	212,3	:84,7
1983	:	2 834,7	29,7	42,6	342,4	533,6	880,1	395,4	117,0	1 253,9	1,68	39,7	:	78,7
1985	:	2 729,4	28,4	37,1	317,0	537,1	:	316,6	114,4	1 272,3	1,48	39,1	:	65,9

From 6 to less than 8 ESU — **De 6 à moins de 8 UDE**

YEAR	EUR 12	EUR 10	B	DK	D	EL	ES	F	IRL	I	L	NL	P	UK
1975	:	:	73,0	92,9	556,6	:	:	891,7	105,6	601,3	3,42	74,8	:	145,0
1979/80	:	2 839,2	41,3	57,5	431,1	463,2	:	562,4	118,2	1 025,4	2,05	49,9	138,1	88,1
1983	:	2 626,3	34,2	50,7	383,9	429,2	762,7	459,7	115,3	1 025,4	1,75	45,3	:	80,8
1985	:	2 622,5	31,7	43,9	353,1	489,3	:	412,2	113,0	1 056,7	1 59	47,5	:	73,5

From 8 to less than 12 ESU — **De 8 à moins de 12 UDE**

YEAR	EUR 12	EUR 10	B	DK	D	EL	ES	F	IRL	I	L	NL	P	UK
1975	:	:	180,6	216,5	1 172,0	:	:	1 918,2	155,7	786,9	8,54	203,1	:	298,8
1979/80	:	5 257,8	103,3	138,4	922,1	627,8	:	1 378,5	215,4	1 570,3	4,74	111,1	171,6	186,2
1983	:	4 776,7	86,4	119,0	808,0	564,6	1 212,4	1 159,5	196,4	1 570,3	3,91	98,3	:	170,3
1985	:	4 773,1	76,2	101,5	742,8	756,5	:	1 034,6	204,6	1 733,8	3,76	103,4	:	15,9

From 12 to less than 16 ESU — **De 12 à moins de 16 UDE**

YEAR	EUR 12	EUR 10	B	DK	D	EL	ES	F	IRL	I	L	NL	P	UK
1975	:	:	188,5	234,6	1 085,7	:	:	1 619,6	94,3	536,7	10,60	275,1	:	304,4
1979/80	:	5 010,2	134,4	162,8	999,1	352,5	:	1 640,6	186,0	1 188,3	6,29	129,1	101,9	211,1
1983	:	4 456,3	110,3	131,8	887,4	300,8	848,4	1 356,9	177,5	1 188,3	4,97	107,8	:	190,5
1985	:	4 454,0	84,8	114,6	798,5	515,4	:	1 194,3	179,9	1 277,8	4,51	112,7	:	171,5

From 16 to less than 40 ESU — **De 16 à moins de 40 UDE**

YEAR	EUR 12	EUR 10	B	DK	D	EL	ES	F	IRL	I	L	NL	P	UK
1975	:	:	532,4	673,4	2 492,0	:	:	4 016,7	153,6	1 304,5	31,60	1 569,6	:	1 241,5
1979/80	:	23 087,7	966,6	1 054,5	5 168,0	564,4	:	8 177,0	544,7	3 686,7	52,82	1 314,4	266,7	1 558,6
1983	:	21 934,2	879,5	896,0	4 924,7	407,6	2 016,9	8 070,2	553,6	3 686,7	46,16	1 045,5	:	1 424,2
1985	:	23 468,9	807,1	821,4	4 997,5	956,9	:	8 218,4	699,5	4 547,9	43,03	1 052,1	:	1 325,1

From 40 to less than 100 ESU — **De 40 à moins de 100 UDE**

YEAR	EUR 12	EUR 10	B	DK	D	EL	ES	F	IRL	I	L	NL	P	UK
1975	:	:	152,6	186,2	646,7	:	:	1 741,5	29,8	871,1	2,22	537,4	:	1 059,5
1979/80	:	18 292,2	623,8	880,1	2 403,5	114,3	:	5 521,3	183,6	2 807,2	26,80	2 949,7	204,1	2 781,9
1983	:	20 096,3	737,1	973,7	2 907,2	55,7	1 264,3	6 335,7	206,3	2 807,2	30,18	3 168,4	:	2 874,8
1985	:	24 802,1	962,7	1 185,5	4 063,7	185,1	:	7 868,9	338,3	4 010,9	25,47	3 099,7	:	3 061,8

100 ESU and over — **100 UDE et plus**

YEAR	EUR 12	EUR 10	B	DK	D	EL	ES	F	IRL	I	L	NL	P	UK
1975	:	:	29,6	86,2	291,6	:	:	881,2	14,5	733,8	0,00	115,9	:	932,5
1979/80	:	11 827,2	152,0	281,5	798,4	93,4	:	2 852,6	48,4	2 819,0	0,90	1 229,3	345,0	3 551,7
1983	:	12 967,9	185,3	328,6	862,0	43,7	1 920,5	3 284,3	56,0	2 819,0	1,18	1 467,2	:	3 920,6
1985	:	19 046,9	286,4	532,5	1 140,9	84,0	:	4 528,7	91,0	5 485,7	0,61	1 481,9	:	5 415,2

TOTAL — **TOTAL**

YEAR	EUR 12	EUR 10	B	DK	D	EL	ES	F	IRL	I	L	NL	P	UK
1975	:	:	1 296,0	1 635,5	7 460,5	:	:	12 605,2	931,5	8 411,1	63,5	2 899,2	:	4 287,6
1979/80	:	74 755,8	2 104,7	2 668,8	11 630,9	3 818,2	:	21 224,6	1 614,4	17 169,6	97,7	5 850,5	2 304,5	8 576,4
1983	:	74 807,9	2 104,1	2 567,5	11 555,9	3 312,7	10 674,7	21 569,2	1 605,9	17 169,6	91,7	5 995,6	:	8 835,7
1985	:	86 623,6	2 316,6	2 855,0	12 819,1	4 405,6	:	24 040,9	1 910,6	22 052,5	82,4	5 953,8	:	10 187,1

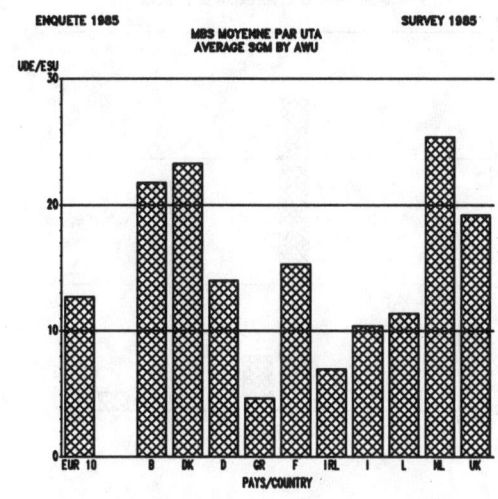

ENQUÊTE 1985 — SURVEY 1985 — MBS MOYENNE PAR UTA / AVERAGE SGM BY AWU — UDE/ESU — PAYS/COUNTRY

1966/67 TO 1985

1966/67 À 1985

DATA IN 1000

DONNÉES EN 1000

YEAR ANNÉE	EUR 12	EUR 10	B	DK	D	EL	ES	F	IRL	I	L	NL	P	UK
FARM TYPE OF HOLDING (1)										**ORIENTATION TECHNICO-ÉCONOMIQUE DES EXPLOITATIONS** (1)				
Farm type 11 - Cereals												OTE 11 – Céréales		
1975	:	:	1,7	27,4	37,9	:	:	68,3	2,8	248,6	0,09	0,5	:	18,8
1979/80		629,9	1,8	28,6	52,9	112,4	:	88,9	5,9	318,8	0,14	0,6	6,3	19,9
1983		597,6	1,8	23	52,8	100,3	168,2	75,9	4,2	318,8	0,13	0,5	:	20,2
1985	:	560,7	1,4	17,7	44,1	92	:	74,6	4,2	305,2	0,19	0,4	:	20,9
Farm type 12 – Other fields crops												OTE 12 – Autres cultures agricoles		
1975	:	:	11,1	18,6	89,4	:	:	86,4	3,3	397,4	0,11	16,8	:	20,1
1979/80		1418,1	9	43	137,6	295,1	:	176,3	11,7	706,5	0,28	15,2	49,3	23,4
1983	:	1412,7	9,2	39,2	128,6	285,1	137,7	177,1	9,6	706,5	0,24	15,9	:	41,3
1985	:	877,5	8,8	21	75,9	198,2	:	96,4	5,5	429,9	0,08	17,2	:	24,5
Farm type 20 – Horticulture												OTE 20 – Horticulture		
1975	:	:	8,2	3,1	17	:	:	35,1	0,7	29,8	0,05	20	:	11,8
1979/80		154,9	10,4	2,6	16,8	26,4	:	33,1	0,2	36	0,08	21,1	44,3	8,2
1983		137,3	9	2,2	14,3	17,5	104,5	30,3	0,1	36	0,06	20,2	:	7,6
1985		140,0	8,4	1,9	14,6	18,9	:	24,7	0,2	45,1	0,06	18,9	:	7,2
Farm type 31 – Vineyards												OTE 31 – Viticulture		
1975	:	:	0	0	34,2	:	:	169,7	0	280,4	0,82	0	:	0
1979/80		633,7	0	0	40,2	43,7	:	161,7	0	387,2	0,90	0	51,9	0
1983		619,9	0	0	37,9	51,2	107,6	142,8	0	387,2	0,79	0	:	0
1985		519,5	0	0	37,7	42,5	:	117,1	0	321,5	0,74	0	:	0
Farm type 32 – Fruit and citrus fruit												OTE 32 – Fruits et autres cultures permanentes		
1975	:	:	:	:	:	:	:	:	:	:	:	:	:	:
1979/80	:	:	:	:	:	:	:	:	:	:	:	:	:	:
1983	:	:	:	:	:	:	:	:	:	:	:	:	:	:
1985	:	378,9	1,9	0,5	8,8	86	:	18	0,2	257,7	0,00	3,1	:	2,7
Farm type 33 – Olives												OTE 33 – Olives		
1975	:	:	–	–	–	:	:	1,7	–	118,4	–	–	:	–
1979/80		355,5	–	–	–	128,3	:	1,9	–	225,3	–	–	11,2	–
1983		371,1	–	–	–	144,1	143,7	1,7	–	225,3	–	–	:	–
1985		437,5	–	–	–	158,7	:	0,9	–	277,9	–	–	:	–
Farm type 34 – Other permanent crops												OTE 34 – Autres cultures permanentes		
1975	:	:	:	:	:	:	:	:	:	:	:	:	:	:
1979/80	:	:	:	:	:	:	:	:	:	:	:	:	:	:
1983	:	:	:	:	:	:	:	:	:	:	:	:	:	:
1985	:	343,6	1,3	0,4	6,4	100,6	:	14,1	0	217	0,01	2,7	:	1,1
Farm type 41 — Cattle, dairying												OTE 41 – Bovins, lait		
1975	:	:	19,8	18,7	166,4	:	:	303,4	57,1	106	1,21	61,4	:	52,5
1979/80		767,8	23,2	20,6	198,1	1,7	:	267	62,8	92,7	0,73	54,1	4,2	46,9
1983		722,2	21	19,6	197	0,9	70,9	239,8	59,3	92,7	0,85	48,7	:	42,3
1985		660,9	18	17,5	185,2	2,8	:	193	57,7	100,7	1,14	45,2	:	39,7
Farm type 42 – Cattle, rearing/fattening												OTE 42 – Bovins, élevage/viande		
1975	:	:	8	0,7	9,8	:	:	80,8	66,4	21,8	0,22	5,2	:	53,3
1979/80		254,9	9,6	0,7	13,4	1,2	:	89,4	65,6	21,7	0,22	6,1	1,5	47
1983		267,4	10	0,4	13,9	0,6	20,4	97,9	73,5	21,7	0,26	7,2	:	41,9
1985		276,3	9,4	0,2	15,7	1,2	:	97	75,9	28	0,31	3,8	:	44,8

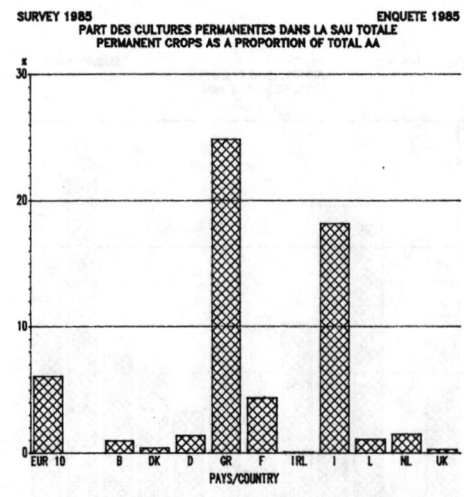

SURVEY 1985
ENQUÊTE 1985
PART DES CULTURES PERMANENTES DANS LA SAU TOTALE
PERMANENT CROPS AS A PROPORTION OF TOTAL AA

(1) The « type of farming » of a holding shall be determined by the relative contribution of different enterprises to its total standard gross margin.

(1) L'« orientation technico-économique » (OTE) d'une exploitation est déterminée par la contribution relative des différentes spéculations de cette exploitation à sa marge brute standard totale.

DATA IN 1000 **DONNÉES EN 1000**

YEAR ANNÉE	EUR 12	EUR 10	B	DK	D	EL	ES	F	IRL	I	L	NL	P	UK
Farm type 43 – Cattle mixed													OTE 43 –	Bovins mixtes
1975	:	:	15,1	1,2	49,8	:	:	57,5	46,4	46,4	1,82	10	:	10,8
1979/80	:	178,1	9,9	0,7	39	0,5	:	48,8	27,3	37,7	1,00	7,2	4,3	6,0
1983	:	148,0	8,5	0,6	34,4	0,5	23	36,4	19,6	37,7	0,83	5,5	:	4,0
1985	:	130,3	7,8	0,3	32,5	0,7	:	29,9	16,2	35,7	0,68	2,3	:	4,2
Farm type 44 – Other grazing livestock													OTE 44 –	Autres herbivores
1975	:	:	10,1	1,8	31,1	:	:	103,9	23,6	95,4	0,12	4,8	:	40,7
1979/80	:	423,4	7,5	2,4	43,7	46	:	137,3	22,7	109,1	0,09	6	14,9	48,6
1983	:	404,0	7,2	0,7	38,6	48,6	166,7	120,2	24,1	109,1	0,10	6,4	:	49,0
1985	:	474,7	7,2	0,8	44,8	66,8	:	95,0	44,6	137,8	0,16	12	:	65,5
Farm type 50 – Granivores													OTE 50 –	Granivores
1975	:	:	9,1	1	17,6	:	:	11,5	1,7	22,5	0,04	11,3	:	11,6
1979/80	:	85,7	6,5	4,3	15,8	7,8	:	15,5	1,5	11,9	0,05	12,1	25	10,2
1983	:	82,4	5,7	3,5	17,7	7,1	27,2	14,5	1,4	11,9	0,04	12,0	:	8,6
1985	:	87,3	5,4	3,7	18,8	5,5	:	13,6	1,6	17,1	0,06	12,8	:	8,7
Farm type 60 – Mixed cropping, other													OTE 60 -	Polycultures
1975	:	:	6,9	7,8	56,1	:	:	82,2	0,7	454,9	0,08	3,6	:	7,1
1979/80	:	737,3	4,9	6,5	46,8	169,9	:	65,3	0,7	432,1	0,82	4,4	290,5	5,9
1983	:	674,5	3,8	4,1	37	132,6	210,7	54,6	0,5	432,1	0,63	4,0	:	5,2
1985	:	620,7	4,3	3,5	36,5	115,6	:	84,1	0,7	367,1	0,06	3,4	:	5,4
Farm type 71 – Grazing livestock partially dominant													OTE 71 –	Herbivores partiellement dominants
1975	:	:	9,3	17,5	127,9	:	:	80,7	3,1	131,4	0,57	2,8	:	3,1
1979/80	:	240,3	6,4	10,3	82,6	18,5	:	49,4	1,7	67	0,84	1,4	74,8	2,2
1983	:	198,2	4,5	5,3	63,3	19,1	101	34,8	1,1	67	0,56	0,9	:	1,6
1985	:	211,8	3,6	4,6	57	18,5	:	62,5	0,7	61,1	0,19	1,0	:	2,6
Farm type 72 – Mixed livestock, other													OTE 72 –	Autres polyélevages
1975	:	:	8	1,2	22,9	:	:	16,9	1,1	20,7	0,10	10,4	:	5,3
1979/80	:	57,8	5,1	2	16,6	2,6	:	14,1	0,6	5,3	0,06	7,8	38,9	3,6
1983	:	52,9	4,4	1	15	3,1	15,7	14,5	0,8	5,3	0,07	6,0	:	2,7
1985	:	63,9	3,9	1,1	20	2,7	:	14	0,6	12,8	0,07	6,6	:	2,1
Farm type 81 – Field crops, grazing livestock													OTE 81 –	Agriculture générale et herbivores
1975	:	:	20,6	20,8	190,4	:	:	149,9	10,8	179,9	0,87	6,1	:	22,5
1979/80	:	478,3	14,9	12,3	139,9	30,4	:	130,7	14,1	110,8	0,03	3,8	41,1	21,4
1983	:	412,3	12,8	8,7	114,1	26,3	64,3	106,1	12,0	110,8	0,03	3,3	:	18,2
1985	:	373,7	13,3	7,7	97,8	32,1	:	91,2	10,7	98,7	0,57	4,0	:	17,6
Farm type 82 – Other crops - livestock													OTE 82 –	Autres cultures / élevages
1975	:	:	3,3	10,7	42,1	:	:	24,4	0,9	91,4	0,07	2,7	:	3,9
1979/80	:	172,3	2,8	15,9	41,4	22,7	:	23,4	0,3	60,5	0,01	2,9	73,6	2,4
1983	:	166,2	2,3	12,4	40,1	25,7	169,9	19,7	0,2	60,5	0,01	2,6	:	2,7
1985	:	185,7	2,8	11,4	44,7	25,7	:	30,7	0,3	65,5	0,04	2,6	:	2,0
TOTAL														**TOTAL**
1975	:	:	137,2	132,2	907,7	:	:	1 314,2	218,9	2 662,0	6,20	162,2	:	268,6
1979/80	:	6 756,1	114,5	122,7	850	990	:	1 253,5	209,5	2 815,4	5,10	148,7	765,8	246,7
1983	:	6 435,6	102	98,7	767,6	953	1 818,2	1 125,3	202,2	2 815,4	4,50	138,5	:	228,4
1985	:	6 342,9	97,5	92,3	740,5	968,5	:	1 056,8	219,1	2 778,8	4,36	136,0	:	249,0

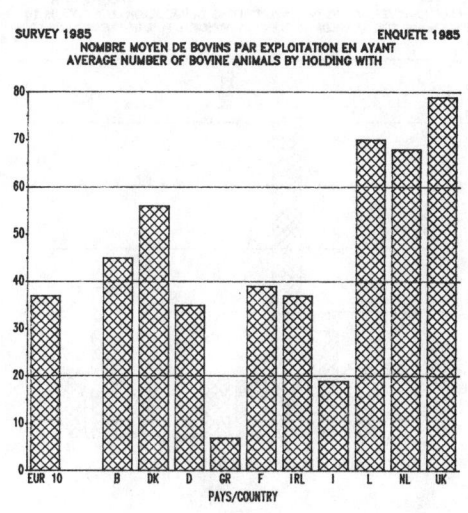

SURVEY 1985 — ENQUETE 1985
NOMBRE MOYEN DE BOVINS PAR EXPLOITATION EN AYANT
AVERAGE NUMBER OF BOVINE ANIMALS BY HOLDING WITH

PAYS/COUNTRY

1966/67 TO 1985

1966/67 À 1985

DATA IN 1000

DONNÉES EN 1000

YEAR ANNÉE	EUR 12	EUR 10	B	DK	D	EL	ES	F	IRL	I	L	NL	P	UK
DISTRIBUTION OF THE SGM BY FARM TYPE												**RÉPARTITION DE LA MBS PAR OTE**		
Farm type 11 - Cereals													OTE 11 – Céréales	
1975	:	:	4,0	176,6	149,2	:	:	994,1	13,8	588,8	0,2	3,4	:	436,4
1979/80	:	5 543,4	6,8	292,7	321,6	269,4	:	1 988,9	63,1	1 578,7	0,6	12,1	39,8	1 009,5
1983	:	5 532,8	8,1	297,0	310,6	234,1	842,0	1 867,4	55,1	1 578,7	0,5	9,2	:	1 172,2
1985	:	6 174,2	8,2	238,6	293,8	271,1	:	2 221,1	58,3	1 628,4	0,7	9,3	:	1 444,8
Farm type 12 – Other fields crops													OTE 12 – Autres cultures agricoles	
1975	:	:	147,1	307,3	765,3	:	:	1 560,0	14,4	1 110,2	0,3	349,2	:	745,4
1979/80	:	10 679,6	213,2	372,8	1 241,3	961,7	:	2 694,7	54,7	2 641,9	1,0	658,1	110,6	1 840,2
1983	:	11 432,1	228,9	422,0	1 330,2	980,1	1 071,4	3 241,7	54,2	2 642,0	0,8	694,4	:	1 837,8
1985	:	14 907,3	292,4	584,5	1 524,9	1 518,0	:	3 799,8	66,3	3 734,7	0,5	828,9	:	2 557,3
Farm type 20 – Horticulture													OTE 20 – Horticulture	
1975	:	:	112,2	48,5	420,1	:	:	916,8	4,4	360,7	0,4	402,1	:	245,2
1979/80	:	5 073,2	231,9	93,3	518,1	170,3	:	1 541,9	6,9	1 183,7	0,8	1 176,0	78,3	150,3
1983	:	5 252,5	233,4	84,8	473,2	99,0	607,8	1 779,4	1,9	1 183,7	0,5	1 256,7	:	139,9
1985	:	7 120,3	254,6	103,0	555,5	158,3	:	1 446,8	7,4	2 993,1	0,6	1 286,5	:	314,6
Farm type 31 – Vineyards													OTE 31 – Viticulture	
1975	:	:	—	—	195,6	:	:	1 300,0	—	548,6	3,6	—	:	—
1979/80	:	3 967,7	—	—	513,8	135,5	:	2 213,9	—	1 093,2	11,3	—	229,6	—
1983	:	4 034,5	—	—	530,3	184,4	265,0	2 215,4	—	1 093,2	11,2	—	:	—
1985	:	4 743,4	—	—	582,6	174,8	:	2 824,5	—	1 153,8	7,7	—	:	—
Farm type 32 – Fruit and citrus fruit													OTE 32 – Fruits et autres cultures permanentes	
1975	:	:	:	:	:	:	:	:	:	:	:	:	:	:
1979/80	:	:	:	:	:	:	:	:	:	:	:	:	:	:
1983	:	:	:	:	:	:	:	:	:	:	:	:	:	:
1985	:	3 502,0	50,1	14,7	71,6	405,9	:	496,7	4,9	2 263,7	0,1	99,3	0,0	95,1
Farm type 33 – Olives													OTE 33 – Olives	
1975	:	:	—	—	—	:	:	0,4	—	276,5	—	—	:	—
1979/80	:	765,8	—	—	—	140,3	:	1,0	—	624,5	—	—	23,3	—
1983	:	793,6	—	—	—	167,7	299,5	1,4	—	624,5	—	—	:	—
1985	:	872,4	—	—	—	184,5	:	1,9	—	685,9	—	—	:	—
Farm type 34 – Other permanent crops													OTE 34 – Autres cultures permanentes	
1975	:	:	:	:	:	:	:	:	:	:	:	:	:	:
1979/80	:	:	:	:	:	:	:	:	:	:	:	:	:	:
1983	:	:	:	:	:	:	:	:	:	:	:	:	:	:
1985	:	2 608,9	41,3	21,7	363,2	317,1	0,0	485,1	0,0	1 222,1	0,3	102,2	0,0	55,8
Farm type 41 — Cattle, dairying													OTE 41 – Bovins, lait	
1975	:	:	154,1	275,1	1 251,8	:	:	2 163,7	311,2	602,0	15,7	1 163,2	:	768,2
1979/80	:	13 901,0	436,1	619,9	2 943,7	4,3	:	3 819,3	743,2	1 077,1	19,4	2 303,2	10,1	1 934,8
1983	:	14 928,0	460,7	664,7	3 319,2	4,3	528,5	4 084,7	779,0	1 077,1	25,4	2 520,8	:	1 992,1
1985	:	15 802,0	435,1	666,0	3 631,3	11,3	:	4 058,5	964,2	1 636,8	34,5	2 220,0	:	2 144,3
Farm type 42 – Cattle, rearing/fattening													OTE 42 – Bovins, élevage/viande	
1975	:	:	31,9	1,7	35,3	:	:	501,2	180,2	115,2	1,1	76,0	:	233,7
1979/80	:	2 214,8	70,7	3,1	99,3	4,8	:	946,3	213,3	390,0	2,1	94,6	12,4	390,6
1983	:	2 480,3	81,8	2,7	120,5	1,6	173,3	1 166,2	227,6	390,0	2,4	108,5	:	379,0
1985	:	2 842,7	90,5	1,3	154,1	6,4	:	1 281,8	257,6	484,6	2,5	97,6	:	466,4

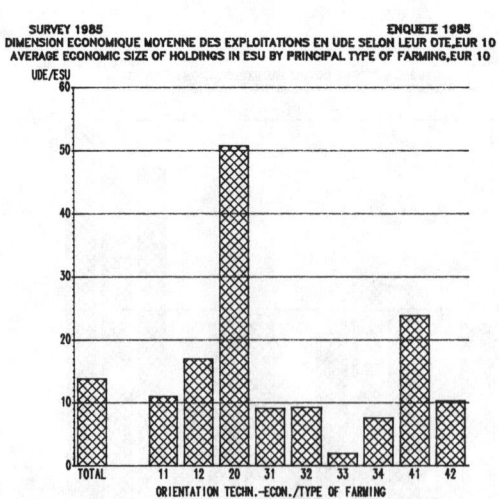

SURVEY 1985   ENQUETE 1985
DIMENSION ECONOMIQUE MOYENNE DES EXPLOITATIONS EN UDE SELON LEUR OTE, EUR 10
AVERAGE ECONOMIC SIZE OF HOLDINGS IN ESU BY PRINCIPAL TYPE OF FARMING, EUR 10

DATA IN 1000

DONNÉES EN 1000

YEAR ANNÉE	EUR 12	EUR 10	B	DK	D	EL	ES	F	IRL	I	L	NL	P	UK
Farm type 43 – Cattle mixed													OTE 43 – Bovins mixtes	
1975	:	:	142,3	18,4	434,2	:	:	588,6	187,9	209,0	26,8	124,6	:	148,7
1979/80	:	2 671,7	184,3	18,3	590,2	1,7	:	849,5	172,9	518,4	27,3	134,2	21,0	174,9
1983	:	2343,0	180,7	16,4	545,8	2,0	191,7	693,9	125,6	518,4	24,2	96,6	:	139,3
1985	:	2 456,5	184,8	10,9	609,0	2,8	:	683,8	127,9	588,9	19,4	55,2	:	173,8
Farm type 44 – Other grazing livestock													OTE 44 – Autres herbivores	
1975	:	:	14,0	6,1	35,7	:	:	495,8	83,7	245,0	0,2	32,8	:	292,1
1979/80	:	2 962,0	17,9	7,4	74,1	285,0	:	978,5	133,0	425,8	0,7	64,5	38,7	975,1
1983	:	2 935,0	15,5	4,5	63,4	314,2	1 187,0	838,6	157,3	425,8	0,5	64,9	:	1050,2
1985	:	3 451,0	20,3	5,7	87,5	417,0	:	982,1	185,4	561,2	0,3	130,7	:	1 061,0
Farm type 50 – Granivores													OTE 50 – Granivores	
1975	:	:	97,4	16,2	176,6	:	:	180,3	19,9	333,9	0,2	181,9	:	194,5
1979/80	:	2 142,1	120,7	133,1	255,3	85,2	:	482,5	32,0	412,0	0,7	354,3	214,5	266,3
1983	:	2 000,0	133,9	169,3	282,5	64,5	673,8	535,4	33,5	412,0	0,5	433,9	:	273,4
1985	:	2 886,6	174,0	224,8	373,0	78,5	:	667,2	38,6	626,3	0,4	517,0	:	186,9
Farm type 60 – Mixed cropping, other													OTE 60 – Polycultures	
1975	:	:	71,1	86,1	463,7	:	:	699,1	7,0	1 271,4	0,4	58,2	:	269,5
1979/80	:	5 224,5	98,0	105,1	573,6	686,9	:	1 007,9	13,5	2 187,5	13,8	224,3	731,4	313,9
1983	:	4 738,9	84,4	75,0	492,7	423,2	901,7	918,4	11,6	2 187,5	10,3	196,5	:	339,4
1985	:	5 396,2	115,2	87,9	551,8	480,4	:	1 249,3	30,7	2 304,5	0,7	127,4	:	448,3
Farm type 71 – Grazing livestock partially dominant													OTE 71 – Herbivores partiellement dominants	
1975	:	:	96,4	238,1	1 129,3	:	:	629,8	18,3	412,2	5,9	44,9	:	66,2
1979/80	:	3 095,9	132,5	266,9	1 278,9	81,1	:	700,7	16,2	473,6	18,6	44,3	168,2	83,1
1983	:	2 476,2	103,8	155,4	1 049,0	70,8	527,9	497,6	9,6	473,6	13,1	28,0	:	75,4
1985	:	2 655,6	93,4	159,5	1 053,4	86,8	:	655,3	11,3	498,3	4,6	27,9	:	65,2
Farm type 72 – Mixed livestock, other													OTE 72 – Autres polyélevages	
1975	:	:	93,2	16,9	257,0	:	:	265,0	11,2	79,4	0,9	179,3	:	71,4
1979/80	:	1 337,4	113,0	55,7	287,0	10,5	:	456,2	13,9	86,0	1,0	234,2	123,1	79,9
1983	:	1 352,2	112,4	39,7	289,1	8,7	125,7	514,6	17,7	86,0	1,5	203,8	:	78,6
1985	:	1 568,9	126,5	48,0	465,8	13,3	:	495,3	18,3	88,5	1,8	252,2	:	59,3
Farm type 81 – Field crops, grazing livestock													OTE 81 – Agriculture générale et herbivores	
1975	:	:	246,7	291,2	1 545,5	:	:	1 669,6	72,1	757,2	6,5	114,1	:	555,5
1979/80	:	7 743,3	351,6	286,0	1 896,4	174,1	:	2 454,2	144,1	1 111,6	0,1	123,3	115,5	1 201,9
1983	:	6 983,1	331,0	231,0	1 663,0	134,4	470,4	2 178,4	127,2	1 111,6	0,1	98,7	:	1 107,7
1985	:	7 312,7	370,6	251,7	1 551,0	190,9	:	2 270,5	131,9	1 177,0	7,3	109,9	:	1 251,9
Farm type 82 – Other crops - livestock													OTE 82 – Autres cultures / élevages	
1975	:	:	36,9	134,2	375,2	:	:	221,3	4,1	235,2	0,7	42,6	:	115,6
1979/80	:	2 156,6	51,9	381,2	656,4	76,7	:	394,0	4,1	364,8	0,1	92,4	180,3	135,0
1983	:	2 199,5	52,7	376,4	708,7	65,0	1 690,0	385,4	3,0	364,9	0,1	88,2	:	155,1
1985	:	2 641,3	69,4	436,8	950,5	88,4	:	466,7	7,9	404,8	0,8	89,7	:	126,4
TOTAL													**TOTAL**	
1975	:	:	1 296,1	1 635,5	7 461,4	:	:	12 605,4	931,5	8 411,1	63,5	2 899,3	:	4 297,8
1979/80	:	74 756,2	2 104,7	2 668,6	11 631,9	3 818,2	:	21 224,7	1 613,9	17 169,7	97,7	5 850,5	2 304,4	8 576,4
1983	:	74 808,8	2 104,2	2 567,6	11 556,4	3 312,7	10 710,4	21 569,3	1 606,0	17 169,7	91,6	5 995,6	:	8 835,8
1985	:	86 941,1	2 326,5	2 854,9	12 818,9	4 404,3	:	24 086,4	1 910,6	22 052,5	82,3	5 953,8	:	10 450,9

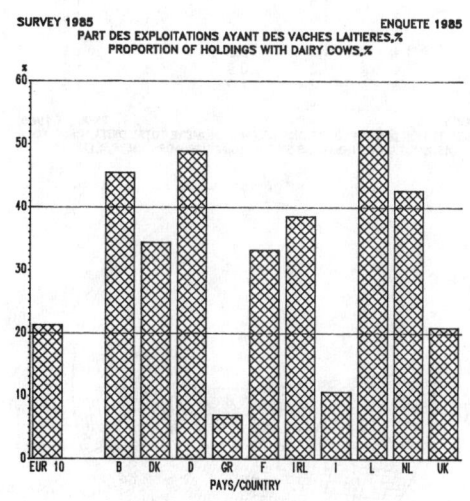

SURVEY 1985   ENQUETE 1985
PART DES EXPLOITATIONS AYANT DES VACHES LAITIERES,%
PROPORTION OF HOLDINGS WITH DAIRY COWS,%

**EC SURVEY ON THE STRUCTURE
OF AGRICULTURAL HOLDINGS**

| I C 7 |

**ENQUÊTE CE SUR LA STRUCTURE
DES EXPLOITATIONS AGRICOLES**

1966/67 TO 1985

1966/67 À 1985

LABOUR FORCE **MAIN-D'ŒUVRE**

YEAR ANNÉE	EUR 12	EUR 10	B	DK	D	EL	ES	F	IRL	I	L	NL	P	UK

TOTAL LABOUR FORCE (Number of persons) / **MAIN-D'ŒUVRE TOTALE (Nombre de personnes)**
(Data in 1000) / (Données en 1000)

	EUR 12	EUR 10	B	DK	D	EL	ES	F	IRL	I	L	NL	P	UK
1966/67	:	:	421,8	:	3 497,0	:	:	4 307,5	:	6 426,4	23,64	476,9	:	:
1970/71	:	:	281,6	:	2 734,5	:	:	3 846,7	:	5 668,7	19,40	363,9	:	:
1975	:	:	221,2	235,6	2 215,2	:	:	3 069,4	473,8	5 389,8	15,78	331,5	:	757,6
1977	:	:	199,5	243,1	2 084,2	:	:	2 881,0	442,7	5 373,4	13,85	322,5	:	648,0
1979/80	:	13 711,7	186,1	234,1	1 983,3	1 841,2	:	2 659,1	468,7	5 300,8	12,27	302,4	1 949,8	723,7
1983	:	13 425,7	164,6	185,7	1 783,6	2 128,0	3 179,8	2 405,8	418,9	5 300,8	10,50	304,7	:	723,1
1985	:	12 977,0	156,8	157,9	1 739,9	2 070,4	:	2 245,8	428,1	5 134,4	10,29	296,8	:	736,6

LABOUR FORCE BY 100 HA AA / **MAIN-D'ŒUVRE PAR 100 HA SAU**
(Number of persons) / (Nombre de personnes)

	EUR 12	EUR 10	B	DK	D	EL	ES	F	IRL	I	L	NL	P	UK
1966/67	:	:	26,5	:	27,4	:	:	14,3	:	35,8	17,6	21,4	:	:
1970/71	:	:	18,3	:	21,6	:	:	12,8	:	33,0	14,4	17,0	:	:
1975	:	:	15,1	7,9	17,9	:	:	10,4	9,3	32,7	11,6	15,9	:	4,6
1977	:	:	13,8	8,3	17,1	:	:	9,8	8,7	32,5	10,5	15,7	:	3,8
1979/80	:	15,4	13,1	8,0	16,2	51,9	:	9,1	9,3	34,0	9,4	14,8	58,8	4,2
1983	:	15,2	11,8	6,5	15,0	54,5	13,5	8,4	8,3	34,0	8,2	15,2	:	4,3
1985	:	14,7	11,4	5,6	14,7	50,3	:	7,9	8,6	32,9	8,2	14,6	:	4,4

LABOUR FORCE BY 100 HOLDINGS / **MAIN-D'ŒUVRE PAR 100 EXPLOITATIONS**
(Number of persons) / (Nombre de personnes)

	EUR 12	EUR 10	B	DK	D	EL	ES	F	IRL	I	L	NL	P	UK
1966/67	:	:	196	:	281	:	:	252	:	216	275	193	:	:
1970/71	:	:	153	:	254	:	:	242	:	199	255	197	:	:
1975	:	:	160	178	244	:	:	233	208	202	254	204	:	270
1977	:	:	158	190	245	:	:	231	197	204	241	209	:	239
1979/80	:	201	162	191	233	184	:	212	210	187	237	203	253	269
1983	:	206	160	188	232	222	175	213	189	187	230	220	:	276
1985	:	204	160	171	235	218	:	212	194	183	233	218	:	285

TOTAL LABOUR FORCE / **MAIN-D'ŒUVRE TOTALE**
Labour volume in 1000 AWU / Volume de travail en 1000 UTA

	EUR 12	EUR 10	B	DK	D	EL	ES	F	IRL	I	L	NL	P	UK
1966/67	:	:	271,2	:	2 329,9	:	:	3 032,3	:	4 127,2	17,04	341,7	:	:
1970/71	:	:	188,6	:	1 611,0	:	:	2 368,8	:	2 989,9	12,27	289,7	:	:
1975	:	:	139,6	176,7	1 233,6	:	:	1 949,7	324,7	2 826,5	12,37	253,7	:	625,7
1977	:	:	:	:	:	:	:	:	:	:	:	:	:	:
1979/80	:	7 293,3	123,9	171,6	1 050,9	797,4	:	1 847,5	310,3	2 157,6	9,05	242,2	1 155,6	582,8
1983	:	6 966,5	111,8	140,3	945,9	863,3	1 432,5	1 658,2	276,1	2 157,6	7,75	243,4	:	562,1
1985	:	6 833,3	106,9	122,4	917,9	931,2	:	1 568,8	275,8	2 125,7	7,23	234,4	:	543,0

Labour force: number of AWU by 100 ha AA / Main-d'œuvre: nombre d'UTA par 100 ha SAU

	EUR 12	EUR 10	B	DK	D	EL	ES	F	IRL	I	L	NL	P	UK
1966/67	:	:	17,0	:	18,2	:	:	10,1	:	23,0	12,72	15,3	:	:
1970/71	:	:	12,2	:	12,7	:	:	7,9	:	17,4	9,08	13,5	:	:
1975	:	:	9,5	6,0	9,0	:	:	6,6	6,4	17,1	9,09	12,2	:	3,8
1977	:	:	:	:	:	:	:	:	:	:	:	:	:	:
1979/80	:	8,2	8,7	5,9	8,6	22,5	:	6,3	6,1	13,8	6,96	11,9	34,9	3,4
1983	:	7,9	8,0	4,9	7,9	22,1	6,1	5,8	5,5	13,8	6,08	12,1	:	3,3
1985	:	7,7	7,7	4,3	7,7	22,6	:	5,5	5,5	13,6	5,73	11,6	:	3,2

Labour force: number of AWU per person / Main-d'œuvre: nombre d'UTA par personne

	EUR 12	EUR 10	B	DK	D	EL	ES	F	IRL	I	L	NL	P	UK
1966/67	:	:	0,64	:	0,67	:	:	0,70	:	0,64	0,72	0,72	:	:
1970/71	:	:	0,67	:	0,59	:	:	0,62	:	0,53	0,63	0,80	:	:
1975	:	:	0,63	0,75	0,56	:	:	0,64	0,69	0,52	0,78	0,77	:	0,83
1977	:	:	:	:	:	:	:	:	:	:	:	:	:	:
1979/80	:	:	0,67	0,73	0,53	:	:	0,69	0,66	0,41	0,74	0,80	0,59	0,81
1983	:	0,52	0,68	0,76	0,53	0,41	0,45	0,69	0,66	0,41	0,74	0,80	:	0,78
1985	:	0,53	0,68	0,78	0,53	0,45	:	0,70	0,64	0,41	0,70	0,79	:	0,74

Labour force: average number of AWU by holding / Nombre moyen d'UTA par exploitation

	EUR 12	EUR 10	B	DK	D	EL	ES	F	IRL	I	L	NL	P	UK
1966/67	:	:	1,3	:	1,9	:	:	1,8	:	1,4	2,0	1,4	:	:
1970/71	:	:	1,0	:	1,5	:	:	1,5	:	1,0	1,6	1,6	:	:
1975	:	:	1,0	1,3	1,4	:	:	1,5	1,4	1,1	2,0	1,6	:	2,2
1977	:	:	:	:	:	:	:	:	:	:	:	:	:	:
1979/80	:	1,1	1,1	1,4	1,2	0,8	:	1,5	1,4	0,8	1,8	1,6	1,5	2,2
1983	:	1,1	1,1	1,4	1,2	0,9	0,8	1,5	1,2	0,8	1,7	1,8	:	2,1
1985	:	1,1	1,1	1,3	1,2	1,0	:	1,5	1,3	0,8	1,6	1,7	:	2,1

SURVEY 1985 ENQUETE 1985
REPARTITION DES EXPLOITATIONS SELON LE NOMBRE TOTAL D'UTA,%,EUR 10
DISTRIBUTION OF HOLDINGS BY TOTAL ANNUAL WORK UNITS,%,EUR 10

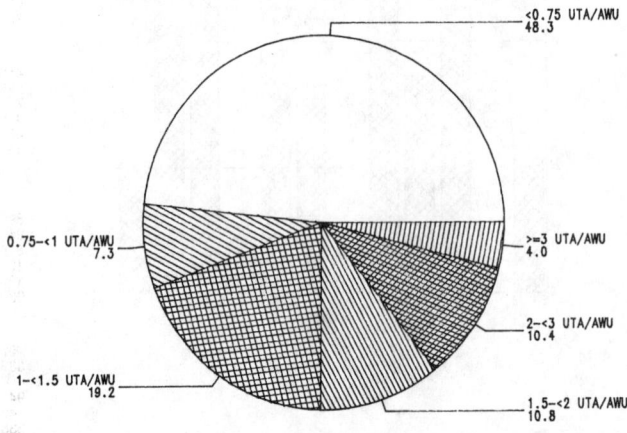

DATA IN 1000   **DONNÉES EN 1000**

USE OF LAND / UTILISATION DU SOL
Number of holdings / Nombre d'exploitations

YEAR ANNÉE	EUR 12	EUR 10	B	DK	D	EL	ES	F	IRL	I	L	NL	P	UK
1966/67	:	:	214,6	:	1 245,8	:	:	1 708,4	:	2 964,0	8,61	246,7	:	:
1970/71	:	:	184,0	:	1 074,6	:	:	1 587,6	277,4	2 849,0	7,91	184,6	:	326,7
1975	:	:	138,1	132,3	907,9	:	:	1 315,1	228,0	2 664,2	6,21	162,6	:	279,3
1979/80	:	6 810,3	115,1	112,7	849,9	998,9	:	1 255,3	223,5	2 832,4	5,17	148,7	769,4	268,6
1983	:	6 505,5	102,6	98,7	767,5	958,6	1 818,2	1 129,6	211,1	2 832,4	4,55	138,5	:	261,9
1985	:	6 359,3	97,8	92,4	740,5	951,6	:	1 056,9	220,2	2 801,1	4,41	135,9	:	258,5

Area / Superficie

YEAR ANNÉE	EUR 12	EUR 10	B	DK	D	EL	ES	F	IRL	I	L	NL	P	UK
1966/67	:	:	1 666,2	:	15 807,4	:	:	35 469,2	:	22 519,6	152,97	2 448,8	:	:
1970/71	:	:	1 602,9	:	15 236,1	:	:	35 039,2	5 646,6	23 650,3	153,27	2 342,3	:	17 998,7
1975	:	:	1 521,9	3 321,0	14 712,8	:	:	33 480,6	5 297,7	22 401,3	152,24	2 296,2	:	16 858,1
1979/80	:	103 226	1 463,0	3 241,0	14 486,4	3 549,8	:	33 164,4	5 237,7	22 139,3	143,92	2 232,1	4 730,1	17 568,4
1983	:	102 166	1 435,7	3 148,2	14 088,5	4 091,3	42 056,7	32 313,9	5 191,8	22 139,3	140,10	2 207,4	:	17 409,6
1985	:	101 358	1 423,3	3 125,9	14 055,2	4 322,5	:	31 826,7	5 155,6	21 747,7	138,38	2 202,7	:	17 360,1

WOODLAND / SUPERFICIE BOISÉE
Number of holdings / Nombre d'exploitations

YEAR ANNÉE	EUR 12	EUR 10	B	DK	D	EL	ES	F	IRL	I	L	NL	P	UK
1966/67	:	:	8,9	:	480,1	:	:	740,3	:	695,9	4,06	:	:	:
1970/71	:	:	8,7	:	474,5	:	:	658,9	:	:	3,67	6,8	:	:
1975	:	:	6,2	25,0	405,7	:	:	543,0	9,9	558,4	3,29	4,4	:	42,3
1979/80	:	:	4,8	18,8	393,6	:	:	537,2	9,8	675,4	2,74	4,5	360,0	44,1
1983	:	1 622,5	3,3	19,4	363,7	29,7	372,9	468,4	6,4	675,4	2,45	6,5	:	47,2
1985	:	1 501,0	3,0	19,3	353,5	20,3	:	430,6	6,6	610,8	2,38	4,9	:	49,6

Area / Superficie

YEAR ANNÉE	EUR 12	EUR 10	B	DK	D	EL	ES	F	IRL	I	L	NL	P	UK
1966/67	:	:	19,2	:	2 288,9	:	:	3 145,6	:	:	17,14	:	:	:
1970/71	:	:	15,0	:	1 832,7	:	:	3 083,1	:	4 422,6	16,89	42,1	:	:
1975	:	:	15,0	174,1	1 656,9	:	:	2 488,2	38,8	3 827,8	15,08	41,1	:	208,1
1979/80	:	:	10,0	140,3	1 658,9	:	:	2 401,6	36,6	4 562,9	12,80	38,6	1 477,4	259,8
1983	:	8 981,7	8,4	144,1	1 591,5	32,6	9 473,9	2 261,4	38,0	4 562,9	11,60	42,2	:	289,0
1985	:	8 713,7	7,5	141,8	1 599,4	58,3	:	2 109,5	37,4	4 408,5	11,16	30,8	:	309,3

AGRICULTURAL AREA IN USE (AA) / SUPERFICIE AGRICOLE UTILISÉE (SAU)
Number of holdings / Nombre d'exploitations

YEAR ANNÉE	EUR 12	EUR 10	B	DK	D	EL	ES	F	IRL	I	L	NL	P	UK
1966/67	:	:	211,9	:	1 233,8	978,1	:	1 705,7	:	2 963,7	8,61	242,1	:	:
1970/71	:	7 635,0	179,5	146,0	1 071,0	1 035,5	:	1 583,3	275,1	2 832,6	7,58	181,1	:	323,3
1975	:	:	134,8	132,2	904,2	:	:	1 313,6	228,0	2 652,1	6,21	159,0	:	278,5
1979/80	:	6 820,3	115,1	122,7	849,9	998,9	:	1 255,3	223,5	2 832,4	5,17	148,7	769,4	268,6
1983	:	6 515,6	102,6	98,7	767,6	958,6	1 818,2	1 129,6	221,1	2 832,4	4,55	138,5	:	261,9
1985	:	6 359,3	97,8	92,4	740,5	951,6	:	1 056,9	220,2	2 801,1	4,41	135,9	:	258,5

Area / Superficie

YEAR ANNÉE	EUR 12	EUR 10	B	DK	D	EL	ES	F	IRL	I	L	NL	P	UK
1966/67	:	:	1 593,1	:	12 678,2	4 093,8	:	30 115,2	:	17 928,3	133,95	2 232,5	:	:
1970/71	:	92 566,1	1 540,3	2 965,5	12 651,1	3 565,1	:	29 940,0	4 737,2	17 178,8	135,14	2 142,6	:	17 710,5
1975	:	:	1 467,5	2 966,0	12 398,6	:	:	29 463,6	5 076,6	16 485,5	136,07	2 086,3	:	16 469,0
1979/80	:	89 553,0	1 421,0	2 920,3	12 212,3	3 549,8	:	29 277,7	5 048,5	15 857,8	130,06	2 037,1	3 314,0	17 098,4
1983	:	88 744,7	1 392,8	2 846,5	11 922,6	3 907,7	23 506,0	28 759,6	5 036,6	15 857,8	127,40	2 010,1	:	16 883,6
1985	:	88 281,3	1 381,2	2 834,6	11 884,0	4 116,3	:	28 486,8	4 995,6	15 600,7	126,09	2 026,2	:	16 829,8

ARABLE LAND / TERRES ARABLES
Number of holdings / Nombre d'exploitations

YEAR ANNÉE	EUR 12	EUR 10	B	DK	D	EL	ES	F	IRL	I	L	NL	P	UK
1966/67	:	:	166,1	:	1 127,9	807,6	:	1 425,5	:	2 273,6	7,96	168,1	:	:
1970/71	:	6 351,6	131,8	142,0	956,2	805,9	:	1 285,0	239,0	2 449,2	6,63	121,3	:	214,6
1975	:	:	105,4	129,6	806,8	:	:	1 069,9	161,9	1 981,8	5,48	99,6	:	199,0
1979/80	:	5 014,8	89,3	117,7	731,1	774,6	:	992,1	144,9	1 893,1	4,24	90,3	737,8	177,5
1983	:	4 659,2	78,5	96,5	651,8	669,7	1 316,4	891,8	121,3	1 893,1	3,73	85,1	:	167,7
1985	:	4 449,1	75,0	90,2	620,9	642,1	:	837,5	117,0	1 812,8	3.51	86,0	:	164,1

Area / Superficie

YEAR ANNÉE	EUR 12	EUR 10	B	DK	D	EL	ES	F	IRL	I	L	NL	P	UK
1966/67	:	:	806,0	:	7 143,5	2 326,7	:	13 326,5	:	9 317,6	67,33	877,1	:	:
1970/71	:	47 475,4	783,2	2 651,4	7 310,2	2 221,4	:	16 014,4	1 767,5	8 715,9	64,23	817,6	:	7 129,6
1975	:	:	749,8	2 673,1	7 266,6	:	:	16 710,3	971,6	8 638,0	61,12	804,4	:	6 999,6
1979/80	:	46 661,1	738,4	2 644,6	7 273,6	2 462,2	:	16 508,0	1 085,3	8 398,6	57,14	828,4	2 636,3	6 664,9
1983	:	46 549,2	728,6	2 598,7	7 190,9	2 124,7	13 786,6	16 659,9	1 041,1	8 398,6	55,13	835,9	:	6 915,7
1985	:	46 777,0	727,6	2 602,7	7 214,1	2 188,8	:	16 776,7	1 030,5	8 320,7	54,31	862,8	:	6 998,8

PERMANENT PASTURE AND MEADOW / PRAIRIES PERMANENTES ET PÂTURAGES
Number of holdings / Nombre d'exploitations

YEAR ANNÉE	EUR 12	EUR 10	B	DK	D	EL	ES	F	IRL	I	L	NL	P	UK
1966/67	:	:	177,9	:	1 077,6	119,4	:	1 353,9	:	1 202,8	7,65	176,3	:	:
1970/71	:	:	146,9	69,5	929,9	:	:	1 207,6	258,2	852,0	6,64	136,2	:	281,7
1975	:	:	114,4	57,6	769,6	:	:	975,0	226,2	720,9	5,41	118,1	:	239,2
1979/80	:	:	96,4	55,0	699,5	:	:	906,8	216,5	639,6	4,26	105,8	74,9	232,1
1983	:	2 870,2	85,3	44,7	620,8	137,5	5 515,1	807,2	214,4	639,6	3,71	97,2	:	219,8
1985	:	2 807,8	80,8	41,2	594,3	110,6	:	747,3	211,2	708,0	3,57	93,6	:	217,2

Area / Superficie

YEAR ANNÉE	EUR 12	EUR 10	B	DK	D	EL	ES	F	IRL	I	L	NL	P	UK
1966/67	:	:	758,1	:	5 294,0	918,9	:	12 100,9	:	5 450,3	64,54	1 294,4	:	:
1970/71	:	:	727,1	300,1	5 114,4	:	:	12 329,9	2 966,2	5 423,2	69,09	1 282,4	:	10 502,4
1975	:	:	698,7	279,0	4 924,3	:	:	11 238,5	4 101,7	4 746,9	73,28	1 240,6	:	9 384,2
1979/80	:	:	667,1	262,7	4 729,1	:	:	11 381,1	3 959,4	4 499,0	71,25	1 171,7	134,9	10 211,8
1983	:	36 545,1	649,1	230,1	4 533,6	721,6	5 531,7	10 782,0	3 992,1	4 499,0	70,67	1 142,9	:	9 924,0
1985	:	35 998,9	635,7	220,6	4 471,8	884,9	:	10 416,4	3,961,2	4 426,8	70,14	1 132,6	:	9 778,8

PERMANENT CROPS / CULTURES PERMANENTES
Number of holdings / Nombre d'exploitations

YEAR ANNÉE	EUR 12	EUR 10	B	DK	D	EL	ES	F	IRL	I	L	NL	P	UK
1966/67	:	:	31,1	:	209,9	:	:	849,1	:	1 893,1	1,62	33,2	:	:
1970/71	:	:	16,3	:	153,4	:	:	720,8	:	1 957,8	1,49	21,6	:	:
1975	:	:	11,0	3,6	121,8	:	:	565,2	3,7	1 819,9	1,11	15,3	:	14,7
1979/80	:	3 462,5	7,6	2,6	114,4	700,0	:	490,5	2,2	2 120,3	1,04	12,5	521,6	11,4
1983	:	3 325,6	5,8	1,9	99,1	666,3	970,5	408,5	1,3	2 120,3	0,90	10,8	:	10,7
1985	:	3 080,6	5,1	1,7	95,1	655,1	:	370,2	1,2	1 930,9	0,87	10,3	:	10,1

Area / Superficie

YEAR ANNÉE	EUR 12	EUR 10	B	DK	D	EL	ES	F	IRL	I	L	NL	P	UK
1966/67	:	:	24,4	:	164,6	827,4	:	1 598,2	:	3 902,0	1,67	54,4	:	:
1970/71	:	5 714,8	21,1	14,0	159,5	855,0	:	1 488,4	13,5	3 039,8	1,44	42,9	:	79,2
1975	:	:	17,4	13,3	158,3	:	:	1 448,9	2,7	3 084,4	1,41	39,2	:	69,2
1979/80	:	5 583,5	14,4	12,4	168,8	1 019,6	:	1 322,0	2,7	2 943,2	1,45	35,2	710,2	63,7
1983	:	5 527,7	13,5	11,1	163,9	1 047,6	4 187,6	1 258,9	2,1	2 943,2	1,43	29,8	:	56,2
1985	:	5 381,4	13,5	10,9	167,0	1 026,4	:	1 237,8	3,0	2 838,5	1,45	29,7	:	53,1

DATA IN 1000   **DONNÉES EN 1000**

CEREALS — Number of holdings / CÉRÉALES — Nombre d'exploitations

YEAR / ANNÉE	EUR 12	EUR 10	B	DK	D	EL	ES	F	IRL	I	L	NL	P	UK
1966/67	:	:	133,1	:	1 064,2	:	:	1 190,5	:	1 911,3	7,40	109,5	:	
1970/71	:	:	104,4	136,8	896,1	:	:	1 052,0	131,8	1 621,8	6,15	73,2	:	140,8
1975	:	:	77,2	123,8	757,8	:	:	875,6	99,2	1 474,6	5,10	39,6	:	127,4
1979/80	:	3 768,1	65,0	112,7	681,3	518,6	:	793,0	73,5	1 382,5	3,91	28,8	521,4	108,8
1983	:	3 449,0	54,2	91,2	601,6	449,6	863,5	696,6	52,2	1 382,5	3,31	21,9	:	95,9
1985	:	3 235,5	48,7	85,7	568,6	428,4	:	669,3	50,1	1 267,1	3,17	19,6	:	94,8

Area / Superficie

YEAR / ANNÉE	EUR 12	EUR 10	B	DK	D	EL	ES	F	IRL	I	L	NL	P	UK
1966/67	:	:	502,9	:	4 782,8	:	:	8 999,4	:	5 054,5	47,30	450,8	:	
1970/71	:	:	460,9	1 743,0	5 130,9	:	:	9 200,9	381,0	4 835,8	45,34	359,6	:	3 716,5
1975	:	:	398,3	1 740,6	5 156,1	:	:	9 460,4	323,6	4 673,6	43,02	244,3	:	3 721,1
1979/80	:	28 391,0	395,2	1 850,2	5 156,1	1 594,5	:	9 654,4	414,3	5 177,6	39,54	237,9	906,3	3 871,3
1983	:	27 151,6	371,5	1 697,9	5 020,2	1 302,0	8 163,5	9 042,5	348,1	5 177,6	30,98	206,2	:	3 954,6
1985	:	26 936,4	339,6	1 600,6	4 869,3	1 339,7	:	9 310,8	340,2	4 908,1	34,22	183,6	:	4 010,3

COMMON WHEAT — Number of holdings / BLÉ — Nombre d'exploitations

YEAR / ANNÉE	EUR 12	EUR 10	B	DK	D	EL	ES	F	IRL	I	L	NL	P	UK
1966/67	:	:	:	:	:	:	:	:	:	:	:	:	:	:
1970/71	:	:	60,2	20,9	659,8	:	:	762,2	20,5	1 411,3	4,38	24,5	:	48,7
1975	:	:	47,2	14,7	555,7	:	:	596,5	8,3	1 215,0	3,28	17,1	:	43,3
1979/80	:	2 602,8	42,9	12,3	503,2	415,1	:	564,6	5,7	997,8	2,67	16,8	104,4	41,7
1983	:	2 381,1	38,3	23,6	443,6	256,8	342,9	520,9	5,9	1 031,7	1,97	15,3	:	43,0
1985	:	2 232,8	34,3	36,1	413,9	299,3	:	489,4	6,0	892,3	1,92	13,4	:	46,2

Area / Superficie

YEAR / ANNÉE	EUR 12	EUR 10	B	DK	D	EL	ES	F	IRL	I	L	NL	P	UK
1966/67	:	:	216,0	:	1 352,6	:	:	3 763,4	:	3 777,9	16,79	141,8	:	
1970/71	:	:	180,6	114,7	1 499,7	:	:	3 669,5	96,5	3 650,7	11,46	141,5	:	1 010,1
1975	:	:	180,3	102,7	1 519,1	:	:	3 821,8	41,6	3 292,9	8,83	106,9	:	1 046,0
1979/80	:	11 910,5	189,3	114,3	1 623,3	1 099,0	:	4 130,3	52,3	3 181,7	8,92	140,7	311,4	1 370,7
1983	:	12 659,4	196,0	241,8	1 644,1	843,9	2 679,1	4 649,4	55,3	3 181,7	6,18	148,2	:	1 692,8
1985	:	12 588,7	187,0	338,5	1 618,4	819,1	:	4 594,6	71,2	2 925,5	6,36	128,1	:	1 899,9

GRAIN MAIZE — Number of holdings / MAÏS-GRAIN — Nombre d'exploitations

YEAR / ANNÉE	EUR 12	EUR 10	B	DK	D	EL	ES	F	IRL	I	L	NL	P	UK
1966/67	:	:	:	:	:	:	:	:	:	:	:	:	:	:
1970/71	:	:	2,1	:	56,3	:	:	352,1	—	659,4	—	0,4	:	0,1
1975	:	:	3,8	—	37,6	:	:	328,8	—	575,8	—	0,5	:	0,1
1979/80	:	1 047,4	3,5	—	35,8	127,4	:	300,4	—	580,1	—	0,2	410,5	—
1983	:	1003,7	2,4	—	37,8	121,9	298,3	261,4	—	580,1	—	0,06	:	—
1985	:	951,0	3,1	—	37,2	131,5	:	258,9	—	520,2	—	0,1	:	—

Area / Superficie

YEAR / ANNÉE	EUR 12	EUR 10	B	DK	D	EL	ES	F	IRL	I	L	NL	P	UK
1966/67	:	:	:	:	:	:	:	:	:	:	:	:	:	:
1970/71	:	:	2,0	:	114,0	:	:	1 441,5	—	682,8	—	1,0	:	0,4
1975	:	:	6,4	—	92,8	:	:	1 831,9	—	753,5	—	1,3	:	1,1
1979/80	:	3 243,3	6,0	—	115,2	139,0	:	1 845,6	—	1 136,9	—	0,6	177,4	—
1983	:	3 101,4	5,2	—	169,5	149,9	340,1	1 639,6	—	1 136,9	—	0,3	:	—
1985	:	3239,2	7,0	—	180,8	178,6	:	1 804,1	—	1 068,3	—	0,4	:	—

PULSES — Number of holdings / LÉGUMES SECS — Nombre d'exploitations

YEAR / ANNÉE	EUR 12	EUR 10	B	DK	D	EL	ES	F	IRL	I	L	NL	P	UK
1966/67	:	:	9,3	:	39,0	:	:	134,9	:	352,4	0,52	8,8	:	
1970/71	:	:	4,8	6,1	26,7	:	:	114,0	:	290,2	0,36	6,4	:	10,5
1975	:	:	2,9	1,1	24,8	:	:	75,2	0,7	215,5	0,14	4,3	:	7,3
1979/80	:	321,8	1,1	0,7	10,6	146,4	:	39,5	0,1	113,7	0,05	3,0	420,5	6,6
1983	:	263,4	0,7	4,2	7,8	81,9	112,3	44,9	0,1	113,6	0,04	3,5	:	6,7
1985	:	232,0	0,6	19,3	15,2	53,7	:	46,6	0,2	78,9	0,05	6,2	:	11,2

Area / Superficie

YEAR / ANNÉE	EUR 12	EUR 10	B	DK	D	EL	ES	F	IRL	I	L	NL	P	UK
1966/67	:	:	9,8	:	39,8	:	:	75,8	:	269,7	0,56	18,4	:	
1970/71	:	:	6,5	23,4	29,1	:	:	59,7	:	199,0	0,42	16,7	:	106,2
1975	:	:	4,5	4,1	27,5	:	:	86,0	1,4	140,9	0,24	11,9	:	76,0
1979/80	:	329,9	2,0	3,8	12,8	80,2	:	82,4	0,1	61,6	0,09	8,3	111,6	78,6
1983	:	419,3	1,4	22,4	12,6	37,8	220,9	191,4	—	61,6	0,06	12,1	:	79,9
1985	:	658,8	14,1	128,8	34,0	27,5	:	245,4	0,5	46,0	0,12	25,4	:	137,0

POTATOES — Number of holdings / POMMES DE TERRE — Nombre d'exploitations

YEAR / ANNÉE	EUR 12	EUR 10	B	DK	D	EL	ES	F	IRL	I	L	NL	P	UK
1966/67	:	:	:	:	:	:	:	:	:	:	:	:	:	:
1970/71	:	:	95,4	24,0	758,8	:	:	895,0	155,8	485,3	4,78	76,2	:	82,9
1975	:	:	64,4	16,7	567,9	:	:	637,0	121,9	444,0	3,29	43,9	:	59,0
1979/80	:	:	49,7	12,7	435,0	:	:	447,6	97,6	289,2	2,30	34,3	609,9	50,8
1983	:	1 225,2	37,1	8,5	329,7	84,1	304,7	334,1	72,4	289,2	1,60	27,9	:	40,6
1985	:	1 013,0	35,2	7,5	290,1	59,6	:	278,1	65,7	208,9	1,65	27,7	:	38,5

Area / Superficie

YEAR / ANNÉE	EUR 12	EUR 10	B	DK	D	EL	ES	F	IRL	I	L	NL	P	UK
1966/67	:	:	52,2	:	682,4	:	:	407,7	:	180,4	3,38	129,9	:	
1970/71	:	:	46,8	37,8	490,2	:	:	311,0	55,1	100,1	2,46	157,1	:	270,6
1975	:	:	36,1	32,2	363,0	:	:	225,0	40,7	114,1	1,42	151,2	:	202,0
1979/80	:	:	36,4	31,7	273,1	:	:	204,2	35,3	70,9	1,13	166,3	135,1	201,8
1983	:	946,5	34,7	30,4	221,7	29,5	145,9	172,9	28,7	70,9	0,94	163,4	:	193,4
1985	:	964,9	41,3	30,4	217,5	42,1	:	180,4	29,3	63,6	0,84	169,0	:	190,5

SUGAR-BEET — Number of holdings / BETTERAVES SUCRIÈRES — Nombre d'exploitations

YEAR / ANNÉE	EUR 12	EUR 10	B	DK	D	EL	ES	F	IRL	I	L	NL	P	UK
1966/67	:	:	:	:	:	:	:	:	:	:	:	:	:	:
1970/71	:	:	32,7	14,4	115,6	:	:	55,1	17,3	136,1	—	33,2	:	20,8
1975	:	:	26,7	14,9	93,6	:	:	54,9	11,3	116,9	—	30,2	:	17,1
1979/80	:	:	22,3	12,4	80,4	:	:	49,3	7,4	79,5	0,02	22,7	:	14,0
1983	:	293,7	19,8	10,5	71,7	26,2	55,7	46,5	7,2	79,5	0,01	20,5	:	11,8
1985	:	279,2	19,8	9,8	69,4	23,5	:	44,6	6,2	73,7	0,03	20,7	:	11,5

Area / Superficie

YEAR / ANNÉE	EUR 12	EUR 10	B	DK	D	EL	ES	F	IRL	I	L	NL	P	UK
1966/67	:	:	68,4	:	295,2	:	:	312,1	:	309,2	0,02	101,7	:	
1970/71	:	:	89,4	47,3	313,8	:	:	399,7	26,8	234,2	—	103,9	:	187,6
1975	:	:	118,9	93,1	418,5	:	:	593,4	34,0	260,3	—	136,5	:	206,9
1979/80	:	:	115,0	77,9	392,2	39,2	:	536,1	32,3	252,6	0,02	123,6	:	213,7
1983	:	1 708,42	108,6	72,4	389,9	36,2	231,0	491,1	36,1	252,6	0,01	122,8	:	198,7
1985	:	1 739,3	117,4	72,8	402,8	36,0	:	487,8	31,0	256,0	0,01	130,5	:	205,0

DATA IN 1000 — **DONNÉES EN 1000**

FORAGE ROOTS AND TUBERS / PLANTES SARCLÉES FOURRAGÈRES

Number of holdings / Nombre d'exploitations

YEAR ANNÉE	EUR 12	EUR 10	B	DK	D	EL	ES	F	IRL	I	L	NL	P	UK
1966/67	:	:	:	:	:	:	:	:	:	:	:	:	:	:
1970/71	:	:	80,0	89,8	621,9	:	:	773,1	79,7	—	2,81	29,7	:	58,2
1975	:	:	54,8	66,7	457,8	:	:	528,7	51,0	56,0	1,38	10,6	:	52,5
1979/80	:	:	38,4	46,9	336,8	:	:	370,7	44,4	29,9	0,66	5,3	:	36,7
1983	:	666,2	29,2	36,6	245,4	0,3	66,5	263,8	27,5	29,9	0,32	4,5	:	28,7
1985	:	556,9	27,5	32,4	207,9	1,0	:	216,3	23,0	15,0	0,37	4,4	:	29,0

Area / Superficie

YEAR ANNÉE	EUR 12	EUR 10	B	DK	D	EL	ES	F	IRL	I	L	NL	P	UK
1966/67	:	:	38,1	:	415,6	:	:	806,8	:	30,8	1,44	16,7	:	:
1970/71	:	:	33,5	204,9	329,9	:	:	671,3	55,7	—	0,79	9,5	:	174,1
1975	:	:	27,0	180,6	248,8	:	:	464,2	31,8	59,0	0,36	3,6	:	180,5
1979/80	:	:	18,5	136,9	177,6	:	:	325,0	24,5	39,9	0,18	1,8	:	133,7
1983	:	672,4	15,6	130,6	124,9	0,06	23,7	229,0	19,6	39,9	0,09	2,2	:	110,4
1985	:	505,9	15,2	124,0	106,7	1,0	:	181,3	20,1	22,6	0,18	2,6	:	111,6

FORAGE PLANTS / PLANTES FOURRAGÈRES

Number of holdings / Nombre d'exploitations

YEAR ANNÉE	EUR 12	EUR 10	B	DK	D	EL	ES	F	IRL	I	L	NL	P	UK
1966/67	:	:	54,2	:	572,1	:	:	1 060,4	:	1 131,3	5,00	31,1	:	:
1970/71	:	:	52,8	97,8	490,0	:	:	891,8	228,0	950,8	4,07	24,1	:	145,4
1975	:	:	45,5	77,5	405,8	:	:	729,6	91,4	843,8	3,32	42,6	:	147,8
1979/80	:	:	44,4	60,4	357,7	:	:	630,3	77,9	651,0	2,68	46,2	366,8	120,3
1983	:	2 104,6	42,9	45,2	331,5	225,6	238,2	571,0	74,3	651,0	2,29	46,5	:	114,3
1985	:	556,9	27,5	32,4	207,9	1,0	:	216,3	23,0	15,0	0,37	4,4	:	29,0

Area / Superficie

YEAR ANNÉE	EUR 12	EUR 10	B	DK	D	EL	ES	F	IRL	I	L	NL	P	UK
1966/67	:	:	82,2	:	749,8	:	:	4 678,1	:	2 606,8	13,36	57,1	:	:
1970/71	:	:	104,2	500,7	811,7	:	:	4 309,8	1 237,4	2 383,7	13,53	60,7	:	2 356,3
1975	:	:	114,1	462,7	854,3	:	:	4 883,0	530,7	2 366,4	15,25	126,4	:	2 233,3
1979/80	:	:	133,9	416,3	969,2	:	:	4 719,7	570,8	1 990,7	15,49	171,3	432,4	1 959,8
1983	:	11 339,5	146,2	400,3	1 006,1	189,3	607,2	4 898,2	622,2	1 990,6	15,85	197,3	:	1 873,4
1985	:	11 316,5	159,4	356,6	1 218,9	197,0	:	4 669,6	599,2	2 061,4	17,99	217,5	:	1 818,9

FRESH VEGETABLES, MELONS, STRAWBERRIES UNDER GLASS / LÉGUMES, MELONS, FRAISES EN CULTURES MARAÎCHÈRES

Number of holdings / Nombre d'exploitations

YEAR ANNÉE	EUR 12	EUR 10	B	DK	D	EL	ES	F	IRL	I	L	NL	P	UK
1966/67	:	:	:	:	:	:	:	:	:	:	:	:	:	:
1970/71	:	:	:	:	:	:	:	:	:	:	:	:	:	:
1975	:	:	8,7	2,2	11,0	:	:	37,6	:	21,1	0,06	9,2	:	13,2
1979/80	:	:	:	:	:	:	:	:	:	:	:	:	1,6	:
1983	:	57,79	3,4	0,7	4,5	9,3	12,5	10,5	0,09	15,5	0,03	7,3	:	6,4
1985	:	70,1	3,2	0,7	4,5	13,1	:	14,1	0,2	21,3	0,03	7,0	:	6,0

Area / Superficie

YEAR ANNÉE	EUR 12	EUR 10	B	DK	D	EL	ES	F	IRL	I	L	NL	P	UK
1966/67	:	:	:	:	:	:	:	:	:	:	:	:	:	:
1970/71	:	:	:	:	:	:	:	:	:	:	:	:	:	:
1975	:	:	3,0	3,9	10,8	:	:	37,9	1,6	13,5	0,05	12,3	:	69,5
1979/80	:	:	:	:	:	:	:	:	:	:	:	:	0,6	:
1983	:	18,6	1,1	0,3	0,8	0,2	2,0	3,8	—	7,2	0,02	4,6	:	0,6
1985	:	26,9	1,1	0,2	0,9	3,5	:	4,5	0,01	10,8	—	4,6	:	1,3

FRUIT AND BERRY PLANTATIONS / PLANTATIONS D'ARBRES FRUITIERS ET BAIES

Number of holdings / Nombre d'exploitations

YEAR ANNÉE	EUR 12	EUR 10	B	DK	D	EL	ES	F	IRL	I	L	NL	P	UK
1966/67	:	:	23,7	:	117,8	:	:	235,5	:	358,4	0,59	28,2	:	:
1970/71	:	:	11,0	:	46,9	:	:	139,2	7,5	319,7	0,46	14,6	:	18,0
1975	:	:	7,6	2,6	67,6	:	:	129,2	3,5	376,0	0,19	10,9	:	13,3
1979/80	:	988,0	5,1	1,9	60,0	263,0	:	113,9	1,7	524,2	0,16	8,3	85,0	9,7
1983	:	884,7	3,7	1,3	49,6	191,6	347,8	98,1	0,7	523,9	0,01	6,9	:	8,9
1985	:	813,4	3,3	1,2	46,4	177,3	:	88,8	0,9	480,6	0,09	6,5	:	8,3

Area / Superficie

YEAR ANNÉE	EUR 12	EUR 10	B	DK	D	EL	ES	F	IRL	I	L	NL	P	UK
1966/67	:	:	20,4	:	73,7	:	:	288,7	:	541,9	0,29	47,1	:	:
1970/71	:	:	18,8	10,3	52,3	:	:	230,0	3,5	442,4	0,23	37,8	:	75,2
1975	:	:	14,9	10,9	56,0	:	:	213,3	2,5	560,4	0,15	31,9	:	64,2
1979/80	:	1 159,9	11,8	8,8	54,1	158,9	:	196,8	2,6	641,7	0,11	27,5	102,3	57,6
1983	:	1 120,4	10,7	7,7	47,7	146,5	884,2	190,4	1,8	641,7	0,07	23,7	:	50,1
1985	:	1 069,8	10,6	7,3	46,9	140,3	:	193,4	2,8	598,2	0,08	23,3	:	46,9

VINEYARDS / VIGNES

Number of holdings / Nombre d'exploitations

YEAR ANNÉE	EUR 12	EUR 10	B	DK	D	EL	ES	F	IRL	I	L	NL	P	UK
1966/67	:	:	—	—	108,5	:	:	727,0	—	1 304,4	1,43	—	:	—
1970/71	:	:	—	—	110,2	:	:	659,9	—	1 359,2	1,35	—	:	—
1975	:	:	—	—	61,9	:	:	507,1	—	1 257,3	1,05	—	:	—
1979/80	:	2 329,7	—	—	62,1	305,0	:	430,9	—	1 530,7	1,00	—	408,4	—
1983	:	2 245,6	—	—	56,3	302,1	396,5	355,8	—	1 530,6	0,80	—	:	—
1985	:	1 893,3	—	—	55,1	268,0	:	319,8	—	1 249,6	0,84	—	:	—

Area / Superficie

YEAR ANNÉE	EUR 12	EUR 10	B	DK	D	EL	ES	F	IRL	I	L	NL	P	UK
1966/67	:	:	—	—	74,2	:	:	1 232,1	—	1 219,5	1,35	—	:	—
1970/71	:	:	—	—	84,3	:	:	1 200,2	—	1 153,5	1,18	—	:	—
1975	:	:	—	—	83,8	:	:	1 191,0	—	1 240,5	1,22	—	:	—
1979/80	:	2 465,8	—	—	92,0	162,3	:	1 084,0	—	1 126,2	1,30	—	270,4	—
1983	:	2 432,6	—	—	93,8	181,4	1 265,7	1 029,9	—	1 126,2	1,31	—	:	—
1985	:	2 347,2	—	—	97,0	143,1	:	1 010,0	—	1 095,8	1,33	—	:	—

CROPS UNDER GLASS / CULTURES SOUS VERRE

Number of holdings / Nombre d'exploitations

YEAR ANNÉE	EUR 12	EUR 10	B	DK	D	EL	ES	F	IRL	I	L	NL	P	UK
1966/67	:	:	14,7	:	23,9	:	:	23,4	:	15,3	0,25	21,1	:	:
1970/71	:	:	:	:	:	:	:	:	:	:	:	:	:	:
1975	:	:	8,6	3,2	14,9	:	:	19,8	0,9	18,0	0,05	17,6	:	7,7
1979/80	:	:	7,6	2,5	14,7	:	:	17,4	0,4	24,5	0,07	15,9	1,9	9,3
1983	:	97,2	6,7	1,9	12,6	10,0	13,4	17,6	0,09	24,5	0,06	15,2	:	8,5
1985	:	114,4	6,2	1,8	13,0	13,6	:	21,2	0,2	35,0	0,06	15,0	:	8,3

Area / Superficie

YEAR ANNÉE	EUR 12	EUR 10	B	DK	D	EL	ES	F	IRL	I	L	NL	P	UK
1966/67	:	:	2,0	:	2,5	:	:	4,9	:	5,8	0,02	6,6	:	:
1970/71	:	:	:	:	:	:	:	:	:	:	:	:	:	:
1975	:	:	1,8	0,6	2,9	:	:	6,9	0,1	7,2	:	7,9	:	1,7
1979/80	:	:	1,8	0,6	3,3	:	:	5,0	0,3	10,2	0,01	8,5	0,7	2,1
1983	:	34,2	1,7	0,5	3,0	2,4	11,9	5,5	0,09	10,2	0,06	8,8	:	1,9
1985	:	42,7	1,7	0,5	3,2	3,6	:	6,2	—	16,6	—	9,0	:	1,9

DATA IN 1000   **DONNÉES EN 1000**

YEAR ANNÉE	EUR 12	EUR 10	B	DK	D	EL	ES	F	IRL	I	L	NL	P	UK

BREEDING STOCK — ÉLEVAGE DES ANIMAUX
HOLDINGS WITH ANIMALS — EXPLOITATIONS AVEC ANIMAUX

YEAR	EUR 12	EUR 10	B	DK	D	EL	ES	F	IRL	I	L	NL	P	UK
1966/67	:	:	:	:	:	:	:	:	:	:	:	:	:	:
1970/71	:	:	:	:	:	:	:	:	:	:	:	:	:	:
1975	:	:	118,3	114,3	793,0	:	:	1 121,7	214,1	1 605,6	5,57	125,9	:	240,8
1979/80	:	:	97,6	102,3	710,7	:	:	1 047,3	2 202,4	1 271,1	4,31	112,5	675,0	217,7
1983	:	4 230,0	86,5	79,5	639,2	722,3	920,1	929,8	196,1	1 271,1	3,81	101,6	:	200,1
1985	:	3 877,3	81,5	72,3	612,2	707,5	:	856,5	194,5	1 055,9	6,34	98,5	:	192,1

BOVINE ANIMALS — BOVINS TOTAL
Number of holdings — Nombre d'exploitations

YEAR	EUR 12	EUR 10	B	DK	D	EL	ES	F	IRL	I	L	NL	P	UK
1966/67	:	:	159,0	:	1 006,5	277,1	:	1 218,6	:	1 243,1	7,10	157,8	:	:
1970/71	:	3 850,8	127,9	103,2	793,4	242,8	:	1 051,5	227,6	939,5	6,12	130,8	:	228,0
1975	:	:	95,7	81,6	633,6	:	:	842,4	209,4	785,4	4,98	108,2	:	209,3
1979/80	:	2 530,0	81,2	65,7	537,1	137,1	:	733,4	195,9	500,9	3,85	90,9	268,5	183,9
1983	:	2 281,3	71,9	51,5	474,9	98,8	443,6	642,5	190,1	500,9	3,39	80,3	:	167,0
1985	:	2 132.8	67,9	46,3	448,7	93,9	:	590,0	187,0	458,2	3,17	76,6	:	161,0

Number of animals — Nombre d'animaux

YEAR	EUR 12	EUR 10	B	DK	D	EL	ES	F	IRL	I	L	NL	P	UK
1966/67	:	:	2 658,0	:	14 176,2	882,3	:	21 058,9	:	9 501,3	171,29	3 598,7	:	:
1970/71	:	74 430,7	2 886,7	2 840,6	14 674,0	872,4	:	21 400,1	5 975,5	8 701,4	192,77	4 314,5	:	12 572,7
1975	:	:	2 983,6	3 068,0	14 320,6	:	:	23 652,6	7 150,1	8 952,3	226,39	4 956,3	:	15 090,5
1979/80	:	78 994,3	3 042,9	3 035,4	14 937,7	824,1	:	22 843,6	6 870,8	8 527,0	224,80	5 148,6	1 174,1	13 539,4
1983	:	79 262,4	3 077,5	2 851,6	15 023,3	616,1	4 539,4	23 425,3	6 899,8	8 527,0	224,64	5 410,9	:	13 206,3
1985	:	79 028,1	3 080,3	2 617,7	15 576,0	674,3	:	23 140,8	6 964,6	8 711,8	223,11	5 247,7	:	12 791,8

DAIRY COWS — VACHES LAITIÈRES
Number of holdings — Nombre d'exploitations

YEAR	EUR 12	EUR 10	B	DK	D	EL	ES	F	IRL	I	L	NL	P	UK
1966/67	:	:	140,6	:	917,3	166,1	:	1 145,3	:	783,7	6,46	143,7	:	:
1970/71	:	:	101,4	96,4	713,4	:	:	815,5	108,6	604,4	5,50	116,3	:	109,6
1975	:	:	74,6	63,3	565,8	:	:	633,8	127,5	517,5	4,52	93,7	:	83,0
1979/80	:	1 747,3	57,9	46,6	452,4	91,9	:	517,4	104,6	331,5	2,98	74,8	136,3	67,2
1983	:	1 514,2	48,7	35,5	396,9	66,2	302,9	420,4	91,4	331,5	2,51	63,5	:	57,6
1985	:	1 353,0	44,5	31,8	361,9	66,2	:	351,0	84,7	298,6	2,30	58,0	:	54,0

Number of animals — Nombre d'animaux

YEAR	EUR 12	EUR 10	B	DK	D	EL	ES	F	IRL	I	L	NL	P	UK
1966/67	:	:	1 060,8	:	5 830,7	313,9	:	9 342,2	:	3 459,4	56,68	1 734,2	:	:
1970/71	:	:	994,8	1 152,4	5 480,4	:	:	7 280,4	1 311,2	2 861,2	62,05	1 865,6	:	3 243,6
1975	:	:	990,2	1 101,9	5 365,1	:	:	7 551,1	1 477,0	2 912,1	73,94	2 258,8	:	3 289,9
1979/80	:	24 920,8	977,2	1 071,4	5 428,9	256,9	:	7 270,0	1 614,9	2 576,5	67,83	2 369,0	343,8	3 288,2
1983	:	25 143,8	982,1	1 002,9	5 530,6	214,7	1 499,5	7 215,3	1 668,1	2 576,5	68,77	2 557,2	:	3 327,6
1985	:	24 313,0	969,9	896,4	5 567,2	222,0	:	6 609,3	1 684,2	2 782,3	68,35	2 366,6	:	3 146,7

OTHER COWS — AUTRES VACHES
Number of holdings — Nombre d'exploitations

YEAR	EUR 12	EUR 10	B	DK	D	EL	ES	F	IRL	I	L	NL	P	UK
1966/67	:	:	:	:	:	:	:	:	:	:	:	:	:	:
1970/71	:	:	:	:	:	:	:	:	:	:	:	:	:	:
1975	:	:	9,0	13,4	36,6	:	:	246,7	99,4	160,8	1,18	—	:	109,5
1979/80	:	563,0	13,9	10,5	38,8	35,2	:	233,5	79,7	63,8	1,75	—	71,7	85,8
1983	:	516,9	14,0	8,7	32,6	28,1	176,2	222,5	72,6	63,8	1,79	—	:	72,8
1985	:	553,9	15,6	8,6	41,1	25,4	:	232,5	73,8	76,7	1,85	6,4	:	71,9

Number of animals — Nombre d'animaux

YEAR	EUR 12	EUR 10	B	DK	D	EL	ES	F	IRL	I	L	NL	P	UK
1966/67	:	:	:	:	:	:	:	:	:	:	:	:	:	:
1970/71	:	:	:	:	:	:	:	:	:	:	:	:	:	:
1975	:	:	74,3	86,8	125,4	:	:	2 668,5	665,1	625,0	4,58	—	:	1 951,7
1979/80	:	5 626,9	129,7	72,5	146,6	117,4	:	2 832,3	465,2	316,8	12,03	—	249,4	1 534,4
1983	:	5 645,3	149,5	57,8	126,1	88,9	1 199,1	3 145,7	404,5	316,8	14,37	—	:	1 341,6
1985	:	6 221,0	172,4	54,3	171,7	122,5	:	3 430,7	408,3	480,6	14,87	45,9	:	1 319,7

SHEEP — OVINS
Number of holdings — Nombre d'exploitations

YEAR	EUR 12	EUR 10	B	DK	D	EL	ES	F	IRL	I	L	NL	P	UK
1966/67	:	:	:	:	:	294,3	:	:	:	:	:	:	:	:
1970/71	:	877,3	12,8	4,8	28,3	265,5	:	173,7	65,3	211,0	0,31	19,8	:	95,8
1975	:	:	11,6	3,9	35,4	:	:	168,0	53,5	203,9	0,27	21,7	:	89,3
1979/80	:	793,7	9,2	3,9	38,4	221,0	:	200,0	43,6	170,4	0,27	22,6	124,4	84,3
1983	:	723,3	8,8	10,5	36,4	242,4	160,8	172,4	28,0	170,4	0,34	20,4	:	33,7
1985	:	721,4	8,9	4,4	39,5	188,7	:	161,2	48,0	163,0	0,28	19,7	:	87,7

Number of animals — Nombre d'animaux

YEAR	EUR 12	EUR 10	B	DK	D	EL	ES	F	IRL	I	L	NL	P	UK
1966/67	:	:	:	:	:	6 822,7	:	:	:	:	:	:	:	:
1970/71	:	54 696,4	113,3	68,6	970,5	7 677,7	:	9 052,4	4 169,0	5 986,8	3,46	574,7	:	26 079,9
1975	:	:	115,9	71,6	954,8	:	:	10 179,5	3 754,9	6 452,7	5,57	760,1	:	27 887,1
1979/80	:	63 292,0	119,6	54,0	959,4	8 553,7	:	13 120,8	3 301,3	6 426,6	3,57	895,4	2 057,3	29 857,6
1983	:	64 346,6	130,0	52,0	905,9	6 681,9	15 953,9	11 420,1	4 049,5	6 426,6	3,54	772,3	:	33 904,8
1985	:	67 902,2	161,4	70,4	1 068,1	7 214,6	:	11 181,1	4 404,6	7 521,8	5,08	814,3	:	35 460,8

TOTAL PIGS — PORCINS TOTAL
Number of holdings — Nombre d'exploitations

YEAR	EUR 12	EUR 10	B	DK	D	EL	ES	F	IRL	I	L	NL	P	UK
1966/67	:	:	105,2	:	1 004,0	279,4	:	831,1	:	999,1	7,11	97,8	:	:
1970/71	:	2 840,6	83,7	118,4	751,1	139,2	:	656,6	67,9	857,6	4,77	75,8	:	85,5
1975	:	:	57,4	89,4	612,6	:	:	497,5	26,5	827,2	2,93	55,2	:	47,5
1979/80	:	1 653,5	43,7	73,3	506,7	80,3	:	318,4	12,1	533,7	1,74	47,4	360,2	36,2
1983	:	1 536,7	34,8	51,6	435,3	119,2	476,4	287,8	10,1	533,7	1,40	35,5	:	27,3
1985	:	1 291,8	29,8	44,2	402,5	102,2	:	249,1	7,4	396,1	1,10	36,1	:	23,3

Number of animals — Nombre d'animaux

YEAR	EUR 12	EUR 10	B	DK	D	EL	ES	F	IRL	I	L	NL	P	UK
1966/67	:	:	:	:	:	519,9	:	:	:	:	:	:	:	:
1970/71	:	63 972,9	3 727,8	8 297,7	19 898,0	597,6	:	10 703,2	1 189,1	5 834,6	103,43	5 533,3	:	8 088,2
1975	:	:	4 618,3	7 687,2	19 336,0	:	:	10 579,6	882,1	8 421,8	81,51	7 279,1	:	7 356,7
1979/80	:	76 058,5	5 099,9	9 341,8	21 917,0	1 268,0	:	11 027,0	1 009,2	8 755,6	79,32	9 721,8	2 410,7	7 838,9
1983	:	77 244,0	5 299,5	9 253,1	21 696,5	1 047,2	9 642,2	11 308,5	1 050,5	8 775,6	71,90	10 656,1	:	8 085,1
1985	:	79 981,5	5 340,8	9 089,0	23 200,7	1 023,2	:	11 271,4	960,2	8 816,1	69,95	12 382,6	:	7 827,5

EC SURVEY ON THE STRUCTURE
OF AGRICULTURAL HOLDINGS

IC 9

ENQUÊTE CE SUR LA STRUCTURE
DES EXPLOITATIONS AGRICOLES

1966/67 TO 1985

1966/67 À 1985

DATA IN 1000　　　　　　　　　　　　　　　　　　　　　　　　　　　　　　　　　　**DONNÉES EN 1000**

YEAR ANNÉE	EUR 12	EUR 10	B	DK	D	EL	ES	F	IRL	I	L	NL	P	UK
BREEDING SOWS Number of holdings													**TRUIES (⩾ 50 kg)** Nombre d'exploitations	
1966/67	:	:	:	:	:	:		:	:	:	:	:		:
1970/71		1 086,5	53,3	94,7	349,3	37,2		229,2	42,0	165,3	2,71	46,0		66,8
1975		:	39,1	68,3	261,0	:		149,6	18,9	125,2	1,55	32,1		37,3
1979/80		533,8	29,9	53,2	210,0	23,1		93,8	7,9	58,8	1,12	27,2	129,1	28,8
1983		432,6	23,7	36,5	174,7	23,4	200,6	66,5	7,0	58,8	0,90	20,0		21,1
1985	:	379,7	20,5	31,3	160,8	21,6	:	56,1	4,5	47,4	0,76	18,8	:	17,9
Number of animals													Nombre d'animaux	
1966/67	:	:	:	:	:	:		:	:	:	:	:		:
1970/71		7 329,5	587,0	989,7	2 111,7	126,5		1 131,9	140,7	549,9	16,06	737,2		938,8
1975		:	589,4	988,4	2 152,8	:		1 307,4	106,2	732,2	9,30	872,5		865,0
1979/80		8 843,7	643,6	1 183,0	2 564,1	217,0		1 269,9	117,3	716,7	13,36	1 186,4	362,9	932,3
1983		8 753,4	643,2	1 033,5	2 528,7	151,0	1 970,3	1 205,1	122,4	716,7	12,10	1 417,4		923,3
1985	:	9 412,8	645,5	1 052,2	2 733,9	148,6	:	1 209,8	110,5	955,3	11,91	1 643,1	:	902,0
OTHER PIGS Number of holdings													**AUTRES PORCS (⩾ 20 kg)** Nombre d'exploitations	
1966/67	:	:	:	:	:	:		:	:	:	:	:		:
1970/71		2 479,7	65,1	107,8	641,1	107,4		586,8	34,8	805,7	3,81	58,8		68,4
1975		:	45,9	79,7	563,9	:		457,4	15,6	786,5	2,61	45,4		38,6
1979/80		1 489,6	36,3	66,9	469,5	33,2		284,5	8,3	517,7	1,40	41,4	311,8	30,4
1983		1 413,9	29,6	47,9	405,8	85,2	360,1	271,0	6,7	517,7	1,11	26,6		22,3
1985	:	1 179,9	25,8	41,0	375,4	68,4	:	233,8	5,3	383,9	0,90	26,5	:	18,9
Number of animals													Nombre d'animaux	
1966/67	:	:	:	:	:	:		:	:	:	:	:		:
1970/71		37 279,5	1 990,4	4 986,6	11 490,6	419,9		6 025,3	527,7	3 834,6	48,52	3 005,5		4 950,4
1975		:	2 661,7	4 098,5	11 833,7	:		6 461,7	573,5	5 804,9	36,55	4 109,9		4 597,1
1979/80		46 078,6	3 033,8	5 059,8	13 380,4	500,9		6 693,3	670,0	6 458,0	32,80	5 217,8	2 047,8	5 031,8
1983		46 904,0	3 142,7	5 217,3	13 329,5	529,8	5 077,8	7 065,5	690,0	6 457,9	28,86	5 500,4		4 942,0
1985	:	47 476,3	3 222,8	5 130,8	13 955,5	460,2	:	6 962,7	635,0	5 965,4	27,92	6 331,9	:	4 784,1
TOTAL POULTRY Number of holdings													**VOLAILLES TOTAL** Nombre d'exploitations	
1966/67	:	:	:	:	:	760,1		:	:	:	:	:		:
1970/71		:	:	:	:	:		:	:	:	:	:		:
1975		:	55,8	43,7	531,2	:		1 018,7	128,9	1 290,2	3,99	25,9		99,4
1979/80		3 213,9	40,2	32,0	411,0	648,7		882,3	87,2	1 026,2	2,63	9,7	593,3	74,0
1983		2 983,1	27,1	21,7	344,0	650,3	640,2	774,2	68,5	1 026,2	2,22	7,7		61,2
1985	:	2 578,7	22,8	18,0	317,0	644,6	:	693,4	61,8	755,7	2,03	7,4	:	56,0
Number of animals													Nombre d'animaux	
1966/67	:	:	:	:	:	21 435,1		:	:	:	:	:		:
1970/71		:	:	:	:	:		:	:	:	:	:		:
1975		:	27 300,9	13 154,3	67 432,7	:		153 057	11 103,7	121 850	247,32	70 258,3		103 102
1979/80		736 141	24 391,0	16 385,0	76 595,0	31 561,0		185 408	9 604,0	178 259	131,00	79 847,0	37 926,0	133 960
1983		742 727	21 761,2	16 132,1	71 365,9	26 718,4	116 690	208 001	9 531,2	178 259	101,50	83 542,4		127 314
1985	:	732 063	21 299,0	15 219,0	70 929,0	28 160,0	:	217 594	9 440,0	149 347	101,90	91 444,0	:	128 529
TABLE FOWL Number of holdings													**POULETS DE CHAIR** Nombre d'exploitations	
1966/67	:	:	:	:	:	:		:	:	:	:	:		:
1970/71		:	12,1	6,4	30,1	:		775,2	10,4	852,5	0,38	2,8		8,2
1975		:	8,2	4,3	120,4	:		631,8	9,9	816,9	0,22	2,3		4,5
1979/80		1 275,8	4,4	2,8	76,4	142,2		458,0	7,9	577,4	0,87	1,9	443,9	3,9
1983		1 258,3	3,1	2,3	58,4	173,4	170,9	430,6	7,0	577,4	0,83	1,5		3,8
1985	:	1 080,2	2,8	2,0	56,1	179,8	:	405,8	7,9	420,6	0,83	1,5	:	2,9
Number of animals													Nombre d'animaux	
1966/67	:	:	:	:	:	:		:	:	:	:	:		:
1970/71		:	10 981,0	6 969,0	:	:		54 704,0	3 200,0	59 618,0	30,00	30 060,0		49 783,0
1975		:	10 031,7	6 794,1	12 534,9	:		61 735,6	4 988,2	67 717,8	35,36	39 249,9		37 465,2
1979/80		312 302	9 981,7	8 400,5	20 256,3	13 672,7		75 465,3	5 204,2	84 632,0	10,02	38 387,4	24 328,0	56 292,2
1983		321 890	9 933,0	8 304,2	14 373,2	10 220,9	61 180,0	96 452,1	4 444,4	84 632,0	9,20	35 108,0		58 413,2
1985	:	326 333	10 383,0	8 490,0	19 717,0	12 066,0	:	101 119,0	4 775,0	70 158,0	15,00	38 383,0	:	61 227,0
LAYING HENS Number of holdings													**POULES PONDEUSES** Nombre d'exploitations	
1966/67	:	:	:	:	:	:		:	:	:	:	:		:
1970/71		:	87,5	66,6	725,3	:		1 203,9	159,1	1 304,6	4,91	48,7		136,6
1975		:	:	:	:	:		:	:	:	:	:		:
1979/80		3 043,2	37,6	30,8	399,3	627,6		863,3	82,6	923,6	2,56	7,5	574,1	68,3
1983		2 814,3	24,7	20,7	333,6	631,9	624,5	751,5	64,7	923,6	2,15	6,0		55,4
1985	:	2 449,6	20,9	17,2	305,6	629,5	:	669,6	57,1	692,1	1,96	5,7	:	49,9
Number of animals													Nombre d'animaux	
1966/67	:	:	:	:	:	:		:	:	:	:	:		:
1970/71		:	14 996,0	6 141,0	50 508,0	:		43 156,0	4 162,0	43 013,0	222,00	17 846,0		87 424,0
1975		:	16 779,8	5 965,0	53 216,7	:		63 775,3	5 625,3	43 200,0	209,43	28 802,8		59 466,6
1979/80		347 635	13 899,3	6 560,1	53 757,9	17 452,6		73 035,0	3 692,3	69 665,0	119,71	39 682,0	12 115,0	69 771,0
1983		335 908	11 497,1	8 304,2	54 481,2	10 220,9	45 931,0	71 665,0	4 444,4	69 665,0	90,30	47 126,6		58 413,3
1985	:	325 459	10 594,0	5 533,0	48 115,0	14 806,0	:	72 099,0	4 101,0	60 823,0	84,60	51 505,0	:	57 798,0

1975 TO 1985

DATA IN 1000

	Number of holdings Nombre d'exploitations				AA / SAU				SGM / MBS	
	1975	1979/80	1983	1985	1975	1979/80	1983	1985	1975	1979/80

MAIN SURVEY RESULTS BY REGION

Belgie/Belgique	138,1	115,1	102,6	97,6	1 467,5	1 421,0	1 392,8	1 381,0	1 296,1	2 104,7
Danmark	132,3	122,7	98,7	92,4	2 966,0	2 920,0	2 846,5	2 834,6	1 635,5	2 668,6
Bundesrepublik Deutschland										
Schleswig-Holstein	37,6	35,5	32,2	31,3	1 119,0	1 101,4	1 081,5	1 089,9	644,1	:
Niedersachsen	138,2	130,0	117,2	114,6	2 756,5	2 749,6	2 720,4	2 706,0	1 567,1	2 484,1
Nordrhein-Westfalen	118,1	107,3	97,0	94,1	1 713,9	1 670,8	1 606,7	1 608,5	1 198,1	1 856,1
Hessen	73,8	66,9	58,4	56,2	827,6	797,1	769,4	776,5	472,3	709,0
Rheinland-Pfalz	79,1	74,7	66,3	61,7	783,6	760,3	735,8	718,0	543,8	956,8
Baden-Württemberg	159,7	152,3	136,3	130,7	1 548,5	1 532,1	1 492,0	1 492,0	956,7	1 411,2
Bayern	290,9	274,3	253,2	245,3	3 538,4	3 495,6	3 424,8	3 400,6	1 969,2	3 033,4
Saarland	6,6	5,7	4,2	3,8	81,9	76,2	65,0	65,4	43,6	:
Hamburg, Bremen und Berlin	3,7	3,2	2,8	2,7	29,2	29,2	27,1	27,2	66,3	:
Total	907,7	849,9	767,6	740,5	12 399	12 212	11 923	11 884	7 461,2	10 451
Ellas										
Central Greece and Euboa	:	172,4	153,9	154,1	:	558,0	575,5	567,9	:	:
Peloponesos	:	172,9	174,1	171,4	:	652,5	695,7	679,9	:	:
Ionian Islands	:	33,7	33,4	32,6	:	70,1	73,8	90,0	:	:
Epirus	:	54,3	55,4	56,0	:	118,7	149,7	143,6	:	:
Thessaly	:	109,6	104,7	106,6	:	470,8	452,3	487,9	:	:
Macedonia	:	235,2	220,7	217,0	:	985,2	886,3	946,5	:	:
Thrace	:	56,8	52,6	50,5	:	256,9	270,7	264,5	:	:
Aegean Islands	:	64,5	63,0	63,6	:	167,5	328,6	402,7	:	:
Crete	:	99,5	100,8	96,7	:	270,1	475,1	530,1	:	:
Total	:	998,9	958,6	948,4	:	3 549,8	3 907,7	4 113,1	:	:
France										
Île de France	11,6	11,2	10,4	9,7	602,8	600,7	586,4	581,1	374,0	620,3
Champagne	33,8	36,9	34,9	34,1	1 568,3	1 560,7	1 553,0	1 547,3	699,0	1 201,6
Picardie	27,7	27,8	25,0	23,2	1 374,5	1 361,7	1 348,8	1 343,6	684,1	1 146,1
Haute-Normandie	30,8	28,1	26,3	24,7	822,8	823,5	813,4	795,9	371,0	615,6
Centre	68,2	66,0	58,8	55,9	2 495,1	2 512,6	2 479,5	2 470,8	946,0	1 587,6
Basse-Normandie	67,5	64,6	58,8	55,5	1 361,1	1 375,8	1 368,6	1 365,5	511,8	860,4
Bourgogne	49,3	46,5	41,2	38,6	1 829,0	1 798,9	1 778,3	1 771,3	607,7	1 032,1
Nord	39,7	38,3	33,1	30,9	898,5	896,3	874,5	857,2	567,5	938,4
Lorraine	35,9	33,7	29,0	27,1	1 129,8	1 125,1	1 106,9	1 099,2	324,5	554,3
Alsace	29,3	27,5	24,3	23,1	332,8	337,4	342,5	346,4	189,6	314,3
Franche-Comté	24,9	24,5	22,2	20,7	718,3	691,1	691,9	674,7	202,0	340,7
Pays de la Loire	112,3	110,4	98,9	92,3	2 431,3	2 419,2	2 376,7	2 361,1	1 030,5	1 753,6
Bretagne	124,2	118,2	109,1	100,7	1 886,8	1 861,4	1 839,0	1 817,5	1 064,4	1 906,5
Poitou-Charentes	72,7	69,6	61,2	57,0	1 847,3	1 828,7	1 782,3	1 777,4	687,4	1 132,9
Aquitaine	101,1	97,9	85,5	80,4	1 600,1	1 579,1	1 517,0	1 495,5	770,4	1 264,6
Midi-Pyrénées	112,1	104,1	95,9	90,1	2 465,6	2 471,3	2 454,6	2 405,6	786,1	1 276,3
Limousin	39,0	36,5	33,0	30,6	932,9	920,1	889,6	878,3	261,8	427,6
Rhône-Alpes	117,2	110,1	99,0	93,7	1 715,3	1 715,2	1 650,0	1 629,9	715,1	1 217,3
Auvergne	59,0	56,6	51,6	48,0	1 528,7	1 597,4	1 558,9	1 523,9	426,5	720,8
Languedoc	90,4	83,5	75,5	70,1	1 090,6	1 056,4	1 026,5	1 031,0	699,1	1 156,5
Provence-Côte d'Azur	60,5	96,4	50,2	45,2	704,6	622,7	614,9	602,8	622,7	1 056,2
Corse	8,0	7,0	5,7	5,1	127,5	122,8	116,5	110,7	64,0	101,2
Total	1 315,2	1 295,4	1 129,6	1 056,7	29 464	29 278	28 770	28 487	12 605	21 225

ENQUÊTE CE SUR LA STRUCTURE DES EXPLOITATIONS AGRICOLES

1975 À 1985

DONNÉES EN 1000

PRINCIPAUX RÉSULTATS D'ENQUÊTE PAR RÉGION

SGM / MBS		AWU / UTA				Number of persons Nombre de personnes				
1983	1985	1975	1979/80	1983	1985	1975	1979/80	1983	1985	
2 104,2	2 326,5	139,6	123,9	111,8	105,2	331,6	302,4	304,7	157,3	Belgie/Belgique
2 567,6	2 854,9	176,7	171,6	140,3	121,6	235,6	234,1	185,7	157,2	Danmark
										Bundesrepublik Deutschland
1 031,6	1 138,3	58,5	52,8	48,8	47,4	88,3	79,6	71,9	71,0	Schleswig-Holstein
2 538,7	2 772,3	192,1	171,3	150,5	148,0	327,6	298,1	264,7	258,9	Niedersachsen
1 838,7	2 046,7	155,1	131,7	120,3	119,2	268,8	234,1	212,6	212,0	Nordrhein-Westfalen
685,0	730,6	91,8	73,7	65,0	62,8	190,6	160,9	140,6	135,9	Hessen
944,6	1 008,3	101,5	88,8	81,3	76,1	186,2	168,2	153,9	141,1	Rheinland-Pfalz
1 373,5	1 544,9	201,6	168,4	143,3	146,9	392,2	359,2	320,9	316,7	Baden-Württemberg
3 022,0	3 441,8	418,4	352,1	320,7	307,1	736,2	662,4	601,2	587,5	Bayern
49,3	52,4	7,2	5,4	4,3	4,1	15,3	11,8	8,7	8,3	Saarland
72,9	83,6	7,4	6,6	6,7	6,4	10,1	9,1	9,2	8,5	Hamburg, Bremen und Berlin
11 556	12 819	1 233,6	1 050,8	940,9	918,0	2 215,3	1 983,4	1 783,7	1 739,9	Total
										Ellas
452,5	616,9	:	130,0	140,5	150,9	:	301,5	349,2	351,8	Central Greece and Euboa
563,1	707,0	:	152,4	184,9	176,4	:	324,3	393,0	385,3	Peloponesos
60,7	64,8	:	22,8	28,3	23,4	:	66,0	71,1	66,8	Ionian Islands
145,6	180,7	:	45,4	54,8	58,9	:	95,3	124,6	122,6	Epirus
525,3	791,7	:	101,0	102,5	111,6	:	209,0	239,3	239,8	Thessaly
899,9	1 174,6	:	205,4	214,2	213,8	:	456,4	459,5	459,2	Macedonia
196,7	290,7	:	51,7	47,2	62,4	:	111,1	114,3	114,3	Thrace
142,3	171,5	:	45,1	52,3	56,0	:	107,7	125,6	124,1	Aegean Islands
326,5	406,6	:	74,4	93,0	90,2	:	175,0	217,8	201,2	Crete
3 312,6	4 404,5	:	828,2	917,7	943,6	:	1 846,3	2 094,4	2 065,1	Total
										France
627,8	600,8	29,7	27,8	23,6	22,6	35,6	32,4	28,1	25,4	Île de France
1 224,5	1 639,2	55,0	57,0	55,6	53,7	84,0	79,5	74,4	73,9	Champagne
1 135,4	1 352,4	57,1	55,3	50,6	47,6	75,3	67,4	62,0	58,6	Picardie
617,0	646,9	42,8	39,0	34,9	33,6	66,4	57,9	51,4	49,7	Haute-Normandie
1 651,8	2 158,9	102,2	96,7	87,3	84,1	154,5	138,4	122,7	116,7	Centre
879,2	934,3	96,3	93,6	81,8	76,5	145,0	129,1	114,9	107,2	Basse-Normandie
1 059,9	1 100,8	76,2	73,7	65,3	61,9	114,5	101,6	89,1	83,1	Bourgogne
916,1	923,6	67,2	62,6	54,0	51,3	94,8	83,5	69,8	64,8	Nord
554,0	603,6	47,8	46,1	40,1	38,8	84,7	72,9	63,0	60,3	Lorraine
325,7	400,6	42,8	35,6	32,7	31,0	78,2	63,9	56,8	54,3	Alsace
332,6	372,7	36,2	36,0	32,0	30,3	56,6	14,7	45,7	43,0	Franche-Comté
1 813,2	1 960,0	170,9	166,6	149,5	141,0	252,6	263,6	206,9	190,1	Pays de la Loire
1 990,1	2 123,0	178,4	171,7	159,7	148,1	281,6	247,6	225,6	206,1	Bretagne
1 123,9	1 290,4	112,2	103,1	85,9	81,1	173,0	145,8	128,5	117,8	Poitou-Charentes
1 315,1	1 566,7	163,8	157,5	139,4	131,5	254,0	221,5	201,3	190,4	Aquitaine
1 352,1	1 471,2	163,8	154,2	143,3	133,9	269,6	223,7	210,1	194,4	Midi-Pyrénées
440,4	425,8	59,1	53,0	46,5	43,2	97,4	85,3	73,8	67,0	Limousin
1 195,4	1 340,4	147,4	140,5	125,4	121,1	265,6	226,2	206,4	193,7	Rhône-Alpes
713,9	686,6	87,4	79,2	70,5	66,3	139,0	118,1	108,0	100,6	Auvergne
1 112,2	1 290,8	112,2	104,9	94,9	91,1	194,9	159,7	151,5	141,6	Languedoc
1 096,9	1 110,0	91,9	84,1	77,2	72,6	134,6	114,7	105,3	96,9	Provence-Côte d'Azur
92,2	87,7	9,4	9,2	8,0	71,1	16,1	13,1	10,7	9,6	Corse
21 569	24 086	1 949,8	1 847,4	1 658,2	1 632,4	3 068,0	2 660,6	2 406,0	2 245,2	Total

1975 TO 1985

DATA IN 1000

	Number of holdings Nombre d'exploitations				AA / SAU				SGM / MBS	
	1975	1979/80	1983	1985	1975	1979/80	1983	1985	1975	1979/80

MAIN SURVEY RESULTS BY REGION

Ireland	228,0	223,5	221,1	219,1	5 076,6	5 048,5	5 036,6	4 989,8	931,5	1 613,9
Italia										
Piemonte	204,5	193,2	193,2	192,8	1 217,9	1 224,3	1 224,3	1 194,5	678,9	1 390,2
Val D'Aosta	7,3	8,8	8,8	8,8	94,9	93,8	93,8	98,2	15,0	26,2
Lombardia	146,5	142,3	142,3	139,0	1 174,0	1 150,6	1 150,6	1 145,5	870,2	1 684,0
Veneto	188,4	217,8	217,8	215,1	930,1	906,1	906,1	912,5	693,6	1 519,1
Friuli-Venezia Giulia	58,6	58,0	58,0	54,3	284,1	266,8	266,8	268,5	145,6	346,6
Liguria	57,2	50,2	50,2	49,5	129,2	113,7	113,7	103,3	125,0	330,6
Emilia Romagna	174,8	165,3	165,3	160,3	1 324,7	1 272,4	1 272,4	1 263,1	1 059,7	2 078,1
Toscana	128,0	129,6	129,6	128,2	1 033,9	1 008,2	1 008,2	968,4	513,2	981,2
Umbria	49,8	54,2	54,2	53,1	403,5	424,0	424,0	413,9	168,4	288,0
Marche	83,4	80,9	80,9	80,4	597,1	563,3	563,3	566,2	272,0	470,9
Lazio	172,2	197,1	197,1	193,5	923,6	845,1	845,1	852,7	444,5	852,4
Abruzzi	99,6	105,1	105,1	104,2	565,1	526,0	526,0	541,4	195,3	406,6
Molise	42,8	42,0	42,0	41,5	263,1	263,5	263,5	253,9	72,6	153,7
Campania	245,2	257,4	257,4	253,0	762,6	728,9	728,9	685,2	563,1	1 323,8
Puglia	268,8	329,0	329,0	326,8	1 491,6	1 469,0	1 469,0	1 492,0	700,7	1 675,7
Basilicata	76,8	75,6	75,6	74,6	639,5	639,4	639,4	612,2	149,9	337,2
Calabria	174,0	180,8	180,8	178,3	795,4	752,7	752,7	707,9	382,5	686,4
Sicilia	342,4	386,8	386,8	369,9	1 799,4	1 722,1	1 722,1	1 650,1	915,0	1 705,6
Sardegna	90,5	108,3	108,3	106,4	1 643,7	1 453,5	1 453,5	1 433,8	307,5	596,4
Bolzano Bozen	22,0	23,6	23,6	23,0	257,6	258,3	258,3	253,6	77,1	188,2
Trento	31,2	26,3	26,3	25,8	154,2	149,1	149,1	144,8	61,5	128,8
Total	2 664,0	2 832,3	2 832,3	2 778,5	16 485	15 831	15 831	15 562	8 411	17 170
Luxembourg	6,21	5,17	4,60	4,38	136,10	130,10	127,40	126,05	63,50	97,68
Nederland	162,6	148,7	138,5	135,9	2 086,3	2 037,1	2 010,2	2 026,2	2 899,3	5 850,5
United Kingdom										
North	12,9	12,5	11,9	11,6	1 034,3	1 036,9	1 027,9	1 021,9	193,9	:
Yorkshire and Humberside	19,3	18,2	17,0	16,7	1 121,5	1 086,6	1 078,2	1 077,6	365,8	:
East Midlands	20,4	19,0	17,7	17,0	1 233,8	1 223,6	1 217,6	1 216,1	502,1	:
East Anglia	16,4	14,7	13,7	13,0	1 011,7	979,0	975,0	973,4	495,8	:
South East	28,9	27,9	26,9	26,4	1 663,9	1 644,2	1 631,9	1 625,0	691,2	:
South West	39,4	38,8	36,4	35,5	1 833,6	1 796,5	1 780,0	1 777,9	566,6	:
West Midlands	21,6	21,2	19,8	19,4	1 013,9	959,3	951,1	947,5	343,2	:
North West	14,7	13,8	12,7	12,5	477,2	450,3	444,7	444,1	183,4	:
Wales	32,5	31,5	30,0	29,7	1 462,6	1 456,2	1 445,4	1 449,7	247,3	:
Northern Ireland	42,7	40,0	45,0	35,9	1 029,4	1 014,8	1 018,5	1 010,1	203,3	:
Scotland	32,0	31,0	30,9	31,1	4 587,3	5 451,0	5 313,3	5 283,8	505,2	:
Total	280,8	268,6	262,0	248,8	16 469	17 098	16 884	16 827	4 297,8	:
EUR 10	:	6 860,3	6 515,6	6 322,3	:	89 526	88 728	88 230	:	:

52

**ENQUÊTE CE SUR LA STRUCTURE
DES EXPLOITATIONS AGRICOLES**

1975 À 1985

DONNÉES EN 1000

SGM / MBS		AWU / UTA				Number of persons Nombre de personnes				
1983	1985	1975	1979/80	1983	1985	1975	1979/80	1983	1985	

PRINCIPAUX RÉSULTATS D'ENQUÊTE PAR RÉGION

SGM / MBS 1983	1985	1975	1979/80	1983	1985	1975	1979/80	1983	1985	
1 606,0	1 910,6	324,7	310,3	276,1	275,3	473,8	468,7	418,9	426,7	Ireland
										Italia
1 390,2	1 682,8	230,4	180,1	180,1	172,5	426,0	390,6	390,6	368,3	Piemonte
26,2	27,5	8,2	6,2	6,2	6,2	17,5	18,6	18,6	18,7	Val D'Aosta
1 684,0	2 230,3	188,6	142,0	142,0	145,8	315,2	285,2	285,2	290,8	Lombardia
1 519,1	2 006,9	241,3	186,7	186,7	181,9	442,9	451,1	451,1	437,1	Veneto
346,6	438,5	60,0	43,7	43,7	41,4	128,8	119,1	119,1	110,0	Friuli-Venezia Giulia
330,6	496,1	58,1	43,0	43,0	44,2	117,7	97,5	97,5	85,7	Liguria
2 078,1	2 762,6	276,5	194,4	194,4	167,4	416,0	357,8	357,8	341,1	Emilia Romagna
981,2	1 313,6	175,6	129,6	129,6	121,6	289,5	262,5	262,5	243,1	Toscana
288,0	360,1	65,8	42,2	42,2	45,4	114,9	108,1	108,1	92,2	Umbria
470,9	558,2	121,8	78,8	78,8	67,4	201,0	170,7	170,7	160,7	Marche
852,4	1 295,2	168,6	131,8	131,8	137,3	364,4	380,8	380,8	364,4	Lazio
406,6	482,7	108,6	80,6	80,6	73,5	218,4	212,7	212,7	194,7	Abruzzi
153,7	167,1	43,3	26,4	26,4	28,7	89,0	79,5	79,5	83,9	Molise
1 323,8	1 696,7	268,3	211,6	211,6	231,2	525,8	511,5	511,5	556,5	Campania
1 675,7	2 147,7	218,1	190,5	190,5	189,2	467,2	557,6	557,6	530,9	Puglia
337,2	384,2	69,7	44,5	44,5	45,9	148,7	136,9	136,9	129,5	Basilicata
686,4	869,1	140,9	95,6	95,6	109,7	304,3	305,8	305,8	254,6	Calabria
1 705,6	1 988,0	237,3	204,6	204,6	188,4	524,2	550,5	550,5	563,3	Sicilia
596,4	695,6	87,4	72,3	72,3	75,2	168,5	186,7	186,7	177,4	Sardegna
188,2	244,0	32,4	32,8	32,8	31,6	568,0	62,1	62,1	60,8	Bolzano Bozen
128,8	206,4	25,4	19,9	19,9	17,3	63,4	55,7	55,7	43,8	Trento
17 170	22 053	2 826,3	2 157,3	2 157,3	2 121,8	5 911,4	5 301,0	5 301,0	5 107,5	Total
91,63	82,35	12,37	9,05	7,75	7,21	15,79	12,26	10,47	10,11	Luxembourg
5 995,6	5 953,8	253,7	242,2	243,4	234,4	331,6	302,4	304,7	295,2	Nederland
										United Kingdom
473,9	523,7	29,2	28,3	25,2	25,7	34,7	33,6	32,6	32,9	North
762,0	908,6	48,9	42,7	39,7	38,6	57,3	50,6	50,6	48,8	Yorkshire and Humberside
942,0	1 177,9	56,1	45,4	43,3	43,8	65,5	54,6	55,7	54,3	East Midlands
885,6	1 102,0	53,0	48,7	41,2	35,7	59,6	55,3	50,2	44,4	East Anglia
1 250,9	1 497,8	97,3	79,8	81,7	78,2	110,2	92,8	101,9	98,2	South East
1 222,5	1 355,3	88,1	84,8	74,8	73,3	109,8	109,4	100,8	99,0	South West
738,5	839,6	51,8	45,7	42,9	41,9	60,4	55,2	56,3	53,2	West Midlands
351,0	406,9	33,1	28,4	25,4	27,3	40,2	34,8	33,6	35,3	North West
679,2	686,3	56,5	54,2	49,5	51,8	69,0	67,4	65,6	67,5	Wales
383,3	534,8	52,4	52,0	52,7	47,8	79,4	77,6	78,9	17,4	Northern Ireland
1 147,0	1 297,2	59,2	72,7	83,3	73,8	71,5	92,5	76,7	100,2	Scotland
8 835,9	10 330	625,6	582,7	559,7	537,9	757,6	723,8	702,9	651,2	Total
74 809	86 821	:	7 323,5	7 013,2	6 897,4	:	13 835	13 512	12 855	EUR 10

DATA IN 1000

	Farm type 1 – Field crops OTE 1 – Agriculture générale				Farm type 2 – Horticulture OTE 2 – Horticulture			
	1975	1979/80	1983	1985	1975	1979/80	1983	1985

DISTRIBUTION OF THE HOLDINGS BY TYPE OF FARMING

	1975	1979/80	1983	1985	1975	1979/80	1983	1985
Belgie/Belgique	12,8	9,0	9,2	10,2	8,2	10,4	9,0	8,4
Danmark	46,0	43,0	39,2	38,7	3,1	2,6	2,2	1,9
Bundesrepublik Deutschland								
Schleswig-Holstein	3,3	:	4,3	4,1	0,7	–	0,4	0,6
Niedersachsen	20,7	22,7	20,2	19,2	1,8	1,9	1,5	1,6
Nordrhein-Westfalen	15,6	16,3	14,8	14,2	4,8	5,2	4,4	4,1
Hessen	11,8	15,0	14,1	13,1	1,4	1,0	0,9	1,1
Rheinland-Pfalz	10,3	10,5	10,0	8,3	1,0	1,1	1,0	0,9
Baden-Württemberg	20,7	21,2	19,7	18,5	3,0	2,8	2,3	2,5
Bayern	43,0	45,7	44,6	41,4	2,3	2,4	2,2	2,3
Saarland	1,8	:	0,9	0,9	0,2	–	0,1	0,1
Hamburg, Bremen und Berlin	0,2	:	0,1	0,1	1,7	–	1,4	1,3
Total	127,3	137,6	128,6	120,0	17,0	16,8	14,3	14,6
Ellas								
Central Greece and Euboa	:	47,0	36,4	43,7	:	4,0	3,4	2,3
Peloponesos	:	10,0	10,9	11,3	:	5,6	1,9	3,0
Ionian Islands	:	0,6	0,5	0,4	:	0,7	0,5	0,6
Epirus	:	9,9	5,8	9,8	:	1,3	0,7	1,9
Thessaly	:	51,8	48,2	52,5	:	1,5	1,6	1,5
Macedonia	:	129,2	132,7	127,6	:	7,3	3,3	3,1
Thrace	:	42.2	46,4	41,3	:	1,4	0,1	0,4
Aegean Islands	:	3,1	3,5	2,7	:	2,9	1,9	1,2
Crete	:	1,3	0,8	0,8	:	1,6	4,2	5,0
Total	:	295,1	285,1	290,2	:	26,4	17,5	18,9
France								
Île de France	7,1	7,2	7,0	6,5	1,8	1,6	1,4	1,2
Champagne	9,9	10,9	10,9	10,9	0,6	0,2	0,2	0,2
Picardie	9,6	11,2	10,5	10,5	0,5	0,4	0,3	0,3
Haute-Normandie	3,1	3,9	4,2	4,0	0,5	0,4	0,5	0,4
Centre	27,8	28,4	25,4	23,7	1,2	1,2	1,1	1,0
Basse-Normandie	2,2	3,1	3,2	3,6	0,4	0,3	0,3	0,3
Bourgogne	6,7	7,2	7,3	6,9	1,5	1,4	1,3	1,1
Nord	10,2	12,6	11,5	11,5	1,6	1,3	1,2	0,9
Lorraine	2,2	3,0	2,7	2,6	0,6	0,5	0,4	0,3
Alsace	3,8	4,8	5,1	5,6	0,8	1,0	0,7	0,6
Franche-Comté	0,8	0,8	1,1	0,8	0,3	0,2	0,2	0,2
Pays de la Loire	4,8	6,1	6,5	6,6	3,1	3,1	2,5	2,1
Bretagne	10,2	12,8	14,3	12,1	1,1	1,3	1,1	1,2
Poitou-Charentes	6,8	7,6	9,7	10,2	0,7	0,6	0,8	0,7
Aquitaine	13,9	16,6	16,6	17,3	1,5	1,8	2,1	1,3
Midi-Pyrénées	15,9	18,1	19,6	19,2	2,0	1,4	1,3	1,0
Limousin	0,5	0,2	0,3	0,1	0,4	0,2	0,2	0,1
Rhône-Alpes	9,1	10,1	9,1	8,6	1,8	2,3	2,0	1,6
Auvergne	3,0	3,7	4,0	3,3	0,5	0,3	0,3	0,2
Languedoc	1,7	2,6	2,8	2,7	3,3	2,5	2,5	2,2
Provence-Côte-d'Azur	4,8	5,0	5,1	4,3	10,4	10,7	9,5	7,5
Corse	0,2	0,1	0,3	0,0	0,3	0,3	0,3	0,3
Total	154,7	176,3	177,1	171,0	35,1	33,1	30,3	24,7

NOMBRE D'EXPLOITATIONS PAR OTE

Farm type 3 – Permanent crops OTE 3 – Cultures permanentes				Farm type 4 – Grazing livestock OTE 4 – Herbivores				
1975	1979/80	1983	1985	1975	1979/80	1983	1985	
5,9	4,3	3,5	3,2	53,0	50,2	46,7	42,4	Belgie/Belgique
1,6	1,5	1,0	0,9	22,5	24,4	21,3	18,8	Danmark
								Bundesrepublik Deutschland
1,1	–	0,7	0,8	18,9	–	18,6	17,9	Schleswig-Holstein
2,5	2,6	2,7	2,4	36,8	42,1	41,2	42,0	Niedersachsen
1,5	1,9	1,4	1,5	28,5	30,4	29,2	29,0	Nordrhein-Westfalen
2,2	2,1	1,6	1,8	9,8	12,1	12,0	11,6	Hessen
23,9	27,3	25,2	23,9	12,6	13,9	12,3	11,9	Rheinland-Pfalz
14,3	18,4	17,6	17,7	42,1	45,9	43,3	41,9	Baden-Württemberg
3,0	4,1	3,6	4,2	106,3	129,0	125,1	122,1	Bayern
0,3	–	0,2	0,2	1,0	–	1,4	1,1	Saarland
0,4	–	0,3	0,3	1,0	–	0,8	0,6	Hamburg, Bremen und Berlin
49,1	58,1	53,5	52,9	257,1	294,3	283,9	278,2	Total
								Ellas
:	60,1	58,3	59,7	:	9,6	8,9	6,9	Central Greece and Euboa
:	98,9	113,7	117,4	:	5,8	5,3	6,9	Peloponesos
:	21,5	22,4	22,4	:	0,7	0,4	0,4	Ionian Islands
:	12,9	19,2	14,3	:	6,8	9,6	7,9	Epirus
:	25,2	27,9	21,7	:	7,5	7,9	11,1	Thessaly
:	40,1	36,5	40,8	:	9,9	8,1	9,5	Macedonia
:	2,1	0,4	1,1	:	2,3	1,7	2,1	Thrace
:	32,2	29,0	34,6	:	3,9	5,1	3,9	Aegean Islands
:	74,1	78,3	75,7	:	2,9	3,7	2,7	Crete
:	367,1	386,0	387,8	:	49,4	50,5	51,4	Total
								France
0,7	0,9	0,5	0,6	0,5	0,4	0,4	0,3	Île de France
8,8	11,5	11,5	11,5	8,1	8,8	7,2	5,8	Champagne
0,7	0,8	0,8	0,7	7,1	7,5	6,6	5,3	Picardie
0,3	0,4	0,4	0,2	20,6	18,0	16,1	14,0	Haute-Normandie
7,9	7,8	6,7	4,8	9,1	10,4	10,5	9,0	Centre
0,1	0,2	0,2	0,2	60,7	57,0	51,6	46,1	Basse-Normandie
5,8	6,2	5,3	4,9	21,6	21,2	19,1	16,1	Bourgogne
0,2	0,1	0,1	0,1	8,4	8,8	7,9	7,3	Nord
2,1	2,0	1,5	0,9	20,0	19,2	15,6	12,7	Lorraine
7,2	6,9	6,4	5,9	6,1	5,9	5,5	3,9	Alsace
0,8	1,0	0,9	0,7	18,7	18,6	17,1	14,9	Franche-Comté
11,1	12,5	10,3	5,8	69,0	68,3	62,9	54,1	Pays de la Loire
0,4	0,7	0,6	0,3	76,7	71,3	66,4	54,5	Bretagne
15,1	15,1	12,2	7,9	21,1	22,3	18,6	14,9	Poitou-Charentes
16,9	16,5	14,3	13,0	21,9	24,3	22,6	16,1	Aquitaine
7,9	6,9	5,9	4,0	34,6	38,5	37,0	29,5	Midi-Pyrénées
0,4	0,4	0,5	0,3	30,1	31,3	28,0	25,9	Limousin
18,9	17,8	16,3	14,5	54,3	52,2	47,7	38,3	Rhône-Alpes
2,4	1,4	1,1	0,5	41,6	41,9	38,8	34,3	Auvergne
71,6	64,8	58,3	51,7	7,1	7,3	6,6	5,8	Languedoc
30,3	27,0	23,8	19,8	6,0	6,4	5,8	4,3	Provence-Côte d'Azur
3,5	2,4	1,9	1,6	2,5	2,9	2,4	2,0	Corse
213,1	203,2	179,5	150,1	545,8	542,5	494,2	414,8	Total

1975 TO 1985

DATA IN 1000

	Farm type 1 – Field crops OTE 1 – Agriculture générale				Farm type 2 – Horticulture OTE 2 – Horticulture			
	1975	1979/80	1983	1985	1975	1979/80	1983	1985

DISTRIBUTION OF THE HOLDINGS BY TYPE OF FARMING

Ireland	6,0	11,7	9,6	9,7	0,7	0,2	0,1	0,2
Italia								
Piemonte	36,5	42,6	42,6	45,0	1,6	1,9	1,9	1,4
Val D'Aosta	0,2	0,2	0,2	0,3	—	—	—	—
Lombardia	41,6	43,6	43,6	42,1	1,1	1,6	1,6	2,1
Veneto	40,9	74,2	74,2	77,0	2,4	2,5	2,5	3,1
Friuli-Venezia Giulia	14,2	23,3	23,3	26,2	0,5	0,3	0,3	0,5
Liguria	6,3	3,1	3,1	3,9	7,3	8,9	8,9	10,3
Emilia Romagna	52,8	59,2	59,2	65,2	0,9	1,2	1,2	1,0
Toscana	25,2	28,5	28,5	40,9	3,0	3,3	3,3	4,6
Umbria	12,5	17,3	17,3	21,3	0,1	0,2	0,2	0,5
Marche	30,0	40,5	40,5	44,7	0,9	1,2	1,2	1,0
Lazio	31,0	37,5	37,5	29,2	2,4	2,4	2,4	3,1
Abruzzi	31,0	28,8	28,8	35,1	0,3	0,3	0,3	0,5
Molise	15,6	14,6	14,6	13,7	—	0,1	0,1	0,1
Campania	75,5	81,8	81,8	84,3	3,3	3,3	3,3	5,6
Puglia	57,7	58,0	58,0	55,4	1,0	1,2	1,2	1,4
Basilicata	23,7	25,8	25,8	29,1	0,1	—	—	0,1
Calabria	28,4	26,5	26,5	20,0	0,5	0,2	0,2	0,2
Sicilia	101,8	83,9	83,9	78,3	3,5	6,8	6,8	8,8
Sardegna	17,5	16,2	16,2	21,7	0,8	0,6	0,6	0,7
Bolzano Bozen	0,2	0,2	0,2	0,0	0,0	0,0	0,0	0,0
Trento	3,3	1,1	1,1	1,7	0,0	0,0	0,0	0,1
Total	646,0	706,5	706,5	735,1	29,8	36,0	36,0	45,1
Luxembourg	0,2	0,3	0,2	0,3	0,1	0,1	0,1	0,1
Nederland	17,3	15,2	15,9	17,6	20,0	21,1	20,2	18,9
United Kingdom								
North	0,7	:	1,0	1,3	0,2	:	0,1	0,1
Yorkshire and Humberside	5,2	:	4,9	5,4	0,8	:	0,5	0,5
East Midlands	6,4	:	6,5	6,8	1,9	:	0,8	0,8
East Anglia	9,1	:	8,2	8,2	1,1	:	0,5	0,5
South East	5,6	:	6,5	7,2	3,4	:	2,2	2,1
South West	2,3	:	2,7	3,4	1,7	:	0,9	0,9
West Midlands	2,2	:	2,6	3,2	0,9	:	0,7	0,6
North West	1,1	:	1,1	1,3	1,3	:	1,0	0,9
Wales	0,3	:	0,6	0,8	0,1	:	0,2	0,2
Northern Ireland	1,4	:	1,8	1,7	0,1	:	0,2	0,1
Scotland	4,4	:	5,2	6,0	0,3	:	0,4	0,5
Total	38,7	43,3	41,3	45,3	11,8	8,2	7,6	7,2
EUR 10	1 049,0	:	1 127,6	1 147,8	125,8	:	119,7	121,2

ENQUÊTE CE SUR LA STRUCTURE DES EXPLOITATIONS AGRICOLES

1975 À 1985

DONNÉES EN 1000

NOMBRE D'EXPLOITATIONS PAR OTE

Farm type 3 – Permanent crops OTE 3 – Cultures permanentes				Farm type 4 – Grazing livestock OTE 4 – Herbivores				
1975	1979/80	1983	1985	1975	1979/80	1983	1985	
0,3	0,3	0,1	0,2	193,5	178,5	176,5	194,4	Ireland
								Italia
50,2	55,1	55,1	51,5	35,3	34,8	34,8	41,0	Piemonte
0,5	2,5	2,5	2,6	4,7	4,3	4,3	4,2	Val D'Aosta
17,7	23,8	23,8	22,8	49,9	44,9	44,9	45,6	Lombardia
23,2	35,2	35,2	32,4	28,1	32,0	32,0	37,5	Veneto
3,1	5,9	5,9	2,6	5,6	6,2	6,2	7,9	Friuli-Venezia Giulia
22,7	21,2	21,2	19,3	3,4	4,9	4,9	5,5	Liguria
30,2	37,9	37,9	37,8	30,6	26,3	26,3	26,1	Emilia Romagna
49,0	53,5	53,5	36,9	6,4	5,6	5,6	5,5	Toscana
6,4	12,4	12,4	8,4	2,3	2,2	2,2	2,4	Umbria
3,5	7,0	7,0	5,6	4,6	3,1	3,1	5,0	Marche
65,6	88,1	88,1	88,0	14,7	16,5	16,5	18,5	Lazio
18,9	31,1	31,1	28,9	3,9	4,6	4,6	6,1	Abruzzi
2,7	6,9	6,9	7,2	1,7	1,8	1,8	2,5	Molise
66,2	96,3	96,3	89,8	11,3	8,0	8,0	10,7	Campania
168,2	228,9	228,9	227,5	5,3	3,6	3,6	9,9	Puglia
12,7	19,7	19,7	17,3	4,2	3,9	3,9	4,5	Basilicata
74,2	109,9	109,9	115,8	6,2	4,8	4,8	7,3	Calabria
152,2	216,7	216,7	210,8	22,7	17,2	17,2	25,5	Sicilia
26,7	47,9	47,9	44,2	15,5	17,7	17,7	17,7	Sardegna
8,2	8,9	8,9	8,8	8,8	13,0	13,0	12,9	Bolzano Bozen
13,8	15,1	15,1	15,4	4,5	5,8	5,8	5,8	Trento
815,8	1 124,2	1 124,2	1 073,9	269,6	261,2	261,2	302,1	Total
0,9	0,9	0,8	0,8	3,4	2,0	2,0	2,3	Luxembourg
6,7	6,6	6,0	5,8	81,4	73,4	67,8	63,4	Nederland
								United Kingdom
—	:	—	—	9,4	:	8,5	8,8	North
—	:	—	0,1	8,0	:	6,8	7,5	Yorkshire and Humberside
—	:	0,1	0,1	6,5	:	5,6	6,2	East Midlands
0,8	:	0,5	0,5	0,9	:	1,0	1,4	East Anglia
1,9	:	1,3	1,4	8,5	:	7,6	10,2	South East
0,7	:	0,4	0,5	25,8	:	22,6	24,7	South West
0,6	:	0,3	0,4	11,8	:	10,3	11,3	West Midlands
0,1	:	0,1	0,1	8,6	:	7,1	8,1	North West
0,0	:	0,0	0,1	28,4	:	24,3	26,6	Wales
0,3	:	0,3	0,4	29,6	:	26,3	29,8	Northern Ireland
0,3	:	0,2	0,2	19,4	:	17,2	19,6	Scotland
4,7	1,1	3,2	3,8	156,9	148,5	137,3	154,2	Total
1 098,1	:	1 371,6	1 291,5	1 583,2	:	1 490,9	1 470,6	EUR 10

1975 TO 1985

DATA IN 1000

	Farm type 5 – Pigs and poultry OTE 5 – Granivores				Farm type 6 – Mixed cropping OTE 6 – Polyculture			
	1975	1979/80	1983	1985	1975	1979/80	1983	1985

DISTRIBUTION OF THE HOLDINGS BY TYPE OF FARMING

	1975	1979/80	1983	1985	1975	1979/80	1983	1985
Belgie/Belgique	9,1	6,5	5,7	5,4	6,9	4,9	3,8	4,3
Danmark	1,0	4,3	3,5	3,7	7,8	6,5	4,1	3,5
Bundesrepublik Deutschland								
Schleswig-Holstein	1,7	–	1,6	1,3	0,8	–	0,6	0,7
Niedersachsen	6,2	5,6	6,1	7,2	7,0	5,9	4,1	3,7
Nordrhein-Westfalen	5,4	4,3	5,1	5,5	6,0	5,5	4,4	4,2
Hessen	0,5	0,4	0,6	0,5	5,8	5,6	4,3	4,5
Rheinland-Pfalz	0,7	0,5	0,6	0,6	8,1	5,6	4,4	4,3
Baden-Württemberg	1,2	1,0	1,4	1,6	15,3	13,9	11,5	10,7
Bayern	1,8	1,7	2,3	2,1	12,5	9,1	7,4	8,1
Saarland	0,1	–	0,0	0,1	0,6	–	0,2	0,2
Hamburg, Bremen und Berlin	0,1	–	0,0	0,0	0,1	–	0,1	–
Total	17,6	15,8	17,7	18,8	56,1	46,8	37,0	36,5
Ellas								
Central Greece and Euboa	:	1,6	1,9	1,6	:	33,5	28,2	26,6
Peloponesos	:	0,7	0,9	0,7	:	39,0	31,2	22,0
Ionian Islands	:	0,1	0,0	0,0	:	8,2	8,2	7,4
Epirus	:	1,0	1,0	0,8	:	12,0	9,5	10,0
Thessaly	:	0,8	1,0	0,8	:	13,6	9,5	9,2
Macedonia	:	2,6	1,4	0,8	:	30,3	24,3	19,6
Thrace	:	0,2	0,1	0,2	:	4,8	1,0	1,8
Aegean Islands	:	0,4	0,4	0,2	:	14,2	12,2	11,8
Crete	:	0,4	0,3	0,4	:	14,3	8,6	7,2
Total	:	7,8	7,1	5,5	:	169,9	132,6	115,6
France								
Île de France	0,1	0,1	0,2	0,1	0,4	0,5	0,3	0,5
Champagne	0,1	0,3	0,2	0,1	1,1	1,0	0,7	0,9
Picardie	0,2	0,5	0,3	0,2	0,7	0,4	0,2	0,4
Haute-Normandie	0,3	0,2	0,2	0,2	0,2	0,2	0,2	0,5
Centre	0,5	0,5	0,5	0,3	5,8	4,9	3,6	5,8
Basse-Normandie	0,2	0,2	0,1	0,2	0,2	0,2	0,2	0,4
Bourgogne	0,2	0,5	0,3	0,2	1,8	1,3	1,0	1,7
Nord	0,7	0,7	0,6	0,5	3,2	2,6	1,8	1,9
Lorraine	0,2	0,3	0,3	0,2	1,6	0,7	1,0	1,5
Alsace	0,1	0,1	0,1	0,1	2,5	1,9	1,8	2,6
Franche-Comté	0,3	0,3	0,3	0,2	0,2	0,2	0,2	0,5
Pays de la Loire	1,1	1,1	1,1	1,1	3,7	3,1	2,7	5,8
Bretagne	3,7	5,6	6,2	6,2	1,3	1,3	1,6	4,1
Poitou-Charentes	0,6	0,5	0,4	0,7	9,6	7,7	6,8	9,8
Aquitaine	0,5	0,9	0,7	0,6	13,5	10,5	8,0	11,7
Midi-Pyrénées	0,7	0,8	0,7	0,7	13,6	10,3	8,9	12,1
Limousin	0,1	0,2	0,1	0,1	0,7	0,3	0,3	0,3
Rhône-Alpes	1,0	1,4	1,2	1,0	10,6	8,2	7,7	9,8
Auvergne	0,3	0,2	0,2	0,2	1,6	1,2	1,2	2,1
Languedoc	0,2	0,3	0,2	0,2	4,0	4,3	3,3	5,6
Provence-Côte d'Azur	0,3	0,6	0,5	0,4	5,7	4,3	3,0	5,8
Corse	0,1	0,2	0,2	0,1	0,3	0,2	0,1	0,3
Total	11,5	15,5	14,5	13,6	82,2	65,3	54,6	84,1

Farm type 7 – Mixed livestock OTE 7 – Polyélevage				Farm type 8 – Crops-livestock OTE 8 – Cultures-élevage				
1975	1979/80	1983	1985	1975	1979/80	1983	1985	
								NOMBRE D'EXPLOITATIONS PAR OTE
17,3	11,6	8,9	7,6	23,9	17,7	15,1	16,0	Belgie/Belgique
18,7	12,3	6,4	5,7	31,5	28,2	21,1	19,2	Danmark
								Bundesrepublik Deutschland
5,0	–	1,9	1,7	6,1	–	4,0	4,4	Schleswig-Holstein
32,1	21,4	16,7	17,5	31,0	27,7	24,7	20,8	Niedersachsen
29,4	19,4	16,4	15,4	26,9	24,4	21,3	20,1	Nordrhein-Westfalen
16,6	9,6	7,2	7,2	25,7	21,0	17,8	16,4	Hessen
6,5	3,7	2,9	2,6	16,0	12,2	9,8	9,2	Rheinland-Pfalz
27,9	19,6	15,4	14,8	35,2	29,5	25,1	23,0	Baden-Württemberg
32,8	22,4	17,6	17,5	89,3	59,8	50,3	47,6	Bayern
0,5	–	0,3	0,3	2,0	0,0	1,0	0,9	Saarland
0,1	–	0,1	0,1	0,1	0,0	0,1	0,1	Hamburg, Bremen und Berlin
150,8	99,2	78,4	77,0	232,5	181,3	154,2	142,5	Total
								Ellas
:	4,7	5,7	3,6	:	9,4	9,9	9,6	Central Greece and Euboa
:	4,9	3,4	4,0	:	7,1	6,3	6,0	Peloponesos
:	0,5	0,5	0,5	:	1,3	0,9	0,9	Ionian Islands
:	2,9	3,6	4,1	:	6,9	5,5	7,2	Epirus
:	1,9	1,2	2,8	:	6,5	6,5	7,0	Thessaly
:	2,0	1,7	1,8	:	10,9	10,9	13,9	Macedonia
:	0,3	0,1	0,2	:	3,2	2,7	3,3	Thrace
:	3,0	4,8	3,2	:	4,3	5,7	6,1	Aegean Islands
:	1,1	1,1	0,9	:	3,5	3,6	3,9	Crete
:	21,2	22,2	21,1	:	53,0	52,0	57,9	Total
								France
0,0	0,1	0,0	0,0	0,8	0,6	0,4	0,5	Île de France
0,5	0,3	0,2	0,6	4,7	3,8	3,5	4,1	Champagne
0,7	0,3	0,4	0,7	8,2	6,6	5,8	5,1	Picardie
0,8	0,5	0,4	1,0	5,1	4,4	4,3	4,4	Haute-Normandie
2,6	1,9	1,5	3,2	13,1	10,8	9,2	8,2	Centre
0,9	0,5	0,3	2,0	2,7	3,1	3,0	2,7	Basse-Normandie
2,8	1,1	0,9	1,9	8,9	7,5	5,5	5,8	Bourgogne
3,4	2,4	1,7	1,9	12,0	9,8	8,2	6,7	Nord
2,5	1,5	1,3	3,3	6,6	6,4	6,1	5,6	Lorraine
2,3	1,4	0,8	1,1	6,4	5,5	3,8	3,4	Alsace
0,9	0,6	0,4	1,5	2,9	2,7	2,0	1,9	Franche-Comté
8,3	5,5	4,4	6,5	11,0	10,4	8,2	10,2	Pays de la Loire
19,8	14,0	10,0	12,2	11,1	10,9	8,6	10,2	Bretagne
5,7	3,2	2,4	3,6	13,0	12,4	10,0	9,2	Poitou-Charentes
11,9	8,1	6,1	7,2	20,9	18,8	14,7	13,3	Aquitaine
16,9	11,0	8,6	10,9	20,3	17,0	13,8	12,6	Midi-Pyrénées
3,4	1,5	1,4	2,2	3,4	2,3	2,2	1,5	Limousin
8,3	5,9	5,0	10,0	13,3	12,0	9,7	9,8	Rhône-Alpes
3,9	2,6	2,2	4,3	5,6	5,2	3,6	3,1	Auvergne
0,6	0,1	0,3	0,8	1,7	1,6	1,4	1,1	Languedoc
0,8	0,6	0,6	1,0	2,0	1,8	1,5	2,1	Provence-Côte d'Azur
0,4	0,4	0,2	0,4	0,7	0,5	0,3	0,4	Corse
97,5	63,5	49,3	76,5	174,3	154,1	125,8	121,9	Total

1975 TO 1985

DATA IN 1000

	Farm type 5 – Pigs and poultry OTE 5 – Granivores				Farm type 6 – Mixed cropping OTE 6 – Polyculture			
	1975	1979/80	1983	1985	1975	1979/80	1983	1985

DISTRIBUTION OF THE HOLDINGS BY TYPE OF FARMING

	1975	1979/80	1983	1985	1975	1979/80	1983	1985
Ireland	1,7	1,5	1,4	1,6	0,7	0,7	0,5	0,7
Italia								
Piemonte	1,9	1,3	1,3	2,0	38,7	28,7	28,7	25,1
Val D'Aosta	0,0	0,0	0,0	0,0	0,4	0,6	0,6	0,6
Lombardia	3,5	2,9	2,9	4,1	9,4	7,7	7,7	6,1
Veneto	2,0	1,2	1,2	3,0	32,6	35,6	35,6	28,3
Friuli-Venezia Giulia	0,4	0,3	0,3	0,4	12,8	10,7	10,7	7,2
Liguria	0,1	0,1	0,1	0,4	11,5	7,9	7,9	6,4
Emilia Romagna	3,5	2,4	2,4	1,6	27,6	23,5	23,5	18,7
Toscana	1,1	0,4	0,4	1,1	26,3	28,4	28,4	27,0
Umbria	2,1	0,4	0,4	1,3	10,3	15,2	15,2	12,9
Marche	1,1	0,4	0,4	0,6	16,5	19,4	19,4	16,3
Lazio	0,6	0,4	0,4	0,6	29,6	32,5	32,5	32,0
Abruzzi	0,3	0,2	0,2	0,2	25,5	27,9	27,9	21,2
Molise	0,2	0,1	0,1	0,1	14,0	12,3	12,3	11,7
Campania	0,6	0,4	0,4	0,4	51,6	46,7	46,7	40,7
Puglia	0,2	0,1	0,1	0,1	28,0	30,6	30,6	27,0
Basilicata	0,4	0,1	0,1	0,6	20,3	17,9	17,9	13,4
Calabria	2,1	0,2	0,2	0,1	38,9	30,0	30,0	24,5
Sicilia	1,3	0,4	0,4	0,1	40,5	41,2	41,2	35,5
Sardegna	1,0	0,5	0,5	0,4	15,7	13,7	13,7	11,9
Bolzano Bozen	0,1	0,1	0,1	0,0	0,6	0,2	0,2	0,0
Trento	0,1	0,0	0,0	0,1	4,3	1,6	1,6	0,6
Total	22,5	11,9	11,9	17,1	454,9	432,1	432,1	367,1
Luxembourg	0,0	0,1	0,0	0,1	0,1	0,8	0,6	0,1
Nederland	11,3	12,1	12,0	12,8	3,6	4,4	4,0	3,4
United Kingdom								
North	0,2	:	0,2	0,2	0,0	:	0,1	0,1
Yorkshire and Humberside	1,2	:	0,9	0,9	0,6	:	0,4	0,4
East Midlands	1,0	:	0,7	0,6	1,0	:	0,7	0,6
East Anglia	1,4	:	0,9	0,8	1,2	:	0,6	0,6
South East	2,1	:	1,5	1,4	1,5	:	1,2	1,3
South West	1,5	:	1,2	1,3	0,7	:	0,5	0,7
West Midlands	0,7	:	0,7	0,7	0,9	:	0,6	0,6
North West	1,1	:	0,7	0,7	0,4	:	0,4	0,4
Wales	0,2	:	0,4	0,5	0,1	:	0,1	0,1
Northern Ireland	1,4	:	1,1	0,9	0,2	:	0,3	0,1
Scotland	0,8	:	0,5	0,5	0,5	:	0,4	0,4
Total	11,6	10,2	8,6	8,7	7,1	5,9	5,2	5,4
EUR 10	86,3	:	75,3	81,8	619,4	:	542,0	505,0

Farm type 7 – Mixed livestock OTE 7 – Polyélevage				Farm type 8 – Crops-livestock OTE 8 – Cultures-élevage				
1975	1979/80	1983	1985	1975	1979/80	1983	1985	

NOMBRE D'EXPLOITATIONS PAR OTE

1975	1979/80	1983	1985	1975	1979/80	1983	1985	
4,3	2,3	1,8	1,3	11,6	14,4	12,2	11,0	Ireland
								Italia
13,2	0,0	0,0	7,7	27,2	21,6	21,6	10,2	Piemonte
0,6	0,3	0,3	0,2	0,8	1,0	1,0	0,8	Val D'Aosta
8,0	3,8	3,8	4,9	15,3	13,2	13,2	11,2	Lombardia
26,2	13,6	13,6	12,4	33,0	23,3	23,3	21,5	Veneto
7,2	3,2	3,2	2,7	14,8	8,0	8,0	6,7	Friuli-Venezia Giulia
1,9	0,9	0,9	1,1	3,9	3,1	3,1	2,4	Liguria
9,4	4,6	4,6	2,8	19,8	10,0	10,0	7,2	Emilia Romagna
5,6	3,0	3,0	2,8	11,3	6,5	6,5	9,3	Toscana
6,6	2,2	2,2	2,2	9,4	4,3	4,3	4,1	Umbria
7,4	2,1	2,1	1,6	19,5	7,3	7,3	5,5	Marche
10,9	6,4	6,4	8,0	17,4	12,5	12,5	14,1	Lazio
5,6	4,2	4,2	4,8	14,2	8,0	8,0	7,4	Abruzzi
2,8	1,8	1,8	1,3	5,9	4,3	4,3	4,9	Molise
12,2	6,5	6,5	7,7	24,3	13,8	13,8	13,6	Campania
2,9	1,4	1,4	0,8	5,4	4,0	4,0	4,8	Puglia
6,8	2,4	2,4	3,8	8,8	5,4	5,4	5,9	Basilicata
9,5	2,5	2,5	2,2	14,3	6,0	6,0	8,1	Calabria
5,1	2,4	2,4	2,4	13,7	8,9	8,9	8,4	Sicilia
6,0	3,8	3,8	3,8	7,4	7,6	7,6	6,1	Sardegna
2,8	0,2	0,2	0,5	1,3	0,8	0,8	0,8	Bolzano Bozen
1,4	0,6	0,6	0,3	3,8	2,0	2,0	1,9	Trento
152,0	72,3	72,3	73,9	271,3	171,3	171,3	164,2	Total
0,7	0,9	0,6	0,3	1,0	:	:	0,6	Luxembourg
13,2	9,3	6,8	7,5	8,8	6,7	5,9	6,6	Nederland
								United Kingdom
0,2	:	0,1	0,1	1,1	:	1,0	1,0	North
0,6	:	0,4	0,4	2,5	:	1,8	1,5	Yorkshire and Humberside
0,5	:	0,2	0,2	2,5	:	1,7	1,6	East Midlands
0,3	:	0,1	0,2	1,6	:	0,9	0,7	East Anglia
0,8	:	0,5	0,6	3,2	:	2,4	2,2	South East
1,3	:	0,7	0,9	3,4	:	2,8	3,1	South West
0,9	:	0,4	0,4	2,6	:	2,2	2,1	West Midlands
0,8	:	0,3	0,3	0,8	:	0,5	0,6	North West
0,5	:	0,2	0,5	0,9	:	0,8	0,9	Wales
3,1	:	1,1	0,8	3,7	:	2,6	2,1	Northern Ireland
0,7	:	0,3	0,2	4,8	:	4,3	3,8	Scotland
9,7	5,7	4,3	4,6	27,1	23,8	20,9	19,6	Total
464,2	:	228,9	254,4	782,0	:	526,6	501,6	EUR 10

1975 TO 1985

DATA IN 1000

	Farm type 1 – Field crops OTE 1 – Agriculture générale				Farm type 2 – Horticulture OTE 2 – Horticulture			
	1975	1979/80	1983	1985	1975	1979/80	1983	1985

DISTRIBUTION OF THE SGM BY TYPE OF FARMING

	1975	1979/80	1983	1985	1975	1979/80	1983	1985
Belgie/Belgique	151,1	220,0	236,9	300,6	112,2	231,9	233,4	254,6
Danmark	483,9	665,5	719,1	823,1	48,5	93,3	84,8	103,0
Bundesrepublik Deutschland								
Schleswig-Holstein	75,0	–	200,9	234,6	16,9	–	18,7	29,2
Niedersachsen	260,3	453,0	478,5	519,6	36,6	56,1	52,2	66,1
Nordrhein-Westfalen	148,4	254,2	251,5	286,0	139,7	178,7	156,5	175,0
Hessen	51,0	98,4	106,2	107,7	28,9	33,0	29,3	37,4
Rheinland-Pfalz	57,0	79,6	87,8	88,1	17,3	20,7	25,8	23,1
Baden-Württemberg	71,6	108,4	119,5	126,6	67,8	85,0	71,3	88,6
Bayern	244,9	367,2	390,0	449,5	59,8	67,0	69,0	77,2
Saarland	5,0	–	4,6	5,0	6,6	–	3,4	3,7
Hamburg, Bremen und Berlin	1,5	–	1,7	1,6	46,6	–	47,0	55,3
Total	914,5	1 562,8	1 640,7	1 818,7	420,1	518,1	473,2	555,5
Ellas								
Central Greece and Euboa	:	192,8	160,2	297,3	:	27,1	22,7	21,6
Peloponesos	:	47,7	66,1	102,9	:	42,8	8,7	25,6
Ionian Islands	:	1,4	0,2	0,5	:	1,5	0,4	0,3
Epirus	:	27,7	7,6	32,7	:	3,8	1,3	10,7
Thessaly	:	279,5	295,7	425,0	:	11,4	8,9	6,8
Macedonia	:	509,6	511,8	691,6	:	54,4	19,4	23,3
Thrace	:	157,4	165,1	228,7	:	15,0	1,1	3,7
Aegean Islands	:	12,6	6,I	8,0	:	10,7	7,3	5,1
Crete	:	2,4	1,5	2,3	:	3,8	29,3	61,1
Total	:	1 231,1	1 214,2	1 789,2	:	170,3	99,0	158,3
France								
Île de France	252,3	437,4	444,5	463,9	70,5	108,2	123,9	70,3
Champagne	310,3	549,2	581,2	715,5	11,4	11,2	10,4	6,2
Picardie	390,6	705,1	727,4	860,9	12,7	13,9	13,0	60,8
Haute-Normandie	102,3	202,0	207,4	220,9	14,2	19,2	18,8	8,6
Centre	546,6	939,6	983,2	1 042,3	43,8	77,5	122,3	432,5
Basse-Normandie	37,6	83,9	98,2	106,6	10,3	13,7	14,1	5,3
Bourgogne	132,4	237,9	278,7	297,7	26,0	38,4	45,3	22,2
Nord	184,4	370,5	377,6	378,6	31,1	48,8	58,6	32,0
Lorraine	22,6	59,0	79,2	94,6	17,1	19,4	15,4	8,2
Alsace	25,5	53,1	62,9	102,6	14,2	19,4	25,9	14,0
Franche-Comté	8,4	17,7	23,1	24,1	4,9	7,4	6,2	3,7
Pays de la Loire	38,1	71,8	90,6	138,0	147,7	237,4	252,3	140,7
Bretagne	57,3	109,5	124,4	131,4	35,8	76,5	96,7	49,9
Poitou-Charentes	69,2	136,4	189,7	313,6	14,0	19,0	28,2	16,5
Aquitaine	109,2	216,2	252,6	375,9	40,5	72,4	104,5	54,9
Midi-Pyrénées	126,9	245,4	326,0	422,5	28,7	35,3	66,4	23,2
Limousin	2,2	2,0	1,9	2,3	6,2	7,9	5,8	3,0
Rhône-Alpes	56,0	100,4	97,0	124,1	36,1	77,7	86,3	57,0
Auvergne	29,1	53,4	63,8	61,2	9,9	15,5	14,8	3,6
Languedoc	16,6	43,0	41,9	59,2	63,9	110,1	114,2	73,5
Provence-Côte d'Azur	35,9	49,7	57,0	84,2	274,0	506,0	547,3	355,0
Corse	0,5	0,5	0,8	0,8	4,0	7,0	9,1	5,6
Total	2 554,1	4 683,6	5 109,1	6 020,9	916,8	1 541,9	1 779,4	1 446,8

DONNÉES EN 1000

Farm type 3 – Permanent crops OTE 3 – Cultures permanentes				Farm type 4 – Grazing livestock OTE 4 – Herbivores				
1975	1979/80	1983	1985	1975	1979/80	1983	1985	

DISTRIBUTION DE LA MBS OTE

1975	1979/80	1983	1985	1975	1979/80	1983	1985	
48,7	76,1	77,0	91,4	342,3	709,0	738,6	730,7	Belgie/Belgique
19,2	33,1	28,7	36,3	301,4	648,6	688,3	683,9	Danmark
								Bundesrepublik Deutschland
44,0	—	78,4	85,2	251,9	—	495,1	498,9	Schleswig-Holstein
51,7	92,4	100,4	97,0	315,3	714,3	822,9	942,5	Niedersachsen
29,2	62,3	68,5	84,5	161,5	370,8	421,6	464,8	Nordrhein-Westfalen
16,1	38,1	34,3	44,0	55,4	127,6	145,1	163,0	Hessen
155,1	408,8	414,5	450,5	70,8	151,3	152,4	171,5	Rheinland-Pfalz
87,6	143,5	147,7	165,2	211,2	414,5	432,4	487,0	Baden-Württemberg
27,5	53,6	53,2	74,0	677,6	1 446,0	1 547,7	1 724,0	Bayern
3,1	—	2,4	5,2	7,2	—	21,4	21,6	Saarland
8,1	—	9,1	11,8	6,0	—	10,1	8,6	Hamburg, Bremen und Berlin
422,5	895,8	908,6	1 017,4	1 757,0	3 707,3	4 048,7	4 481,9	Total
								Ellas
:	115,2	78,9	68,1	:	51,4	46,3	45,7	Central Greece and Euboa
:	292,7	285,2	378,8	:	39,5	60,4	58,6	Peloponesos
:	47,1	41,5	40,1	:	4,7	3,1	3,6	Ionian Islands
:	33,5	38,4	33,1	:	26,1	37,5	32,1	Epirus
:	121,5	92,5	104,9	:	51,8	48,6	134,8	Thessaly
:	151,9	132,1	182,2	:	61,7	50,5	62,1	Macedonia
:	5,6	0,4	0,5	:	13,1	10,6	14,6	Thrace
:	38,1	39,9	53,0	:	17,7	24,3	29,6	Aegean Islands
:	200,8	201,8	221,4	:	29,7	40,9	56,1	Crete
:	1 006,3	910,6	1 082,3	:	295,8	322,2	437,4	Total
								France
15,1	31,7	23,4	27,9	3,9	5,5	4,5	5,2	Île de France
164,0	290,9	303,6	559,0	87,8	151,0	143,5	143,3	Champagne
18,3	40,6	34,6	45,3	65,8	115,1	126,4	135,9	Picardie
5,7	12,1	12,4	12,1	132,3	208,8	206,6	222,9	Haute-Normandie
43,2	88,0	89,3	171,6	59,7	115,5	128,7	172,1	Centre
2,5	10,4	7,0	7,8	405,5	660,0	662,0	690,3	Basse-Normandie
89,1	163,4	171,6	200,0	185,0	327,1	340,8	339,8	Bourgogne
4,2	7,2	6,2	9,5	63,6	115,4	131,0	169,8	Nord
4,6	8,6	9,1	10,2	165,6	287,3	283,0	300,8	Lorraine
41,1	69,8	75,4	112,5	29,1	57,9	67,1	63,7	Alsace
2,9	6,8	5,7	12,9	148,9	254,4	248,6	278,9	Franche-Comté
60,5	127,0	113,7	142,9	543,3	943,7	1 011,3	1 085,3	Pays de la Loire
6,1	13,2	22,4	25,5	487,0	859,5	928,6	1 021,3	Bretagne
130,0	216,1	197,7	190,7	175,0	326,4	307,2	295,8	Poitou-Charentes
172,8	282,1	291,9	422,4	119,3	207,1	232,6	200,5	Aquitaine
53,3	72,8	73,8	104,0	214,0	432,7	437,5	415,6	Midi-Pyrénées
7,1	11,9	12,0	6,7	199,9	358,9	369,3	363,5	Limousin
144,6	253,6	260,7	352,8	270,4	456,4	453,3	413,6	Rhône-Alpes
6,0	5,4	3,5	4,7	295,3	532,0	530,3	504,1	Auvergne
509,4	810,8	770,5	915,7	50,6	94,4	92,0	90,2	Languedoc
199,7	329,2	331,9	430,1	35,7	59,1	54,8	67,0	Provence-Côte d'Azur
39,8	58,5	51,2	43,9	12,0	25,5	24,3	26,4	Corse
1 719,9	2 910,0	2 867,5	3 808,3	3 749,4	6 593,6	6 783,5	7 006,1	Total

1975 TO 1985

DATA IN 1000

	Farm type 1 – Field crops OTE 1 – Agriculture générale				Farm type 2 – Horticulture OTE 2 – Horticulture			
	1975	1979/80	1983	1985	1975	1979/80	1983	1985

DISTRIBUTION OF THE SGM BY TYPE OF FARMING

	1975	1979/80	1983	1985	1975	1979/80	1983	1985
Ireland	28,3	117,8	109,3	124,6	4,4	6,9	1,9	7,4
Italia								
Piemonte	126,3	331,6	331,6	445,6	16,2	64,3	64,3	59,0
Val D'Aosta	0,5	0,8	0,8	0,4	0,0	0,0	0,0	0,0
Lombardia	118,9	359,5	359,5	509,7	21,7	75,4	75,4	137,6
Veneto	135,1	451,5	451,5	568,8	15,3	69,2	69,2	209,1
Friuli-Venezia Giulia	30,5	97,8	97,8	140,7	2,8	11,8	11,8	43,8
Liguria	6,3	7,2	7,2	10,9	61,1	217,6	217,6	392,9
Emilia Romagna	203,3	503,2	503,2	698,5	11,4	55,5	55,5	304,0
Toscana	77,3	214,2	214,2	313,7	30,8	103,6	103,6	282,1
Umbria	37,9	105,6	105,6	148,9	0,3	4,7	4,7	13,3
Marche	84,1	230,2	230,2	301,9	4,9	12,5	12,5	8,0
Lazio	95,7	205,0	205,0	256,1	65,1	115,2	115,2	385,6
Abruzzi	43,1	89,5	89,5	118,0	1,8	6,7	6,7	18,7
Molise	32,5	67,4	67,4	72,3	0,1	0,9	0,9	0,3
Campania	172,4	454,2	454,2	533,1	25,7	142,7	142,7	288,8
Puglia	202,2	470,0	470,0	533,7	13,0	53,2	53,2	365,2
Basilicata	63,9	173,7	173,7	195,4	1,8	–	–	1,7
Calabria	38,0	67,8	67,8	88,0	6,6	8,7	8,7	68,1
Sicilia	147,2	229,4	229,4	215,9	65,6	219,2	219,2	392,9
Sardegna	79,6	160,2	160,3	209,2	14,9	21,0	21,0	15,2
Bolzano Bozen	0,8	0,3	0,3	0,0	1,4	1,0	1,0	0,5
Trento	3,5	1,7	1,7	2,2	0,3	0,6	0,6	6,4
Total	1 699,0	4 220,7	4 220,7	5 363,1	360,7	1 183,7	1 183,7	2 993,1
Luxembourg	0,5	1,6	1,3	1,3	0,4	0,8	0,5	0,6
Nederland	352,7	670,2	703,6	838,1	402,1	1 176,0	1 256,7	1 286,5
United Kingdom								
North	27,9	:	64,8	102,0	1,6	:	1,4	2,7
Yorkshire and Humberside	165,1	:	366,6	515,9	12,0	:	9,9	21,3
East Midlands	219,7	:	575,6	721,7	83,1	:	22,0	65,3
East Anglia	291,0	:	663,5	846,2	36,5	:	10,4	37,7
South East	206,7	:	587,4	743,5	48,9	:	42,5	88,9
South West	58,0	:	170,1	224,9	24,4	:	14,3	29,2
West Midlands	65,1	:	182,9	256,6	13,1	:	13,3	20,6
North West	15,6	:	33,5	54,0	16,1	:	16,4	32,0
Wales	4,2	:	12,9	19,3	2,1	:	1,5	3,5
Northern Ireland	8,1	:	22,5	32,9	4,7	:	4,3	5,1
Scotland	117,1	:	330,1	459,1	2,4	:	3,9	4,2
Total	1 178,5	2 849,7	3 009,9	3 976,0	244,9	150,3	139,9	310,6
EUR 10	7 362,6	:	15 750,6	19 266,4	2 510,1	:	5 153,5	6 958,0

ENQUÊTE CE SUR LA STRUCTURE DES EXPLOITATIONS AGRICOLES

1975 À 1985

DONNÉES EN 1000

Farm type 3 – Permanent crops OTE 3 – Cultures permanentes				Farm type 4 – Grazing livestock OTE 4 – Herbivores				
1975	1979/80	1983	1985	1975	1979/80	1983	1985	

DISTRIBUTION DE LA MBS PAR OTE

1975	1979/80	1983	1985	1975	1979/80	1983	1985	
3,3	3,7	2,7	4,9	762,9	1 262,4	1 289,5	1 535,1	Ireland
								Italia
116,5	240,3	240,3	269,8	144,7	327,7	327,7	468,4	Piemonte
0,5	3,1	3,1	3,9	11,8	19,7	19,7	20,9	Val D'Aosta
37,7	104,0	104,0	132,4	408,4	676,2	676,2	879,9	Lombardia
93,9	191,5	191,5	252,7	98,8	309,2	309,2	422,6	Veneto
13,4	35,6	35,6	51,1	6,3	27,3	27,3	40,3	Friuli-Venezia Giulia
29,9	61,1	61,1	47,4	4,1	12,6	12,6	10,9	Liguria
206,1	500,4	500,4	646,9	157,6	344,1	344,1	394,6	Emilia Romagna
180,7	307,5	307,5	307,9	17,3	30,0	30,0	64,4	Toscana
9,3	29,5	29,5	22,3	17,7	19,9	19,9	27,4	Umbria
12,6	34,1	34,1	32,7	15,2	25,8	25,8	48,3	Marche
95,1	214,7	214,7	260,1	43,6	97,8	97,8	142,0	Lazio
40,3	123,2	123,2	133,0	14,8	34,6	34,6	56,3	Abruzzi
2,6	13,8	13,8	13,6	3,3	7,3	7,3	15,2	Molise
153,0	380,5	380,5	409,5	33,9	50,8	50,8	78,6	Campania
323,6	833,9	833,9	894,0	16,5	35,3	35,3	53,8	Puglia
11,8	46,1	46,1	67,5	10,2	20,7	20,7	22,7	Basilicata
196,2	436,1	436,1	494,4	14,5	23,5	23,5	45,6	Calabria
465,4	893,0	893,0	939,8	42,1	87,5	87,5	122,1	Sicilia
32,4	87,9	87,9	67,0	71,8	151,7	151,7	218,6	Sardegna
37,9	103,3	103,3	139,7	26,2	75,1	75,1	93,8	Bolzano Bozen
32,2	78,7	78,7	140,0	12,5	34,5	34,5	44,7	Trento
2 091,0	4 718,3	4 718,3	5 325,5	1 171,2	2 411,3	2 411,4	3 271,4	Total
4,2	11,8	11,7	8,1	43,8	49,4	52,6	56,7	Luxembourg
127,1	335,0	195,5	201,5	1 396,6	2 596,5	2 790,8	2 503,6	Nederland
								United Kingdom
0,3	:	0,2	0,7	114,9	:	312,9	322,7	North
0,0	:	0,4	2,8	68,1	:	185,7	187,8	Yorkshire and Humberside
2,6	:	1,0	5,5	60,5	:	142,2	156,5	East Midlands
21,4	:	14,4	21,1	7,6	:	16,3	17,1	East Anglia
104,9	:	56,9	73,4	89,0	:	177,4	186,9	South East
5,2	:	6,2	10,8	302,8	:	738,9	765,9	South West
11,2	:	10,3	18,8	113,9	:	308,9	311,0	West Midlands
4,5	:	0,9	4,8	94,1	:	229,3	239,3	North West
0,2	:	1,1	1,6	214,2	:	617,1	612,7	Wales
2,4	:	1,5	6,6	125,4	:	290,9	399,9	Northern Ireland
2,8	:	3,1	2,9	251,3	:	540,9	575,4	Scotland
155,5	21,0	95,9	149,0	1 441,8	3 475,4	3 560,6	3 775,3	Total
4 591,4	:	8 905,9	10 642,4	10 966,4	:	22 364,1	24 044,7	EUR 10

I C 10

DATA IN 1000

	Farm type 5 – Pigs and poultry OTE 5 – Granivores				Farm type 6 – Mixed cropping OTE 6 – Polyculture			
	1975	1979/80	1983	1985	1975	1979/80	1983	1985

DISTRIBUTION OF THE SGM BY TYPE OF FARMING

	1975	1979/80	1983	1985	1975	1979/80	1983	1985
Belgie/Belgique	97,4	120,7	133,8	174,0	71,1	98,0	84,3	115,2
Danmark	16,1	133,1	169,3	224,8	86,1	105,3	75,0	87,9
Bundesrepublik Deutschland								
Schleswig-Holstein	11,8	–	12,0	14,8	22,3	–	23,1	30,5
Niedersachsen	69,2	78,7	87,7	112,1	91,4	114,0	90,7	93,4
Nordrhein-Westfalen	54,4	88,9	105,2	126,3	62,1	84,4	67,7	79,5
Hessen	7,3	12,3	11,4	13,4	32,8	41,5	38,7	43,4
Rheinland-Pfalz	8,4	11,1	10,6	15,7	82,8	100,9	91,9	97,3
Baden-Württemberg	10,7	20,3	27,9	44,7	79,5	106,0	99,1	109,8
Bayern	12,9	26,2	25,2	42,7	89,4	92,7	79,2	94,4
Saarland	1,2	–	1,8	2,4	2,1	–	1,2	1,8
Hamburg, Bremen und Berlin	0,6	–	0,7	0,8	1,5	–	1,1	1,6
Total	176,6	255,3	282,5	373,0	463,7	573,5	492,7	551,8
Ellas								
Central Greece and Euboa	:	34,6	20,9	31,9	:	100,6	75,5	94,7
Peloponesos	:	8,0	5,7	5,2	:	162,0	103,5	91,8
Ionian Islands	:	0,5	0,1	0,0	:	16,1	12,8	16,2
Epirus	:	10,2	16,7	14,1	:	30,8	17,7	22,0
Thessaly	:	6,2	4,8	7,2	:	86,7	36,2	53,1
Macedonia	:	17,2	10,3	15,1	:	183,7	117,9	116,8
Thrace	:	1,5	0,6	0,7	:	32,9	2,7	14,2
Aegean Islands	:	2,8	2,7	0,4	:	34,7	27,7	37,5
Crete	:	4,4	2,8	3,8	:	39,4	29,2	34,0
Total	:	85,2	64,5	78,5	:	686,9	423,2	480,4
France								
Île de France	1,7	1,9	1,6	1,8	11,2	17,0	14,6	14,5
Champagne	1,4	2,0	2,2	2,7	25,4	42,0	37,0	52,6
Picardie	2,1	4,7	1,2	3,0	25,1	30,3	27,7	23,3
Haute-Normandie	2,8	3,9	4,5	5,3	5,3	11,0	11,3	14,6
Centre	6,0	10,2	7,1	8,8	48,2	79,3	60,2	77,7
Basse-Normandie	2,5	4,6	5,3	9,1	3,8	5,1	7,2	6,1
Bourgogne	3,1	10,0	3,1	3,8	17,0	28,8	24,0	36,9
Nord	4,8	14,3	16,4	15,4	59,6	86,8	64,4	52,2
Lorraine	1,5	3,5	4,8	7,7	4,4	7,5	6,4	7,3
Alsace	1,7	1,3	2,9	2,8	14,3	19,4	20,1	25,7
Franche-Comté	2,3	6,7	8,0	8,6	1,1	0,9	2,8	1,9
Pays de la Loire	17,0	37,5	43,6	58,4	32,4	46,4	40,7	60,0
Bretagne	85,1	263,7	310,3	381,9	16,0	19,1	25,8	23,5
Poitou-Charentes	5,6	13,6	13,9	21,5	89,2	133,6	127,2	172,2
Aquitaine	6,1	14,2	23,4	28,5	96,2	123,4	115,2	169,0
Midi-Pyrénées	11,8	18,7	16,8	20,3	84,2	118,0	107,1	148,9
Limousin	0,7	1,1	1,5	5,0	5,2	4,3	4,0	3,5
Rhône-Alpes	13,0	42,1	41,6	49,7	59,0	80,4	76,5	107,5
Auvergne	2,6	5,7	6,2	9,1	7,5	9,3	11,2	13,0
Languedoc	2,8	6,4	6,5	7,6	40,2	70,9	65,2	115,3
Provence-Côte d'Azur	5,7	15,4	13,3	15,5	52,0	72,1	68,9	120,0
Corse	0,2	1,1	1,1	0,6	1,6	2,3	1,0	3,7
Total	180,3	482,5	535,3	667,2	699,1	1 008,0	918,4	1 249,3

Farm type 7 – Mixed livestock OTE 7 – Polyélevage				Farm type 8 – Crops-livestock OTE 8 – Cultures-élevage				
1975	1979/80	1983	1985	1975	1979/80	1983	1985	

DISTRIBUTION DE LA MBS PAR OTE

189,7	245,5	216,3	219,9	283,6	403,5	383,8	440,0	Belgie/Belgique
255,0	322,6	195,1	207,4	425,4	667,2	607,4	688,5	Danmark
								Bundesrepublik Deutschland
89,4	–	47,6	52,6	132,8	–	155,8	192,4	Schleswig-Holstein
370,2	421,1	365,9	441,0	372,3	554,4	540,3	500,5	Niedersachsen
321,8	387,0	358,3	391,8	281,0	429,6	409,5	438,7	Nordrhein-Westfalen
117,2	124,7	103,1	109,1	163,7	233,3	216,9	212,6	Hessen
50,2	52,3	42,4	42,7	102,3	132,1	119,0	119,4	Rheinland-Pfalz
208,4	242,0	200,4	223,3	219,9	291,5	275,2	299,7	Baden-Württemberg
223,1	266,0	214,5	253,1	634,2	714,3	643,1	727,0	Bayern
5,1	–	4,6	4,1	13,2	–	9,9	8,7	Saarland
0,8	–	1,1	1,5	1,2	–	2,0	2,3	Hamburg, Bremen und Berlin
1 386,3	1 565,9	1 338,0	1 519,2	1 920,7	2 552,8	2 371,6	2 501,4	Total
								Ellas
:	17,0	15,2	14,5	–	45,4	33,0	42,9	Central Greece and Euboa
:	24,5	14,5	16,8	–	33,4	19,1	27,4	Peloponesos
:	1,5	1,3	2,3	–	2,2	1,3	1,8	Ionian Islands
:	9,5	11,5	12,1	–	27,6	14,9	23,8	Epirus
:	10,3	4,6	18,3	–	43,4	34,2	41,8	Thessaly
:	9,4	7,1	11,4	–	54,1	50,8	72,2	Macedonia
:	2,2	0,2	1,0	–	18,1	16,1	27,3	Thrace
:	10,9	19,2	15,7	–	11,0	15,1	22,1	Aegean Islands
:	6,3	6,0	7,9	–	15,5	14,9	20,0	Crete
:	91,7	79,5	100,1	–	250,8	199,4	279,3	Total
								France
0,8	0,2	0,2	–	18,6	18,5	15,2	17,1	Île de France
6,8	8,4	4,1	6,8	92,0	146,9	142,5	152,9	Champagne
9,6	11,9	11,9	12,2	159,9	224,7	193,2	211,1	Picardie
11,8	12,2	11,3	10,4	96,6	146,5	144,7	152,0	Haute-Normandie
23,4	28,3	29,9	43,6	175,0	249,2	231,2	210,4	Centre
13,6	18,4	18,7	31,1	36,0	64,3	66,8	78,1	Basse-Normandie
26,4	24,3	17,5	24,5	128,7	202,3	178,8	175,8	Bourgogne
44,3	55,9	50,4	47,8	175,5	239,2	211,6	218,2	Nord
20,9	20,0	14,1	27,1	87,8	149,1	142,1	147,8	Lorraine
12,0	13,6	10,4	13,9	51,8	79,7	61,0	65,5	Alsace
5,4	6,2	4,0	10,4	28,2	40,6	34,3	32,3	Franche-Comté
90,0	123,2	116,6	138,0	101,5	166,6	144,4	196,8	Pays de la Loire
273,7	408,0	348,8	341,1	103,4	157,1	133,2	148,5	Bretagne
56,3	55,8	48,1	55,3	148,2	232,0	211,8	224,8	Poitou-Charentes
75,1	104,6	82,8	84,6	151,2	244,5	212,1	230,8	Aquitaine
113,1	135,4	114,7	128,9	154,1	218,0	209,6	207,7	Midi-Pyrénées
22,9	20,6	24,5	26,6	17,7	21,1	21,3	15,1	Limousin
46,7	57,3	55,9	83,4	89,4	149,3	124,2	152,4	Rhône-Alpes
30,6	36,7	37,7	45,4	45,7	62,9	46,6	45,5	Auvergne
3,7	2,7	3,9	7,4	11,8	18,1	17,9	21,9	Languedoc
5,1	10,1	4,8	9,2	14,6	14,5	18,8	28,9	Provence-Côte d'Azur
2,6	3,2	2,1	2,8	3,2	3,3	2,6	3,8	Corse
894,8	1 157,0	1 012,3	1 150,6	1 890,9	2 848,2	2 563,8	2 737,3	Total

1975 TO 1985

DATA IN 1000

	Farm type 5 – Pids and poultry OTE 5 – Granivores				Farm type 6 – Mixed cropping OTE 6 – Polyculture			
	1975	1979/80	1983	1985	1975	1979/80	1983	1985

DISTRIBUTION OF THE SGM BY TYPE OF FARMING

Ireland	19,9	32,0	33,5	38,6	7,0	13,0	11,6	30,7
Italia								
Piemonte	23,2	32,1	32,1	38,4	93,7	141,2	141,2	128,6
Val D'Aosta	:	:	:	:	0,3	0,4	0,4	0,8
Lombardia	97,3	131,9	131,9	249,5	18,2	53,2	53,2	42,8
Veneto	43,7	57,8	57,8	89,8	109,1	156,0	156,0	178,4
Friuli-Venezia Giulia	4,0	12,5	12,5	6,0	32,3	70,6	70,6	52,7
Liguria	0,3	0,6	0,6	0,0	17,1	24,4	24,4	23,2
Emilia Romagna	71,0	115,7	115,7	142,7	193,7	327,3	327,3	373,4
Toscana	15,3	6,4	6,4	21,3	126,7	212,4	212,4	204,9
Umbria	22,0	11,5	11,5	19,9	28,8	58,7	58,7	76,8
Marche	14,0	12,3	12,3	8,9	51,0	90,5	90,5	102,5
Lazio	6,0	5,7	5,7	5,8	60,1	98,9	98,9	127,9
Abruzzi	3,0	3,3	3,3	3,1	45,4	86,7	86,7	83,1
Molise	0,8	1,0	1,0	2,4	18,2	37,9	37,9	35,6
Campania	4,5	7,6	7,6	26,8	101,2	198,7	198,7	235,8
Puglia	1,5	2,4	2,4	0,4	104,1	212,8	212,8	229,0
Basilicata	2,7	0,7	0,7	1,9	30,1	54,0	54,0	49,8
Calabria	7,5	1,5	1,5	3,1	74,6	109,4	109,4	97,3
Sicilia	8,6	3,1	3,1	1,7	114,2	181,1	181,1	191,7
Sardegna	6,4	4,5	4,5	3,6	45,7	68,3	68,3	67,4
Bolzano Bozen	0,4	0,3	0,3	—	2,2	1,9	1,9	0,0
Trento	1,8	1,2	1,2	0,9	4,7	3,1	3,1	2,5
Total	333,8	412,0	412,0	626,3	1 271,4	2 187,5	2 187,5	2 304,5
Luxembourg	0,2	0,7	0,5	0,4	0,4	13,8	10,3	0,7
Nederland	181,9	354,4	433,9	517,0	58,1	224,3	196,4	127,4
United Kingdom								
North	3,7	:	6,7	3,7	1,8	:	5,1	6,2
Yorkshire and Humberside	27,8	:	41,8	33,2	22,7	:	34,2	33,1
East Midlands	12,0	:	30,6	16,4	51,5	:	52,7	83,9
East Anglia	31,3	:	42,5	26,7	52,5	:	60,6	79,4
South East	37,8	:	46,1	25,0	57,7	:	88,3	118,3
South West	26,5	:	29,9	19,2	21,6	:	17,0	26,2
West Midlands	11,5	:	20,8	11,6	33,0	:	35,8	46,0
North West	14,3	:	16,0	10,4	9,3	:	18,6	24,0
Wales	4,5	:	7,6	4,4	2,0	:	2,7	3,4
Northern Ireland	15,8	:	12,7	23,0	2,4	:	4,3	3,4
Scotland	9,0	:	18,7	10,2	14,8	:	20,0	21,4
Total	194,2	266,3	273,4	183,8	269,3	313,8	339,3	445,3
EUR 10	1 200,4	:	2 274,3	2 805,0	2 926,2	:	4 315,7	4 912,8

Farm type 7 – Mixed livestock OTE 7 – Polyélevage				Farm type 8 – Crops-livestock OTE 8 – Cultures-élevage				
1975	1979/80	1983	1985	1975	1979/80	1983	1985	

DISTRIBUTION DE LA MBS PAR OTE

29,5	30,1	27,3	29,6	76,2	148,1	130,2	139,8	Ireland
								Italia
49,4	50,2	50,2	68,8	108,9	202,8	202,8	204,3	Piemonte
0,7	0,3	0,3	0,1	1,3	1,9	1,9	1,4	Val D'Aosta
50,7	71,7	71,7	60,4	117,2	212,2	212,2	217,9	Lombardia
74,4	88,8	88,8	84,6	123,3	194,8	194,8	201,0	Veneto
13,4	25,8	25,8	23,6	42,9	65,2	65,2	80,3	Friuli-Venezia Giulia
1,9	1,7	1,7	4,1	4,3	5,4	5,4	6,7	Liguria
67,3	70,8	70,8	51,5	149,1	161,2	161,2	150,9	Emilia Romagna
24,4	33,9	33,9	38,5	40,9	73,2	73,2	80,8	Toscana
23,4	21,3	21,3	17,3	29,2	36,7	36,7	34,3	Umbria
21,6	12,0	12,0	12,5	68,5	53,5	53,5	43,3	Marche
26,3	26,2	26,2	40,1	52,7	89,0	89,0	77,5	Lazio
12,6	24,5	24,5	25,9	34,3	38,1	38,1	43,8	Abruzzi
4,0	7,1	7,1	6,4	11,1	18,3	18,3	21,2	Molise
22,8	25,8	25,8	37,4	49,7	63,6	63,6	86,7	Campania
13,2	16,9	16,9	14,0	26,7	51,1	51,1	57,6	Puglia
11,9	10,2	10,2	12,9	17,6	31,9	31,9	32,3	Basilicata
17,3	12,5	12,5	18,7	27,8	26,9	26,9	53,8	Calabria
20,6	22,0	22,0	22,5	51,3	70,4	70,4	101,4	Sicilia
29,3	35,4	35,4	43,5	27,3	67,3	67,3	71,2	Sardegna
4,8	0,9	0,9	2,8	3,3	5,4	5,4	7,2	Bolzano Bozen
1,6	1,5	1,5	1,2	5,0	7,5	7,5	8,4	Trento
491,7	559,6	559,6	586,8	992,3	1 476,4	1 476,5	1 581,8	Total
6,8	19,6	14,5	6,5	7,2	0,2	0,2	8,1	Luxembourg
224,2	278,5	231,7	280,1	156,7	215,7	186,9	199,6	Nederland
								United Kingdom
3,9	:	5,3	3,3	29,7	:	77,3	82,3	North
9,5	:	13,8	10,8	60,8	:	109,4	103,9	Yorkshire and Humberside
3,0	:	7,3	5,1	69,1	:	110,6	123,6	East Midlands
3,8	:	5,2	5,8	51,8	:	72,7	68,0	East Anglia
14,6	:	16,6	12,4	132,3	:	235,6	249,3	South East
28,5	:	39,2	31,5	99,5	:	206,8	247,4	South West
18,0	:	19,9	12,5	77,4	:	146,6	162,6	West Midlands
11,7	:	12,2	8,3	17,6	:	24,2	34,2	North West
4,9	:	6,7	3,5	14,8	:	29,8	37,9	Wales
24,3	:	14,8	20,4	20,0	:	32,2	43,5	Northern Ireland
14,8	:	12,9	9,5	93,2	:	217,5	214,5	Scotland
137,0	162,9	154,0	122,8	666,2	1 336,9	1 262,8	1 367,2	Total
3 615,0	:	3 748,8	4 122,9	6 419,2	:	8 983,0	9 663,7	EUR 10

DATA IN 1000 — DONNÉES EN 1000

NUMBER OF HOLDINGS BY SIZE GROUPS — NOMBRE D'EXPLOITATIONS PAR CLASSES DE GRANDEURS

YEAR ANNÉE	EUR 12	EUR 10	B	DK	D	EL	ES	F	IRL	I	L	NL	P	UK
From 1 to less than 5 ha														**1 à moins de 5 ha**
1960	:	4 029,6	96,3	34,8	617,4	658,4	:	464,3	56,9	1 880,0	3,26	87,7	:	130,5
1967	:	:	54,7	21,8	487,6	:	:	374,9	55,7	1 700,7	1,90	70,5	:	118,0
1970	:	3 087,4	44,2	16,6	405,8	596,0	:	325,7	54,6	1 542,9	1,48	42,5	:	57,6
1975	:	2 728,5	31,6	15,5	311,7	544,0	:	248,0	34,4	1 467,6	1,07	35,8	:	38,8
1977	:	2 682,4	29,0	14,4	287,5	519,0	:	228,0	33,5	1 501,1	0,99	33,0	:	35,9
1978	:	:	28,2	13,9	281,2	:	:	221,0	:	:	0,96	32,5	:	36,1
1979	:	:	26,9	13,6	261,4	:	:	237,0	:	:	0,95	31,9	:	37,6
1980	:	:	25,9	12,9	257,8	:	:	234,0	34,0	:	0,91	31,0	:	29,4
1981	:	:	25,2	12,2	250,9	541,3	:	228,0	:	:	0,76	29,2	:	27,7
1982	:	:	24,5	11,7	243,6	:	849,5	218,0	:	1 312,3	0,74	29,5	:	28,8
1983	:	:	24,1	2,2	232,9	484,1	:	214,0	34,2	:	0,75	29,5	:	30,4
1984	:	:	23,8	2,1	228,8	:	:	206,0	:	:	0,77	29,6	:	27,7
1985	:	:	23,5	1,9	224,2	491,7	:	195,0	35,2	1 272,7	0,76	29,2	:	29,4
1986	:	:	22,0	1,8	219,3	:	:	185,0	:	:	0,75	28,9	:	:
From 5 to less than 10 ha														**De 5 à moins de 10 ha**
1960	:	1 712,0	52,7	54,3	343,0	172,7	:	375,8	65,8	525,0	1,90	62,2	:	58,4
1967	:	:	39,4	37,5	271,8	:	:	306,9	59,5	450,2	1,24	49,2	:	50,6
1970	:	1 244,0	33,1	30,1	232,7	164,3	:	250,5	56,4	397,4	0,99	39,6	:	39,3
1975	:	1 044,0	23,4	25,1	179,0	155,2	:	185,0	37,7	373,7	0,68	30,7	:	34,0
1977	:	1 012,0	20,9	23,2	165,7	150,6	:	174,0	37,6	377,4	0,60	28,9	:	32,9
1978	:	:	19,9	22,5	161,2	:	:	169,0	:	:	0,58	28,0	:	32,8
1979	:	:	19,0	21,6	153,2	:	:	167,0	:	:	0,54	27,1	:	32,6
1980	:	:	18,1	20,5	149,1	:	:	165,0	35,4	:	0,51	26,1	:	31,2
1981	:	:	17,4	19,5	144,4	149,9	:	151,0	:	:	0,49	25,2	:	30,0
1982	:	:	16,8	18,5	140,5	:	274,2	147,0	:	322,3	0,44	24,6	:	30,0
1983	:	:	16,4	17,3	136,0	149,0	:	140,0	33,9	:	0,41	24,3	:	29,9
1984	:	:	15,9	16,1	133,0	:	:	135,0	:	:	0,41	23,7	:	30,2
1985	:	:	15,4	15,4	130,0	138,8	:	130,0	34,7	318,1	0,40	22,9	:	30,0
1986	:	:	14,9	14,7	126,3	:	:	125,0	:	:	0,39	22,2	:	:
From 10 to less than 20 ha														**De 10 à moins de 20 ha**
1960	:	1 329,0	35,2	54,5	286,5	38,9	:	472,7	83,5	230,0	2,74	53,9	:	72,1
1967	:	:	35,2	51,0	288,6	:	:	413,2	82,5	207,4	1,96	55,4	:	59,7
1970	:	1 115,5	33,5	44,0	267,8	42,8	:	354,8	81,5	187,5	1,55	52,1	:	49,8
1975	:	936,0	28,5	36,7	211,7	46,2	:	275,0	70,6	179,2	1,03	44,0	:	43,3
1977	:	895,0	26,7	34,3	199,4	47,9	:	252,0	67,4	183,8	0,85	41,2	:	41,4
1978	:	:	25,9	33,5	194,1	:	:	243,0	:	:	0,80	39,9	:	40,7
1979	:	:	25,0	32,1	186,5	:	:	243,0	:	:	0,73	38,6	:	40,2
1980	:	:	24,3	30,8	181,3	:	:	240,0	67,7	:	0,68	37,3	:	39,8
1981	:	:	23,6	29,2	176,4	46,6	:	228,0	:	:	0,63	36,1	:	39,2
1982	:	:	22,9	28,1	172,1	:	183,1	223,0	:	166,8	0,59	35,1	:	38,5
1983	:	:	22,3	26,9	167,0	53,5	:	218,0	65,7	:	0,01	34,3	:	38,3
1984	:	:	21,7	25,5	163,3	:	:	210,0	:	:	0,60	33,3	:	38,2
1985	:	:	21,0	24,1	159,3	53,1	:	200,0	63,8	168,1	0,52	32,2	:	37,7
1986	:	:	20,2	22,7	155,1	:	:	190,0	:	:	0,50	31,0	:	:
From 20 to less than 50 ha														**De 20 à moins de 50 ha**
1960	:	820,0	12,3	43,7	122,0	6,9	:	362,9	57,6	88,2	2,27	24,5	:	99,4
1967	:	:	15,5	44,4	141,0	:	:	371,8	58,5	84,4	2,52	25,9	:	86,1
1970	:	850,0	17,1	44,1	157,6	8,8	:	369,6	59,4	82,2	2,62	27,9	:	80,5
1975	:	867,0	18,8	42,4	176,1	11,3	:	361,0	65,6	86,6	2,29	30,1	:	72,7
1977	:	865,0	19,1	41,8	178,9	12,6	:	352,0	67,0	91,4	2,11	30,4	:	70,1
1978	:	:	19,1	41,4	178,0	:	:	347,0	:	:	1,96	30,4	:	69,1
1979	:	:	19,1	40,9	178,5	:	:	347,0	:	:	1,90	30,6	:	68,1
1980	:	:	19,1	40,4	177,9	:	:	345,0	66,6	:	1,81	30,8	:	67,6
1981	:	:	19,0	39,7	176,4	12,4	:	339,0	:	:	1,67	30,9	:	66,6
1982	:	:	19,0	38,9	174,4	:	132,8	339,0	:	86,9	1,60	31,0	:	65,7
1983	:	:	19,1	37,9	173,1	18,3	:	330,0	67,5	:	1,50	31,3	:	64,8
1984	:	:	19,1	37,0	171,4	:	:	325,0	:	:	1,49	31,6	:	64,4
1985	:	:	19,0	35,9	170,0	18,1	:	321,0	66,8	92,7	1,34	31,9	:	63,5
1986	:	:	19,0	35,1	168,4	:	:	316,0	:	:	1,30	32,0	:	:
50 ha and over														**50 ha et plus**
1960	:	265,0	2,2	6,4	16,3	0,7	:	97,8	14,7	33,1	0,18	2,0	:	82,7
1967	:	:	2,4	7,8	17,4	:	:	109,1	14,8	34,6	0,25	2,2	:	78,6
1970	:	291,0	2,6	8,7	19,3	0,9	:	120,4	14,9	37,5	0,30	2,5	:	84,3
1975	:	325,0	3,4	10,1	26,2	1,3	:	140,0	19,6	37,5	0,52	3,2	:	82,8
1977	:	330,0	3,6	10,7	28,3	1,5	:	143,0	19,5	38,2	0,65	3,5	:	81,5
1978	:	:	3,7	11,0	29,1	:	:	146,0	:	:	0,69	3,6	:	81,4
1979	:	:	3,8	11,5	30,3	:	:	149,0	:	:	0,75	3,7	:	81,4
1980	:	:	3,8	11,8	31,3	:	:	151,0	19,7	:	0,79	3,8	:	81,3
1981	:	:	3,9	12,2	32,4	1,6	:	152,0	:	:	0,85	4,0	:	81,0
1982	:	:	4,0	12,6	33,5	:	84,4	153,0	:	38,0	0,87	4,1	:	81,0
1983	:	:	4,1	13,1	34,8	3,8	:	158,0	19,7	:	0,91	4,2	:	80,9
1984	:	:	4,2	13,8	36,0	:	:	169,0	:	:	0,90	4,4	:	81,1
1985	:	:	4,3	14,1	37,3	4,6	:	176,0	19,6	40,0	0,98	4,6	:	81,1
1986	:	:	4,4	14,5	38,6	:	:	184,0	:	:	1,00	4,8	:	:
Total														**Total**
1960	:	8 147,3	198,7	193,7	1 385,2	877,6	:	1 773,5	278,5	2 756,3	10,4	230,3	:	443,1
1967	:	:	147,2	162,5	1 206,4	:	:	1 575,9	271,0	2 477,3	7,9	203,2	:	393,0
1970	:	6 588,3	130,5	143,5	1 083,2	812,8	:	1 421,0	266,8	2 247,5	6,9	164,6	:	311,5
1975	:	5 900,7	105,7	129,8	904,7	758,0	:	1 209,0	227,9	2 144,6	5,6	143,8	:	271,6
1977	:	5 785,0	99,3	124,4	859,8	731,6	:	1 149,0	225,0	2 191,9	5,2	137,0	:	261,8
1978	:	:	96,8	122,3	843,6	:	:	1 126,0	:	:	5,0	134,4	:	260,1
1979	:	:	93,8	119,7	809,9	:	:	1 143,0	:	:	4,9	131,9	:	259,9
1980	:	:	91,2	116,4	797,4	:	:	1 135,0	223,4	:	4,7	129,0	:	249,3
1981	:	:	89,1	112,8	780,5	751,8	:	1 098,0	:	:	4,4	125,4	:	244,5
1982	:	:	87,2	109,8	764,1	:	1 524,0	1 080,0	:	1 926,3	4,2	124,3	:	244,0
1983	:	:	86,0	97,4	743,8	708,7	:	1 060,0	221,0	:	4,2	123,6	:	244,3
1984	:	:	84,7	94,5	732,5	:	:	1 045,0	:	:	4,2	122,6	:	241,6
1985	:	:	83,2	91,4	720,8	706,3	:	1 022,0	220,1	1 891,6	4,0	120,8	:	241,7
1986	:	:	80,5	88,8	707,7	:	:	1 000,0	:	:	3,9	118,9	:	:

DATA IN 1000   DONNÉES EN 1000

YEAR ANNÉE	EUR 12	EUR 10	B	DK	D	EL	ES	F	IRL	I	L	NL	P	UK
AA BY SIZE OF HOLDINGS														**SAU PAR CLASSES DE GRANDEUR**
From 1 to less than 5 ha														*De 1 à moins de 5 ha*
1960	:	10 297,0	257,0	105,5	1 622,0	1 658,3	:	1 252,5	170,0	4 660,0	8,44	223,0	:	339,3
1967	:	:	147,9	62,7	1 268,2	:		1 014,7	165,0	4 210,3	5,10	175,6		312,5
1970	:	7 658,0	118,5	47,0	1 058,0	1 495,1		871,4	161,8	3 632,0	3,93	114,4		156,1
1975	:	6 630,0	81,6	44,4	802,7	1 310,0		666,0	100,2	3 413,6	2,84	95,5		112,9
1977	:	6 464,0	74,5	41,4	737,3	1 217,1		590,0	93,8	3 512,8	2,65	88,5		105,7
1978	:	:	72,2	40,0	720,1			560,0			2,54	86,8		106,3
1979	:	:	69,1	38,9	670,7			621,0			2,51	84,6		109,5
1980	:	:	66,7	37,1	659,5			620,0	98,0		2,43	82,1		82,9
1981	:	:	65,1	35,0	641,1	1 342,0		605,0			2,06	79,0		76,2
1982	:	:	63,3	33,7	622,8		2 007,0	578,0		3 022,5	2,00	77,8		78,8
1983	:	:	62,5	7,0	596,4	1 209,0		560,0	97,5		2,11	77,6		83,1
1984	:	:	61,7	5,8	585,4			496,0			2,11	77,7		75,5
1985	:	:	60,7	5,7	572,7	1 213,9		473,0	99,6	2 907,3	2,08	76,3		79,6
1986	:	:	59,7	5,1	559,7	:		450,0			2,06	75,2		:
From 5 to less than 10 ha														*De 5 à moins de 10 ha*
1960	:	12 259,0	375,6	389,4	2 483,2	1 143,2	:	2 779,7	490,0	3 700,0	13,98	456,6	:	427,2
1967	:	:	285,8	272,0	1 976,7			2 260,7	440,0	3 176,3	9,08	364,0		375,9
1970	:	8 839,0	241,0	211,7	1 691,4	1 092,6		1 845,6	420,9	2 747,1	7,31	290,2		281,3
1975	:	7 319,0	171,3	183,4	1 301,6	990,0		1 340,0	284,9	2 570,1	5,00	226,0		247,0
1977	:	7 049,0	153,3	169,2	1 205,3	938,5		1 270,0	283,0	2 572,6	4,41	212,7		240,0
1978	:	:	145,7	164,4	1 173,3			1 220,0			4,25	205,7		238,4
1979	:	:	139,5	157,6	1 115,3			1 219,0			3,92	199,1		237,6
1980	:	:	132,6	150,0	1 086,0			1 215,0	264,9		3,76	191,7		230,8
1981	:	:	127,7	142,4	1 051,7	1 004,2		1 132,0			3,55	185,1		222,6
1982	:	:	123,2	135,2	1 023,9		1 894,7	1 102,0		2 229,4	3,22	180,6		221,8
1983	:	:	120,4	127,0	991,3	1 005,6		1 005,0	256,0		2,96	177,7		221,0
1984	:	:	116,4	118,1	969,2			950,0			2,97	173,4		224,0
1985	:	:	112,3	113,1	947,1	931,7		260,5	260,5	2 187,5	2,85	167,6		221,7
1986	:	:	108,0	107,2	920,0	:		900,0			2,83	162,0		:
From 10 to less than 20 ha														*De 10 à moins de 20 ha*
1960	:	18 724,0	487,8	770,0	3 990,5	498,1	:	6 784,5	1 180,0	3 170,0	40,06	749,8	:	1 053,0
1967	:	:	493,0	702,5	4 101,2			5 959,6	1 170,0	2 861,9	29,16	773,7		871,0
1970	:	15 855,0	472,1	628,5	3 847,9	553,0		5 164,6	1 156,6	2 548,7	22,98	736,7		724,0
1975	:	13 296,0	407,1	530,2	3 073,8	565,0		3 990,0	1 019,0	2 436,7	15,20	630,3		628,8
1977	:	12 706,0	383,4	497,6	2 892,3	571,0		3 690,0	975,9	2 485,3	12,58	591,4		606,1
1978	:	:	372,0	485,0	2 816,5			3 570,0			11,84	573,6		595,8
1979	:	:	360,0	465,7	2 711,3			3 559,0			10,84	555,0		588,9
1980	:	:	349,7	447,5	2 635,2			3 550,0	977,7		10,13	536,6		581,4
1981	:	:	340,8	424,3	2 564,1	609,0		3 420,0			9,54	520,8		570,9
1982	:	:	331,4	408,7	2 502,9		2 522,9	3 345,0		2 278,9	8,94	507,0		560,5
1983	:	:	322,4	391,1	2 429,8	699,7		3 150,0	948,9		9,04	494,8		558,6
1984	:	:	314,1	369,9	2 376,2			2 950,0			9,10	481,5		555,8
1985	:	:	304,7	349,5	2 319,0	702,0		2 800,0	923,9	2 287,3	7,71	465,3		546,9
1986	:	:	293,6	329,2	2 256,9	:		2 780,0			7,30	448,7		:
From 20 to less than 50 ha														*De 20 à moins de 50 ha*
1960	:	24 561,0	347,8	1 240,5	3 504,5	185,3	:	10 931,9	1 730,0	2 640,0	64,99	701,9	:	3 214,6
1967	:	:	439,8	1 283,0	4 009,2			11 274,4	1 760,0	2 531,5	76,38	739,3		2 785,9
1970	:	25 591,0	487,3	1 310,0	4 494,9	243,2		11 345,2	1 786,0	2 440,1	81,41	794,0		2 610,3
1975	:	26 397,0	548,5	1 290,7	5 200,1	282,0		11 220,0	2 005,1	2 559,4	75,35	866,6		2 368,9
1977	:	26 581,0	561,1	1 280,0	5 281,2	301,8		11 110,0	2 048,9	2 738,9	70,41	881,0		2 308,0
1978	:	:	563,0	1 273,1	5 300,5			11 050,0			66,44	885,5		2 276,0
1979	:	:	565,9	1 262,6	5 340,5			10 962,0			64,22	893,3		2 246,1
1980	:	:	566,0	1 248,7	5 342,9			10 960,0	2 037,6		61,85	902,6		2 228,9
1981	:	:	566,8	1 233,4	5 320,7	340,8		10 900,1			57,20	908,5		2 194,8
1982	:	:	568,3	1 213,9	5 276,1		4 070,2	10 900,0		2 594,7	55,05	914,4		2 169,0
1983	:	:	570,4	1 187,7	5 249,9	531,7		10 874,0	2 067,4		52,20	925,7		2 143,2
1984	:	:	572,1	1 161,7	5 215,5			10 500,0			52,51	938,9		2 127,8
1985	:	:	572,7	1 133,3	5 188,6	507,8		10 160,0	2 037,4	2 584,4	46,68	951,5		2 099,2
1986	:	:	573,7	1 112,2	5 154,7	:		10 060,0			45,54	955,5		
50 ha and over														**50 ha et plus**
1960	:	25 516,0	166,0	545,0	1 334,6	56,3	:	8 413,2	1 190,0	4 490,9	11,72	151,8	:	9 157,3
1967	:	:	182,6	733,3	1 416,4			9 532,4	1 200,0	4 815,3	15,45	175,8		9 365,7
1970	:	34 054,0	197,8	757,1	1 552,6	188,9		10 596,5	1 206,5	5 513,3	19,24	197,6		13 922,7
1975	:	36 806,0	253,8	887,1	2 083,8	94,0		12 230,0	1 667,4	5 207,9	33,12	255,3		14 093,8
1977	:	36 983,0	271,5	937,8	2 227,8	96,3		12 590,0	1 666,3	4 961,3	42,09	278,9		13 910,9
1978	:	:	280,2	960,3	2 294,9			12 750,0			44,55	286,2		13 946,6
1979	:	:	285,8	994,2	2 365,8			12 483,0			48,71	294,1		13 947,9
1980	:	:	292,0	1 020,7	2 448,8			13 050,0	1 670,2		51,68	300,2		13 999,2
1981	:	:	298,5	1 060,9	2 534,4	133,4		13 200,0			55,69	310,2		13 910,3
1982	:	:	308,4	1 095,1	2 619,9		12 881,4	13 306,0		5 279,6	57,60	318,6		13 904,3
1983	:	:	315,1	1 133,0	2 716,5	343,8		13 650,0	1 666,8		60,95	326,2		13 880,5
1984	:	:	322,9	1 199,3	2 806,0			14 371,0			61,30	337,8		13 893,5
1985	:	:	331,5	1 232,6	2 905,0	642,7		14 850,0	1 674,2	4 982,0	66,61	351,7		13 890,4
1986	:	:	340,3	1 265,2	3 018,2	:		14 050,0			69,05	364,6		
Total														**Total**
1960	:	91 356	1 634	3 050	12 935	3 541	:	30 162	4 760	18 661	139,2	2 283	:	14 191
1967	:	:	1 549	3 054	12 272			30 042	4 735	17 595	135,2	2 228		13 711
1970	:	91 997	1 517	2 954	12 645	3 573		29 823	4 732	16 881	134,9	2 133		17 694
1975	:	90 448	1 462	2 936	12 462	3 241		29 446	5 077	16 188	131,5	2 074		17 451
1977	:	89 783	1 444	2 926	12 344	3 125		29 250	5 068	16 271	132,1	2 053		17 171
1978	:	:	1 433	2 923	12 305			29 150			129,6	2 038		17 163
1979	:	:	1 420	2 919	12 204			28 844			130,2	2 026		17 130
1980	:	:	1 407	2 904	12 172			29 395	5 048		129,9	2 013		17 123
1981	:	:	1 399	2 896	12 112	3 429		29 257			128,0	2 004		16 975
1982	:	:	1 395	2 887	12 046		23 376	29 231		15 405	126,8	1 998		16 934
1983	:	:	1 391	2 846	11 984	3 790		29 239	5 037		127,3	2 002		16 886
1984	:	:	1 387	2 855	11 952			29 267			128,0	2 009		16 877
1985	:	:	1 382	2 834	11 932	3 998		29 193	4 996	14 949	125,9	2 012		16 838
1986	:	:	1 375	2 819	11 910	:		28 240	:	:	126,8	2 006		:

YEAR ANNÉE	EUR 12	EUR 10	B	DK	D	EL	ES	F	IRL	I	L	NL	P	UK
INVENTORY OF FARM MACHINERY Tractors in 1000													**PARC DE MACHINES AGRICOLES** Tracteurs en 1000	
1958	:	:	35,5	:	699,2	:	:	623,0	:	207,1	5,80	53,6	:	:
1965	:	:	64,6	164,0	1 164,1	:	:	996,0	60,2	419,9	7,32	104,7	:	517,0
1970	:	4 342,0	90,9	175,0	1 356,0	102,3	:	1 265,0	84,3	614,7	8,16	135,3	:	511,0
1975	:	4 896,0	95,4	187,2	1 438,0	152,9	:	1 390,0	114,2	819,3	8,79	156,5	:	534,0
1977	:	5 066,0	101,2	191,3	1 460,0	181,6	:	1 420,0	125,4	909,6	8,81	164,0	:	504,0
1978	:		101,1	189,9	1 457,0	195,4	:	1 430,0	:	953,2	8,60	169,0	:	504,0
1979	:		104,9	189,7	1 466,0	:	:	1 485,0	:	1 006,1	8,66	173,6	:	502,0
1980	:		107,0	189,4	1 469,0	221,9	:	1 475,0	154,1	1 072,2	8,85	:	:	500,0
1981	:		104,9	181,3	1 468,0	238,1	:	1 485,0	:	1 106,2	8,51	:	:	503,2
1982	:		106,9	183,1	1 472,0	248,4	537,0	1 493,0	:	:	8,70	:	:	509,8
1983	:		101,9	:	1 483,0	260,8	:	1 495,0	:	1 141,4	8,62	:	82,7	517,6
1984	:		108,9	169,7	1 483,0	273,4	:	1 491,0	:	1 198,0	:	:	81,1	512,6
1985	:		114,3	166,3	1 483,0	:	:	1 428,0	:	1 227,1	8,93	103,4	78,6	515,2
1986	:		114,5	168,6	1 479,0	:	:	1 485,0	:	:	:	:	75,6	:
Tractors per 100 ha AA													Tracteurs pour 100 ha SAU	
1958	:	:	2,1	:	4,9	:	:	1,8	:	1,0	4,1	2,3	:	:
1965	:	:	3,9	5,4	8,4	:	:	2,9	1,0	2,1	5,4	4,6	:	2,4
1970	:	4,1	5,7	5,9	10,0	1,1	:	3,9	1,4	3,1	6,0	6,1	:	2,4
1975	:	4,7	6,2	6,4	10,8	1,7	:	4,3	2,0	4,6	6,7	7,5	:	2,6
1977	:	4,9	6,9	6,5	11,0	2,0	:	4,4	2,5	5,1	6,7	7,9	:	2,5
1978	:		7,0	6,5	11,1	2,1	:	4,4	:	5,3	6,8	8,2	:	2,5
1979	:		7,3	6,5	11,9	:	:	4,6	:	5,6	6,9	8,5	:	2,5
1980	:		7,4	6,5	12,0	2,4	:	4,6	2,5	6,0	6,8	:	:	2,7
1981	:		7,3	6,3	12,0	2,6	:	4,7	:	6,2	6,6	:	:	2,7
1982	:		7,5	6,3	12,1	2,7	2,3	4,7	:	:	6,9	:	:	2,7
1983	:		7,1	:	12,3	4,5	:	4,7	:	:	6,7	:	1,8	2,8
1984	:		7,5	5,9	12,3	4,8	:	5,1	:	:	:	:	1,8	2,7
1985	:		8,2	5,9	12,4	:	:	5,1	:	:	7,09	5,1	1,7	3,1
1986	:		7,9	6,0	12,4	:	:	5,1	:	:	:	:	1,6	:
Combine harvesters in 1000													Moissonneuses-batteuses en 1000	
1958	:	:	1,9	:	26,0	:	:	42,0	:	2,0	0,26	2,5	:	:
1965	:	:	5,6	31,0	120,0	:	:	102,1	5,8	13,2	1,19	6,1	:	65,0
1970	:	438,0	8,1	41,0	140,4	4,1	:	139,0	6,3	24,1	1,97	7,5	:	66,0
1975	:	489,0	8,4	43,0	177,1	5,2	:	153,0	4,9	27,8	1,87	6,8	:	61,4
1977	:		8,4	41,2	:	5,3	:	145,0	5,5	29,6	1,85	6,4	:	57,8
1978	:		8,3	40,3	:	5,7	:	148,0	:	30,6	1,89	6,2	:	57,8
1979	:		7,7	39,2	:	:	:	148,0	:	33,8	1,91	6,0	:	57,3
1980	:		:	38,8	:	6,1	:	149,0	5,3	35,2	1,85	:	:	57,3
1981	:		8,1	38,4	151,0	6,4	:	150,0	:	36,8	1,78	:	:	57,2
1982	:		7,9	37,6	:	6,5	26,0	151,0	:	:	1,75	:	:	56,8
1983	:		7,3	:	:	6,3	:	152,0	:	:	1,74	:	:	56,8
1984	:		7,4	35,4	139,0	6,5	:	158,0	:	:	1,69	:	:	55,0
1985	:		7,7	34,6	:	:	:	154,7	:	:	1,63	4,0	5,1	54,5
1986	:		7,2	34,1	:	:	:	145,4	:	:	:	:	:	:
Combine harvesters by 100 ha AA													Moissonneuses-batteuses pour 100 ha SAU	
1958	:	:	0,4	:	0,5	:	:	0,5	:	0,0	0,5	0,5	:	:
1965	:	:	1,1	1,9	2,4	:	:	1,1	1,5	0,2	2,4	1,3	:	1,8
1970	:	1,5	1,7	2,4	2,7	0,3	:	1,5	1,7	0,5	4,3	2,1	:	1,8
1975	:	1,8	2,1	2,5	3,3	0,3	:	1,6	1,4	0,6	4,5	2,8	:	1,7
1977	:		2,1	2,3	:	0,4	:	1,5	:	0,7	4,6	2,7	:	1,5
1978	:		2,1	2,2	:	0,4	:	1,5	:	0,7	4,7	2,6	:	1,5
1979	:		1,9	2,1	:	:	:	1,5	:	0,7	4,8	2,5	:	1,5
1980	:		:	2,1	:	0,4	:	1,5	1,2	0,7	4,7	:	:	1,5
1981	:		4,6	2,1	3,0	0,4	:	1,6	2,1	1,3	1,4	2,2	:	
1982	:		2,2	2,1	:	0,4	:	1,6	:	:	4,7	:	:	1,4
1983	:		2,0	:	:	0,4	:	1,6	:	:	5,6	:	:	1,4
1984	:		2,0	2,1	2,8	0,4	:	1,6	:	:	4,8	:	:	1,4
1985	:		2,0	2,1	:	:	:	1,6	:	:	:	2,2	:	1,4
1986	:		2,0	2,1	:	:	:	1,6	:	:	:	:	:	
Mechanical milking equipment in 1000													Installations de traite mécanique en 1000	
1958	:	:	26,9	:	176,0	:	:	110,3	:	:	4,22	22,7	:	:
1965	:	:	43,7	:	440,0	:	:	185,7	:	52,0	4,94	78,2	:	:
1970	:	:	51,0	:	479,3	:	:	295,0	8,2	69,6	4,68	85,5	:	:
1975	:	:	49,1	65,6	457,6	:	:	360,2	19,5	105,2	3,96	77,8	:	86,2
1977	:	:	47,4	:	:	:	:	382,9	21,9	106,2	3,59	70,0	:	64,7
1978	:	:	45,8	:	:	:	:	392,0	:	:	3,37	66,0	:	:
1979	:	:	45,0	:	:	:	:	361,0	:	:	3,24	62,6	:	:
1980	:	:	43,9	:	:	:	:	375,0	20,2	:	3,07	:	:	:
1981	:	:	44,5	:	:	:	:	378,0	:	:	2,91	:	:	:
1982	:	:	38,3	:	:	:	92,0	377,0	:	:	2,75	:	:	:
1983	:	:	43,0	:	:	:	:	373,0	:	:	2,65	:	:	:
1984	:	:	40,8	:	:	:	:	347,0	:	:	2,61	:	:	:
1985	:	:	41,0	:	:	:	:	324,4	:	:	2,50	:	:	:
1986	:	:	37,2	:	:	:	:	313,3	:	:	:	:	:	:
Number by 100 dairy cows													Nombre pour 100 vaches laitières	
1958	:	:	2,7	:	3,1	:	:	1,6	:	:	8,1	1,5	:	:
1965	:	:	4,3	:	7,5	:	:	2,6	:	1,5	8,9	4,6	:	:
1970	:	:	5,1	:	8,6	:	:	3,8	0,7	2,2	7,5	4,5	:	:
1975	:	:	5,0	5,9	8,5	:	:	4,8	1,4	3,6	5,7	3,5	:	2,7
1977	:	:	4,9	:	:	:	:	5,1	1,5	3,6	5,3	3,2	:	1,9
1978	:	:	4,7	:	:	:	:	5,2	:	:	5,0	2,9	:	:
1979	:	:	4,6	:	:	:	:	4,8	:	:	4,8	2,7	:	:
1980	:	:	4,5	:	:	:	:	5,3	1,4	:	4,4	:	:	:
1981	:	:	4,6	:	:	:	:	5,4	:	:	4,3	:	:	:
1982	:	:	4,0	:	:	:	6,1	5,3	:	:	4,1	:	:	:
1983	:	:	4,4	:	:	:	:	5,3	:	:	3,8	:	:	:
1984	:	:	4,1	:	:	:	:	5,0	:	:	3,7	:	:	:
1985	:	:	4,2	:	:	:	:	4,9	:	:	:	:	:	:
1986	:	:	3,8	:	:	:	:	4,7	:	:	:	:	:	:

1000 t   1000 t

YEAR ANNÉE	EUR 12	EUR 10	B	DK	D	EL	ES	F	IRL	I	L	NL	P	UK

CONSUMPTION OF COMMERCIAL FERTILIZERS (pure nutrient content)   **CONSOMMATION D'ENGRAIS CHIMIQUES (éléments fertilisants)**

Nitrogenous fertilizers (N)   Engrais azotés

YEAR ANNÉE	EUR 12	EUR 10	B	DK	D	EL	ES	F	IRL	I	L	NL	P	UK
1956/60	:	:	92	:	555	:	:	452	:	289	3,9	202	:	:
1965/66	:	147	:	192	874	:	:	867	32	462	6,8	312	:	690
1969/70	:	4 726	182	271	1 085	145	:	1 230	70	550	10,4	387	:	796
1974/75	:	5 669	175	300	1 201	258	:	1 555	133	673	11,9	435	:	927
1976/77	:	6 350	176	350	1 323	254	:	1 813	167	713	14,8	430	:	1 110
1977/78	:	6 661	179	375	1 325	270	:	1 832	230	812	13,7	447	:	1 177
1978/79	:	7 184	184	380	1 354	305	:	2 012	264	1 006	14,0	443	:	1 222
1979/80	:	7 725	185	394	1 477	338	:	2 221	248	1 047	14,6	486	:	1 314
1980/81	7 539		184	381	1 551	352	895	2 147	275	911	14,5	483	185	1 240
1981/82	7 503		184	376	1 323	374	815	2 193	275	900	14,9	477	162	1 386
1982/83	:		186	391	1 465	410	785	2 196	296	:	14,8	457	175	1 560
1983/84	:		187	412	1 378	401	778	2 320	331	908	15,6	478	136	1 601
1984/85	:		:	398	1 452	:	907	2 337	328	974	15,9	505	164	1 580
1985/86	:	:	:	382	1 516	:	827	2 408	323	993	17,1	500	161	1 668

Phosphatic fertilizers (P$_2$O$_5$)   Engrais phosphatés (P$_2$O$_5$)

YEAR ANNÉE	EUR 12	EUR 10	B	DK	D	EL	ES	F	IRL	I	L	NL	P	UK
1956/60	:	:	102	:	604	:	:	825	:	396	5,6	112	:	:
1965/66	:	:	113	127	833	:	:	1 286	107	453	6,1	115	:	429
1969/70	:	4 184	145	127	857	107	:	1 710	167	486	6,6	108	:	470
1974/75	:	3 966	149	114	877	171	:	1 711	116	370	6,5	93	:	368
1976/77	:	4 238	118	135	887	163	:	1 796	150	501	6,8	92	:	389
1977/78	:	4 377	80	141	873	166	:	1 840	175	609	6,7	87	:	399
1978/79	:	4 682	112	136	906	197	:	1 950	185	697	6,4	81	:	412
1979/80	:	4 713	101	133	913	171	:	1 984	156	718	6,6	84	:	446
1980/81	4 206		104	111	837	158	447	1 774	146	596	5,8	83	142	392
1981/82	4 023		93	105	753	166	412	1 677	142	563	6,2	81	130	437
1982/83	:		102	113	740	176	385	1 631	146	:	5,9	77	133	452
1983/84	:		123	119	745	199	397	1 679	152	602	6,2	87	105	461
1984/85	:		:	111	732	:	446	1 580	152	626	4,9	89	124	469
1985/86	:	:	:	106	737	:	445	1 466	134	610	5,7	81	124	439

Potash fertilizers (K$_2$O)   Engrais potassiques (K$_2$O)

YEAR ANNÉE	EUR 12	EUR 10	B	DK	D	EL	ES	F	IRL	I	L	NL	P	UK
1956/60	:	:	152	:	955	:	:	647	:	75	5,7	154	:	:
1965/66	:	:	169	185	1 190	:	:	970	89	168	7,0	139	:	436
1969/70	:	3 666	187	183	1 120	13	:	1 280	139	195	7,7	122	:	419
1974/75	:	3 767	171	160	1 170	17	:	1 413	112	232	7,9	113	:	371
1976/77	:	4 011	155	168	1 195	26	:	1 494	170	270	8,5	114	:	411
1977/78	:	4 126	144	177	1 183	26	:	1 558	204	299	8,1	111	:	416
1978/79	:	4 375	161	173	1 178	35	:	1 690	221	376	7,9	107	:	426
1979/80	:	4 519	143	171	1 206	41	:	1 786	189	390	7,9	124	:	461
1980/81	4 216		151	142	1 144	36	274	1 689	180	342	7,6	114	80	410
1981/82	4 152		128	137	1 055	41	255	1 700	178	330	7,0	106	74	470
1982/83	:		123	148	1 042	48	240	1 744	184	:	7,1	102	75	521
1983/84	:		138	157	1 014	47	251	1 834	194	359	6,7	117	57	542
1984/85	:		:	150	988	:	291	1 863	197	352	6,8	125	64	541
1985/86	:	:	:	146	932	:	295	1 820	174	339	7,8	120	62	517

TOTAL   **TOTAL**

YEAR ANNÉE	EUR 12	EUR 10	B	DK	D	EL	ES	F	IRL	I	L	NL	P	UK
1956/60	:	:	346	:	2 114	:	:	1 924	:	760	15,2	468	:	:
1965/66	:	:	429	504	2 897	:	:	3 123	228	1 083	19,9	566	:	1 555
1969/70	:	12 576	514	581	3 062	265	:	4 220	376	1 231	24,7	617	:	1 685
1974/75	:	13 402	495	574	3 248	446	:	4 679	361	1 275	26,3	641	:	1 666
1976/77	:	14 599	449	653	3 405	443	:	5 103	487	1 484	30,1	636	:	1 910
1977/78	:	15 164	403	693	3 381	462	:	5 230	609	1 720	28,5	645	:	1 992
1978/79	:	16 241	457	689	3 438	537	:	5 652	670	2 079	28,3	631	:	2 060
1979/80	:	16 957	429	698	3 596	550	:	5 991	593	2 155	29,1	694	:	2 221
1980/81	15 961		439	634	3 532	546	1 616	5 610	601	1 849	27,9	680	407	2 042
1981/82	15 678		405	618	3 131	581	1 482	5 570	595	1 793	28,1	664	366	2 293
1982/83	:		411	652	3 247	634	1 410	5 571	626	:	27,8	636	383	2 533
1983/84	:		448	688	3 137	647	1 426	5 833	677	1 869	28,5	682	298	2 604
1984/85	:	:		659	3 172	:	1 644	5 780	677	1 952	27,6	719	352	2 590
1985/86	:	:		634	3 185	:	1 567	5 694	631	1 942	30,6	701	337	2 524

Straight fertilizers   Engrais simples

YEAR ANNÉE	EUR 12	EUR 10	B	DK	D	EL	ES	F	IRL	I	L	NL	P	UK
1956/60	:	:	:	:	:	:	:	:	:	:	:	:	:	:
1965/66	:	:	272	186	1 678	:	:	1 414	94	622	18,6	415	:	:
1969/70	:	:	251	198	1 548	89	:	1 569	118	716	20,8	440	:	:
1974/75	:	5 735	256	148	1 584	179	:	1 622	114	732	22,4	483	:	595
1976/77	:	6 188	268	195	1 683	156	:	1 903	122	712	27,4	475	:	647
1977/78	:	6 297	217	200	1 611	162	:	1 971	154	796	25,6	484	:	676
1978/79	:	6 897	239	197	1 604	179	:	2 283	158	978	25,2	474	:	730
1979/80	:	7 360	208	200	1 762	218	:	2 455	150	1 021	26,3	527	:	803
1980/81	7 152		196	212	1 752	227	865	2 426	170	889	25,0	514	116	741
1981/82	6 966		184	209	1 476	240	827	2 411	169	887	25,1	503	96	862
1982/83	:		177	192	1 654	252	774	2 423	176	:	24,7	488	103	1 013
1983/84	:	:		169	1 566	253	764	2 589	205	907	25,7	518	82	1 068
1984/85	:	:		172	1 587	:	874	2 574	199	962	24,6	533	100	1 087
1985/86	:	:		205	1 591	:	788	2 724	195	972	26,3	529	92	1 132

Compound fertilizers   Engrais composés

YEAR ANNÉE	EUR 12	EUR 10	B	DK	D	EL	ES	F	IRL	I	L	NL	P	UK
1956/60	:	:	:	:	:	:	:	:	:	:	:	:	:	:
1965/66	:	:	157	317	1 219	:	:	1 710	134	460	1,3	151	:	:
1969/70	:	:	263	383	1 513	175	:	2 651	258	515	3,9	177	:	:
1974/75	:	7 667	239	426	1 665	258	:	3 057	247	543	3,9	158	:	1 071
1976/77	:	8 410	181	457	1 723	286	:	3 201	365	772	2,7	160	:	1 263
1977/78	:	8 886	186	493	1 770	300	:	3 259	455	924	2,9	160	:	1 316
1978/79	:	9 373	218	491	1 835	359	:	3 369	510	1 101	3,0	157	:	1 330
1979/80	:	9 596	221	498	1 835	332	:	3 546	442	1 134	2,8	167	:	1 418
1980/81	8 802		243	422	1 774	319	751	3 183	431	960	2,6	166	290	1 301
1981/82	8 713		221	409	1 655	342	683	3 159	426	906	3,0	161	270	1 431
1982/83	:		234	461	1 592	382	632	3 149	450	:	3,1	149	280	1 520
1983/84	:	:		518	1 571	394	663	3 244	473	962	2,8	164	215	1 536
1984/85	:	:		487	1 585	:	770	3 206	477	990	3,0	177	133	1 503
1985/86	:	:		428	1 593	:	779	2 970	435	971	4,3	172	245	1 392

KG PER HA AA | KG/HA SAU

Nitrogenous fertilizers (N) — Engrais azotés

YEAR ANNÉE	EUR 12	EUR 10	B	DK	D	EL	ES	F	IRL	I	L	NL	P	UK
1956/60	:	:	53	:	39	:	:	13	:	15	28	87	:	:
1965/66	:	:	89	64	63	:	:	26	7	24	51	138	:	35
1969/70	:	44	114	91	80	16	:	38	12	28	77	175	:	42
1974/75	:	54	114	102	90	28	:	48	23	38	90	208	:	49
1976/77	:	61	121	119	100	28	:	56	29	40	112	208	:	59
1977/78	:	64	124	128	101	29	:	57	40	45	106	218	:	63
1978/79	:	70	126	130	110	33	:	63	46	56	107	217	:	65
1979/80	:	75	128	136	121	37	:	70	43	59	112	240	:	71
1980/81	:	74	128	132	127	38	:	67	48	51	113	239	:	68
1981/82	:	74	128	130	109	41	:	69	48	50	117	238	:	74
1982/83	:	:	130	137	121	45	:	70	52	:	116	227	:	83
1983/84	:	:	:	143	114	:	:	74	59	:	122	236	:	86
1984/85	:	:	:	139	122	:	33	73	57	55	126	249	36	85
1985/86	:	:	:	135	126	:	30	77	57	57	126	247	33	84

Phosphatic fertilizers (P_2O_5) — Engrais phosphatés (P_2O_5)

YEAR ANNÉE	EUR 12	EUR 10	B	DK	D	EL	ES	F	IRL	I	L	NL	P	UK
1956/60	:	:	59	:	42	:	:	24	:	20	40	48	:	:
1965/66	:	:	69	42	60	:	:	38	22	23	45	51	:	22
1969/70	:	39	91	43	63	12	:	53	29	25	49	49	:	25
1974/75	:	38	97	39	66	17	:	53	20	21	49	44	:	19
1976/77	:	41	81	46	67	18	:	56	26	28	51	44	:	21
1977/78	:	42	55	48	66	18	:	57	31	34	52	42	:	21
1978/79	:	46	77	47	74	21	:	61	32	39	49	40	:	22
1979/80	:	46	70	46	75	19	:	62	27	40	51	41	:	24
1980/81	:	41	72	38	68	17	:	56	25	33	45	41	:	21
1981/82	:	40	65	36	62	18	:	53	25	32	49	40	:	23
1982/83	:	:	71	40	61	19	:	52	26	:	46	38	:	24
1983/84	:	:	:	41	62	:	:	53	27	:	48	43	:	25
1984/85	:	:	:	39	61	:	16	49	27	35	39	44	27	25
1985/86	:	:	:	37	61	:	16	47	23	35	39	40	27	24

Potash fertilizers (K_2O) — Engrais potassiques (K_2O)

YEAR ANNÉE	EUR 12	EUR 10	B	DK	D	EL	ES	F	IRL	I	L	NL	P	UK
1956/60	:	:	88	:	67	:	:	19	:	4	41	66	:	:
1965/66	:	:	102	61	86	:	:	29	19	9	52	61	:	22
1969/70	:	34	117	62	82	1	:	39	24	10	57	55	:	22
1974/75	:	36	111	54	88	2	:	44	20	13	60	54	:	19
1976/77	:	39	106	57	90	3	:	46	30	15	64	55	:	22
1977/78	:	40	100	60	90	3	:	48	36	17	62	54	:	22
1978/79	:	43	110	59	96	4	:	53	39	21	61	52	:	23
1979/80	:	44	99	59	98	4	:	56	33	22	61	61	:	25
1980/81	:	41	105	49	94	4	:	53	32	19	59	57	:	22
1981/82	:	41	89	47	87	4	:	54	31	19	55	53	:	25
1982/83	:	:	86	52	86	5	:	55	33	:	55	51	:	28
1983/84	:	:	:	55	84	:	:	58	34	:	62	58	:	29
1984/85	:	:	:	52	83	:	11	58	35	20	54	62	14	29
1985/86	:	:	:	51	78	:	11	58	30	19	54	59	14	28

TOTAL — TOTAL

YEAR ANNÉE	EUR 12	EUR 10	B	DK	D	EL	ES	F	IRL	I	L	NL	P	UK
1956/60	:	:	200	:	148	:	:	56	:	39	109	201	:	:
1965/66	:	:	260	167	209	:	:	93	48	56	148	250	:	79
1969/70	:	117	322	196	225	29	:	130	65	63	183	279	:	89
1974/75	:	128	322	195	244	47	:	145	63	72	199	306	:	87
1976/77	:	141	308	222	257	49	:	158	85	83	227	307	:	102
1977/78	:	146	279	236	257	50	:	162	107	96	220	314	:	106
1978/79	:	159	313	236	280	58	:	177	117	116	217	309	:	110
1979/80	:	165	297	241	294	60	:	188	103	121	224	342	:	120
1980/81	:	156	305	219	289	59	:	176	105	103	217	337	:	111
1981/82	:	155	282	213	258	63	:	176	104	101	221	331	:	122
1982/83	:	:	287	229	268	69	:	177	111	:	217	316	:	135
1983/84	:	:	:	239	260	:	:	185	120	:	222	337	:	140
1984/85	:	:	:	230	266	:	60	181	119	111	219	355	78	139
1985/86	:	:	:	223	265	:	58	181	110	111	219	346	74	135

Straight fertilizers — Engrais simples

YEAR ANNÉE	EUR 12	EUR 10	B	DK	D	EL	ES	F	IRL	I	L	NL	P	UK
1956/60	:	:	:	:	:	:	:	:	:	:	:	:	:	:
1965/66	:	:	165	62	121	:	:	42	20	32	138	184	:	:
1969/70	:	:	157	67	114	10	:	48	20	36	154	199	:	:
1974/75	:	55	167	50	119	19	:	50	20	41	170	231	:	31
1976/77	:	60	184	67	127	17	:	59	21	40	207	230	:	34
1977/78	:	61	150	68	122	18	:	61	27	45	197	236	:	36
1978/79	:	67	164	67	130	19	:	71	28	55	193	232	:	39
1979/80	:	72	144	69	144	24	:	77	26	57	202	260	:	44
1980/81	:	70	136	73	144	25	:	76	30	50	195	255	:	40
1981/82	:	68	128	72	122	26	:	76	30	50	197	251	:	46
1982/83	:	:	124	67	137	28	:	77	31	:	194	242	:	54
1983/84	:	:	:	59	130	:	:	82	36	:	200	256	:	57
1984/85	:	:	:	60	133	:	32	81	35	54	195	263	22	58
1985/86	:	:	:	72	132	:	29	87	34	55	195	261	20	61

Compound fertilizers — Engrais composés

YEAR ANNÉE	EUR 12	EUR 10	B	DK	D	EL	ES	F	IRL	I	L	NL	P	UK
1956/60	:	:	:	:	:	:	:	:	:	:	:	:	:	:
1965/66	:	:	95	105	88	:	:	51	28	24	10	67	:	:
1969/70	:	:	165	129	111	19	:	81	44	26	29	80	:	:
1974/75	:	74	156	145	125	28	:	94	43	31	30	76	:	56
1976/77	:	81	124	156	130	31	:	99	64	43	20	77	:	67
1977/78	:	86	129	168	134	32	:	101	80	52	22	78	:	70
1978/79	:	91	149	168	149	39	:	105	89	61	22	77	:	71
1979/80	:	94	153	171	150	36	:	111	77	63	22	82	:	77
1980/81	:	87	169	146	145	35	:	100	75	54	20	82	:	71
1981/82	:	86	154	142	136	37	:	100	74	51	24	80	:	76
1982/83	:	:	164	162	132	41	:	100	80	:	24	74	:	81
1983/84	:	:	:	180	130	:	:	103	84	:	22	81	:	82
1984/85	:	:	:	170	132	:	28	100	84	56	23	87	51	80
1985/86	:	:	:	151	133	:	29	94	76	55	34	85	54	75

I D

Crop production

Production végétale

ID 1

HARVESTED CROPS AREA | SUPERFICIES RECOLTEES

1000 HA

YEAR ANNÉE	EUR 12	EUR 10	B	DK	D	GR	E	F	IRL	I	L	NL	P	UK
CEREALS (INCL.RICE)													**CEREALES (Y.C. RIZ)**	
1983	36 294 *	27 798 *	373 *	1 698	5 044 *	1 571	7 433	9 389	395	5 129	31	206	1 063	3 962 *
1984	36 552 *	27 980 *	361 *	1 669	4 941 *	1 534	7 584	9 724	406	5 077	35	196 *	988	4 038 *
1985	36 038 *	27 487 *	345	1 612	4 884	1 476 *	7 591	9 713 *	400	4 822 *	35	183 *	960	4 017 *
1986	35 826 *	27 152 *	350	1 588	4 812	1 463 *	7 671 *	9 499	380	4 831 *	34	171 *	1 004 *	4 025 *
CEREALS (EXCL.RICE)													**CEREALES (N.C. RIZ)**	
1983	36 022 *	27 594 *	373 *	1 698	5 044 *	1 556	7 392	9 382	395	4 946	31	206	1 037	3 962 *
1984	36 244 *	27 775 *	361 *	1 669	4 941 *	1 518	7 511	9 715	406	4 897	35	196 *	958	4 038 *
1985	35 719 *	27 273 *	345	1 612	4 884	1 460 *	7 517	9 701 *	400	4 636 *	35	183 *	930	4 017 *
1986	35 498 *	26 934 *	350	1 588	4 812	1 446 *	7 592 *	9 487	380	4 642	34	171 *	973 *	4 025 *
WHEAT AND SPELT													**BLE ET EPEAUTRE**	
1983	16 082 *	13 145 *	197	242	1 655 *	984	2 604	4 825	59	3 333	6	148	334	1 695
1984	16 167 *	13 568 *	186	332	1 634 *	867	2 306	5 107	77	3 274	8	143	293	1 939
1985	15 301 *	12 973 *	188	340	1 624	875	2 043	4 797	78	3 034	7	128	285	1 902 *
1986	15 685 *	13 292 *	189	354	1 648	905	2 096	4 865	76	3 133	7	118	298	1 997
COMMON WHEAT AND SPELT													**BLE TENDRE ET EPEAUTRE**	
1983	13 722 *	10 973	197	242	1 654	682	2 431	4 713	59	1 576	6	148	317 *	1 695
1984	13 744 *	11 319	186	332	1 629	553	2 154	4 976	77	1 476	8	143	270 *	1 939
1985	12 814 *	10 642 *	188	340	1 609	469	1 911	4 632	78	1 295	7	128	262	1 896 *
1986	12 918	10 654	189	353	1 623	426	1 990	4 604	76	1 271	7	118	274	1 987
WINTER COMMON WHEAT													**BLE TENDRE D'HIVER**	
1983	:	:	189	232	1 554	682	:	4 663	:	1 574	5	142	:	:
1984	:	:	182	322	1 553	553	:	4 932	:	1 474	7	139	:	:
1985	:	:	182	330	1 537	469	:	4 570	:	1 294 *	4	121	:	:
1986	:	:	186	343	1 556	426	:	4 560	:	1 270	5	112	:	:
SPRING COMMON WHEAT													**BLE TENDRE DE PRINTEMPS**	
1983	:	:	8	10	100	—	—	51	:	2	1	6	—	:
1984	:	:	4	10	76	—	—	44	:	2	2	4	—	:
1985	:	:	6	10	72	—	—	63	:	1 *	3	7	—	:
1986	:	:	4	10	67	—	—	44	:	1	2	6	—	:
DURUM WHEAT													**BLE DUR**	
1983	2 361 *	2 172 *	—	—	1 *	302	172	112	—	1 757	—	—	17 *	—
1984	2 423 *	2 249 *	—	—	6 *	314	151	131	—	1 798	—	—	23 *	—
1985	2 487 *	2 331 *	—	—	15	406	133	165	—	1 739	—	—	23	6 *
1986	2 767 *	2 638 *	—	1	25	478	105	261	—	1 862	—	—	24	10 *
RYE													**SEIGLE**	
1983	1 011	662	6	77	445	7	217	101	—	11	1	7	133	7
1984	1 061	701	7	122	439	10	231	100	—	9	1	6	130	6
1985	1 011 *	677 *	5	127	426	10	211	87	—	9	1	5	123	8 *
1986	998 *	652	4	121	414	13	223	80	—	8	1	4	123 *	7
MASLIN													**METEIL**	
1983	20	16	—	—	12	0	4	4	—	—	0	—	—	—
1984	21	16	—	—	11	1	5	4	—	—	—	—	—	—
1985	25	18	—	—	12	0	7	6	—	—	—	—	—	—
1986	22 *	17	—	—	11	0	5 *	6	—	—	—	—	—	—
OATS AND MIXED GRAIN													**AVOINE ET MELANGES DE CEREALES D'ETE**	
1983	2 389	1 744	26	32	729	43	454	546	23	207	8	14	191	116
1984	2 348 *	1 674 *	24	34	669	43	479	554	25	190	10	12 *	194	114
1985	2 364 *	1 715 *	24	41	692	43	459	547	23	182	10	12 *	190	141 *
1986	1 998 *	1 421 *	16	25	605	43	384	407	21	184	8	7 *	194	104

SOURCE: CRONOS-ZPA1 DATA BANK, AGRICULTURAL PRODUCTS

SOURCE: BANQUE DE DONNEES CRONOS-ZPA1, PRODUITS AGRICOLES

| ID 1 |

HARVESTED PRODUCTION

PRODUCTION RECOLTEE

YEAR ANNÉE	EUR 12	EUR 10	B	DK	D	GR	E	F	IRL	I	L	NL	P	UK
1000 T														
CEREALS (INCL.RICE)													**CEREALES (Y.C. RIZ)**	
1983	140 047 *	125 142 *	1 876 *	6 380	23 011 *	4 604	13 759	46 510	1 991 *	18 087	68	1 308	1 146	21 307 *
1984	174 932 *	152 452 *	2 369 *	9 283	26 489	5 512	21 032	58 188	2 513	19 939	134	1 407 *	1 448	26 618 *
1985	162 481 *	140 134 *	2 065	7 956	25 914	4 531 *	20 972	55 812 *	2 095	18 029	132	1 129 *	1 374	22 471 *
1986	155 850 *	137 938 *	2 258	7 968	25 590	5 285 *	16 289 *	50 558	1 954	18 450 *	125	1 265 *	1 623 *	24 486 *
CEREALS (EXCL.RICE)													**CEREALES (N.C. RIZ)**	
1983	138 563 *	123 991 *	1 876 *	6 380	23 011 *	4 518	13 535	46 472	1 991 *	17 060	68	1 308	1 037	21 307 *
1984	173 207 *	151 301 *	2 369 *	9 283	26 489	5 417	20 592	58 153	2 513	18 919	134	1 407 *	1 314	26 618 *
1985	160 571 *	138 834 *	2 065	7 956	25 914	4 429 *	20 510	55 750 *	2 095	16 892	132	1 129 *	1 228	22 471 *
1986	153 923 *	136 658 *	2 258	7 968	25 590	5 164 *	15 795 *	50 498	1 954	17 350 *	125	1 265 *	1 470 *	24 486 *
WHEAT AND SPELT													**BLE ET EPEAUTRE**	
1983	64 008 *	59 411 *	1 043	1 548	8 998 *	2 059	4 268	24 795	387	8 717	19	1 043	330	10 802
1984	82 622	76 101	1 294	2 446	10 223	2 316	6 052	33 026	602	10 057	37	1 131	468	14 970
1985	71 248 *	65 522 *	1 187	1 972	9 866	1 789	5 329	28 823	495	8 461	28	851	397	12 050 *
1986	72 003 *	67 211 *	1 295	2 177	10 406	2 389	4 292	26 570	424	9 070	30	940	500	13 910 *
COMMON WHEAT AND SPELT													**BLE TENDRE ET EPEAUTRE**	
1983	59 704 *	55 386	1 043	1 548	8 993	1 477	4 005	24 397	387	5 677	19	1 043	313 *	10 802
1984	75 999	70 019	1 294	2 446	10 197	1 456	5 550	32 448	602	5 439	37	1 131	430	14 970
1985	65 376	60 053	1 187	1 972	9 779	1 013	4 958	28 091	495	4 610	28	851	365	12 026
1986	64 838	60 340	1 295	2 171	10 286	1 124	4 038	25 541	424	4 685	30	940	460	13 845
WINTER COMMON WHEAT													**BLE TENDRE D'HIVER**	
1983	:	:	1 009	1 514	8 568	1 477	:	24 199	:	5 674	16	1 012	:	:
1984	:	:	1 272	2 402	9 797	1 456	:	32 224	:	5 436	29	1 108	:	:
1985	:	:	1 159	1 928	9 422	1 013	:	27 769	:	4 608	17	813	:	:
1986	:	:	1 276	2 119	9 954	1 124	:	25 367	:	4 682	23	903	:	:
SPRING COMMON WHEAT													**BLE TENDRE DE PRINTEMPS**	
1983	:	:	34	34	425	—	—	197	:	3	3	31	—	:
1984	:	:	22	44	400	—	—	223	:	3	7	23	—	:
1985	:	:	28	44	357	—	—	322	:	2	11	38	—	:
1986	:	:	19	52	333	—	—	174	:	2	6	38	—	:
DURUM WHEAT													**BLE DUR**	
1983	4 304 *	4 025 *	—	—	5	582	263	398	—	3 040	—	—	17 *	—
1984	6 623	6 082	—	—	26	860	503	578	—	4 618	—	—	38	—
1985	5 873 *	5 469 *	—	—	87	776	371	732	—	3 851	—	—	32	24
1986	7 165 *	6 871 *	—	6	120	1 266	254	1 029	—	4 385	—	—	40	65
RYE													**SEIGLE**	
1983	2 669 *	2 324 *	25	315	1 599	13	253	293	— *	27	3	26	92	24
1984	3 436	3 018	32	608	1 931	18	315	347	—	24	5	25	103	28
1985	3 175	2 805	23	565	1 821	19	273	297	—	23	3	19	97	35
1986	2 981 *	2 665	19	546	1 768	29	220	226	—	22	3	19	96 *	32
MASLIN													**METEIL**	
1983	62	59	—	—	47	0	3	11	—	—	0	—	—	—
1984	74	68	—	—	52	1	7	15	—	—	—	—	—	—
1985	84	75	—	—	55	0	9	20	—	—	—	—	—	—
1986	72 *	66 *	—	—	49	0 *	6 *	17	—	—	—	—	—	—
OATS AND MIXED GRAIN												**AVOINE ET MELANGES DE CEREALES D'ETE**		
1983	6 043	5 480	99	93	2 489	62	464	1 750	101	313	11	61	99	501
1984	7 789 *	6 849 *	117	158	2 973	66	788	2 327	141	430	31	58 *	152	550
1985	7 835 *	7 036 *	108	168	3 278	65	680	2 203	106	363	39	59 *	119	646
1986	6 001 *	5 426 *	71	111	2 687	70	422	1 384	102	397	28	42 *	153	534

SOURCE: CRONOS-ZPA1 DATA BANK, AGRICULTURAL PRODUCTS

SOURCE: BANQUE DE DONNEES CRONOS-ZPA1, PRODUITS AGRICOLES

HARVESTED CROPS AREA | SUPERFICIES RECOLTEES

YEAR ANNÉE	EUR 12	EUR 10	B	DK	D	GR	E	F	IRL	I	L	NL	P	UK
					1000 HA									
BARLEY														**ORGE**
1983	12 707	8 889	139	1 347	2 035	329	3 735	2 143	313	385	16	37	83	2 144
1984	12 669	8 562	136	1 181	2 006	365	4 023	2 108	304	434	16	34	84	1 979
1985	12 857	8 526	118	1 104	1 949	310	4 246	2 256	298	468	17	39	86	1 966
1986	12 673	8 252	128	1 088	1 947	266	4 334	2 097	283	466	18	42	87	1 917
WINTER BARLEY														**ORGE D'HIVER**
1983	:	:	122	96	1 260	329	:	1 361	:	:	4	10	:	:
1984	:	:	125	204	1 337	365	:	1 446	:	:	4	11	:	:
1985	:	:	101	60	1 189	310	:	1 393	:	:	3	7	:	:
1986	:	:	114	61	1 266	266	:	1 411	:	:	4	9	:	:
SPRING BARLEY														**ORGE DE PRINTEMPS**
1983	:	:	17	1 251	775	–	–	782	:	:	12	27	–	:
1984	:	:	11	976	669	–	–	662	:	:	11	23	–	:
1985	:	:	17	1 044	760	–	–	863	:	:	14	32	–	:
1986	:	:	14	1 027	681	–	–	686	:	:	14	33	–	:
GRAIN MAIZE														**MAIS GRAIN**
1983	3 683 *	3 033 *	5	–	169	192	354	1 685	–	982	–	0	295	– *
1984	3 821 *	3 125 *	8	–	182	231	440	1 743	–	961	–	0 *	257	– *
1985	3 995 *	3 223 *	7	–	181	221	526	1 891 *	–	923	–	0 *	246	– *
1986	3 925 *	3 129 *	7	–	187	218	525	1 884	–	833	–	0 *	271 *	–
SORGHUM														**SORGHO**
1983	100	79	–	–	–	1	20	54	–	25	–	–	–	–
1984	101	81	–	–	–	1	21	57	–	23	–	–	–	–
1985	80 *	60 *	–	–	–	1 *	21	44 *	–	15 *	–	–	–	–
1986	77 *	58 *	–	–	–	1 *	19	45	–	12	–	–	–	–
TRITICALE														**TRITICALE**
1983	18 *	:	– *	–	–	–	–	17	–	2	–	–	–	–
1984	40 *	:	– *	–	–	–	–	37	–	3	–	–	–	–
1985	63	:	2	–	–	–	–	57	–	4	–	–	–	–
1986	96	:	4	–	–	–	–	88	–	4	–	–	–	–
RICE (PADDY)														**RIZ (PADDY)**
1983	272	204	–	–	–	14	41	7	–	183	–	–	26	–
1984	308	205	–	–	–	15	73	9	–	180	–	–	30	–
1985	319	214	–	–	–	17	75	11	–	186	–	–	30	–
1986	328 *	218 *	–	–	–	18	79	12	–	188 *	–	–	31	–
DRIED PULSES														**LEGUMES SECS**
1983	1 308 *	587 *	1	22 *	13	56	434	204	1	200 *	0	12	287	78 *
1984	1 364 *	673 *	1	57 *	16	50	425	232	1	212	0	16	266 *	88
1985	1 483 *	822 *	1	127 *	34	42	411	254	2 *	200	0	25	250 *	136 *
1986	1 675 *	988 *	3	140 *	69	43	417 *	354	2 *	195	0	32	270 *	150 *
PEAS OTHER THAN FIELDPEAS													**POIS SECS AUTRES QUE POIS FOURRAGERS**	
1983	176 *	56 *	1	0	–	8	92	10	0 *	14	0	8	29	15 *
1984	176 *	57 *	0	–	1 *	5	93	10	0 *	14	– *	11	26	14
1985	186 *	69 *	1	0	1 *	5	91	16	0 *	13 *	0	20	26	13 *
1986	192 *	78 *	2	0	2 *	5	90	19	0 *	12 *	0	22	24 *	15 *
FIELDPEAS														**POIS FOURRAGERS**
1983	168 *	165 *	–	21 *	–	0	3	115	:	–	–	–	:	29
1984	226 *	223 *	–	53 *	5 *	0	3	123	:	–	–	–	:	42
1985	393 *	390 *	–	123 *	14 *	0	4	175	:	– *	–	–	:	78 *
1986	522 *	517 *	–	135	33 *	0	5	273	:	– *	–	–	:	76 *

ID 1

HARVESTED PRODUCTION

PRODUCTION RECOLTEE

YEAR ANNÉE	EUR 12	EUR 10	B	DK	D	GR	E	F	IRL	I	L	NL	P	UK
						1000 T								
BARLEY														**ORGE**
1983	43 033	36 317	670	4 423	8 944	624	6 662	8 773	1 503	1 188	35	177	54	9 980
1984	55 186	44 306	873	6 072	10 284	854	10 789	11 512	1 770	1 618	61	192	91	11 070
1985	51 560	40 797	685	5 251	9 690	606	10 698	11 442	1 494	1 630	61	197	65	9 740
1986	46 839	39 418	793	5 134	9 377	681	7 331	10 120	1 428	1 548	65	262	90	10 010
WINTER BARLEY														**ORGE D'HIVER**
1983	:	:	618	:	6 402	624	:	6 529	:	:	11	56	:	:
1984	:	:	825	:	7 533	854	:	8 461	:	:	18	67	:	:
1985	:	:	617	:	6 351	606	:	7 664	:	:	12	37	:	:
1986	:	:	738	:	6 537	681	:	7 786	:	:	16	61	:	:
SPRING BARLEY														**ORGE DE PRINTEMPS**
1983	:	:	52	:	2 542	—	—	2 243	:	:	24	121	—	:
1984	:	:	48	:	2 751	—	—	3 051	:	:	43	125	—	:
1985	:	:	68	:	3 339	—	—	3 778	:	:	49	160	—	:
1986	:	:	55	:	2 840	—	—	2 334	:	:	49	202	—	:
GRAIN MAIZE														**MAIS GRAIN**
1983	22 221 *	19 956 *	39	—	934	1 758	1 803	10 525	—	6 699	—	2	461	— *
1984	23 436 *	20 407 *	53	—	1 026	2 162	2 529	10 493	—	6 672	—	1 *	499	—
1985	25 972 *	22 008 *	50	—	1 204	1 948	3 414	12 448	—	6 357	—	2 *	550	—
1986	25 273 *	21 237 *	57	—	1 302	1 994	3 405	11 636	—	6 247	—	1 *	631 *	—
SORGHUM														**SORGHO**
1983	437	359	—	—	—	2	79	248	—	109	—	—	—	—
1984	460	364	—	—	—	1	95	258	—	105	—	—	—	—
1985	362 *	263 *	—	—	—	1 *	98	206	—	56	—	—	—	—
1986	340 *	234 *	—	—	—	1 *	106	172	—	61	—	—	—	—
TRITICALE														**TRITICALE**
1983	74 *	74 *	— *	—	—	—	—	68	—	6	—	—	—	—
1984	179 *	179 *	— *	—	—	—	—	168	—	11	—	—	—	—
1985	280	280	11	—	—	—	—	255	—	14	—	—	—	—
1986	361	361	22	—	—	—	—	325	—	15	—	—	—	—
RICE (PADDY)														**RIZ (PADDY)**
1983	1 478	1 145	—	—	—	86	224	38	—	1 021	—	—	109	—
1984	1 714	1 139	—	—	—	95	440	36	—	1 009	—	—	134	—
1985	1 896	1 287	—	—	—	103	462	62	—	1 123	—	—	147	—
1986	1 913	1 266	—	—	—	121	494	60	—	1 085	—	—	153	—
DRIED PULSES														**LEGUMES SECS**
1983	1 841 *	1 496 *	5 *	78 *	36 *	69	276	752	0 *	268	0 *	44	70	243
1984	2 478 *	2 062 *	4 *	285 *	55 *	66	336	921	1 *	304	0 *	74	79	352
1985	3 049 *	2 632 *	5 *	523 *	125 *	60	338	1 138	1 *	265	0	91	79	425 *
1986	3 589 *	3 183 *	11 *	534 *	264 *	68	325 *	1 329 *	1 *	252	0	164	81 *	560 *
PEAS OTHER THAN FIELDPEAS														**POIS SECS AUTRES QUE POIS FOURRAGERS**
1983	211 *	153 *	3	0	—	8	50	40	0 *	17	0 *	32	8	53
1984	271 *	194 *	2	0	4 *	6	63	49	1 *	19	— *	56	14	57
1985	310 *	239 *	2	0	5 *	6	58	81	1 *	17	—	71	13	55 *
1986	357 *	286 *	8	0	7 *	6	59 *	69	1 *	16	0	124	12 *	55 *
FIELDPEAS														**POIS FOURRAGERS**
1983	661 *	659 *	—	75	—	0	2	499	—	—	—	:	:	85
1984	1 056 *	1 053 *	—	265	17 *	1	3	601	—	—	—	:	:	170
1985	1 653 *	1 649 *	—	506	47 *	0	4	881	—	—	—	:	:	215
1986	2 009 *	2 003 *	—	514	127 *	1	6	1 087	—	—	—	:	:	275 *

ID 1

HARVESTED CROPS AREA

SUPERFICIES RECOLTEES

YEAR ANNÉE	EUR 12	EUR 10	B	DK	D	GR	E	F	IRL	I	L	NL	P	UK
						1000 HA								
BEANS													**HARICOTS,FEVES,FEVEROLES**	
1983	758 *	337 *	1	— *	6	30	163	68	—	195	0	4	259	34
1984	753 *	346 *	1	— *	9 *	28	167	85	—	186	0	5	240 *	32
1985	696 *	316 *	1	— *	16 *	27	155	53	—	168	0	5	225 *	46
1986	751 *	349 *	1	— *	30 *	26	155	53	—	171	0	9	246 *	60
OTHER DRIED PULSES													**AUTRES LEGUMES SECS**	
1983	232 *	56 *	0	1 *	7	17	176	12	—	19 *	0	—	:	—
1984	207 *	46 *	0	4 *	1 *	16	161	12	—	12	0	—	:	—
1985	200 *	39 *	0	4 *	3 *	10	161	9	—	12	— *	—	:	—
1986	210 *	42 *	0	5 *	4 *	11	167 *	10 *	—	12	— *	—	:	—
POTATOES													**POMMES DE TERRE**	
1983	1 577	1 105	43	30	224	64	340	204	34	147	1	163	132	196
1984	1 570 *	1 094 *	44	31	219	59	348	205 *	36	139	1	160	129	200
1985	1 563	1 100	49	30	220	56	331	211	33	138	1	169	132	192
1986	1 477	1 056	48	31	210	56	289	201	31	133	1	167	131	179
EARLY POTATOES													**POMMES DE TERRE HATIVES**	
1983	:	:	4	:	19	24	51	23	:	29	0	:	:	16
1984	:	:	4	:	20	22	53	23	:	27	0	:	:	21
1985	:	:	5	:	22	16	50	24	:	29	0	:	:	17
1986	:	:	4	:	20	15	39	21	:	28 *	0	:	:	17
OTHER POTATOES													**AUTRES POMMES DE TERRE**	
1983	:	:	39	:	205	40	288	180	:	118	1	:	:	180
1984	:	:	40	:	199	38	295	182	:	112	1	:	:	179
1985	:	:	45	:	198	40	281	187	:	109	1	:	:	176
1986	:	:	44	:	189	41	250	180	:	105 *	1	:	:	162
SUGAR BEET													**BETTERAVES SUCRIERES**	
1983	1 936	1 686	109	72	393	38	249	490	36	232	0	117	1	199
1984	1 959	1 738	117	74	405	29	220	526	35	225	0	129	1	198
1985	1 904 *	1 723 *	118	73	403	41	180	491	33	232	0	131	1	202 *
1986	1 913	1 717	113	70	390	42	195	449	37	277	0	138	1	201
FODDER BEET													**BETTERAVES FOURRAGERES**	
1983	437	419	15	121	120	0	17	271	6	15	0	2	:	5
1984	431 *	414 *	15	124	111	0 *	17	262	6	15	0	2	:	8
1985	405 *	388 *	15	120	102	0 *	17	232	6	15	0	2	:	12 *
1986	381 *	365 *	14	117	94	0 *	16 *	209	7	15 *	0	2	:	12
OTHER ROOT CROPS													**AUTRES PLANTES SARCLEES**	
1983	:	:	26	10	6	0	94	402	14	24 *	0	:	:	105
1984	:	:	25 *	8	6	0	93	361	14	32	—	:	:	103
1985	:	:	21 *	5	6	0 *	88	308	14 *	31 *	0	:	:	99 *
1986	:	:	24 *	0	6	0 *	88 *	286	13	31 *	0	:	:	92
OILSEEDS													**PLANTES OLEAGINEUSES**	
1983	2 924 *	1 902	11	165	232	193	1 001	959	3	97	1	19	22 *	222
1984	3 284 *	2 144	15	195	254	255	1 101	1 009	4	122	1	20	40 *	269
1985	3 619 *	2 491 *	13	219	266	285	1 087	1 196	4	195	1	15 *	41 *	296 *
1986	4 000 *	2 916 *	10	230 *	308	313 *	1 043 *	1 380 *	2	364	1	9	41 *	299
RAPE AND TURNIP RAPE													**COLZA ET NAVETTE**	
1983	1 120	1 107	4	162	232	—	13	470	3	0	1	13	—	222
1984	1 181	1 173	5	191	254	—	8	433	4	2	1	13	—	269
1985	1 287	1 277	2	218	266	—	10	474	4	6	1	10	—	296
1986	1 259 *	1 254 *	3	227	308	—	5	386 *	2	23	1	6	—	299 *

SOURCE: CRONOS-ZPA1 DATA BANK, AGRICULTURAL PRODUCTS

SOURCE: BANQUE DE DONNEES CRONOS-ZPA1, PRODUITS AGRICOLES

HARVESTED PRODUCTION

PRODUCTION RECOLTEE

YEAR ANNÉE	EUR 12	EUR 10	B	DK	D	GR	E	F	IRL	I	L	NL	P	UK
								1000 T						
BEANS													**HARICOTS,FEVES,FEVEROLES**	
1983	:	:	2	– *	17	40	118	194	–	237	0	13	61	105
1984	:	:	2	– *	31 *	40	140	248	–	271	0	17	65	125
1985	:	:	2	– *	60 *	39	131	157	–	235	0	19	66	155 *
1986	:	:	2	– *	114 *	47	128	152	–	224	0	39	69 *	230
OTHER DRIED PULSES													**AUTRES LEGUMES SECS**	
1983	181 *	:	1 *	4 *	18 *	20	106	19	–	13	:	–	:	–
1904	212 *	:	1 *	20 *	4 *	20	130	22	–	14	:	–	:	–
1985	220 *	:	1 *	17 *	12 *	14	144	19	–	13	:	–	:	–
1986	217 *	:	1 *	20 *	15 *	15	132 *	21 *	–	12	:	–	:	–
POTATOES													**POMMES DE TERRE**	
1983	34 787	28 617	1 194	853	5 669	1 135	5 163	5 317	661	2 502	17	5 412	1 007	5 857
1984	41 693	34 610	1 614	1 121	7 272	1 051	5 981	6 125	870	2 450	36	6 673	1 102	7 398
1985	43 021	35 879	1 805	1 100	7 905	1 009	5 927	6 913	686	2 390	29	7 150	1 215	6 892
1986	39 639	33 668	1 667	1 129	7 390	971	4 857	6 021	619	2 547	25	6 854	1 114	6 445
EARLY POTATOES													**POMMES DE TERRE HATIVES**	
1983	:	:	71	:	424	443	778	443	:	449	1 *	:	:	322
1984	:	:	89	:	540	381	911	437	:	443	:	:	:	397
1985	:	:	106	:	630	350	850	478	:	455	:	:	:	403
1986	:	:	85	:	556	316	702	386	:	498	:	:	:	365
OTHER POTATOES													**AUTRES POMMES DE TERRE**	
1983	:	:	1 123	:	5 245	692	4 385	4 874	:	2 053	16 *	:	:	5 535
1984	:	:	1 525	:	6 733	670	5 070	5 688	:	2 007	:	:	:	7 001
1985	:	:	1 699	:	7 276	659	5 077	6 435	:	1 934	:	:	:	6 489
1986	:	:	1 582	:	6 835	654	4 155	5 634	:	2 048	:	:	:	6 080
SUGAR BEET													**BETTERAVES SUCRIERES**	
1983	87 079 *	77 418 *	5 120	2 616	16 295	2 413	9 619	26 320	1 630	10 084	1 *	5 445	42	7 494
1984	97 281 *	89 120 *	5 763	3 614	20 060	1 775	8 095	28 752	1 694	11 490	1 *	6 955	66	9 015
1985	94 352 *	87 702 *	5 952	3 515	20 813	2 506	6 619	29 989	1 309	9 567	0 *	6 335	31	7 715
1986	96 438	88 707	5 886	3 195	20 260	2 458	7 701	24 848	1 274	14 959	0	7 707	30	8 120
FODDER BEET													**BETTERAVES FOURRAGERES**	
1983	25 852	25 313	1 305	5 553	9 715	0	540	14 928	288	525	3	165	:	296
1984	30 193 *	29 638 *	1 409	8 195	10 884	0 *	554	15 014	340	552	10	171	:	570
1985	28 779 *	28 243 *	1 355	7 534	10 810	0 *	536	13 367	345	500	11	189	:	815
1986	26 484 *	25 934 *	1 316	7 105	9 798	0 *	550 *	11 691	343	500 *	10	171	:	845
OTHER ROOT CROPS													**AUTRES PLANTES SARCLEES**	
1983	:	:	:	:	437 *	2	1 774	8 682	:	:	:	:	:	:
1984	:	:	:	:	522 *	4	1 802	6 692	:	:	:	:	:	:
1985	:	:	:	:	663 *	4 *	1 678	5 976	:	:	:	:	:	:
1986	:	:	:	:	600 *	4 *	1 707 *	5 922	:	:	:	:	:	:
OILSEEDS													**PLANTES OLEAGINEUSES**	
1983	4 715 *	3 862 *	16	312 *	599	257	842	1 869	8	192	1	45	11 *	563
1984	6 400 *	5 133	19	478	662	312	1 237	2 412	15	263	2	47	30 *	925
1985	7 256 *	6 163 *	14	548	803	362	1 064	3 026	14	463	1	37 *	29 *	895
1986	8 298 *	7 253 *	14	625 *	969	506 *	1 014 *	3 027	6	1 114	2	25 *	30 *	965
RAPE AND TURNIP RAPE													**COLZA ET NAVETTE**	
1983	2 504	2 496	10	309	599	–	8	967	8	1	1	38	–	563
1984	3 499	3 490	11	474	662	–	10	1 358	15	5	2	38	–	925
1985	3 737	3 725	6	544	803	–	12	1 419	14	13	1	31	–	895
1986	3 685 *	3 673 *	8	613	969	–	12	1 046 *	6	44	2	20	–	965

CROP PRODUCTS (EXC.VEGETABLES & FRUITS)

I D 1

PRODUITS VEGETAUX (EXC. LEGUMES ET FRUITS)

HARVESTED CROPS AREA

SUPERFICIES RECOLTEES

1000 HA

YEAR ANNÉE	EUR 12	EUR 10	B	DK	D	GR	E	F	IRL	I	L	NL	P	UK
SUNFLOWER SEEDS													**GRAINES DE TOURNESOL**	
1983	1 464	517	–	–	–	13	926	431	–	72	–	–	21	–
1984	1 675	630	–	–	–	43	1 007	504	–	83	–	–	38	–
1985	1 811	783	–	–	–	50	989	639	–	95	–	–	40	–
1986	2 061	1 085	–	–	–	79	936	901	–	104	–	–	40	–
OILFLAX													**LIN OLEAGINEUX**	
1983	51 *	51 *	7	0	–	–	–	39	–	0 *	–	3	– *	–
1984	61 *	61 *	10	0	–	–	0	46	–	1 *	–	4	– *	–
1985	69 *	69 *	11	0	–	–	–	53	–	1 *	–	4 *	– *	–
1986	53 *	53 *	8	1 *	–	–	–	41 *	–	0 *	–	3 *	– *	–
SOYABEANS													**GRAINES DE SOJA**	
1983	37	36	–	–	–	–	1	13	–	23	–	–	–	–
1984	61	58	–	–	–	0	3	22	–	36	–	–	–	–
1985	124	121	–	–	–	0	2	27	–	94	–	–	–	–
1986	286 *	283 *	–	–	–	0 *	3 *	47	–	236	–	–	–	–
OTHER OILSEEDS													**AUTRES PLANTES OLEAGINEUSES**	
1983	252 *	190 *	0	3	–	180	60	5	–	1 *	–	2	1	–
1984	306 *	222 *	0	3	–	211	82	4	–	1 *	–	2	2	–
1985	328 *	241 *	0	0	–	235	86	4	–	1 *	–	1 *	2	– *
1986	342 *	242 *	0	3 *	–	234	99 *	4 *	–	1 *	–	0 *	1	– *
FLAX (STRAW)													**LIN (PAILLE)**	
1983	53 *	53 *	7	–	–	0	0	42	–	0 *	–	3	– *	–
1984	64 *	64 *	10	–	–	0	0	50	–	1 *	–	4	– *	–
1985	74 *	74 *	11	–	–	0	0	59	–	1 *	–	4	– *	–
1986	58 *	58 *	8	–	–	0	0 *	47	–	0 *	–	3	– *	–
HEMP (STRAW)													**CHANVRE (PAILLE)**	
1983	5 *	5 *	–	–	–	–	0	5	–	0 *	–	–	–	–
1984	5	5	–	–	–	–	0	5	–	0	–	–	–	–
1985	7 *	6 *	–	–	–	–	0	6	–	– *	–	–	–	–
1986	6 *	6 *	–	–	–	–	0	6	–	0 *	–	–	–	–
TOBACCO													**TABAC**	
1983	204 *	181 *	0	–	3	91	22	14	–	71 *	–	–	1	–
1984	209	185	1	–	3	92	22	14	–	76	–	–	1	–
1985	223 *	197 *	1	–	3	98	25	15	–	81 *	–	–	2	–
1986	220	196	1	–	3	97	22	15	–	80	–	–	2	–
HOPS													**HOUBLON**	
1983	29 *	27 *	1	–	20	– *	2	1	0	–	–	–	:	6
1984	28 *	26 *	1	–	19	– *	2	1	0	–	–	–	:	5
1985	28 *	26 *	1	–	19	0 *	2	1	0	–	–	–	:	5
1986	27 *	25 *	1	–	20	0 *	2	1	0	–	–	–	:	4 *
CHICORY													**CHICOREE A CAFE**	
1983	7	6	1	–	–	–	1	5	–	–	–	–	0	–
1984	6	5	1	–	–	–	1	4	–	–	–	–	0	–
1985	8	6	1	–	–	–	1	5	–	–	–	–	0	–
1986	8 *	7	1	–	–	–	1	5	–	–	–	–	0	–
CARAWAY													**CUMIN**	
1983	3	3	–	1	–	–	0	–	–	–	–	2	–	–
1984	3 *	3 *	–	1 *	–	–	0	–	–	–	–	2	–	–
1985	4	4	–	1	–	–	0	–	–	–	–	2	–	–
1986	4 *	3 *	–	2 *	–	–	0	–	–	–	–	2	–	–

SOURCE: CRONOS-ZPA1 DATA BANK, AGRICULTURAL PRODUCTS

SOURCE: BANQUE DE DONNEES CRONOS-ZPA1, PRODUITS AGRICOLES

HARVESTED PRODUCTION

PRODUCTION RECOLTEE

1000 T

YEAR ANNÉE	EUR 12	EUR 10	B	DK	D	GR	E	F	IRL	I	L	NL	P	UK
SUNFLOWER SEEDS													**GRAINES DE TOURNESOL**	
1983	1 760	999	–	–	–	27	750	841	–	131	–	–	11	–
1984	2 321	1 193	–	–	–	69	1 100	978	–	146	–	–	28	–
1985	2 704	1 760	–	–	–	85	915	1 513	–	162	–	–	28	–
1986	3 150	2 277	–	–	–	164	844	1 858	–	255	–	–	29	–
OILFLAX													**LIN OLEAGINEUX**	
1983	34 *	34 *	6	0 *	–	–	–	23	–	0	–	4	– *	–
1984	41 *	41	8	–	–	–	0	27	–	0	–	6	– *	–
1985	49 *	49 *	8	0 *	–	–	–	34	–	0	–	6 *	– *	–
1986	37 *	37 *	6	0 *	–	–	–	25 *	–	0 *	–	5 *	– *	–
SOYABEANS													**GRAINES DE SOJA**	
1983	91	89	–	–	–	–	2	30	–	59	–	–	–	–
1984	160	155	–	–	–	0	5	46	–	110	–	–	–	–
1985	348	343	–	–	–	0	5	56	–	286	–	–	–	–
1986	915 *	909 *	–	–	–	0 *	6 *	95	–	814	–	–	–	–
OTHER OILSEEDS												**AUTRES PLANTES OLEAGINEUSES**		
1983	326 *	244 *	–	3 *	–	230	82	7	–	1	–	3	0	–
1984	379	254	–	4	–	243	123	3	–	1	–	3	1	–
1985	418 *	286 *	–	4 *	–	277	131	3	–	1	–	1	1	–
1986	511 *	358 *	–	12 *	–	342	152	3 *	–	1 *	–	0	1	–
FLAX (STRAW)													**LIN (PAILLE)**	
1983	346 *	346 *	43	–	–	0 *	–	281	–	0	–	21	– *	–
1984	475 *	475 *	65	–	–	– *	–	378	–	0	–	32	– *	–
1985	566 *	566 *	70	–	–	– *	–	460	–	0	–	36	– *	–
1986	:	:	48	–	–	– *	– *	282	–	:	–	25	– *	–
HEMP (STRAW)													**CHANVRE (PAILLE)**	
1983	25	25	–	–	–	–	0	25	–	0	–	–	–	–
1984	30	29	–	–	–	–	1	29	–	0	–	–	–	–
1985	37	36	–	–	–	–	2	36	–	–	–	–	–	–
1986	34 *	32 *	–	–	–	–	2 *	32	–	– *	–	–	–	–
TOBACCO													**TABAC**	
1983	362	316	2	–	7	116	43	36	–	156	–	–	2	–
1984	397	351	2	–	7	145	43	35	–	161	–	–	3	–
1985	408	362	2	–	8	150	42	36	–	166	–	–	3	–
1986	410 *	363	2	–	8	161	43 *	36	–	156	–	–	4	–
HOPS													**HOUBLON**	
1983	52 *	49 *	1	–	37	– *	3	1	0	–	–	–	:	9
1984	49 *	46 *	1	–	36	– *	3	1	0	–	–	–	:	8
1985	47 *	44 *	1	–	36	0 *	3	1	0	–	–	–	:	6
1986	44 *	41 *	1	–	34	0 *	3	1	0	–	–	–	:	5
CHICORY													**CHICOREE A CAFE**	
1983	210	183	42	–	–	–	20	141	–	–	–	–	7	–
1984	192	156	36	–	–	–	20	120	–	–	–	–	15	–
1985	267	229	46	–	–	–	27	183	–	–	–	–	11	–
1986	266 *	235	50	–	–	–	20	186	–	–	–	–	11	–
CARAWAY													**CUMIN**	
1983	4 *	4 *	–	1 *	–	–	0	–	–	–	–	3	–	–
1984	3 *	3 *	–	1 *	–	–	0	–	–	–	–	1	–	–
1985	4 *	4 *	–	1 *	–	–	0	–	–	–	–	3	–	–
1986	5 *	5 *	–	1 *	–	–	0	–	–	–	–	4	–	–

| ID 1 |

HARVESTED CROPS AREA

SUPERFICIES RECOLTEES

YEAR ANNÉE	EUR 12	EUR 10	B	DK	D	GR	E	F	IRL	I	L	NL	P	UK
						1000 HA								
FODDER (TOTAL)													**FOURRAGES (TOTAL)**	
1983	:	54 934 *	799	636	5 734	2 116 *	:	17 748	5 209 *	7 688	87	1 341	1 231 *	13 575
1984	:	54 347 *	799	616	5 782	2 001 *	:	17 441	5 190 *	7 596	89	1 347	1 231 *	13 486
1985	:	54 037 *	800	577	5 790	2 030 *	:	17 220	5 207 *	7 592	89	1 344	1 231 *	13 387 *
1986	:	53 874 *	795	570	5 791	2 009 *	:	17 189	5 204 *	7 547	90	1 345 *	1 231 *	13 333
ANNUAL GREEN FODDER													**FOURRAGES VERTS ANNUELS**	
1983	:	:	109 *	:	1 993 *	173 *	518	2 092	:	1 372	7	160 *	:	40 *
1984	:	:	118 *	:	2 140 *	65 *	522	2 035	:	1 375	9	167 *	:	36 *
1985	:	:	129	:	:	66 *	502	2 041	:	1 345	10	179 *	:	40 *
1986	:	:	:	:	:	66 *	507 *	2 193	:	1 273	10	199 *	:	43 *
GREEN MAIZE													**MAIS FOURRAGE**	
1983	3 061 *	2 958	101	16	807	3	102	1 409	—	444	5	157	:	15
1984	3 147 *	3 040	108	21	869	3	106	1 405	—	448	6	164	:	16
1985	3 288 *	3 181 *	119	20	932	4 *	107	1 462	—	442	7	176	:	20
1986	3 444 *	3 336 *	120	25	947	4 *	107	1 619	—	396	7	196	:	23
PERENNIAL GREEN FODDER													**FOURRAGES VERTS PLURANNUELS**	
1983	9 282	8 648	37	320	291	:	:	3 556	586	1 823	9	41	:	1 832
1984	9 090	8 466	37	314	301	:	:	3 470	592	1 778	9	40	:	1 779
1985	8 986 *	8 377 *	31	282	287	:	:	3 372	595	1 805	9	41	:	1 780 *
1986	8 757 *	8 146 *	32	268	301	:	:	3 293	591 *	1 750	9	40 *	:	1 708
CLOVER AND MIXTURES													**TREFLES ET MELANGES**	
1983	625	:	2	:	160	—	—	112	—	335	1	0	—	:
1984	:	:	1	:	158	—	—	104	—	:	0	0	—	:
1985	:	:	1	:	153	—	—	97	—	:	0	0	—	:
1986	:	:	2	:	157	—	—	95	—	:	0	0	—	:
LUCERNE													**LUZERNE**	
1983	2 135 *	1 808 *	1	3	29	:	:	567	—	1 050 *	0	2	:	—
1984	2 092	1 771	1	4	30	:	:	548	—	1 039	0	3	:	—
1985	:	:	1	4	28	:	:	514	—	:	0	3	:	0 *
1986	:	:	1	5	27	:	:	496	—	:	0	3	:	0
OTHER LEGUMES													**AUTRES LEGUMINEUSES**	
1983	:	:	—	—	—	:	:	52	—	240 *	—	—	:	:
1984	:	:	—	—	—	:	:	56	—	263	—	—	:	:
1985	:	:	—	—	—	:	:	55	—	:	—	—	:	:
1986	:	:	—	—	—	:	:	50	—	:	—	—	:	:
TEMPORARY GRASSES AND GRAZINGS													**PRAIRIES ET PATURAGES TEMPORAIRES**	
1983	6 214 *	5 979 *	34	317	102	—	—	2 824	586	238 *	8	38	—	1 832
1984	6 119	5 885	34	311	113	—	—	2 762	592	249	8	37	—	1 779
1985	:	:	28	278	105	—	—	2 707	595	:	8	38	—	1 780
1986	:	:	29	264	117	—	—	2 652	591 *	:	9	37 *	—	1 708
PERMANENT GRASSLAND													**SUPERFICIES TOUJOURS COUVERTES D'HERBE**	
1983	49 791	42 385	653	236	4 630	1 789	6 645	12 535	4 622	5 002	71	1 143	761	11 704
1984	49 528	42 121	644	228	4 607	1 789	6 646	12 362	4 597	5 012	71	1 141	761	11 670
1985	49 153 *	41 746	640	221	4 566	1 789	6 646 *	12 200	4 612	4 954	71	1 127	761	11 567
1986	48 995 *	41 589	632	219	4 537	1 789	6 645 *	12 094	4 612	4 944	70	1 108	761	11 583
PERMANENT MEADOWS													**PRAIRIES PERMANENTES**	
1983	:	:	237	:	3 418	:	1 452	3 893	935	1 094	32	:	33 *	:
1984	:	:	238	:	3 404	:	1 440	3 825	937	1 085	28	:	33 *	:
1985	:	:	242	:	2 389	:	1 450 *	3 767	948	1 090	29	:	33 *	:
1986	:	:	246	:	2 370	:	1 450 *	3 800 *	940 *	1 088	28	:	33 *	:

SOURCE: CRONOS-ZPA1 DATA BANK, AGRICULTURAL PRODUCTS

SOURCE: BANQUE DE DONNEES CRONOS-ZPA1, PRODUITS AGRICOLES

HARVESTED PRODUCTION　　　　　　　　　　　　　　　　　　　　　　PRODUCTION RECOLTEE

YEAR ANNÉE	EUR 12	EUR 10	B	DK	D	GR	E	F	IRL	I	L	NL	P	UK
						1000 T								
FODDER (TOTAL)														**FOURRAGES (TOTAL)**
1983	:	361 648 *	6 434 *	11 644	50 904 *	13 582 *	:	95 160	37 000 *	32 720	452	24 760 *	:	88 993 *
1984	:	356 700 *	6 734 *	12 415	54 434 *	13 542 *	:	85 783	37 000 *	32 672	499	24 621 *	:	89 000 *
1985	:	:	:	11 846	46 761	13 769 *	:	91 448	37 000 *	30 952 *	472 *	25 012 *	:	89 048 *
1986	:	:	:	11 425 *	47 101 *	13 612 *	:	89 220 *	37 000 *	31 385 *	461 *	25 689 *	:	4 169 *
ANNUAL GREEN FODDER														**FOURRAGES VERTS ANNUELS**
1983	:	:	4 868 *	3 456	57 316 *	:	:	76 373	:	42 669	225	7 039 *	:	1 571 *
1984	:	:	4 920 *	4 225	63 419 *	:	:	72 467	:	43 271	350	6 485 *	:	1 600 *
1985	:	:	:	3 848	67 727	:	:	76 415	:	41 722 *	377	8 050 *	:	1 790 *
1986	:	:	:	3 848	70 637 *	:	:	76 837	:	40 000	373	10 757 *	:	1 935 *
GREEN MAIZE														**MAIS FOURRAGE**
1983	127 278	:	4 567	540	33 416	38	3 641	56 320	—	21 089	178	6 938	:	551
1984	129 151	:	4 580	842	37 919	35	3 676	53 705	—	21 115	290	6 408	:	580
1985	143 180 *	:	5 262	855	44 387	45 *	3 935	59 621	—	20 022	312	7 971	:	770
1986	148 020 *	:	6 091	887	45 427	45 *	3 861	61 056	—	18 754	307	10 676	:	915
PERENNIAL GREEN FODDER														**FOURRAGES VERTS PLURIANNUELS**
1983	:	:	392	2 770	:	1 573	:	25 549	:	14 066	43	:	:	3 600 *
1984	:	:	413	3 208	:	1 533	:	17 863	:	13 973	44	:	:	3 600 *
1985	:	:	323	2 807	:	1 758	:	23 084	:	13 139	48	:	:	3 600 *
1986	:	:	303	2 463	:	1 601	:	20 511	:	12 958 *	45	:	:	3 600 *
CLOVER AND MIXTURES														**TREFLES ET MELANGES**
1983	4 859	:	13	:	1 221	:	97	782	:	2 744	3	—	:	:
1984	4 586	:	11	:	1 332	:	91	744	:	2 406	2	—	:	:
1985	4 387	:	9	:	1 300	:	89	642	:	2 346	2	—	:	:
1986	4 258 *	:	12	:	1 336	:	90 *	567	:	2 250	2	—	:	:
LUCERNE														**LUZERNE**
1983	17 578	:	13	39	226	1 573	3 371	4 396	:	7 960	2	:	:	:
1984	18 082	:	15	43	259	1 533	3 495	4 518	:	8 218	0	:	:	:
1985	16 917	:	11	49	241	1 758	3 354	3 969	:	7 535	0	:	:	:
1986	16 377 *	:	11	53	240	1 601	3 515	3 457	:	7 500 *	0	:	:	:
OTHER LEGUMES														**AUTRES LEGUMINEUSES**
1983	:	:	:	:	:	:	124	365	:	1 033	:	:	:	:
1984	:	:	:	:	:	:	136	370	:	1 215	:	:	:	:
1985	:	:	:	:	:	:	146	348	:	1 097	:	:	:	:
1986	:	:	:	:	:	:	136 *	276	:	1 100 *	:	:	:	:
TEMPORARY GRASSES AND GRAZINGS														**PRAIRIES ET PATURAGES TEMPORAIRES**
1983	:	:	367	2 731	761	—	—	20 007	:	2 330	:	:	—	:
1984	:	:	386	3 165	983	—	—	12 230	:	2 134	:	:	—	:
1985	:	:	303	2 758	924	—	—	18 125	:	2 162	:	:	—	:
1986	:	:	280	2 410	996	—	—	16 210	:	2 108	:	:	—	:
PERMANENT GRASSLAND														**SUPERFICIES TOUJOURS COUVERTES D'HERBE**
1983	:	:	4 824	8 010	34 368 *	12 000 *	:	50 518	:	7 987	353	23 000 *	:	85 000 *
1984	:	:	5 091	8 151	36 005 *	12 000 *	:	49 803	:	7 881	367	23 000 *	:	85 000 *
1985	:	:	5 099 *	8 077	27 364	12 000 *	:	49 260	:	7 382	330 *	23 000 *	:	85 000 *
1986	:	:	5 039 *	8 000 *	26 870	12 000 *	:	49 500 *	:	8 427	322 *	23 000 *	:	85 *
PERMANENT MEADOWS														**PRAIRIES PERMANENTES**
1983	:	:	1 975	:	25 368	:	:	19 164	:	5 253	157	:	:	:
1984	:	:	2 126	:	27 005	:	:	18 538	:	4 816	142	:	:	:
1985	:	:	2 099	:	18 769	:	:	18 661	:	4 620	130	:	:	:
1986	:	:	2 039	:	18 510	:	:	18 500 *	:	5 441	122	:	:	:

SOURCE: CRONOS-ZPA1 DATA BANK, AGRICULTURAL PRODUCTS　　　　　　　SOURCE: BANQUE DE DONNEES CRONOS-ZPA1, PRODUITS AGRICOLES

I D 1

YIELD

RENDEMENT

100 KG/H

YEAR ANNÉE	EUR 12	EUR 10	B	DK	D	GR	E	F	IRL	I	L	NL	P	UK
COMMON WHEAT AND SPELT													**BLE TENDRE ET EPEAUTRE**	
1983	43,5 *	50,5	53,0	64,0	54,4	21,7	16,5	51,8	65,6	36,0	29,9	70,4	9,9 *	63,7
1984	55,3 *	61,9	69,5	73,6	62,6	26,3	25,8	65,2	78,0	36,9	43,7	78,9	15,9 *	77,2
1985	51,0 *	56,4 *	63,1	58,0	60,8	21,6	25,9	60,6	63,4	35,6	43,1	66,5	14,0	63,4 *
1986	50,2	56,6	68,3	61,5	63,4	26,4	20,3	55,5	55,7	36,9	41,8	80,0	16,8	69,7
WINTER COMMON WHEAT													**BLE TENDRE D'HIVER**	
1983	:	:	53,4	65,2	55,1	21,7	:	51,9	:	36,0	33,0	71,4	:	:
1984	:	:	70,0	74,5	63,1	26,3	:	65,3	:	36,9	45,0	79,5	:	:
1985	:	:	63,7	58,4	61,3	21,6	:	60,8	:	35,6 *	45,0	67,0	:	:
1986	:	:	68,7	61,8	64,0	26,4	:	55,6	:	36,9	42,8	80,7	:	:
SPRING COMMON WHEAT													**BLE TENDRE DE PRINTEMPS**	
1983	:	:	42,1	35,4	42,4	–	–	39,0	:	18,3	18,6	48,3	–	:
1984	:	:	51,7	44,9	52,9	–	–	50,6	:	19,3	39,2	57,2	–	:
1985	:	:	46,9	44,4	49,7	–	–	51,4	:	18,7 *	40,5	56,6	–	:
1986	:	:	49,7	52,0	49,4	–	–	39,6	:	19,2	38,5	66,4	–	:
DURUM WHEAT													**BLE DUR**	
1983	18,2 *	18,5 *	–	–	50,0 *	19,3	15,2	35,6	–	17,3	–	–	9,9 *	–
1984	27,3 *	27,0 *	–	–	45,6 *	27,4	33,2	44,2	–	25,7	–	–	16,5 *	–
1985	23,6 *	23,5 *	–	–	58,0	19,1	28,0	44,3	–	22,1	–	–	13,9	40,0 *
1986	25,9 *	26,0 *	–	60,0	48,0	26,5	24,2	39,4	–	23,5	–	–	16,7	65,0 *
RYE													**SEIGLE**	
1983	26,4 *	35,1 *	38,3	41,2	36,0	18,6	11,6	28,9	– *	23,7	30,3	38,7	7,0	36,8
1984	32,4	43,1	45,7	49,9	43,9	18,2	13,7	34,8	–	26,2	34,1	42,9	8,0	45,4
1985	31,4 *	41,4 *	43,7	44,5	42,8	19,4	12,9	34,0	–	25,2	39,5	42,2	7,9	45,0 *
1986	29,9 *	40,9	43,2	45,1	42,7	22,7	9,9	28,2	–	26,5	34,3	48,6	7,8 *	46,4
BARLEY													**ORGE**	
1983	33,9	40,9	48,3	32,8	44,0	19,0	17,8	40,9	48,0	30,9	22,0	47,4	6,5	46,5
1984	43,6	51,7	64,3	51,4	51,3	23,4	26,8	54,6	58,2	37,3	38,6	56,5	10,9	55,9
1985	40,1	47,9	58,0	47,6	49,7	19,5	25,2	50,7	50,1	34,8	36,1	51,0	7,6	49,5
1986	37,0	47,8	62,0	47,2	48,2	25,6	16,9	48,3	50,5	33,2	35,7	62,4	10,3	52,2
WINTER BARLEY													**ORGE D'HIVER**	
1983	:	:	50,6	:	50,8	19,0	:	48,0	:	:	28,4	55,0	:	:
1984	:	:	66,1	:	56,3	23,4	:	58,5	:	:	40,1	63,4	:	:
1985	:	:	60,9	:	53,4	19,5	:	55,0	:	:	41,0	55,2	:	:
1986	:	:	64,7	:	51,6	25,6	:	55,2	:	:	39,0	65,1	:	:
SPRING BARLEY													**ORGE DE PRINTEMPS**	
1983	:	:	31,6	:	32,8	–	–	28,7	:	:	20,0	44,6	–	:
1984	:	:	44,1	:	41,1	–	–	46,1	:	:	38,0	53,3	–	:
1985	:	:	40,3	:	43,9	–	–	43,8	:	:	35,1	50,1	–	:
1986	:	:	39,7	:	41,7	–	–	34,0	:	:	34,7	61,6	–	:
OATS													**AVOINE**	
1983	24,5	31,4	38,0	29,5	34,4	14,4	10,2	32,6	44,7	15,1	13,5	45,2	5,2	43,3
1984	32,3	41,0	48,9	46,7	45,2	15,1	16,4	42,6	56,6	22,6	32,2	48,0	7,8	48,6
1985	32,3	41,1	44,7	41,0	48,1	15,2	14,8	40,9	45,5	20,0	37,9	51,6	6,3	45,9
1986	29,1	38,3	43,8	44,4	45,0	16,1	11,0	34,2	48,8	21,6	32,9	61,1	7,9	52,1
GRAIN MAIZE													**MAIS (GRAIN)**	
1983	60,3 *	65,8 *	75,3	–	55,3	91,5	50,9	62,5	–	68,2	–	48,0	15,6	– *
1984	61,3 *	65,3 *	67,6	–	56,5	93,4	57,5	60,2	–	69,5	–	50,0 *	19,4	– *
1985	65,0 *	68,3 *	71,4	–	66,5	88,3	64,9	65,8 *	–	68,9	–	50,0 *	22,3	– *
1986	64,4 *	67,9 *	79,4	–	69,6	91,6	64,9	61,8	–	75,0	–	50,0 *	23,3 *	–

SOURCE: CRONOS-ZPA1 DATA BANK, AGRICULTURAL PRODUCTS

SOURCE: BANQUE DE DONNEES CRONOS-ZPA1, PRODUITS AGRICOLES

ID 1

YIELD   RENDEMENT

YEAR ANNÉE	EUR 12	EUR 10	B	DK	D	GR	E	F	IRL	I	L	NL	P	UK

100 KG/H

RICE (PADDY) / **RIZ (PADDY)**

YEAR ANNÉE	EUR 12	EUR 10	B	DK	D	GR	E	F	IRL	I	L	NL	P	UK
1983	54,4	56,0	:	:	:	59,6	54,9	50,6	:	56,0	:	:	41,2	:
1984	55,7	55,6	:	:	:	61,8	60,4	38,6	:	55,9	:	:	44,8	:
1985	59,5	60,1	:	:	:	60,6	62,0	55,0	:	60,4	:	:	48,4	:
1986	58,4 *	58,2 *	:	:	:	68,5	62,5	51,3	:	57,6 *	:	:	49,4	:

PEAS OTHER THAN FIELDPEAS / **POIS SECS AUTRES QUE POIS FOURRAGERS**

YEAR ANNÉE	EUR 12	EUR 10	B	DK	D	GR	E	F	IRL	I	L	NL	P	UK
1983	12,0 *	27,3 *	37,3	10,0	—	10,0	5,5	40,3	26,7 *	11,8	36,4 *	41,8	2,9	35,3 *
1984	15,4 *	34,2 *	40,9	0,0	31,1 *	10,4	6,8	47,1	32,5 *	13,7	— *	51,5	5,3	40,7
1985	16,7 *	34,7 *	39,1	10,0	37,5 *	11,3	6,4	49,3	40,0 *	13,6 *	—	36,5	5,2	42,3 *
1986	18,6 *	36,9 *	44,4	10,0	34,2 *	11,7	6,5 *	36,5	40,0 *	13,4 *	10,0	55,5	5,0 *	36,7 *

BEANS / **HARICOTS, FEVES, FEVEROLES**

YEAR ANNÉE	EUR 12	EUR 10	B	DK	D	GR	E	F	IRL	I	L	NL	P	UK
1983	:	:	32,7	— *	29,9	13,6	7,2	28,5	—	12,2	24,9	31,8	2,4	31,0
1984	:	:	30,9	— *	35,1 *	14,3	8,4	29,0	—	14,6	24,3	33,9	2,7 *	39,1
1985	:	:	32,9	— *	38,6 *	14,8	8,5	29,4	—	13,9	25,0	35,9	2,9 *	34,0 *
1986	:	:	31,1	— *	38,1 *	18,3	8,2	28,6	—	13,1	23,6	43,2	2,8 *	38,5

POTATOES / **POMMES DE TERRE**

YEAR ANNÉE	EUR 12	EUR 10	B	DK	D	GR	E	F	IRL	I	L	NL	P	UK
1983	220,6	258,9	279,8	280,1	253,0	178,0	151,9	261,0	197,3	170,5	180,0	331,3	76,5	298,7
1984	265,5 *	316,4 *	365,3	361,0	331,5	177,5	172,1	299,3 *	243,7	176,6	350,0	417,0	85,6	370,3
1985	275,2	326,2	366,8	362,0	359,3	178,9	179,1	328,0	207,9	173,3	320,0	423,4	91,9	358,4
1986	268,5	318,7	345,5	364,2	352,4	174,8	168,1	299,1	203,0	190,9	315,0	410,6	85,0	360,3

SUGAR BEET / **BETTERAVES SUCRIERES**

YEAR ANNÉE	EUR 12	EUR 10	B	DK	D	GR	E	F	IRL	I	L	NL	P	UK
1983	449,8 *	459,2 *	469,4	361,4	414,7	629,9	386,2	537,0	451,5	435,5	472,2 *	466,5	415,8	377,0
1984	496,7 *	512,8 *	492,6	489,6	494,7	621,9	367,7	547,1	485,4	510,6	650,0 *	537,9	819,1	454,8
1985	495,5 *	509,0 *	505,0	483,1	516,3	616,0	367,0	610,8	396,7	412,0	444,4 *	485,4	499,9	381,9 *
1986	504,1	516,6	522,0	456,4	518,8	580,5	394,9	553,9	344,3	539,7	400,0	559,7	300,0	404,0

RAPE AND TURNIP RAPE / **COLZA ET NAVETTE**

YEAR ANNÉE	EUR 12	EUR 10	B	DK	D	GR	E	F	IRL	I	L	NL	P	UK
1983	22,3	22,5	25,7	19,0	25,9	—	6,0	20,6	24,7	18,4	20,0	28,8	—	25,3
1984	29,6	29,8	21,1	24,8	26,0	—	11,7	31,4	33,7	23,8	25,0	28,7	—	34,4
1985	29,0	29,2	25,3	25,0	30,2	—	12,2	29,9	31,5	21,3	19,0	30,3	—	30,2
1986	29,3 *	29,3 *	30,6	27,0	31,5	—	24,4 *	27,1 *	29,7	19,2	28,5	34,6	—	32,3 *

TOBACCO / **TABAC**

YEAR ANNÉE	EUR 12	EUR 10	B	DK	D	GR	E	F	IRL	I	L	NL	P	UK
1983	17,7 *	17,5 *	33,8	—	22,8	12,7	19,4	25,2	—	21,8 *	—	—	18,8	—
1984	19,0	18,9	34,2	—	23,8	15,8	19,6	24,8	—	21,4	—	—	20,9	—
1985	18,3 *	18,4 *	34,9	—	27,2	15,4	17,2	24,6	—	20,6 *	—	—	21,9	—
1986	18,7 *	18,5	35,7	—	24,7	16,6	19,5 *	24,3	—	19,5	—	—	20,0	—

HOPS / **HOUBLON**

YEAR ANNÉE	EUR 12	EUR 10	B	DK	D	GR	E	F	IRL	I	L	NL	P	UK
1983	17,9 *	18,1 *	18,0	—	18,8	— *	14,9	18,8	14,5	—	—	—	—	16,0
1984	17,5 *	17,7 *	19,1	—	18,2	— *	14,6	18,7	15,3	—	—	—	—	15,4
1985	17,1 *	17,2 *	17,4	—	18,3	10,0 *	16,7	19,4	11,6	—	—	—	—	12,2
1986	16,7 *	16,7 *	18,3	—	17,5	10,0 *	16,9	19,8	4,1	—	—	—	—	12,2 *

GREEN MAIZE / **MAIS FOURRAGER**

YEAR ANNÉE	EUR 12	EUR 10	B	DK	D	GR	E	F	IRL	I	L	NL	P	UK
1983	415,9 *	:	452,6	334,4	414,0	113,7	356,5	399,7	—	475,0	350,0	442,8	:	364,5
1984	410,3 *	:	423,4	409,8	436,2	114,5	346,7	382,2	—	471,7	450,0	390,5	:	367,0
1985	435,4 *	:	443,5	419,9	476,5	128,6 *	368,6	407,9	—	453,0	475,0	451,6	:	386,3
1986	429,8 *	:	508,4	358,9	479,7	128,6 *	360,3	377,2	—	473,8	450,0	544,0	:	396,1

PERMANENT MEADOWS / **PRAIRIES PERMANENTES**

YEAR ANNÉE	EUR 12	EUR 10	B	DK	D	GR	E	F	IRL	I	L	NL	P	UK
1983	:	:	83,5	:	74,2	:	:	49,2	:	52,3	49,1	:	:	:
1984	:	:	89,2	:	79,3	:	:	48,5	:	44,4	49,9	:	:	:
1985	:	:	86,9	:	78,6	:	:	49,5	:	42,5	45,0	:	:	:
1986	:	:	82,8	:	78,1	:	:	48,7 *	:	50,0 *	43,0	:	:	:

YEAR ANNÉE	EUR 12	EUR 10	B	DK	D	GR	E	F	IRL	I	L	NL	P	UK

1000 HA

FRESH VEGETABLES (TOTAL,INC.KITCHEN GARDENS) — **LEGUMES FRAIS (TOTAL,Y.C.JARDINS)**

1983	:	:	:	:	96,7	152,4	454,4	575,0	:	627,2 *	:	:	89,0 *	:
1984	:	:	:	:	101,4	153,0	477,8	579,3	:	630,5 *	:	:	94,0 *	:
1985	:	:	:	:	103,6	150,5 *	472,2	577,1	:	619,9 *	:	:	94,0 *	:
1986	:	:	:	:	103,3	139,8 *	459,7 *	572,4 *	:	582,2 *	:	:	94,0 *	:

FRESH VEG.OF KITCHEN GARDENS — **LEGUMES FRAIS DES JARDINS**

1983	:	:	:	:	49,0	:	—	254,7	:	84,3	:	:	—	:
1984	:	:	:	:	49,0	:	—	253,6	:	86,1	:	:	—	:
1985	:	:	:	:	49,0	:	—	249,3	:	86,5	:	:	—	:
1986	:	:	:	:	49,0	:	—	249,7	:	86,9 *	:	:	—	:

FRESH VEGETABLES (AGRIC.HOLDINGS) — **LEGUMES FRAIS (EXPL.AGRICOLES)**

1983	1 902,7 *	1 359,2 *	43,9	14,1 *	47,7	152,4	454,4	320,3	7,3	542,9 *	0,2	71,9	89,0 *	158,5
1984	1 954,3 *	1 382,5 *	45,9	16,5 *	52,4	153,0	477,8	325,7	7,5	544,4 *	0,2	72,4	94,0 *	164,4
1985	1 958,5 *	1 392,2 *	50,4	18,7 *	54,6	150,5 *	472,2	327,8	7,5	533,3 *	0,2	77,1	94,0 *	172,2
1986	:	:	52,7	:	54,3	139,8 *	459,7 *	322,8 *	8,0	495,2 *	0,1	76,5	94,0 *	171,7

ALL BRASSICAS (EX.ROOTS) — **CHOUX POTAGERS**

1983	240,5 *	200,9 *	4,5	2,3 *	14,8	11,5	30,9	54,4	3,2	51,2	0,0	11,7	8,7 *	47,4
1984	242,2 *	202,6 *	5,0	2,3 *	15,8	11,5	30,8	55,5	3,1	47,6	0,0	12,1	8,8 *	49,7
1985	250,3 *	209,3	7,8	2,3	17,3	11,2	32,2	57,8	2,9	47,1	0,0	12,1	8,8 *	50,9
1986	:	:	9,1	:	16,2	11,4	30,6 *	57,0	3,3	43,5	0,0	12,5	:	51,9

VEGET.LEAFY OR STALKED — **LEGUMES FEUILLUS ET A TIGE SAUF CHOUX**

1983	386,7 *	304,6	16,4	0,8	14,1	16,3	80,7	91,1	0,4	135,5	0,1	17,3	1,3 *	12,5
1984	394,5 *	307,9 *	17,3	0,8 *	14,7	16,4	85,2	90,2	0,4	137,6	0,1	18,0	1,4 *	12,5
1985	393,7 *	305,0 *	18,5	0,8 *	14,6	15,9 *	87,3	89,0	0,4	133,1	0,1	19,7	1,4 *	13,0
1986	:	:	20,0	:	15,1	15,9 *	86,5 *	91,1 *	0,4	129,5	0,0	19,7	—	13,0

VEGET.CULTIVATED FOR FRUIT — **LEGUMES CULTIVES POUR LE FRUIT**

1983	583,9 *	367,8	1,7	0,1	1,7	91,2	196,3	39,3	0,1	228,1	0,0	4,5	19,8 *	1,0
1984	606,3 *	373,4	1,8	0,1	1,6	92,3	206,6	39,6	0,1	232,6	0,0	4,3	26,2 *	1,0
1985	596,8 *	372,5 *	1,9	0,1 *	1,7	93,3	198,2	40,6	0,1	229,4	0,0	4,4	26,0 *	1,0
1986	:	:	2,0	:	2,0	83,7	196,1 *	38,4 *	0,1	203,4	0,0	5,1	:	1,0

ROOT AND TUBER VEGETABLES — **RACINES,BULBES ET TUBERCULES**

1983	258,5 *	169,8	5,8	2,6	8,0	18,3	83,6	44,2	2,3	39,0	0,0	19,4	5,2 *	30,0
1984	274,1 *	177,4 *	6,1	2,6 *	9,6	17,7	91,2	46,0	2,6	39,1	0,0	21,4	5,5 *	32,2
1985	276,0 *	180,4 *	5,8	2,6 *	10,3	16,5	90,2	46,3	2,7	39,0	0,0	22,9	5,5 *	34,2
1986	:	:	5,5	:	9,8	15,5	85,5 *	44,6 *	2,8	37,0	0,0	21,5	:	34,8

PULSES — **LEGUMES A COSSE**

1983	346,0 *	290,4	14,9	7,3	7,2	15,2	52,6	85,1	1,3	88,5	0,0	14,3	3,0 *	56,6
1984	350,3 *	293,0	15,4	9,7	8,0	15,1	54,3	86,5	1,2	86,9	0,0	13,4	3,0 *	56,8
1985	350,1 *	292,2	16,1	11,2	7,9	13,6	54,9	84,6	1,3	84,1	0,0	14,6	3,0 *	58,8
1986	:	:	15,8	:	7,9	13,3	51,8	82,1 *	1,2	81,2	0,0	14,3	—	57,6

CULTIVATED MUSHROOMS — **CHAMPIGNONS DE CULTURE**

1983	:	:	0,0	0,0	:	—	0,2	0,0	0,0	0,0	—	0,1	—	0,4
1984	:	:	0,0	0,0 *	:	—	0,3	0,0	0,0	0,0	—	0,1	—	0,5
1985	:	:	0,0	0,0 *	:	—	0,3	0,0	0,0	0,0	—	0,1	—	0,5
1986	:	:	0,0	0,0 *	:	—	0,3	0,0	0,0	0,0	—	0,1	—	0,5

FRESH VEGETABLES N.O.S. — **LEGUMES FRAIS N.D.A.**

1983	86,2 *	:	0,3	0,9	1,8	:	10,1	6,1	0,1	0,6 *	0,0	4,7	51,0 *	10,6
1984	86,0 *	:	0,3	1,0 *	2,8	:	9,4	7,9	0,1	0,6 *	0,0	3,1	49,1 *	11,7
1985	90,5 *	:	0,3	1,5	2,9	:	9,2	9,6	0,1	0,6 *	0,0	3,3	49,3 *	13,7
1986	:	:	0,3	:	3,3	:	9,1 *	9,5 *	0,2	0,6 *	0,0	3,3	:	12,9

HARVESTED PRODUCTION   PRODUCTION RECOLTEE

YEAR ANNÉE	EUR 12	EUR 10	B	DK	D	GR	E	F	IRL	I	L	NL	P	UK
						1000 T								
FRESH VEGETABLES (TOTAL,INC.KITCHEN GARDENS)													**LEGUMES FRAIS (TOTAL,Y.C.JARDINS)**	
1983	44 296 *	33 941 *	980	226	1 759	3 795 *	8 704	6 552	279	14 577	13	2 730	1 650 *	3 029
1984	46 930 *	35 760 *	1 062	251 *	1 985	4 365 *	9 291	6 388	304	15 071 *	13	2 839	1 880 *	3 481
1985	48 115 *	36 715 *	1 199	278	2 195	4 201 *	9 500	7 088 *	293 *	14 945 *	13	2 942	1 900 *	3 561
1986	:	:	1 242 *	:	2 175	3 690 *	9 262 *	6 734 *	303 *	12 956 *	12	3 136	1 700 *	3 639
FRESH VEG.OF KITCHEN GARDENS													**LEGUMES FRAIS DES JARDINS**	
1983	:	:	144	0	586	:	—	1 634	74	1 887	10	200	—	:
1984	:	:	152	0	621	:	—	1 437	76	1 880	10	200	—	:
1985	:	:	179	0	669	:	—	1 550 *	73 *	1 884	10	200	—	:
1986	:	:	185 *	0 *	664	:	—	1 480 *	75 *	1 875 *	9	200	—	:
FRESH VEGETABLES (AGRIC.HOLDINGS)													**LEGUMES FRAIS (EXPL.AGRICOLES)**	
1983	39 760 *	29 406 *	836	226	1 173	3 795 *	8 704	4 918	205	12 690	3	2 530	1 650 *	3 029
1984	42 555 *	31 384 *	911	251 *	1 364	4 365 *	9 291	4 951	228	13 192 *	3	2 639	1 880 *	3 481
1985	43 551 *	32 151 *	1 020	278	1 526	4 201 *	9 500	5 538	220	13 061 *	3	2 742	1 900 *	3 561
1986	:	:	1 057 *	:	1 511	3 690 *	9 262 *	5 254 *	228	11 081 *	3	2 936	1 700 *	3 639
ALL BRASSICAS (EX.ROOTS)													**CHOUX POTAGERS**	
1983	4 868 *	3 966	98	50	511	228	744	796	73	935	1	303	158 *	971
1984	4 919 *	4 005 *	121	58 *	614	234	751	640	75	769	1	310	163 *	1 184
1985	5 324 *	4 394	171	62	711	227	767	813	69	829	1	320	163 *	1 191
1986	:	:	178	:	695	217	781 *	827	79	871	1	379	:	1 216
VEGET.LEAFY OR STALKED													**LEGUMES FEUILLUS ET A TIGE SAUF CHOUX**	
1983	6 085 *	4 870 *	321	17	217	239 *	1 184	1 250	11	2 086	1	395	30 *	334
1984	6 087 *	4 788 *	328	18 *	230	254 *	1 268	1 171	11	2 026	1	399	30 *	350
1985	6 181 *	4 878 *	362	19	237	256 *	1 273	1 263	10	1 908	1	426	30 *	396
1986	:	:	400	:	233	259 *	1 310 *	1 275	10	1 985	1	458	—	393
VEGET.CULTIVATED FOR FRUIT													**LEGUMES CULTIVES POUR LE FRUIT**	
1983	19 390 *	13 812	171	25	79	2 973	4 811	1 226	23	8 194	0	939	767 *	182
1984	21 121 *	15 176	184	27	63	3 514	5 041	1 327	19	8 907	0	934	904 *	199
1985	21 220 *	15 220	207	26	77	3 360	5 092	1 471	15	8 887	0	986	908 *	190
1986	:	:	225	:	96	2 852	4 965 *	1 283	13	6 810	0	1 071	:	207
ROOT AND TUBER VEGETABLES													**RACINES,BULBES ET TUBERCULES**	
1983	5 973 *	4 431	137	94	214	249	1 404	994	81	940	1	687	138 *	1 034
1984	6 613 *	4 820 *	157	100 *	272	250	1 649	1 067	97	946	1	784	143 *	1 147
1985	6 917 *	5 030 *	154	113	316	253 *	1 746	1 184	97	921	1	778	141 *	1 212
1986	:	:	140	:	297	261 *	1 639 *	1 070 *	100	896	1	788	:	1 227
PULSES													**LEGUMES A COSSE**	
1983	1 982 *	1 572	91	31	61	106	383	397	7	472	0	118	28 *	289
1984	2 156 *	1 721 *	105	40 *	66	113	406	457	8	477	0	105	29 *	350
1985	2 157 *	1 680	107	48	63	104	447	478	7	451	0	120	30 *	302
1986	:	:	94	:	66	102 *	395	464 *	5	453	0	119	—	321
CULTIVATED MUSHROOMS													**CHAMPIGNONS DE CULTURE**	
1983	472	432	13	8	35	—	40	165	9	45	—	80	—	77
1984	521 *	478 *	12	9 *	35	—	43	177	14	50	—	94	—	87
1985	568	520	15	9	35	—	48	188	18	51	—	105	—	100
1986	:	:	15 *	:	35	—	50	190 *	17	52	—	110	—	100
FRESH VEGETABLES N.O.S.													**LEGUMES FRAIS N.D.A.**	
1983	975 *	:	5	0	57	:	135	80	2	15	1	8	529 *	143
1984	1 122 *	:	4	0	82	:	127	104	3	15 *	1	13	611 *	164
1985	1 175 *	:	4	0	86	:	124	138	4	14 *	1	7	628 *	171
1986	:	:	4	:	88	:	120 *	140 *	4	13 *	1	12	:	175

SOURCE: CRONOS-ZPA1 DATA BANK, AGRICULTURAL PRODUCTS   SOURCE: BANQUE DE DONNEES CRONOS-ZPA1, PRODUITS AGRICOLES

| I D 2 |

YEAR ANNÉE	EUR 12	EUR 10	B	DK	D	GR	E	F	IRL	I	L	NL	P	UK

1000 HA

WILD PRODUCTS   **PRODUITS DE CUEILLETTE (LEGUMES)**

1983	:	–	–	–	–	–	–	–	–	–	–	–	–	–
1984	:	–	–	–	–	–	–	–	–	–	–	–	–	–
1985	:	–	–	–	–	–	–	–	–	–	–	–	–	–
1986	:	–	–	–	–	–	–	–	–	–	–	–	–	–

ALL BRASSICAS (EX.ROOTS)   **CHOUX POTAGERS**

1983	240,5 *	200,9 *	4,5	2,3 *	14,8	11,5	30,9	54,4	3,2	51,2	0,0	11,7	8,7 *	47,4
1984	242,2 *	202,6 *	5,0	2,3 *	15,8	11,5	30,8	55,5	3,1	47,6	0,0	12,1	8,8 *	49,7
1985	250,3 *	209,3	7,8	2,3	17,3	11,2	32,2	57,8	2,9	47,1	0,0	12,1	8,8 *	50,9
1986	:	:	9,1	:	16,2	11,4	30,6 *	57,0	3,3	43,5	0,0	12,5	:	51,9

CAULIFLOWER   **CHOUX FLEURS**

1983	116,8 *	106,6	2,0	0,9	3,6	3,0	9,5	43,3	0,9	34,4	–	2,5	0,7 *	16,0
1984	116,4 *	106,0 *	2,3	0,9 *	3,3	3,0	9,6	44,3	0,9	31,9	–	2,7	0,8 *	16,7
1985	121,6 *	110,4	4,1	0,9	3,4	3,4	10,4	46,4	0,9	31,2	–	2,5	0,8 *	17,6
1986	:	:	4,7	:	3,6	3,5	10,4	46,2	0,9	29,0	–	2,6	:	18,2

BRUSSELS SPROUTS   **CHOUX DE BRUXELLES**

1983	23,7 *	:	1,6	0,2 *	0,4	:	0,6	2,7	0,3	0,2	–	6,0	–	11,7
1984	23,6 *	:	1,6	0,2 *	0,4	:	0,6	2,6	0,3	0,3	–	6,0	–	11,6
1985	23,9	:	2,3	0,2	0,4	:	0,7	2,5	0,3	0,4	–	6,2	–	11,0
1986	:	:	3,1	:	0,4	:	0,6 *	2,4	0,3	0,4	–	6,3	–	10,7

CABBAGE   **CHOUX BLANCS**

1983	54,9	45,2	0,1	0,7	5,8	8,5	9,6	1,2	1,5	6,2	0,0	1,6	–	19,7
1984	55,0 *	47,6 *	0,2	0,7 *	6,7	8,4	7,5	1,2	1,3	5,9	0,0	1,7	–	21,4
1985	55,9	47,9	0,3	0,7	6,8	7,8	7,9	1,4	1,1	5,7	0,0	1,8	–	22,3
1986	:	:	0,3	:	6,2	7,9	7,1 *	1,1	1,5	5,6	0,0	1,7	–	23,0

BRASSICAS N.O.S.(EX.ROOTS)   **AUTRES CHOUX,N.D.A.**

1983	45,2 *	:	0,8	0,5 *	4,9	:	11,2	7,2	0,5	10,4	–	1,6	8,0 *	–
1984	47,2 *	:	0,9	0,5 *	5,4	:	13,1	7,4	0,6	9,5	–	1,8	8,0 *	–
1985	48,9 *	:	1,1	0,5	6,6	:	13,1	7,5	0,6	9,8	–	1,7	8,0 *	–
1986	:	:	1,0	:	5,9	:	12,5 *	7,3	0,5	8,5	–	1,9	–	–

VEGET.LEAFED OR STALKED   **LEGUMES FEUILLUS ET A TIGE SAUF CHOUX**

1983	386,7 *	304,6	16,4	0,8	14,1	16,3	80,7	91,1	0,4	135,5	0,1	17,3	1,3 *	12,5
1984	394,5 *	307,9 *	17,3	0,8 *	14,7	16,4	85,2	90,2	0,4	137,6	0,1	18,0	1,4 *	12,5
1985	393,7 *	305,0 *	18,5	0,8 *	14,6	15,9 *	87,3	89,0	0,4	133,1	0,1	19,7	1,4 *	13,0
1986	:	:	20,0	:	15,1	15,9 *	86,5 *	91,1 *	0,4	129,5	0,0	19,7	–	13,0

CELERIAC AND CELERY   **CELERIS (RAVE + BRANCHE)**

1983	14,9	13,3	1,1	0,2	1,3	0,7	1,6	3,2	0,0	4,5	0,0	1,2	–	1,1
1984	15,1 *	13,5 *	1,1	0,2 *	1,4	0,8	1,6	3,1	0,0	4,5	0,0	1,3	–	1,1
1985	15,3	13,8	1,1	0,2	1,6	0,7	1,6	3,0	0,0	4,5	0,0	1,5	–	1,2
1986	:	:	1,2	:	1,5	0,6	1,6 *	3,0	0,0	4,2	0,0	1,6	–	1,1

LEEKS   **POIREAUX**

1983	24,2	21,6	2,4	0,4	1,6	1,8	2,6	10,0	0,0	1,1	0,0	2,3	–	2,1
1984	25,0 *	22,1 *	2,6	0,4 *	1,7	1,8	2,8	9,6	0,0	1,2	0,0	2,5	–	2,3
1985	26,1	23,2	3,1	0,4	1,5	1,7	2,9	9,7	0,0	1,3	0,0	2,9	–	2,6
1986	:	:	3,3	:	1,7	1,8	2,9 *	9,8	0,0	1,3	0,0	2,8	–	2,7

LETTUCE   **LAITUES**

1983	79,7 *	55,6	2,5	0,2	4,1	2,9	22,8	14,3	0,3	19,4	0,0	3,8	1,3 *	8,0
1984	79,3 *	54,3 *	2,5	0,2 *	4,0	3,0	23,6	13,4	0,3	19,6	0,0	3,5	1,4 *	7,8
1985	80,1 *	54,2 *	2,5	0,2 *	3,7	2,7	24,4	13,5	0,3	19,4	0,0	3,8	1,4 *	8,0
1986	:	:	2,5	:	3,6	2,9	24,6	13,1	0,2	19,2	0,0	3,6	–	7,9

YEAR ANNÉE	EUR 12	EUR 10	B	DK	D	GR	E	F	IRL	I	L	NL	P	UK
						1000 T								

WILD PRODUCTS — PRODUITS DE CUEILLETTE (LEGUMES)

YEAR ANNÉE	EUR 12	EUR 10	B	DK	D	GR	E	F	IRL	I	L	NL	P	UK
1983	:	11	–	–	–	–	3	9	–	2	–	–	–	–
1984	:	11	–	–	–	–	5	9	–	2	–	–	–	–
1985	:	4	–	–	–	–	5	3	–	1	–	–	–	–
1986	:	7 *	–	–	–	–	3	5 *	–	2 *	–	–	–	–

ALL BRASSICAS (EX.ROOTS) — CHOUX POTAGERS

YEAR ANNÉE	EUR 12	EUR 10	B	DK	D	GR	E	F	IRL	I	L	NL	P	UK
1983	4 868 *	3 966	98	50	511	228	744	796	73	935	1	303	158 *	971
1984	4 919 *	4 005 *	121	58 *	614	234	751	640	75	769	1	310	163 *	1 184
1985	5 324 *	4 394	171	62	711	227	767	813	69	829	1	320	163 *	1 191
1986	:	:	178	:	695	217	781 *	827	79	871	1	379	:	1 216

CAULIFLOWER — CHOUX FLEURS

YEAR ANNÉE	EUR 12	EUR 10	B	DK	D	GR	E	F	IRL	I	L	NL	P	UK
1983	1 907 *	1 663	35	10	81	52	228	543	15	572	–	56	16 *	299
1984	1 671 *	1 428 *	35	10 *	75	60	226	372	15	457	–	60	18 *	344
1985	1 887 *	1 646	62	11	79	50	222	526	14	500	–	49	18 *	356
1986	:	:	71	:	86	53	235	553	12	565	–	62	:	360

BRUSSELS SPROUTS — CHOUX DE BRUXELLES

YEAR ANNÉE	EUR 12	EUR 10	B	DK	D	GR	E	F	IRL	I	L	NL	P	UK
1983	310 *	:	19	2 *	5	:	11	29	5	4	–	83	–	154
1984	317 *	:	24	2 *	5	:	13	25	5	4	–	71	–	169
1985	329	:	35	2	6	:	14	28	4	5	–	83	–	152
1986	:	:	41	:	6	:	13 *	27	4	5	–	100	–	157

CABBAGE — CHOUX BLANCS

YEAR ANNÉE	EUR 12	EUR 10	B	DK	D	GR	E	F	IRL	I	L	NL	P	UK
1983	1 573	1 344	9	22	282	176	230	67	41	131	1	97	–	518
1984	1 816 *	1 613 *	15	29 *	362	174	204	96	41	116	1	109	–	670
1985	1 892	1 665	16	30	397	177	227	104	35	115	1	108	–	683
1986	:	:	16	:	400	164	213 *	89	49	117	1	126	–	698

BRASSICAS N.O.S.(EX.ROOTS) — AUTRES CHOUX,N.D.A.

YEAR ANNÉE	EUR 12	EUR 10	B	DK	D	GR	E	F	IRL	I	L	NL	P	UK
1983	1 078 *	:	36	16 *	144	:	276	157	12	228	–	68	142 *	0
1984	1 114 *	:	47	17 *	172	:	309	147	15	192	–	70	145 *	–
1985	1 216 *	:	59	19	230	:	303	155	16	208	–	80	145 *	–
1986	:	:	50	:	203	:	320 *	158	14	184	–	92	–	0

VEGET.LEAFED OR STALKED — LEGUMES FEUILLUS ET A TIGE SAUF CHOUX

YEAR ANNÉE	EUR 12	EUR 10	B	DK	D	GR	E	F	IRL	I	L	NL	P	UK
1983	6 085 *	4 870 *	321	17	217	239 *	1 184	1 250	11	2 086	1	395	30 *	334
1984	6 087 *	4 788 *	328	18 *	230	254 *	1 268	1 171	11	2 026	1	399	30 *	350
1985	6 181 *	4 878 *	362	19	237	256 *	1 273	1 263	10	1 908	1	426	30 *	396
1986	:	:	400	:	233	259 *	1 310 *	1 275	10	1 985	1	458	–	393

CELERIAC AND CELERY — CELERIS (RAVE + BRANCHE)

YEAR ANNÉE	EUR 12	EUR 10	B	DK	D	GR	E	F	IRL	I	L	NL	P	UK
1983	472	428	49	4	32	12	44	102	3	132	0	43	–	53
1984	487 *	441 *	43	4 *	38	14	46	93	3	139	0	43	–	66
1985	470	430	44	6	47	12	41	99	2	104	0	53	–	63
1986	:	:	44	:	43	12	42 *	98	3	123	0	59	–	64

LEEKS — POIREAUX

YEAR ANNÉE	EUR 12	EUR 10	B	DK	D	GR	E	F	IRL	I	L	NL	P	UK
1983	567	522	72	6	34	35	45	234	0	30	0	67	–	44
1984	571 *	515 *	74	7 *	39	38	56	218	1	32	0	53	–	53
1985	611	555	87	7	39	37	56	229	1	30	0	66	–	60
1986	:	:	107	:	43	37	55 *	227	1	30	0	75	–	61

LETTUCE — LAITUES

YEAR ANNÉE	EUR 12	EUR 10	B	DK	D	GR	E	F	IRL	I	L	NL	P	UK
1983	1 810 *	1 252	81	7	81	54	529	330	6	369	0	119	30	203
1984	1 834 *	1 230 *	77	7 *	81	64	574	308	6	368	0	117	30	201
1985	1 893 *	1 268	76	7	77	58	595	323	6	361	0	118	30	243
1986	:	:	76	:	71	60	566	218	5	367	0	122	–	237

ID 2

YEAR ANNÉE	EUR 12	EUR 10	B	DK	D	GR	E	F	IRL	I	L	NL	P	UK

1000 HA

ENDIVE | | | | | | | | | | | | | **CHICOREES FRISEES ET SCAROLES**

1983	:	:	0,2	:	0,3	1,9	3,6	5,9	:	12,8	0,0	0,9	—	:
1984	:	:	0,2	:	0,3	2,0	3,5	6,0	:	12,9	0,0	0,9	—	:
1985	:	:	0,2	:	0,3	1,8	3,8	6,4	:	13,1	0,0	0,9	—	:
1986	:	:	0,2	:	0,3	1,8	3,8 *	6,1	:	12,5	0,0	0,9	—	:

SPINACH | | | | | | | | | | | | | | **EPINARDS**

1983	:	:	0,8	0,0	3,0	2,8	3,6	6,8	:	7,5	—	2,2	—	:
1984	:	:	1,1	0,0	2,8	2,4	3,3	7,0	:	7,6	—	2,4	—	:
1985	:	:	1,3	0,0	2,8	2,5	3,2	6,9	:	7,2	—	2,5	—	:
1986	:	:	1,3	:	3,1	2,3	3,2 *	6,8	:	7,4	—	2,0	—	:

ASPARGUS | | | | | | | | | | | | | | **ASPERGES**

1983	45,9	28,6	0,1	0,0	3,4	0,7	17,3	16,6	0,0	4,9	—	2,6	—	0,4
1984	48,4	29,4	0,1	0,0	3,8	1,1	19,0	16,5	0,0	4,8	—	2,7	—	0,4
1985	48,7	29,9	0,2	0,0	3,9	1,3	18,8	16,5	0,0	4,7	—	2,8	—	0,5
1986	49,9	30,1	0,2	0,0	4,1	1,6	19,7	16,1	0,0	4,9	—	2,8	—	0,5

CHICORY | | | | | | | | | | | | | **CHICOREES (ENDIVES)**

1983	41,9	41,7	9,0	—	—	—	0,1	15,3	—	13,2	0,0	4,3	—	—
1984	44,2	44,1	9,3	—	—	—	0,1	16,1	—	14,0	0,0	4,7	—	—
1985	44,2	44,0	9,8	—	—	—	0,2	15,2	—	13,7	0,0	5,3	—	—
1986	48,0 *	47,8	11,0	—	—	—	0,3 *	17,8	—	12,8	0,0	6,2	—	

GLOBE ARTICHOKE | | | | | | | | | | | | | | **ARTICHAUTS**

1983	91,9	68,4	—	—	—	3,5	23,5	14,2	—	50,7	—	—	—	—
1984	93,6	67,9	—	—	—	3,4	25,6	14,3	—	50,3	—	—	—	—
1985	92,0	64,4	—	—	—	3,2	27,6	13,2	—	48,0	—	—	—	—
1986	90,0	65,0	—	—	—	2,8	25,0	14,0	—	48,2	—	—	—	—

OTHER VEG.LEAFED OR STACKED N.O.S. | | | | | | | | | **AUTRES LEG. FEULLUS OU A TIGE N.D.A.**

1983	35,7	30,1	0,3	—	0,6	2,0	5,6	4,8	0,1	21,4	—	0,0	—	0,9
1984	36,4 *	30,9 *	0,3	— *	0,7	2,0	5,5	4,3	0,1	22,6	—	0,0	—	0,9
1985	34,2 *	29,6 *	0,3	— *	0,7	2,0 *	4,7	4,4	0,0	21,3	—	0,0	—	0,8
1986	:	:	0,3	:	0,8	2,0 *	5,4 *	4,4 *	0,0	19,1	—	0,0	—	0,8

VEGET. CULTIVATED FOR FRUIT | | | | | | | | | **LEGUMES CULTIVES POUR FRUITS**

1983	583,9 *	367,8	1,7	0,1	1,7	91,2	196,3	39,3	0,1	228,1	0,0	4,5	19,8 *	1,0
1984	606,3 *	373,4	1,8	0,1	1,6	92,3	206,6	39,6	0,1	232,6	0,0	4,3	26,2 *	1,0
1985	596,8 *	372,5 *	1,9	0,1 *	1,7	93,3	198,2	40,6	0,1	229,4	0,0	4,4	26,0 *	1,0
1986	:	:	2,0	:	2,0	83,7	196,1 *	38,4 *	0,1	203,4	0,0	5,1	:	1,0

TOMATOES | | | | | | | | | | | | | | **TOMATES**

1983	285,4	206,5	1,0	0,1	0,4	47,2	59,6	16,0	0,1	138,5	0,0	2,5	19,2	0,7
1984	307,0	216,2	1,1	0,1	0,4	50,0	65,1	16,3	0,1	145,3	0,0	2,3	25,7	0,7
1985	298,9 *	212,8 *	1,1	0,1 *	0,3	48,6	60,6	16,7	0,1	143,1	0,0	2,1	25,5 *	0,7
1986	:	:	1,2	:	0,3	40,8	58,0	13,3	0,1	118,8	0,0	2,3	:	0,7

CUCUMBERS | | | | | | | | | | | | | | **CONCOMBRES**

1983	14,4	8,6	0,1	0,0	0,5	2,5	5,9	0,7	0,0	3,6	—	1,0	—	0,2
1984	14,4	8,7	0,1	0,0	0,4	2,7	5,8	0,7	0,0	3,6	—	1,0	—	0,2
1985	14,7 *	8,7 *	0,1	0,0 *	0,4	2,5	6,0	0,6	0,0	3,7	—	1,1	—	0,2
1986	:	:	0,1	:	0,5	2,6	5,9 *	0,6	0,0	3,4	—	1,4	—	0,2

GHERKINS | | | | | | | | | | | | | | **CORNICHONS**

1983	7,4	5,7	0,7	0,0	0,8	—	1,6	1,7	—	1,9	—	0,6	—	—
1984	6,7	4,7	0,6	0,0	0,9	—	2,0	1,3	—	1,3	—	0,5	—	—
1985	8,2	5,3	0,8	0,0	0,9	—	2,9	1,5	—	1,6	—	0,6	—	—
1986	:	:	0,7	:	1,2	—	3,0 *	1,5 *	—	1,7	—	0,8	—	—

SOURCE: CRONOS-ZPA1 DATA BANK, AGRICULTURAL PRODUCTS   SOURCE: BANQUE DE DONNEES CRONOS-ZPA1, PRODUITS AGRICOLES

YEAR ANNÉE	EUR 12	EUR 10	B	DK	D	GR	E	F	IRL	I	L	NL	P	UK
							1000 T							

ENDIVE — **CHICOREES FRISEES ET SCAROLES**

	EUR 12	EUR 10	B	DK	D	GR	E	F	IRL	I	L	NL	P	UK
1983	:	:	7	:	7	29	74	121	:	250	0	41	−	:
1984	:	:	10	:	7	34	73	99	:	243	0	46	−	:
1985	:	:	10	:	7	33	77	134	:	232	0	45	−	:
1986	:	:	9	:	6	36	75 *	137	:	220	0	41	−	:

SPINACH — **EPINARDS**

	EUR 12	EUR 10	B	DK	D	GR	E	F	IRL	I	L	NL	P	UK
1983	:	:	21	0	42	33	56	86	:	96	−	53	−	:
1984	:	:	27	0	42	28	54	86	:	92	−	59	−	:
1985	:	:	32	0	41	38	52	90	:	81	−	59	−	:
1986	:	:	32	:	42	39	50 *	88	:	93	−	56	−	:

ASPARGUS — **ASPERGES**

	EUR 12	EUR 10	B	DK	D	GR	E	F	IRL	I	L	NL	P	UK
1983	148	93	0	0	11	3	56	44	0	26	−	9	−	1
1984	155	101	0	0	12	4	55	49	0	25	−	10	−	1
1985	170	100	0	0	14	4	69	51	0	21	−	10	−	1
1986	176	108	1	0	15	3	68	54	0	23	−	12	−	1

CHICORY — **CHICOREES (ENDIVES)**

	EUR 12	EUR 10	B	DK	D	GR	E	F	IRL	I	L	NL	P	UK
1983	495	493	86	−	−	−	2	172	−	191	0	45	−	−
1984	511	509	93	−	−	−	1	165	−	200	0	51	−	−
1985	560	557	108	−	−	−	4	205	−	187	0	57	−	−
1986	598 *	594	126	−	−	−	5 *	211	−	182	0	75	−	−

GLOBE ARTICHOKE — **ARTICHAUTS**

	EUR 12	EUR 10	B	DK	D	GR	E	F	IRL	I	L	NL	P	UK
1983	892	634	−	−	−	33	258	74	−	527	−	−	−	−
1984	911	622	−	−	−	31	289	79	−	512	−	−	−	−
1985	777	508	−	−	−	35	269	55	−	418	−	−	−	−
1986	935	601	−	−	−	31	334	· 66	−	504	−	−	−	−

OTHER VEG.LEAFED OR STACKED N.O.S. — **AUTRES LEG. FEULLUS OU A TIGE N.D.A.**

	EUR 12	EUR 10	B	DK	D	GR	E	F	IRL	I	L	NL	P	UK
1983	784 *	663 *	6	−	10	40 *	121	87	2	467	−	18	−	33
1984	719 *	598 *	5	− *	12	42 *	121	75	2	415	−	19	−	30
1985	770 *	659 *	5	−	12	40 *	111	77	2	474	−	19	−	30
1986	:	:	5	:	13	40 *	116 *	176	1	443	−	19	−	30

VEGET. CULTIVATED FOR FRUIT — **LEGUMES CULTIVES POUR FRUITS**

	EUR 12	EUR 10	B	DK	D	GR	E	F	IRL	I	L	NL	P	UK
1983	19 390 *	13 812	171	25	79	2 973	4 811	1 226	23	8 194	0	939	767 *	182
1984	21 121 *	15 176	184	27	63	3 514	5 041	1 327	19	8 907	0	934	904 *	199
1985	21 220 *	15 220	207	26	77	3 360	5 092	1 471	15	8 887	0	986	908 *	190
1986	:	:	225	:	96	2 852	4 965 *	1 283	13	6 810	0	1 071	:	207

TOMATOES — **TOMATES**

	EUR 12	EUR 10	B	DK	D	GR	E	F	IRL	I	L	NL	P	UK
1983	12 296 *	9 202	125	16	26	1 869	2 349	762	20	5 790	0	475	745 *	118
1984	13 995	10 604	145	17	21	2 388	2 511	833	17	6 564	0	488	881	129
1985	13 909	10 595	160	17	23	2 238	2 429	940	14	6 563	0	525	885	116
1986	10 840	7 828	174	17	26	1 700	2 306	712	12	4 516	0	547	706	125

CUCUMBERS — **CONCOMBRES**

	EUR 12	EUR 10	B	DK	D	GR	E	F	IRL	I	L	NL	P	UK
1983	1 055	795	15	8	34	141	261	84	2	99	−	350	−	61
1984	1 052 *	812 *	16	8 *	29	139	240	96	2	99	−	355	−	68
1985	1 087	829	14	9	32	159	258	94	1	98	−	350	−	71
1986	:	:	17	:	39	140	250 *	95	2	90	−	393	−	80

GHERKINS — **CORNICHONS**

	EUR 12	EUR 10	B	DK	D	GR	E	F	IRL	I	L	NL	P	UK
1983	166	145	30	0	19	−	21	14	−	34	−	49	−	−
1984	117	95	23	0	14	−	22	11	−	21	−	27	−	−
1985	162	132	34	0	22	−	30	12	−	25	−	39	−	−
1986	:	:	34	:	31	−	30 *	13 *	−	30	−	45	−	−

1000 HA

MELONS / MELONS

YEAR ANNÉE	EUR 12	EUR 10	B	DK	D	GR	E	F	IRL	I	L	NL	P	UK
1983	103,0	39,6	0,0	0,0	–	8,7	63,4	15,0	–	15,9	–	–	–	–
1984	105,1	39,0	0,0	0,0	–	7,7	66,1	15,5	–	15,8	–	–	–	–
1985	104,2 *	40,4 *	0,0	0,0 *	–	9,1	63,8	15,5	–	15,9	–	–	–	–
1986	:	:	0,0	:	–	8,9	65,9	16,8	–	15,9	–	–	–	–

WATERMELONS / PASTEQUES

YEAR ANNÉE	EUR 12	EUR 10	B	DK	D	GR	E	F	IRL	I	L	NL	P	UK
1983	72,1 *	42,7	–	–	–	19,0	29,0	0,2	–	23,5	–	–	0,3 *	–
1984	70,9 *	41,3	–	–	–	17,5	29,2	0,2	–	23,6	–	–	0,3 *	–
1985	69,9 *	41,6	–	–	–	18,6	28,0	0,3	–	22,7	–	–	0,3 *	–
1986	65,9 *	39,9 *	–	–	–	17,2	26,0	0,3 *	–	22,4	–	–	:	–

EGGPLANT,PUMPKINS,MARROWS / AUBERGINES,COURGES,COURGETTES,CITROUILLES

YEAR ANNÉE	EUR 12	EUR 10	B	DK	D	GR	E	F	IRL	I	L	NL	P	UK
1983	48,5 *	37,9 *	–	0,0	–	8,0	10,6	4,3	–	25,6	–	0,1 *	–	–
1984	47,9 *	37,5 *	–	0,0	–	8,1	10,5	4,1	–	25,2	–	0,1 *	–	–
1985	47,4 *	37,2 *	–	0,0	–	7,6	10,3	4,5	–	24,9	–	0,1 *	–	–
1986	:	:	–	:	–	7,7	10,2 *	4,4 *	–	23,6	–	0,1 *	–	–

EGGPLANT / AUBERGINES

YEAR ANNÉE	EUR 12	EUR 10	B	DK	D	GR	E	F	IRL	I	L	NL	P	UK
1983	21,2 *	16,5	–	–	–	3,2	4,7	1,1	–	12,2	–	0,1 *	–	–
1984	20,8 *	16,1	–	–	–	3,3	4,6	0,9	–	11,9	–	0,1 *	–	–
1985	20,3	15,8	–	–	–	3,1	4,4	1,1	–	11,6	–	0,1	–	–
1986	19,9 *	15,5 *	–	–	–	3,0	4,4 *	1,1 *	–	11,3	–	0,1	–	–

PEPPERS / POIVRONS

YEAR ANNÉE	EUR 12	EUR 10	B	DK	D	GR	E	F	IRL	I	L	NL	P	UK
1983	50,6 *	24,1	0,0	0,0	–	3,3	26,3	1,5	0,0	19,0	–	0,3	0,2	0,1
1984	51,8 *	23,7	0,0	0,0	–	4,0	27,9	1,5	0,0	17,7	–	0,5	0,2	0,1
1985	51,1 *	24,2 *	0,0	0,0 *	–	4,6	26,7	1,5	0,0	17,5	–	0,5	0,2	0,1
1986	:	:	0,0	:	–	4,2	27,0	1,5 *	0,0	17,6	–	0,5	–	0,1

ROOT AND TUBER VEGETABLES / RACINES,BULBES ET TUBERCULES

YEAR ANNÉE	EUR 12	EUR 10	B	DK	D	GR	E	F	IRL	I	L	NL	P	UK
1983	258,5 *	169,8	5,8	2,6	8,0	18,3	83,6	44,2	2,3	39,0	0,0	19,4	5,2 *	30,0
1984	274,1 *	177,4 *	6,1	2,6 *	9,6	17,7	91,2	46,0	2,6	39,1	0,0	21,4	5,5 *	32,2
1985	276,0 *	180,4 *	5,8	2,6 *	10,3	16,5	90,2	46,3	2,7	39,0	0,0	22,9	5,5 *	34,2
1986	:	:	5,5	:	9,8	15,5	85,5 *	44,6 *	2,8	37,0	0,0	21,5	:	34,8

KOHL-RABI / CHOUX RAVES

YEAR ANNÉE	EUR 12	EUR 10	B	DK	D	GR	E	F	IRL	I	L	NL	P	UK
1983	1,6	1,6	–	–	1,5	:	–	–	–	–	–	0,1	–	–
1984	1,7	1,7	–	–	1,6	:	–	–	–	–	–	0,1	–	–
1985	1,7	1,7	–	–	1,7	:	–	–	–	–	–	0,1	–	–
1986	1,8	1,8	–	–	1,7	:	–	–	–	–	–	0,0	–	–

TURNIPS / NAVETS POTAGERS

YEAR ANNÉE	EUR 12	EUR 10	B	DK	D	GR	E	F	IRL	I	L	NL	P	UK
1983	13,1	11,6	–	–	–	:	1,6	3,3	0,9	3,4	–	0,0	–	4,1
1984	13,7	12,3	–	–	–	:	1,4	3,2	1,1	3,5	–	0,0	–	4,5
1985	13,5	12,2	–	–	–	:	1,4	3,4	1,1	3,4	–	0,0	–	4,3
1986	13,1 *	11,8	–	–	–	:	1,3 *	3,4	1,2	2,4	–	0,0	–	4,8

CARROTS / CAROTTES

YEAR ANNÉE	EUR 12	EUR 10	B	DK	D	GR	E	F	IRL	I	L	NL	P	UK
1983	59,5 *	51,4	2,3	1,2	3,8	1,3	5,0	17,9	1,0	7,4	0,0	3,4	3,0	13,1
1984	64,2 *	55,7 *	2,5	1,2 *	4,5	1,1	5,4	19,7	1,1	7,8	0,0	4,1	3,0	13,8
1985	66,6 *	57,9	2,7	1,2	4,8	1,0	5,7	19,7	1,1	8,4	0,0	4,9	3,0	14,1
1986	:	:	2,6	:	4,3	1,0	5,7 *	17,8	1,1	8,1	0,0	4,6	–	13,8

GARLIC / AIL

YEAR ANNÉE	EUR 12	EUR 10	B	DK	D	GR	E	F	IRL	I	L	NL	P	UK
1983	56,8	15,9	–	–	–	3,1	40,9	7,3	–	5,5	–	–	–	–
1984	60,6	15,7	–	–	–	3,0	44,9	7,4	–	5,3	–	–	–	–
1985	56,2	14,5	–	–	–	2,8	41,7	6,8	–	4,9	–	–	–	–
1986	53,9 *	13,9 *	–	–	–	2,2	40,0	7,0 *	–	4,7	–	–	–	–

YEAR ANNÉE	EUR 12	EUR 10	B	DK	D	GR	E	F	IRL	I	L	NL	P	UK

1000 T

MELONS | **MELONS**

YEAR	EUR 12	EUR 10	B	DK	D	GR	E	F	IRL	I	L	NL	P	UK
1983	1 451 *	694	0	0	—	110	738	222	—	357	—	5	19 *	—
1984	1 525 *	707 *	0	0 *	—	119	799	234	—	347	—	6	20 *	—
1985	1 588 *	723	0	1	—	113	846	254	—	351	—	3	20 *	—
1986	:	:	0	:	—	130	843	279	—	368	—	4	:	—

WATERMELONS | **PASTEQUES**

YEAR	EUR 12	EUR 10	B	DK	D	GR	E	F	IRL	I	L	NL	P	UK
1983	1 986 *	1 412	—	—	—	609	572	4	—	798	—	—	2 *	—
1984	1 958 *	1 397	—	—	—	596	558	5	—	797	—	—	2 *	—
1985	1 935 *	1 364	—	—	—	575	569	6	—	783	—	—	2 *	—
1986	1 918 *	1 397 *	—	—	—	610	521	7 *	—	781	—	—	:	—

EGGPLANT,PUMPKINS,MARROWS | **AUBERGINES,COURGES,COURGETTES,CITROUILLES**

YEAR	EUR 12	EUR 10	B	DK	D	GR	E	F	IRL	I	L	NL	P	UK
1983	1 204	941	—	0	—	153	262	113	—	662	—	14	—	—
1984	1 212	942	—	0	—	162	270	116	—	650	—	14	—	—
1985	1 237	951	—	0	—	162	287	132	—	638	—	18	—	—
1986	:	:	—	:	—	157	290 *	145 *	—	608	—	23	—	—

EGGPLANT | **AUBERGINES**

YEAR	EUR 12	EUR 10	B	DK	D	GR	E	F	IRL	I	L	NL	P	UK
1983	548	423	—	—	—	69	125	28	—	314	—	12	—	—
1984	534	414	—	—	—	72	120	22	—	307	—	12	—	—
1985	535	413	—	—	—	71	122	29	—	297	—	15	—	—
1986	540 *	420 *	—	—	—	70	120 *	28 *	—	304	—	19	—	—

PEPPERS | **POIVRONS**

YEAR	EUR 12	EUR 10	B	DK	D	GR	E	F	IRL	I	L	NL	P	UK
1983	1 215 *	606	0	1	—	73	608	26	1	456	—	46	1 *	3
1984	1 244 *	602 *	0	1 *	—	93	641	31	0	430	—	45	1 *	3
1985	1 288 *	612	0	1	—	97	675	32	0	428	—	51	1 *	3
1986	:	:	0	:	—	94	725	33 *	0	417	—	59	—	3

ROOT AND TUBER VEGETABLES | **RACINES,BULBES ET TUBERCULES**

YEAR	EUR 12	EUR 10	B	DK	D	GR	E	F	IRL	I	L	NL	P	UK
1983	5 973 *	4 431	137	94	214	249	1 404	994	81	940	1	687	138 *	1 034
1984	6 613 *	4 820 *	157	100 *	272	250	1 649	1 067	97	946	1	784	143 *	1 147
1985	6 917 *	5 030 *	154	113	316	253 *	1 746	1 184	97	921	1	778	141 *	1 212
1986	:	:	140	:	297	261 *	1 639 *	1 070 *	100	896	1	788	:	1 227

KOHL-RABI | **CHOUX RAVES**

YEAR	EUR 12	EUR 10	B	DK	D	GR	E	F	IRL	I	L	NL	P	UK
1983	41	41	—	—	36	:	—	—	—	—	—	6	—	—
1984	43	43	—	—	38	:	—	—	—	—	—	5	—	—
1985	47	47	—	—	43	:	—	—	—	—	—	4	—	—
1986	45	45	—	—	41	:	—	—	—	—	—	4	—	—

TURNIPS | **NAVETS POTAGERS**

YEAR	EUR 12	EUR 10	B	DK	D	GR	E	F	IRL	I	L	NL	P	UK
1983	331	306	—	—	—	:	25	68	33	56	—	14	—	135
1984	353	331	—	—	—	:	22	70	43	65	—	10	—	143
1985	355	333	—	—	—	:	22	73	43	60	—	14	—	143
1986	362 *	340	—	—	—	:	22 *	76	48	41	—	14	—	160

CARROTS | **CAROTTES**

YEAR	EUR 12	EUR 10	B	DK	D	GR	E	F	IRL	I	L	NL	P	UK
1983	2 043 *	1 822	65	58	119	38	141	508	36	266	1	176	80 *	554
1984	2 188 *	1 964 *	84	60 *	149	36	143	542	40	269	1	213	81 *	572
1985	2 376 *	2 134	92	63	173	26	161	644	41	271	1	224	81 *	600
1986	:	:	85	:	148	31	170	533	39	271	0	225	—	589

GARLIC | **AIL**

YEAR	EUR 12	EUR 10	B	DK	D	GR	E	F	IRL	I	L	NL	P	UK
1983	357	134	—	—	—	18	223	64	—	52	—	—	—	—
1984	398	128	—	—	—	18	270	63	—	48	—	—	—	—
1985	361	113	—	—	—	16	249	53	—	44	—	—	—	—
1986	348	113	—	—	—	13	235	55	—	45	—	—	—	—

YEAR ANNÉE	EUR 12	EUR 10	B	DK	D	GR	E	F	IRL	I	L	NL	P	UK
							1000 HA							

ONIONS — **OIGNONS**

	EUR 12	EUR 10	B	DK	D	GR	E	F	IRL	I	L	NL	P	UK
1983	100,4 *	65,7	0,5	1,1	1,0	12,9	32,4	7,1	0,2	20,1	0,0	14,9	2,2 *	8,0
1984	105,0 *	67,0 *	0,5	1,1 *	1,7	12,5	35,5	6,9	0,2	19,8	0,0	16,1	2,5 *	8,1
1985	109,0 *	69,2	0,5	1,1	1,9	11,7	37,3	7,4	0,2	19,6	0,0	16,7	2,5 *	10,2
1986	:	:	0,5	:	2,1	11,3	34,4	7,6	0,2	19,4	0,0	15,5	:	10,5

SHALLOTS — **ECHALOTTES**

	EUR 12	EUR 10	B	DK	D	GR	E	F	IRL	I	L	NL	P	UK
1983	2,3	2,3	0,0	0,0	—	:	—	2,3	—	—	—	0,0	—	—
1984	2,5 *	2,5 *	0,0	0,0 *	—	:	—	2,5	—	—	—	0,0	—	—
1985	2,4	2,4	0,0	0,0	—	:	—	2,3	—	—	—	0,0	—	—
1986	:	:	0,0	:	—	:	—	2,4 *	—	—	—	0,0	—	—

BEETROOT — **BETTERAVES POTAGERES**

	EUR 12	EUR 10	B	DK	D	GR	E	F	IRL	I	L	NL	P	UK
1983	9,3	8,6	—	0,2	0,6	0,7	0,7	2,9	0,0	1,3	—	0,4	—	2,4
1984	10,4 *	9,7 *	—	0,3 *	0,7	0,8	0,7	3,0	0,0	1,3	—	0,5	—	3,1
1985	10,3	9,6	—	0,3	0,8	0,7	0,7	3,0	0,0	1,4	—	0,6	—	2,9
1986	:	:	—	:	0,5	0,7	0,6 *	3,0 *	0,0	1,1	—	0,5	—	2,8

SALSIFY AND SCORZONERA — **SALSIFIS ET SCORSONERES**

	EUR 12	EUR 10	B	DK	D	GR	E	F	IRL	I	L	NL	P	UK
1983	4,6	4,6	3,0	—	—	—	—	0,9	—	—	—	0,7	—	—
1984	4,5	4,5	3,0	—	—	—	—	0,8	—	—	—	0,7	—	—
1985	4,1	4,1	2,5	—	—	—	—	0,8	—	—	—	0,8	—	—
1986	3,9	3,9	2,2	—	—	—	—	0,8	—	—	—	0,9	—	—

RADISH — **RADIS**

	EUR 12	EUR 10	B	DK	D	GR	E	F	IRL	I	L	NL	P	UK
1983	5,1	4,2	0,0	0,0	0,1	0,3	0,9	2,4	0,0	1,4	—	0,0	—	0,0
1984	5,4	4,4	0,0	:	0,1	0,3	1,1	2,5	:	1,4	—	0,0	—	—
1985	5,3	4,3	0,0	:	0,1	0,3	1,0	2,5	:	1,3	—	0,0	—	—
1986	5,2 *	4,2	0,0	:	0,1	0,3	1,0 *	2,5	:	1,3	—	0,0	—	:

OTHER N.O.S. — **AUTRES N.D.A.**

	EUR 12	EUR 10	B	DK	D	GR	E	F	IRL	I	L	NL	P	UK
1983	5,8	3,8	—	0,0	1,0	:	2,0	0,1	0,3	—	—	0,0	—	2,4
1984	6,2 *	4,0 *	—	0,0 *	1,0	:	2,2	0,1	0,3	—	—	—	—	2,6
1985	6,9 *	4,5 *	—	0,0 *	1,1	:	2,5	0,4	0,3	—	—	0,0	—	2,8
1986	:	:	—	:	1,1	:	2,4 *	0,1 *	0,3	—	—	0,0	—	2,9

PULSES — **LEGUMES A COSSE**

	EUR 12	EUR 10	B	DK	D	GR	E	F	IRL	I	L	NL	P	UK
1983	346,0 *	290,4	14,9	7,3	7,2	15,2	52,6	85,1	1,3	88,5	0,0	14,3	3,0 *	56,6
1984	350,3 *	293,0	15,4	9,7	8,0	15,1	54,3	86,5	1,2	86,9	0,0	13,4	3,0 *	56,8
1985	350,1 *	292,2	16,1	11,2	7,9	13,6	54,9	84,6	1,3	84,1	0,0	14,6	3,0 *	58,8
1986	:	:	15,8	:	7,9	13,3	51,8	82,1 *	1,2	81,2	0,0	14,3	—	57,6

PEAS — **PETITS POIS**

	EUR 12	EUR 10	B	DK	D	GR	E	F	IRL	I	L	NL	P	UK
1983	169,1	158,4	10,7	7,3	2,9	4,1	10,7	43,8	1,2	34,9	0,0	7,7	—	45,8
1984	170,3	160,3	10,6	9,7	3,6	3,9	10,0	45,0	1,1	34,1	0,0	6,8	—	45,5
1985	165,5	154,2	11,1	11,2	3,2	3,1	11,3	36,8	1,2	33,1	0,0	6,9	—	47,6
1986	160,7	149,7	10,7	11,7	2,9	2,9	11,0	33,7	1,1	32,8	0,0	6,5	—	47,3

BEANS RUNNER AND FRENCH — **HARICOTS VERTS**

	EUR 12	EUR 10	B	DK	D	GR	E	F	IRL	I	L	NL	P	UK
1983	119,7 *	158,4	4,2	0,0	3,6	9,3	26,2	27,5	0,1	34,0	—	4,9	3,0 *	7,0
1984	121,9 *	160,3	4,8	0,0	3,5	9,4	27,0	28,1	0,1	33,6	—	5,0	3,0 *	7,4
1985	126,3 *	154,2	5,0	0,0	3,7	9,1	26,5	33,4	0,1	32,2	—	6,0	3,0 *	7,3
1986	:	149,7	5,1	:	4,0	9,0	25,8	34,3	0,2	29,7	—	6,3	—	6,9

OTHER PULSES — **AUTRES LEGUMES A COSSE**

	EUR 12	EUR 10	B	DK	D	GR	E	F	IRL	I	L	NL	P	UK
1983	57,2	41,5	—	—	0,7	1,9	15,7	13,8	0,0	19,6	—	1,7	—	3,8
1984	58,1	40,8	—	—	0,9	1,8	17,2	13,4	0,0	19,2	—	1,6	—	3,9
1985	58,3	41,2	—	—	1,0	1,4	17,1	14,4	0,0	18,8	—	1,7	—	3,9
1986	:	:	—	:	1,0	1,4	15,0	14,0 *	0,0	18,7	—	1,5	—	3,4

YEAR ANNÉE	EUR 12	EUR 10	B	DK	D	GR	E	F	IRL	I	L	NL	P	UK
								1000 T						

ONIONS   **OIGNONS**

YEAR	EUR 12	EUR 10	B	DK	D	GR	E	F	IRL	I	L	NL	P	UK
1983	2 582	1 566	17	27	33	174	959	180	5	499	0	432	58	200
1984	2 949 *	1 732 *	18	31 *	56	175	1 155	204	4	497	0	486	62	260
1985	3 092 *	1 783	17	40	68	192	1 249	222	5	483	0	463	60 *	293
1986	:	:	16	:	80	195	1 149	208	4	485	0	469	:	309

SHALLOTS   **ECHALOTTES**

YEAR	EUR 12	EUR 10	B	DK	D	GR	E	F	IRL	I	L	NL	P	UK
1983	27	27	0	0	—	:	—	27	—	—	—	0	—	—
1984	34	34	0	0	—	:	—	34	—	—	—	0	—	—
1985	33	33	0	0	—	:	—	33	—	—	—	0	—	—
1986	:	:	0	:	—	:	—	30 *	—	—	—	0	—	—

BEETROOT   **BETTERAVES POTAGERES**

YEAR	EUR 12	EUR 10	B	DK	D	GR	E	F	IRL	I	L	NL	P	UK
1983	286	274	—	9	18	14	12	88	1	28	—	22	—	94
1984	328 *	315 *	—	9 *	22	17	13	98	1	29	—	26	—	115
1985	332	318	—	10	25	14	13	101	0	29	—	25	—	114
1986	:	:	—	:	20	16	13 *	95 *	0	21	—	25	—	104

SALSIFY AND SCORZONERA   **SALSIFIS ET SCORSONERES**

YEAR	EUR 12	EUR 10	B	DK	D	GR	E	F	IRL	I	L	NL	P	UK
1983	82	82	54	—	—	—	—	14	—	—	—	14	—	—
1984	82	82	54	—	—	—	—	11	—	—	—	16	—	—
1985	75	75	45	—	—	—	—	11	—	—	—	19	—	—
1986	70	70	38	—	—	—	—	11	—	—	—	21	—	—

RADISH   **RADIS**

YEAR	EUR 12	EUR 10	B	DK	D	GR	E	F	IRL	I	L	NL	P	UK
1983	125	112	0	0	3	4	13	43	0	40	—	22	—	0
1984	133	118	0	:	2	5	15	42	:	40	—	28	—	:
1985	128 *	114 *	0	:	2	5 *	14	44	:	34	—	29	—	:
1986	130 *	115 *	0	:	2	6 *	15 *	44	:	33	—	30	—	:

OTHER N.O.S.   **AUTRES N.D.A.**

YEAR	EUR 12	EUR 10	B	DK	D	GR	E	F	IRL	I	L	NL	P	UK
1983	98	67	—	—	7	:	32	2	6	0	—	1	—	51
1984	106 *	75 *	—	— *	6	:	31	2	8	0	—	1	—	57
1985	119	81	—	—	6	:	38	4	8	0	—	1	—	62
1986	:	:	—	:	7	:	35 *	18 *	8	0	—	1	—	64

PULSES   **LEGUMES A COSSE**

YEAR	EUR 12	EUR 10	B	DK	D	GR	E	F	IRL	I	L	NL	P	UK
1983	1 982 *	1 572	91	31	61	106	383	397	7	472	0	118	28 *	289
1984	2 156 *	1 721 *	105	40 *	66	113	406	457	8	477	0	105	29 *	350
1985	2 157 *	1 680	107	48	63	104	447	478	7	451	0	120	30 *	302
1986	:	:	94	:	66	102 *	395	464 *	5	453	0	119	—	321

PEAS   **PETITS POIS**

YEAR	EUR 12	EUR 10	B	DK	D	GR	E	F	IRL	I	L	NL	P	UK
1983	629	608	48	31	14	18	21	174	6	73	0	37	—	207
1984	751 *	731 *	57	40 *	17	20	20	221	7	77	0	39	—	252
1985	695	672	66	48	17	18	23	186	6	72	0	42	—	217
1986	:	:	64	:	15	16	23	168	4	73	0	33	—	240

BEANS RUNNER AND FRENCH   **HARICOTS VERTS**

YEAR	EUR 12	EUR 10	B	DK	D	GR	E	F	IRL	I	L	NL	P	UK
1983	915 *	608	43	0	36	76	242	168	1	185	—	71	28 *	65
1984	956 *	731 *	47	0	37	82	258	184	1	187	—	54	29 *	77
1985	1 003 *	672	41	0	41	74	280	231	1	175	—	65	30 *	66
1986	:	:	30	:	46	76	244	237	1	175	—	74	—	65

OTHER PULSES   **AUTRES LEGUMES A COSSE**

YEAR	EUR 12	EUR 10	B	DK	D	GR	E	F	IRL	I	L	NL	P	UK
1983	438	318	—	—	10	11	120	55	0	214	—	11	—	17
1984	450 *	322 *	—	— *	12	11	128	52	0	213	—	12	—	21
1985	458	314	—	—	5	12	144	61	0	204	—	13	—	19
1986	:	:	—	:	5	10 *	127	60 *	0	205	—	12	—	16

ID 2

100 KG/H

YEAR ANNÉE	EUR 12	EUR 10	B	DK	D	GR	E	F	IRL	I	L	NL	P	UK
CAULIFLOWER														**CHOUX FLEURS**
1983	163 *	156	170	118	224	174	241	125	166	166	—	226	229 *	187
1984	144 *	135 *	150	115 *	231	197	234	84	163	143	—	226	225 *	206
1985	155 *	149	150	127	234	146	214	113	159	160	—	195	225 *	202
1986	:	:	149	:	237	151	227	120	133	194	—	234	:	198
BRUSSELS SPROUTS														**CHOUX DE BRUXELLES**
1983	131 *	:	120	94 *	107	:	186	107	144	167	—	138	:	131
1984	135 *	:	150	97 *	120	:	209	96	149	148	—	118	:	146
1985	137	:	150	109	134	:	201	111	141	152	—	135	:	138
1986	:	:	130	:	134	:	217 *	112	136	142	—	158	:	147
CELERIAC														**CELERIS (RAVE + BRANCHE)**
1983	317	322	435	196	256	162	271	319	613	295	375	364	:	471
1984	321 *	326 *	396	200 *	272	178	279	303	616	306	375	331	:	578
1985	306	312	395	267	297	168	258	326	628	234	375	362	:	542
1986	:	:	360	:	291	189	263 *	326	565	297	400	371	:	558
LEEKS														**POIREAUX**
1983	234	241	300	140	219	200	175	235	263	265	219	286	:	212
1984	229 *	233 *	279	163 *	238	208	196	227	271	265	219	215	:	231
1985	234	239	281	158	261	221	192	235	283	228	222	230	:	233
1986	:	:	320	:	256	206	190 *	232	254	225	220	269	:	228
LETTUCE														**LAITUES**
1983	227 *	225	319	349	201	184	232	231	221	190	200	311	222 *	255
1984	231 *	227 *	303	350 *	203	215	243	229	223	188	200	335	214 *	259
1985	236 *	234 *	302	340 *	210	213	243	238	217	186	200	307	214 *	302
1986	:	:	303	:	194	205	230	166	208	191	200	339	:	299
ENDIVE														**CHICOREES FRISEES ET SCAROLES**
1983	:	:	400	:	215	154	206	203	:	194	200	447	:	:
1984	:	:	503	:	207	170	207	166	:	189	200	539	:	:
1985	:	:	500	:	208	188	201	209	:	178	200	476	:	:
1986	:	:	500	:	204	202	197 *	223	:	176	200	484	:	:
SPINACH														**EPINARDS**
1983	:	:	249	10	141	120	156	127	:	128	—	242	:	:
1984	:	:	250	10	147	116	162	123	:	120	—	241	:	:
1985	:	:	255	10	146	149	159	131	:	112	—	234	:	:
1986	:	:	256	:	137	167	156 *	129	:	127	—	279	:	:
ASPARGUS														**ASPERGES**
1983	32	32	30	10	32	36	32	26	10	52	—	36	:	15
1984	32	34	28	10	31	37	29	30	10	51	—	38	:	18
1985	35	34	28	10	35	26	37	31	10	45	—	34	:	17
1986	35	36	28	10	36	22	34	33	10	47	—	42	:	18
CHICORY														**CHICOREES (ENDIVES)**
1983	118	118	96	—	—	:	143	112	—	145	150	105	:	—
1984	115	115	100	—	—	:	151	103	—	142	150	108	:	—
1985	127	127	110	—	—	:	155	135	—	136	150	109	:	—
1986	125 *	124	115	—	—	:	180 *	119	—	141	150	122	:	—
GLOBE ARTICHOKE														**ARTICHAUTS**
1983	97	93	—	—	—	95	110	52	—	104	—	—	:	—
1984	97	92	—	—	—	91	113	55	—	102	—	—	:	—
1985	84	79	—	—	—	111	97	42	—	87	—	—	:	—
1986	104	93	—	—	—	110	133	47	—	105	—	—	:	—

YEAR ANNÉE	EUR 12	EUR 10	B	DK	D	GR	E	F	IRL	I	L	NL	P	UK
100 KG/H														

TOMATOES — **TOMATES**

	EUR 12	EUR 10	B	DK	D	GR	E	F	IRL	I	L	NL	P	UK
1983	431 *	446	1 267	2 688	698	396	394	476	1 577	418	150	1 868	388 *	1 603
1984	456	490	1 321	2 804	598	478	386	510	1 530	452	150	2 157	343	1 760
1985	465 *	498 *	1 445	2 783 *	743	461	401	563	1 495	459	150	2 479	347 *	1 731
1986	:	:	1 480	:	901	417	398	536	1 597	380	150	2 335	:	1 916

CUCUMBERS — **CONCOMBRES**

	EUR 12	EUR 10	B	DK	D	GR	E	F	IRL	I	L	NL	P	UK
1983	731	926	1 800	3 604	722	576	445	1 290	1 889	273	—	3 418	:	2 590
1984	730 *	937 *	1 800	3 212 *	705	524	418	1 451	1 950	275	—	3 609	:	3 004
1985	740 *	952 *	2 000	3 401 *	728	634	432	1 463	1 950	269	—	3 121	:	3 096
1986	:	:	2 000	:	786	538	424 *	1 471	1 822	267	—	2 869	:	3 335

GHERKINS — **CORNICHONS**

	EUR 12	EUR 10	B	DK	D	GR	E	F	IRL	I	L	NL	P	UK
1983	226	254	448	10	235	:	130	84	:	172	:	775	:	:
1984	175	204	352	10	160	:	108	86	:	155	:	517	:	:
1985	196	247	447	10	238	:	103	82	:	156	:	666	:	:
1986	:	:	493	:	262	:	100 *	83 *	:	177	:	559	:	:

MELONS — **MELONS**

	EUR 12	EUR 10	B	DK	D	GR	E	F	IRL	I	L	NL	P	UK
1983	141 *	175	667	862	:	126	116	148	:	224	:	48	190 *	:
1984	145 *	181 *	70	870 *	:	156	121	151	:	220	:	55	200 *	:
1985	152 *	179 *	700	1 030 *	:	124	133	164	:	222	:	34	200 *	:
1986	:	:	700	:	:	146	128	166	:	231	:	44	:	:

WATERMELONS — **PASTEQUES**

	EUR 12	EUR 10	B	DK	D	GR	E	F	IRL	I	L	NL	P	UK
1983	276 *	330	:	:	:	321	197	224	:	339	:	:	57 *	:
1984	276 *	338	:	:	:	340	191	248	:	337	:	:	57 *	:
1985	277 *	328	:	:	:	309	203	236	:	344	:	:	57 *	:
1986	291 *	350 *	:	:	:	354	200	233 *	:	348	:	:	:	:

EGGPLANTS — **AUBERGINES**

	EUR 12	EUR 10	B	DK	D	GR	E	F	IRL	I	L	NL	P	UK
1983	258 *	256	:	:	:	212	269	256	:	259	:	1 696 *	:	:
1984	257 *	257	:	:	:	220	263	237	:	259	:	1 553 *	:	:
1985	263	261	:	:	:	232	275	257	:	256	:	2 065	:	:
1986	271 *	272 *	:	:	:	230	273 *	250 *	:	268	:	2 430	:	:

CARROTS — **CAROTTES**

	EUR 12	EUR 10	B	DK	D	GR	E	F	IRL	I	L	NL	P	UK
1983	343 *	354	285	471	310	302	280	283	375	359	261	521	267 *	422
1984	341 *	352 *	339	486 *	333	328	263	276	380	345	260	519	270 *	413
1985	357 *	368	336	511	359	269	285	326	382	322	260	460	270 *	427
1986	:	:	321	:	348	318	298 *	300	352	336	280	488	:	426

ONIONS — **OIGNONS**

	EUR 12	EUR 10	B	DK	D	GR	E	F	IRL	I	L	NL	P	UK
1983	257 *	238	338	249	329	136	296	252	251	248	200	290	265 *	250
1984	281 *	259 *	340	283 *	323	140	326	296	224	251	200	302	250 *	320
1985	284 *	258	335	366	354	164	335	301	226	247	200	278	240 *	287
1986	:	:	297	:	374	173	334	274	203	249	167	303	:	294

PEAS — **PETITS POIS**

	EUR 12	EUR 10	B	DK	D	GR	E	F	IRL	I	L	NL	P	UK
1983	37	38	44	43	49	45	20	40	50	21	30	48	:	45
1984	44 *	46 *	54	41 *	47	50	20	49	63	23	25	57	:	55
1985	42	44	60	43	53	59	20	50	50	22	25	61	:	46
1986	:	:	60	:	51	54	21	50	40	22	80	50	:	51

BEANS RUNNER AND FRENCH — **HARICOTS VERTS**

	EUR 12	EUR 10	B	DK	D	GR	E	F	IRL	I	L	NL	P	UK
1983	76 *	38	102	10	100	82	92	61	94	54	—	144	93 *	93
1984	78 *	46 *	98	10	105	87	96	65	96	56	—	108	97 *	104
1985	79 *	44	82	10	112	81	106	69	83	54	—	108	100 *	90
1986	:	:	58	:	115	85	95	69	66	59	—	118	:	94

YEAR ANNÉE	EUR 12	EUR 10	B	DK	D	GR	E	F	IRL	I	L	NL	P	UK

1000 HA

TOTAL FRESH FRUIT / **TOTAL FRUITS FRAIS**

1983	11 807,3 *	6 055,4 *	11,6	9,2	157,5	1 011,6 *	4 894,0	1 336,9	2,0 *	3 441,4	1,5	25,8	857,9	58,0 *
1984	11 717,9 *	6 036,7 *	11,6	9,1 *	157,9	1 019,4 *	4 822,7	1 317,9	2,0 *	3 435,8	1,5	25,7 *	858,5 *	55,7 *
1985	11 625,7 *	5 951,1 *	11,4	8,7	157,5	1 020,3 *	4 817,5	1 304,5	2,0	3 365,2	1,5	25,4 *	857,2 *	54,6 *
1986	11 541,9 *	5 874,1 *	11,3	8,1 *	157,2	1 023,5 *	4 810,6 *	1 289,9 *	2,0	3 303,0 *	1,5	24,4 *	857,2 *	53,2 *

FRUIT TREES (EX.OLIVES AND CITRUS) / **ARBRES FRUITIERS (EX.OLIVES ET AGRUMES)**

1983	2 415,4 *	1 321,1 *	10,6	6,7	48,7	140,4 *	854,8	207,2	1,3 *	842,2	0,1	23,1	239,5	40,7 *
1984	2 411,3 *	1 320,5 *	10,7	6,6 *	47,6	142,3	851,1	207,3	1,3 *	842,2	0,1	23,1	239,7	39,2 *
1985	2 422,1 *	1 319,0 *	10,5	6,3	47,5	142,9 *	865,3	206,6	1,3	842,5	0,1	22,8	237,8	38,5 *
1986	2 422,8 *	1 317,1 *	10,4	5,6 *	47,1	143,9 *	868,1 *	205,9 *	1,3	843,1 *	0,1	21,7	237,6 *	37,8 *

STRAWBERRIES / **FRAISES**

1983	45,8	39,1	0,7	1,4	6,3	0,8	6,0	9,4	0,4	10,7	0,0	2,1	0,7	7,2
1984	45,9 *	37,9	0,7	1,4	7,0	0,8	7,3	8,9	0,4	9,8	0,0	2,0	0,7 *	6,9
1985	47,9 *	38,6	0,7	1,4	7,1	0,5	8,7	8,8	0,4	10,8	0,0	2,0	0,7 *	6,9
1986	48,7 *	38,4 *	0,8	1,4	7,4	0,4	9,6	8,6 *	0,4	10,6	0,0	2,2	0,7 *	6,6

SOFT FRUIT / **BAIES**

1983	43,0	31,3	0,1	1,0	2,0	0,1	10,2	4,6	0,2	13,0	0,0	0,6	1,4	9,7
1984	45,7 *	33,9 *	0,1	1,0 *	2,0	0,1	10,3	5,2	0,2	15,5	0,0	0,6	1,4	9,2
1985	49,8 *	36,8 *	0,1	1,1	2,0	0,1 *	11,5	6,3	0,2	17,6	0,0	0,6	1,5	8,9
1986	53,7 *	40,1 *	0,1	1,1	2,0	0,1 *	12,0 *	6,7 *	0,2	21,0 *	0,0	0,6	1,5 *	8,4

CITRUS FRUITS / **AGRUMES**

1983	500,5 *	235,5 *	—	—	—	49,9 *	235,7	2,4	—	183,2	—	—	29,3	—
1984	512,3 *	237,2 *	—	—	—	50,3 *	245,4	2,4	—	184,5	—	—	29,7	—
1985	519,6 *	237,0 *	—	—	—	50,8 *	252,4	2,2	—	184,0	—	—	30,2	—
1986	525,4 *	238,1 *	—	—	—	51,6 *	256,9 *	2,2 *	—	184,3	—	—	30,4 *	—

GRAPES / **RAISINS**

1983	4 480,1 *	2 512,5	0,1	—	100,4	177,7	1 696,8	1 094,6	—	1 138,3	1,3	0,0	270,4	0,3 *
1984	4 386,8 *	2 483,0 *	0,1	—	101,4	174,5	1 633,0	1 076,2	—	1 129,4	1,3	0,0 *	270,4	0,4
1985	4 303,1 *	2 439,3 *	0,1	—	100,9	171,0 *	1 592,9	1 063,2	—	1 102,8	1,3	0,0 *	270,4	0,4 *
1986	4 262,9 *	2 418,1 *	0,1	—	100,7	170,0 *	1 574,0 *	1 049,2	—	1 096,8	1,3	0,0 *	270,4	0,4 *

WINE GRAPES / **RAISINS DE CUVE**

1983	4 202,1 *	2 319,3 *	0,0	—	100,4	94,4	1 618,5	1 065,9	—	1 057,0	1,3	—	264,3	0,3 *
1984	4 109,5	2 292,0	0,0	—	101,4	92,0	1 553,2	1 048,6	—	1 048,3	1,3	—	264,3	0,4
1985	4 032,9 *	2 251,9 *	0,0	—	100,9	90,0 *	1 516,7	1 036,9	—	1 022,3	1,3	—	264,3	0,4 *
1986	3 989,9 *	2 226,7 *	0,0	—	100,7	90,0 *	1 499,0 *	1 023,6	—	1 010,6	1,3	—	264,3	0,4 *

OLIVES / **OLIVES**

1983	4 322,6	1 915,5	—	—	—	642,8	2 090,5	18,8	—	1 254,0	—	—	316,6	—
1984	4 315,9	1 923,8	—	—	—	651,5	2 075,6	17,9	—	1 254,4	—	—	316,6	—
1985	4 283,2 *	1 879,9 *	—	—	—	655,0 *	2 086,7	17,5	—	1 207,4	—	—	316,6	—
1986	4 228,5 *	1 821,9 *	—	—	—	657,5 *	2 090,0 *	17,3	—	1 147,2	—	—	316,6	—

OLIVES FOR OIL / **OLIVES POUR HUILE**

1983	:	:	—	—	—	521,3	1 935,5	10,3	—	:	—	—	307,8	—
1984	:	:	—	—	—	530,2	1 917,1	10,1	—	:	—	—	307,8	—
1985	:	:	—	—	—	534,0 *	1 929,1	10,1	—	:	—	—	307,8	—
1986	:	:	—	—	—	537,0 *	1 933,0 *	10,1	—	:	—	—	307,8	—

WILD PRODUCTS / **PRODUITS DE CUEILLETTE**

1983	:	—	—	—	—	—	—	—	—	—	—	—	—	—
1984	:	—	—	—	—	—	—	—	—	—	—	—	—	—
1985	:	—	—	—	—	—	—	—	—	—	—	—	—	—
1986	:	—	—	—	—	—	—	—	—	—	—	—	—	—

SOURCE: CRONOS-ZPA1 DATA BANK, AGRICULTURAL PRODUCTS

SOURCE: BANQUE DE DONNEES CRONOS-ZPA1, PRODUITS AGRICOLES

YEAR ANNÉE	EUR 12	EUR 10	B	DK	D	GR	E	F	IRL	I	L	NL	P	UK
						1000 T								

TOTAL FRESH FRUIT — **TOTAL FRUITS FRAIS**

	EUR 12	EUR 10	B	DK	D	GR	E	F	IRL	I	L	NL	P	UK
1983	20 563 *	16 554	364	75	2 601	2 193	3 587	3 085	19	7 069	6	611	422 *	529
1984	21 453 *	17 425	360	81	3 251	2 200	3 653	3 630	19	6 695	7	634	375 *	548
1985	19 959 *	15 822 *	350	73	2 687	2 161 *	3 756	3 386	19 *	6 175	8	469	381 *	494
1986	20 962 *	17 330 *	413 *	83 *	3 571	2 135 *	3 304 *	3 390 *	17 *	6 589 *	10	622	328 *	501

FRUIT TREES (EX.OLIVES AND CITRUS) — **ARBRES FRUITIERS (EX.OLIVES ET AGRUMES)**

	EUR 12	EUR 10	B	DK	D	GR	E	F	IRL	I	L	NL	P	UK
1983	17 777 *	14 104 *	325	61	2 338	1 340	3 271	3 314	8	5 743	5	549	402	421 *
1984	19 468 *	15 823 *	322	66	2 977	1 326	3 287	4 419	10	5 670	6	573	357	455 *
1985	17 560 *	13 760 *	315	61	2 420	1 296	3 448	3 724	9	5 114	7	417	352	397 *
1986	18 477 *	15 280 *	376	70 *	3 297	1 374 *	2 870 *	3 949	8	5 236 *	9	558	327 *	403 *

STRAWBERRIES — **FRAISES**

	EUR 12	EUR 10	B	DK	D	GR	E	F	IRL	I	L	NL	P	UK
1983	511 *	409	25	9	43	10	100	84	3	151	0	26	2 *	58
1984	558 *	414	25	10	46	10	142	90	3	145	0	26	2 *	59
1985	584 *	417	23	9	47	8	165	92	4	161	0	17	2 *	56
1986	619 *	428 *	25	9 *	50	6	189	92	3	168	0	23	2	51

SOFT FRUIT — **BAIES**

	EUR 12	EUR 10	B	DK	D	GR	E	F	IRL	I	L	NL	P	UK
1983	539	469	5	5	230	6	66	23	1	127	0	5	5	66
1984	573 *	486	5	4	239	6	82	29	2	140	0	5	5 *	55
1985	526 *	453 *	5	4	228	7 *	67	27	2	120	0	3	6 *	58
1986	574 *	493 *	5	4 *	237	8 *	75 *	39	1	132 *	0	4	6 *	62

CITRUS FRUITS — **AGRUMES**

	EUR 12	EUR 10	B	DK	D	GR	E	F	IRL	I	L	NL	P	UK
1983	8 636	4 630	–	–	–	918	3 874	31	–	3 681	–	–	132	–
1984	6 400	3 743	–	–	–	1 057	2 520	27	–	2 659	–	–	138	–
1985	7 998	4 349	–	–	–	879	3 514	37	–	3 434	–	–	136	–
1986	8 793 *	4 785 *	–	–	–	1 122 *	3 867	40	–	3 623	–	–	141 *	–

GRAPES — **RAISINS**

	EUR 12	EUR 10	B	DK	D	GR	E	F	IRL	I	L	NL	P	UK
1983	31 886 *	25 553 *	4	–	1 790 *	1 716	5 119	9 041	–	12 975	24	1	1 214	2 *
1984	28 944 *	22 082 *	4	–	1 190	1 746	5 632	8 370	–	10 751	20	1	1 230	1 *
1985	27 870 *	21 016 *	3	–	820	1 624 *	5 450	8 969	–	9 584	14	1	1 404	1 *
1986	30 681 *	23 793 *	3 *	–	1 320	1 488 *	5 788	9 335	–	11 623	23	1	1 100	1 *

WINE GRAPES — **RAISINS DE CUVE**

	EUR 12	EUR 10	B	DK	D	GR	E	F	IRL	I	L	NL	P	UK
1983	28 462 *	22 698 *	1	–	1 790 *	764	4 614	8 912	–	11 206	24	–	1 150	2 *
1984	25 837 *	19 590 *	1	–	1 190	781	5 072	8 236	–	9 361	20	–	1 175	1 *
1985	24 719 *	18 499 *	1	–	820	670 *	4 880	8 813	–	8 181	14	–	1 340	1 *
1986	27 311 *	21 018 *	1	–	1 320	630 *	5 233	9 200	–	9 844	23	–	1 060	1 *

OLIVES — **OLIVES**

	EUR 12	EUR 10	B	DK	D	GR	E	F	IRL	I	L	NL	P	UK
1983	7 071	5 652	–	–	–	1 431	1 328	16	–	4 206	–	–	91	–
1984	7 056	3 167	–	–	–	1 307	3 525	16	–	1 845	–	–	363	–
1985	7 065 *	4 836 *	–	–	–	1 439 *	1 989	8	–	3 388	–	–	240	–
1986	5 818 *	3 006 *	–	–	–	979 *	2 551	7	–	2 020	–	–	261	–

OLIVES FOR OIL — **OLIVES POUR HUILE**

	EUR 12	EUR 10	B	DK	D	GR	E	F	IRL	I	L	NL	P	UK
1983	6 706	5 441	–	–	–	1 298	1 194	14	–	4 128	–	–	72	–
1984	6 555	2 976	–	–	–	1 167	3 237	14	–	1 795	–	–	343	–
1985	6 625 *	4 580 *	–	–	–	1 275 *	1 825	7	–	3 298	–	–	219	–
1986	5 324 *	2 791 *	–	–	–	848 *	2 292	5	–	1 937	–	–	241	–

WILD PRODUCTS — **PRODUITS DE CUEILLETTE**

	EUR 12	EUR 10	B	DK	D	GR	E	F	IRL	I	L	NL	P	UK
1983	24	19	–	–	–	–	5	5	–	14	–	–	–	–
1984	14	10	–	–	–	–	3	5	–	5	–	–	–	–
1985	15	10	–	–	–	–	5	5	–	5	–	–	–	–
1986	16 *	12 *	–	–	–	–	4	5 *	–	7 *	–	–	–	–

SOURCE: CRONOS-ZPA1 DATA BANK, AGRICULTURAL PRODUCTS

SOURCE: BANQUE DE DONNEES CRONOS-ZPA1, PRODUITS AGRICOLES

PURE STAND AREAS

CULTURES PURES

1000 HA

YEAR ANNÉE	EUR 12	EUR 10	B	DK	D	GR	E	F	IRL	I	L	NL	P	UK
TOTAL TABLE FRUIT													**TOTAL FRUITS DE TABLE**	
1983	3 500,0 *	1 875,3 *	11,6	9,2	54,7	332,2 *	1 338,8	255,8	2,0 *	1 130,4	0,2	25,8	285,9	53,4
1984	3 513,0 *	1 875,2 *	11,6	9,1 *	54,2	334,2 *	1 351,3	254,2	2,0 *	1 133,0	0,2	25,7 *	286,5 *	51,0
1985	3 529,4 *	1 873,7 *	11,4	8,7	54,3	334,3 *	1 370,6	252,0	2,0	1 135,4	0,2	25,4 *	285,1 *	50,0
1986	3 542,8 *	1 880,1 *	11,1	8,5 *	54,2	335,5 *	1 377,6 *	250,2 *	2,0	1 145,3 *	0,2	24,4 *	285,1 *	48,9
DESSERT APPLES & PEARS													**POMMES ET POIRES DE TABLE**	
1983	471,3	339,9	8,4	4,6	26,1	26,2	96,7	87,1	0,7	136,3	0,1	21,4	34,7	29,0
1984	466,7	338,3	8,5	4,5	26,1	26,1	94,8	86,2	0,7	136,4	0,1	21,3	33,5	28,3
1985	459,2 *	334,9 *	8,6	4,1	26,1	26,0 *	93,2	85,7	0,7	134,6	0,1	21,2	31,2	27,9
1986	454,8 *	332,1 *	8,2	4,1	26,1	25,9 *	92,0 *	84,5 *	0,7	134,7	0,1	20,2	30,7 *	27,5
FRESH GRAPES													**RAISINS FRAIS**	
1983	278,0	193,5	0,1	—	—	83,4	78,3	28,8	—	81,3	—	0,0	6,1	—
1984	277,3 *	191,3 *	0,1	—	—	82,6	79,9	27,6	—	81,1	—	0,0 *	6,1	—
1985	270,2 *	187,9 *	0,1	—	—	81,0 *	76,2	26,3	—	80,5	—	0,0 *	6,1	—
1986	273,0 *	191,9 *	0,1	—	—	80,0 *	75,0 *	25,6	—	86,3	—	0,0 *	6,1	—
FRESH FRUITS OF KITCHEN GARDENS													**FRUITS FRAIS DES JARDINS**	
1983	:	:	:	:	:	:	—	:	:	:	:	:	—	:
1984	:	:	:	:	:	:	—	:	:	:	:	:	—	:
1985	:	:	:	:	:	:	—	:	:	:	:	:	—	:
1986	:	:	:	:	:	:	—	:	:	:	:	:	—	:
FRUIT TREES (EX.OLIVES AND CITRUS)													**ARBRES FRUITIERS (EX.OLIVES ET AGRUMES)**	
1983	2 415,4 *	1 321,1 *	10,6	6,7	48,7	140,4 *	854,8	207,2	1,3 *	842,2	0,1	23,1	239,5	40,7 *
1984	2 411,3 *	1 320,5 *	10,7	6,6 *	47,6	142,3	851,1	207,3	1,3 *	842,2	0,1	23,1	239,7	39,2 *
1985	2 422,1 *	1 319,0 *	10,5	6,3	47,5	142,9 *	865,3	206,6	1,3	842,5	0,1	22,8	237,8	38,5 *
1986	2 422,8 *	1 317,1 *	10,4	5,6 *	47,1	143,9 *	868,1 *	205,9 *	1,3	843,1 *	0,1	21,7	237,6 *	37,8 *
APPLES													**POMMES**	
1983	342,6 *	255,9 *	5,6	4,1	26,4	18,9	61,4	70,5	0,6	85,0	0,1	15,8	25,2	28,8 *
1984	340,4 *	256,3 *	5,7	4,0	26,4	18,8	60,2	70,5	0,7	86,1	0,1	15,8	24,0	28,3 *
1985	335,2 *	255,4 *	5,7	3,6	26,4	18,8 *	58,2	71,3	0,7	85,5	0,1	15,6	21,6	27,8 *
1986	332,2 *	254,2 *	5,7	3,3	26,4	18,8 *	57,0 *	71,0 *	0,7	86,0	0,1	15,0	21,0 *	27,3 *
TABLE APPLES													**POMMES DE TABLE**	
1983	330,4	245,0	5,6	4,1	24,3	18,9	60,2	65,6	0,6	85,0	0,1	15,8	25,2	24,9
1984	328,2	245,2	5,7	4,0	24,3	18,8	59,0	65,5	0,7	86,1	0,1	15,8	24,0	24,2
1985	322,5 *	243,9 *	5,7	3,6	24,3	18,8 *	57,0	65,8	0,7	85,5	0,1	15,6	21,6	23,9
1986	319,4 *	242,4 *	5,5	3,6	24,3	18,8 *	56,0 *	65,0 *	0,7	86,0	0,1	15,0	21,0 *	23,5
GOLDEN DELICIOUS													**GOLDEN DELICIOUS**	
1983	:	:	:	:	:	:	25,0	:	:	:	:	:	—	:
1984	:	:	:	:	:	:	23,9	:	:	:	:	:	—	:
1985	:	:	:	:	:	:	23,5	:	:	:	:	:	—	:
1986	:	:	:	:	:	:	23,0 *	:	:	:	:	:	—	:
PEARS													**POIRES**	
1983	141,4 *	95,5 *	2,9	0,4	2,1	7,3	36,5	21,4	0,0	51,3	0,0	5,6	9,5	4,4 *
1984	139,1 *	93,7 *	2,8	0,5	2,1	7,2	35,8	20,7	0,0	50,4	0,0	5,6	9,5	4,3 *
1985	137,2 *	91,5 *	2,8	0,4	2,1	7,2 *	36,0	19,9	0,0	49,1	0,0	5,6	9,6	4,3 *
1986	135,9 *	90,2 *	2,8	0,4	2,1	7,2 *	36,0 *	19,5 *	0,0	48,7	0,0	5,3	9,7 *	4,2 *
TABLE PEARS													**POIRES DE TABLE**	
1983	140,9	94,9	2,9	0,4	1,8	7,3	36,5	21,4	0,0	51,3	0,0	5,6	9,5	4,1
1984	138,5	93,1	2,8	0,5	1,8	7,2	35,8	20,7	0,0	50,4	0,0	5,6	9,5	4,1
1985	136,7 *	91,0 *	2,8	0,4	1,8	7,2 *	36,2	19,9	0,0	49,1	0,0	5,6	9,6	4,0
1986	135,4 *	89,7 *	2,8	0,4	1,8	7,2 *	36,0 *	19,5 *	0,0	48,7	0,0	5,3	9,7 *	4,0

SOURCE: CRONOS-ZPA1 DATA BANK, AGRICULTURAL PRODUCTS

SOURCE: BANQUE DE DONNEES CRONOS-ZPA1, PRODUITS AGRICOLES

1000 T

YEAR ANNÉE	EUR 12	EUR 10	B	DK	D	GR	E	F	IRL	I	L	NL	P	UK
TOTAL TABLE FRUIT													**TOTAL FRUITS DE TABLE**	
1983	30 775 *	22 259	359	75	2 611	3 358	7 893	3 166	12	11 562	5	581	623 *	529
1984	29 538 *	22 136	355	81	3 262	3 502	6 824	3 704	15	10 058	6	604	579 *	548
1985	29 621 *	21 174 *	346	73	2 694	3 309 *	7 867	3 471	15	10 325	7	439	581 *	494
1986	31 511 *	23 193 *	409 *	83 *	3 584	3 499 *	7 782 *	3 481 *	13	11 029 *	9	586	536 *	501
DESSERT APPLES & PEARS													**POMMES ET POIRES DE TABLE**	
1983	10 366	8 618	302	51	1 670	453	1 564	1 989	8	3 237	4	538	183	366
1984	11 301	9 675	298	58	2 197	425	1 468	2 454	10	3 275	6	559	158	395
1985	10 011	8 260	294	49	1 707	406	1 599	2 210	9	2 820	6	407	152	352
1986	10 849	9 534	343	60	2 589	436	1 189	2 223	8	2 970	7	548	126	349
FRESH GRAPES													**RAISINS FRAIS**	
1983	3 424	2 854	3	—	—	951	505	130	—	1 769	—	1	64	—
1984	3 107	2 492	3	—	—	965	560	134	—	1 390	—	1	55	—
1985	3 151	2 516	3	—	—	954	570	156	—	1 402	—	1	64	—
1986	3 370 *	2 775 *	2 *	—	—	858	555	135	—	1 779	—	1	40	—
FRESH FRUITS OF KITCHEN GARDENS													**FRUITS FRAIS DES JARDINS**	
1983	44	44	6	0	—	—	—	—	7	0	1	30	—	—
1984	41	41	5	0	—	—	—	—	5	0	1	30	—	—
1985	40 *	40 *	5	0	—	—	—	—	4 *	0	1	30	—	—
1986	46 *	46 *	5	0	—	—	—	—	4 *	0	1	36	—	—
FRUIT TREES (EX.OLIVES AND CITRUS)													**ARBRES FRUITIERS (EX.OLIVES ET AGRUMES)**	
1983	17 777 *	14 104 *	325	61	2 338	1 340	3 271	3 314	8	5 743	5	549	402	421 *
1984	19 468 *	15 823 *	322	66	2 977	1 326	3 287	4 419	10	5 670	6	573	357	455 *
1985	17 560 *	13 760 *	315	61	2 420	1 296	3 448	3 724	9	5 114	7	417	352	397 *
1986	18 477 *	15 280 *	376	70 *	3 297	1 374 *	2 870 *	3 949	8	5 236 *	9	558	327 *	403 *
APPLES													**POMMES**	
1983	7 803 *	6 612 *	200	47	1 300	308	1 076	1 985	8	2 032	3	403	115	325 *
1984	9 454 *	8 340 *	225	54	1 766	304	1 028	2 969	10	2 210	5	431	86	365 *
1985	8 068 *	6 903 *	216	45	1 383	267	1 070	2 348	9	2 014	6	300	95	315 *
1986	9 096 *	8 155	262	57	2 115	306	865 *	2 649	8	1 990	7	445	76	315
TABLE APPLES													**POMMES DE TABLE**	
1983	7 316	6 188	200	47	1 300	308	1 013	1 575	8	2 032	3	403	115	312
1984	8 413	7 357	225	54	1 766	304	969	2 005	10	2 210	5	431	86	347
1985	7 434	6 334	216	45	1 383	267	1 004	1 793	9	2 014	6	300	95	301
1986	8 276	7 372	262	57	2 115	306	828	1 878	8	1 990	7	445	76	303
GOLDEN DELICIOUS													**GOLDEN DELICIOUS**	
1983	:	:	93	6	:	28	495	1 057	2	860	1	130	—	:
1984	:	:	91	7	:	33	444	1 306	3	950	2	123	40	:
1985	:	:	85	6	:	30	452	1 148	1	879	1	92	45	:
1986	:	:	89	7	:	29	385 *	1 139	2	890	2	118,	45	:
PEARS													**POIRES**	
1983	3 063 *	2 444 *	102	4	371	145	551	425	0	1 205	0	135	68	57 *
1984	2 930 *	2 359 *	72	3	432	122	499	487	0	1 064	0	128	71	51 *
1985	2 596 *	1 944 *	78	4	324	139	595	433	0	806	0	107	57	53 *
1986	2 587 *	2 176 *	81	4	474	129	361	355	0	980	0	103	50	50 *
TABLE PEARS													**POIRES DE TABLE**	
1983	3 049	2 430	102	4	371	145	551	414	0	1 205	0	135	68	54
1984	2 889	2 318	72	3	432	122	499	449	0	1 064	0	128	71	48
1985	2 577	1 925	78	4	324	139	595	417	0	806	0	107	57	51
1986	2 574	2 163	81	4	474	129	361	345	0	980	0	103	50	47

SOURCE: CRONOS-ZPA1 DATA BANK, AGRICULTURAL PRODUCTS

SOURCE: BANQUE DE DONNEES CRONOS-ZPA1, PRODUITS AGRICOLES

I D 3

YEAR ANNÉE	EUR 12	EUR 10	B	DK	D	GR	E	F	IRL	I	L	NL	P	UK
						1000 HA								
STONE FRUIT													**FRUITS A NOYAU**	
1983	432,3 *	309,7 *	2,1	2,2	13,8	43,8 *	106,6	87,2	0,0	154,2	0,0	1,7	15,9	4,7
1984	443,4 *	313,9 *	2,1	2,1 *	13,8	45,9	113,1	87,8	0,0	156,1	0,0	1,7	16,4	4,3
1985	452,8 *	317,6 *	1,9	2,2	13,8	46,9 *	118,4	87,4	0,0	159,7	0,0	1,6	16,7	4,0
1986	457,3 *	319,7 *	1,8	1,9 *	13,8	48,0 *	120,5 *	87,5 *	0,0	161,2	0,0	1,4	17,0 *	4,0
PEACHES													**PECHES**	
1983	202,3 *	144,5	0,0	—	0,1	29,6	49,7 *	29,8	—	85,0	—	0,0	8,1	—
1984	208,2 *	145,4	0,0	—	0,1	31,1	54,3 *	29,9	—	84,3	—	0,0	8,4	—
1985	209,7 *	143,6 *	0,0	—	0,1	31,5 *	57,6 *	28,8	—	83,2	—	0,0	8,5	—
1986	210,6 *	142,9 *	0,0	—	0,1	32,0 *	59,0 *	28,5 *	—	82,2	—	0,0	8,7 *	—
NECTARINES													**NECTARINES**	
1983	:	23,1 *	—	—	—	1,2	2,4	6,6	—	15,3	—	—	—	—
1984	:	26,9	—	—	—	1,5	2,5	7,5	—	18,0	—	—	—	—
1985	:	32,4	—	—	—	2,0	3,0	7,9	—	22,4	—	—	—	—
1986	:	35,5 *	—	—	—	2,5	3,5	8,5 *	—	24,5	—	—	—	—
APRICOTS													**ABRICOTS**	
1983	59,7	36,1	—	—	0,1	6,6	21,3	13,6	—	15,9	—	—	2,3	—
1984	59,8	36,3	—	—	0,1	6,6	21,2	13,7	—	15,9	—	—	2,3	—
1985	60,3 *	37,0 *	—	—	0,1	6,6 *	20,8	14,1	—	16,2	—	—	2,5	—
1986	59,9 *	36,9 *	—	—	0,1	6,7 *	20,5 *	14,0 *	—	16,2	—	—	2,5 *	—
CHERRIES													**CERISES**	
1983	83,8	63,5	1,7	1,9	9,8	5,6	16,8	18,2	—	24,3	0,0	0,9	3,6	1,1
1984	84,7 *	63,0 *	1,7	1,9	9,8	6,0	18,0	17,7	—	24,0	0,0	0,9 *	3,6	1,0
1985	85,5 *	62,6 *	1,6	2,0	9,8	6,0 *	19,2	17,2	—	24,3	0,0	0,7	3,7	1,0
1986	86,2 *	63,0 *	1,5	1,7	9,8	6,0 *	19,5 *	17,0 *	—	25,4	0,0	0,6	3,7 *	1,0
PLUMS													**PRUNES**	
1983	60,1	41,7	0,4	0,2	3,8	0,7	16,4	19,0	0,0	13,2	0,0	0,8	2,0	3,6
1984	60,5 *	41,4 *	0,4	0,2 *	3,8	0,7	17,1	19,1	0,0	13,3	0,0	0,8 *	2,0	3,2
1985	61,0 *	41,0 *	0,3	0,2	3,8	0,7 *	17,8	19,3	0,0	12,9	0,0	0,7	2,1	3,0
1986	60,6 *	40,4 *	0,3	0,2 *	3,8	0,7 *	18,0 *	19,5 *	0,0	12,1	0,0	0,7	2,1 *	3,1
OTHER STONE FRUIT N.O.S.													**AUTRES FRUITS A NOYAU N.D.A.**	
1983	0,8 *	0,8	—	0,1	—	0,1	0,0 *	—	—	0,6	—	0,1	0,0	—
1984	0,9 *	0,9 *	—	0,1 *	—	0,1	— *	—	—	0,7	—	0,1 *	0,0	—
1985	1,0 *	1,0 *	—	0,1	—	0,1 *	— *	—	—	0,7	—	0,1	0,0	—
1986	1,0 *	1,0 *	—	0,1 *	—	0,1 *	— *	— *	—	0,7	—	0,1	— *	—
NUTS													**FRUITS A COQUE**	
1983	1 329,5	624,0	0,0	—	0,1	59,7	607,0	26,9	—	537,3	—	—	98,4	—
1984	1 319,7	621,3	0,0	—	0,1	59,7	599,9	27,2	—	534,2	—	—	98,5	—
1985	1 331,1 *	620,0 *	0,0	—	0,1	59,5 *	612,4	27,0	—	533,3	—	—	98,8	—
1986	1 333,2 *	619,5 *	0,0	—	0,1	59,6 *	614,9 *	26,9 *	—	533,0 *	—	—	98,8 *	—
WALNUTS													**NOIX**	
1983	39,7	36,0	0,0	—	0,1	7,9	1,4	14,1	—	14,0	—	—	2,3	—
1984	40,1	36,5	0,0	—	0,1	8,1	1,3	14,4	—	13,9	—	—	2,3	—
1985	40,3 *	36,1 *	0,0	—	0,1	8,1 *	1,8	14,1	—	13,8	—	—	2,4	—
1986	36,7 *	32,4 *	0,0	—	0,1	8,2 *	1,8 *	14,0	—	10,2	—	—	2,4 *	—
HAZELNUTS													**NOISETTES**	
1983	118,8	80,7	—	—	—	7,1	37,1	1,7	—	72,0	—	—	1,0	—
1984	117,2	78,8	—	—	—	6,5	37,4	1,7	—	70,6	—	—	1,0	—
1985	118,6 *	79,8 *	—	—	—	6,5 *	37,7	1,8	—	71,5	—	—	1,1	—
1986	119,5 *	80,4 *	—	—	—	6,4 *	38,0 *	1,8 *	—	72,2	—	—	1,1 *	—

SOURCE: CRONOS-ZPA1 DATA BANK, AGRICULTURAL PRODUCTS

SOURCE: BANQUE DE DONNEES CRONOS-ZPA1, PRODUITS AGRICOLES

YEAR ANNÉE	EUR 12	EUR 10	B	DK	D	GR	E	F	IRL	I	L	NL	P	UK
						1000 T								

STONE FRUIT / **FRUITS A NOYAU**

	EUR 12	EUR 10	B	DK	D	GR	E	F	IRL	I	L	NL	P	UK
1983	5 268	4 362	23	10	658	688	839	848	0	2 084	1	11	68	39
1984	5 528	4 554	24	8	769	712	923	911	0	2 076	1	14	51	39
1985	5 282	4 321	21	11	706	713	906	889	0	1 941	2	10	56	29
1986	5 242 *	4 328 *	32	10 *	695	751 *	858	891	0	1 899 *	1	10	56	38

PEACHES / **PECHES**

	EUR 12	EUR 10	B	DK	D	GR	E	F	IRL	I	L	NL	P	UK
1983	2 830 *	2 318 *	0 *	–	28	479	476	393	–	1 418	–	–	36 *	–
1984	2 815 *	2 297	0	–	31	547	494	394	–	1 324	–	0	24 *	–
1985	2 667	2 109	0	–	18	509	532	391	–	1 191	–	0	26	–
1986	2 658	2 145	0	–	31	577	492	364	–	1 174	–	0	21	–

NECTARINES / **NECTARINES**

	EUR 12	EUR 10	B	DK	D	GR	E	F	IRL	I	L	NL	P	UK
1983	314 *	297	–	–	–	16	15	78	–	203	–	–	2 *	–
1984	359 *	342	–	–	–	23	15	89	–	230	–	–	3 *	–
1985	378	360	–	–	–	29	16	98	–	234	–	–	3	–
1986	447	402	–	–	–	28	35	113	–	261	–	–	10	–

APRICOTS / **ABRICOTS**

	EUR 12	EUR 10	B	DK	D	GR	E	F	IRL	I	L	NL	P	UK
1983	552	395	–	–	2	137	151	102	–	154	–	–	7	–
1984	586	373	–	–	2	94	208	82	–	196	–	–	5	–
1985	584	428	–	–	2	128	151	102	–	196	–	–	5	–
1986	554	398	–	–	2	97	150	114	–	186	–	–	6	–

CHERRIES / **CERISES**

	EUR 12	EUR 10	B	DK	D	GR	E	F	IRL	I	L	NL	P	UK
1983	659	571	17	9	265	40	74	98	–	137	0	3	14	3
1984	720	629	19	7	282	34	78	119	–	159	0	4	13	5
1985	658	565	15	10	238	36	80	101	–	157	0	2	14	5
1986	617 *	538 *	26	9 *	239	38	67	92	–	127	0	3	12 *	4

PLUMS / **PRUNES**

	EUR 12	EUR 10	B	DK	D	GR	E	F	IRL	I	L	NL	P	UK
1983	899	767	6	1	364	6	124	177	0	168	1	8	8	36
1984	1 034	899	5	1	454	5	129	228	0	162	1	10	6	34
1985	983	848	6	1	448	6	128	197	0	157	2	9	7	24
1986	953 *	832	7	1	422	4	114	209	0	146	1	7	7 *	34

OTHER STONE FRUIT N.O.S. / **AUTRES FRUITS A NOYAU N.D.A.**

	EUR 12	EUR 10	B	DK	D	GR	E	F	IRL	I	L	NL	P	UK
1983	14 *	14 *	– *	–	0	10	–	0	–	5	–	–	0 *	–
1984	14 *	14	–	–	0	8	– 0	0	–	6	–	–	– *	–
1985	13	11	–	–	0	5	0	0	–	6	–	–	2	–
1986	12 *	12 *	–	– *	0	7 *	–	0	–	6 *	–	–	– *	–

NUTS / **FRUITS A COQUE**

	EUR 12	EUR 10	B	DK	D	GR	E	F	IRL	I	L	NL	P	UK
1983	825	543	1	–	10	114	231	49	–	371	–	–	51	–
1984	756	426	1	–	12	106	285	45	–	263	–	–	45	–
1985	853	457	1	–	7	104	353	48	–	297	–	–	43	–
1986	813 *	490	1	–	13	111	276 *	49	–	317	–	–	47 *	–

WALNUTS / **NOIX**

	EUR 12	EUR 10	B	DK	D	GR	E	F	IRL	I	L	NL	P	UK
1983	109	97	1	–	10	28	6	25	–	33	–	–	6	–
1984	111	97	1	–	12	28	8	24	–	34	–	–	6	–
1985	115	99	1	–	7	29	8	27	–	35	–	–	7	–
1986	102 *	90	1	–	13	21	6 *	28	–	27	–	–	6 *	–

HAZELNUTS / **NOISETTES**

	EUR 12	EUR 10	B	DK	D	GR	E	F	IRL	I	L	NL	P	UK
1983	176	143	–	–	–	9	31	2	–	132	–	–	1	–
1984	103	89	–	–	–	10	13	2	–	77	–	–	1	–
1985	155	123	–	–	–	6	30	2	–	116	–	–	1	–
1986	155 *	132	–	–	–	10	21	2	–	120	–	–	1 *	–

SOURCE: CRONOS-ZPA1 DATA BANK, AGRICULTURAL PRODUCTS

SOURCE: BANQUE DE DONNEES CRONOS-ZPA1, PRODUITS AGRICOLES

ID 3

YEAR ANNÉE	EUR 12	EUR 10	B	DK	D	GR	E	F	IRL	I	L	NL	P	UK
						1000 HA								

ALMONDS | | | | | | | | | | | | | | **AMANDES**

1983	774,4	164,7	–	–	–	32,4	568,6	2,2	–	130,1	–	–	41,1	–
1984	765,3	162,9	–	–	–	32,2	561,2	2,2	–	128,5	–	–	41,2	–
1985	775,1 *	161,0 *	–	–	–	32,0 *	572,8	2,2	–	126,7	–	–	41,3	–
1986	779,8 *	163,5 *	–	–	–	31,9 *	575,0	2,3 *	–	129,3	–	–	41,3 *	–

CHESTNUTS | | | | | | | | | | | | | | **CHATAIGNES**

1983	387,2	333,2	–	–	–	7,2	0,0	8,9	–	317,0	–	–	54,0	–
1984	387,3	333,3	–	–	–	7,4	0,0	8,9	–	317,0	–	–	54,0	–
1985	387,3 *	333,3 *	–	–	–	7,4 *	0,0	8,9	–	317,0	–	–	54,0 *	–
1986	387,3 *	333,3 *	–	–	–	7,4 *	0,0	8,8 *	–	317,0 *	–	–	54,0 *	–

OTHER NUTS N.O.S. | | | | | | | | | | | | | | **AUTRES FRUITS A COQUE N.D.A.**

1983	9,4	9,4	–	–	–	5,1	−0,0	–	–	4,3	–	–	–	–
1984	9,8	9,8	–	–	–	5,5	−0,0	–	–	4,3	–	–	–	–
1985	9,8 *	9,8 *	–	–	–	5,5 *	−0,0	–	–	4,3	–	–	– *	–
1986	10,0 *	10,0 *	–	–	–	5,7 *	−0,0 *	– *	–	4,3 *	–	–	– *	–

OTHER FRUIT OF WOODY PLANTS | | | | | | | | | | | | | | **AUTRES FRUITS DE PLANTES LIGNEUSES**

1983	169,7 *	35,9 *	0,1	–	6,3	10,7	43,2	1,1	0,6 *	14,3	–	–	90,5	2,8
1984	168,7 *	35,3 *	0,1	–	5,3	10,6	42,2	1,0	0,6 *	15,3	–	–	91,2	2,4
1985	165,9 *	34,5 *	0,1	–	5,2	10,4 *	40,3	1,0	0,6	14,8	–	–	91,1	2,4
1986	164,2 *	33,5 *	0,1	–	4,8	10,4 *	39,8 *	1,0 *	0,6	14,3	–	–	91,0 *	2,4

FIGS | | | | | | | | | | | | | | **FIGUES**

1983	131,7	24,1	–	–	–	10,1	21,7	0,5	–	13,5	–	–	85,9	–
1984	131,7	24,9	–	–	–	9,9	20,9	0,5	–	14,4	–	–	85,9	–
1985	130,4 *	24,2 *	–	–	–	9,8 *	20,3	0,5	–	13,9	–	–	85,9 *	–
1986	129,5 *	23,6 *	–	–	–	9,8 *	20,0 *	0,5 *	–	13,3	–	–	85,9 *	–

QUINCES | | | | | | | | | | | | | | **COINGS**

1983	3,1	0,7	–	–	–	0,3	0,6	0,3	–	0,1	–	–	1,7	–
1984	3,1	0,7	–	–	–	0,3	0,6	0,3	–	0,1	–	–	1,7	–
1985	3,1 *	0,7 *	–	–	–	0,3 *	0,7	0,3	–	0,1	–	–	1,7	–
1986	3,1 *	0,7 *	–	–	–	0,3 *	0,8 *	0,3 *	–	0,1	–	–	1,7 *	–

OTHER N.O.S. | | | | | | | | | | | | | | **AUTRES FRUITS N.D.A.**

1983	34,8 *	11,1 *	0,1	–	6,3	0,3	20,9	0,2	0,6 *	0,7	–	–	2,9	2,8
1984	33,9 *	9,7 *	0,1	–	5,3	0,4	20,6	0,2	0,6 *	0,8	–	–	3,6	2,4
1985	32,4 *	9,6 *	0,1	–	5,2	0,4 *	19,2	0,2	0,6	0,8	–	–	3,5 *	2,4
1986	31,7 *	9,3 *	0,1	–	4,8	0,4 *	19,0 *	0,2 *	0,6	0,8	–	–	3,4 *	2,4

SOFT FRUIT | | | | | | | | | | | | | | **BAIES**

1983	43,0	31,3	0,1	1,0	2,0	0,1	10,2	4,6	0,2	13,0	0,0	0,6	1,4	9,7
1984	45,7 *	33,9 *	0,1	1,0 *	2,0	0,1	10,3	5,2	0,2	15,5	0,0	0,6	1,4	9,2
1985	49,8 *	36,8 *	0,1	1,1	2,0	0,1 *	11,5	6,3	0,2	17,6	0,0	0,6	1,5	8,9
1986	53,7 *	40,1 *	0,1	1,1	2,0	0,1 *	12,0 *	6,7 *	0,2	21,0 *	0,0	0,6	1,5 *	8,4

CURRANTS (BLACK,RED AND WHITE) | | | | | | | | | | | | | | **GROSEILLES ET CASSIS**

1983	7,5	7,5	0,1	0,9	1,2	–	0,0	1,7	0,1	0,1	0,0	0,0	–	3,5
1984	7,4	7,4	0,1	0,9	1,2	–	0,0	1,8	0,1	0,1	0,0	0,0	–	3,2
1985	7,8 *	7,8	0,0	0,9	1,2	–	0,0 *	2,1	0,1	0,1	0,0	0,0	–	3,3
1986	7,9 *	7,9 *	0,0	1,0 *	1,2	–	0,0	2,1 *	0,1	0,1 *	0,0	0,2	–	3,1

RASPBERRIES | | | | | | | | | | | | | | **FRAMBOISES**

1983	6,2	6,2	0,0	0,1	0,1	–	–	1,3	0,1	0,3	–	0,0	–	4,2
1984	6,0 *	6,0 *	0,0	0,1 *	0,1	–	–	1,4	0,1	0,3	–	0,0	–	4,1
1985	6,0	6,0	0,0	0,1	0,1	–	–	1,4	0,1	0,3	–	0,0	–	4,0
1986	5,9 *	5,9 *	0,0	0,1 *	0,1	–	–	1,4 *	0,1	0,3 *	–	0,0	–	3,9

SOURCE: CRONOS-ZPA1 DATA BANK, AGRICULTURAL PRODUCTS   SOURCE: BANQUE DE DONNEES CRONOS-ZPA1, PRODUITS AGRICOLES

YEAR ANNÉE	EUR 12	EUR 10	B	DK	D	GR	E	F	IRL	I	L	NL	P	UK

1000 T

ALMONDS   **AMANDES**

YEAR	EUR 12	EUR 10	B	DK	D	GR	E	F	IRL	I	L	NL	P	UK
1983	378	191	—	—	—	59	166	5	—	127	—	—	21	—
1984	411	158	—	—	—	54	236	4	—	101	—	—	17	—
1985	470	166	—	—	—	57	287	4	—	106	—	—	16	—
1986	429 *	180	—	—	—	52	229	4	—	123	—	—	20 *	—

CHESTNUTS   **CHATAIGNES**

YEAR	EUR 12	EUR 10	B	DK	D	GR	E	F	IRL	I	L	NL	P	UK
1983	154	107	—	—	—	14	28	17	—	77	—	—	19	—
1984	124	77	—	—	—	12	29	15	—	51	—	—	18	—
1985	108	64	—	—	—	11	28	14	—	39	—	—	17	—
1986	123 *	86 *	—	—	—	26	20 *	15	—	45 *	—	—	17 *	—

OTHER NUTS N.O.S.   **AUTRES FRUITS A COQUE N.D.A.**

YEAR	EUR 12	EUR 10	B	DK	D	GR	E	F	IRL	I	L	NL	P	UK
1983	8	5	—	—	—	3	—	—	—	2	—	—	3	—
1984	6	4	—	—	—	4	—0	—	—	0	—	—	3	—
1985	5	4	—	—	—	2	—0	—	—	2	—	—	2	—
1986	6 *	3 *	—	—	—	2	— *	—	—	1 *	—	—	2 *	—

OTHER FRUIT OF WOODY PLANTS   **AUTRES FRUITS DE PLANTES LIGNEUSES**

YEAR	EUR 12	EUR 10	B	DK	D	GR	E	F	IRL	I	L	NL	P	UK
1983	817	143	—	—	—	85	574	6	0	51	—	—	100	0
1984	800	144	—	—	—	82	551	6	0	56	—	—	104	0
1985	760	135	—	—	0	73	524	6	0	56	—	—	101	0
1986	740 *	132 *	—	—	0	76 *	510 *	5	0	51 *	—	—	98 *	0

FIGS   **FIGUES**

YEAR	EUR 12	EUR 10	B	DK	D	GR	E	F	IRL	I	L	NL	P	UK
1983	197	113	—	—	—	66	39	3	—	45	—	—	45	—
1984	202	114	—	—	—	63	42	2	—	49	—	—	46	—
1985	201	106	—	—	—	55	50	2	—	49	—	—	45	—
1986	190 *	100	—	—	—	54	45 *	2	—	44	—	—	45 *	—

QUINCES   **COINGS**

YEAR	EUR 12	EUR 10	B	DK	D	GR	E	F	IRL	I	L	NL	P	UK
1983	39	19	—	—	—	14	11	3	—	2	—	—	9	—
1984	36	19	—	—	—	13	11	4	—	2	—	—	7	—
1985	34	15	—	—	—	9	12	4	—	2	—	—	7	—
1986	29 *	13 *	—	—	—	8 *	9 *	2	—	2	—	—	7 *	—

OTHER N.O.S.   **AUTRES FRUITS N.D.A.**

YEAR	EUR 12	EUR 10	B	DK	D	GR	E	F	IRL	I	L	NL	P	UK
1983	581	10	—	—	—	6	524	0	0	4	—	—	47	0
1984	562	12	—	—	—	7	499	0	0	5	—	—	51	0
1985	526	15	—	—	0	9	462	0	0	5	—	—	49	0
1986	521 *	19 *	—	—	0	14	456 *	1	0	5 *	—	—	46 *	0

SOFT FRUIT   **BAIES**

YEAR	EUR 12	EUR 10	B	DK	D	GR	E	F	IRL	I	L	NL	P	UK
1983	539	469	5	5	230	6	66	23	1	127	0	5	5	66
1984	573 *	486	5	4	239	6	82	29	2	140	0	5	5 *	55
1985	526 *	453 *	5	4	228	7 *	67	27	2	120	0	3	6 *	58
1986	574 *	493 *	5	4 *	237	8 *	75 *	39	1	132 *	0	4	6 *	62

CURRANTS (BLACK, RED AND WHITE)   **GROSEILLES ET CASSIS**

YEAR	EUR 12	EUR 10	B	DK	D	GR	E	F	IRL	I	L	NL	P	UK
1983	181	181	5	4	130	—	0	7	0	1	0	3	—	32
1984	172	172	5	4	134	—	0	7	1	1	0	3	—	18
1985	167	167	4	3	127	—	0	7	1	1	0	3	—	22
1986	181 *	181 *	5	3 *	132	—	0	10	1	1	0	3	—	28

RASPBERRIES   **FRAMBOISES**

YEAR	EUR 12	EUR 10	B	DK	D	GR	E	F	IRL	I	L	NL	P	UK
1983	56	56	0	0	24	—	—	6	0	2	—	1	—	22
1984	60	59	0	0	25	—	—	7	1	2	—	1	—	24
1985	108	108	0	0	76	—	—	6	1	2	—	0	—	23
1986	58 *	58 *	0	0 *	25	—	—	6	0	2	—	0	—	24

SOURCE: CRONOS-ZPA1 DATA BANK, AGRICULTURAL PRODUCTS   SOURCE: BANQUE DE DONNEES CRONOS-ZPA1, PRODUITS AGRICOLES

YEAR ANNÉE	EUR 12	EUR 10	B	DK	D	GR	E	F	IRL	I	L	NL	P	UK
1000 HA														
GOOSEBERRIES														**GROSEILLES A MAQUEREAU**
1983	1,7	1,7	0,0	0,0	0,7	—	0,0	—	0,0	0,0	—	0,0	—	0,9
1984	1,6	1,6	0,0	0,0	0,7	—	0,0	—	0,0	0,0	—	0,0	—	0,9
1985	1,5 *	1,5	0,0	0,0	0,7	—	0,0	—	0,0	0,0	—	0,0	—	0,8
1986	1,5 *	1,5 *	0,0	0,0	0,7	—	0,0	—	0,0	0,0 *	—	0,0	—	0,7
OTHER SOFT FRUIT														**AUTRES BAIES**
1983	24,1	12,5	0,0	0,1	—	0,1	10,2	0,0	0,0	10,7	—	0,6	1,4	1,1
1984	24,6 *	12,9 *	0,0	0,1 *	—	0,1	10,3	0,0	0,0	11,1	—	0,6	1,4	1,0
1985	25,5 *	12,6 *	0,0	0,0	—	0,1 *	11,5 *	0,0	0,0	11,0	—	0,6	1,5	0,8
1986	25,1 *	11,6 *	0,0	0,1 *	—	0,1 *	12,0 *	0,0 *	0,0	10,5 *	—	0,3	1,5 *	0,6
CITRUS FRUITS														**AGRUMES**
1983	500,5 *	235,5 *	—	—	—	49,9 *	235,7	2,4	—	183,2	—	—	29,3	—
1984	512,3 *	237,2 *	—	—	—	50,3 *	245,4	2,4	—	184,5	—	—	29,7	—
1985	519,6 *	237,0 *	—	—	—	50,8 *	252,4	2,2	—	184,0	—	—	30,2	—
1986	525,4 *	238,1 *	—	—	—	51,6 *	256,9 *	2,2 *	—	184,3	—	—	30,4 *	—
ORANGES														**ORANGES**
1983	285,9 *	141,5 *	—	—	—	32,7 *	125,2	0,2	—	108,7	—	—	19,2	—
1984	289,1 *	141,8 *	—	—	—	32,8 *	127,9	0,2	—	108,8	—	—	19,3	—
1985	293,8 *	142,6 *	—	—	—	33,5 *	131,6	0,2	—	109,0	—	—	19,6	—
1986	296,7 *	143,1 *	—	—	—	34,0 *	134,0 *	0,1 *	—	109,0	—	—	19,6 *	—
MANDARINS														**MANDARINES**
1983	44,2	20,1	—	—	—	3,8	19,6	0,0	—	16,3	—	—	4,5	—
1984	45,5	20,7	—	—	—	4,1	20,1	0,0	—	16,6	—	—	4,6	—
1985	45,5 *	20,2 *	—	—	—	4,2 *	20,6	0,0	—	16,0	—	—	4,7	—
1986	45,6 *	20,4 *	—	—	—	4,5 *	20,5 *	0,0 *	—	15,8	—	—	4,8 *	—
CLEMENTINES														**CLEMENTINES**
1983	56,4	16,6	—	—	—	—	38,5	2,1	—	14,5	—	—	1,4	—
1984	58,3	17,2	—	—	—	—	39,6	2,1	—	15,1	—	—	1,4	—
1985	59,6	17,7	—	—	—	—	40,5	1,9	—	15,8	—	—	1,5	—
1986	61,1 *	18,6 *	—	—	—	—	41,0	1,9 *	—	16,7	—	—	1,5	—
LEMONS														**CITRONS**
1983	104,4	52,7	—	—	—	13,0	47,6	0,1	—	39,7	—	—	4,0	—
1984	110,0	53,0	—	—	—	13,0	52,8	0,1	—	39,9	—	—	4,2	—
1985	112,2 *	52,7 *	—	—	—	12,8 *	55,2	0,0	—	39,8	—	—	4,3	—
1986	113,7 *	52,4 *	—	—	—	12,8 *	57,0 *	0,0 *	—	39,5	—	—	4,3 *	—
GRAPEFRUIT														**PAMPLEMOUSSES**
1983	1,1	0,3	—	—	—	—	0,6	0,0	—	0,3	—	—	0,2	—
1984	1,2	0,3	—	—	—	—	0,8	0,0	—	0,3	—	—	0,2	—
1985	1,1	0,3	—	—	—	—	0,6	0,0	—	0,3	—	—	0,2	—
1986	1,1 *	0,3 *	—	—	—	—	0,6	0,0 *	—	0,3	—	—	0,2	—
OTHER CITRUS FRUIT N.O.S.														**AUTRES AGRUMES**
1983	8,5	4,3	—	—	—	0,4	4,2	0,0	—	3,9	—	—	—	—
1984	8,3	4,2	—	—	—	0,4	4,1	0,0	—	3,8	—	—	—	—
1985	7,3 *	3,5 *	—	—	—	0,3 *	3,9	0,0	—	3,1	—	—	— 0,0	—
1986	7,2 *	3,4 *	—	—	—	0,3 *	3,8 *	0,0 *	—	3,0	—	—	— *	—
TABLE OLIVES														**OLIVES DE TABLE**
1983	:	:	—	—	—	121,5	155,0	8,4	—	:	—	—	8,8	—
1984	:	:	—	—	—	121,3	158,4	7,9	—	:	—	—	8,8	—
1985	:	:	—	—	—	121,0 *	157,6	7,4	—	:	—	—	8,8	—
1986	:	:	—	—	—	120,5 *	157,0 *	7,2	—	:	—	—	8,8	—

SOURCE: CRONOS-ZPA1 DATA BANK, AGRICULTURAL PRODUCTS

SOURCE: BANQUE DE DONNEES CRONOS-ZPA1, PRODUITS AGRICOLES

ID 3

YEAR ANNÉE	EUR 12	EUR 10	B	DK	D	GR	E	F	IRL	I	L	NL	P	UK
						1000 T								

GOOSEBERRIES — **GROSEILLES A MAQUEREAU**

YEAR ANNÉE	EUR 12	EUR 10	B	DK	D	GR	E	F	IRL	I	L	NL	P	UK
1983	85,5	85,5	0,5	0,0	76,5	—	0,0	—	0,4	0,0	—	0,2	—	7,9
1984	88,9	88,9	0,4	0,0	79,8	—	0,0	—	0,3	0,0	—	0,2	—	8,2
1985	32,7	32,7	0,4	0,0	25,2	—	0,0	—	0,2	0,0	—	—	—	7,0
1986	88,0	88,0	0,5	0,0	80,6	—	0,0	—	0,2	0,0	—	0,5	—	6,2

OTHER SOFT FRUIT — **AUTRES BAIES**

YEAR ANNÉE	EUR 12	EUR 10	B	DK	D	GR	E	F	IRL	I	L	NL	P	UK
1983	197,0	126,3	0,1	0,3	—	4,8	65,7	0,2	—	115,3	—	1,0	5,0	4,6
1984	213,6	126,1	0,1	0,2	—	4,7	82,1	0,2	—	114,7	—	0,8	5,4	5,4
1985	178,8 *	106,0 *	0,0	0,2	—	4,5 *	67,1	0,2	—	94,7	—	0,2	5,6	6,2
1986	190,7 *	110,0 *	0,1	0,3 *	—	4,8 *	75,0 *	0,2	—	100,0 *	—	0,6	5,7 *	4,2

CITRUS FRUITS — **AGRUMES**

YEAR ANNÉE	EUR 12	EUR 10	B	DK	D	GR	E	F	IRL	I	L	NL	P	UK
1983	8 635,7	4 630,1	—	—	—	918,1	3 873,9	30,6	—	3 681,4	—	—	131,7	—
1984	6 400,3	3 742,5	—	—	—	1 056,7	2 519,5	27,2	—	2 658,7	—	—	138,3	—
1985	7 998,4	4 349,0	—	—	—	878,8	3 513,8	36,6	—	3 433,5	—	—	135,5	—
1986	8 793,0 *	4 785,1 *	—	—	—	1 121,8 *	3 867,0	40,2	—	3 623,1	—	—	140,9 *	—

ORANGES — **ORANGES**

YEAR ANNÉE	EUR 12	EUR 10	B	DK	D	GR	E	F	IRL	I	L	NL	P	UK
1983	5 124,2	2 963,6	—	—	—	663,3	2 067,2	1,6	—	2 298,7	—	—	93,4	—
1984	3 799,3	2 362,4	—	—	—	803,5	1 338,8	1,5	—	1 557,4	—	—	98,0	—
1985	4 813,8	2 772,6	—	—	—	607,9	1 945,1	2,6	—	2 162,1	—	—	96,1	—
1986	5 180,4	3 058,4	—	—	—	837,5	2 023,0	2,7	—	2 218,3	—	—	99,0	—

MANDARINS — **MANDARINES**

YEAR ANNÉE	EUR 12	EUR 10	B	DK	D	GR	E	F	IRL	I	L	NL	P	UK
1983	864,8	315,8	—	—	—	59,3	534,2	0,3	—	256,3	—	—	14,8	—
1984	684,6	250,3	—	—	—	65,5	418,8	0,2	—	184,6	—	—	15,6	—
1985	795,3	308,1	—	—	—	67,7	471,9	0,2	—	240,2	—	—	15,3	—
1986	840,4 *	347,4	—	—	—	76,9	476,0	0,2	—	270,3	—	—	17,0 *	—

CLEMENTINES — **CLEMENTINES**

YEAR ANNÉE	EUR 12	EUR 10	B	DK	D	GR	E	F	IRL	I	L	NL	P	UK
1983	948,2	241,6	—	—	—	—	700,2	28,0	—	213,6	—	—	6,3	—
1984	659,9	203,1	—	—	—	—	450,1	24,6	—	178,5	—	—	6,7	—
1985	864,2	278,8	—	—	—	—	578,9	33,2	—	245,6	—	—	6,5	—
1986	1 018,2 *	320,2	—	—	—	—	690,0	36,5	—	283,7	—	—	8,0	—

LEMONS — **CITRONS**

YEAR ANNÉE	EUR 12	EUR 10	B	DK	D	GR	E	F	IRL	I	L	NL	P	UK
1983	1 606,0	1 045,2	—	—	—	189,9	544,5	0,6	—	854,8	—	—	16,3	—
1984	1 187,5	881,5	—	—	—	181,9	288,9	0,6	—	699,1	—	—	17,1	—
1985	1 428,6	930,2	—	—	—	192,1	481,6	0,4	—	737,7	—	—	16,8	—
1986	1 660,8	999,8	—	—	—	199,5	645,0	0,5	—	799,8	—	—	16,0	—

GRAPEFRUIT — **PAMPLEMOUSSES**

YEAR ANNÉE	EUR 12	EUR 10	B	DK	D	GR	E	F	IRL	I	L	NL	P	UK
1983	22,3	8,4	—	—	—	—	13,2	0,0	—	8,3	—	—	0,8	—
1984	17,3	8,0	—	—	—	—	8,4	0,1	—	7,9	—	—	0,9	—
1985	21,9	8,3	—	—	—	—	12,8	0,1	—	8,1	—	—	0,8	—
1986	27,1 *	8,2	—	—	—	—	18,0	0,2	—	8,0	—	—	0,9	—

OTHER CITRUS FRUIT N.O.S. — **AUTRES AGRUMES**

YEAR ANNÉE	EUR 12	EUR 10	B	DK	D	GR	E	F	IRL	I	L	NL	P	UK
1983	70,2	55,5	—	—	—	5,7	14,7	0,2	—	49,6	—	—	—	—
1984	51,7	37,2	—	—	—	5,8	14,5	0,2	—	31,2	—	—	—	—
1985	74,6	51,0	—	—	—	11,0	23,6	0,1	—	39,8	—	—	—	—
1986	66,1 *	51,1 *	—	—	—	7,9 *	15,0	0,2	—	43,0	—	—	— *	—

TABLE OLIVES — **OLIVES DE TABLE**

YEAR ANNÉE	EUR 12	EUR 10	B	DK	D	GR	E	F	IRL	I	L	NL	P	UK
1983	365,2	211,6	—	—	—	132,1	134,9	1,8	—	77,7	—	—	18,7	—
1984	500,7	191,3	—	—	—	139,5	288,7	2,4	—	49,4	—	—	20,7	—
1985	440,4	255,5	—	—	—	164,8	164,2	1,1	—	89,6	—	—	20,7	—
1986	494,9	215,9	—	—	—	131,0	259,0	2,1	—	82,8	—	—	20,0	—

SOURCE: CRONOS-ZPA1 DATA BANK, AGRICULTURAL PRODUCTS

SOURCE: BANQUE DE DONNEES CRONOS-ZPA1, PRODUITS AGRICOLES

Supply balance sheets

Bilans d'approvisionnement

ID 4

YEAR ANNÉE	EUR 12	EUR 10	UEBL BLEU	DK	D	GR	E	F	IRL	I	NL	P	UK

1000 T

USABLE PRODUCTION / PRODUCTION UTILISABLE

1982/83	145 241 *	131 392 *	2 187 *	7 993 *	24 625 *	5 375 *	12 746 *	48 678 *	2 177 *	17 331 *	1 377 *	1 103 *	21 649 *
1983/84	138 154 *	123 576 *	1 944 *	6 380 *	23 011 *	4 358 *	13 535 *	46 468 *	1 990 *	16 809 *	1 309 *	1 043 *	21 307 *
1984/85	173 258 *	151 329 *	2 503	9 284	26 489 *	5 440	20 592	58 142	2 502 *	18 973	1 406	1 337 *	26 590
1985/86	160 431 *	138 685 *	2 197	7 956	25 915	4 298	20 511	55 687 *	2 095 *	16 941	1 130	1 235 *	22 466

IMPORTS / IMPORTATIONS

1982/83	20 052 *	10 210 *	5 140 *	340 *	5 880 *	512 *	6 716 *	2 613 *	550 *	5 077 *	4 826 *	3 260 *	3 840 *
1983/84	16 274 *	8 481 *	5 273 *	551 *	5 785 *	287 *	5 111 *	1 930 *	739 *	6 051 *	4 897 *	3 109 *	3 545 *
1984/85	13 434 *	6 870 *	5 385	316	6 893 *	486	3 750	1 812	473 *	7 772	5 027	2 971 *	2 776 *
1985/86	10 915 *	5 785 *	5 457	432	7 169	905	3 120	1 659 *	711 *	7 685 *	5 130	2 452 *	4 460

RESOURCES = USES / RESSOURCES = EMPLOIS

1982/83	165 293 *	141 602 *	7 327 *	8 333 *	30 505 *	5 887 *	19 462 *	51 291 *	2 727 *	22 408 *	6 203 *	4 363 *	25 489 *
1983/84	154 429 *	132 057 *	7 217 *	6 931 *	28 796 *	4 645 *	18 646 *	48 398 *	2 729 *	22 860 *	6 206 *	4 152 *	24 852 *
1984/85	186 692 *	158 199 *	7 888	9 600	33 382 *	5 926	24 342	59 954	2 975 *	26 745	6 433	4 308 *	29 366 *
1985/86	171 346 *	144 470 *	7 654	8 388	33 084	5 203	23 631	57 346 *	2 806 *	24 626 *	6 260	3 687 *	26 926

EXPORTS / EXPORTATIONS

1982/83	23 443 *	22 885 *	3 611 *	1 078 *	3 408 *	893 *	682 *	22 376 *	348 *	2 397 *	1 680 *	10 *	5 662 *
1983/84	22 688 *	23 027 *	3 097 *	924 *	4 412 *	1 321 *	86 *	24 570 *	310 *	1 878 *	1 629 *	1 *	5 463 *
1984/85	29 251 *	29 185 *	3 664	2 000	3 676 *	1 466	223	30 756	518 *	3 115	1 838	0 *	6 222 *
1985/86	27 520 *	25 743 *	3 548	1 632	5 440	1 325	2 220	30 454 *	368 *	3 257 *	1 724	— *	5 817

FINAL STOCK / STOCK FINAL

1982/83	:	:	:	1 213 *	6 828 *	:	:	5 476 *	:	:	631 *	:	2 413 *
1983/84	:	:	:	634 *	5 394 *	:	:	3 182 *	:	:	425 *	:	1 522 *
1984/85	:	:	:	1 278 *	8 485 *	:	:	5 909	:	:	478	:	5 495 *
1985/86	:	:	:	1 360	8 975	:	:	:	:	:	544	:	7 171

OF WHICH: MARKET / DONT: MARCHE

1982/83	:	:	:	947 *	6 316 *	:	:	5 476 *	:	:	631 *	:	2 333 *
1983/84	:	:	:	526 *	5 002 *	:	:	3 182 *	:	:	425 *	:	1 432 *
1984/85	:	:	:	1 034 *	7 669 *	:	:	5 909	:	:	478	:	5 405 *
1985/86	:	:	:	1 109	8 507	:	:	:	:	:	544	:	7 081

CHANGE IN STOCKS / VARIATION DES STOCKS

1982/83	3 854 *	4 855 *	18 *	620 *	1 454 *	7 *	− 1 023 *	2 076 *	— *	− 94 *	174 *	22 *	600 *
1983/84	− 9 061 *	− 6 988 *	− 69 *	− 579 *	− 1 434 *	− 1 190 *	− 2 073 *	− 2 295 *	15 *	− 339 *	− 206 *	— *	− 891 *
1984/85	12 587 *	10 489 *	96	644	3 091 *	− 472	1 948 *	2 727	— *	377	53	150 *	3 973 *
1985/86	474 *	1 888 *	13	82	490	− 261	− 939	− 349 *	— *	171 *	66	− 475 *	1 676

OF WHICH: MARKET / DONT: MARCHE

1982/83	:	4 850 *	36 *	557 *	1 470 *	7 *	:	2 076 *	— *	− 90 *	174 *	:	620 *
1983/84	:	− 6 554 *	− 65 *	− 421 *	− 1 314 *	− 1 190 *	:	− 2 295 *	15 *	− 177 *	− 206 *	:	− 901 *
1984/85	:	9 930 *	97	508	2 667 *	− 472 *	:	2 727	— *	377	53	:	3 973 *
1985/86	:	2 230 *	14	75	838	− 261 *	:	− 349 *	— *	171 *	66	:	1 676

TOTAL DOMESTIC USES / UTILISATION INTERIEURE TOTALE

1982/83	137 996 *	113 862 *	3 698 *	6 635 *	25 643 *	4 987 *	19 803 *	26 839 *	2 379 *	20 105 *	4 349 *	4 331 *	19 227 *
1983/84	140 804 *	116 020 *	4 189 *	6 586 *	25 820 *	4 514 *	20 633 *	26 123 *	2 404 *	21 321 *	4 783 *	4 151 *	20 280 *
1984/85	144 854 *	118 525 *	4 128	6 956	26 615 *	4 932	22 171 *	26 471	2 457 *	23 253	4 542	4 158 *	19 171 *
1985/86	143 352 *	116 840 *	4 093	6 674	27 154	4 139	22 350	27 241 *	2 438 *	21 198 *	4 470	4 162 *	19 433

SEEDS / SEMENCES

1982/83	5 582 *	4 366 *	54 *	306 *	843 *	292 *	1 115 *	1 375 *	65 *	767 *	35 *	101 *	629 *
1983/84	5 719 *	4 520 *	53 *	300 *	832 *	295 *	1 106 *	1 486 *	70 *	797 *	36 *	93 *	651 *
1984/85	5 860 *	4 669 *	51	289	821 *	350	1 103 *	1 590 *	70 *	818	33	88 *	647
1985/86	5 754 *	4 566 *	53	286	803	329 *	1 096	1 553 *	64 *	788 *	32	92 *	658

LOSSES / PERTES

1982/83	1 860 *	1 840 *	18 *	240 *	620 *	196 *	— *	405 *	139 *	61 *	34 *	20 *	126 *
1983/84	1 767 *	1 750 *	21 *	191 *	587 *	— *	— *	400 *	87 *	52 *	37 *	17 *	374 *
1984/85	2 061 *	2 044 *	18	279	650 *	—	— *	477	91 *	38	37	17 *	453
1985/86	1 940 *	1 921 *	21	239	645	—	—	415 *	129 *	51 *	34	19 *	386

SUPPLY BALANCE SHEET

CEREALS (TOTAL)

BILAN D'APPROVISIONNEMENT

CEREALES (TOTAL)

YEAR ANNÉE	EUR 12	EUR 10	UEBL BLEU	DK	D	GR	E	F	IRL	I	NL	P	UK
					1000 T								

ANIMAL FEED / ALIMENTATION ANIMALE

	EUR 12	EUR 10	UEBL BLEU	DK	D	GR	E	F	IRL	I	NL	P	UK
1982/83	85 797 *	69 170 *	1 986 *	5 454 *	15 831 *	2 849 *	13 871 *	18 582 *	1 604 *	9 744 *	2 364 *	2 756 *	10 756 *
1983/84	87 536 *	70 218 *	2 288 *	5 444 *	15 986 *	2 674 *	14 679 *	17 560 *	1 654 *	11 272 *	2 668 *	2 639 *	10 672 *
1984/85	90 677 *	71 943 *	2 212	5 717	16 657 *	2 949 *	16 105	17 536 *	1 706 *	12 569	2 526	2 629 *	10 071 *
1985/86	88 770 *	69 906 *	1 984	5 477	17 161	2 250	16 230	18 257 *	1 649 *	10 729 *	2 495	2 634 *	9 904

OF WHICH:DOMESTIC ORIGIN / DONT: ORIGINE INTERIEURE

	EUR 12	EUR 10	UEBL BLEU	DK	D	GR	E	F	IRL	I	NL	P	UK
1982/83	:	65 946 *	1 067 *	5 136 *	13 826 *	2 374 *	:	18 566 *	1 322 *	7 194 *	491 *	:	10 021 *
1983/84	:	66 985 *	1 086 *	5 131 *	13 794 *	2 514 *	:	17 545 *	1 317 *	8 386 *	595 *	:	10 237 *
1984/85	:	69 194 *	1 267	5 542 *	14 514 *	2 756 *	:	17 536 *	1 482 *	9 401	586	:	9 649 *
1985/86	:	67 958 *	1 023	5 374 *	14 411	2 054 *	13 545 *	18 244 *	1 241 *	8 624 *	557	:	9 549

OF WHICH:ON FARM WHERE GROWN / DONT: A LA FERME(AUTOCONSOMMATION)

	EUR 12	EUR 10	UEBL BLEU	DK	D	GR	E	F	IRL	I	NL	P	UK
1982/83	:	30 625 *	532 *	2 955 *	10 727 *	1 038 *	:	10 339 *	527 *	1 819 *	7 *	:	2 681 *
1983/84	:	30 565 *	424 *	2 720 *	10 528 *	876 *	:	8 756 *	537 *	2 003 *	6 *	:	4 715 *
1984/85	:	31 574 *	501	2 835 *	11 023 *	944	:	10 546 *	590 *	2 041	6	:	3 088
1985/86	:	31 510 *	462	2 505 *	11 426	821	5 597 *	10 590 *	483 *	2 128	7	:	3 088

INDUSTRIAL USES / USAGES INDUSTRIELS

	EUR 12	EUR 10	UEBL BLEU	DK	D	GR	E	F	IRL	I	NL	P	UK
1982/83	:	:	684 *	202 *	2 756 *	130 *	1 079 *	903 *	154 *	484 *	833 *	75 *	:
1983/84	:	:	843 *	202 *	2 786 *	100 *	1 101 *	909 *	153 *	473 *	887 *	60 *	:
1984/85	:	:	882	202	2 786	100	1 109	1 156	155 *	502	841	60 *	:
1985/86	:	:	1 076	202	2 704	100	1 149	1 260 *	151 *	536	811	70 *	:

OF WHICH: ALCOHOL / DONT: ALCOOL

	EUR 12	EUR 10	UEBL BLEU	DK	D	GR	E	F	IRL	I	NL	P	UK
1982/83	:	1 240 *	0 *	— *	124 *	— *	:	— *	76 *	— *	17 *	— *	1 023 *
1983/84	:	1 483 *	0 *	— *	125 *	— *	:	10 *	75 *	— *	13 *	— *	1 260 *
1984/85	:	806 *	0	—	120 *	—	:	15	77 *	—	11	— *	583 *
1985/86	:	338 *	0	—	104	—	:	15 *	73 *	—	4	— *	142 *

OF WHICH: BEER / DONT: BIERE

	EUR 12	EUR 10	UEBL BLEU	DK	D	GR	E	F	IRL	I	NL	P	UK
1982/83	:	4 912 *	391 *	200 *	2 181 *	60 *	:	477 *	71 *	210 *	429 *	75 *	893 *
1983/84	:	5 206 *	406 *	200 *	2 155 *	50 *	:	400 *	71 *	200 *	380 *	60 *	1 344 *
1984/85	:	4 791 *	404	200	2 131 *	50	:	324	71 *	230	398	60 *	983 *
1985/86	:	3 948 *	398	200	2 165	50	:	435 *	71 *	250	379	70 *	— *

PROCESSING / TRANSFORMATION

	EUR 12	EUR 10	UEBL BLEU	DK	D	GR	E	F	IRL	I	NL	P	UK
1982/83	:	:	— :	— *	— *	— *	— *	19 *	— *	:	— *	100 *	:
1983/84	:	:	— :	— *	— *	— *	— *	41 *	— *	:	— *	100 *	:
1984/85	:	:	— :	—	— *	—	—	38	— *	:	—	100 *	:
1985/86	:	:	:	—	—	—	—	40 *	— *	:	—	100 *	:

HUMAN CONSUMPTION / CONSOMMATION HUMAINE

	EUR 12	EUR 10	UEBL BLEU	DK	D	GR	E	F	IRL	I	NL	P	UK
1982/83	35 233 *	30 216 *	956 *	433 *	5 593 *	1 520 *	3 738 *	5 555 *	417 *	9 049 *	1 083 *	1 279 *	5 610 *
1983/84	35 377 *	30 388 *	984 *	449 *	5 629 *	1 445 *	3 747 *	5 727 *	440 *	8 727 *	1 155 *	1 242 *	5 832 *
1984/85	36 382 *	31 264 *	965	469	5 701 *	1 533	3 854	5 674	435 *	9 326	1 105	1 264 *	6 056 *
1985/86	36 689 *	31 566 *	959	470	5 841	1 460	3 876	5 716 *	445 *	9 094	1 098	1 247 *	6 483 *

NETT HUMAN CONSUMPTION / CONSOMMATION HUMAINE NETTE

	EUR 12	EUR 10	UEBL BLEU	DK	D	GR	E	F	IRL	I	NL	P	UK
1982/83	26 319 *	22 485 *	724 *	341 *	4 362 *	1 069 *	2 784 *	4 279 *	304 *	6 547 *	848 *	1 050 *	4 011 *
1983/84	26 470 *	22 653 *	743 *	352 *	4 399 *	1 033 *	2 794 *	4 417 *	321 *	6 323 *	898 *	1 023 *	4 167 *
1984/85	27 169 *	23 258 *	734	366 *	4 438 *	1 095	2 872 *	4 376	317 *	6 740	862	1 039 *	4 330 *
1985/86	27 381 *	23 464 *	726	365 *	4 533	1 044	2 890	4 411 *	321 *	6 573	852	1 027 *	4 639 *

SELF-SUFFICIENCY (%) / AUTO-APPROVISIONNEMENT (%)

	EUR 12	EUR 10	UEBL BLEU	DK	D	GR	E	F	IRL	I	NL	P	UK
1982/83	105,3 *	115,4 *	59,1 *	120,5 *	96,0 *	107,8 *	64,4 *	181,4 *	91,5 *	86,2 *	31,7 *	25,5 *	112,6 *
1983/84	98,1 *	106,5 *	46,4 *	96,9 *	89,1 *	96,5 *	65,6 *	177,9 *	82,8 *	78,8 *	27,4 *	25,1 *	105,1 *
1984/85	119,6 *	127,7 *	60,6	133,5	99,5 *	110,3	92,9 *	219,6	101,8 *	81,6	31,0	32,2 *	138,7 *
1985/86	111,9 *	118,7 *	53,7	119,2	95,4	103,8	91,8	204,4 *	85,9 *	79,9 *	25,3	29,7 *	115,6

NETT HUMAN CONSUMP.(KG/HD/YEAR) / CONS.HUMAINE NETTE (KG/TETE/AN)

	EUR 12	EUR 10	UEBL BLEU	DK	D	GR	E	F	IRL	I	NL	P	UK
1982/83	82,2 *	82,6 *	70,8 *	66,6 *	70,9 *	108,8 *	73,1 *	78,3 *	86,9 *	115,4 *	59,1 *	105,3 *	71,1 *
1983/84	82,5 *	83,1 *	72,7 *	68,9 *	71,8 *	104,6 *	73,0 *	80,6 *	91,1 *	111,1 *	62,4 *	101,8 *	73,8 *
1984/85	84,5 *	85,2 *	71,8	71,6 *	72,7 *	110,4	74,6 *	79,5	89,7 *	118,1	59,6	102,6 *	76,6 *
1985/86	85,0 *	85,8 *	71,0	71,3 *	74,3	104,9	74,9	79,8 *	90,8 *	114,9	58,6	100,8 *	81,8 *

SOURCE: CRONOS-ZPA1 DATA BANK, AGRICULTURAL PRODUCTS

SOURCE: BASE DE DONNEES CRONOS-ZPA1, PRODUITS AGRICOLES

ID 5

YEAR ANNÉE	EUR 12	EUR 10	UEBL BLEU	DK	D	GR	E	F	IRL	I	NL	P	UK

1000 T

USABLE PRODUCTION — **PRODUCTION UTILISABLE**

1982/83	60 231 *	55 718 *	1 063	1 207	8 630 *	2 236	4 130	24 997	400 *	6 036	967	383	10 182
1983/84	59 641 *	55 322 *	1 062	1 548	8 993 *	1 477	4 005	24 397	387 *	5 613	1 043	314 *	10 802
1984/85	76 195 *	70 213 *	1 330	2 446	10 197 *	1 717	5 550	32 448	602 *	5 410	1 130	432 *	14 933
1985/86	65 531 *	60 205 *	1 215	1 972	9 779	1 114	4 958	28 092 *	495 *	4 665	851	368 *	12 022

IMPORTS — **IMPORTATIONS**

1982/83	3 301 *	2 667 *	1 137	107	1 820	11	67	828	277 *	1 447	1 521	580	1 502
1983/84	3 219 *	2 554 *	1 494	125	1 676	43	198	417	408 *	2 377	1 529	566 *	1 262
1984/85	2 819 *	2 034 *	1 430	161	2 697	242	211	391	287 *	3 825	1 557	618 *	1 014
1985/86	2 662 *	2 025 *	1 468	273	2 897	503	66	406 *	493 *	4 124	1 693	744 *	2 429

RESOURCES = USES — **RESSOURCES = EMPLOIS**

1982/83	63 532 *	58 385 *	2 200	1 314	10 450 *	2 247	4 197	25 825	677 *	7 483	2 488	963	11 684
1983/84	62 860 *	57 876 *	2 556	1 673	10 669 *	1 520	4 203	24 814	795 *	7 990	2 572	880 *	12 064
1984/85	79 014 *	72 247 *	2 760	2 607	12 894 *	1 959	5 761	32 839	889 *	9 235	2 687	1 050 *	15 947
1985/86	68 193 *	62 230 *	2 683	2 245	12 676	1 617	5 024	28 498 *	988 *	8 789	2 544	1 112 *	14 451

EXPORTS — **EXPORTATIONS**

1982/83	14 520 *	13 952 *	714	195	1 530	450	580	13 156	77 *	601	770	1	2 442
1983/84	15 326 *	15 379 *	926	396	2 685	571	46	14 277	33 *	459	842	— *	1 967
1984/85	17 707 *	17 600 *	1 029	617	1 904	953	151	19 001	110 *	495	893	— *	2 168
1985/86	14 203 *	14 245 *	978	546	3 152	243	131	17 522 *	109 *	531	750	— *	2 675

FINAL STOCK — **STOCK FINAL**

1982/83	:	:	248	435	4 378	:	814	3 052	:	240	383	:	1 153
1983/84	:	:	179	223	3 475	:	252	1 903	:	287	177	:	837
1984/85	:	:	275	495	5 014	:	297	3 900	:	220	234	:	4 131
1985/86	:	:	343	321	4 655	:	101	:	:	380	227	:	4 801

OF WHICH: MARKET — *DONT: MARCHE*

1982/83	:	:	217	431	4 244	:	:	3 052	:	185	383	:	1 143
1983/84	:	:	152	215	3 329	:	:	1 903	:	287	177	:	817
1984/85	:	:	249	460	4 767	:	:	3 900	:	220	234	:	4 111
1985/86	:	:	313	304	4 542	:	:	:	:	380	227	:	4 781

CHANGE IN STOCKS — **VARIATION DES STOCKS**

1982/83	2 778 *	3 541 *	18	301	1 191	265	− 763	1 483	− *	− 69	152	− *	200
1983/84	− 4 600 *	− 4 038 *	− 69	− 212	− 903	− 673	− 562	− 1 149	− *	− 510	− 206	− *	− 316
1984/85	6 709 *	6 664 *	96	272	1 539	− 524	45	1 997	− *	− 67	57	− *	3 294
1985/86	− 679 *	− 483 *	13	− 174	− 359	14	− 196	− 800 *	− *	160	− 7	− *	670

OF WHICH: MARKET — *DONT: MARCHE*

1982/83	:	3 629 *	36	298	1 240	265	:	1 483	− *	− 65	152	:	220
1983/84	:	− 3 898 *	− 65	− 216	− 915	− 673	:	− 1 149	− *	− 348	− 206	:	− 326
1984/85	:	6 537 *	97	245	1 438	− 524 *	:	1 997	− *	− 67	57	:	3 294
1985/86	:	− 330 *	14	− 156	− 225	14	:	− 800 *	− *	160	− 7	:	670

TOTAL DOMESTIC USES — **UTILISATION INTERIEURE TOTALE**

1982/83	46 234 *	40 892 *	1 468	818	7 729	1 532	4 380	11 186	600 *	6 951	1 566	962 *	9 042
1983/84	52 135 *	46 536 *	1 699	1 489	8 889	1 621	4 719	11 686	762 *	8 041	1 936	880 *	10 413
1984/85	54 598 *	47 983 *	1 635	1 718	9 451	1 530	5 565	11 841	779 *	8 807	1 737	1 050 *	10 485
1985/86	54 669 *	48 468 *	1 692	1 873	9 883	1 360	5 089	11 776 *	879 *	8 098	1 801	1 112 *	11 106

SEEDS — *SEMENCES*

1982/83	2 462 *	2 031 *	31	43	299	170	˙389	842	10 *	320	22	42 *	294
1983/84	2 530 *	2 142 *	30	60	299	161	349	893	15 *	320	22	39 *	342
1984/85	2 521 *	2 156 *	30	62	302	180	330	913	20 *	300	19	35 *	330
1985/86	2 461 *	2 110 *	31	64	302	160	316	910 *	15 *	260	17	35 *	351

LOSSES — *PERTES*

1982/83	625 *	623 *	11	36	211	22	—	196	30 *	50	22	2 *	55
1983/84	735 *	735 *	14	46	218	—	—	197	14 *	42	14	− *	190
1984/85	910 *	908 *	10	73	243	—	—	263	25 *	33	13	2 *	248
1985/86	813 *	813 *	15	59	233	—	—	220 *	31 *	34	12	− *	209

SOURCE: CRONOS-ZPA1 DATA BANK, AGRICULTURAL PRODUCTS

SOURCE: BASE DE DONNEES CRONOS-ZPA1, PRODUITS AGRICOLES

SUPPLY BALANCE SHEET

SOFT WHEAT

ID 5

BILAN D'APPROVISIONNEMENT

BLE TENDRE

YEAR ANNÉE	EUR 12	EUR 10	UEBL BLEU	DK	D	GR	E	F	IRL	I	NL	P	UK
						1000 T							
ANIMAL FEED											*ALIMENTATION ANIMALE*		
1982/83	15 496 *	14 873 *	463	445	3 299	80	505	5 566	200 *	230	475	118 *	4 115
1983/84	21 065 *	20 159 *	678	1 081	4 394	260	865	6 018	360 *	1 509	770	41 *	5 089
1984/85	23 160 *	21 307 *	631	1 278	4 876	150	1 640	6 070	360 *	2 374	670	213 *	4 898
1985/86	22 792 *	21 357 *	545	1 443	5 311	—	1 158	6 081 *	453 *	1 804	730	277 *	4 990
OF WHICH:DOMESTIC ORIGIN											*DONT: ORIGINE INTERIEURE*		
1982/83	:	14 603 *	300	413 *	2 515	80 *	:	5 566	116 *	200	250	:	3 933
1983/84	:	19 874 *	282	1 010 *	3 565	260 *	:	6 018	230 *	1 479	500	:	5 087
1984/85	:	21 133 *	468	1 200 *	3 780	150 *	:	6 070	280 *	2 326	454	:	4 807
1985/86	:	21 120 *	328	1 400 *	3 419	—	1 150 *	6 081 *	176 *	1 750	428	:	4 910
OF WHICH:ON FARM WHERE GROWN											*DONT: A LA FERME(AUTOCONSOMMATION)*		
1982/83	:	5 686 *	42	100 *	2 275	20	:	2 911	34 *	130	1	:	173
1983/84	:	6 434 *	55	250 *	2 674	20	:	2 568	37 *	330	0	:	500
1984/85	:	6 992 *	60	300 *	2 745	90	:	3 061	56 *	330	0	:	350
1985/86	:	7 161 *	57	300 *	2 800	—	310 *	3 000 *	53 *	600	1	:	350
INDUSTRIAL USES											*USAGES INDUSTRIELS*		
1982/83	560 *	549 *	84	—	168	10	11	122	— *	50	98	— *	17
1983/84	676 *	656 *	100	—	217	—	20	161	— *	50	102	— *	26
1984/85	869 *	849 *	117	—	237	—	20	174	— *	50	55	— *	216
1985/86	1 125 *	1 105 *	256	—	243	—	20	165 *	— *	50	67	— *	324
OF WHICH: ALCOHOL											*DONT: ALCOOL*		
1982/83	:	76 *	0	—	69	—	:	—	— *	—	7	— *	—
1983/84	:	73 *	0	—	69	—	:	—	— *	—	4	— *	—
1984/85	:	77 *	0	—	73	—	:	—	— *	—	4	— *	—
1985/86	:	66 *	0	—	62	—	:	— *	— *	—	4	— *	—
OF WHICH: BEER											*DONT: BIERE*		
1982/83	:	79 *	6	—	64	—	:	—	— *	—	—	— *	9
1983/84	:	82 *	6	—	62	—	:	—	— *	—	—	— *	14
1984/85	:	87 *	4	—	75	—	:	—	— *	—	—	— *	8
1985/86	:	93 *	4	—	89	—	:	— *	— *	—	—	— *	—
PROCESSING											*TRANSFORMATION*		
1982/83	— *	— *	—	—	—	—	—	—	— *	—	—	— *	—
1983/84	— *	— *	—	—	—	—	—	—	— *	—	—	— *	—
1984/85	— *	— *	—	—	—	—	—	—	— *	—	—	— *	—
1985/86	— *	— *	—	—	—	—	—	— *	— *	—	—	— *	—
HUMAN CONSUMPTION											*CONSOMMATION HUMAINE*		
1982/83	27 091 *	22 816 *	879	294	3 752	1 250	3 475	4 460	360 *	6 301	959	800 *	4 561
1983/84	27 129 *	22 844 *	877	302	3 761	1 200	3 485	4 417	373 *	6 120	1 028	800 *	4 766
1984/85	27 138 *	22 763 *	847	305	3 793	1 200	3 575	4 421	374 *	6 050	980	800 *	4 793
1985/86	27 478 *	23 083 *	845	307	3 794	1 200	3 595	4 400 *	380 *	5 950	975	800 *	5 232
NETT HUMAN CONSUMPTION											*CONSOMMATION HUMAINE NETTE*		
1982/83	20 318 *	17 072 *	668	229 *	2 968	893	2 606	3 434	263 *	4 600	759	640 *	3 258
1983/84	20 344 *	17 090 *	664	235 *	2 982	857	2 614	3 401	272 *	4 470	805	640 *	3 404
1984/85	20 348 *	17 027 *	648	237 *	2 996	857	2 681	3 404	273 *	4 418	770	640 *	3 424
1985/86	20 589 *	17 253 *	645	238 *	3 005	857	2 696	3 388 *	274 *	4 344	765	640 *	3 737
SELF-SUFFICIENCY (%)											*AUTO-APPROVISIONNEMENT (%)*		
1982/83	130,3 *	136,3 *	72,4	147,6	111,7 *	146,0	94,3	223,5	66,7 *	86,8	61,7	39,8 *	112,6
1983/84	114,4 *	118,9 *	62,5	104,0	101,2 *	91,1	84,9	208,8	50,8 *	69,8	53,9	35,7 *	103,7
1984/85	139,6 *	146,3 *	81,3	142,4	107,9 *	112,2	99,7	274,0	77,3 *	61,4	65,1	41,1 *	142,4
1985/86	119,9 *	124,2 *	71,8	105,3	98,9	81,9	97,4	238,6 *	56,3 *	57,6	47,3	33,1 *	108,2
NETT HUMAN CONSUMP.(KG/HD/YEAR)											*CONS.HUMAINE NETTE (KG/TETE/AN)*		
1982/83	63,4 *	62,7 *	65,3	44,8 *	48,2	90,9	68,5	62,9	75,2 *	81,1	52,9	64,2 *	57,8
1983/84	63,4 *	62,7 *	65,0	46,0 *	48,6	86,8	68,3	62,0	77,2 *	78,5	55,9	63,7 *	60,3
1984/85	63,3 *	62,4 *	63,4	46,4 *	49,1	86,4	69,6	61,8	77,2 *	77,4	53,3	63,2 *	60,5
1985/86	63,9 *	63,1 *	63,1	46,5 *	49,2	86,1	69,9	61,3 *	77,4 *	75,9	52,7	62,8 *	65,9

SOURCE: CRONOS-ZPA1 DATA BANK, AGRICULTURAL PRODUCTS

SOURCE: BASE DE DONNEES CRONOS-ZPA1, PRODUITS AGRICOLES

SUPPLY BALANCE SHEET

HARD WHEAT

I D 6

BILAN D'APPROVISIONNEMENT

BLE DUR

YEAR ANNÉE	EUR 12	EUR 10	UEBL BLEU	DK	D	GR	E	F	IRL	I	NL	P	UK
						1000 T							
USABLE PRODUCTION												**PRODUCTION UTILISABLE**	
1982/83	4 377 *	4 054 *	—	—	2 *	747	281	372	— *	2 933	—	42	—
1983/84	4 169 *	3 889 *	—	—	5 *	585	263	398	— *	2 901	—	17 *	—
1984/85	6 668 *	6 127 *	—	—	26 *	904	503	578	— *	4 595	—	38 *	24
1985/86	5 755 *	5 352 *	—	—	87	661	371	729 *	— *	3 851	—	32 *	24
IMPORTS												**IMPORTATIONS**	
1982/83	1 256 *	1 210 *	91	—	245	5	62	441	7 *	981	27	47	102
1983/84	773 *	733 *	94	—	250	6	0	406	17 *	723	9	40 *	93
1984/85	828 *	677 *	114	—	259	6	0	343	12 *	784	12	175 *	47
1985/86	551 *	545 *	111	—	186	34	14	339 *	16 *	1 179	10	18 *	36
RESOURCES = USES												**RESSOURCES = EMPLOIS**	
1982/83	5 633 *	5 264 *	91	—	247 *	752	343	813	7 *	3 914	27	89	102
1983/84	4 942 *	4 622 *	94	—	255 *	591	263	804	17 *	3 624	9	57 *	93
1984/85	7 496 *	6 804 *	114	—	285 *	910	503	921	12 *	5 379	12	213 *	71
1985/86	6 306 *	5 897 *	111	—	273	695	385	1 068 *	16 *	5 030	10	50 *	60
EXPORTS												**EXPORTATIONS**	
1982/83	1 514 *	1 490 *	55	—	42	419	85	264	1 *	1 367	21	2	10
1983/84	1 203 *	1 186 *	34	—	51	673	17	180	1 *	1 092	3	— *	17
1984/85	1 846 *	1 847 *	46	—	58	498	23	273	2 *	1 861	6	— *	3
1985/86	1 873 *	1 824 *	43	—	59	498	75	446 *	2 *	2 138	4	— *	—
FINAL STOCK												**STOCK FINAL**	
1982/83	:	:	4	—	141	:	262	125	:	385	3	:	—
1983/84	:	:	4	—	130	:	55	97	:	556	2	:	—
1984/85	:	:	4	—	128	:	120	107	:	1 000	1	:	—
1985/86	:	:	5	—	118	:	29	:	:	960	1	:	—
OF WHICH: MARKET												*DONT: MARCHE*	
1982/83	:	:	4	—	141	:	:	125	:	385	3	:	—
1983/84	:	:	4	—	130	:	:	97	:	556	2	:	—
1984/85	:	:	4	—	128	:	:	107	:	1 000	1	:	—
1985/86	:	:	5	—	118	:	:	:	:	960	1	:	—
CHANGE IN STOCKS												**VARIATION DES STOCKS**	
1982/83	− 41 *	− 27 *	0	—	− 8	7	− 36	− 3	— *	− 25	2	22 *	—
1983/84	− 478 *	− 271 *	0	—	− 11	− 402	− 207	− 28	— *	171	− 1	— *	—
1984/85	665 *	450 *	0	—	− 2	− 1	65	10	— *	444	− 1	150 *	—
1985/86	− 312 *	− 211 *	0	—	− 10	− 143	− 91	− 18 *	— *	− 40	—	− 10 *	—
OF WHICH: MARKET												*DONT: MARCHE*	
1982/83	:	− 27 *	0	—	− 8	7	:	− 3	— *	− 25	2	:	—
1983/84	:	− 271 *	0	—	− 11	− 402	:	− 28	— *	171	− 1	:	—
1984/85	:	450 *	0	—	− 2	− 1 *	:	10	— *	444	− 1	:	—
1985/86	:	− 211 *	0	—	− 10	− 143 *	:	− 18 *	— *	− 40	—	:	—
TOTAL DOMESTIC USES												**UTILISATION INTERIEURE TOTALE**	
1982/83	4 160 *	3 801 *	36	—	213 *	326	294	552	6 *	2 572	4	65 *	92
1983/84	4 217 *	3 707 *	60	—	215 *	320	453	652	16 *	2 361	7	57 *	76
1984/85	4 985 *	4 507 *	68	—	229 *	413	415	638	10 *	3 074	7	63 *	68
1985/86	4 745 *	4 284 *	68	—	224	340	401	640 *	14 *	2 932	6	60 *	60
SEEDS												*SEMENCES*	
1982/83	422 *	395 *	—	—	0 *	60	· 22	15	— *	320	—	5 *	—
1983/84	447 *	425 *	—	—	0 *	70	20	34	— *	320	—	2 *	1
1984/85	503 *	480 *	—	—	1 *	90	20	27	— *	360	—	3 *	2
1985/86	529 *	506 *	—	—	4	90	20	40 *	— *	370	—	3 *	2
LOSSES												*PERTES*	
1982/83	27 *	27 *	0	—	2	6	—	19	— *	0	0	— *	—
1983/84	28 *	28 *	1	—	2	—	—	25	— *	0	—	— *	—
1984/85	7 *	7 *	1	—	2	—	—	4	— *	0	0	— *	—
1985/86	4 *	4 *	0	—	4	—	—	— *	— *	0	—	— *	—

SOURCE: CRONOS-ZPA1 DATA BANK, AGRICULTURAL PRODUCTS

SOURCE: BASE DE DONNEES CRONOS-ZPA1, PRODUITS AGRICOLES

YEAR ANNÉE	EUR 12	EUR 10	UEBL BLEU	DK	D	GR	E	F	IRL	I	NL	P	UK
1000 T													
ANIMAL FEED												ALIMENTATION ANIMALE	
1982/83	116 *	46 *	–	–	–	–	70	–	– *	40	–	– *	6
1983/84	270 *	30 *	–	–	–	10	240	–	– *	20	–	– *	–
1984/85	235 *	48 *	–	–	–	–	187	–	– *	48	–	– *	–
1985/86	206 *	30 *	–	–	–	–	176	– *	– *	30	–	– *	
OF WHICH:DOMESTIC ORIGIN												DONT: ORIGINE INTERIEURE	
1982/83	:	41 *	–	–	–	–	:	–	– *	40	–	:	–
1983/84	:	30 *	–	–	–	10 *	:	–	*	20	–	:	–
1984/85	:	48 *	–	–	–	–	:	–	– *	48	–	:	–
1985/86	:	30 *	–	–	–	–	170 *	– *	– *	30	–	:	–
OF WHICH:ON FARM WHERE GROWN												DONT: A LA FERME(AUTOCONSOMMATION)	
1982/83	:	40 *	–	–	–	–	:	–	– *	40	–	:	–
1983/84	:	25 *	–	–	–	10 *	–	–	– *	15	–	:	–
1984/85	:	40 *	–	–	–	–	:	–	– *	40	–	:	–
1985/86	:	30 *	–	–	–	–	70 *	– *	– *	30	–	:	–
INDUSTRIAL USES												USAGES INDUSTRIELS	
1982/83	2 *	– *	–	–	–	–	2	–	– *	–	–	– *	–
1983/84	3 *	– *	–	–	–	–	3	–	– *	–	–	– *	–
1984/85	2 *	– *	–	–	–	–	2	–	– *	–	–	– *	–
1985/86	2 *	– *	–	–	–	–	2	– *	– *	–	–	– *	–
OF WHICH: ALCOHOL												DONT: ALCOOL	
1982/83	:	– *	–	–	–	–	:	–	– *	–	–	– *	–
1983/84	:	– *	–	–	–	–	:	–	– *	–	–	– *	–
1984/85	:	– *	–	–	–	–	:	–	– *	–	–	– *	–
1985/86	:	– *	–	–	–	–	:	– *	– *	–	–	– *	–
OF WHICH: BEER												DONT: BIERE	
1982/83	:	– *	–	–	–	–	:	–	– *	–	–	– *	–
1983/84	:	– *	–	–	–	–	:	–	– *	–	–	– *	–
1984/85	:	– *	–	–	–	–	:	–	– *	–	–	– *	–
1985/86	:	– *	–	–	–	–	:	– *	– *	–	–	– *	–
PROCESSING												TRANSFORMATION	
1982/83	– *	– *	–	–	–	–	–	–	– *	–	–	– *	–
1983/84	– *	– *	–	–	–	–	–	–	– *	–	–	– *	–
1984/85	– *	– *	–	–	–	–	–	–	– *	–	–	– *	–
1985/86	– *	– *	–	–	–	–	–	– *	– *	–	–	– *	–
HUMAN CONSUMPTION												CONSOMMATION HUMAINE	
1982/83	3 593 *	3 333 *	36	–	211 *	260	200	518	6 *	2 212	4	60 *	86
1983/84	3 469 *	3 224 *	59	–	213 *	240	190	593	16 *	2 021	7	55 *	75 *
1984/85	4 238 *	3 972 *	67	–	226 *	323	206	607	10 *	2 666	7	60 *	66
1985/86	4 004 *	3 744 *	68	–	216	250	203	600 *	14 *	2 532	6	57 *	58
NETT HUMAN CONSUMPTION												CONSOMMATION HUMAINE NETTE	
1982/83	2 527 *	2 359 *	29	–	147 *	168	120	399	4 *	1 548	3	48 *	61
1983/84	2 472 *	2 314 *	46	–	153 *	172	114	457	12 *	1 415	5	44 *	54
1984/85	3 006 *	2 834 *	52	–	160 *	230	124	467	7 *	1 866	5	48 *	47
1985/86	2 835 *	2 666 *	51	–	147	179	122	462 *	10 *	1 772	4	47 *	41
SELF-SUFFICIENCY (%)												AUTO-APPROVISIONNEMENT (%)	
1982/83	105,2 *	106,7 *	–	–	0,9 *	229,1	95,6	67,4	– *	114,0	–	64,6 *	–
1983/84	98,9 *	104,9 *	–	–	2,3 *	182,8	58,1	61,0	– *	122,9	–	29,8 *	–
1984/85	133,8 *	135,9 *	–	–	11,4 *	218,9	121,2	90,6	– *	149,5	–	60,3 *	35,3
1985/86	121,3 *	124,9 *	–	–	38,8	194,4	92,5	113,9 *	– *	131,3	–	53,3 *	40,0
NETT HUMAN CONSUMP.(KG/HD/YEAR)												CONS.HUMAINE NETTE (KG/TETE/AN)	
1982/83	7,9 *	8,7 *	2,8	–	2,4 *	17,1	3,2	7,3	1,1 *	27,3	0,2	4,8 *	1,1
1983/84	7,7 *	8,5 *	4,5	–	2,5 *	17,4	3,0	8,3	3,4 *	24,9	0,3	4,4 *	1,0
1984/85	9,3 *	10,4 *	5,1	–	2,6 *	23,2	3,2	8,5	2,0 *	32,7	0,3	4,7 *	0,8
1985/86	8,8 *	9,7 *	5,0	–	2,4	18,0	3,2	8,4 *	2,8 *	31,0	0,3	4,6 *	0,7

SOURCE: CRONOS-ZPA1 DATA BANK, AGRICULTURAL PRODUCTS   SOURCE: BASE DE DONNEES CRONOS-ZPA1, PRODUITS AGRICOLES

SUPPLY BALANCE SHEET

BARLEY

ID 7

BILAN D'APPROVISIONNEMENT

ORGE

YEAR ANNÉE	EUR 12	EUR 10	UEBL BLEU	DK	D	GR	E	F	IRL	I	NL	P	UK
1000 T													
USABLE PRODUCTION											**PRODUCTION UTILISABLE**		
1982/83	46 674 *	41 353 *	814	6 357	9 460	852	5 270	10 036	1 676 *	1 074	247	51	10 837
1983/84	42 973 *	36 257 *	705	4 423	8 944	578	6 662	8 773	1 503 *	1 174	177	54 *	9 980
1984/85	55 136 *	44 256 *	935	6 072	10 284	818	10 789	11 512	1 770 *	1 618	192	91 *	11 055
1985/86	51 571 *	40 808 *	747	5 251	9 690	619	10 698	11 440 *	1 494 *	1 630	197	65 *	9 740
IMPORTS											**IMPORTATIONS**		
1982/83	2 053 *	324 *	1 266	24	1 384	91	1 709	408	43 *	1 291	767	63	114
1983/84	592 *	578 *	1 262	221	1 351	42	314	290	85 *	1 290	835	15 *	154
1984/85	322 *	289 *	1 881	9	1 338	26	22	155	12 *	1 193	726	43 *	140
1985/86	118 *	103 *	1 790	49	1 395	65	61	80 *	21 *	938	785	70 *	423
RESOURCES = USES											**RESSOURCES = EMPLOIS**		
1982/83	48 727 *	41 677 *	2 080	6 381	10 844	943	6 979	10 444	1 719 *	2 365	1 014	114	10 951
1983/84	43 565 *	36 835 *	1 967	4 644	10 295	620	6 976	9 063	1 588 *	2 464	1 012	69 *	10 134
1984/85	55 458 *	44 545 *	2 816	6 081	11 622	844	10 811	11 667	1 782 *	2 811	918	134 *	11 195
1985/86	51 689 *	40 911 *	2 537	5 300	11 085	684	10 759	11 520 *	1 515 *	2 568	982	135 *	10 163
EXPORTS											**EXPORTATIONS**		
1982/83	5 764 *	5 799 *	952	799	1 210	20	1	4 151	259 *	90	213	7	3 169
1983/84	4 722 *	5 035 *	824	417	983	17	2	3 896	267 *	73	136	0 *	3 374
1984/85	9 135 *	9 149 *	1 659	1 175	1 004	1	18	5 901	392 *	50	121	0 *	4 037
1985/86	9 583 *	7 699 *	1 640	961	1 153	0	2 000	5 850 *	250 *	15	148	— *	3 125
FINAL STOCK											**STOCK FINAL**		
1982/83	:	:	:	669	1 169	:	1 100	219	:	:	104	:	1 093
1983/84	:	:	:	339	817	:	15	−44	:	:	100	:	584
1984/85	:	:	:	506	1 769	:	1 618	255	:	:	96	:	1 257
1985/86	:	:	:	538	2 473	:	916	:	:	35	106	:	2 129
OF WHICH: MARKET											*DONT: MARCHE*		
1982/83	:	:	:	410	987	:	:	219	:	:	104	:	1 033
1983/84	:	:	:	243	694	:	:	−44	:	:	100	:	524
1984/85	:	:	:	312	1 473	:	:	255	:	:	96	:	1 197
1985/86	:	:	:	317	2 350	:	:	:	:	35	106	:	2 069
CHANGE IN STOCKS											**VARIATION DES STOCKS**		
1982/83	1 328 *	1 378 *	—	326	378	−5	−50	290	— *	—	24	— *	365
1983/84	−2 612 *	−1 527 *	—	−330	−352	−84	−1 085	−263	15 *	—	−4	— *	−509
1984/85	3 773 *	2 170 *	—	167	952	83	1 603	299	— *	—	−4	— *	673
1985/86	925 *	1 627 *	—	32	704	−26	−702	— *	— *	35	10	— *	872
OF WHICH: MARKET											*DONT: MARCHE*		
1982/83	:	1 298 *	—	264	360	−5	:	290	— *	—	24	:	365
1983/84	:	−1 305 *	—	−167	−293	−84	:	−263	15 *	—	−4	:	−509
1984/85	:	1 899 *	—	69	779	83	:	299	— *	—	−4	:	673
1985/86	:	1 773 *	—	5	877	−26 *	:	— *	— *	35	10	:	872
TOTAL DOMESTIC USES											**UTILISATION INTERIEURE TOTALE**		
1982/83	41 635 *	34 500 *	1 128	5 256	9 256	928	7 028	6 003	1 460 *	2 275	777	107 *	7 417
1983/84	41 456 *	33 328 *	1 143	4 557	9 664	688	8 059	5 430	1 306 *	2 391	880	69 *	7 269
1984/85	42 550 *	33 226 *	1 157	4 739	9 666	760	9 190	5 467	1 390 *	2 761	801	134 *	6 485
1985/86	41 181 *	31 585 *	897	4 307	9 228	710	9 461	5 670 *	1 265 *	2 518	824	135 *	6 166
SEEDS											*SEMENCES*		
1982/83	2 014 *	1 410 *	18	243	312	50	596	360	50 *	60	4	8 *	313
1983/84	2 009 *	1 377 *	17	212	310	50	623	368	50 *	80	4	9 *	286
1984/85	2 071 *	1 418 *	15	197	305	66	645	409	45 *	90	4	8 *	287
1985/86	2 034 *	1 377 *	17	196	297	65	650	380 *	45 *	90	5	7 *	282
LOSSES											*PERTES*		
1982/83	737 *	737 *	5	191	234	8	—	120	103 *	3	6	— *	67
1983/84	719 *	719 *	5	133	222	—	—	110	67 *	3	7	— *	172
1984/85	835 *	835 *	6	183	241	—	—	146	59 *	2	6	— *	192
1985/86	788 *	788 *	5	158	237	—	—	125 *	93 *	2	7	— *	161

SOURCE: CRONOS-ZPA1 DATA BANK, AGRICULTURAL PRODUCTS

SOURCE: BASE DE DONNEES CRONOS-ZPA1, PRODUITS AGRICOLES

SUPPLY BALANCE SHEET

BARLEY

ID 7

BILAN D'APPROVISIONNEMENT

ORGE

YEAR ANNÉE	EUR 12	EUR 10	UEBL BLEU	DK	D	GR	E	F	IRL	I	NL	P	UK

1000 T

ANIMAL FEED — ALIMENTATION ANIMALE

YEAR	EUR 12	EUR 10	UEBL BLEU	DK	D	GR	E	F	IRL	I	NL	P	UK
1982/83	33 157 *	27 192 *	744	4 621	6 563	810	5 936	5 109	1 163 *	1 990	484	29 *	5 708
1983/84	32 480 *	25 535 *	776	4 011	7 003	588	6 935	4 611	1 046 *	2 098	589	10 *	4 813
1984/85	33 990 *	25 895 *	807	4 158	7 036	644	8 024	4 660	1 141 *	2 429	495	71 *	4 525
1985/86	32 572 *	24 238 *	552	3 752	6 564	595	8 271	4 800 *	986 *	2 166	524	63 *	4 299

OF WHICH:DOMESTIC ORIGIN — DONT: ORIGINE INTERIEURE

YEAR	EUR 12	EUR 10	UEBL BLEU	DK	D	GR	E	F	IRL	I	NL	P	UK
1982/83	:	26 788 *	475	4 500 *	6 055	810 *	:	5 109	1 128 *	710	150	:	5 618
1983/84	:	25 080 *	030	3 900 *	0 418	500 *	:	4 011	1 009 *	010	05	:	4 709
1984/85	:	25 675 *	574	4 158 *	6 603	644 *	:	4 660	1 101 *	1 500	101	:	4 472
1985/86	:	24 003 *	477	3 752 *	6 048	595 *	8 000 *	4 800 *	980 *	1 500	98	:	4 209

OF WHICH:ON FARM WHERE GROWN — DONT: A LA FERME(AUTOCONSOMMATION)

YEAR	EUR 12	EUR 10	UEBL BLEU	DK	D	GR	E	F	IRL	I	NL	P	UK
1982/83	:	14 988 *	268	2 750 *	4 471	445	:	3 722	448 *	560	2	:	2 322
1983/84	:	15 835 *	228	2 365 *	4 760	400	:	3 059	455 *	550	3	:	4 015
1984/85	:	15 606 *	267	2 450 *	4 890	400	:	4 012	474 *	550	3	:	2 560
1985/86	:	14 999 *	229	2 100 *	4 892	370	3 350 *	4 000 *	380 *	465	3	:	2 560

INDUSTRIAL USES — USAGES INDUSTRIELS

YEAR	EUR 12	EUR 10	UEBL BLEU	DK	D	GR	E	F	IRL	I	NL	P	UK
1982/83	5 631 *	5 081 *	359	200	2 122	60	495	394	144 *	210	279	55 *	1 313
1983/84	6 147 *	5 607 *	343	200	2 097	50	500	320	143 *	200	274	40 *	1 980
1984/85	5 543 *	4 983 *	327	200	2 060	50	520	232	145 *	230	291	40 *	1 448
1985/86	5 670 *	5 080 *	319	200	2 079	50	540	345 *	141 *	250	284	50 *	1 412

OF WHICH: ALCOHOL — DONT: ALCOOL

YEAR	EUR 12	EUR 10	UEBL BLEU	DK	D	GR	E	F	IRL	I	NL	P	UK
1982/83	:	518 *	—	—	5	—	:	—	74 *	—	—	— *	439 *
1983/84	:	737 *	—	—	4	—	:	—	73 *	—	—	— *	660 *
1984/85	:	562 *	—	—	4	—	:	—	75 *	—	—	— *	483 *
1985/86	:	74 *	—	—	3	—	:	— *	71 *	—	—	— *	—

OF WHICH: BEER — DONT: BIERE

YEAR	EUR 12	EUR 10	UEBL BLEU	DK	D	GR	E	F	IRL	I	NL	P	UK
1982/83	:	4 561 *	359	200	2 117	60	:	392	70 *	210	279	55 *	874 *
1983/84	:	4 844 *	343	200	2 093	50	:	294	70 *	200	274	40 *	1 320 *
1984/85	:	4 407 *	327	200	2 056	50	:	218	70 *	230	291	40 *	965 *
1985/86	:	3 579 *	319	200	2 076	50	:	330 *	70 *	250	284	50 *	—

PROCESSING — TRANSFORMATION

YEAR	EUR 12	EUR 10	UEBL BLEU	DK	D	GR	E	F	IRL	I	NL	P	UK
1982/83	— *	— *	—	—	—	—	—	—	— *	—	—	— *	—
1983/84	— *	— *	—	—	—	—	—	—	— *	—	—	— *	—
1984/85	— *	— *	—	—	—	—	—	—	— *	—	—	— *	—
1985/86	— *	— *	—	—	—	—	—	— *	— *	—	—	— *	—

HUMAN CONSUMPTION — CONSOMMATION HUMAINE

YEAR	EUR 12	EUR 10	UEBL BLEU	DK	D	GR	E	F	IRL	I	NL	P	UK
1982/83	96 *	80 *	2	1	25	—	1	20	0 *	12	4	15 *	16
1983/84	101 *	90 *	2	1	32	—	1	21	0 *	10	6	10 *	18
1984/85	111 *	95 *	2	1	24	—	1	20	0 *	10	5	15 *	33
1985/86	118 *	102 *	4	1	51	—	1	20 *	0 *	10	4	15 *	12

NETT HUMAN CONSUMPTION — CONSOMMATION HUMAINE NETTE

YEAR	EUR 12	EUR 10	UEBL BLEU	DK	D	GR	E	F	IRL	I	NL	P	UK
1982/83	55 *	44 *	1	1 *	13	—	1	11	0 *	7	2	10 *	9
1983/84	59 *	51 *	2	1 *	16	—	1	12	0 *	6	4	7 *	10
1984/85	63 *	52 *	1	1	12	—	1	11	0 *	6	3	10 *	18
1985/86	67 *	56 *	2	1 *	26	—	1	11 *	0 *	6	3	10 *	7

SELF-SUFFICIENCY (%) — AUTO-APPROVISIONNEMENT (%)

YEAR	EUR 12	EUR 10	UEBL BLEU	DK	D	GR	E	F	IRL	I	NL	P	UK
1982/83	112,1 *	119,9 *	72,2	120,9	102,2	91,8	75,0	167,2	114,8 *	47,2	31,8	47,7 *	146,1
1983/84	103,7 *	108,8 *	61,7	97,1	92,5	84,0	82,7	161,6	115,1 *	49,1	20,1	78,3 *	137,3
1984/85	129,6 *	133,2 *	80,8	128,1	106,4	107,6	117,4	210,6	127,3 *	58,6	24,0	67,9 *	170,5
1985/86	125,2 *	129,2 *	83,3	121,9	105,0	87,2	113,1	201,8 *	118,1 *	64,7	23,9	48,1 *	158,0

NETT HUMAN CONSUMP.(KG/HD/YEAR) — CONS.HUMAINE NETTE (KG/TETE/AN)

YEAR	EUR 12	EUR 10	UEBL BLEU	DK	D	GR	E	F	IRL	I	NL	P	UK
1982/83	0,2 *	0,2 *	0,1	0,2 *	0,2	—	0,0	0,2	0,0 *	0,1	0,1	1,0 *	0,2
1983/84	0,2 *	0,2 *	0,2	0,2 *	0,3	—	0,0	0,2	0,0 *	0,1	0,3	0,7 *	0,2
1984/85	0,2 *	0,2 *	0,1	0,2	0,2	—	0,0	0,2	0,0 *	0,1	0,2	1,0 *	0,3
1985/86	0,2 *	0,2 *	0,2	0,2 *	0,4	—	0,0	0,2 *	0,0 *	0,1	0,2	1,0 *	0,1

SOURCE: CRONOS-ZPA1 DATA BANK, AGRICULTURAL PRODUCTS

SOURCE: BASE DE DONNEES CRONOS-ZPA1, PRODUITS AGRICOLES

I D 8

YEAR ANNÉE	EUR 12	EUR 10	UEBL BLEU	DK	D	GR	E	F	IRL	I	NL	P	UK

1000 T

USABLE PRODUCTION — **PRODUCTION UTILISABLE**

1982/83	22 501 *	19 749 *	52	—	1 054	1 449	2 330	10 400	— *	6 793	1	422	—
1983/84	22 089 *	19 819 *	39	—	934	1 654	1 803	10 520	— *	6 670	2	467 *	—
1984/85	23 302 *	20 252 *	53	—	1 026	1 913	2 529	10 483	— *	6 776	1	521 *	—
1985/86	25 816 *	21 832 *	51	—	1 204	1 822	3 414	12 441 *	— *	6 309	5	570 *	—

IMPORTS — **IMPORTATIONS**

1982/83	12 681 *	5 754 *	2 412	180	2 161	403	4 601	899	219 *	1 252	2 358	2 340	2 065
1983/84	10 222 *	4 166 *	2 196	157	2 176	195	3 757	781	222 *	1 568	2 312	2 310 *	1 958
1984/85	8 637 *	3 478 *	1 734	117	2 152	210	3 183	879	159 *	1 813	2 505	2 014 *	1 518
1985/86	7 199 *	2 797 *	1 867	73	2 376	300	2 956	790 *	177 *	1 306	2 435	1 565 *	1 521

RESOURCES = USES — **RESSOURCES = EMPLOIS**

1982/83	35 182 *	25 503 *	2 464	180	3 215	1 852	6 931	11 299	219 *	8 045	2 359	2 762	2 065
1983/84	32 311 *	23 985 *	2 235	157	3 110	1 849	5 560	11 301	222 *	8 238	2 314	2 777 *	1 958
1984/85	31 939 *	23 730 *	1 787	117	3 178	2 123	5 712	11 362	159 *	8 589	2 506	2 535 *	1 518
1985/86	33 015 *	24 629 *	1 918	73	3 580	2 122	6 370	13 231 *	177 *	7 615	2 440	2 135 *	1 521

EXPORTS — **EXPORTATIONS**

1982/83	1 586 *	1 593 *	1 860	17	557	4	7	4 379	9 *	337	595	0	30
1983/84	1 350 *	1 349 *	1 283	17	596	60	11	5 891	6 *	252	552	1 *	91
1984/85	412 *	432 *	907	18	656	14	18	4 986	7 *	704	737	0 *	12
1985/86	1 697 *	1 802 *	857	18	907	584	14	6 146 *	5 *	572	745	— *	16

FINAL STOCK — **STOCK FINAL**

1982/83	:	:	:	18	302	:	479	2 040	:	400	125	:	127
1983/84	:	:	:	30	242	:	200	1 194	:	400	130	:	75
1984/85	:	:	:	26	207	:	415	1 459	:	400	125	:	70
1985/86	:	:	:	26	346	:	481	:	:	400	178	:	208

OF WHICH: MARKET — *DONT: MARCHE*

1982/83	:	:	:	18	281	:	:	2 040	:	400	125	:	127
1983/84	:	:	:	30	219	:	:	1 194	:	400	130	:	75
1984/85	:	:	:	26	177	:	:	1 459	:	400	125	:	70
1985/86	:	:	:	26	325	:	:	:	:	400	178	:	208

CHANGE IN STOCKS — **VARIATION DES STOCKS**

1982/83	− 37 *	19 *	—	—	− 71	− 260	− 56	317	— *	—	− 2	— *	35
1983/84	− 1 251 *	− 972 *	—	12	− 60	− 31	− 279	− 846	— *	—	5	— *	− 52
1984/85	383 *	168 *	—	− 4	− 35	− 48	215	265	— *	—	− 5	— *	− 5
1985/86	294 *	693 *	—	—	139	− 122	66	485 *	— *	—	53	− 465 *	138

OF WHICH: MARKET — *DONT: MARCHE*

1982/83	:	25 *	—	—	− 65	− 260	:	317	— *	—	− 2	:	35
1983/84	:	− 974 *	—	12	− 62	− 31	:	− 846	— *	—	5	:	− 52
1984/85	:	161 *	—	− 4	− 42	− 48 *	:	265	— *	—	− 5	:	− 5
1985/86	:	702 *	—	—	148	− 122 *	:	485 *	— *	—	53	:	138

TOTAL DOMESTIC USES — **UTILISATION INTERIEURE TOTALE**

1982/83	33 633 *	23 891 *	604	163	2 729	2 108	6 980	6 603	210 *	7 708	1 766	2 762 *	2 000
1983/84	32 212 *	23 608 *	952	128	2 574	1 820	5 828	6 256	216 *	7 986	1 757	2 776 *	1 919
1984/85	31 144 *	23 130 *	880	103	2 557	2 157	5 479	6 111	152 *	7 885	1 774	2 535 *	1 511
1985/86	31 024 *	22 134 *	1 061	55	2 534	1 660	6 290	6 600 *	172 *	7 043	1 642	2 600 *	1 367

SEEDS — *SEMENCES*

1982/83	182 *	156 *	0	—	37	4	13	78	— *	32	5	13 *	—
1983/84	227 *	202 *	0	—	41	5	15	109	— *	40	7	10 *	—
1984/85	220 *	197 *	0	—	44	5	13	105	— *	35	8	10 *	—
1985/86	227 *	198 *	0	—	45	5 *	14	105 *	— *	35	8	15 *	—

LOSSES — *PERTES*

1982/83	293 *	279 *	1	—	41	160	—	55	— *	7	15	14 *	—
1983/84	133 *	119 *	1	—	39	—	—	58	— *	7	14	14 *	—
1984/85	120 *	110 *	1	—	42	—	—	49	— *	3	15	10 *	—
1985/86	145 *	130 *	1	—	45	—	—	55 *	— *	15	14	15 *	—

SOURCE: CRONOS-ZPA1 DATA BANK, AGRICULTURAL PRODUCTS

SOURCE: BASE DE DONNEES CRONOS-ZPA1, PRODUITS AGRICOLES

ID 8

YEAR ANNÉE	EUR 12	EUR 10	UEBL BLEU	DK	D	GR	E	F	IRL	I	NL	P	UK

1000 T

ANIMAL FEED / *ALIMENTATION ANIMALE*

1982/83	27 059 *	18 358 *	338	149	1 674	1 874	6 386	5 564	160 *	6 926	1 250	2 315 *	423
1983/84	25 307 *	17 752 *	520	118	1 503	1 760	5 223	4 981	166 *	7 145	1 185	2 332 *	374
1984/85	24 170 *	17 188 *	410	86	1 430	2 092	4 887	4 586	102 *	7 030	1 211	2 095 *	241
1985/86	23 922 *	16 097 *	537	31	1 388	1 595	5 675	5 000 *	122 *	6 159	1 115	2 150 *	150

OF WHICH:DOMESTIC ORIGIN / *DONT: ORIGINE INTERIEURE*

1982/83	:	15 948 *	52	—	1 031	1 400 *	:	5 564	— *	5 787	1	:	—
1983/84	:	15 581 *	39	—	904	1 600 *	:	4 981	— *	5 660	—	:	—
1984/85	:	15 177 *	53	—	989	1 900 *	:	4 586	— *	5 000	0	:	—
1985/86	:	15 079 *	51	—	1 155	1 400 *	3 300 *	5 000 *	— *	4 900	0	:	—

OF WHICH:ON FARM WHERE GROWN / *DONT: A LA FERME(AUTOCONSOMMATION)*

1982/83	:	3 715 *	52	—	504	500	:	1 838	— *	820	1	:	—
1983/84	:	3 357 *	39	—	559	400	:	1 539	— *	820	—	:	—
1984/85	:	3 575 *	53	—	667	400	:	1 635	— *	820	0	:	—
1985/86	:	3 676 *	51	—	705	400	1 270 *	1 700 *	— *	820	0	:	—

INDUSTRIAL USES / *USAGES INDUSTRIELS*

1982/83	:	:	241	—	431	60	563	387	10 *	224	456	20 *	:
1983/84	:	:	400	—	438	50	570	428	10 *	223	511	20 *	:
1984/85	:	:	438	—	452	50	560	750	10 *	222	495	20 *	:
1985/86	:	:	501	—	351	50	580	750 *	10 *	236	460	20 *	:

OF WHICH: ALCOHOL / *DONT: ALCOOL*

1982/83	:	611 *	—	—	15	—	—	—	2 *	—	10	— *	584 *
1983/84	:	639 *	—	—	18	—	:	10	2 *	—	9	— *	600 *
1984/85	:	130 *	—	—	6	—	:	15	2 *	—	7	— *	100 *
1985/86	:	167 *	—	—	8	—	:	15 *	2 *	—	—	— *	142 *

OF WHICH: BEER / *DONT: BIERE*

1982/83	:	272 *	26	—	—	—	:	85	1 *	—	150	20 *	10 *
1983/84	:	280 *	57	—	—	—	:	106	1 *	—	106	20 *	10 *
1984/85	:	297 *	73	—	—	—	:	106	1 *	—	107	20 *	10 *
1985/86	:	276 *	75	—	—	—	:	105 *	1 *	—	95	20 *	— *

PROCESSING / *TRANSFORMATION*

1982/83	:	:	— :	—	—	—	—	19	— *	:	—	100 *	:
1983/84	:	:	— :	—	—	—	—	41	— *	:	—	100 *	:
1984/85	:	:	— :	—	—	—	—	38	— *	:	—	100 *	:
1985/86	:	:	— :	—	—	—	—	40 *	— *	:	—	100 *	:

HUMAN CONSUMPTION / *CONSOMMATION HUMAINE*

1982/83	2 811 *	2 493 *	24	14	546	10	18	500	40 *	519	40	300 *	800 *
1983/84	3 009 *	2 689 *	31	10	553	5	20	639	40 *	571	40	300 *	800 *
1984/85	3 219 *	2 900 *	31	17	589	10	19	583	40 *	595	45	300 *	990 *
1985/86	3 415 *	3 094 *	22	24	705	10	21	650 *	40 *	598	45	300 *	1 000 *

NETT HUMAN CONSUMPTION / **CONSOMMATION HUMAINE NETTE**

1982/83	2 106 *	1 815 *	15	9 *	340	8 *	18	400	30 *	388	25	273 *	600 *
1983/84	2 261 *	1 968 *	20	6 *	344	4	20	511	30 *	428	25	273 *	600 *
1984/85	2 408 *	2 116 *	20	10 *	366	8	19	466	30 *	446	30	273 *	740 *
1985/86	2 546 *	2 252 *	14	14 *	438	8	21	520 *	30 *	448	30	273 *	750 *

SELF-SUFFICIENCY (%) / **AUTO-APPROVISIONNEMENT (%)**

1982/83	66,9 *	82,7 *	8,6	—	38,6	68,7	33,4	157,5	— *	88,1	0,1	15,3 *	—
1983/84	68,6 *	84,0 *	4,1	—	36,3	90,9	30,9	168,2	— *	83,5	0,1	16,8 *	—
1984/85	74,8 *	87,6 *	6,0	—	40,1	88,7	46,2	171,5	— *	85,9	0,1	20,6 *	—
1985/86	83,2 *	98,6 *	4,8	—	47,5	109,8	54,3	188,5 *	— *	89,6	0,3	21,9 *	—

NETT HUMAN CONSUMP.(KG/HD/YEAR) / **CONS.HUMAINE NETTE (KG/TETE/AN)**

1982/83	6,6 *	6,7 *	1,5	1,8 *	5,5	0,8 *	0,5	7,3	8,6 *	6,8	1,7	27,4 *	10,6 *
1983/84	7,0 *	7,2 *	2,0	1,2 *	5,6	0,4	0,5	9,3	8,5 *	7,5	1,7	27,2 *	10,6 *
1984/85	7,5 *	7,8 *	2,0	2,0 *	6,0	0,8	0,5	8,5	8,5 *	7,8	2,1	27,0 *	13,1 *
1985/86	7,9 *	8,2 *	1,4	2,7 *	7,2	0,8	0,5	9,4 *	8,5 *	7,8	2,1	26,8 *	13,2 *

SOURCE: CRONOS-ZPA1 DATA BANK, AGRICULTURAL PRODUCTS

SOURCE: BASE DE DONNEES CRONOS-ZPA1, PRODUITS AGRICOLES

I D 9

YEAR ANNÉE	EUR 12	EUR 10	UEBL BLEU	DK	D	GR	E	F	IRL	I	NL	P	UK

1000 T

USABLE PRODUCTION / **PRODUCTION UTILISABLE**

	EUR 12	EUR 10	UEBL BLEU	DK	D	GR	E	F	IRL	I	NL	P	UK
1982/83	40 540	34 335	1 614	1 107	7 195	993	5 222	6 797	855	2 622	6 319	983	6 833
1983/84	35 227 *	29 032 *	1 209	767	5 795	1 020	5 163	5 731	639 *	2 542	5 491	1 032 *	5 838
1984/85	42 366 *	35 397 *	1 648	1 009	7 406	976	5 981	6 964	844 *	2 467	6 773	988 *	7 310
1985/86	43 806 *	36 743 *	1 831	990	8 008	959	5 927	7 787	663 *	2 389	7 220	1 136 *	6 896

IMPORTS / **IMPORTATIONS**

	EUR 12	EUR 10	UEBL BLEU	DK	D	GR	E	F	IRL	I	NL	P	UK
1982/83	426 *	394	340	24	1 447	18	122	420	33	610	306	136	709
1983/84	648 *	689 *	422	56	1 540	22	86	561	117 *	390	387	68 *	885
1984/85	347 *	358 *	438	26	1 393	6	85	595	120 *	614	398	112 *	664
1985/86	427 *	443 *	610	33	1 366	20	81	459	192 *	503	895	110 *	771

RESOURCES = USES / **RESSOURCES = EMPLOIS**

	EUR 12	EUR 10	UEBL BLEU	DK	D	GR	E	F	IRL	I	NL	P	UK
1982/83	40 966 *	34 729	1 954	1 131	8 642	1 011	5 344	7 217	888	3 232	6 625	1 119	7 542
1983/84	35 875 *	29 721 *	1 631	823	7 335	1 042	5 249	6 292	756 *	2 932	5 878	1 100 *	6 723
1984/85	42 713 *	35 755 *	2 086	1 035	8 799	982	6 066	7 559	964 *	3 081	7 171	1 100 *	7 974
1985/86	44 233 *	37 186 *	2 441	1 023	9 374	979	6 008	8 246	855 *	2 892	8 115	1 246 *	7 667

EXPORTS / **EXPORTATIONS**

	EUR 12	EUR 10	UEBL BLEU	DK	D	GR	E	F	IRL	I	NL	P	UK
1982/83	863 *	1 021	522	35	287	20	64	651	18	229	2 578	4	194
1983/84	745 *	840 *	557	26	351	164	96	452	20 *	394	2 356	4 *	211
1984/85	949 *	1 036 *	590	24	504	26	120	568	28 *	347	2 622	1 *	223
1985/86	1 083 *	1 173 *	635	24	781	50	111	755	23 *	431	2 666	6 *	214

FINAL STOCK / **STOCK FINAL**

	EUR 12	EUR 10	UEBL BLEU	DK	D	GR	E	F	IRL	I	NL	P	UK
1982/83	:	:	:	:	144	180	–	:	:	:	–	:	349
1983/84	:	:	:	:	84	112	–	:	:	:	–	:	135
1984/85	:	:	:	:	190	151	–	:	:	:	–	:	250
1985/86	:	:	:	:	176	193	–	:	:	:	–	:	338

CHANGE IN STOCKS / **VARIATION DES STOCKS**

	EUR 12	EUR 10	UEBL BLEU	DK	D	GR	E	F	IRL	I	NL	P	UK
1982/83	259 *	259	–	–	– 73	80	–	–	–	–	–	– *	252
1983/84	– 344 *	– 344 *	–	–	– 60	– 68	–	–	– *	–	–	– *	– 216
1984/85	260 *	260 *	–	–	106	39	–	–	– *	–	–	– *	115
1985/86	117 *	117 *	–	–	– 14	42	–	–	– *	–	–	– *	89

TOTAL DOMESTIC USES / **UTILISATION INTERIEURE TOTALE**

	EUR 12	EUR 10	UEBL BLEU	DK	D	GR	E	F	IRL	I	NL	P	UK
1982/83	39 844 *	33 449	1 432	1 096	8 428	911	5 280	6 566	870	3 003	4 047	1 115 *	7 096
1983/84	35 474 *	29 225 *	1 074	797	7 044	946	5 153	5 840	736 *	2 538	3 522	1 096 *	6 728
1984/85	41 504 *	34 459 *	1 496	1 011	8 189	917	5 946	6 991	936 *	2 734	4 549	1 099 *	7 636
1985/86	43 033 *	35 896 *	1 806	999	8 607	887	5 897	7 491	832 *	2 461	5 449	1 240 *	7 364

SEEDS / *SEMENCES*

	EUR 12	EUR 10	UEBL BLEU	DK	D	GR	E	F	IRL	I	NL	P	UK
1982/83	3 253 *	2 573	47	75	559	95	510	432	100	250	365	170 *	650
1983/84	3 250 *	2 553 *	48	76	549	95	522	431	108 *	228	360	175 *	658
1984/85	3 226 *	2 561 *	53	78	545	97	485	441	110 *	232	370	180 *	635
1985/86	3 084 *	2 460 *	53	76	520	108	434	423	98 *	226	365	190 *	591

LOSSES / *PERTES*

	EUR 12	EUR 10	UEBL BLEU	DK	D	GR	E	F	IRL	I	NL	P	UK
1982/83	2 084 *	1 838	125	–	205	–	236	1 000	171	212	125	10 *	–
1983/84	1 252 *	1 012 *	84	–	194	–	230	400	130 *	101	103	10 *	–
1984/85	2 261 *	1 838 *	126	–	203	–	413	1 070	200 *	109	130	10 *	–
1985/86	2 201 *	1 950 *	161	–	219	–	241	1 160	170 *	99	141	10 *	–

ANIMAL FEED / *ALIMENTATION ANIMALE*

	EUR 12	EUR 10	UEBL BLEU	DK	D	GR	E	F	IRL	I	NL	P	UK
1982/83	4 535 *	3 962	248	238	1 936	–	523	300	154	190	337	50 *	559
1983/84	2 516 *	1 962 *	33	55	974	–	493	200	58 *	184	310	61 *	148
1984/85	5 476 *	4 730 *	264	136	1 636	–	687	577	176 *	190	736	59 *	1 015
1985/86	6 073 *	4 970 *	590	133	1 534	–	963	755	114 *	110	1 203	140 *	531

OF WHICH:DOMESTIC ORIGIN / *DONT: ORIGINE INTERIEURE*

	EUR 12	EUR 10	UEBL BLEU	DK	D	GR	E	F	IRL	I	NL	P	UK
1982/83	4 535 *	3 962	198	238	1 931	–	523 *	300	154	190	314	50 *	559
1983/84	2 516 *	1 961 *	7	55 *	973	–	493 *	200	58 *	184	301	61 *	148
1984/85	5 476 *	4 730 *	204	136 *	1 635	–	687 *	577	176 *	190 *	713	59 *	1 015
1985/86	6 073 *	4 970 *	386	133 *	1 531	–	963 *	755	114 *	110 *	1 171	140 *	531

SOURCE: CRONOS-ZPA1 DATA BANK, AGRICULTURAL PRODUCTS

SOURCE: BASE DE DONNEES CRONOS-ZPA1, PRODUITS AGRICOLES

POTATOES

POMMES DE TERRE

YEAR ANNÉE	EUR 12	EUR 10	UEBL BLEU	DK	D	GR	E	F	IRL	I	NL	P	UK
1000 T													
INDUSTRIAL USES												*USAGES INDUSTRIELS*	
1982/83	456 *	456	—	21	435	—	—	—	—	—	—	— *	—
1983/84	342 *	342 *	—	9	333	—	—	—	— *	—	—	— *	—
1984/85	423 *	423 *	—	15	408	—	—	—	— *	—	—	— *	—
1985/86	475 *	475 *	—	17	458	—	—	—	— *	—	—	— *	—
OF WHICH: ALCOHOL												*DONT: ALCOOL*	
1982/83	456 *	456	—	21	435	—	—	—	—	—	—	— *	—
1983/84	342 *	342 *	—	0	000	—	—	—	— *	—	—	— *	—
1984/85	423 *	423 *	—	15	408	—	—	—	— *	—	—	— *	—
1985/86	475 *	475 *	—	17	458	—	—	—	— *	—	—	— *	—
PROCESSING												*TRANSFORMATION*	
1982/83	4 019 *	3 989	—	414	753	—	30	765	—	—	2 057	— *	0
1983/84	3 358 *	3 293 *	—	305	697	—	65	712	— *	—	1 579	— *	0
1984/85	4 417 *	4 317 *	—	451	963	—	100	853	— *	—	2 050	— *	0
1985/86	5 170 *	5 050 *	—	446	1 132	—	120	987	— *	—	2 485	— *	0
HUMAN CONSUMPTION												*CONSOMMATION HUMAINE*	
1982/83	25 498 *	20 632	1 012	348	4 540	816	3 981	4 069	446	2 351	1 163	885 *	5 887
1983/84	24 756 *	20 063 *	909	352	4 297	851	3 843	4 097	440 *	2 025	1 170	850 *	5 922
1984/85	25 701 *	20 590 *	1 053	331	4 434	820	4 261	4 050	450 *	2 203	1 263	850 *	5 986
1985/86	26 030 *	20 991 *	1 002	327	4 744	779	4 139	4 166	450 *	2 026	1 255	900 *	6 242
SELF-SUFFICIENCY (%)												*AUTO-APPROVISIONNEMENT (%)*	
1982/83	101,7 *	102,6	112,7	101,0	85,4	109,0	98,9	103,5	98,3	87,3	156,1	88,2 *	96,3
1983/84	99,3 *	99,3 *	112,6	96,2	82,3	107,8	100,2	98,1	86,8 *	100,2	155,9	94,2 *	86,8
1984/85	102,1 *	102,7 *	110,2	99,8	90,4	106,4	100,6	99,6	90,2 *	90,2	148,9	89,9 *	95,7
1985/86	101,8 *	102,4 *	101,4	99,1	93,0	108,1	100,5	104,0	79,7 *	97,1	132,5	91,6 *	93,6
HUMAN CONSUMPTION (KG/HEAD/YEAR)												*CONSOMMATION HUMAINE(KG/TETE/AN)*	
1982/83	79,6 *	75,8	99,0	68,0	73,8	83,1	104,6	74,5	127,5	41,4	81,1	88,8 *	104,4
1983/84	77,1 *	73,6 *	89,0	68,9	70,1	86,2	100,4	74,7	124,9 *	35,6	81,3	84,6 *	104,9
1984/85	79,9 *	75,4 *	103,0	64,8	72,6	82,7	110,7	73,6	127,2 *	38,6	87,4	83,9 *	105,8
1985/86	80,8 *	76,7 *	98,0	63,9	77,7	78,3	107,3	75,4	127,2 *	35,4	86,4	88,4 *	110,1

SOURCE: CRONOS-ZPA1 DATA BANK, AGRICULTURAL PRODUCTS

SOURCE: BASE DE DONNEES CRONOS-ZPA1, PRODUITS AGRICOLES

I D 10

1000 T

YEAR ANNÉE	EUR 12	EUR 10	UEBL BLEU	DK	D	GR	E	F	IRL	I	NL	P	UK
USABLE PRODUCTION												PRODUCTION UTILISABLE	
1982/83	11 720 *	7 052	17	338	535	1 400	4 114 *	1 897	5	2 236	44	554 *	580
1983/84	11 532 *	9 258 *	19	313	599	1 430 *	2 170 *	1 868	8	4 411	48	104 *	562
1984/85	13 276 *	8 142	22	478	662	1 457	4 742	2 424	15	2 114	47	392 *	923
1985/86	:	:	19	622 *	803	2 065	3 053	:	13	3 776	:	297 *	896
IMPORTS												IMPORTATIONS	
1982/83	17 314 *	13 157	1 797	260	5 198	159	3 158 *	1 208	8	1 644	3 557	1 100 *	1 105
1983/84	15 043 *	11 237 *	1 760	260	3 995	143 *	2 698 *	938	6	1 414	3 390	1 212 *	963
1984/85	14 628 *	11 460	1 856	161	4 272	121	2 039	822	5	1 854	3 540	1 246 *	1 028
1985/86	:	:	1 976	167	5 047	195	2 288	:	7	1 797	:	1 179 *	1 074
RESOURCES = USES												RESSOURCES = EMPLOIS	
1982/83	29 034 *	20 209	1 814	598	5 733	1 559	7 272 *	3 105	13	3 880	3 601	1 654 *	1 685
1983/84	26 575 *	20 495 *	1 779	573	4 594	1 573	4 868 *	2 806	14	5 825	3 438	1 316 *	1 525
1984/85	27 904 *	19 602	1 878	639	4 934	1 578	6 781	3 246	20	3 968	3 587	1 638 *	1 951
1985/86	:	:	1 995	789 *	5 850	2 260	5 341	:	20	5 573	:	1 476 *	1 970
EXPORTS												EXPORTATIONS	
1982/83	— *	—	37	290	73	0	101 *	1 066	1	0	216	0 *	96
1983/84	— *	— *	37	263	94	0 *	104 *	1 034	5	0	142	0 *	57
1984/85	— *	—	53	396	128	5	116	1 184	13	0	134	1 *	286
1985/86	:	:	43	383	130	68	113	:	14	1	:	1 *	428
FINAL STOCK												STOCK FINAL	
1982/83	:	:	32	:	139	71	:	125	:	—	83	:	37
1983/84	:	:	19	:	51	23	:	115	:	—	54	:	31
1984/85	:	:	48	:	119	34	:	182	:	—	113	:	29
1985/86	:	:	52	:	220	29	:	:	:	—	:	:	54
CHANGE IN STOCKS												VARIATION DES STOCKS	
1982/83	− 16 *	− 59	− 29	45	− 70	26	6 *	38	—	—	− 40	37 *	− 29
1983/84	− 113 *	− 101 *	− 13	45	− 88	− *	− 32 *	− 10	—	—	− 29	20 *	− 6
1984/85	262 *	248	29	46	38	11	0	67	—	—	59	14 *	− 2
1985/86	:	:	4	180 *	101	4	0	:	—	—	:	− 11 *	25
TOTAL DOMESTIC USES												UTILISATION INTERIEURE TOTALE	
1982/83	29 050 *	20 268	1 806	263	5 730	1 533	7 165 *	2 001	12	3 880	3 425	1 617 *	1 618
1983/84	26 687 *	20 595 *	1 755	265	4 588	1 573 *	4 796 *	1 782	8	5 825	3 325	1 296 *	1 474
1984/85	27 641 *	19 354	1 796	197	4 768	1 562	6 664	1 995	7	3 968	3 394	1 623 *	1 667
1985/86	:	:	1 948	226	5 619	2 189	5 227	:	7	5 572	:	1 486 *	1 517
SEEDS												*SEMENCES*	
1982/83	:	:	1	6 *	14	8	4 *	19	0	0	0	0 *	:
1983/84	:	:	1	6 *	15	10 *	5 *	22	0	0	7	0 *	:
1984/85	:	:	2	11 *	19	13	9	30	0	0	11	0 *	:
1985/86	:	:	1	—	17	15	9	:	0	0	:	0 *	:
LOSSES												*PERTES*	
1982/83	:	:	—	− 6 *	8	—	− *	2	—	15	50	− *	:
1983/84	:	:	—	− 6 *	10	− *	− *	2	—	10	39	− *	:
1984/85	:	:	—	− 11 *	19	—	—	2	—	10	− 23	− *	:
1985/86	:	:	—	—	23	—	—	:	0	10	:	− *	:
ANIMAL FEED												*ALIMENTATION ANIMALE*	
1982/83	:	:	1	—	45	1	− *	0	—	0	333	− *	:
1983/84	:	:	1	—	51	1 *	− *	0	6	0	125	− *	:
1984/85	:	:	1	—	41	1	—	0	6	31	79	− *	:
1985/86	:	:	1	—	46	24	—	:	4	71	:	− *	:
INDUSTRIAL USES												*USAGES INDUSTRIELS*	
1982/83	:	:	—	—	—	—	− *	3	—	—	—	− *	:
1983/84	:	:	—	—	—	− *	− *	2	0	—	—	− *	:
1984/85	:	:	—	—	—	—	—	3	0	5	—	− *	:
1985/86	:	:	—	—	—	—	—	:	0	5	:	− *	:

SOURCE: CRONOS-ZPA1 DATA BANK, AGRICULTURAL PRODUCTS

SOURCE: BASE DE DONNEES CRONOS-ZPA1, PRODUITS AGRICOLES

I D 10

YEAR ANNÉE	EUR 12	EUR 10	UEBL BLEU	DK	D	GR	E	F	IRL	I	NL	P	UK
						1000 T							
PROCESSING												*TRANSFORMATION*	
1982/83	27 753 *	19 246 *	1 802	260 *	5 625	1 425	6 915 *	1 977	10	3 811	2 982	1 592 *	1 354
1983/84	25 690 *	19 770 *	1 751	260 *	4 464	1 461 *	4 646 *	1 756	—	5 735	3 082	1 274 *	1 261
1984/85	26 367 *	18 348	1 791	194	4 644	1 440	6 418	1 960	—	3 857	3 246	1 601 *	1 216
1985/86	:	:	1 944	221	5 485	2 089	5 106	:	—	5 404	:	1 464 *	1 203
HUMAN CONSUMPTION												*CONSOMMATION HUMAINE*	
1982/83	654 *	680 *	2	3 *	38	99	246 *	—	1	54	60	25 *	126
1983/84	515 *	348 *	2	5 *	48	101 *	145 *	—	2	80	72	22 *	38
1984/85	653 *	393 *	2	3 *	45	108	238	0	2	65	81	22 *	87
1985/86	:	:	2	5 *	48	60	113	:	3	82	:	22 *	98
SELF-SUFFICIENCY (%)												**AUTO-APPROVISIONNEMENT (%)**	
1982/83	40,3 *	34,8	0,9	128,5	9,3	91,3	57,4 *	94,8	41,7	57,6	1,3	34,3 *	35,8
1983/84	43,2 *	45,0 *	1,1	118,1	13,1	90,9 *	45,2 *	104,8	100,0	75,7	1,4	8,0 *	38,1
1984/85	48,0 *	42,1	1,2	242,6	13,9	93,3	71,2	121,5	214,3	53,3	1,4	24,2 *	55,4
1985/86	:	:	1,0	275,2 *	14,3	94,3	58,4	:	185,7	67,8	:	20,0 *	59,1
HUMAN CONSUMPTION (KG/HEAD/YEAR)												**CONSOMMATION HUMAINE(KG/TETE/AN)**	
1982/83	2,0 *	1,4 *	0,2	0,6 *	0,6	10,1	6,5 *	—	0,3	1,0	4,2	2,5 *	2,2
1983/84	1,6 *	1,3 *	0,2	1,0 *	0,8	10,2 *	3,8 *	—	0,6	1,4	5,0	2,2 *	0,7
1984/85	2,0 *	1,4 *	0,2	0,6 *	0,7	10,9	6,2	0,0	0,6	1,1	5,6	2,2 *	1,5
1985/86	:	:	0,2	1,0 *	0,8	6,0	2,9	:	0,8	1,4	:	2,2 *	1,7

SOURCE: CRONOS-ZPA1 DATA BANK, AGRICULTURAL PRODUCTS

SOURCE: BASE DE DONNEES CRONOS-ZPA1, PRODUITS AGRICOLES

OILCAKES : TOTAL(EXCL.OLIV.RES.)

TOURTEAUX : TOTAL(NC GRIGN.OLIVES)

YEAR ANNÉE	EUR 12	EUR 10	UEBL BLEU	DK	D	GR	E	F	IRL	I	NL	P	UK

1000 T

USABLE PRODUCTION | | | | | | | | | | | | **PRODUCTION UTILISABLE**

1982/83	15 756 *	12 106	1 405	182	4 052	240	2 874 *	1 422	7	1 416	2 306	776 *	1 076
1983/84	13 974 *	10 596 *	1 351	177	3 125	265 *	2 587 *	1 184	—	1 287	2 355	791 *	852
1984/85	14 506 *	11 303	1 327	121	3 320	264	2 288	1 328	—	1 667	2 473	915 *	803
1985/86	:	:	1 400	138	3 848	352	2 416	:	—	1 770	:	963 *	821

FROM INDIGENOUS PRODUCTS | | | | | | | | | | | *A PARTIR DE MATIERE PREMIERE INDIGENE*

1982/83	2 581 *	2 107 *	10	41	289	127	445 *	465	2	142	13	15 *	175
1983/84	2 936 *	2 471 *	11	36	314	162 *	442 *	506	—	196	17	6 *	333
1984/85	3 841 *	3 159 *	12	47	366	176	648 *	741	—	250	17	16 *	357
1985/86	:	:	12	87	417	205	577 *	:	—	421	:	15 *	289

IMPORTS | | | | | | | | | | | | **IMPORTATIONS**

1982/83	15 582 *	15 373	1 312	2 042	4 853	12	464 *	3 613	469	1 349	3 489	103 *	1 796
1983/84	15 615 *	15 169	1 268	1 972	4 974	11 *	789 *	3 680	441	1 347	3 288	25 *	1 916
1984/85	14 721 *	13 832 *	1 318	1 807	4 375	33	1 148	3 496	335	1 620	3 383	29 *	1 892
1985/86	:	:	1 449	2 120	5 022	54	930	:	440	1 656	:	50 *	2 280

RESOURCES = USES | | | | | | | | | | | | **RESSOURCES = EMPLOIS**

1982/83	31 338 *	27 479	2 717	2 224	8 905	252	3 338 *	5 035	476	2 765	5 795	879 *	2 872
1983/84	29 589 *	25 765 *	2 619	2 149	8 099	276 *	3 376 *	4 864	441	2 634	5 643	816 *	2 768
1984/85	29 227 *	25 135 *	2 645	1 928	7 695	297	3 436	4 824	335	3 287	5 856	944 *	2 695
1985/86	:	:	2 849	2 258	8 870	406	3 346	:	440	3 426	:	1 013 *	3 101

EXPORTS | | | | | | | | | | | | **EXPORTATIONS**

1982/83	2 895 *	2 657	1 162	21	2 389	8	484 *	152	4	138	2 324	112 *	21
1983/84	2 229 *	1 744 *	1 201	19	1 868	84 *	680 *	156	4	128	1 986	173 *	26
1984/85	1 928 *	1 385 *	1 310	23	2 019	30	573	268	3	122	1 995	258 *	42
1985/86	:	:	1 328	23	2 575	70	166	:	5	156	:	299 *	39

FINAL STOCK | | | | | | | | | | | | **STOCK FINAL**

1982/83	:	:	5	130	33	8	:	41	:	:	10	:	33
1983/84	:	:	31	153	31	13	:	56	:	:	14	:	34
1984/85	:	:	16	119	27	24	:	104	:	:	12	:	30
1985/86	:	:	11	207	37	13	:	:	:	:	:	:	90

CHANGE IN STOCKS | | | | | | | | | | | | **VARIATION DES STOCKS**

1982/83	− 26 *	− 26	− 12	− 4	− 1	—	− *	− 4	—	—	− 1	− *	− 4
1983/84	66 *	66 *	26	23	− 2	− *	− *	15	—	—	4	− *	—
1984/85	− 1 *	− 1	− 15	− 34	− 4	11	0	48	—	—	− 2	− *	− 5
1985/86	:	:	− 5	88	10	− 11	—	:	—	—	:	− *	60

TOTAL DOMESTIC USES | | | | | | | | | | | | **UTILISATION INTERIEURE TOTALE**

1982/83	28 469 *	24 848	1 567	2 207	6 517	244	2 854 *	4 887	472	2 627	3 472	767 *	2 855
1983/84	27 294 *	23 955 *	1 392	2 107	6 233	192 *	2 696 *	4 693	437	2 506	3 653	643 *	2 742
1984/85	27 299 *	23 750	1 350	1 939	5 680	256	2 863	4 508	331	3 165	3 863	686 *	2 658
1985/86	:	:	1 526	2 147	6 285	347	3 180	:	436	3 270	:	714 *	3 002

ANIMAL FEED | | | | | | | | | | | | *ALIMENTATION ANIMALE*

1982/83	28 430 *	24 809	1 567	2 207	6 500	242	2 854 *	4 877	472	2 627	3 472	767 *	2 845
1983/84	27 264 *	23 925 *	1 392	2 107	6 216	190 *	2 696 *	4 684	437	2 506	3 653	643 *	2 740
1984/85	27 234 *	23 700	1 350	1 939	5 664	253	2 848	4 499	331	3 165	3 863	686 *	2 636
1985/86	:	:	1 526	2 147	6 265	345	3 162	:	436	3 270	:	714 *	2 993

INDUSTRIAL USES | | | | | | | | | | | | *USAGES INDUSTRIELS*

1982/83	37 *	37	—	—	17	—	− *	10	—	—	—	− *	10
1983/84	28 *	28 *	—	—	17	− *	− *	9	—	—	—	− *	2
1984/85	62 *	47	—	—	16	—	15	9	—	—	—	− *	22
1985/86	:	:	—	—	20	—	18	:	—	—	:	− *	9

SELF-SUFFICIENCY (%) | | | | | | | | | | | | **AUTO-APPROVISIONNEMENT (%)**

1982/83	9,1 *	8,5 *	0,6	1,9	4,4	52,0	15,6 *	9,5	0,4	5,4	0,4	2,0 *	6,1
1983/84	10,8 *	10,3 *	0,8	1,7	5,0	84,4 *	16,4 *	10,8	—	7,8	0,5	0,9 *	12,1
1984/85	14,1 *	13,3 *	0,9	2,4	6,4	68,8	22,6 *	16,4	—	7,9	0,4	2,3 *	13,4
1985/86	:	:	0,8	4,1	6,6	59,1	18,1 *	:	—	12,9	:	2,1 *	9,6

SUPPLY BALANCE SHEET

SUGAR (IN WHITE SUGAR)

ID 12

BILAN D'APPROVISIONNEMENT

SUCRE (EN SUCRE BLANC)

YEAR ANNÉE	EUR 12	EUR 10	UEBL BLEU	DK	D	GR	E	F	IRL	I	NL	P	UK

1000 T

USABLE PRODUCTION — PRODUCTION UTILISABLE

1982/83	15 096	13 952	1 105	537	3 305	296	1 144	4 757	222	1 180	1 130	—	1 420
1983/84	12 262 *	11 022	782	345	2 511	298	1 240	3 834	197	1 247	745	— *	1 063
1984/85	13 589 *	12 515 *	841	547	2 905	218	1 074 *	4 257 *	222	1 276	935	— *	1 314
1985/86	13 631 *	12 728 *	944	530	3 165	317	903	4 248 *	174 *	1 244	896	— *	1 210

IMPORTS — IMPORTATIONS

1982/83	1 488 *	1 277	193	26	400	7	70	319	32	322	153	235	1 184
1983/84	1 752 *	1 511 *	288	31	401	6	61	351	47	347	159	275 *	1 340
1984/85	1 821 *	1 552 *	319	24	420	22	60	335 *	56	361	180	292 *	1 269
1985/86	1 762 *	1 521 *	228	25	432	33	70	493 *	55 *	372	140	320 *	1 070

RESOURCES = USES — RESSOURCES = EMPLOIS

1982/83	16 584 *	15 229	1 298	563	3 705	303	1 214	5 076	254	1 502	1 283	235	2 604
1983/84	14 014 *	12 533 *	1 070	376	2 912	304	1 301	4 185	244	1 594	904	275 *	2 403
1984/85	15 410 *	14 067 *	1 160	571	3 325	240	1 134 *	4 592 *	278	1 637	1 115	292 *	2 583
1985/86	15 393 *	14 249 *	1 172	555	3 597	350	973	4 741 *	229 *	1 616	1 036	320 *	2 280

EXPORTS — EXPORTATIONS

1982/83	4 952 *	4 998	853	305	1 243	22	43	2 569	74	187	657	5	447
1983/84	4 448 *	4 458 *	782	222	1 008	44	53	2 834	101	99	487	32 *	340
1984/85	3 830 *	3 822 *	801	273	915	26	65	2 328 *	111	149	395	26 *	258
1985/86	4 498 *	4 448 *	797	341	1 109	27	182	2 567 *	100 *	127	353	17 *	354

CHANGE IN STOCKS — VARIATION DES STOCKS

1982/83	742 *	693	65	45	219	7	109	541	25	— 166	41	— 60 *	— 84
1983/84	— 752 *	— 937	— 94	— 55	— 191	— 19	232	— 675	5	30	— 81	— 47 *	143
1984/85	865 *	738 *	— 5	69	208	— 43	151	250 *	10	— 165	151	— 24 *	263
1985/86	— 76 *	208 *	— 11	7	220	4	— 297	150 *	— 16 *	— 46	68	13 *	— 168

TOTAL DOMESTIC USES — UTILISATION INTERIEURE TOTALE

1982/83	10 890 *	9 538	380	213	2 243	274	1 062	1 966	155	1 481	585	290 *	2 241
1983/84	10 317 *	9 012	382	209	2 095	279	1 015	2 026	138	1 465	498	290 *	1 920
1984/85	10 713 *	9 505 *	364	229	2 202	256	918	2 014 *	156	1 653	569	290 *	2 062
1985/86	10 971 *	9 593 *	386	207	2 268	319	1 088	2 024 *	145 *	1 535	615	290 *	2 094

ANIMAL FEED — ALIMENTATION ANIMALE

1982/83	19 *	12	—	1	4	1	7	1	0	—	—	— *	5
1983/84	11 *	10	—	1	3	1	1	—	0	—	—	— *	5
1984/85	12 *	11 *	—	1	3	2	1	— *	0	—	—	— *	5
1985/86	13 *	12 *	—	1	3	3	1	— *	— *	—	—	— *	5

INDUSTRIAL USES — USAGES INDUSTRIELS

1982/83	88 *	66	5	—	19	0	12	23	2	—	17	10 *	0
1983/84	103 *	64	6	—	18	1	29	19	2	—	18	10 *	0
1984/85	111 *	70 *	6	—	24	0	31	14 *	—	—	26	10 *	—
1985/86	121 *	79 *	5	—	27	1	32	24 *	— *	—	22	10 *	0

HUMAN CONSUMPTION — CONSOMMATION HUMAINE

1982/83	10 778 *	9 455	375	207	2 220	273	1 043	1 942	153	1 481	568	280 *	2 236
1983/84	10 198 *	8 933	375	205	2 074	277	985	2 007	135	1 465	480	280 *	1 915
1984/85	10 584 *	9 418 *	358	222	2 175	254	886	2 000 *	156	1 653	543	280 *	2 057
1985/86	10 832 *	9 497 *	381	201	2 238	315	1 055	2 000 *	145 *	1 535	593	280 *	2 089

SELF-SUFFICIENCY (%) — AUTO-APPROVISIONNEMENT (%)

1982/83	138,6 *	146,3	290,8	252,1	147,3	108,0	107,7	242,0	143,2	79,7	193,2	— *	63,4
1983/84	118,9 *	122,3	204,7	165,1	119,9	106,8	122,2	189,2	142,8	85,1	149,6	— *	55,4
1984/85	126,8 *	131,7 *	231,0	238,9	131,9	85,2	117,0 *	211,4 *	142,3	77,2	164,3	— *	63,7
1985/86	124,2 *	132,7 *	244,6	256,0	139,6	99,4	83,0	209,9 *	120,0 *	81,0	145,7	— *	57,8

HUMAN CONSUMPTION (KG/HEAD/YEAR) — CONSOMMATION HUMAINE(KG/TETE/AN)

1982/83	33,6 *	34,6	36,7	40,5	36,1	27,8	27,4	35,0	43,7	26,1	39,6	28,1 *	39,7
1983/84	31,8 *	32,6	36,7	40,1	33,8	28,1	25,7	35,9	38,3	25,7	33,3	27,9 *	33,9
1984/85	32,9 *	34,4 *	35,0	43,4	35,6	25,6	23,0	35,6 *	44,1	29,0	37,6	27,6 *	36,4
1985/86	33,6 *	34,6 *	37,3	39,3	36,7	31,7	27,3	35,5 *	41,0 *	26,8	40,8	27,5 *	36,8

SOURCE: CRONOS-ZPA1 DATA BANK, AGRICULTURAL PRODUCTS

SOURCE: BASE DE DONNEES CRONOS-ZPA1, PRODUITS AGRICOLES

I D 13

YEAR ANNÉE	EUR 12	EUR 10	UEBL BLEU	DK	D	GR	E	F	IRL	I	NL	P	UK

1000 T

USABLE PRODUCTION — **PRODUCTION UTILISABLE**

1982/83	43 077 *	32 721	1 023	230	1 796	3 386	8 816	7 012	292	12 809	2 883	1 540 *	3 290
1983/84	43 507	33 153	993	201	1 586	3 402	8 704	6 552	278	14 577	2 730	1 650	2 834
1984/85	45 703 *	34 532 *	1 076	220 *	1 788	3 811	9 291	6 388	297	15 071	2 839	1 880 *	3 042
1985/86	46 495 *	35 063 *	1 213	255	1 979	3 778	9 532	7 048 *	263	14 418	2 943	1 900 *	3 166

IMPORTS — **IMPORTATIONS**

1982/83	1 650 *	2 694	492	132	3 022	9	53	1 164	64	218	587	14 *	1 822
1983/84	1 898 *	3 040	554	145	3 137	14	49	1 534	85	221	646	2 *	2 150
1984/85	2 001 *	3 134	622	145	3 228	23	49	1 326	102	355	753	10 *	2 078
1985/86	2 203 *	3 465 *	643	166	3 256	16	44	1 557 *	113	319	809	3 *	2 276

RESOURCES = USES — **RESSOURCES = EMPLOIS**

1982/83	44 727 *	35 415	1 515	362	4 818	3 395	8 869	8 176	356	13 027	3 470	1 554 *	5 112
1983/84	45 405 *	36 193	1 547	346	4 723	3 416	8 753	8 086	363	14 798	3 376	1 652 *	4 984
1984/85	47 704 *	37 666 *	1 698	365 *	5 016	3 834	9 340	7 714	399	15 426	3 592	1 890 *	5 120
1985/86	48 698 *	38 528 *	1 856	421	5 235	3 794	9 576	8 605 *	376	14 737	3 752	1 903 *	5 442

EXPORTS — **EXPORTATIONS**

1982/83	3 658 *	2 701	656	42	158	1 154	1 673	732	23	2 485	1 974	395 *	293
1983/84	4 504 *	3 199	693	49	189	1 475	1 941	850	28	2 984	2 076	557 *	301
1984/85	5 165 *	3 573	740	57	168	1 392	2 234	733	34	3 169	2 187	550 *	591
1985/86	5 120 *	3 447 *	835	61	216	1 069	2 485	949 *	26	3 468	2 282	497 *	231

CHANGE IN STOCKS — **VARIATION DES STOCKS**

1982/83	50 *	–	–	–	–	–	–	–	–	–	–	50 *	–
1983/84	– 60 *	–	–	–	–	–	–	–	–	–	–	– 60 *	–
1984/85	70 *	–	–	–	–	–	–	–	–	–	–	70 *	–
1985/86	100 *	– *	–	–	–	–	–	– *	–	–	–	100 *	–

TOTAL DOMESTIC USES — **UTILISATION INTERIEURE TOTALE**

1982/83	41 040 *	32 735	859	320	4 660	2 260	7 196	7 444	333	10 542	1 498	1 109 *	4 819
1983/84	40 961 *	32 993	854	297	4 534	1 941	6 813	7 236	334	11 814	1 300	1 155 *	4 683
1984/85	42 470 *	34 094 *	958	308 *	4 848	2 442	7 106	6 981	365	12 257	1 405	1 270 *	4 530
1985/86	43 478 *	35 081 *	1 021	360	5 019	2 725	7 091	7 656 *	350	11 269	1 470	1 306 *	5 211

LOSSES — **PERTES**

1982/83	4 032 *	3 006	43	–	411	339	971	845	57	1 261	50	55 *	–
1983/84	4 385 *	3 369	46	–	385	291	959	810	40	1 764	33	57 *	–
1984/85	4 671 *	3 594	53	–	420	367	1 014	771	64	1 897	22	63 *	–
1985/86	4 556 *	3 419 *	58	–	435	456	1 032	850 *	58	1 530	32	105 *	–

ANIMAL FEED — **ALIMENTATION ANIMALE**

1982/83	545 *	312 *	23	–	–	113 *	206	5	–	112	59	27 *	–
1983/84	490 *	270 *	23	–	–	97 *	191	1	–	124	25	29 *	–
1984/85	743 *	426 *	26	–	–	122 *	286	1	–	250	27	31 *	–
1985/86	730 *	436 *	29	–	–	136 *	262	5 *	–	190	76	32 *	–

HUMAN CONSUMPTION — **CONSOMMATION HUMAINE**

1982/83	36 450 *	29 404	790	320	4 249	1 808	6 019	6 594	277	9 158	1 389	1 027 *	4 819
1983/84	36 073 *	29 341	785	297	4 149	1 553	5 663	6 425	294	9 913	1 242	1 069 *	4 683
1984/85	37 041 *	30 059 *	879	308 *	4 428	1 953	5 806	6 209	301	10 095	1 356	1 176 *	4 530
1985/86	38 583 *	31 617 *	934	360	4 584	2 269	5 797	6 800 *	291	9 806	1 362	1 169 *	5 211

SELF-SUFFICIENCY (%) — **AUTO-APPROVISIONNEMENT (%)**

1982/83	105,0 *	100,0	119,1	71,9	38,5	149,8	122,5	94,2	87,7	121,5	192,5	138,9 *	68,3
1983/84	106,2 *	100,5	116,3	67,7	35,0	175,3	127,8	90,5	83,2	123,4	210,0	142,9 *	60,5
1984/85	107,6 *	101,3 *	112,3	71,4 *	36,9	156,1	130,7	91,5	81,4	123,0	202,1	148,0 *	67,2
1985/86	106,9 *	99,9 *	118,8	70,8	39,4	138,6	134,4	92,1 *	75,1	127,9	200,2	145,5 *	60,8

HUMAN CONSUMPTION (KG/HEAD/YEAR) — **CONSOMMATION HUMAINE(KG/TETE/AN)**

1982/83	113,8 *	108,0	77,3	62,5	69,0	184,1	158,1	120,7	79,2	161,4	96,9	103,0 *	85,5
1983/84	112,4 *	107,6	76,8	58,1	67,7	157,3	147,9	117,2	83,5	174,1	86,3	106,4 *	83,0
1984/85	115,2 *	110,1 *	86,0	60,3 *	72,5	196,9	150,8	112,8	85,1	176,9	93,8	116,1 *	80,1
1985/86	119,7 *	115,6 *	91,3	70,4	75,1	228,1	150,2	123,0 *	82,2	171,4	93,7	114,8 *	91,9

SOURCE: CRONOS-ZPA1 DATA BANK, AGRICULTURAL PRODUCTS

SOURCE: BASE DE DONNEES CRONOS-ZPA1, PRODUITS AGRICOLES

SUPPLY BALANCE SHEET

FRESH FRUITS (EXCL.CITRUS FRUITS

ID 14

BILAN D'APPROVISIONNEMENT

FRUITS FRAIS (SAUF AGRUMES)

1000 T

YEAR ANNÉE	EUR 12	EUR 10	UEBL BLEU	DK	D	GR	E	F	IRL	I	NL	P	UK
USABLE PRODUCTION												**PRODUCTION UTILISABLE**	
1982/83	22 270 *	18 546	437	79	4 021	1 970	3 311	3 515	15	7 321	681	413 *	507
1983/84	20 363 *	16 360	370	72	2 470	2 190	3 587	3 085	16	7 069	611	416 *	477
1984/85	21 166 *	17 138 *	368	77 *	3 088	2 129	3 653	3 630	17	6 695	634	375 *	500
1985/86	19 774 *	15 643	359	71	2 553	2 161	3 751	3 385	17	6 175	475	380 *	447
IMPORTS												**IMPORTATIONS**	
1982/83	3 729 *	3 949	471	138	2 908	8	50	1 175	118	519	758	40 *	1 487
1983/84	3 818 *	4 089	480	164	3 251	7	38	1 243	105	415	845	35 *	1 538
1984/85	4 818 *	5 060	515	156	3 384	6	55	1 184	126	626	947	45 *	2 181
1985/86	4 378 *	4 861 *	567	172	3 522	5	59	1 322 *	116	716	1 035	17 *	1 577
RESOURCES = USES												**RESSOURCES = EMPLOIS**	
1982/83	25 999 *	22 495	908	217	6 929	1 978	3 364	4 690	133	7 840	1 439	453 *	1 994
1983/84	24 181 *	20 449	850	236	5 721	2 197	3 625	4 328	121	7 484	1 456	451 *	2 015
1984/85	25 984 *	22 198 *	883	233 *	6 472	2 135	3 708	4 814	143	7 321	1 581	420 *	2 681
1985/86	24 152 *	20 504 *	926	243	6 075	2 166	3 810	4 707 *	133	6 891	1 510	397 *	2 024
EXPORTS												**EXPORTATIONS**	
1982/83	1 162 *	1 091	225	34	838	347	372	912	22	1 849	432	12 *	65
1983/84	1 041 *	878	248	41	935	414	492	825	16	1 807	480	15 *	71
1984/85	1 643 *	1 409	300	40	1 013	422	566	958	27	2 067	565	10 *	82
1985/86	1 647 *	1 577 *	325	45	1 082	475	625	1 017 *	16	2 195	499	4 *	94
TOTAL DOMESTIC USES												**UTILISATION INTERIEURE TOTALE**	
1982/83	24 817 *	21 384	683	183	6 071	1 631	2 992	3 778	111	5 991	1 007	441 *	1 929
1983/84	23 147 *	19 578	602	195	4 793	1 783	3 133	3 503	105	5 677	976	436 *	1 944
1984/85	24 587 *	21 035 *	583	193 *	5 453	1 713	3 142	4 107	117	5 254	1 016	410 *	2 599
1985/86	22 423 *	18 845 *	601	198	4 911	1 691	3 185	3 690 *	117	4 696	1 011	393 *	1 930
LOSSES												*PERTES*	
1982/83	2 184 *	1 743	58	—	274	222	419	524	5	553	107	22 *	—
1983/84	1 972 *	1 499	51	—	240	204	451	377	5	547	75	22 *	—
1984/85	2 369 *	1 857	52	—	261	213	492	773	5	471	82	20 *	—
1985/86	1 714 *	1 222 *	52	—	248	210	472	510 *	5	140	57	20 *	—
ANIMAL FEED												*ALIMENTATION ANIMALE*	
1982/83	550 *	462 *	38	—	—	38 *	88	202	—	144	40	— *	—
1983/84	309 *	244 *	10	—	—	40 *	65	7	—	185	2	— *	—
1984/85	305 *	236 *	19	—	—	54 *	69	35	—	115	13	— *	—
1985/86	171 *	100 *	15	—	—	—	71	10 *	—	70	5	— *	—
PROCESSING												*TRANSFORMATION*	
1982/83	:	:	—	—	—	652	37	100	:	20	—	15 *	—
1983/84	:	:	—	—	—	741	37	80	:	23	—	15 *	—
1984/85	:	:	—	—	—	704	36	103	:	21	—	15 *	—
1985/86	:	:	—	—	—	745	37	77 *	:	22	—	15 *	—
HUMAN CONSUMPTION												*CONSOMMATION HUMAINE*	
1982/83	20 204 *	17 354	587	183	5 797	719	2 446	2 934	105	4 240	860	404 *	1 929
1983/84	18 900 *	15 923	526	195	4 553	798	2 578	3 039	100	3 869	899	399 *	1 944
1984/85	20 029 *	17 111 *	498	193 *	5 192	744	2 543	2 945	112	3 907	921	375 *	2 599
1985/86	19 212 *	16 251 *	521	198	4 743	737	2 603	3 093 *	111	3 969	949	358 *	1 930
SELF-SUFFICIENCY (%)												**AUTO-APPROVISIONNEMENT (%)**	
1982/83	89,7 *	86,7	64,0	43,2	66,2	120,8	110,7	93,0	13,5	122,2	67,6	93,7 *	26,3
1983/84	88,0 *	83,6	61,5	36,9	51,5	122,8	114,5	88,1	15,2	124,5	62,6	95,4 *	24,5
1984/85	86,1 *	81,5 *	63,1	39,9 *	56,6	124,3	116,3	88,4	14,5	127,4	62,4	91,5 *	19,2
1985/86	88,2 *	83,0 *	59,7	35,9	52,0	127,8	117,8	91,7 *	14,5	131,5	47,0	96,7 *	23,2
HUMAN CONSUMPTION (KG/HEAD/YEAR)												**CONSOMMATION HUMAINE(KG/TETE/AN)**	
1982/83	63,1 *	63,7	57,4	35,8	94,2	73,2	64,3	53,7	30,0	74,7	60,0	40,5 *	34,2
1983/84	58,9 *	58,4	51,5	38,1	74,3	80,8	67,3	55,4	28,4	68,0	62,5	39,7 *	34,4
1984/85	62,3 *	62,7 *	48,7	37,8 *	85,0	75,0	66,1	53,5	31,7	68,4	63,7	37,0 *	46,0
1985/86	59,6 *	59,4 *	50,9	38,7	77,7	74,1	67,5	56,0 *	31,4	69,4	65,3	35,1 *	34,0

SOURCE: CRONOS-ZPA1 DATA BANK, AGRICULTURAL PRODUCTS

SOURCE: BASE DE DONNEES CRONOS-ZPA1, PRODUITS AGRICOLES

SUPPLY BALANCE SHEET

CITRUS FRUITS

ID 15

BILAN D'APPROVISIONNEMENT

AGRUMES

1000 T

YEAR ANNÉE	EUR 12	EUR 10	UEBL BLEU	DK	D	GR	E	F	IRL	I	NL	P	UK
USABLE PRODUCTION												**PRODUCTION UTILISABLE**	
1982/83	6 726	3 534	–	–	–	983	3 024	38	–	2 513	–	168	–
1983/84	8 636	4 630	–	–	–	918	3 874	31	–	3 681	–	132	–
1984/85	6 345	3 687	–	–	–	1 001	2 520	27	–	2 659	–	138	–
1985/86	8 000 *	4 350	–	–	–	879	3 514	37	–	3 434	–	136 *	–
IMPORTS												**IMPORTATIONS**	
1982/83	3 966 *	5 562	287	63	2 453	6	20	1 199	50	106	2 206	–	758
1983/84	3 913 *	5 947	320	73	2 688	3	23	1 326	57	73	2 455	–	839
1984/85	2 542 *	4 847	289	62	2 450	5	20	1 070	59	103	1 827	– *	785
1985/86	4 051 *	5 566 *	371	77	2 465	4	27	1 307 *	62	128	1 996	1 *	839
RESOURCES = USES												**RESSOURCES = EMPLOIS**	
1982/83	10 692 *	9 096	287	63	2 453	989	3 044	1 237	50	2 619	2 206	168	758
1983/84	12 549 *	10 577	320	73	2 688	921	3 897	1 357	57	3 754	2 455	132	839
1984/85	8 887 *	8 534	289	62	2 450	1 006	2 540	1 097	59	2 762	1 827	138 *	785
1985/86	12 051 *	9 916 *	371	77	2 465	883	3 541	1 344 *	62	3 562	1 996	137 *	839
EXPORTS												**EXPORTATIONS**	
1982/83	1 138 *	775	87	21	752	229	1 979	48	2	332	841	– *	29
1983/84	849 *	663	92	26	863	274	2 242	46	4	308	913	1 *	24
1984/85	305 *	718	113	10	810	383	1 912	45	5	509	622	– *	24
1985/86	1 530 *	879 *	131	14	625	416	2 194	57 *	4	546	751	– *	18
CHANGE IN STOCKS												**VARIATION DES STOCKS**	
1982/83	–	–	–	–	–	–	–	–	–	–	–	–	–
1983/84	–	–	–	–	–	–	–	–	–	–	–	–	–
1984/85	– *	–	–	–	–	–	–	–	–	–	–	– *	–
1985/86	– *	– *	–	–	–	–	–	– *	–	–	–	– *	–
TOTAL DOMESTIC USES												**UTILISATION INTERIEURE TOTALE**	
1982/83	9 554 *	8 321	200	42	1 701	760	1 065	1 189	48	2 287	1 365	168 *	729
1983/84	10 390 *	8 604	228	47	1 825	647	1 655	1	53	3 446	1 542	131 *	815
1984/85	8 571 *	7 805	176	52	1 640	612	628	1 052	54	2 253	1 205	138 *	761
1985/86	10 521 *	9 037 *	240	63	1 840	467	1 347	1 287 *	58	3 016	1 245	137 *	821
LOSSES												*PERTES*	
1982/83	776 *	531	4	–	38	123	237	99	2	235	30	8 *	–
1983/84	1 638 *	1 331	4	–	40	279	300	108	2	807	91	7 *	–
1984/85	630 *	400	4	–	35	16	223	88	2	230	25	7 *	–
1985/86	1 148 *	870 *	4	–	37	112	271	105 *	2	585	25	7 *	–
INDUSTRIAL USES												*USAGES INDUSTRIELS*	
1982/83	45	42	–	–	–	–	3	–	–	42	–	–	–
1983/84	154	151	–	–	–	–	3	–	–	151	–	–	–
1984/85	88 *	85	–	–	–	–	3	–	–	85	–	– *	–
1985/86	20 *	20 *	–	–	–	–	–	– *	–	20	–	– *	–
HUMAN CONSUMPTION												*CONSOMMATION HUMAINE*	
1982/83	8 673 *	7 688	196	42	1 663	637	825	1 090	46	1 950	1 335	160 *	729
1983/84	8 271 *	6 795	224	47	1 785	368	1 352	1	51	2 353	1 151	124 *	815
1984/85	7 828 *	7 295	172	52	1 605	596	402	964	52	1 913	1 180	131 *	761
1985/86	9 314 *	8 112 *	236	63	1 803	355	1 072	1 182 *	56	2 376	1 220	130 *	821
SELF-SUFFICIENCY (%)												**AUTO-APPROVISIONNEMENT (%)**	
1982/83	70,4 *	42,5	–	–	–	129,3	283,9	3,2	–	109,9	–	100,0 *	–
1983/84	83,1 *	53,8	–	–	–	141,9	234,1	364,6	–	106,8	–	100,8 *	–
1984/85	74,0 *	47,2	–	–	–	163,6	401,3	2,6	–	118,0	–	100,0 *	–
1985/86	76,0 *	48,1 *	–	–	–	188,2	260,9	2,9 *	–	113,9	–	99,3 *	–
HUMAN CONSUMPTION (KG/HEAD/YEAR)												**CONSOMMATION HUMAINE(KG/TETE/AN)**	
1982/83	27,1 *	28,2	19,2	8,2	27,0	64,9	21,7	20,0	13,2	34,4	93,1	16,0 *	12,9
1983/84	25,8 *	24,9	21,9	9,2	29,1	37,3	35,3	0,0	14,5	41,3	80,0	12,3 *	14,4
1984/85	24,3 *	26,7	16,8	10,2	26,3	60,1	10,4	17,5	14,7	33,5	81,6	12,9 *	13,5
1985/86	28,9 *	29,7 *	23,1	12,3	29,5	35,7	27,8	21,4 *	15,8	41,5	84,0	12,8 *	14,5

SOURCE: CRONOS-ZPA1 DATA BANK, AGRICULTURAL PRODUCTS

SOURCE: BASE DE DONNEES CRONOS-ZPA1, PRODUITS AGRICOLES

SUPPLY BALANCE SHEET

WINE (TOTAL)

ID 16

BILAN D'APPROVISIONNEMENT

VIN (TOTAL)

YEAR ANNÉE	EUR 12	EUR 10	B	DK	D	GR	E	F	IRL	I	L	NL	P	UK
						1000 H								
OFFICIAL PRODUCTION													**PRODUCTION OFFICIELLE**	
1982/83	221 208 *	173 500	3	—	16 133	4 500	39 219	79 953	—	72 648	256	—	8 489 *	7
1983/84	210 549	169 601	2	—	13 397	5 250	32 465	68 547	—	82 200	185	—	8 483	20
1984/85	194 245	149 341	2	—	8 887	5 025	36 249	64 360	—	70 900	152	—	8 655	15
1985/86	189 040	144 636	2	—	6 102	4 782	34 511	71 297	—	62 340	107	—	9 893	6
USABLE PRODUCTION													**PRODUCTION UTILISABLE**	
1982/83	218 675 *	171 935	3	—	16 128	4 500	38 251	79 093	—	71 948	256	—	8 489 *	7
1983/84	207 984	168 243	2	—	13 392	5 250	31 238	67 894	—	81 500	185	—	8 483	20
1984/85	190 498	147 664	2	—	8 882	5 025	34 179	63 418	—	70 170	152	—	8 655	15
1985/86	184 805 *	141 809 *	2	—	6 097	4 782	33 103	70 055	—	60 760 *	107	—	9 893	6
IMPORTS													**IMPORTATIONS**	
1982/83	:	5 082	2 022	879	9 566	5	19	5 472	105	152	146	2 123	:	4 632
1983/84	2 198 *	5 209	2 273	950	9 298	7	20	6 068	113	145	161	2 134	—	5 417
1984/85	1 827 *	5 002	2 155	1 050	9 812	6	27	7 535	123	509	136	2 282	—	5 287
1985/86	2 829 *	3 173 *	1 790 *	989 *	8 335 *	6 *	54 *	4 625 *	118	571 *	137 *	2 133	1	5 036 *
INTRA EUR-10													*INTRA EUR-10*	
1982/83	:	20 020	1 665	695	7 538	5	:	4 928	83	83	143	1 570	:	3 310
1983/84	:	21 357	1 814	767	7 367	6	:	5 478	93	88	154	1 584	:	4 006
1984/85	:	23 893	1 769	853	7 872	6	:	6 924	100	419	129	1 745	:	4 076
1985/86	:	20 567 *	1 712	836 *	7 228	6	:	4 412	95	493	129	1 602	:	4 054
INTRA EUR-12													*INTRA EUR-12*	
1982/83	:	:	1 892	844	7 538	5	3 *	5 248	98	145	145	2 092	:	4 255
1983/84	24 388 *	:	2 082	916	8 051	6	9 *	5 835	107	138	159	2 114	—	4 971
1984/85	27 095 *	:	2 035	1 003	8 404	6	25 *	7 294	115	502	135	2 269	—	5 307
1985/86	20 966 *	:	1 764 *	948 *	7 590 *	5 *	9 *	4 047 *	105	565 *	137 *	2 111	1	3 684 *
RESOURCES = USES													**RESSOURCES = EMPLOIS**	
1982/83	:	177 017	2 025	879	25 694	4 505	38 270	84 565	105	72 100	402	2 123	:	4 639
1983/84	210 162 *	173 452	2 275	950	22 690	5 257	31 258	73 962	113	81 645	346	2 134	8 483	5 437
1984/85	192 325 *	152 666	2 157	1 050	18 694	5 031	34 206	70 953	123	70 679	288	2 282	8 655	5 302
1985/86	187 634 *	144 982 *	1 792 *	989 *	14 432 *	4 788 *	33 157 *	74 680 *	118	61 331 *	244 *	2 133	9 894	5 042 *
EXPORTS													**EXPORTATIONS**	
1982/83	:	8 645	196	22	2 545	212	5 395	9 715	3	15 670	89	54	:	159
1983/84	12 712 *	7 758	167	26	3 036	347	6 539	10 988	2	14 264	87	71	1 446	127
1984/85	16 023 *	11 440	168	34	3 140	1 094	6 358	11 523	2	19 082	85	61	1 427	144
1985/86	15 541 *	8 466 *	111 *	29	2 575 *	970 *	6 052 *	12 374	3	12 719 *	73	44 *	1 422 *	135 *
INTRA EUR-10													*INTRA EUR-10*	
1982/83	:	:	188	10	1 504	152	:	6 887	2	10 802	89	53	:	84
1983/84	:	:	164	16	1 887	271	:	7 472	2	9 859	87	68	:	46
1984/85	:	:	165	16	1 993	661	:	7 817	1	14 040	85	59	:	44
1985/86	:	:	174	:	1 762	691	:	8 610	3	9 717	73	44	:	45
INTRA EUR-12													*INTRA EUR-12*	
1982/83	:	:	188	10	1 504	152	1 663 *	6 990	2	10 802	89	53	:	84
1983/84	:	:	164	16	1 887	271	2 281 *	7 475	2	9 859	87	68	771	52
1984/85	:	:	165	16	1 993	661	1 977 *	7 817	1	14 040	85	59	830	77
1985/86	:	:	109 *	18 *	1 756 *	970 *	1 980 *	8 610	3	9 100 *	73	50	899 *	135 *
FINAL STOCK													**STOCK FINAL**	
1982/83	120 107 *	89 290	387	—	15 941	2 442	23 458 *	47 186	32	21 428	229	500	7 359	1 145
1983/84	134 341 *	109 766 *	389	—	17 107	2 582	18 336 *	47 223	27	40 590 *	256	444	6 239	1 148
1984/85	129 390 *	98 848 *	375 *	—	16 663	2 185	24 769	44 346	29	33 450 *	249 *	486 *	5 773	1 065
1985/86	129 578 *	96 957 *	373 *	—	14 175	2 309	26 508	44 698	29	33 522 *	209 *	523 *	6 113	1 119
OF WHICH: MARKET													*DONT: MARCHE*	
1982/83	:	30 659	385	—	6 861	173	:	12 904	32	8 593	70	500	4 903	1 141
1983/84	:	39 455 *	387	—	7 256	116	:	13 542	27	16 480 *	68	444	4 492	1 135
1984/85	:	33 385	405	—	7 047	174	:	13 937	29	10 172	63	501	3 641	1 057
1985/86	:	31 633	407	—	6 521	153	:	13 103	29	9 706	64	538	3 406	1 112

SOURCE: CRONOS-ZPA1 DATA BANK, AGRICULTURAL PRODUCTS   SOURCE: BASE DE DONNEES CRONOS-ZPA1, PRODUITS AGRICOLES

WINE (TOTAL)　　　　　　　　　　　　　　　　　　　　　　　　　　　VIN (TOTAL)

1000 H

YEAR ANNÉE	EUR 12	EUR 10	B	DK	D	GR	E	F	IRL	I	L	NL	P	UK
CHANGE IN STOCKS												**VARIATION DES STOCKS**		
1982/83	:	12 846	− 27	−	6 011	111	1 375 *	7 274	2	− 677	75	79	:	− 2
1983/84	14 234 *	20 476 *	2	−	1 166	140	− 5 122 *	37	− 5	19 162 *	27	− 56	− 1 120	3
1984/85	− 4 951 *	− 10 918 *	− 14 *	−	− 444	− 397	6 433 *	− 2 877	2	− 7 140 *	− 7 *	42 *	− 466	− 83
1985/86	188 *	− 1 891 *	− 2 *	−	− 2 488	124	1 739	352	−	72 *	− 40 *	37 *	340	54
OF WHICH: MARKET												*DONT: MARCHE*		
1982/83	:	− 1 513	− 26	−	842	− 111	:	8	2	− 2 263	− 40	79	:	− 4
1983/84	:	8 796 *	2	−	395	− 57	:	638	− 5	7 887 *	− 2	− 56	− 411	− 6
1984/85	:	− 6 070 *	18	−	− 209	58	:	395	2	− 6 308 *	− 5	57	− 851	− 78
1985/86	:	− 1 752	2	−	− 526	− 21	:	− 834	−	− 466	1	37	− 235	55
TOTAL DOMESTIC USES												**UTILISATION INTERIEURE TOTALE**		
1982/83	:	155 526	1 856	857	17 138	4 182	31 500	67 576	100	57 107	238	1 990	:	4 482
1983/84	204 121	166 123	2 106	924	18 488	4 770	29 841	62 937	116	69 124	232	2 119	8 157	5 307
1984/85	188 358	151 996	1 971	1 016	15 998	4 334	28 668	62 307	119	58 637	209	2 164	7 694	5 241
1985/86	171 592 *	138 094 *	1 683 *	960 *	14 345 *	3 694 *	25 366 *	61 663 *	115	48 540 *	211 *	2 030 *	8 132 *	4 853 *
LOSSES												*PERTES*		
1982/83	:	963	13	−	−	75	472	584	−	270	1	20	:	−
1983/84	1 344	946	13	−	−	69	398	572	−	270	1	21	−	−
1984/85	1 079	668	12	−	−	70	411	300	−	265	−	21	−	−
1985/86	1 065 *	663 *	12	−	−	69	402	302	−	260	−	20 *	−	−
INDUSTRIAL USES												*USAGES INDUSTRIELS*		
1982/83	:	32 230	2	−	834	494	11 917	20 069	−	10 831	−	−	:	−
1983/84	55 496	44 116	1	−	2 711	1 395	10 494	16 856	−	23 153	−	−	886	−
1984/85	47 211	37 061	1	−	390	1 120	9 559	17 800	−	17 750	−	−	591	−
1985/86	38 281	31 564	1	−	434	675	5 923	17 626	−	12 828	−	−	794	−
OF WHICH: ALCOHOL												*DONT: ALCOOL*		
1982/83	:	31 417	−	−	734	444	11 638	19 809	−	10 430	−	−	:	−
1983/84	54 253	43 262	−	−	2 616	1 350	10 205	16 593	−	22 703	−	−	786	−
1984/85	46 019	36 249	−	−	292	1 080	9 269	17 577	−	17 300	−	−	501	−
1985/86	36 680	30 724	−	−	340	625	5 262	17 381	−	12 378	−	−	694	−
PROCESSING												*TRANSFORMATION*		
1982/83	:	:	−	−	−	−	:	−	−	−	−	−	:	−
1983/84	:	:	−	−	−	−	:	−	−	−	−	−	:	−
1984/85	−	:	−	−	−	−	−	−	−	−	−	−	−	−
1985/86	2 565 *	:	270 *	− *	− *	50 *	366 *	291 *	− *	1 580 *	− *	8 *	− *	− *
HUMAN CONSUMPTION												*CONSOMMATION HUMAINE*		
1982/83	:	122 333	1 841	857	16 304	3 613	19 111	46 923	100	46 006	237	1 970	:	4 482
1983/84	147 281	121 061	2 092	924	15 777	3 306	18 949	45 509	116	45 701	231	2 098	7 271	5 307
1984/85	140 068	114 267	1 958	1 016	15 608	3 144	18 698	44 207	119	40 622	209	2 143	7 103	5 241
1985/86	132 103 *	105 952 *	1 670 *	960 *	13 911 *	2 900 *	18 815	43 735 *	115	35 567	211 *	2 030 *	7 336 *	4 853 *
SELF-SUFFICIENCY (%)												**AUTO-APPROVISIONNEMENT (%)**		
1982/83	:	110,6	0,2	−	94,1	107,6	121,4	117,0	−	126,0	107,6	−	:	0,2
1983/84	101,9	101,3	0,1	−	72,4	110,1	104,7	107,9	−	117,9	79,7	−	104,0	0,4
1984/85	101,1	97,1	0,1	−	55,5	115,9	119,2	101,8	−	119,7	72,7	−	112,5	0,3
1985/86	107,7 *	102,7 *	0,1 *	− *	42,5 *	129,5 *	130,5 *	113,6 *	−	125,2 *	50,7 *	− *	121,7 *	0,1 *
HUMAN CONSUMPTION (KG/HEAD/YEAR)												**CONSOMMATION HUMAINE(KG/TETE/AN)**		
1982/83	:	44,9	18,7	16,7	26,5	36,8	50,2	85,9	2,9	81,1	64,9	13,7	:	7,9
1983/84	45,9	44,4	21,2	18,1	25,7	33,5	49,5	83,0	3,3	80,3	63,1	14,6	72,3	9,4
1984/85	43,6	41,9	19,9	19,9	25,6	31,7	48,6	80,3	3,4	71,2	57,1	14,8	70,1	9,3
1985/86	41,0 *	38,7 *	16,9 *	18,8 *	22,8 *	29,1 *	48,8	79,1 *	3,3	62,2	57,5 *	14,0 *	72,0 *	8,6 *

SOURCE: CRONOS-ZPA1 DATA BANK, AGRICULTURAL PRODUCTS　　　　SOURCE: BASE DE DONNEES CRONOS-ZPA1, PRODUITS AGRICOLES

MIO FU   MIO UF

	EUR 10	B L	DK	D	GR	F	IRL	I	NL	UK
VEGETABLE ORIGIN										**D'ORIGINE VÉGÉTALE**
1981/82	82 452	3 454	5 911	18 384	2 607	20 509	1 649	12 744	6 171	11 023
1982/83	81 774	3 809	5 546	18 534	3 063	20 063	1 711	11 159	5 834	12 055
1983/84	:	3 133	5 564	18 527	2 891	19 309	:	12 536	5 806	11 462
1984/85	:	3 415	5 862	19 597	3 212	:	:	13 978	5 428	11 665
1985/86	:	3 203	5 710	:	2 453	:	:	12 277	7 300	11 335
OF WHICH: CEREALS										*DONT: CÉRÉALES*
1981/82	70 617	2 155	5 713	15 442	2 588	18 761	1 578	12 069	2 650	9 661
1982/83	70 695	2 320	5 454	15 461	3 048	19 012	1 620	10 442	2 498	10 840
1983/84	:	2 332	5 480	15 785	2 860	18 250	:	12 040	2 010	10 735
1984/85	:	2 235	5 748	16 448	3 186	:	:	13 341	1 327	10 176
1985/86	:	2 019	5 488	:	2 425	:	:	11 395	2 626	9 993
PROCESSED BY-PRODUCT										**SOUS-PRODUITS DE TRANSFORMATION**
1981/82	42 804	2 872	2 646	10 412	557	7 104	791	5 705	7 114	5 603
1982/83	44 455	3 099	2 696	10 590	621	7 468	796	5 420	7 911	5 854
1983/84	:	2 797	2 739	10 026	653	6 996	:	5 391	8 345	5 937
1984/85	:	2 550	2 156	9 102	974	:	:	6 126	8 559	5 844
1985/86	:	2 691	2 557	:	719	:	:	6 022	8 651	6 113
OF WHICH: OF THE MILLING INDUSTRY										*DONT: DE MEUNERIE*
1981/82	7 232	657	100	1 286	195	706	189	2 152	783	1 164
1982/83	6 676	604	83	1 176	234	774	188	1 756	764	1 097
1983/84	:	684	69	1 126	234	699	:	1 897	823	1 153
1984/85	:	503	69	1 031	234	:	:	2 036	654	1 068
1985/86	:	501	54	:	234	:	:	1 983	579	1 109
OILCAKES										**TOURTEAUX**
1981/82	23 487	1 322	2 015	6 211	248	4 521	418	2 992	3 135	2 625
1982/83	24 254	1 518	2 041	6 149	269	4 886	385	2 927	3 344	2 735
1983/84	:	1 345	1 928	5 601	288	4 648	:	2 677	3 226	2 550
1984/85	:	1 303	1 657	5 097	262	:	:	3 269	3 279	2 478
1985/86	:	1 465	2 055	:	332	:	:	3 262	3 716	2 559
ANIMAL ORIGIN										**D'ORIGINE ANIMALE**
1981/82	11 364	527	449	2 015	212	3 803	406	1 019	1 701	1 232
1982/83	11 183	585	420	2 092	198	3 813	408	884	1 785	998
1983/84	:	668	407	2 198	160	3 631	:	118	1 152	1 121
1984/85	:	736	421	1 862	143	:	:	794	2 108	612
1985/86	:	:	414	:	114	:	:	859	2 861	659
MILK AND DAIRY PRODUCTS										**LAIT ET PRODUITS DE LAITERIE**
1981/82	7 001	247	278	986	178	2 906	379	915	539	573
1982/83	6 990	324	265	1 037	158	2 866	379	772	600	589
1983/84	:	373	281	1 162	123	2 680	:	0	831	617
1984/85	:	286	258	901	106	:	:	588	948	91
1985/86	:	:	237	:	73	:	:	589	867	96
MARKETABLE FEEDINGSTUFFS										**ALIMENTS COMMERCIALISABLES**
1981/82	136 668	6 853	9 005	30 811	3 375	31 416	2 846	19 468	15 036	17 858
1982/83	137 412	7 493	8 663	31 216	3 883	31 343	2 914	17 463	15 529	18 908
1983/84	:	6 598	8 710	30 742	3 704	29 936	:	18 044	15 303	18 520
1984/85	:	6 700	8 439	30 562	4 328	:	:	20 899	16 095	18 120
1985/86	:	:	8 681	:	3 286	:	:	19 158	18 212	18 108

MIO FU   MIO UF

	EUR 10	B L	DK	D	GR	F	IRL	I	NL	UK
ROOT CROPS										**PLANTES SARCLÉES**
1981/82	6 202	332	930	1 681	3	2 229	38	187	43	759
1982/83	6 187	246	1 103	1 547	4	2 281	38	172	78	718
1983/84	:	257	1 389	1 115	0	1 992	:	151	80	718
1984/85	:	252	123	1 252	0	:	:	190	83	203
1985/86	:	:	1 840	:	0	:	:	159	85	224
GREEN MAIZE										**MAÏS FOURRAGER**
1981/82	19 805	886	0	5 818	16	7 466	0	4 383	1 120	116
1982/83	21 725	773	0	6 422	17	9 070	0	4 225	1 106	112
1983/84	:	794	0	7 238	28	9 180	:	4 055	905	113
1984/85	:	895	0	6 181	28	:	:	4 060	836	66
1985/86	:	:	0	:	26	:	:	3 839	836	113
OTHER GREEN FODDER CROPS										**AUTRES FOURRAGES VERTS**
1981/82	7 857	38	0	2 335	2	2 454	0	2 880	26	122
1982/83	7 336	38	0	1 855	2	2 511	0	2 807	0	123
1983/84	:	43	2 399	2 390	0	2 507	:	2 880	0	123
1984/85	:	61	2 466	2 550	0	:	:	2 984	0	0
1985/86	:	:	2 262	:	0	:	:	2 659	1 136	0
MEADOWS AND GRASSLAND										**PRAIRIES ET PÂTURAGES**
1981/82	12 585	296	0	452	60	10 371	0	1 406	0	0
1982/83	12 584	288	0	495	60	10 353	0	1 388	0	0
1983/84	:	290	0	422	60	11 084	:	0	0	0
1984/85	:	27	0	545	61	:	:	0	0	0
1985/86	:	:	0	:	61	:	:	1 068	0	0
CROP BY-PRODUCTS										**PRODUITS FATALES DES CULTURES**
1981/82	5 399	248	780	1 719	174	339	94	1 129	114	802
1982/83	5 157	231	665	1 639	174	337	92	1 035	77	907
1983/84	:	243	550	1 322	174	310	:	927	93	983
1984/85	:	251	709	1 510	175	:	:	966	65	1 144
1985/86	:	:	662	:	187	:	:	881	70	1 191
OF WHICH: STRAW										*DONT: PAILLE*
1981/82	2 709	29	415	470	132	305	89	760	32	477
1982/83	2 536	26	346	476	132	303	87	660	32	474
1983/84	:	25	324	486	132	282	:	592	40	655
1984/85	:	25	369	495	133	:	:	646	24	760
1985/86	:	:	322	:	145	:	:	592	28	846
NON-MARKETABLE FEEDINGSTUFFS										**ALIMENTS NON COMMERCIALISABLES**
1981/82	168 040	4 526	4 628	31 384	2 808	52 415	12 673	19 493	8 912	30 901
1982/83	168 511	4 255	4 459	31 040	2 783	54 859	12 847	18 807	8 610	30 851
1983/84	:	4 455	4 491	30 388	2 797	53 987	:	16 388	8 666	30 648
1984/85	:	4 632	3 455	31 233	2 825	:	:	14 908	8 635	30 157
1985/86	:	:	4 763	:	2 778	:	:	14 621	9 649	27 800
TOTAL RESOURCES										**RESSOURCES TOTALES**
1981/82	304 709	11 379	13 633	62 195	6 183	83 831	15 819	38 961	23 949	48 759
1982/83	305 923	11 748	13 122	62 256	6 665	86 202	15 761	36 270	24 139	49 760
1983/84	:	11 053	13 201	61 130	6 501	83 923	:	34 432	23 968	49 168
1984/85	:	11 332	11 894	61 794	7 153	:	:	35 807	24 730	48 277
1985/86	:	:	13 444	:	6 063	:	:	33 780	27 861	45 908

% FU   % UF

	EUR 10	B L	DK	D	GR	F	IRL	I	NL	UK
VEGETABLE ORIGIN										**D'ORIGINE VÉGÉTALE**
1981/82	27,06	30,35	43,36	29,56	42,16	24,46	10,42	32,71	25,77	22,61
1982/83	26,73	32,42	42,26	29,77	45,96	23,27	10,86	30,77	24,17	24,23
1983/84	:	28,35	42,15	30,31	44,47	23,01	:	36,41	24,22	23,31
1984/85	:	30,14	49,29	31,71	44,90	:	:	39,04	21,95	24,16
1985/86	:	:	42,47	:	40,46	:	:	36,34	26,20	24,69
OF WHICH: CEREALS										**DONT: CÉRÉALES**
1981/82	23,18	18,94	41,91	24,83	41,86	22,38	9,98	30,98	11,07	19,81
1982/83	23,11	19,75	41,56	24,83	45,73	22,06	10,28	28,79	10,35	21,78
1983/84	:	21,10	41,58	25,82	44,13	21,75	:	34,98	11,72	21,00
1984/85	:	19,72	48,33	26,62	44,54	:	:	37,26	5,37	21,08
1985/86	:	:	40,82	:	40,00	:	:	33,73	9,43	21,77
PROCESSED BY-PRODUCT										**SOUS-PRODUITS DE TRANSFORMATION**
1981/82	14,05	25,24	19,41	16,74	9,01	8,47	5,00	14,64	29,70	11,49
1982/83	14,53	26,38	20,55	17,01	9,32	8,66	5,05	14,94	32,77	11,76
1983/84	:	25,31	20,75	16,40	10,04	8,34	:	15,66	34,82	12,07
1984/85	:	22,50	18,13	14,73	13,62	:	:	17,11	34,61	12,11
1985/86	:	:	19,02	:	11,86	:	:	17,83	31,05	13,32
OF WHICH: OF THE MILLING INDUSTRY										**DONT: DE MEUNERIE**
1981/82	2,37	5,77	0,73	2,07	3,15	0,84	1,19	5,52	3,27	2,39
1982/83	2,18	5,14	0,63	1,89	3,51	0,90	1,19	4,84	3,17	2,20
1983/84	:	6,19	0,52	1,84	3,60	0,83	:	5,51	3,43	2,35
1984/85	:	4,44	0,58	1,67	3,27	:	:	5,69	2,64	2,21
1985/86	:	:	0,40	:	3,86	:	:	5,87	2,08	2,42
OILCAKES										**TOURTEAUX**
1981/82	7,71	11,62	14,78	9,99	4,01	5,39	2,64	7,68	13,09	5,38
1982/83	7,93	12,92	15,55	9,88	4,04	5,67	2,44	8,07	13,85	5,50
1983/84	:	12,17	14,60	9,16	4,43	5,54	:	7,77	13,46	5,19
1984/85	:	11,50	13,93	8,25	3,66	:	:	9,13	13,26	5,13
1985/86	:	:	15,29	:	5,48	:	:	9,66	13,34	5,57
ANIMAL ORIGIN										**D'ORIGINE ANIMALE**
1981/82	3,73	4,63	3,29	3,24	3,43	4,54	2,57	2,62	7,10	2,53
1982/83	3,66	4,98	3,20	3,36	2,97	4,42	2,59	2,44	7,39	2,01
1983/84	:	6,04	3,08	3,58	2,46	4,33	:	0,34	4,81	2,28
1984/85	:	6,49	3,54	3,01	2,00	:	:	2,22	8,52	1,27
1985/86	:	:	3,08	:	1,88	:	:	2,54	10,27	1,44
MILK AND DAIRY PRODUCTS										**LAIT ET PRODUITS DE LAITERIE**
1981/82	2,30	2,17	2,04	1,59	2,88	3,47	2,40	2,35	2,25	1,18
1982/83	2,28	2,76	2,02	1,67	2,37	3,32	2,40	2,13	2,49	1,18
1983/84	:	3,37	2,13	1,90	1,89	3,19	:	0,00	3,47	1,25
1984/85	:	2,52	2,17	1,46	1,48	:	:	1,64	3,83	0,19
1985/86	:	:	1,76	:	1,20	:	:	1,74	3,11	0,21
MARKETABLE FEEDINGSTUFFS										**ALIMENTS COMMERCIALISABLES**
1981/82	44,85	60,22	66,05	49,54	54,59	37,48	17,99	49,97	62,78	36,63
1982/83	44,92	63,78	66,02	50,14	58,26	36,36	18,49	48,15	64,33	38,00
1983/84	:	59,69	65,98	50,29	56,98	35,67	:	52,40	63,85	37,67
1984/85	:	59,12	70,95	49,46	60,51	:	:	58,37	65,08	37,53
1985/86	:	:	64,57	:	54,20	:	:	56,71	65,37	39,44

% FU   % UF

	EUR 10	B L	DK	D	GR	F	IRL	I	NL	UK
ROOT CROPS										**PLANTES SARCLÉES**
1981/82	2,04	2,92	6,82	2,70	0,05	2,66	0,24	0,48	0,18	1,56
1982/83	2,02	2,09	8,41	2,48	0,06	2,65	0,24	0,47	0,32	1,44
1983/84	:	2,33	10,52	1,82	0,00	2,37	:	0,44	0,33	1,46
1984/85	:	2,22	1,03	2,03	0,00	:	:	0,53	0,34	0,42
1985/86	:	:	13,69	:	0,00	:	:	0,47	0,31	0,49
GREEN MAIZE										**MAÏS FOURRAGER**
1981/82	6,50	7,79	0,00	9,35	0,26	8,91	0,00	11,25	4,68	0,24
1982/83	7,10	6,58	0,00	10,32	0,26	10,52	0,00	11,65	4,58	0,23
1983/84	:	7,18	0,00	11,84	0,43	10,94	:	11,78	3,78	0,23
1984/85	:	7,90	0,00	10,00	0,39	:	:	11,34	3,38	0,14
1985/86	:	:	0,00	:	0,43	:	:	11,36	3,00	0,25
OTHER GREEN FODDER CROPS										**AUTRES FOURRAGES VERTS**
1981/82	2,58	0,33	0,00	3,75	0,03	2,93	0,00	7,39	0,11	0,25
1982/83	2,40	0,32	0,00	2,98	0,03	2,91	0,00	7,74	0,00	0,25
1983/84	:	0,39	18,17	3,91	0,00	2,99	:	8,36	0,00	0,25
1984/85	:	0,54	20,73	4,13	0,00	:	:	8,33	0,00	0,00
1985/86	:	:	16,83	:	0,00	:	:	7,87	4,08	0,00
MEADOWS AND GRASSLAND										**PRAIRIES ET PÂTURAGES**
1981/82	4,13	2,60	0,00	0,73	0,97	12,37	0,00	3,61	0,00	0,00
1982/83	4,11	2,45	0,00	0,80	0,90	12,01	0,00	3,83	0,00	0,00
1983/84	:	2,62	0,00	0,69	0,92	13,21	:	0,00	0,00	0,00
1984/85	:	0,24	0,00	0,88	0,85	:	:	0,00	0,00	0,00
1985/86	:	:	0,00	:	1,01	:	:	3,16	0,00	0,00
CROP BY-PRODUCTS										**PRODUITS FATALES DES CULTURES**
1981/82	1,77	2,18	5,72	2,76	2,81	0,40	0,59	2,90	0,48	1,64
1982/83	1,69	1,97	5,07	2,63	2,61	0,39	0,58	2,85	0,32	1,82
1983/84	:	2,20	4,17	2,16	2,68	0,37	:	2,69	0,39	2,00
1984/85	:	2,21	5,96	2,44	2,45	:	:	2,70	0,26	2,37
1985/86	:	:	4,92	:	3,08	:	:	2,61	0,25	2,59
OF WHICH: STRAW										*DONT: PAILLE*
1981/82	0,89	0,25	3,04	0,76	2,13	0,36	0,56	1,95	0,13	0,98
1982/83	0,83	0,22	2,64	0,76	1,98	0,35	0,55	1,82	0,13	0,95
1983/84	:	0,23	2,45	0,80	2,03	0,34	:	1,72	0,17	1,33
1984/85	:	0,22	3,10	0,80	1,86	:	:	1,80	0,10	1,57
1985/86	:	:	2,40	:	2,39	:	:	1,75	0,10	1,84
NON-MARKETABLE FEEDINGSTUFFS										**ALIMENTS NON COMMERCIALISABLES**
1981/82	55,15	39,78	33,95	50,46	45,41	62,52	80,11	50,03	37,21	63,37
1982/83	55,08	36,22	33,98	49,86	41,76	63,64	81,51	51,85	35,67	62,00
1983/84	:	40,31	34,02	49,71	43,02	64,33	:	47,60	36,16	62,33
1984/85	:	40,88	29,05	50,54	39,49	:	:	41,63	34,92	62,47
1985/86	:	:	35,43	:	45,82	:	:	43,28	34,63	60,56
TOTAL RESOURCES										**RESSOURCES TOTALES**
1981/82	100,00	100,00	100,00	100,00	100,00	100,00	100,00	100,00	100,00	100,00
1982/83	100,00	100,00	100,00	100,00	100,00	100,00	100,00	100,00	100,00	100,00
1983/84	:	100,00	100,00	100,00	100,00	100,00	:	100,00	100,00	100,00
1984/85	:	100,00	100,00	100,00	100,00	:	:	100,00	100,00	100,00
1985/86	:	:	100,00	:	100,00	:	:	100,00	100,00	100,00

I E

Animal production

Production animale

1000 HEAD   1000 TETES

YEAR ANNÉE	EUR 12	EUR 10	B	DK	D	EL	ES	F	IRL	I	L	NL	P	UK
TOTAL														**TOTAL**
1985	:	77 550	2 943	2 623	15 627	776	:	22 802	5 779	9 009	220	5 076	:	12 695
1986	80 717	75 763	2 932	2 490	15 305	761	4 954	22 171	5 626	8 866	214	4 922	—	12 476
ANIMALS UNDER 1 YEAR OLD													**ANIMAUX DE MOINS D'1 AN**	
1985	:	22 386	760	998	5 463	281	:	5 756	1 387	2 562	53	1 556	:	3 571
1986	23 427	22 110	772	970	5 385	245	1 317	5 698	1 350	2 514	52	1 578	—	3 547
SLAUGHTER ANIMALS UNDER 1 YEAR OLD											**ANIMAUX DE BOUCHERIE DE MOINS D'1 AN**			
1985	:	2 550	111	6	223	120	:	856	—	549	1	652	:	32
1986	3 006	2 443	99	6	227	106	563	795	—	544	0	636	—	29
OTHER ANIMALS UNDER 1 YEAR OLD (MALES)										**AUTRES ANIMAUX DE MOINS D'1 AN (MALES)**				
1985	:	8 782	228	484	2 556	77	:	1 837	751	856	17	204	:	1 772
1986	9 262	8 968	246	480	2 490	58	294	2 092	738	831	17	267	—	1 749
OTHER ANIMALS UNDER 1 YEAR OLD (FEMALES)										**AUTRES ANIMAUX DE MOINS D'1 AN (FEMELLES)**				
1985	:	11 053	421	508	2 684	84	:	3 063	635	1 157	35	700	:	1 767
1986	11 159	10 699	427	484	2 667	81	460	2 811	612	1 139	34	675	—	1 769
MALES 1 YEAR OLD BUT UNDER 2													**MALES DE 1 A 2 ANS**	
1985	:	6 144	155	71	1 544	51	:	1 189	822	917	13	129	:	1 254
1986	6 187	6 046	161	58	1 440	61	141	1 232	815	911	12	120	—	1 235
SLAUGHTER FEMALES 1 YEAR OLD BUT UNDER 2											**FEMELLES DE BOUCHERIE DE 1 A 2 ANS**			
1985	:	2 380	96	14	366	11	:	489	326	165	6	22	:	885
1986	2 499	2 445	77	14	364	10	54	585	322	165	5	21	—	881
OTHER FEMALES 1 YEAR OLD BUT UNDER 2												**AUTRES FEMELLES DE 1 A 2 ANS**		
1985	:	8 292	400	424	1 716	37	:	2 569	241	980	32	800	:	1 094
1986	8 286	7 847	392	395	1 655	41	439	2 387	229	975	31	751	—	991
MALES 2 YEARS OLD AND OVER													**MALES DE 2 ANS ET PLUS**	
1985	:	2 277	53	9	179	6	:	746	660	124	6	15	:	478
1986	2 202	2 127	50	9	165	6	75	667	631	123	6	14	—	456
SLAUGHTER HEIFERS 2 YEARS OLD AND OVER											**GENISSES DE BOUCHERIE DE 2 ANS ET PLUS**			
1985	:	1 040	107	6	62	6	:	404	171	50	4	12	:	218
1986	1 082	1 048	118	6	60	2	34	400	167	48	4	11	—	232
OTHER HEIFERS 2 YEARS OLD AND OVER												**AUTRES GENISSES DE 2 ANS ET PLUS**		
1985	:	4 695	239	129	673	40	:	1 887	232	651	20	209	:	616
1986	4 488	4 278	226	109	666	27	210	1 647	216	648	18	167	—	554
COWS 2 YEARS OLD AND OVER													**VACHES DE 2 ANS ET PLUS**	
1985	:	30 281	1 133	972	5 625	344	:	9 763	1 942	3 503	86	2 333	:	4 579
1986	32 490	29 806	1 136	929	5 569	368	2 684	9 555	1 897	3 426	86	2 260	—	4 580
DAIRY COWS 2 YEARS OLD AND OVER												**VACHES LAITIERES DE 2 ANS ET PLUS**		
1985	:	24 303	951	913	5 451	219	:	6 506	1 528	3 075	70	2 333	:	3 257
1986	25 638	23 852	939	865	5 391	233	1 786	6 359	1 490	3 004	68	2 260	—	3 242
OTHER COWS 2 YEARS OLD AND OVER (INCL. FEMALE BUFFALOES)										**AUTRES VACHES DE 2 ANS ET PLUS (Y.C. BUFFLONNES)**				
1985	:	5 978	182	59	173	126	:	3 257	415	428	16	—	:	1 323
1986	6 853	5 955	197	64	178	135	898	3 196	407	422	17	—	—	1 338
MALE BUFFALOES													**BUFFLES MALES**	
1985	:	57	—	—	—	—	:	—	—	57	—	—	:	—
1986	57	57	—	—	—	—	—	—	—	57	—	—	—	—

1000 HEAD   **1000 TETES**

YEAR ANNÉE	EUR 12	EUR 10	B	DK	D	EL	ES	F	IRL	I	L	NL	P	UK
TOTAL														**TOTAL**
1985	:	80 676	3 093	2 618	15 959	797	:	23 689	6 907	9 229	225	5 248	:	12 911
1986	85 595	79 233	3 067	2 494	15 806	790	5 029	23 570	6 655	8 971	223	5 123	1 333	12 534
1987	:	:	3 054	:	15 400	793	:	22 274	:	:	217	:	:	12 182
% 87/86	:	:	−0,4	—	−2,6	0,4	:	−5,5	:	:	−2,5	:	:	−2,8
ANIMALS UNDER 1 YEAR OLD														**ANIMAUX DE MOINS D'1 AN**
1985	:	23 268	812	999	5 609	284	:	6 054	1 647	2 569	59	1 624	:	3 612
1986	24 784	22 875	799	952	5 371	259	1 496	6 134	1 613	2 507	59	1 638	413	3 544
1987	:	:	809	:	5 289	261	:	5 672	:	:	56	:	:	3 459
% 87/86	:	:	1,3	:	−1,5	0,8	:	−7,5	:	:	−3,9	:	:	−2,4
SLAUGHTER ANIMALS UNDER 1 YEAR OLD														**ANIMAUX DE BOUCHERIE DE MOINS D'1 AN**
1985	:	2 638	131	6	220	137	:	887	0	585	2	638	:	33
1986	3 441	2 717	119	6	222	125	657	944	0	576	2	690	67	33
1987	:	:	136	:	215	125	:	872	:	:	2	:	:	34
% 87/86	:	:	14,7	:	−3,5	—	:	−1,1	:	:	− 16,6	:	:	4,0
OTHER ANIMALS UNDER 1 YEAR OLD (MALES)														**AUTRES ANIMAUX DE MOINS D'1 AN (MALES)**
1985	:	9 483	251	481	2 663	65	:	2 337	886	772	19	227	:	1 783
1986	9 740	9 242	253	455	2 516	59	334	2 338	871	749	19	227	165	1 756
1987	:	:	252	:	2 486	51	:	2 160	:	:	18	:	:	1 696
% 87/86	:	:	−0,2	:	−1,2	−13,6	:	−7,6	:	:	−3,0	:	:	−3,4
OTHER ANIMALS UNDER 1 YEAR OLD (FEMALES)														**AUTRES ANIMAUX DE MOINS D'1 AN (FEMELLES)**
1985	:	11 148	430	512	2 727	82	:	2 830	761	1 212	39	759	:	1 797
1986	11 603	10 917	428	491	2 631	76	505	2 851	743	1 182	38	721	181	1 756
1987	:	:	415	:	2 589	85	:	2 601	:	:	36	:	:	1 730
% 87/86	:	:	−2,9	:	−1,6	11,8	:	−8,8	:	:	−3,6	:	:	−1,5
MALES 1 YEAR OLD BUT UNDER 2														**MALES DE 1 A 2 ANS**
1985	:	6 810	190	68	1 555	63	:	1 531	999	991	13	142	:	1 258
1986	7 027	6 815	193	58	1 580	78	110	1 555	1 021	966	12	159	103	1 193
1987	:	:	195	:	1 598	80	:	1 493	:	:	12	:	:	1 165
% 87/86	:	:	0,9	:	1,1	2,6	:	−4,0	:	:	−4,0	:	:	−2,3
SLAUGHTER FEMALES 1 YEAR OLD BUT UNDER 2														**FEMELLES DE BOUCHERIE DE 1 A 2 ANS**
1985	:	2 674	102	14	356	12	:	630	415	197	4	24	:	921
1986	2 697	2 640	100	14	351	11	36	625	428	185	5	28	21	893
1987	:	:	91	:	399	13	:	587	:	:	5	:	:	896
% 87/86	:	:	−9,3	:	13,6	18,2	:	−6,1	:	:	7,3	:	:	0,4
OTHER FEMALES 1 YEAR OLD BUT UNDER 2														**AUTRES FEMELLES DE 1 A 2 ANS**
1985	:	8 666	416	450	1 833	42	:	2 622	300	978	31	826	:	1 170
1986	8 770	8 192	392	422	1 845	42	476	2 451	261	950	30	743	102	1 057
1987	:	:	394	:	1 727	40	:	2 376	:	:	29	:	:	999
% 87/86	:	:	0,6	:	−6,4	−4,8	:	−3,0	:	:	−2,7	:	:	−5,5
MALES 2 YEARS OLD AND OVER														**MALES DE 2 ANS ET PLUS**
1985	:	2 776	63	11	207	5	:	827	979	142	7	16	:	519
1986	2 697	2 594	63	10	212	7	64	756	912	137	7	18	39	474
1987	:	:	61	:	197	6	:	746	:	:	6	:	:	449
% 87/86	:	:	−3,0	:	−6,8	−14,3	:	−1,2	:	:	− 12,4	:	:	−5,2
SLAUGHTER HEIFERS 2 YEARS OLD AND OVER														**GENISSES DE BOUCHERIE DE 2 ANS ET PLUS**
1985	:	1 189	106	6	64	2	:	471	254	41	5	15	:	226
1986	1 229	1 206	115	6	68	3	15	492	232	40	5	28	8	218
1987	:	:	115	:	76	1	:	499	:	:	5	:	:	220
% 87/86	:	:	−0,1	:	12,0	−66,7	:	1,6	:	:	2,3	:	:	1,0
OTHER HEIFERS 2 YEARS OLD AND OVER														**AUTRES GENISSES DE 2 ANS ET PLUS**
1985	:	4 877	262	119	740	23	:	1 930	237	636	22	188	:	721
1986	5 064	4 852	260	112	796	18	166	1 914	204	644	22	174	46	709
1987	:	:	240	:	737	21	:	1 736	:	:	22	:	:	619
% 87/86	:	:	−7,6	:	−7,3	16,7	:	−9,3	:	:	−2,8	:	:	−12,7
COWS 2 YEARS OLD AND OVER														**VACHES DE 2 ANS ET PLUS**
1985	:	30 360	1 146	951	5 595	367	:	9 624	2 078	3 620	84	2 412	:	4 483
1986	33 266	29 998	1 146	920	5 586	368	2 666	9 646	1 984	3 486	83	2 334	601	4 446
1987	:	:	1 149	:	5 376	370	:	9 165	:	:	82	:	:	4 375
% 87/86	:	:	0,3	:	−3,8	0,5	:	−5,0	:	:	−1,4	:	:	−1,6
DAIRY COWS 2 YEARS OLD AND OVER														**VACHES LAITIERES DE 2 ANS ET PLUS**
1985	:	24 403	973	897	5 445	225	:	6 398	1 633	3 201	69	2 412	:	3 150
1986	26 165	23 906	943	864	5 419	241	1 875	6 304	1 527	3 069	67	2 334	384	3 138
1987	:	:	918	:	5 189	245	:	5 892	:	:	65	:	:	3 036
% 87/86	:	:	−2,7	:	−4,2	1,7	:	−6,5	:	:	−3,4	:	:	−3,3
OTHER COWS 2 YEARS OLD AND OVER (INCL. FEMALE BUFFALOES)														**AUTRES VACHES DE 2 ANS ET PLUS (Y.C. BUFFLONNES)**
1985	:	5 957	173	54	150	141	:	3 226	446	420	15	—	:	1 333
1986	7 101	6 093	203	56	166	127	791	3 342	457	418	16	—	217	1 308
1987	:	:	231	:	187	125	:	3 273	:	:	17	:	:	1 339
% 87/86	:	:	14,1	:	12,4	−1,6	:	−2,0	:	:	7,2	:	:	2,4
MALE BUFFALOES														**BUFFLES MALES**
1985	:	57	—	—	—	—	:	—	—	57	—	—	:	—
1986	56	56	—	—	—	—	—	—	—	56	—	—	:	—
1987	:	:	—	:	—	—	:	—	:	:	—	:	:	—
% 87/86	:	:	—	:	—	—	:	—	:	:	—	:	:	—

I E 2

1000 HEAD

1000 TETES

YEAR ANNÉE	EUR 12	EUR 10	B	DK	D	EL	ES	F	IRL	I	L	NL	P	UK
TOTAL														**TOTAL**
1985	:	79 820	5 646	9 278	23 965	1 102	:	10 451	1 004	8 365	68	12 008	:	7 933
1986	97 649	82 901	5 595	9 417	24 905	1 068	14 748	11 097	999	8 463	70	13 234	– :	8 052
1987	103 187	84 632	5 652	9 160	24 614	1 143	16 122	11 766	994	8 520	74	14 409	2 433	8 300
% 87/86	:	2,1	1,0	–2,7	–1,2	7,0	:	6,0	–0,5	0,7	4,5	8,9	:	3,1
PIGLETS (<20 KG)													**PORCELETS (<20 KG)**	
1985	:	23 966	1 586	2 952	7 512	394	:	2 710	237	2 169	30	4 196	:	2 180
1986	28 062 :	24 392	1 553	3 032	7 668	390	3 671	2 800	239	1 818	31	4 557	– :	2 304
1987	30 553	25 179	1 685	3 029	7 619	390	4 615	3 087	225	1 820	31	4 952	759	2 341
% 87/86	:	3,2	8,5	–0,1	–0,6	–0,0	:	10,3	–5,7	0,1	2,1	8,7	:	1,6
YOUNG PIGS (20-50 KG)													**JEUNES PORCS (20-50 KG)**	
1985	:	19 895	1 294	2 586	5 558	277	:	3 062	315	2 075	12	2 481	:	2 234
1986	25 334 :	21 018	1 374	2 620	5 795	278	4 317	3 308	295	1 970	13	3 119	– :	2 246
1987	26 725	21 713	1 362	2 751	5 790	286	4 331	3 506	310	1 982	13	3 387	681	2 327
% 87/86	:	3,3	–0,9	5,0	–0,1	3,0	:	6,0	5,2	0,6	1,0	8,6	:	3,6
PIGS FOR FATTENING (>50 KG)													**PORCS A L'ENGRAIS (>50 KG)**	
1985	:	26 490	2 081	2 651	7 966	257	:	3 471	332	3 219	14	3 937	:	2 563
1986	32 898 :	27 864	1 987	2 650	8 411	240	5 034	3 793	348	3 864	15	4 033	– :	2 524
1987	33 676	27 949	1 876	2 291	8 261	302	5 092	3 890	346	3 902	18	4 416	635	2 647
% 87/86	:	0,3	–5,6	–13,5	–1,8	25,8	:	2,6	–0,5	1,0	18,5	9,5	:	4,9
PIGS FOR FATTENING (50-80 KG)													**PORCS A L'ENGRAIS (50-80 KG)**	
1985	:	16 131	1 054	1 982	4 997	175	:	1 908	245	1 409	9	2 501	:	1 851
1986	20 443 :	17 028	1 265	2 067	5 248	166	3 415	2 043	267	1 598	10	2 530	– :	1 833
1987	20 852	17 032	1 161	1 822	5 128	181	3 341	2 161	264	1 613	10	2 770	479	1 921
% 87/86	:	0,0	–8,2	–11,9	–2,3	9,1	:	5,8	–0,9	0,9	–4,4	9,5	:	4,8
PIGS FOR FATTENING (80-110 KG)													**PORCS A L'ENGRAIS (80-110 KG)**	
1985	:	8 872	900	651	2 826	76	:	1 395	69	977	5	1 368	:	605
1986	10 676 :	9 168	712	568	3 011	70	1 508	1 576	66	1 159	5	1 405	– :	596
1987	11 004	9 234	695	455	3 001	100	1 643	1 582	67	1 169	8	1 539	127	618
% 87/86	:	0,7	–2,4	–19,9	–0,4	43,6	:	0,4	2,0	0,9	68,5	9,5	:	3,6
PIGS FOR FATTENING (>110 KG)													**PORCS A L'ENGRAIS (>110 KG)**	
1985	:	1 487	127	18	143	6	:	168	17	833	0	68	:	107
1986	1 779 :	1 668	9	15	152	4	111	173	15	1 107	0	98	– :	94
1987	1 820	1 683	20	14	132	20	108	147	15	1 120	1	107	29	108
% 87/86	:	0,9	122,2	–6,7	–13,1	419,9 .	:	–15,2	–4,0	1,1	19,8	9,2	:	14,3
BREEDING BOARS (>50 KG)													**VERRATS REPRODUCTEURS (>50 KG)**	
1985	:	414	29	38	115	12	:	66	5	52	1	51	:	44
1986	493 :	414	26	40	118	13	79	68	5	45	1	53	– :	46
1987	555	425	25	40	117	13	103	74	5	45	1	57	27	47
% 87/86	:	2,7	–2,0	–	–0,2	3,6	:	9,5	–4,0	0,7	–8,4	7,5	:	1,8
BREEDING SOWS (>50 KG)													**TRUIES D'ELEVAGE (>50 KG)**	
1985	:	9 055	656	1 051	2 814	161	:	1 142	115	850	11	1 343	:	912
1986	10 484 :	9 214	656	1 075	2 914	148	1 271	1 129	113	766	11	1 472	– :	930
1987	11 677	9 365	704	1 049	2 827	153	1 981	1 207	108	771	11	1 597	331	938
% 87/86	:	1,6	7,3	–2,4	–3,0	3,2	:	7,0	–4,0	0,6	–2,6	8,5	:	0,8
MATED SOWS													**TRUIES SAILLIES**	
1985	:	5 778	423	639	1 780	94	:	698	78	592	8	832	:	634
1986	6 815 :	5 976	440	669	1 863	94	838	712	77	569	8	905	– :	640
1987	7 519	6 075	469	650	1 797	96	1 242	767	77	573	7	986	202	654
% 87/86	:	1,7	6,5	–2,8	–3,5	1,7	:	7,7	0,3	0,6	–4,5	9,0	:	2,3
OF WHICH: SOWS MATED FOR THE FIRST TIME													**DONT: TRUIES SAILLIES POUR LA PREMIERE FOIS**	
1985	:	1 318	99	161	398	24	:	148	14	177	2	185	:	111
1986	1 548 :	1 320	103	160	424	22	228	162	15	142	2	181	– :	108
1987	1 610	1 306	112	153	385	21	241	169	15	143	2	197	63	110
% 87/86	:	–1,1	8,6	–4,4	–9,3	–5,3	:	4,4	–2,6	0,5	–14,9	8,8	:	1,6
BREEDING SOWS NOT MATED													**TRUIES NON SAILLIES**	
1985	:	3 278	233	412	1 034	67	:	444	37	258	4	511	:	278
1986	3 670 :	3 237	216	406	1 051	54	432	417	36	197	4	567	– :	291
1987	4 158	3 290	235	399	1 031	57	739	440	32	198	4	611	129	284
% 87/86	:	1,6	9,0	–1,7	–1,9	5,6	:	5,6	–13,0	0,7	1,6	7,8	:	–2,4
OF WHICH: BREEDING GILTS NOT YET MATED													**DONT: JEUNES TRUIES NON SAILLIES**	
1985	:	1 071	89	136	284	7	:	162	10	106	1	189	:	87
1986	1 209 :	1 056	82	130	296	12	154	141	10	83	1	210	– :	92
1987	1 294	1 092	96	135	290	14	171	151	8	83	1	227	31	87
% 87/86	:	:	17,1	3,8	–2,0	:	:	7,5	–15,5	–0,1	13,5	8,1	:	–5,0

1000 HEAD   **1000 TETES**

YEAR / ANNÉE	EUR 12	EUR 10	B	DK	D	EL	ES	F	IRL	I	L	NL	P	UK
TOTAL														**TOTAL**
1985	:	81 854	5 250	9 552	24 813	1 126	:	10 804	1 008	8 890	73	12 379	:	7 958
1986	99 613:	83 827	5 756	9 760	24 959	1 083	15 786	10 755	1 000	8 937	74	13 488	–:	8 017
1987	:	:	:	9 685	24 989	:	:	12 059	995	:	75	13 923	:	:
% 87/86	:	:	:	–0,8	0,1	:	:	12,1	–0,4	:	1,9	3,2	:	:
PIGLETS (<20 KG)														**PORCELETS (<20 KG)**
1985	:	23 511	1 436	2 980	7 462	368	:	2 755	253	1 737	28	4 295	:	2 196
1986	28 234:	24 127	1 542	3 056	7 684	383	4 107	2 615	234	1 759	29	4 575	–:	2 251
1987	:	:	:	3 048	7 389	:	:	3 004	229	:	30	5 020	:	:
% 87/86	:	:	:	–0,3	–3,8	:	:	14,9	–2,3	:	4,2	9,7	:	:
YOUNG PIGS (20-50 KG)														**JEUNES PORCS (20-50 KG)**
1985	:	20 644	1 364	2 758	6 044	298	:	3 087	306	1 939	16	2 538	:	2 295
1986	26 205:	21 612	1 591	3 040	5 845	309	4 593	3 178	291	1 938	16	3 103	–:	2 301
1987	:	:	:	2 991	6 039	:	:	3 722	313	:	17	3 225	:	:
% 87/86	:	:	:	–1,6	3,3	:	:	17,1	7,6	:	2,8	3,9	:	:
PIGS FOR FATTENING (>50 KG)														**PORCS A L'ENGRAIS (>50 KG)**
1985	:	28 221	1 767	2 700	8 317	285	:	3 762	330	4 406	17	4 121	:	2 516
1986	33 631:	28 430	1 914	2 548	8 405	226	5 201	3 762	356	4 428	17	4 274	–:	2 500
1987	:	:	:	2 542	8 647	:	:	4 048	341	:	17	4 456	:	:
% 87/86	:	:	:	–0,2	2,9	:	:	7,6	–4,2	:	1,3	4,3	:	:
PIGS FOR FATTENING (50-80 KG)														**PORCS A L'ENGRAIS (50-80 KG)**
1985	:	17 417	1 117	2 136	5 350	214	:	2 041	245	1 874	12	2 609	:	1 818
1986	21 202:	17 537	1 242	2 005	5 377	166	3 665	2 129	270	1 875	11	2 637	–:	1 825
1987	:	:	:	2 023	5 397	:	:	2 251	261	:	11	2 776	:	:
% 87/86	:	:	:	0,9	0,4	:	:	5,7	–3,4	:	3,3	5,3	:	:
PIGS FOR FATTENING (80-110 KG)														**PORCS A L'ENGRAIS (80-110 KG)**
1985	:	9 001	628	550	2 840	65	:	1 534	67	1 270	5	1 449	:	593
1986	10 545:	9 093	664	530	2 882	56	1 452	1 479	70	1 285	6	1 542	–:	580
1987	:	:	:	506	3 116	:	:	1 665	65	:	6	1 573	:	:
% 87/86	:	:	:	–4,5	8,1	:	:	12,6	–7,5	:	0,7	2,0	:	:
PIGS FOR FATTENING (>110 KG)														**PORCS A L'ENGRAIS (>110 KG)**
1985	:	1 804	22	14	128	6	:	187	18	1 262	0	63	:	104
1986	1 884:	1 800	8	13	146	4	84	154	16	1 268	0	95	–:	95
1987	:	:	:	13	134	:	:	132	16	:	0	107	:	:
% 87/86	:	:	:	–	–8,3	:	:	–14,3	–3,7	:	–39,0	12,6	:	:
BREEDING BOARS (>50 KG)														**VERRATS REPRODUCTEURS (>50 KG)**
1985	:	406	25	39	116	14	:	72	5	46	1	45	:	44
1986	503:	411	27	39	117	12	92	71	5	46	1	49	–:	45
1987	:	:	:	38	117	:	:	75	5	:	1	57	:	:
% 87/86	:	:	:	–2,6	–0,1	:	:	5,6	–2,0	:	–5,2	16,3	:	:
BREEDING SOWS (>50 KG)														**TRUIES D'ELEVAGE (>50 KG)**
1985	:	9 071	658	1 075	2 875	161	:	1 128	114	762	12	1 380	:	907
1986	10 648:	9 249	683	1 077	2 908	152	1 399	1 130	114	766	11	1 487	–:	921
1987	:	:	:	1 066	2 797	:	:	1 211	108	:	11	1 165	:	:
% 87/86	:	:	:	–1,0	–3,8	:	:	7,2	–5,4	:	–6,6	–21,7	:	:
MATED SOWS														**TRUIES SAILLIES**
1985	:	5 877	432	659	1 852	91	:	695	76	571	8	867	:	626
1986	6 929:	6 048	447	671	1 874	96	881	716	79	573	8	939	–:	646
1987	:	:	:	669	1 808	:	:	778	75	:	7	786	:	:
% 87/86	:	:	:	–0,3	–3,5	:	:	8,7	–4,1	:	–8,8	–16,3	:	:
OF WHICH: SOWS MATED FOR THE FIRST TIME														**DONT: TRUIES SAILLIES POUR LA PREMIERE FOIS**
1985	:	1 282	99	152	408	21	:	148	14	141	2	192	:	105
1986	1 498:	1 280	105	147	398	22	217	155	15	143	2	189	–:	105
1987	:	:	:	139	364	:	:	169	14	:	1	196	:	:
% 87/86	:	:	:	–5,4	–8,4	:	:	9,0	–6,7	:	–18,0	3,7	:	:
BREEDING SOWS NOT MATED														**TRUIES NON SAILLIES**
1985	:	3 195	226	416	1 023	70	:	433	38	191	4	513	:	281
1986	3 719:	3 201	235	406	1 034	56	519	414	36	193	4	548	–:	275
1987	:	:	:	397	989	:	:	433	33	:	4	379	:	:
% 87/86	:	:	:	–2,2	–4,4	:	:	4,6	–8,4	:	–2,0	–30,8	:	:
OF WHICH: BREEDING GILTS NOT YET MATED														**DONT: JEUNES TRUIES NON SAILLIES**
1985	:	1 046	93	132	297	16	:	142	10	80	1	190	:	86
1986	1 240:	1 065	95	128	298	14	176	146	10	81	1	204	–:	87
1987	:	:	:	132	286	:	:	146	9	:	1	222	:	:
% 87/86	:	:	:	3,1	–4,1	:	:	–	–6,1	:	–7,1	8,8	:	:

1000 HEAD | **1000 TETES**

YEAR ANNÉE	EUR 12	EUR 10	B	DK	D	EL	ES	F	IRL	I	L	NL	P	UK
TOTAL														**TOTAL**
1985	:	81 923	5 412	9 104	24 282	1 095	:	10 956	994	9 169	72	12 908	:	7 930
1986	100 683:	84 903	5 762	9 422	24 180	1 130	15 780	12 063	980	9 274	74	14 063	—:	7 955
PIGLETS (<20 KG)														**PORCELETS (<20 KG)**
1985	:	22 697	1 448	2 780	6 968	338	:	2 607	241	1 797	27	4 339	:	2 153
1986	27 577:	23 628	1 526	2 924	7 045	346	3 949	2 876	219	1 816	29	4 682	—:	2 165
YOUNG PIGS (20-50 KG)														**JEUNES PORCS (20-50 KG)**
1985	:	21 000	1 480	2 671	5 925	311	:	3 185	285	1 905	13	2 967	:	2 258
1986	25 661:	21 424	1 540	2 952	5 731	285	4 237	3 417	302	1 915	13	3 049	—:	2 221
PIGS FOR FATTENING (>50 KG)														**PORCS A L'ENGRAIS (>50 KG)**
1985	:	28 709	1 814	2 586	8 404	273	:	3 952	351	4 659	20	4 088	:	2 562
1986	35 799:	30 057	1 991	2 450	8 453	328	5 742	4 464	345	4 732	20	4 656	—:	2 617
PIGS FOR FATTENING (50-80 KG)														**PORCS A L'ENGRAIS (50-80 KG)**
1985	:	16 853	1 157	2 029	5 219	176	:	2 129	265	1 467	12	2 523	:	1 877
1986	20 850:	17 615	1 227	1 949	5 240	192	3 235	2 553	265	1 486	12	2 821	—:	1 870
PIGS FOR FATTENING (80-110 KG)														**PORCS A L'ENGRAIS (80-110 KG)**
1985	:	9 322	638	541	2 964	88	:	1 575	67	1 384	7	1 458	:	600
1986	12 188:	9 981	743	487	2 984	127	2 207	1 769	65	1 399	7	1 742	—:	658
PIGS FOR FATTENING (>110 KG)														**PORCS A L'ENGRAIS (>110 KG)**
1985	:	2 534	19	16	221	9	:	248	19	1 809	1	107	:	85
1986	2 761:	2 461	21	14	230	9	300	142	16	1 847	1	93	—:	89
BREEDING BOARS (>50 KG)														**VERRATS REPRODUCTEURS (>50 KG)**
1985	:	399	26	38	115	13	:	67	5	46	1	45	:	45
1986	505:	416	26	39	119	13	89	72	5	46	1	51	—:	45
BREEDING SOWS (>50 KG)														**TRUIES D'ELEVAGE (>50 KG)**
1985	:	9 115	644	1 029	2 871	161	:	1 143	113	763	11	1 469	:	912
1986	11 161:	9 378	680	1 057	2 831	158	1 783	1 234	108	765	11	1 625	—:	908
MATED SOWS														**TRUIES SAILLIES**
1985	:	5 944	431	642	1 842	101	:	709	77	572	8	922	:	639
1986	7 322:	6 193	457	661	1 830	100	1 129	820	76	573	7	1 030	—:	639
OF WHICH: SOWS MATED FOR THE FIRST TIME														**DONT: TRUIES SAILLIES POUR LA PREMIERE FOIS**
1985	:	1 251	102	140	382	24	:	153	15	141	2	191	:	102
1986	1 486:	1 266	106	132	362	22	220	157	15	142	2	223	—:	106
BREEDING SOWS NOT MATED														**TRUIES NON SAILLIES**
1985	:	3 171	213	387	1 029	60	:	434	36	190	4	547	:	272
1986	3 839:	3 185	223	396	1 002	58	654	414	33	192	4	595	—:	269
OF WHICH: BREEDING GILTS NOT YET MATED														**DONT: JEUNES TRUIES NON SAILLIES**
1985	:	1 063	84	127	304	9	:	151	10	81	1	212	:	85
1986	1 255:	1 101	90	132	285	14	154	156	9	81	1	247	—:	86

1000 HEAD   **1000 TETES**

YEAR ANNÉE	EUR 12	EUR 10	B	DK	D	EL	ES	F	IRL	I	L	NL	P	UK
TOTAL														**TOTAL**
1985	:	61 848	124	52	1 296	9 989	16 954	10 791	2 774	11 293	4	985	:	24 540
1986	84 865	64 688	125	69	1 341	11 032	17 177	10 580	2 917	11 659	4	985	3 000	25 976
COVERED & ADULT FEMALES													**FEMELLES SAILLIES ET ADULTES**	
1985	:	44 521	98	38	913	6 684	12 195	8 006	2 047	8 720	3	735	:	17 277
1986	59 668	45 685	100	51	924	7 031	11 983	7 696	2 149	8 803	2	735	2 000	18 194

GOAT POPULATION IN DECEMBER   EFFECTIFS CAPRINS EN DECEMBRE

YEAR ANNÉE	EUR 12	EUR 10	B	DK	D	EL	ES	F	IRL	I	L	NL	P	UK
TOTAL														**TOTAL**
1985	:	8 008	7	—	45	5 696	2 584	1 005	—	1 169	1	38	:	48
1986	12 642:	8 917:	7	—	45	6 600:	2 925	980	—	1 197	1	39	800	48
COVERED & ADULT FEMALES													**FEMELLES SAILLIES ET ADULTES**	
1985	:	5 690:	—	—	—:	3 846	1 819	865	—	979	—	—	—:	—
1986	8 045:	6 233:	—	—	—:	4 420:	1 812	842	—	971	—	—	—:	—

EQUID POPULATION IN DECEMBER   EFFECTIFS D'EQUIDES EN DECEMBRE

YEAR ANNÉE	EUR 12	EUR 10	B	DK	D	EL	ES	F	IRL	I	L	NL	P	UK
TOTAL														**TOTAL**
1985	:	:	26	34 *	:	:	—	:	87 *	398	:	62	—	145 *
1986	:	:	:	:	:	:	—	:	:	:	:	66	—	:
HORSES														**CHEVAUX**
1985	:	:	26	34 *	:	:	—	:	:	248	:	62	—	145 *
1986	:	:	:	:	:	:	—	:	:	:	:	66	—	:
DONKEYS, MULES & HINNIES													**ANES, MULETS & BARDOTS**	
1985	:	:	—	—	—	:	—	:	:	150	—	—	—	—
1986	:	:	:	—	—	:	—	:	:	:	—	—	—	—

POULTRY POPULATION   EFFECTIFS DE VOLAILLE

YEAR ANNÉE	EUR 12	EUR 10	B	DK	D	EL	ES	F	IRL	I	L	NL	P	UK
LAYING HENS														**POULES PONDEUSES**
1985	296 013	296 013	10 854	4 026	51 300	16 784	—	69 600	3 246	47 798	90	40 374	—	51 941
1986	:	:	10 719	4 224	49 700	16 784	—	:	:	:	91	:	—	53 015

1000 LU   **1000 UGB**

	EUR 12	EUR 10	BL	DK	D	GR	F	IRL	I	NL	UK
TOTAL LU											**TOTAL UGB**
1983	:	99 100,6	4 121,6	4 718,6	19 494,1	2 533,6	25 473,0	5 221,9	12 766,3	8 322,5	16 448,9
1984	:	98 992,2	4 158,9	4 615,5	19 607,3	2 482,8	25 153,3	5 268,5	12 938,5	8 466,3	16 301,1
1985	:	:	4 216,6	4 603,5	:	:	24 980,2	5 271,4	12 777,9	8 648,4	16 307,8
1986	:	:	:	:	:	:	:	:	:	:	:
CATTLE											**BOVINS**
1983	:	62 487,1	2 449,2	2 305,0	12 119,4	552,1	18 404,8	4 525,5	6 979,6	4 698,8	10 452,6
1984	:	62 588,6	2 477,3	2 290,6	12 267,2	539,4	18 349,8	4 575,1	7 082,3	4 715,3	10 291,6
1985	:	:	2 500,7	2 174,3	12 256,0	:	18 170,7	4 569,5	6 952,8	4 651,2	10 144,8
1986	:	:	2 501,9	:	:	:	:	:	:	4 553,4	:
PIGS											**PORCINS**
1983	:	19 488,8	1 320,5	2 188,3	5 854,3	273,5	2 792,2	278,4	2 278,1	2 515,2	1 988,3
1984	:	19 275,3	1 334,2	2 107,9	5 816,4	252,1	2 693,3	264,8	2 290,1	2 614,9	1 901,5
1985	:	19 790,0	1 370,5	2 210,9	5 880,0	264,4	2 714,1	256,8	2 281,8	2 814,4	1 970,0
1986	:	20 453,7	1 441,4	2 253,7	5 943,1	256,9	2 869,8	257,2	2 329,8	3 127,0	1 974,8
SHEEP AND GOATS											**OVINS ET CAPRINS**
1983	:	6 802,8	25,1	7,0	160,7	988,2	1 618,1	242,4	1 368,2	92,5	2 300,5
1984	:	6 811,1	26,4	7,2	164,4	1 001,0	1 518,7	253,7	1 411,0	88,5	2 340,1
1985	:	6 920,1	30,1	7,3	172,8	1 007,6	1 471,2	269,0	1 466,1	93,0	2 402,8
1986	:	:	32,6	8,5	171,8	1 003,0	:	:	:	:	2 461,6
EQUIDAE											**ÉQUIDÉS**
1983	:	1 513,0	25,7	32,8	295,3	315,2	264,0	74,4	337,4	47,4	120,8
1984	:	1 473,2	24,8	30,4	282,9	298,4	265,3	72,8	331,1	48,3	119,2
1985	:	:	23,3	28,0	:	:	265,8	71,2	320,9	51,5	117,6
1986	:	:	:	27,2	:	:	:	69,6	318,2	49,7	116,0
POULTRY											**VOLAILLES**
1983	:	8 809,0	301,1	185,4	1 064,6	404,7	2 393,9	101,2	1 803,0	968,4	1 586,7
1984	:	8 843,9	296,2	179,3	1 076,4	391,9	2 326,3	102,0	1 823,9	999,2	1 648,6
1985	:	8 852,0	292,0	182,9	1 078,1	395,7	2 358,4	104,8	1 756,3	1 011,2	1 672,5
1986	:	:	293,6	186,6	1 079,7	384,6	:	:	:	:	1 747,0

NUMBER OF HOLDERS (1000)   **NOMBRE DE DETENTEURS (1000)**

YEAR ANNÉE	EUR 12	EUR 10	B	DK	D	EL	ES	F	IRL	I	L	NL	P	UK
TOTAL HOLDERS													**ENSEMBLE DES DETENTEURS**	
1985	:	2 150,1	68,6	46,3	464,7	:	98,7	566,9	174,9	490,7	3,3	76,6	:	159,6
1987		:	:	:	431,1	:	:	:	:	:	:	:	:	:
% 87/85		:	:	:	*−7,2*	:	:	:	:	:	:	:	:	:
HOLDERS WITH 1-2 ANIMALS													**DETENTEURS AVEC 1-2 ANIMAUX**	
1985	:	195,0	3,9	2,4	22,6	:	36,5	24,7	3,5	95,4	0,1	2,0	:	4,0
1987		:	:	:	20,2	:	:	:	:	:	:	:	:	:
% 87/85		:	:	:	*−10,8*	:	:	:	:	:	:	:	:	:
HOLDERS WITH 3-4 ANIMALS													**DETENTEURS AVEC 3-4 ANIMAUX**	
1985	:	191,4	4,0	2,1	31,1	:	25,0	29,4	8,9	82,8	0,1	2,2	:	5,8
1987		:	:	:	27,7	:	:	:	:	:	:	:	:	:
% 87/85		:	:	:	*−10,9*	:	:	:	:	:	:	:	:	:
HOLDERS WITH 5-9 ANIMALS													**DETENTEURS AVEC 5-9 ANIMAUX**	
1985	:	316,0	6,7	4,1	67,6	:	20,5	66,1	27,4	107,6	0,2	5,5	:	12,2
1987		:	:	:	59,8	:	:	:	:	:	:	:	:	:
% 87/85		:	:	:	*−11,5*	:	:	:	:	:	:	:	:	:
HOLDERS WITH 10-14 ANIMALS													**DETENTEURS AVEC 10-14 ANIMAUX**	
1985	:	226,6	5,2	3,2	51,4	:	6,7	51,8	26,2	66,6	0,2	4,9	:	10,4
1987		:	:	:	46,5	:	:	:	:	:	:	:	:	:
% 87/85		:	:	:	*−9,5*	:	:	:	:	:	:	:	:	:
HOLDERS WITH 15-19 ANIMALS													**DETENTEURS AVEC 15-19 ANIMAUX**	
1985	:	162,7	4,4	2,7	40,3	:	2,8	45,8	18,3	35,7	0,2	3,7	:	8,8
1987		:	:	:	36,1	:	:	:	:	:	:	:	:	:
% 87/85		:	:	:	*−10,5*	:	:	:	:	:	:	:	:	:
HOLDERS WITH 20-29 ANIMALS													**DETENTEURS AVEC 20-29 ANIMAUX**	
1985	:	236,4	7,8	4,6	62,6	:	2,6	74,3	27,3	35,0	0,3	6,5	:	15,5
1987		:	:	:	56,9	:	:	:	:	:	:	:	:	:
% 87/85		:	:	:	*−9,2*	:	:	:	:	:	:	:	:	:
HOLDERS WITH 30-39 ANIMALS													**DETENTEURS AVEC 30-39 ANIMAUX**	
1985	:	174,0	6,8	3,8	46,1	:	1,2	57,9	17,2	22,6	0,2	5,8	:	12,2
1987		:	:	:	42,6	:	:	:	:	:	:	:	:	:
% 87/85		:	:	:	*−7,6*	:	:	:	:	:	:	:	:	:
HOLDERS WITH 40-49 ANIMALS													**DETENTEURS AVEC 40-49 ANIMAUX**	
1985	:	135,0	5,8	3,4	36,0	:	1,1	47,4	11,8	13,1	0,2	5,8	:	10,3
1987		:	:	:	34,0	:	:	:	:	:	:	:	:	:
% 87/85		:	:	:	*−5,5*	:	:	:	:	:	:	:	:	:
HOLDERS WITH 50-59 ANIMALS													**DETENTEURS AVEC 50-59 ANIMAUX**	
1985	:	103,4	4,9	2,9	27,2	:	0,8	39,4	8,2	5,5	0,2	5,4	:	8,9
1987		:	:	:	26,5	:	:	:	:	:	:	:	:	:
% 87/85		:	:	:	*−2,7*	:	:	:	:	:	:	:	:	:
HOLDERS WITH 60-99 ANIMALS													**DETENTEURS AVEC 60-99 ANIMAUX**	
1985	:	240,5	12,3	8,5	55,3	:	0,8	87,6	16,5	13,8	0,8	18,0	:	26,8
1987		:	:	:	55,3	:	:	:	:	:	:	:	:	:
% 87/85		:	:	:	*−0,1*	:	:	:	:	:	:	:	:	:
HOLDERS WITH 100-199 ANIMALS													**DETENTEURS AVEC 100-199 ANIMAUX**	
1985	:	135,8	6,0	7,3	22,2	:	0,6	38,9	8,1	8,2	0,8	13,9	:	29,7
1987		:	:	:	23,0	:	:	:	:	:	:	:	:	:
% 87/85		:	:	:	*4,0*	:	:	:	:	:	:	:	:	:
HOLDERS WITH 200-299 ANIMALS													**DETENTEURS AVEC 200-299 ANIMAUX**	
1985	:	21,1	0,5	0,9	1,7	:	0,1	3,4	1,0	2,4	0,1	1,6	:	9,5
1987		:	:	:	1,9	:	:	:	:	:	:	:	:	:
% 87/85		:	:	:	*10,5*	:	:	:	:	:	:	:	:	:
HOLDERS WITH 300 ANIMALS AND MORE													**DETENTEURS AVEC 300 ANIMAUX ET PLUS**	
1985	:	10,8	0,2	0,2	0,4	:	0,0	0,9	0,4	2,0	0,0	1,1	:	5,4
1987		:	:	:	0,5	:	:	:	:	:	:	:	:	:
% 87/85		:	:	:	*21,2*	:	:	:	:	:	:	:	:	:
HOLDERS WITH 100 ANIMALS AND MORE													**DETENTEURS AVEC 100 ANIMAUX ET PLUS**	
1985	:	167,7	6,7	8,4	24,3	:	0,7	43,2	9,5	12,5	0,8	16,7	:	44,7
1987		:	:	:	25,4	:	:	:	:	:	:	:	:	:
% 87/85		:	:	:	*4,7*	:	:	:	:	:	:	:	:	:

NUMBER OF ANIMALS (1000)   **NOMBRE D'ANIMAUX (1000)**

YEAR ANNÉE	EUR 12	EUR 10	B	DK	D	EL	ES	F	IRL	I	L	NL	P	UK
TOTAL HOLDERS													**ENSEMBLE DES DETENTEURS**	
1985	:	77 809,6	3 091,7	2 617,7	15 672,7	:	775,9	22 802,1	5 779,0	8 907,8	220,4	5 247,6	:	12 694,8
1987	:	:	:	:	15 291,2	:	:	:	:	:	:	:	:	:
% 87/85					−2,4									
HOLDERS WITH 1-2 ANIMALS													**DETENTEURS AVEC 1-2 ANIMAUX**	
1985	:	325,8	6,5	3,8	38,4	:	56,6	42,5	6,3	161,5	0,2	3,2	:	6,7
1987	:	:	:	:	34,2	:	:	:	:	:	:	:	:	:
% 87/85	:	:	:	:	−11,0	:	:	:	:	:	:	:	:	:
HOLDERS WITH 3-4 ANIMALS													**DETENTEURS AVEC 3-4 ANIMAUX**	
1985	:	671,5	14,1	7,6	110,1	:	86,9	103,4	32,1	289,8	0,4	7,7	:	19,6
1987	:	:	:	:	97,9	:	:	:	:	:	:	:	:	:
% 87/85	:	:	:	:	−11,1	:	:	:	:	:	:	:	:	:
HOLDERS WITH 5-9 ANIMALS													**DETENTEURS AVEC 5-9 ANIMAUX**	
1985	:	2 155,9	45,5	28,5	465,8	:	134,6	450,1	191,4	717,8	1,3	38,4	:	82,5
1987	:	:	:	:	412,1	:	:	:	:	:	:	:	:	:
% 87/85	:	:	:	:	−11,5	:	:	:	:	:	:	:	:	:
HOLDERS WITH 10-14 ANIMALS													**DETENTEURS AVEC 10-14 ANIMAUX**	
1985	:	2 688,0	62,1	38,5	609,4	:	77,9	619,0	308,0	791,7	2,2	58,6	:	120,6
1987	:	:	:	:	551,3	:	:	:	:	:	:	:	:	:
% 87/85	:	:	:	:	−9,5	:	:	:	:	:	:	:	:	:
HOLDERS WITH 15-19 ANIMALS													**DETENTEURS AVEC 15-19 ANIMAUX**	
1985	:	2 735,9	74,7	45,2	681,4	:	46,6	778,5	306,9	592,1	3,1	63,2	:	144,3
1987	:	:	:	:	609,7	:	:	:	:	:	:	:	:	:
% 87/85	:	:	:	:	−10,5	:	:	:	:	:	:	:	:	:
HOLDERS WITH 20-29 ANIMALS													**DETENTEURS AVEC 20-29 ANIMAUX**	
1985	:	5 696,1	188,6	112,2	1 513,4	:	59,6	1 797,4	652,6	843,9	6,5	157,7	:	364,3
1987	:	:	:	:	1 375,1	:	:	:	:	:	:	:	:	:
% 87/85	:	:	:	:	−9,1	:	:	:	:	:	:	:	:	:
HOLDERS WITH 30-39 ANIMALS													**DETENTEURS AVEC 30-39 ANIMAUX**	
1985	:	5 912,9	234,1	131,8	1 576,7	:	42,8	1 989,2	580,8	743,7	8,3	200,7	:	404,7
1987	:	:	:	:	1 456,6	:	:	:	:	:	:	:	:	:
% 87/85	:	:	:	:	−7,6	:	:	:	:	:	:	:	:	:
HOLDERS WITH 40-49 ANIMALS													**DETENTEURS AVEC 40-49 ANIMAUX**	
1985	:	5 953,3	256,0	151,7	1 591,6	:	49,1	2 092,1	520,5	582,7	9,3	256,8	:	443,5
1987	:	:	:	:	1 505,1	:	:	:	:	:	:	:	:	:
% 87/85	:	:	:	:	−5,4	:	:	:	:	:	:	:	:	:
HOLDERS WITH 50-59 ANIMALS													**DETENTEURS AVEC 50-59 ANIMAUX**	
1985	:	5 583,4	263,6	157,3	1 474,3	:	46,4	2 136,9	443,8	291,2	9,9	293,6	:	466,4
1987	:	:	:	:	1 435,2	:	:	:	:	:	:	:	:	:
% 87/85	:	:	:	:	−2,7	:	:	:	:	:	:	:	:	:
HOLDERS WITH 60-99 ANIMALS													**DETENTEURS AVEC 60-99 ANIMAUX**	
1985	:	18 224,9	942,2	661,5	4 169,8	:	60,9	6 630,3	1 242,8	1 030,4	60,6	1 409,7	:	2 016,7
1987	:	:	:	:	4 172,4	:	:	:	:	:	:	:	:	:
% 87/85	:	:	:	:	0,1	:	:	:	:	:	:	:	:	:
HOLDERS WITH 100-199 ANIMALS													**DETENTEURS AVEC 100-199 ANIMAUX**	
1985	:	17 849,0	776,6	981,9	2 848,1	:	81,8	5 020,9	1 064,3	1 080,1	98,9	1 826,4	:	4 070,0
1987	:	:	:	:	2 970,0	:	:	:	:	:	:	:	:	:
% 87/85	:	:	:	:	4,3	:	:	:	:	:	:	:	:	:
HOLDERS WITH 200-299 ANIMALS													**DETENTEURS AVEC 200-299 ANIMAUX**	
1985	:	4 959,3	115,0	207,2	390,8	:	13,4	783,3	241,5	561,8	16,2	378,7	:	2 251,3
1987	:	:	:	:	431,0	:	:	:	:	:	:	:	:	:
% 87/85	:	:	:	:	10,3	:	:	:	:	:	:	:	:	:
HOLDERS WITH 300 ANIMALS AND MORE												**DETENTEURS AVEC 300 ANIMAUX ET PLUS**		
1985	:	4 967,4	112,6	90,6	202,8	:	17,2	358,6	187,9	1 137,1	3,6	553,0	:	2 304,0
1987	:	:	:	:	240,7	:	:	:	:	:	:	:	:	:
% 87/85	:	:	:	:	18,7	:	:	:	:	:	:	:	:	:
HOLDERS WITH 100 ANIMALS AND MORE												**DETENTEURS AVEC 100 ANIMAUX ET PLUS**		
1985	:	27 775,8	1 004,2	1 279,7	3 441,7	:	112,4	6 162,8	1 493,7	2 779,0	118,8	2 758,2	:	8 625,3
1987	:	:	:	:	3 641,7	:	:	:	:	:	:	:	:	:
% 87/85	:	:	:	:	5,8	:	:	:	:	:	:	:	:	:

NUMBER OF HOLDERS (1000)   **NOMBRE DE DETENTEURS (1000)**

YEAR ANNÉE	EUR 12	EUR 10	B	DK	D	EL	ES	F	IRL	I	L	NL	P	UK
TOTAL HOLDERS													**ENSEMBLE DES DETENTEURS**	
1985	:	1 378,5	44,8	31,8	368,9	:	73,4	328,7	76,8	337,7	2,3	61,3	:	52,9
1987	:	:	:	:	337,3	:	:	:	:	:	:	:	:	:
% 87/85	:	:	:	:	−8,6	:	:	:	:	:	:	:	:	:
HOLDERS WITH 1-2 ANIMALS													**DETENTEURS AVEC 1-2 ANIMAUX**	
1985	:	261,7	3,2	1,7	37,6	:	50,2	26,4	13,2	121,6	0,1	4,9	:	2,7
1987	:	:	:	:	31,9	:	:	:	:	:	:	:	:	:
% 87/85	:	:	:	:	−15,3	:	:	:	:	:	:	:	:	:
HOLDERS WITH 3-4 ANIMALS													**DETENTEURS AVEC 3-4 ANIMAUX**	
1985	:	145,5	2,2	0,9	38,5	:	12,1	20,4	5,9	62,9	0,1	2,0	:	0,5
1987	:	:	:	:	31,2	:	:	:	:	:	:	:	:	:
% 87/85	:	:	:	:	−18,8	:	:	:	:	:	:	:	:	:
HOLDERS WITH 5-9 ANIMALS													**DETENTEURS AVEC 5-9 ANIMAUX**	
1985	·	235,5	6,3	3,0	84,7	:	9,0	49,2	11,4	68,2	0,2	0,1	:	1,4
1987	:	:	:	:	72,4	:	:	:	:	:	:	:	:	:
% 87/85	:	:	:	:	−14,5	:	:	:	:	:	:	:	:	:
HOLDERS WITH 10-14 ANIMALS													**DETENTEURS AVEC 10-14 ANIMAUX**	
1985	:	170,3	7,0	3,9	61,1	:	1,8	51,4	10,4	29,0	0,2	3,6	:	1,8
1987	:	:	:	:	55,9	:	:	:	:	:	:	:	:	:
% 87/85	:	:	:	:	−8,6	:	:	:	:	:	:	:	:	:
HOLDERS WITH 15-19 ANIMALS													**DETENTEURS AVEC 15-19 ANIMAUX**	
1985	:	126,7	5,7	3,5	44,5	:	0,5	42,0	7,2	17,1	0,2	4,0	:	2,0
1987	:	:	:	:	42,3	:	:	:	:	:	:	:	:	:
% 87/85	:	:	:	:	−4,9	:	:	:	:	:	:	:	:	:
HOLDERS WITH 20-29 ANIMALS													**DETENTEURS AVEC 20-29 ANIMAUX**	
1985	:	180,1	8,7	6,1	55,7	:	0,5	65,8	10,6	17,8	0,4	8,9	:	5,4
1987	:	:	:	:	55,7	:	:	:	:	:	:	:	:	:
% 87/85	:	:	:	:	0,0	:	:	:	:	:	:	:	:	:
HOLDERS WITH 30-39 ANIMALS													**DETENTEURS AVEC 30-39 ANIMAUX**	
1985	:	100,5	5,2	4,8	24,3	:	0,2	37,7	6,7	7,1	0,5	8,1	:	6,0
1987	:	:	:	:	25,1	:	:	:	:	:	:	:	:	:
% 87/85	:	:	:	:	3,5	:	:	:	:	:	:	:	:	:
HOLDERS WITH 40-49 ANIMALS													**DETENTEURS AVEC 40-49 ANIMAUX**	
1985	:	58,7	3,0	3,3	11,2	:	0,1	19,6	4,3	4,3	0,3	7,0	:	5,7
1987	:	:	:	:	11,7	:	:	:	:	:	:	:	:	:
% 87/85	:	:	:	:	4,5	:	:	:	:	:	:	:	:	:
HOLDERS WITH 50-59 ANIMALS													**DETENTEURS AVEC 50-59 ANIMAUX**	
1985	:	34,8	1,6	1,9	5,8	:	0,1	8,6	2,5	3,2	0,2	6,2	:	4,7
1987	:	:	:	:	6,0	:	:	:	:	:	:	:	:	:
% 87/85	:	:	:	:	2,9	:	:	:	:	:	:	:	:	:
HOLDERS WITH 60-99 ANIMALS													**DETENTEURS AVEC 60-99 ANIMAUX**	
1985	:	48,5	1,6	2,2	5,1	:	0,0	7,0	3,6	4,3	0,2	11,1	:	13,4
1987	:	:	:	:	4,7	:	:	:	:	:	:	:	:	:
% 87/85	:	:	:	:	−8,4	:	:	:	:	:	:	:	:	:
HOLDERS WITH 100 ANIMALS AND MORE											**DETENTEURS AVEC 100 ANIMAUX ET PLUS**			
1985	:	16,3	0,2	0,4	0,4	:	0,0	0,6	0,9	2,0	0,0	2,4	:	9,4
1987	:	:	:	:	0,4	:	:	:	:	:	:	:	:	:
% 87/85	:	:	:	:	−13,3	:	:	:	:	:	:	:	:	:

NUMBER OF ANIMALS (1000)   **NOMBRE D'ANIMAUX (1000)**

YEAR ANNÉE	EUR 12	EUR 10	B	DK	D	EL	ES	F	IRL	I	L	NL	P	UK
TOTAL HOLDERS												**ENSEMBLE DES DETENTEURS**		
1985	:	24 517,8	973,0	896,4	5 581,0	:	218,9	6 506,1	1 527,7	3 075,4	70,3	2 412,4	:	3 256,5
1987	:	:	:	:	5 390,0	:	:	:	:	:	:	:	:	:
% 87/85	:	:	:	:	−3,4	:	:	:	:	:	:	:	:	:
HOLDERS WITH 1-2 ANIMALS												**DETENTEURS AVEC 1-2 ANIMAUX**		
1985	:	372,2	4,5	2,4	57,1	:	70,7	40,4	18,5	168,2	0,1	6,8	:	3,5
1987	:	:	:	:	47,6	:	:	:	:	:	:	:	:	:
% 87/85	:	:	:	:	−16,5	:	:	:	:	:	:	:	:	:
HOLDERS WITH 3-4 ANIMALS												**DETENTEURS AVEC 3-4 ANIMAUX**		
1985	:	505,9	7,9	3,2	135,4	:	41,0	71,4	20,5	217,7	0,2	6,8	:	1,8
1987	:	:	:	:	110,0	:	:	:	:	:	:	:	:	:
% 87/85	:	:	:	:	−18,8	:	:	:	:	:	:	:	:	:
HOLDERS WITH 5-9 ANIMALS												**DETENTEURS AVEC 5-9 ANIMAUX**		
1985	:	1 579,9	44,1	21,8	579,9	:	49,0	343,5	77,6	431,8	1,2	21,7	:	9,3
1987	:	:	:	:	498,6	:	:	:	:	:	:	:	:	:
% 87/85	:	:	:	:	−14,0	:	:	:	:	:	:	:	:	:
HOLDERS WITH 10-14 ANIMALS												**DETENTEURS AVEC 10-14 ANIMAUX**		
1985	:	2 007,3	83,5	47,0	722,0	:	19,7	611,1	121,6	335,6	2,6	42,8	:	21,3
1987	:	:	:	:	660,6	:	:	:	:	:	:	:	:	:
% 87/85	:	:	:	:	−8,5	:	:	:	:	:	:	:	:	:
HOLDERS WITH 15-19 ANIMALS												**DETENTEURS AVEC 15-19 ANIMAUX**		
1985	:	2 128,5	95,4	59,7	747,4	:	8,0	710,4	119,2	284,5	3,4	67,4	:	33,1
1987	:	:	:	:	711,0	:	:	:	:	:	:	:	:	:
% 87/85	:	:	:	:	−4,9	:	:	:	:	:	:	:	:	:
HOLDERS WITH 20-29 ANIMALS												**DETENTEURS AVEC 20-29 ANIMAUX**		
1985	:	4 271,3	206,9	147,1	1 319,3	:	12,7	1 577,8	246,2	406,8	10,9	219,1	:	124,5
1987	:	:	:	:	321,0	:	:	:	:	:	:	:	:	:
% 87/85	:	:	:	:	−75,7	:	:	:	:	:	:	:	:	:
HOLDERS WITH 30-39 ANIMALS												**DETENTEURS AVEC 30-39 ANIMAUX**		
1985	:	3 384,4	172,5	162,8	813,0	:	6,6	1 275,0	222,5	238,6	16,0	278,3	:	199,1
1987	:	:	:	:	840,8	:	:	:	:	:	:	:	:	:
% 87/85	:	:	:	:	3,4	:	:	:	:	:	:	:	:	:
HOLDERS WITH 40-49 ANIMALS												**DETENTEURS AVEC 40-49 ANIMAUX**		
1985	:	2 547,8	128,2	142,7	486,2	:	3,1	854,1	185,0	183,3	13,5	310,7	:	241,0
1987	:	:	:	:	508,1	:	:	:	:	:	:	:	:	:
% 87/85	:	:	:	:	4,5	:	:	:	:	:	:	:	:	:
HOLDERS WITH 50-59 ANIMALS												**DETENTEURS AVEC 50-59 ANIMAUX**		
1985	:	1 855,9	86,6	102,4	312,0	:	3,0	464,0	130,5	165,5	9,1	337,2	:	245,4
1987	:	:	:	:	320,6	:	:	:	:	:	:	:	:	:
% 87/85	:	:	:	:	2,8	:	:	:	:	:	:	:	:	:
HOLDERS WITH 60-99 ANIMALS												**DETENTEURS AVEC 60-99 ANIMAUX**		
1985	:	3 534,3	115,7	159,4	357,9	:	2,6	488,7	260,4	321,5	10,9	815,6	:	1 001,7
1987	:	:	:	:	327,7	:	:	:	:	:	:	:	:	:
% 87/85	:	:	:	:	−8,4	:	:	:	:	:	:	:	:	:
HOLDERS WITH 100 ANIMALS AND MORE											**DETENTEURS AVEC 100 ANIMAUX ET PLUS**			
1985	:	2 330,7	28,3	47,7	51,0	:	2,7	69,7	125,6	321,9	2,4	305,9	:	1 375,5
1987	:	:	:	:	44,0	:	:	:	:	:	:	:	:	:
% 87/85	:	:	:	:	−13,6	:	:	:	:	:	:	:	:	:

NUMBER OF HOLDERS (1000)   **NOMBRE DE DETENTEURS (1000)**

YEAR ANNÉE	EUR 12	EUR 10	B	DK	D	EL	ES	F	IRL	I	L	NL	P	UK
TOTAL HOLDERS												**ENSEMBLE DES DETENTEURS**		
1985	:	560,5	15,7	8,6	42,9	:	20,8	238,9	73,0	82,6	1,8	–	:	76,1
1987					42,4									
% 87/85	:	:	:	:	− 1,3	:	:	:	:	:	:	:	:	:
HOLDERS WITH 1-2 ANIMALS												**DETENTEURS AVEC 1-2 ANIMAUX**		
1985	:	176,1	4,1	3,5	25,9	:	13,1	41,5	23,4	47,7	0,5	–	:	16,4
1987					24,8									
% 87/85	:	:	:	:	− 4,0	:	:	:	:	:	:	:	:	:
HOLDERS WITH 3-4 ANIMALS												**DETENTEURS AVEC 3-4 ANIMAUX**		
1985	:	90,8	2,5	1,6	8,3	:	3,2	28,6	20,4	15,4	0,4	–	:	10,2
1987					8,7									
% 87/85	:	:	:	:	4,1	:	:	:	:	:	:	:	:	:
HOLDERS WITH 5-9 ANIMALS												**DETENTEURS AVEC 5-9 ANIMAUX**		
1985	:	107,0	3,3	1,9	5,1	:	1,7	51,3	17,8	11,6	0,5	–	:	13,8
1987					5,2									
% 87/85	:	:	:	:	2,2	:	:	:	:	:	:	:	:	:
HOLDERS WITH 10-14 ANIMALS												**DETENTEURS AVEC 10-14 ANIMAUX**		
1985	:	58,2	2,0	0,8	1,6	:	0,5	35,5	6,2	2,1	0,1	–	:	9,3
1987					1,6									
% 87/85	:	:	:	:	− 3,7	:	:	:	:	:	:	:	:	:
HOLDERS WITH 15-19 ANIMALS												**DETENTEURS AVEC 15-19 ANIMAUX**		
1985	:	37,5	1,1	0,3	0,8	:	0,5	24,1	2,1	3,2	0,1	–	:	5,4
1987					0,7									
% 87/85	:	:	:	:	− 1,8	:	:	:	:	:	:	:	:	:
HOLDERS WITH 20-29 ANIMALS												**DETENTEURS AVEC 20-29 ANIMAUX**		
1985	:	43,6	1,3	0,3	0,7	:	0,7	30,5	1,8	0,9	0,1	–	:	7,2
1987					0,7									
% 87/85	:	:	:	:	8,1	:	:	:	:	:	:	:	:	:
HOLDERS WITH 30-39 ANIMALS												**DETENTEURS AVEC 30-39 ANIMAUX**		
1985	:	21,2	0,7	0,1	0,2	:	0,6	14,1	0,7	0,5	0,0	–	:	4,3
1987					0,3									
% 87/85	:	:	:	:	16,9	:	:	:	:	:	:	:	:	:
HOLDERS WITH 40-49 ANIMALS												**DETENTEURS AVEC 40-49 ANIMAUX**		
1985	:	10,2	0,3	0,0	0,1	:	0,1	6,2	0,3	0,3	0,0	–	:	2,7
1987					0,2									
% 87/85	:	:	:	:	12,7	:	:	:	:	:	:	:	:	:
HOLDERS WITH 50-59 ANIMALS												**DETENTEURS AVEC 50-59 ANIMAUX**		
1985	:	6,1	0,2	0,0	0,1	:	0,1	3,6	0,1	0,2	0,0	–	:	1,8
1987					0,1									
% 87/85	:	:	:	:	− 19,0	:	:	:	:	:	:	:	:	:
HOLDERS WITH 60-99 ANIMALS												**DETENTEURS AVEC 60-99 ANIMAUX**		
1985	:	7,4	0,2	0,0	0,1	:	0,2	3,2	0,1	0,3	0,0	–	:	3,3
1987					0,1									
% 87/85	:	:	:	:	5,7	:	:	:	:	:	:	:	:	:
HOLDERS WITH 100 ANIMALS AND MORE												**DETENTEURS AVEC 100 ANIMAUX ET PLUS**		
1985	:	2,3	0,0	0,0	0,0	:	0,0	0,3	–	0,2	0,0	–	:	1,6
1987					0,0									
% 87/85	:	:	:	:	22,7	:	:	:	:	:	:	:	:	:

NUMBER OF ANIMALS (1000) **NOMBRE D'ANIMAUX (1000)**

YEAR ANNÉE	EUR 12	EUR 10	B	DK	D	EL	ES	F	IRL	I	L	NL	P	UK
TOTAL HOLDERS												**ENSEMBLE DES DETENTEURS**		
1985	:	5 917,5	173,0	54,3	171,5	:	125,6	3 256,8	414,6	383,3	15,9	—	:	1 322,5
1987	:	:	:	:	175,2	:	:	:	:	:	:	:	:	:
% 87/85	:	:	:	:	*2,1*	:	:	:	:	:	.	:	:	:
HOLDERS WITH 1-2 ANIMALS												**DETENTEURS AVEC 1-2 ANIMAUX**		
1985	:	265,3	6,1	5,0	37,0	:	21,3	63,8	38,0	69,7	0,9	—	:	23,5
1987	:	:	:	:	36,0	:	:	:	:	:	:	:	:	:
% 87/85	:	:	:	:	*−2,7*	:	:	:	:	:	:	:	:	:
HOLDERS WITH 3-4 ANIMALS												**DETENTEURS AVEC 3-4 ANIMAUX**		
1985	:	311,7	8,7	5,6	28,1	:	11,0	99,4	70,5	52,4	1,6	—	:	34,4
1987	:	:	:	:	29,4	:	:	:	:	:	:	:	:	:
% 87/85	:	:	:	:	*4,4*	:	:	:	:	:	:	:	:	:
HOLDERS WITH 5-9 ANIMALS												**DETENTEURS AVEC 5-9 ANIMAUX**		
1985	:	701,8	22,1	12,3	32,2	:	11,1	348,8	113,7	68,7	3,7	—	:	89,3
1987	:	:	:	:	32,7	:	:	:	:	:	:	:	:	:
% 87/85	:	:	:	:	*1,8*	:	:	:	:	:	:	:	:	:
HOLDERS WITH 10-14 ANIMALS												**DETENTEURS AVEC 10-14 ANIMAUX**		
1985	:	676,3	22,6	8,9	18,7	:	6,0	418,8	69,5	25,1	1,8	—	:	104,8
1987	:	:	:	:	18,0	:	:	:	:	:	:	:	:	:
% 87/85	:	:	:	:	*−3,6*	:	:	:	:	:	:	:	:	:
HOLDERS WITH 15-19 ANIMALS												**DETENTEURS AVEC 15-19 ANIMAUX**		
1985	:	623,9	17,4	5,5	12,7	:	7,9	406,2	34,5	51,6	1,1	—	:	87,0
1987	:	:	:	:	12,4	:	:	:	:	:	:	:	:	:
% 87/85	:	:	:	:	*−2,5*	:	:	:	:	:	:	:	:	:
HOLDERS WITH 20-29 ANIMALS												**DETENTEURS AVEC 20-29 ANIMAUX**		
1985	:	1 026,6	31,1	7,4	16,1	:	16,8	727,6	40,4	22,2	1,9	—	:	163,1
1987	:	:	:	:	17,4	:	:	:	:	:	:	:	:	:
% 87/85	:	:	:	:	*7,9*	:	:	:	:	:	:	:	:	:
HOLDERS WITH 30-39 ANIMALS												**DETENTEURS AVEC 30-39 ANIMAUX**		
1985	:	710,3	21,8	3,8	7,8	:	19,7	478,0	21,5	17,3	1,4	—	:	139,1
1987	:	:	:	:	8,9	:	:	:	:	:	:	:	:	:
% 87/85	:	:	:	:	*15,2*	:	:	:	:	:	:	:	:	:
HOLDERS WITH 40-49 ANIMALS												**DETENTEURS AVEC 40-49 ANIMAUX**		
1985	:	437,0	14,4	2,0	5,9	:	6,2	267,1	12,0	14,6	1,1	—	:	113,8
1987	:	:	:	:	6,6	:	:	:	:	:	:	:	:	:
% 87/85	:	:	:	:	*11,8*	:	:	:	:	:	:	:	:	:
HOLDERS WITH 50-59 ANIMALS												**DETENTEURS AVEC 50-59 ANIMAUX**		
1985	:	323,1	9,2	1,1	4,3	:	8,0	190,9	4,8	9,5	0,7	—	:	94,7
1987	:	:	:	:	3,4	:	:	:	:	:	:	:	:	:
% 87/85	:	:	:	:	*−19,9*	:	:	:	:	:	:	:	:	:
HOLDERS WITH 60-99 ANIMALS												**DETENTEURS AVEC 60-99 ANIMAUX**		
1985	:	527,3	16,9	2,0	6,2	:	12,2	221,5	9,7	19,6	1,3	—	:	237,9
1987	:	:	:	:	6,6	:	:	:	:	:	:	:	:	:
% 87/85	:	:	:	:	*6,5*	:	:	:	:	:	:	:	:	:
HOLDERS WITH 100 ANIMALS AND MORE											**DETENTEURS AVEC 100 ANIMAUX ET PLUS**			
1985	:	314,2	2,8	0,9	2,6	:	5,3	34,6	—	32,6	0,4	—	:	234,9
1987	:	:	:	:	3,7	:	:	:	:	:	:	:	:	:
% 87/85	:	:	:	:	*40,6*	:	:	:	:	:	:	:	:	:

NUMBER OF HOLDERS (1000) **NOMBRE DE DETENTEURS (1000)**

YEAR ANNÉE	EUR 12	EUR 10	B	DK	D	EL	ES	F	IRL	I	L	NL	P	UK
TOTAL HOLDERS												**ENSEMBLE DES DETENTEURS**		
1985	:	1 395,9	30,0	44,2	432,4	:	56,5	165,6	7,1	598,5	1,9	36,1	:	23,6
1987		:	:	:	392,4	:	:	:	:	:	:	:	:	:
% 87I85	:	:	:	:	− 9,3	:	:	:	:	:	:	:	:	:
HOLDERS WITH 1-2 ANIMALS												**DETENTEURS AVEC 1-2 ANIMAUX**		
1985	:	673,9	3,6	1,3	89,2	:	43,6	83,7	2,4	446,0	0,4	0,8	:	2,9
1987		:	:	:	78,8	:	:	:	:	:	:	:	:	:
% 87I85	:	:	:	:	− 11,6	:	:	:	:	:	:	:	:	:
HOLDERS WITH 3-9 ANIMALS												**DETENTEURS AVEC 3-9 ANIMAUX**		
1985	:	280,6	3,7	3,2	124,5	:	5,5	33,1	1,4	104,1	0,6	1,4	:	3,3
1987		:	:	:	108,2	:	:	:	:	:	:	:	:	:
% 87I85	:	:	:	:	− 13,0	:	:	:	:	:	:	:	:	:
HOLDERS WITH 10-19 ANIMALS												**DETENTEURS AVEC 10-19 ANIMAUX**		
1985	:	101,8	2,5	4,1	53,1	:	2,3	9,6	1,3	24,7	0,2	1,3	:	2,7
1907		:	:	:	48,3	:	:	:	:	:	:	:	:	:
% 87I85	:	:	:	:	− 12,7	:	:	:	:	:	:	:	:	:
HOLDERS WITH 20-49 ANIMALS												**DETENTEURS AVEC 20-49 ANIMAUX**		
1985	:	111,5	4,5	8,5	65,8	:	1,9	11,3	0,9	11,8	0,3	3,4	:	3,2
1987	:	:	:	:	59,1	:	:	:	:	:	:	:	:	:
% 87I85	:	:	:	:	− 10,2	:	:	:	:	:	:	:	:	:
HOLDERS WITH 50-99 ANIMALS												**DETENTEURS AVEC 50-99 ANIMAUX**		
1985	:	71,3	4,3	7,5	40,5	:	1,5	6,2	0,3	3,3	0,2	5,2	:	2,4
1987		:	:	:	38,0	:	:	:	:	:	:	:	:	:
% 87I85	:	:	:	:	− 6,2	:	:	:	:	:	:	:	:	:
HOLDERS WITH 100-199 ANIMALS												**DETENTEURS AVEC 100-199 ANIMAUX**		
1985	:	59,2	4,3	6,8	28,7	:	0,9	6,8	0,2	2,1	0,1	7,0	:	2,3
1987	:	:	:	:	28,2	:	:	:	:	:	:	:	:	:
% 87I85	:	:	:	:	− 1,6	:	:	:	:	:	:	:	:	:
HOLDERS WITH 200-399 ANIMALS												**DETENTEURS AVEC 200-399 ANIMAUX**		
1985	:	46,7	3,5	6,0	18,7	:	0,3	6,5	0,1	2,2	0,0	7,0	:	2,2
1987	:	:	:	:	19,7	:	:	:	:	:	:	:	:	:
% 87I85	:	:	:	:	5,0	:	:	:	:	:	:	:	:	:
HOLDERS WITH 400-999 ANIMALS												**DETENTEURS AVEC 400-999 ANIMAUX**		
1985	:	39,4	2,9	5,4	11,2	:	0,4	6,9	0,2	2,5	0,0	7,5	:	2,5
1987	:	:	:	:	13,1	:	:	:	:	:	:	:	:	:
% 87I85	:	:	:	:	17,3	:	:	:	:	:	:	:	:	:
HOLDERS WITH 1000 ANIMALS AND MORE												**DETENTEURS AVEC 1000 ANIMAUX ET PLUS**		
1985	:	11,5	0,8	1,4	0,9	:	0,1	1,6	0,2	1,8	0,0	2,6	:	2,1
1987	:	:	:	:	0,9	:	:	:	:	:	:	:	:	:
% 87I85	:	:	:	:	7,0	:	:	:	:	:	:	:	:	:

NUMBER OF ANIMALS (1000)   NOMBRE D'ANIMAUX (1000)

YEAR ANNÉE	EUR 12	EUR 10	B	DK	D	EL	ES	F	IRL	I	L	NL	P	UK
TOTAL HOLDERS												**ENSEMBLE DES DETENTEURS**		
1985	:	80 615,6	5 364,8	9 089,0	23 563,0	:	1 095,1	10 956,3	994,1	9 169,1	71,8	12 382,6	:	7 929,9
1987					24 469,7									
% 87/85					3,8									
HOLDERS WITH 1-2 ANIMALS												**DETENTEURS AVEC 1-2 ANIMAUX**		
1985	:	1 018,5	6,0	2,1	153,0	:	55,5	127,8	3,5	663,9	0,8	1,3	:	4,6
1987					135,9									
% 87/85					− 11,2									
HOLDERS WITH 3-9 ANIMALS												**DETENTEURS AVEC 3-9 ANIMAUX**		
1985	:	1 330,5	18,2	19,1	615,3	:	27,8	149,2	7,2	465,4	2,9	7,4	:	17,9
1987					533,8									
% 87/85					− 13,3									
HOLDERS WITH 10-19 ANIMALS												**DETENTEURS AVEC 10-19 ANIMAUX**		
1985	:	1 375,8	34,7	57,3	728,3	:	33,0	132,9	16,6	313,4	2,5	19,0	:	38,1
1987					635,8									
% 87/85					− 12,7									
HOLDERS WITH 20-49 ANIMALS												**DETENTEURS AVEC 20-49 ANIMAUX**		
1985	:	3 533,8	148,2	281,0	2 089,7	:	62,6	363,6	27,2	337,9	9,3	114,4	:	99,9
1987					1 880,1									
% 87/85					− 10,0									
HOLDERS WITH 50-99 ANIMALS												**DETENTEURS AVEC 50-99 ANIMAUX**		
1985	:	5 087,7	303,1	534,3	2 885,5	:	109,4	443,2	19,6	232,9	11,8	378,3	:	169,7
1987					2 682,9									
% 87/85					− 7,0									
HOLDERS WITH 100-199 ANIMALS												**DETENTEURS AVEC 100-199 ANIMAUX**		
1985	:	8 363,0	607,3	964,8	4 024,2	:	118,9	975,2	27,0	302,7	11,8	1 003,5	:	327,6
1987					3 963,6									
% 87/85					− 1,5									
HOLDERS WITH 200-399 ANIMALS												**DETENTEURS AVEC 200-399 ANIMAUX**		
1985	:	13 256,4	993,7	1 705,6	5 278,2	:	89,5	1 866,4	42,7	662,3	11,5	1 979,9	:	626,6
1987					5 545,9									
% 87/85					5,1									
HOLDERS WITH 400-999 ANIMALS												**DETENTEURS AVEC 400-999 ANIMAUX**		
1985	:	24 083,4	1 752,9	3 323,4	6 524,6	:	236,3	4 188,7	140,0	1 581,6	18,7	4 687,6	:	1 629,7
1987					7 718,5									
% 87/85					18,3									
HOLDERS WITH 1000 ANIMALS AND MORE												**DETENTEURS AVEC 1000 ANIMAUX ET PLUS**		
1985	:	22 595,2	1 500,2	2 201,5	1 293,4	:	362,2	2 709,1	710,4	4 609,0	2,4	4 191,2	:	5 015,8
1987					1 373,3									
% 87/85					6,2									

STRUCTURE OF SOW HOLDINGS (> = 50 KG)   I E 6   STRUCTURE DES ELEVAGES DE TRUIES (> = 50 KG)

NUMBER OF HOLDERS (1000)   **NOMBRE DE DETENTEURS (1000)**

YEAR ANNÉE	EUR 12	EUR 10	B	DK	D	EL	ES	F	IRL	I	L	NL	P	UK
TOTAL HOLDERS													**ENSEMBLE DES DETENTEURS**	
1985	:	399,9	20,6	31,3	166,6	:	11,1	48,8	4,3	79,9	0,7	18,6	:	18,0
1987					150,6									
% 87/85					−9,6									
HOLDERS WITH 1 ANIMAL													**DETENTEURS AVEC 1 ANIMAL**	
1985	:	81,4	0,9	1,9	21,9	:	3,6	7,4	1,0	42,1	0,1	0,5	:	2,1
1987					17,8									
% 87/85					−18,9									
HOLDERS WITH 2 ANIMALS													**DETENTEURS AVEC 2 ANIMAUX**	
1985	:	48,6	1,1	2,3	18,7	:	1,2	5,8	1,0	15,9	0,1	0,5	:	2,0
1987					15,1									
% 87/85					−19,1									
HOLDERS WITH 3-4 ANIMALS													**DETENTEURS AVEC 3-4 ANIMAUX**	
1985	:	49,1	1,8	3,7	22,2	:	1,4	5,8	0,9	10,3	0,1	0,8	:	2,0
1987					19,1									
% 87/85					−14,0									
HOLDERS WITH 5-9 ANIMALS													**DETENTEURS AVEC 5-9 ANIMAUX**	
1985	:	56,7	3,1	5,8	29,3	:	1,7	7,4	0,5	4,9	0,2	1,5	:	2,5
1987					25,6									
% 87/85					−12,6									
HOLDERS WITH 10-19 ANIMALS													**DETENTEURS AVEC 10-19 ANIMAUX**	
1985	:	55,2	4,1	5,4	30,5	:	1,4	6,4	0,3	2,6	0,2	2,2	:	2,2
1987					27,6									
% 87/85					−9,5									
HOLDERS WITH 20-49 ANIMALS													**DETENTEURS AVEC 20-49 ANIMAUX**	
1985	:	60,2	5,6	5,8	30,4	:	1,1	8,6	0,2	1,5	0,1	4,1	:	2,7
1987					29,9									
% 87/85					−1,7									
HOLDERS WITH 50-99 ANIMALS													**DETENTEURS AVEC 50-99 ANIMAUX**	
1985	:	30,8	2,9	3,6	11,4	:	0,4	5,6	0,1	1,0	0,0	3,8	:	1,9
1987					12,6									
% 87/85					10,7									
HOLDERS WITH 100 ANIMALS AND MORE													**DETENTEURS AVEC 100 ANIMAUX ET PLUS**	
1985	:	17,8	1,2	2,7	2,2	:	0,2	1,8	0,3	1,6	0,0	5,1	:	2,6
1987					2,9									
% 87/85					30,1									

NUMBER OF ANIMALS (1000)   **NOMBRE D'ANIMAUX (1000)**

YEAR ANNÉE	EUR 12	EUR 10	B	DK	D	EL	ES	F	IRL	I	L	NL	P	UK
TOTAL HOLDERS												**ENSEMBLE DES DETENTEURS**		
1985	:	8 986,4	647,9	1 052,2	2 757,3	:	160,8	1 143,6	112,6	762,6	11,2	1 426,4	:	911,8
1987		:	:	:	2 851,2	:	:	:	:	:	:	:	:	:
% 87/85	:	:	:	:	3,4	:	:	:	:	:	:	:	:	:
HOLDERS WITH 1 ANIMAL												**DETENTEURS AVEC 1 ANIMAL**		
1985	:	79,9	0,9	1,9	21,9	:	3,6	5,8	1,0	42,1	0,1	0,5	:	2,1
1987		:	:	:	17,8	:	:	:	:	:	:	:	:	:
% 87/85	:	:	:	:	− 19,0	:	:	:	:	:	:	:	:	:
HOLDERS WITH 2 ANIMALS												**DETENTEURS AVEC 2 ANIMAUX**		
1985	:	97,0	2,2	4,5	37,4	:	2,4	11,6	1,9	31,7	0,1	1,1	:	4,0
1987		:	:	:	30,2	:	:	:	:	:	:	:	:	:
% 87/85	:	:	:	:	− 19,2	:	:	:	:	:	:	:	:	:
HOLDERS WITH 3-4 ANIMALS												**DETENTEURS AVEC 3-4 ANIMAUX**		
1985	:	169,0	6,5	12,9	76,4	:	4,9	19,9	3,2	35,1	0,3	2,8	:	7,0
1987		:	:	:	65,6	:	:	:	:	:	:	:	:	:
% 87/85	:	:	:	:	− 14,1	:	:	:	:	:	:	:	:	:
HOLDERS WITH 5-9 ANIMALS												**DETENTEURS AVEC 5-9 ANIMAUX**		
1985	:	374,5	20,6	39,1	195,6	:	10,5	49,2	3,4	29,0	1,1	10,1	:	15,9
1987		:	:	:	171,4	:	:	:	:	:	:	:	:	:
% 87/85	:	:	:	:	− 12,4	:	:	:	:	:	:	:	:	:
HOLDERS WITH 10-19 ANIMALS												**DETENTEURS AVEC 10-19 ANIMAUX**		
1985	:	754,0	56,3	73,8	417,8	:	20,7	85,4	3,4	32,8	2,4	31,1	:	30,1
1987		:	:	:	378,7	:	:	:	:	:	:	:	:	:
% 87/85	:	:	:	:	− 9,4	:	:	:	:	:	:	:	:	:
HOLDERS WITH 20-49 ANIMALS												**DETENTEURS AVEC 20-49 ANIMAUX**		
1985	:	1 880,3	176,1	183,8	930,9	:	31,6	281,1	5,7	48,2	3,7	135,1	:	84,2
1987		:	:	:	922,6	:	:	:	:	:	:	:	:	:
% 87/85	:	:	:	:	− 0,9	:	:	:	:	:	:	:	:	:
HOLDERS WITH 50-99 ANIMALS												**DETENTEURS AVEC 50-99 ANIMAUX**		
1985	:	2 135,9	201,2	256,6	766,8	:	26,9	385,3	10,8	72,4	2,7	277,7	:	135,6
1987		:	:	:	857,6	:	:	:	:	:	:	:	:	:
% 87/85	:	:	:	:	11,8	:	:	:	:	:	:	:	:	:
HOLDERS WITH 100 ANIMALS AND MORE											**DETENTEURS AVEC 100 ANIMAUX ET PLUS**			
1985	:	3 494,3	184,3	479,6	310,4	:	60,1	303,7	83,2	471,3	0,8	968,0	:	632,9
1987		:	:	:	407,3	:	:	:	:	:	:	:	:	:
% 87/85	:	:	:	:	31,2	:	:	:	:	:	:	:	:	:

NUMBER OF HOLDERS (1000)　　　　　　　　　　　　　　　　　　　　　　　　**NOMBRE DE DETENTEURS (1000)**

YEAR ANNÉE	EUR 12	EUR 10	B	DK	D	EL	ES	F	IRL	I	L	NL	P	UK
TOTAL HOLDERS												**ENSEMBLE DES DETENTEURS**		
1985	:	1 120,0	14,2	29,9	313,7	:	33,2	134,7	3,4	556,8	1,6	19,6	:	12,9
1987	:	:	:	:	290,3	:	:	:	:	:	:	:	:	:
% 87/85	:	:	:	:	−7,5	:	:	:	:	:	:	:	:	:
HOLDERS WITH 1-2 ANIMALS												**DETENTEURS AVEC 1-2 ANIMAUX**		
1985	:	694,3	2,8	2,1	104,1	:	29,3	87,6	1,4	463,8	0,6	0,8	:	1,9
1987	:	:	:	:	91,9	:	:	:	:	:	:	:	:	:
% 87/85	:	:	:	:	−11,7	:	:	:	:	:	:	:	:	:
HOLDERS WITH 3-9 ANIMALS												**DETENTEURS AVEC 3-9 ANIMAUX**		
1985	:	227,5	2,3	4,9	109,3	:	2,2	27,2	0,8	76,3	0,8	1,6	:	2,1
1987	:	:	:	:	100,1	:	:	:	:	:	:	:	:	:
% 87/85	:	:	:	:	−8,4	:	:	:	:	:	:	:	:	:
HOLDERS WITH 10-19 ANIMALS												**DETENTEURS AVEC 10-19 ANIMAUX**		
1985	:	55,0	1,2	4,7	35,2	:	0,4	3,2	0,3	7,3	0,1	1,3	:	1,4
1987	:	:	: !	:	00,Ω	:	:	:	:	:	:	:	:	:
% 87/85	:	:	:	:	−5,7	:	:	:	:	:	:	:	:	:
HOLDERS WITH 20-49 ANIMALS												**DETENTEURS AVEC 20-49 ANIMAUX**		
1985	:	48,8	1,8	6,8	29,7	:	0,4	2,6	0,2	2,7	0,1	2,8	:	1,7
1987	:	:	:	:	28,3	:	:	:	:	:	:	:	:	:
% 87/85	:	:	:	:	−4,9	:	:	:	:	:	:	:	:	:
HOLDERS WITH 50-99 ANIMALS												**DETENTEURS AVEC 50-99 ANIMAUX**		
1985	:	30,2	1,7	4,7	14,5	:	0,3	2,6	0,1	1,5	0,0	3,5	:	1,4
1987	:	:	:	:	14,5	:	:	:	:	:	:	:	:	:
% 87/85	:	:	:	:	−0,3	:	:	:	:	:	:	:	:	:
HOLDERS WITH 100-199 ANIMALS												**DETENTEURS AVEC 100-199 ANIMAUX**		
1985	:	28,0	1,8	3,8	10,7	:	0,3	4,6	0,2	1,2	0,0	3,9	:	1,5
1987	:	:	:	:	10,9	:	:	:	:	:	:	:	:	:
% 87/85	:	:	:	:	1,9	:	:	:	:	:	:	:	:	:
HOLDERS WITH 200-399 ANIMALS												**DETENTEURS AVEC 200-399 ANIMAUX**		
1985	:	22,7	1,5	2,2	7,4	:	0,2	4,9	0,1	1,4	0,0	3,6	:	1,3
1987	:	:	:	:	8,2	:	:	:	:	:	:	:	:	:
% 87/85	:	:	:	:	10,8	:	:	:	:	:	:	:	:	:
HOLDERS WITH 400-999 ANIMALS												**DETENTEURS AVEC 400-999 ANIMAUX**		
1985	:	11,2	0,8	0,7	2,7	:	0,1	1,9	0,1	1,7	0,0	2,0	:	1,2
1987	:	:	:	:	3,1	:	:	:	:	:	:	:	:	:
% 87/85	:	:	:	:	14,0	:	:	:	:	:	:	:	:	:
HOLDERS WITH 1000 ANIMALS AND MORE											**DETENTEURS AVEC 1000 ANIMAUX ET PLUS**			
1985	:	2,3	0,3	0,0	0,2	:	0,0	0,2	0,1	0,8	−	0,2	:	0,5
1987	:	:	:	:	0,2	:	:	:	:	:	:	:	:	:
% 87/85	:	:	:	:	−	:	:	:	:	:	:	:	:	:

NUMBER OF ANIMALS (1000)   **NOMBRE D'ANIMAUX (1000)**

YEAR ANNÉE	EUR 12	EUR 10	B	DK	D	EL	ES	F	IRL	I	L	NL	P	UK
TOTAL HOLDERS												**ENSEMBLE DES DETENTEURS**		
1985	:	27 555,1	1 856,1	2 183,3	8 305,7	:	272,6	3 952,8	351,1	4 659,0	20,1	3 392,1	:	2 562,3
1987	:	:	:	:	8 631,6	:	:	:	:	:	:	:	:	:
% 87/85	:	:	:	:	3,9	:	:	:	:	:	:	:	:	:
HOLDERS WITH 1-2 ANIMALS												**DETENTEURS AVEC 1-2 ANIMAUX**		
1985	:	1 017,9	4,4	3,2	169,0	:	33,7	132,1	2,1	668,1	1,1	1,3	:	3,0
1987	:	:	:	:	150,6	:	:	:	:	:	:	:	:	:
% 87/85	:	:	:	:	− 10,9	:	:	:	:	:	:	:	:	:
HOLDERS WITH 3-9 ANIMALS												**DETENTEURS AVEC 3-9 ANIMAUX**		
1985	:	1 057,1	11,5	28,3	530,9	:	11,2	113,5	3,8	333,4	3,4	8,8	:	12,4
1987	:	:	:	:	486,0	:	:	:	:	:	:	:	:	:
% 87/85	:	:	:	:	− 8,5	:	:	:	:	:	:	:	:	:
HOLDERS WITH 10-19 ANIMALS												**DETENTEURS AVEC 10-19 ANIMAUX**		
1985	:	727,3	15,6	62,7	463,2	:	5,4	41,4	4,2	97,9	0,9	17,0	:	19,0
1987	:	:	:	:	437,9	:	:	:	:	:	:	:	:	:
% 87/85	:	:	:	:	− 5,5	:	:	:	:	:	:	:	:	:
HOLDERS WITH 20-49 ANIMALS												**DETENTEURS AVEC 20-49 ANIMAUX**		
1985	:	1 501,5	56,9	215,0	901,3	:	10,9	83,4	6,9	81,1	1,5	90,5	:	54,0
1987	:	:	:	:	856,6	:	:	:	:	:	:	:	:	:
% 87/85	:	:	:	:	− 5,0	:	:	:	:	:	:	:	:	:
HOLDERS WITH 50-99 ANIMALS												**DETENTEURS AVEC 50-99 ANIMAUX**		
1985	:	2 090,8	120,2	320,3	1 001,1	:	18,8	183,4	7,1	98,1	1,7	245,8	:	94,2
1987	:	:	:	:	999,7	:	:	:	:	:	:	:	:	:
% 87/85	:	:	:	:	− 0,1	:	:	:	:	:	:	:	:	:
HOLDERS WITH 100-199 ANIMALS												**DETENTEURS AVEC 100-199 ANIMAUX**		
1985	:	3 919,7	249,4	517,1	1 491,3	:	36,4	670,0	25,4	160,1	3,0	553,0	:	214,0
1987	:	:	:	:	1 520,9	:	:	:	:	:	:	:	:	:
% 87/85	:	:	:	:	2,0	:	:	:	:	:	:	:	:	:
HOLDERS WITH 200-399 ANIMALS												**DETENTEURS AVEC 200-399 ANIMAUX**		
1985	:	6 238,4	408,6	598,7	2 039,8	:	54,6	1 360,3	25,9	391,1	4,1	979,1	:	376,2
1987	:	:	:	:	2 261,3	:	:	:	:	:	:	:	:	:
% 87/85	:	:	:	:	10,9	:	:	:	:	:	:	:	:	:
HOLDERS WITH 400-999 ANIMALS												**DETENTEURS AVEC 400-999 ANIMAUX**		
1985	:	6 397,1	489,9	379,9	1 458,2	:	41,4	1 060,9	69,9	1 037,2	4,5	1 121,8	:	733,5
1987	:	:	:	:	1 660,5	:	:	:	:	:	:	:	:	:
% 87/85	:	:	:	:	13,9	:	:	:	:	:	:	:	:	:
HOLDERS WITH 1000 ANIMALS AND MORE												**DETENTEURS AVEC 1000 ANIMAUX ET PLUS**		
1985	:	4 606,2	499,6	58,2	251,9	:	60,1	307,8	205,8	1 792,0	−	374,7	:	1 056,0
1987	:	:	:	:	258,2	:	:	:	:	:	:	:	:	:
% 87/85	:	:	:	:	2,5	:	:	:	:	:	:	:	:	:

NUMBER OF HATCHERIES   **NOMBRE DE COUVOIRS**

YEAR ANNÉE	EUR 12	EUR 10	B	DK	D	EL	ES	F	IRL	I	L	NL	P	UK
TOTAL														**TOTAL**
1985	:	:	64	36	203	55	:	331	22	128	:	104	:	89
1986	:	:	61	31	193	49	—	306	:	128	:	96	—	88
HATCHERIES WITH A CAPACITY OF 1001-10000 EGGS										**COUVOIRS AYANT UNE CAPACITE DE 1001-10000 OEUFS**				
1985	:	:	—	6	63	—	:	51	3	8	:	—		—:
1986	:	:	—	5	64	—	—	48	:	8	:	—		—:
HATCHERIES WITH A CAPACITY OF 10001-20000 EGGS										**COUVOIRS AYANT UNE CAPACITE DE 10001-20000 OEUFS**				
1985	:	:	7	6	53	—	:	53	3	10	:	2	:	9
1986	:	:	6	4	48	1	—	48	:	10	:	1	—	9
HATCHERIES WITH A CAPACITY OF 20001-50000 EGGS										**COUVOIRS AYANT UNE CAPACITE DE 20001-50000 OEUFS**				
1985	:	:	7	11	31	6	:	55	3	20	:	10	:	5
1986	:	:	6	10	29	9	—	49	:	20	:	6	—	5
HATCHERIES WITH A CAPACITY OF 50001-100000 EGGS										**COUVOIRS AYANT UNE CAPACITE DE 50001-100000 OEUFS**				
1985	:	:	14	1	15	9	:	52	2	11	:	7	.	
1986	:	:	13	1	13	15	—	52	:	11	:	9	.	—:
HATCHERIES WITH A CAPACITY OF 100001-200000 EGGS										**COUVOIRS AYANT UNE CAPACITE DE 100001-200000 OEUFS**				
1985	:	:	9	3	9	19	:	30	4	19	:	17	:	6
1986	:	:	9	3	8	15	—	27	:	19	:	14	—	6
HATCHERIES WITH A CAPACITY OF 200001-500000 EGGS										**COUVOIRS AYANT UNE CAPACITE DE 200001-500000 OEUFS**				
1985	:	:	18	5	18	16	:	43	5	21	:	34	:	25
1986	:	:	19	4	17	16	—	38	:	21	:	33	—	25
HATCHERIES WITH A CAPACITY OF MORE THAN 500000 EGGS										**COUVOIRS AYANT UNE CAPACITE SUPERIEURE A 500000 OEUFS**				
1985	:	:	9	4	14	5	:	47	2	39	:	34	:	44
1986	:	:	9	4	14	5	—	44	:	39	:	33	—	43
HATCHERIES WITH A CAPACITY OF MORE THAN 200000 EGGS										**COUVOIRS AYANT UNE CAPACITE SUPERIEURE A 200000 OEUFS**				
1985	:	:	27	9	32	21	:	90	7	60	:	68	:	69
1986	:	:	27	8	31	20	—	82	:	60	:	66	—	68

STRUCTURE AND UTILISATION OF HATCHERIES
(HENS EGGS)

I E 7

STRUCTURE ET UTILISATION DES COUVOIRS
(ŒUFS DES POULES)

CAPACITY OF HATCHERIES (1000 EGGS)   **CAPACITE DES COUVOIRS (1000 OEUFS)**

YEAR ANNÉE	EUR 12	EUR 10	B	DK	D	EL	ES	F	IRL	I	L	NL	P	UK
TOTAL														**TOTAL**
1985	:	:	15 826	8 355	:	13 192	:	84 424	3 630	43 892	:	47 394	:	49 732
1986	:	:	15 153	7 670	:	11 889	—	79 163	:	43 892	:	48 013	—	49 050
HATCHERIES WITH A CAPACITY OF 1001-10000 EGGS										**COUVOIRS AYANT UNE CAPACITE DE 1001-10000 OEUFS**				
1985	:	:	—	41	377 *	—	:	323	18	50	:	—	:	—:
1986	:	:	—	33	390	—	—	304	:	50	:	—		—:
HATCHERIES WITH A CAPACITY OF 10001-20000 EGGS										**COUVOIRS AYANT UNE CAPACITE DE 10001-20000 OEUFS**				
1985	:	:	112	90	822 *	—	:	814	42	188	:	11	:	101
1986	:	:	97	64	741	11	—	749	:	188	:	11	—	110
HATCHERIES WITH A CAPACITY OF 20001-50000 EGGS										**COUVOIRS AYANT UNE CAPACITE DE 20001-50000 OEUFS**				
1985	:	:	252	381	1 027 *	193	:	1 874	117	711	:	383	:	146
1986	:	:	222	350	967	134	—	1 677	:	711	:	238	—	146
HATCHERIES WITH A CAPACITY OF 50001-100000 EGGS										**COUVOIRS AYANT UNE CAPACITE DE 50001-100000 OEUFS**				
1985	:	:	1 055	60	1 088 *	782	:	3 719	173	588	:	500	:	—:
1986	:	:	1 008	60	961	773	—	3 737	:	950	:	602	—	—:
HATCHERIES WITH A CAPACITY OF 100001-200000 EGGS										**COUVOIRS AYANT UNE CAPACITE DE 100001-200000 OEUFS**				
1985	:	:	1 332	440	1 329 *	3 130	:	4 667	708	3 776	:	2 451	:	811
1986	:	:	1 360	440	1 248	2 497	—	4 190	:	3 414	:	2 078	—	811
HATCHERIES WITH A CAPACITY OF 200001-500000 EGGS										**COUVOIRS AYANT UNE CAPACITE DE 200001-500000 OEUFS**				
1985	:	:	6 487	1 659	5 640 *	5 118	:	14 106	1 395	7 632	:	11 807	:	8 645
1986	:	:	6 888	1 449	5 339	4 505	—	12 470	:	7 632	:	11 178	—	8 645
HATCHERIES WITH A CAPACITY OF MORE THAN 500000 EGGS										**COUVOIRS AYANT UNE CAPACITE SUPERIEURE A 500000 OEUFS**				
1985	:	:	6 588	5 274	21 463 *	3 969	:	58 921	1 176	30 947	:	32 242	:	40 029
1986	:	:	5 578	5 274	22 048	3 969	—	56 036	:	30 947	:	33 906	—	39 338
HATCHERIES WITH A CAPACITY OF MORE THAN 200000 EGGS										**COUVOIRS AYANT UNE CAPACITE SUPERIEURE A 200000 OEUFS**				
1985	:	:	13 075	6 933	:	9 087	:	73 027	2 572	38 579	:	44 049	:	48 674
1986	:	:	12 466	6 723	:	8 474	—	68 506	:	38 579	:	48 013	—	47 983

STRUCTURE AND UTILISATION OF HATCHERIES (HENS EGGS)

I E 7

STRUCTURE ET UTILISATION DES COUVOIRS (ŒUFS DES POULES)

INCUBATIONS (1000 EGGS) — INCUBATIONS (1000 OEUFS)

YEAR ANNÉE	EUR 12	EUR 10	B	DK	D	EL	ES	F	IRL	I	L	NL	P	UK
TOTAL														**TOTAL**
1985	:		146 691	115 944	390 770	105 832	:	939 593	45 654	482 817	:	564 119	:	726 711
1986	:		158 434	114 659	388 040	109 209	−	948 338	:	431 519	:	586 728	−	772 882
HATCHERIES WITH A CAPACITY OF 1001-10000 EGGS													COUVOIRS AYANT UNE CAPACITE DE 1001-10000 OEUFS	
1985	:		−	65	939	−	:	1 023	34	571	:	−	:	−:
1986	:		−	32	929	−	−	1 028	:	38	:	−	−	−:
HATCHERIES WITH A CAPACITY OF 10001-20000 EGGS													COUVOIRS AYANT UNE CAPACITE DE 10001-20000 OEUFS	
1985	:		150	92	2 305		:	2 872	157	2 064	:	−	:	243
1986	:		203	80	2 312	126	−	2 637	:	1 028	:	−	−	329
HATCHERIES WITH A CAPACITY OF 20001-50000 EGGS													COUVOIRS AYANT UNE CAPACITE DE 20001-50000 OEUFS	
1985	:		214	522	3 674	1 846	:	5 900	1 618	7 816	:	372	:	502
1986	:		326	426	3 880	1 955	−	5 782	:	1 770	:	419	−	610
HATCHERIES WITH A CAPACITY OF 50001-100000 EGGS													COUVOIRS AYANT UNE CAPACITE DE 50001-100000 OEUFS	
1985	:		7 916	381	6 502	14 345	:	22 856	3 092	6 469	:	2 701	:	−:
1986	:		8 970	315	5 127	16 868	−	22 272	:	12 323	:	2 746	−	−:
HATCHERIES WITH A CAPACITY OF 100001-200000 EGGS													COUVOIRS AYANT UNE CAPACITE DE 100001-200000 OEUFS	
1985	:		9 933	3 683	12 154	15 551	:	37 965	9 246	41 488	:	18 616	:	7 426
1986	:		9 527	4 052	7 383	18 184	−	39 569	:	12 576	:	19 784	−	8 282
HATCHERIES WITH A CAPACITY OF 200001-500000 EGGS													COUVOIRS AYANT UNE CAPACITE DE 200001-500000 OEUFS	
1985	:		60 501	22 968	65 646	29 873	:	155 367	17 926	83 960	:	122 577	:	119 804
1986	:		74 005	22 232	67 443	27 948	−	139 487	:	66 614	:	104 354	−	124 767
HATCHERIES WITH A CAPACITY OF MORE THAN 500000 EGGS													COUVOIRS AYANT UNE CAPACITE SUPERIEURE A 500000 OEUFS	
1985	:		67 977	88 233	300 549	55 149	:	713 580	13 582	340 450	:	419 853	:	598 736
1986	:		65 403	87 522	301 028	56 713	−	737 563	:	319 699	:	459 425	−	638 894
HATCHERIES WITH A CAPACITY OF MORE THAN 200000 EGGS													COUVOIRS AYANT UNE CAPACITE SUPERIEURE A 200000 OEUFS	
1985	:		128 478	111 201	366 196	85 022	:	868 947	31 507	424 410	:	542 431	:	:
1986	:		139 408	109 754	368 660	84 661	−	928 589	:	403 784	:	563 779	−	:

STRUCTURE AND UTILISATION OF HATCHERIES (HENS EGGS)

I E 7

STRUCTURE ET UTILISATION DES COUVOIRS (ŒUFS DES POULES)

INCUBATIONS (LAYING STOCK / 1000 EGGS) — INCUBATIONS (RACE PONTE / 1000 OEUFS)

YEAR ANNÉE	EUR 12	EUR 10	B	DK	D	EL	ES	F	IRL	I	L	NL	P	UK
TOTAL														**TOTAL**
1985	:	:	38 372	11 164	108 845	7 931	:	128 061	6 910	55 412	:	116 077	:	100 959
1986	:	:	40 325	10 344	102 751	8 082	−	119 193	:	56 960	:	111 851	−	97 465
HATCHERIES WITH A CAPACITY OF 1001-10000 EGGS													COUVOIRS AYANT UNE CAPACITE DE 1001-10000 OEUFS	
1985	:	:	−	65	790	−	:	9	19	63	:	−	:	−:
1986	:	:	−	32	778	−	−	18	:	:	:	−	−	−:
HATCHERIES WITH A CAPACITY OF 10001-20000 EGGS													COUVOIRS AYANT UNE CAPACITE DE 10001-20000 OEUFS	
1985	:	:	131	92	1 799		:	146	34	257	:	−	:	228
1986	:	:	109	80	1 802	−	−	157	:	6	:	−	−	287
HATCHERIES WITH A CAPACITY OF 20001-50000 EGGS													COUVOIRS AYANT UNE CAPACITE DE 20001-50000 OEUFS	
1985	:	:	133	492	3 017	60	:	529	641	888	:	326	:	211
1986	:	:	205	391	3 195	−	−	501	:	28	:	385	−	243
HATCHERIES WITH A CAPACITY OF 50001-100000 EGGS													COUVOIRS AYANT UNE CAPACITE DE 50001-100000 OEUFS	
1985	:	:	947	381	5 722	1 000	:	4 291	−	752	:	2 648	:	−:
1986	:	:	1 241	315	4 304	932	−	4 182	:	134	:	2 525	−	−:
HATCHERIES WITH A CAPACITY OF 100001-200000 EGGS													COUVOIRS AYANT UNE CAPACITE DE 100001-200000 OEUFS	
1985	:	:	3 945	1 921	8 409	2 000	:	738	155	4 716	:	9 141	:	3 795
1986	:	:	3 331	2 328	4 329	2 189	−	723	:	137	:	7 833	−	3 849
HATCHERIES WITH A CAPACITY OF 200001-500000 EGGS													COUVOIRS AYANT UNE CAPACITE DE 200001-500000 OEUFS	
1985	:	:	17 161	8 213	42 390	4 871	:	15 637	6 062	9 654	:	54 719	:	37 711
1986	:	:	24 891	7 198	43 632	4 961	−	14 415	:		:	35 239	−	36 224
HATCHERIES WITH A CAPACITY OF MORE THAN 500000 EGGS													COUVOIRS AYANT UNE CAPACITE SUPERIEURE A 500000 OEUFS	
1985	:	:	16 055	−	46 718	−	:	106 711	−	39 082	:	49 243	:	59 014
1986	:	:	10 548	−	44 771	−	−	99 197	:	39 082	:	65 869	−	56 862
HATCHERIES WITH A CAPACITY OF MORE THAN 200000 EGGS													COUVOIRS AYANT UNE CAPACITE SUPERIEURE A 200000 OEUFS	
1985	:	:	33 216	8 213	89 108	4 871	:	122 348	6 062	48 735	:	103 963	:	96 725
1986	:	:	35 439	7 198	88 403	4 961	−	119 193	:	56 655	:	101 108	−	93 086

STRUCTURE AND UTILISATION OF HATCHERIES (HENS EGGS) — I E 7 — STRUCTURE ET UTILISATION DES COUVOIRS (ŒUFS DES POULES)

INCUBATIONS (MEAT STOCK / 1000 EGGS) — INCUBATIONS (RACE CHAIR / 1000 OEUFS)

YEAR ANNÉE	EUR 12	EUR 10	B	DK	D	EL	ES	F	IRL	I	L	NL	P	UK
TOTAL														**TOTAL**
1985	:	:	108 319	104 780	281 925	89 949	:	776 590	38 744	403 362		448 042	:	625 752
1986	:	:	118 109	104 315	285 289	91 647	−	789 570		363 828		474 877	−	675 417
HATCHERIES WITH A CAPACITY OF 1001-10000 EGGS												**COUVOIRS AYANT UNE CAPACITE DE 1001-10000 OEUFS**		
1985	:	:	−	−	149	−	:	375	15	480		−	:	−:
1986	:	:	−	−	151	−	−	343	:	13		−	−	−:
HATCHERIES WITH A CAPACITY OF 10001-20000 EGGS												**COUVOIRS AYANT UNE CAPACITE DE 10001-20000 OEUFS**		
1985	:	:	19	−	506	−	:	1 041	123	1 705		−	:	15
1986	:	:	94	−	510	−	−	893	:	648		−	−	42
HATCHERIES WITH A CAPACITY OF 20001-50000 EGGS												**COUVOIRS AYANT UNE CAPACITE DE 20001-50000 OEUFS**		
1985	:	:	81	30	657	569	:	3 151	977	6 558		46	:	291
1986	:	:	121	35	685	936	−	2 644	:	599		34	−	367
HATCHERIES WITH A CAPACITY OF 50001-100000 EGGS												**COUVOIRS AYANT UNE CAPACITE DE 50001-100000 OEUFS**		
1985	:	:	6 969	−	780	12 932	:	13 514	3 092	5 404		53	:	−:
1986	:	:	7 729	−	822	14 774	−	13 317	:	11 157		221	−	−:
HATCHERIES WITH A CAPACITY OF 100001-200000 EGGS												**COUVOIRS AYANT UNE CAPACITE DE 100001-200000 OEUFS**		
1985	:	:	5 988	1 762	3 745	12 932	:	28 937	9 091	34 684		9 475	:	3 631
1986	:	:	6 196	1 724	3 053	14 744	−	28 761	:	9 824		11 951	−	4 433
HATCHERIES WITH A CAPACITY OF 200001-500000 EGGS												**COUVOIRS AYANT UNE CAPACITE DE 200001-500000 OEUFS**		
1985	:	:	43 340	14 755	23 257	21 299	:	135 397	11 864	70 126		67 858	:	82 093
1986	:	:	49 114	15 034	23 811	19 254	−	119 341	:	61 201		69 115	−	88 543
HATCHERIES WITH A CAPACITY OF MORE THAN 500000 EGGS												**COUVOIRS AYANT UNE CAPACITE SUPERIEURE A 500000 OEUFS**		
1985	:	:	51 922	88 233	253 831	55 149	:	594 175	13 582	284 405		370 610	:	539 722
1986	:	:	54 855	87 522	256 257	56 713	−	624 271	:	280 386		393 556	−	582 032
HATCHERIES WITH A CAPACITY OF MORE THAN 200000 EGGS												**COUVOIRS AYANT UNE CAPACITE SUPERIEURE A 200000 OEUFS**		
1985	:	:	95 262	102 988	277 088	76 448	:	729 572	25 446	354 532		438 468	:	621 815
1986	:	:	103 969	102 556	280 257	75 967	−	789 570	:	341 587		462 671	−	670 575

STRUCTURE AND UTILISATION OF HATCHERIES (HENS EGGS) — I E 7 — STRUCTURE ET UTILISATION DES COUVOIRS (ŒUFS DES POULES)

INCUBATIONS (MIXED STOCK / 1000 EGGS) — INCUBATIONS (RACE MIXTE / 1000 OEUFS)

YEAR ANNÉE	EUR 12	EUR 10	B	DK	D	EL	ES	F	IRL	I	L	NL	P	UK
TOTAL														**TOTAL**
1985	:	:	−	−	−	7 952	:	34 942	−	24 043		−	:	−
1986	:	:	−	−	−	9 480	−	39 575	:	10 731		−	−	−
HATCHERIES WITH A CAPACITY OF 1001-10000 EGGS												**COUVOIRS AYANT UNE CAPACITE DE 1001-10000 OEUFS**		
1985	:	:	−	−	−	−	:	639	−	27		−	:	−
1986	:	:	−	−	−	−	−	667	:	25		−	−	−
HATCHERIES WITH A CAPACITY OF 10001-20000 EGGS												**COUVOIRS AYANT UNE CAPACITE DE 10001-20000 OEUFS**		
1985	:	:	−	−	−	−	:	1 685	−	103		−	:	−
1986	:	:	−	−	−	126	−	1 587	:	374		−	−	−
HATCHERIES WITH A CAPACITY OF 20001-50000 EGGS												**COUVOIRS AYANT UNE CAPACITE DE 20001-50000 OEUFS**		
1985	:	:	−	−	−	1 217	:	2 220	−	370		−	:	−
1986	:	:	−	−	−	1 019	−	2 637	:	1 143		−	−	−
HATCHERIES WITH A CAPACITY OF 50001-100000 EGGS												**COUVOIRS AYANT UNE CAPACITE DE 50001-100000 OEUFS**		
1985	:	:	−	−	−	413	:	5 051	−	312		−	:	−
1986	:	:	−	−	−	1 162	−	4 773	:	1 032		−	−	−
HATCHERIES WITH A CAPACITY OF 100001-200000 EGGS												**COUVOIRS AYANT UNE CAPACITE DE 100001-200000 OEUFS**		
1985	:	:	−	−	−	2 619	:	8 290	−	2 088		−	:	−
1986	:	:	−	−	−	3 440	−	10 085	:	2 615		−	−	−
HATCHERIES WITH A CAPACITY OF 200001-500000 EGGS												**COUVOIRS AYANT UNE CAPACITE DE 200001-500000 OEUFS**		
1985	:	:	−	−	−	3 703	:	4 333	−	4 180		−	:	−
1986	:	:	−	−	−	3 733	−	5 731	:	5 311		−	−	−
HATCHERIES WITH A CAPACITY OF MORE THAN 500000 EGGS												**COUVOIRS AYANT UNE CAPACITE SUPERIEURE A 500000 OEUFS**		
1985	:	:	−	−	−	−	:	12 694	−	16 963		−	:	−
1986	:	:	−	−	−	−	−	14 095	:	231		−	−	−
HATCHERIES WITH A CAPACITY OF MORE THAN 200000 EGGS												**COUVOIRS AYANT UNE CAPACITE SUPERIEURE A 200000 OEUFS**		
1985	:	:	−	−	−	3 703	:	17 027	−	21 143		−	:	−
1986	:	:	−	−	−	3 733	−	19 826	:	5 542		−	:	−

STRUCTURE AND UTILISATION OF HATCHERIES (DUCK EGGS)
STRUCTURE ET UTILISATION DES COUVOIRS (ŒUFS DE CANES)

YEAR ANNÉE	EUR 12	EUR 10	B	DK	D	EL	ES	F	IRL	I	L	NL	P	UK
NUMBER OF HATCHERIES														**NOMBRE DE COUVOIRS**
1985	:	:	6	18	31	2	:	100	−:	8	:	19	:	10
1986	:	:	6	19	34	3	−	101	:	9	:	16	−	10
CAPACITY OF HATCHERIES (1000 EGGS)														**CAPACITE DES COUVOIRS (1000 ŒUFS)**
1985	:	:	411	1 425	:	221	:	6 562	:	849	:	951	:	1 606
1986	:	:	389	1 519	:	1 085	−	6 791	:	976	:	831	−	1 606
INCUBATIONS (1000 EGGS)														**INCUBATIONS (1000 ŒUFS)**
1985	:	:	159	6 243	6 972	14	:	58 782	:	1 935	:	4 182	:	13 848
1986	:	:	112	6 185	8 267	66	−	67 078	:	1 259	:	4 681	−	13 922

STRUCTURE AND UTILISATION OF HATCHERIES (GEESE EGGS)
STRUCTURE ET UTILISATION DES COUVOIRS (OEUFS D'OIES)

YEAR ANNÉE	EUR 12	EUR 10	B	DK	D	EL	ES	F	IRL	I	L	NL	P	UK
NUMBER OF HATCHERIES														**NOMBRE DE COUVOIRS**
1985	:	:	6	18	40	−	:	53	−:	6	:	−	:	S
1986	:	:	7	18	37	−	−	55	:	6	:	−	−	S
CAPACITY OF HATCHERIES (1000 EGGS)														**CAPACITE DES COUVOIRS (1000 OEUFS)**
1985	:	:	452	991	:	−	:	684	:	769	:	−	:	S
1986	:	:	532	986	:	−	−	738	:	769	:	−	−	S
INCUBATIONS (1000 EGGS)														**INCUBATIONS (1000 OEUFS)**
1985	:	:	104	296	663	−	:	1 987	:	286	:	−	:	S
1986	:	:	100	323	694	−	−	1 963	:	204	:	−	−	S

STRUCTURE AND UTILISATION OF HATCHERIES (TURKEY EGGS)
STRUCTURE ET UTILISATION DES COUVOIRS (OEUFS DE DINDES)

YEAR ANNÉE	EUR 12	EUR 10	B	DK	D	EL	ES	F	IRL	I	L	NL	P	UK
NUMBER OF HATCHERIES														**NOMBRE DE COUVOIRS**
1985	:	:	13	3	9	6	:	54	−:	12	:	14	:	34
1986	:	:	13	2	9	4	−	52	:	15	:	14	−	34
CAPACITY OF HATCHERIES (1000 EGGS)														**CAPACITE DES COUVOIRS (1000 OEUFS)**
1985	:	:	1 957	688	:	858	:	8 729	:	5 851	:	541	:	5 667
1986	:	:	1 912	288	:	440	−	9 277	:	5 851	:	653	−	5 718
INCUBATIONS (1000 EGGS)														**INCUBATIONS (1000 OEUFS)**
1985	:	:	1 703	1 510	11 826	419	:	82 322	:	30 911	:	3 088	:	44 166
1986	:	:	1 668	1 451	12 953	514	−	88 009	:	29 062	:	3 774	−	48 755

STRUCTURE AND UTILISATION OF HATCHERIES (GUINEA-FOWL EGGS)
STRUCTURE ET UTILISATION DES COUVOIRS (OEUFS DE PINTADES)

YEAR ANNÉE	EUR 12	EUR 10	B	DK	D	EL	ES	F	IRL	I	L	NL	P	UK
NUMBER OF HATCHERIES														**NOMBRE DE COUVOIRS**
1985	:	:	5	−	4	−	:	58	:	5	:	−	:	S
1986	:	:	8	−	4	−	−	54	:	6	:	−	−	S
CAPACITY OF HATCHERIES (1000 EGGS)														**CAPACITE DES COUVOIRS (1000 OEUFS)**
1985	:	:	998	−	:	−	:	7 321	:	2 601	:	−	:	S
1986	:	:	1 595	−	:	−	−	7 355	:	6 621	:	−	−	S
INCUBATIONS (1000 EGGS)														**INCUBATIONS (1000 OEUFS)**
1985	:	:	1 210	−	2	−	:	75 156	:	23 666	:	−	:	S
1986	:	:	1 388	−	1	−	−	74 196	:	26 413	:	−	−	S

	EUR 10	EUR 12	B L	DK	D	GR	ES	F	IRL	I	NL	P	UK
1000 HEAD													**1000 TÊTES**
CATTLE													**BOVINS**
1983	27 720	− :	1 004	1 062	5 544	367	− :	8 999	1 677	2 678	2 410	− :	3 979
1984	29 972	− :	1 138	1 100	5 968	363	− :	9 540	1 750	3 027	2 754	− :	4 331
1985	28 948	− :	1 205	1 043	5 787	329	− :	9 132	1 806	2 869	2 571	− :	4 207
1986	− :	31 333	1 162	1 021	6 137	325	1 859	9 255	1 955	2 753	2 510	471	3 884
PIGS													**PORCINS**
1983	127 483	− :	7 986	15 207	37 512	2 284	− :	17 951	2 295	10 375	17 356	− :	16 516
1984	127 783	− :	7 896	14 815	38 285	2 259	− :	18 205	2 154	10 823	18 110	− :	15 237
1985	129 025	− :	7 771	15 219	38 018	2 225	− :	18 320	2 070	10 257	19 711	− :	15 434
1986	− :	150 622	7 761	16 117	39 983	2 345	14 694	18 756	2 162	9 370	21 372	2 420	15 642
SHEEP AND GOATS													**OVINS ET CAPRINS**
1983	46 554 :	− :	183 :	27	1 006	11 198	− :	10 305	1 629	6 231	860	− :	15 114 :
1984	46 727 :	− :	135 :	30	1 055	11 369	− :	10 168	1 670	6 613	689	− :	14 998 :
1985	47 639 :	− :	172 :	36	1 090	11 428	− :	9 963	2 131	6 299	760	− :	15 759 :
1986	− :	60 122 :	147 :	40	1 040	9 924	11 840	9 540	3 636	6 489	729	1 268	15 469 :
EQUIDAE													**ÉQUIDÉS**
1983	242	− :	10	4	33	3	− :	47	9	84	23	− :	29
1984	248	− :	8	4	32	3	− :	45	9	95	24	− :	28
1985	195 :	− :	9	3	31	3	− :	46	7	71	23	− :	2 :
1986	− :	278 :	6	3	28	6	50	55	6	97	19	8	1 :
1000 TONNES													**1000 TONNES**
CATTLE													**BOVINS**
1983	6 935	− :	294	240	1 528	81	− :	1 937	465	921	451	− :	1 019
1984	7 542	− :	331	247	1 636	80	− :	2 123	506	987	524	− :	1 108
1985	7 396	− :	343	237	1 596	74	− :	2 040	534	965	510	− :	1 099
1986	− :	7 997	347	243	1 739	73	421	2 069	572	915	523	101	994
PIGS													**PORCINS**
1983	10 364	− :	678	1 051	3 146	149	− :	1 564	146	1 115	1 476	− :	1 040
1984	10 418	− :	679	1 039	3 161	148	− :	1 576	138	1 166	1 543	− :	966
1985	10 524	− :	667	1 086	3 151	142	− :	1 570	132	1 121	1 677	− :	979
1986	− :	12 183	705	1 146	3 287	153	1 111	1 591	237	1 052	1 737	170	993
SHEEP AND GOATS													**OVINS ET CAPRINS**
1983	726 :	− :	5 :	1	24	119	− :	178	40	51	21	− :	288 :
1984	728 :	− :	1 :	1	24	129	− :	174	41	54	17	− :	288 :
1985	742 :	− :	4 :	1	24	122	− :	172	49	48	18	− :	304 :
1986	− :	850	6 :	1	23	106	134	162	47	49	17	13	292 :
EQUIDAE													**ÉQUIDÉS**
1983	56	− :	3	1	8	− :	− :	14	2	15	5	− :	7
1984	58	− :	3	1	8	− :	− :	14	2	16	5	− :	7
1985	45 :	− :	2	1	8	− :	− :	15	2	12	5	− :	0 :
1986	− :	56 :	2 :	1	7	1	7	14	1	17	4	1	1 :

MEAT (TOTAL)   **VIANDE (TOTAL)**

YEAR ANNÉE	EUR 12	EUR 10	UEBL BLEU	DK	D	GR	E	F	IRL	I	NL	P	UK
						1000 T							
GROSS INDIGENOUS PRODUCTION											**PRODUCTION INDIGENE BRUTE**		
1984	:	25 135	1 244	1 461	5 535	552	2 807	5 878	835	3 627	2 617	505	3 386
1985	:	25 092:	1 243	1 503	5 481	552:	2 761	5 776	869	3 519	2 711	486	3 438
1986	23 302:	:	1 277	1 578	5 803	529	3 096	—:	815	3 413	2 848	531	3 412
EXPORTS OF LIVE ANIMALS											**EXPORTATIONS D'ANIMAUX VIVANTS**		
1984	:	135	98	4	119	1	1	192	133	8	327	—	37
1985	:	97	84	3	114	1	—	215	114	5	365	—	42
1986	406:	:	113	2	145	1	—	—:	92	3	394	—	62
INTRA EUR													*INTRA EUR*
1984	:	:	97	4	83	—	:	177	74	1	312		36
1985	:	:	82	3	83	—	:	203	78	2	355	:	41
1986	:	:	110	2	128	1	—	—	—	—	388	:	60
IMPORTS OF LIVE ANIMALS											**IMPORTATIONS D'ANIMAUX VIVANTS**		
1984	:	204	168	—	171	7	8	190	20	343	22	2	68
1985	:	240	159	—	201	9	17	173	16	424	33	5	71
1986	598:	:	184	—	156	9	12	—:	31	482	51	4	75
INTRA EUR													*INTRA EUR*
1984	:	784	163	—	104	1	:	169	20	241	21	2	68
1985	:	845	153	—	133	2	:	156	16	285	33	:	71
1986	406:	:	179	—	100	1	—	—	—	—	50	—	76
USABLE PRODUCTION (SLAUGHTERINGS)											**PRODUCTION UTILISABLE (ABBATAGES)**		
1984	28 526	25 205	1 314	1 457	5 587	559	2 814	5 876	722	3 962	2 312	507	3 416
1985	28 505:	25 236:	1 318	1 500	5 568	560:	2 778	5 734	771	3 938	2 379	491	3 467
1986	23 495:	19 852:	1 348	1 576	5 814	537	3 108	—:	754	3 892	2 505	535	3 426
IMPORTS											**IMPORTATIONS**		
1984	:	1 164	201	9	1 158	211	93	912	38	861	197	13	1 128
1985	:	1 278	209	19	1 207	227	111	1 000	38	1 069	204	41	1 167
1986	2 035:	:	217	27	1 184	241	101	—:	38	1 051	206	41	1 180
INTRA EUR													*INTRA EUR*
1984	:	3 551	148	7	915	182	:	746	37	674	127	:	715
1985	:	3 863	150	16	947	194	:	839	38	820	136	:	723
1986	2 251:	:	154	23	958	201	—	—	—	—	141	—	774
RESOURCES = USES											**RESSOURCES = EMPLOIS**		
1984	:	26 369	1 515	1 466	6 745	769	2 907	6 788	760	4 823	2 509	520	4 544
1985	:	26 514:	1 527	1 519	6 775	787:	2 889	6 734	809	5 007	2 583	532	4 634
1986	25 530:	:	1 565	1 603	6 998	778	3 209	—:	792	4 943	2 711	576	4 606
EXPORTS											**EXPORTATIONS**		
1984	:	1 712	492	1 038	626	2	33	835	348	169	1 384	9	368
1985	:	1 576	473	1 061	617	1	18	880	406	213	1 438	10	349
1986	2 804:	:	546	1 085	783	1	24	—:	479	210	1 543	10	374
INTRA EUR													*INTRA EUR*
1984	:	:	446	629	430	1	:	330	232	100	1 244	:	272
1985	:	:	435	639	436	—	:	321	250	151	1 301	:	273
1986	:	:	501	667	527	1	—	—	—	—	1 382	—	279
CHANGE IN STOCKS											**VARIATION DES STOCKS**		
1984	286	316	−2	−1	66	−0	−25	98	71	41	15	−5	28
1985	211:	216:	25	−3	29	4:	−3	32	64	8	3	−2	54
1986	− 105:	− 105:	−13	−1	−13	−4	−8	—:	19	−71	16	8	−38
TOTAL DOMESTIC USES											**UTILISATION INTERIEURE TOTALE**		
1984	:	24 341	1 025	429	6 053	768	2 899	5 855	341	4 613	1 110	516	4 147
1985	:	24 722:	1 029	461	6 129	782:	2 874	5 822	339	4 786	1 142	524	4 232
1986	22 831:	:	1 032	519	6 228	781	3 193	—:	294	4 804	1 152	558	4 270
HUMAN CONSUMPTION (1)											*CONSOMMATION HUMAINE (1)*		
1984	27 756	24 341	1 025	429	6 053	768	2 899	5 855	341	4 613	1 110	516	4 147
1985	28 120:	24 722:	1 029	461	6 129	782:	2 874	5 822	339	4 786	1 142	524	4 232
1986	22 831:	19 080:	1 032	519	6 228	781	3 193	—:	294	4 804	1 152	558	4 270
SELF-SUFFICIENCY (%)											**AUTO-APPROVISIONNEMENT (%)**		
1984	:	103,3	121,4	340,6	91,4	71,9	96,8	100,4	244,9	78,6	235,8	97,9	81,6
1985	:	101,5:	120,8	326,0	89,4	70,6:	96,1	99,2	256,3	73,5	237,4	92,7	81,2
1986	102,1:	:	123,7	304,0	93,2	67,7	97,0	:	277,2	71,0	247,2	95,2	79,9
HUMAN CONSUMPTION (KG/HEAD/YEAR)											**CONSOMMATION HUMAINE(KG/TETE/AN)**		
1984	86,4	89,2	100,3	83,9	98,9	77,6	75,5	106,6	96,6	80,9	77,0	51,1	73,4
1985	87,4:	90,5:	100,6	90,1	100,4	78,7:	74,6	105,5	95,8	83,8	78,8	51,6	74,7
1986	70,7:	69,7:	100,9	101,3	102,0	78,4	82,6	—:	83,1	83,9	79,1	54,7	75,2

(1) QUANTITIES AVAILABLE FOR HUMAN CONSUMPTION   (1) QUANTITES DISPONIBLES POUR LA CONSOMMATION HUMAINE

I E 10

MEAT : TOTAL CATTLE   **VIANDE BOVINE (TOTALE)**

YEAR ANNÉE	EUR 12	EUR 10	UEBL BLEU	DK	D	GR	E	F	IRL	I	NL	P	UK
1000 T													
GROSS INDIGENOUS PRODUCTION											**PRODUCTION INDIGENE BRUTE**		
1984	:	7 535	330	247	1 637	80	381	2 121	505	987	524	101	1 104
1985	:	7 385	333	236	1 596	75	384	2 039	533	967	509	98	1 097
1986	5 945 :	:	336	243	1 739	73	423	— :	570	919	523	102	1 016
EXPORTS OF LIVE ANIMALS											**EXPORTATIONS D'ANIMAUX VIVANTS**		
1984	:	114	23	—	73	0	—	151	109	7	22	—	13
1985	:	75	27	—	68	—	—	167	88	3	22	—	10
1986	125 :	:	32	—	80	—	—	— :	86	1	21	—	31
INTRA EUR													*INTRA EUR*
1984	:	:	23	—	42	—	:	138	60	—	18	:	13
1985	:	:	27	—	40	—	:	156	62	—	17	:	9
1986	:	:	32	—	64						10		31
IMPORTS OF LIVE ANIMALS											**IMPORTATIONS D'ANIMAUX VIVANTS**		
1984	:	81	12	—	50	5	8	21	5	202	13	2	56
1985	:	102	11	—	48	8	17	21	3	241	23	5	57
1986	331 :	:	13	—	36	9	12	— :	25	261	37	4	61
INTRA EUR													*INTRA EUR*
1984	:	284	12	—	17	1	:	21	5	159	13	:	56
1985	:	309	11	—	17	2	:	21	3	175	23	:	57
1986	126 :	:	13	—	14	1	—	—	—	—	37	—	61
USABLE PRODUCTION (SLAUGHTERINGS)											**PRODUCTION UTILISABLE (ABBATAGES)**		
1984	7 994	7 502	319	247	1 614	85	389	1 991	401	1 182	515	103	1 148
1985	7 916	7 412	317	236	1 576	82	401	1 893	448	1 205	510	103	1 145
1986	6 151 :	5 610 :	317	243	1 695	82	435	— :	509	1 179	539	106	1 046
IMPORTS											**IMPORTATIONS**		
1984	:	388	35	6	285	128	31	281	12	432	61	5	315
1985	:	449	32	12	301	132	39	322	9	535	69	13	327
1986	832 :	:	30	18	300	140	7	— :	8	485	77	17	380
INTRA EUR													*INTRA EUR*
1984	:	1 167	29	6	191	121	:	267	12	340	47	:	154
1985	:	1 289	24	12	208	122	:	306	9	403	52	:	153
1986	630 :	:	25	17	194	127	—	—	—	—	57	—	210
RESOURCES = USES											**RESSOURCES = EMPLOIS**		
1984	:	7 890	354	253	1 899	213	420	2 272	413	1 614	576	108	1 463
1985	:	7 861	349	248	1 877	214	440	2 215	457	1 740	579	116	1 472
1986	6 983 :	:	347	261	1 995	222	442	— :	517	1 664	616	123	1 426
EXPORTS											**EXPORTATIONS**		
1984	:	823	89	176	449	0	14	405	258	105	293	2	215
1985	:	807	86	165	437	0	1	460	316	141	301	2	190
1986	1 362 :	:	99	189	579	0	1	— :	414	148	366	3	192
INTRA EUR													*INTRA EUR*
1984	:	:	76	106	280	—	:	218	149	45	235	:	130
1985	:	:	79	108	277	—	:	192	166	90	241	:	128
1986	:	:	89	99	343	—	—	—	—	—	278	—	113
CHANGE IN STOCKS											**VARIATION DES STOCKS**		
1984	332	365	3	9	72	−2	−28	112	71	41	15	−5	44
1985	194 :	200 :	2	11	30	3 :	−4	33	64	8	3	−2	46
1986	− 100 :	− 98 :	4	−14	−16	−2	−4	— :	19	−71	12	2	−30
TOTAL DOMESTIC USES											**UTILISATION INTERIEURE TOTALE**		
1984	:	6 701	262	68	1 378	214	434	1 755	84	1 468	268	111	1 204
1985	:	6 855 :	261	72	1 410	211 :	443	1 722	77	1 591	275	116	1 236
1986	5 722 :	:	244	86	1 432	224	445	— :	84	1 587	238	118	1 264
HUMAN CONSUMPTION (1)											*CONSOMMATION HUMAINE (1)*		
1984	7 246	6 701	262	68	1 378	214	434	1 755	84	1 468	268	111	1 204
1985	7 414 :	6 855 :	261	72	1 410	211 :	443	1 722	77	1 591	275	116	1 236
1986	5 722 :	5 159 :	244	86	1 432	224	445	— :	84	1 587	238	118	1 264
SELF-SUFFICIENCY (%)											**AUTO-APPROVISIONNEMENT (%)**		
1984	:	112,4	126,0	363,2	118,8	37,2	87,8	120,9	601,2	67,2	195,5	91,0	91,7
1985	:	107,7 :	127,6	327,8	113,2	35,3 :	86,7	118,4	692,2	60,8	185,1	84,5	88,8
1986	103,9 :	:	137,7	282,6	121,4	32,9	95,1	:	678,6	57,9	219,7	86,4	80,4
HUMAN CONSUMPTION (KG/HEAD/YEAR)											**CONSOMMATION HUMAINE(KG/TETE/AN)**		
1984	22,6	24,6	25,6	13,3	22,5	21,6	11,3	31,9	23,8	25,8	18,6	11,0	21,3
1985	23,0 :	25,1 :	25,5	14,1	23,1	21,3 :	11,5	31,2	21,8	27,8	19,0	11,4	21,8
1986	17,7 :	18,8 :	23,9	16,8	23,5	22,4	11,5	— :	23,7	27,7	16,3	11,6	22,3
SLAUGHTER WEIGHT (KG/CARCASS)											**POIDS A L'ABATTAGE (KG/CARCASSE)**		
1984	:	250,2	300,9	226,2	275,9	207,6	:	241,4	288,3	230,2	205,6	:	267,1
1985	:	252,8	305,6	229,2	277,2	210,5	:	243,5	295,8	231,3	209,8	:	269,5
1986	254,0	256,3	314,4	239,9	285,7	215,0	228,0	245,7	297,4	230,5	214,7	216,1	268,0

---

(1) QUANTITIES AVAILABLE FOR HUMAN CONSUMPTION   (1) QUANTITES DISPONIBLES POUR LA CONSOMMATION HUMAINE

I E 10

MEAT : ADULT CATTLE   **VIANDE DE GROS BOVINS**

YEAR / ANNÉE	EUR 12	EUR 10	UEBL BLEU	DK	D	GR	E	F	IRL	I	NL	P	UK
1000 T													
GROSS INDIGENOUS PRODUCTION											**PRODUCTION INDIGENE BRUTE**		
1984	:	6 633	290	243	1 552	74	273	1 703	504	827	349	93	1 091
1985	:	6 496	290	234	1 513	69	274	1 652	533	792	326	89	1 087
1986	5 299:	:	294	241	1 654	68	303	— :	570	740	329	95	1 006
EXPORTS OF LIVE ANIMALS											**EXPORTATIONS D'ANIMAUX VIVANTS**		
1984	:	74	18	—	59	0	—	110	109	7	7	—	6
1985	:	44	21	—	57	—	—	129	88	3	9	—	5
1986	108:	:	26	—	68	—	—	— :	86	1	7	—	24
INTRA EUR													*INTRA EUR*
1984	:	:	18	—	28	—	:	98	60	—	3	:	6
1985	:	:	21	—	29	—	:	118	62	—	4	:	4
1986	:	:	26	—	52	—	—	—	—	—	4	—	24
IMPORTS OF LIVE ANIMALS											**IMPORTATIONS D'ANIMAUX VIVANTS**		
1984	:	74	9	—	38	4	8	13	5	182	9	2	56
1985	:	96	8	—	37	8	17	14	3	221	17	5	57
1986	310:	:	9	—	25	8	12	— :	25	243	27	4	61
INTRA EUR													*INTRA EUR*
1984	:	243	9	—	7	1	:	13	5	143	9	:	56
1985	:	268	8	—	8	2	:	14	3	159	17	:	57
1986	104:	:	9	—	6	1	—	—	—	—	27	—	61
USABLE PRODUCTION (SLAUGHTERINGS)											**PRODUCTION UTILISABLE (ABBATAGES)**		
1984	7 010	6 634	281	243	1 531	78	281	1 606	400	1 002	351	95	1 141
1985	6 934	6 549	277	234	1 493	76	291	1 537	448	1 010	334	94	1 139
1986	5 501:	5 087:	277	241	1 611	76	315	— :	509	982	349	99	1 042
IMPORTS													**IMPORTATIONS**
1984	:	386	31	6	258	86	30	266	12	392	60	4	312
1985	:	446	29	12	274	99	38	301	9	495	66	12	324
1986	794:	:	27	18	277	121	7	— :	8	453	74	15	376
INTRA EUR													*INTRA EUR*
1984	:	1 037	25	6	164	80	:	252	12	301	46	:	151
1985	:	1 162	21	12	181	91	:	285	9	364	49	:	150
1986	582:	:	22	17	172	110	—	—	—	—	56	—	205
RESOURCES = USES											**RESSOURCES = EMPLOIS**		
1984	:	7 020	312	249	1 789	164	311	1 872	412	1 394	411	99	1 454
1985	:	6 995	306	246	1 767	175	329	1 838	457	1 505	400	106	1 463
1986	6 295:	:	304	259	1 888	198	322	— :	517	1 435	423	114	1 418
EXPORTS													**EXPORTATIONS**
1984	:	766	80	176	444	0	14	377	258	104	150	2	214
1985	:	739	75	165	433	0	1	440	316	137	146	2	190
1986	1 228:	:	87	189	576	0	1	— :	414	146	203	3	191
INTRA EUR													*INTRA EUR*
1984	:	:	67	106	275	—	:	195	149	44	100	:	130
1985	:	:	68	108	273	—	:	176	166	86	117	:	128
1986	:	:	77	99	340	—	—	—	—	—	125	—	111
CHANGE IN STOCKS											**VARIATION DES STOCKS**		
1984	332	365	3	9	72	−2	−28	112	71	41	15	−5	44
1985	194	200	2	11	30	3	−4	33	64	8	3	−2	46
1986	− 100:	−98:	4	−14	−16	−2	−4	— :	19	−71	12	2	−30
TOTAL DOMESTIC USES											**UTILISATION INTERIEURE TOTALE**		
1984	:	5 889	229	64	1 273	166	325	1 383	83	1 249	246	102	1 196
1985	:	6 056	229	70	1 304	172	332	1 365	77	1 360	251	106	1 228
1986	5 168:	:	213	84	1 328	199	325	— :	84	1 360	208	109	1 258
INDUSTRIAL USES													*USAGES INDUSTRIELS*
1984	:	:	:	:	:	:	:	:	:	:	:	:	—
1985	:	:	:	:	:	:	:	:	:	:	:	:	5
1986	:	:	:	:	:	:	:	:	:	:	:	:	—
HUMAN CONSUMPTION (1)											*CONSOMMATION HUMAINE (1)*		
1984	6 316	5 889	229	64	1 273	166	325	1 383	83	1 249	246	102	1 196
1985	6 494	6 056	229	70	1 304	172	332	1 365	77	1 360	251	106	1 228
1986	5 168:	4 734:	213	84	1 328	199	325	— :	84	1 360	208	109	1 258
SELF-SUFFICIENCY (%)											**AUTO-APPROVISIONNEMENT (%)**		
1984	:	112,6	126,6	379,7	121,9	44,6	84,0	123,1	607,2	66,2	141,9	91,2	91,3
1985	:	107,3	126,6	334,3	116,0	39,8	82,5	121,0	692,2	58,2	129,9	84,0	88,6
1986	102,5:	:	138,0	286,9	124,5	34,0	93,2	:	678,6	54,4	158,2	87,2	80,0
HUMAN CONSUMPTION (KG/HEAD/YEAR)											**CONSOMMATION HUMAINE(KG/TETE/AN)**		
1984	19,7	21,6	22,4	12,5	20,8	16,8	8,5	25,2	23,5	21,9	17,1	10,1	21,2
1985	20,2	22,2	22,4	13,7	21,4	17,3	8,6	24,7	21,8	23,8	17,3	10,4	21,7
1986	16,0:	17,3:	20,8	16,4	21,7	20,0	8,4	— :	23,7	23,8	14,3	10,7	22,2
SLAUGHTER WEIGHT (KG/CARCASS)											**POIDS A L'ABATTAGE (KG/CARCASSE)**		
1984	:	292,5	364,9	235,1	297,8	222,8	:	326,9	289,0	272,5	281,3	:	274,1
1985	:	294,2	374,6	238,6	300,0	226,7	:	328,4	296,4	271,9	282,1	:	274,6
1986	294,8	298,2	388,6	248,5	308,2	231,4	253,7	330,8	298,0	274,1	284,2	236,4	272,5

(1) QUANTITIES AVAILABLE FOR HUMAN CONSUMPTION   (1) QUANTITES DISPONIBLES POUR LA CONSOMMATION HUMAINE

MEAT : VEAL   **VIANDE DE VEAUX**

YEAR ANNÉE	EUR 12	EUR 10	UEBL BLEU	DK	D	GR	E	F	IRL	I	NL	P	UK
1000 T													
GROSS INDIGENOUS PRODUCTION										**PRODUCTION INDIGENE BRUTE**			
1984	:	902	40	4	85	6	108	418	1	160	175	8	13
1985	:	889	43	2	83	6	110	387	—	175	183	9	10
1986	645:	:	42	2	85	6	120	— :	—	179	194	7	10
EXPORTS OF LIVE ANIMALS										**EXPORTATIONS D'ANIMAUX VIVANTS**			
1984	:	40	5	—	14	—	—	41	—	—	15	—	7
1985	:	31	6	—	11	—	—	38	—	0	13	—	5
1986	17:	:	6	—	12	—	—	— :	—	—	14	—	7
INTRA EUR													*INTRA EUR*
1984	:		5	—	14	—	:	40	—	—	15	:	7
1985	:		6	—	11	—	:	38	—	—	13	:	5
1986	:		6	—	12	—	—	—			14	—	7
IMPORTS OF LIVE ANIMALS										**IMPORTATIONS D'ANIMAUX VIVANTS**			
1984	:	7	3	—	12	1	—	8	—	20	4	—	0
1985	:	6	3	—	11	0	—	7	—	20	6	—	0
1986	21:	:	4	—	11	0	—	— :	—	18	10	—	—
INTRA EUR													*INTRA EUR*
1984	:	41	3	—	10	—	:	8	—	16	4	:	—
1985	:	41	3	—	9	—	:	7	—	16	6	:	—
1986	22:	:	4	—	8	—	—	—	—	—	10	—	—
USABLE PRODUCTION (SLAUGHTERINGS)										**PRODUCTION UTILISABLE (ABBATAGES)**			
1984	984	868	38	4	83	6	108	385	1	180	164	8	6
1985	983	864	40	2	83	6	110	356	—	195	176	9	5
1986	650:	523:	40	2	84	6	120	— :	—	197	190	7	4
IMPORTS												**IMPORTATIONS**	
1984	:	2	4	—	27	42	1	15	—	40	1	1	3
1985	:	3	3	—	27	33	1	21	—	40	3	1	3
1986	38:	:	3	—	23	18	—	— :	—	32	3	2	5
INTRA EUR													*INTRA EUR*
1984	:	130	4	—	27	41	:	15	—	39	1	:	3
1985	:	127	3	—	27	31	:	21	—	39	3	:	3
1986	48:	:	3	—	22	17	—	—	—	—	1	—	5
RESOURCES = USES										**RESSOURCES = EMPLOIS**			
1984	:	870	42	4	110	48	109	400	1	220	165	9	9
1985	:	866	43	2	110	39	111	377	—	235	179	10	9
1986	688:	:	43	2	107	24	120	— :	—	229	193	9	8
EXPORTS												**EXPORTATIONS**	
1984	:	57	9	—	5	0	—	28	—	1	143	—	1
1985	:	67	11	—	4	—	—	20	—	4	155	—	1
1986	134:	:	12	—	3	—	—	— :	—	2	163	—	2
INTRA EUR													*INTRA EUR*
1984	:		9	—	5	—	:	23	—	1	135	:	—
1985	:		11	—	4	—	:	16	—	4	124	:	—
1986	:		12	—	3	—	—	—	—	—	153	—	2
CHANGE IN STOCKS										**VARIATION DES STOCKS**			
1984	—	—	—	—	—	—	—	—	—	—	—	—	—
1985	— :	— :	—	—	—	— :	—	—	—	—	—	—	—
1986	— :	— :	—	—	—	—	—	— :	—	—	—	—	—
TOTAL DOMESTIC USES										**UTILISATION INTERIEURE TOTALE**			
1984	:	813	33	4	105	48	109	372	1	219	22	9	9
1985	:	799:	32	2	106	39:	111	357	—	231	24	10	8
1986	554:	:	31	2	104	24	120	— :	—	227	30	9	7
INDUSTRIAL USES										*USAGES INDUSTRIELS*			
1984	:	:	:	:	:	:	:	:	:	:	:		—
1985	:	:	:	:	:	:	:	:	:	:	:		—
1986	:	:	:	:	:	:	:	:	:	:	:		—
HUMAN CONSUMPTION (1)										*CONSOMMATION HUMAINE (1)*			
1984	931	813	33	4	105	48	109	372	1	219	22	9	9
1985	920:	799:	32	2	106	39:	111	357	—	231	24	10	8
1986	554:	425:	31	2	104	24	120	— :	—	227	30	9	7
SELF-SUFFICIENCY (%)										**AUTO-APPROVISIONNEMENT (%)**			
1984	:	110,9	121,2	100,0	81,0	11,6	99,1	112,4	100,0	73,1	795,5	88,9	148,9
1985	:	111,3:	134,4	100,0	78,3	15,6:	99,1	108,4	:	75,8	762,5	90,0	121,0
1986	116,5:	:	135,5	100,0	81,7	23,3	100,0	:	:	78,9	646,7	77,8	161,5
HUMAN CONSUMPTION (KG/HEAD/YEAR)										**CONSOMMATION HUMAINE(KG/TETE/AN)**			
1984	2,9	3,0	3,2	0,8	1,7	4,9	2,8	6,8	0,3	3,8	1,5	0,9	0,2
1985	2,9:	2,9:	3,1	0,4	1,7	3,9:	2,9	6,5	—	4,0	1,7	1,0	0,1
1986	1,7:	1,6:	3,0	0,4	1,7	2,4	3,1	— :	—	4,0	2,1	0,9	0,1
SLAUGHTER WEIGHT (KG/CARCASS)										**POIDS A L'ABATTAGE (KG/CARCASSE)**			
1984	:	118,8	130,7	62,1	117,1	114,2	:	115,4	146,7	123,7	130,5	:	48,3
1985	:	123,1	132,1	69,6	116,9	112,9	:	115,0	32,3	130,3	143,9	:	53,6
1986	128,7	124,0	132,3	48,6	119,3	113,0	180,9	115,8	26,3	127,4	148,1	95,8	48,5

---

(1) QUANTITIES AVAILABLE FOR HUMAN CONSUMPTION   (1) QUANTITES DISPONIBLES POUR LA CONSOMMATION HUMAINE

MEAT : PORK **VIANDE DE PORCS**

YEAR ANNÉE	EUR 12	EUR 10	UEBL BLEU	DK	D	GR	E	F	IRL	I	NL	P	UK

1000 T

GROSS INDIGENOUS PRODUCTION — PRODUCTION INDIGENE BRUTE

YEAR	EUR 12	EUR 10	UEBL BLEU	DK	D	GR	E	F	IRL	I	NL	P	UK
1984	:	10 399	678	1 039	3 161	146	1 192	1 575	141	1 167	1 544	174	948
1985	:	10 482	668	1 086	3 151	147	1 157	1 571	136	1 112	1 635	164	976
1986	10 776:	:	692	1 146	3 288	153	1 393	—:	138	1 053	1 736	184	993

EXPORTS OF LIVE ANIMALS — EXPORTATIONS D'ANIMAUX VIVANTS

1984	:	0	59	4	26	—	—	12	3	—	239	—	6
1985	:	1	40	3	25	—	—	13	4	0	268	—	14
1986	230:	:	60	2	41	—	—	—:	4	—	295	—	8

INTRA EUR — *INTRA EUR*

1984	:	:	59	4	26	—	:	12	3	—	238	:	6
1985	:	:	40	3	25	—	:	13	4	—	267	:	14
1986	:	:	60	2	41	—	—	—	—	—	295	—	8

IMPORTS OF LIVE ANIMALS — IMPORTATIONS D'ANIMAUX VIVANTS

1984	:	32	109	—	87	0	—	121	9	51	1	—	3
1985	:	31	89	—	117	0	—	104	7	75	1	—	4
1986	145:	:	106	—	89	0	:	—:	4	119	3	—	4

INTRA EUR — *INTRA EUR*

1984	:	349	106	—	69	—	:	116	9	47	1	:	3
1985	:	366	85	—	98	—	:	102	7	69	1	:	4
1986	180:	:	102	—	71	—	—	—	—	—	3	—	4

USABLE PRODUCTION (SLAUGHTERINGS) — PRODUCTION UTILISABLE (ABBATAGES)

1984	11 797	10 431	728	1 035	3 222	146	1 192	1 684	147	1 218	1 306	174	945
1985	11 833	10 512	717	1 083	3 243	147	1 157	1 662	139	1 187	1 368	164	966
1986	10 691:	9 114:	738	1 144	3 336	153	1 393	—:	138	1 172	1 444	184	990

IMPORTS — IMPORTATIONS

1984	:	125	59	1	510	56	21	314	16	358	39	2	478
1985	:	134	66	2	535	64	19	357	17	441	36	21	468
1986	632:	:	66	3	529	68	47	—:	20	478	35	15	455

INTRA EUR — *INTRA EUR*

1984	:	1 706	55	1	465	51	:	306	15	318	38	:	457
1985	:	1 852	58	1	484	59	:	350	17	398	35	:	450
1986	1 083:	:	56	2	502	60	—	—	—	—	34	—	429

RESOURCES = USES — RESSOURCES = EMPLOIS

1984	:	10 556	787	1 036	3 732	202	1 213	1 998	163	1 576	1 345	176	1 423
1985	:	10 647	783	1 085	3 778	212	1 176	2 019	156	1 628	1 404	185	1 433
1986	11 324:	:	804	1 147	3 865	220	1 440	—:	158	1 650	1 479	199	1 444

EXPORTS — EXPORTATIONS

1984	:	449	324	776	114	0	3	54	44	44	750	4	49
1985	:	386	299	808	114	0	4	69	38	53	802	4	54
1986	1 214:	:	348	812	132	0	4	—:	37	46	853	4	61

INTRA EUR — *INTRA EUR*

1984	:	:	309	480	107	—	:	30	38	37	704	:	45
1985	:	:	289	489	111	—	:	39	33	45	762	:	50
1986	:	:	335	528	129	—	—	—	—	—	816	:	58

CHANGE IN STOCKS — VARIATION DES STOCKS

1984	− 20	− 23	− 4	− 11	− 6	1	3	− 2	—	—	− 1	—	1
1985	8	7	22	− 13	− 1	− 0	1	—	—	—	—	—	− 0
1986	− 1:	− 1:	− 17	10	3	—	− 4	—:	—	—	2	4	1

TOTAL DOMESTIC USES — UTILISATION INTERIEURE TOTALE

1984	:	10 130	467	271	3 624	201	1 207	1 946	119	1 532	596	172	1 374
1985	:	10 253	462	290	3 665	212	1 171	1 950	118	1 575	602	181	1 379
1986	10 110:	:	473	325	3 730	220	1 440	—:	121	1 604	624	191	1 382

INDUSTRIAL USES — *USAGES INDUSTRIELS*

1984	:	:	:	:	:	:	:	:	:	:	:	:	4
1985	:	:	:	:	:	:	:	:	:	:	:	:	5
1986	:	:	:	:	:	:	:	:	:	:	:	:	—

HUMAN CONSUMPTION (1) — *CONSOMMATION HUMAINE (1)*

1984	11 509	10 130	467	271	3 624	201	1 207	1 946	119	1 532	596	172	1 374
1985	11 605	10 253	462	290	3 665	212	1 171	1 950	118	1 575	602	181	1 379
1986	10 110:	8 479:	473	325	3 730	220	1 440	—:	121	1 604	624	191	1 382

SELF-SUFFICIENCY (%) — AUTO-APPROVISIONNEMENT (%)

1984	:	102,7	145,2	383,4	87,2	72,6	98,8	80,9	118,5	76,2	259,1	101,2	69,0
1985	:	102,2	144,6	374,5	86,0	69,5	98,8	80,6	115,3	70,6	271,6	90,6	70,7
1986	106,6:	:	146,3	352,6	88,2	69,4	96,7	:	114,0	65,6	278,2	96,3	71,9

HUMAN CONSUMPTION (KG/HEAD/YEAR) — CONSOMMATION HUMAINE (KG/TETE/AN)

1984	35,8	37,1	45,7	53,0	59,2	20,3	31,4	35,4	33,7	26,9	41,3	17,0	24,3
1985	36,1	37,5	45,2	56,7	60,1	21,3	30,4	35,3	33,3	27,6	41,5	17,8	24,4
1986	31,3:	31,0:	46,2	63,5	61,1	22,1	37,2	—:	34,2	28,0	42,8	18,7	24,3

SLAUGHTER WEIGHT (KG/CARCASS) — POIDS A L'ABATTAGE (KG/CARCASSE)

1984	:	81,5	86,1	70,0	83,4	65,7	:	85,5	64,6	106,4	84,2	:	63,4
1985	:	81,5	85,5	71,3	83,7	63,7	:	85,1	64,0	105,7	84,4	:	63,4
1986	80,9	82,0	87,0	71,1	84,6	65,1	73,7	84,9	109,8	105,9	80,7	70,4	63,5

(1) QUANTITIES AVAILABLE FOR HUMAN CONSUMPTION (1) QUANTITES DISPONIBLES POUR LA CONSOMMATION HUMAINE

MEAT : SHEEP AND GOATS   **VIANDE DE MOUTONS ET CHEVRES**

YEAR ANNÉE	EUR 12	EUR 10	UEBL BLEU	DK	D	GR	E	F	IRL	I	NL	P	UK
					1000 T								
GROSS INDIGENOUS PRODUCTION											**PRODUCTION INDIGENE BRUTE**		
1984	:	731	4	1	23	120	137	174	41	54	18	26	295
1985	:	746	3	1	23	121	133	173	49	49	18	25	308
1986	786:	:	4	1	23	106	211	—:	47	49	18	25	302
EXPORTS OF LIVE ANIMALS											**EXPORTATIONS D'ANIMAUX VIVANTS**		
1984	:	9	3	—	4	0	—	2	1	—	8	—	10
1985	:	8	4	—	6	0	—	3	2	0	8	—	10
1986	21:	:	3	—	6	0	—	—:	1	—	7	—	12
INTRA EUR													*INTRA EUR*
1984	:	:	3	—	4	—	:	2	1	—	8	:	10
1985	:	:	4	—	6	—	:	3	2	—	7	:	11
1986	:	:	3	—	6	—	—	—	—	—	7	—	12
IMPORTS OF LIVE ANIMALS											**IMPORTATIONS D'ANIMAUX VIVANTS**		
1984	:	25	7	—	9	2	—	7	1	17	0	—	1
1985	:	28	9	—	10	1	—	8	1	21	1	—	2
1986	28:	:	7	—	9	0	—	—:	—	18	—	—	1
INTRA EUR													*INTRA EUR*
1984	:	19	6	—	1	—	:	5	1	5	—	:	1
1985	:	25	9	—	—	—	:	6	1	6	1	:	2
1986	8:	:	7	—	—	—	—	—:	—	—	—	—	1
USABLE PRODUCTION (SLAUGHTERINGS)											**PRODUCTION UTILISABLE (ABBATAGES)**		
1984	909	746	8	1	28	122	137	179	41	71	10	26	286
1985	923	765	8	1	27	122	133	178	48	70	11	25	300
1986	792:	556:	8	1	26	107	211	—:	46	67	11	25	291
IMPORTS											**IMPORTATIONS**		
1984	:	207	12	2	22	15	1	64	—	15	1	—	153
1985	:	232	13	2	27	16	1	68	—	19	2	—	168
1986	211:	:	14	2	26	18	7	—:	—	19	2	—	137
INTRA EUR													*INTRA EUR*
1984	:	76	9	—	3	—	:	59	—	5	—	:	—
1985	:	83	10	—	3	—	:	62	—	6	1	:	1
1986	14:	:	10	—	3	—	—	—	—	—	1	—	—
RESOURCES = USES											**RESSOURCES = EMPLOIS**		
1984	:	953	20	3	50	136	138	243	41	86	11	26	439
1985	:	998	21	3	54	139	134	246	48	89	13	25	468
1986	1 003:	:	22	3	52	124	218	—:	46	86	13	25	428
EXPORTS											**EXPORTATIONS**		
1984	:	9	4	—	1	1	1	5	17	—	5	—	53
1985	:	6	5	—	1	0	—	4	24	0	6	—	49
1986	83:	:	4	—	1	0	5	—:	22	—	5	—	60
INTRA EUR													*INTRA EUR*
1984	:	:	4	—	1	—	:	4	17	—	5	:	50
1985	:	:	5	—	1	—	:	3	24	—	6	:	45
1986	:	:	4	—	1	—	—	—	—	—	5	—	57
CHANGE IN STOCKS											**VARIATION DES STOCKS**		
1984	— 14	— 14	—	—	—	1	—	—	—	—	—	—	— 15
1985	10	10	—	—	—	— 1	—	—	—	—	—	—	11
1986	— 14:	— 14:	—	—	—	0	—	—:	—	—	—	—	— 15
TOTAL DOMESTIC USES											**UTILISATION INTERIEURE TOTALE**		
1984	:	958	16	3	49	135	137	238	24	86	6	26	401
1985	:	982	16	3	53	139	134	242	24	89	7	25	408
1986	934:	:	18	3	51	124	213	—:	24	86	8	25	382
INDUSTRIAL USES											*USAGES INDUSTRIELS*		
1984	:	:	:	:	:	:	:	:	:	:	:	:	4
1985	:	:	:	:	:	:	:	:	:	:	:	:	4
1986	:	:	:	:	:	:	:	:	:	:	:	:	—
HUMAN CONSUMPTION (1)											*CONSOMMATION HUMAINE (1)*		
1984	1 121	958	16	3	49	135	137	238	24	86	6	26	401
1985	1 141	982	16	3	53	139	134	242	24	89	7	25	408
1986	934:	696:	18	3	51	124	213	—:	24	86	8	25	382
SELF-SUFFICIENCY (%)											**AUTO-APPROVISIONNEMENT (%)**		
1984	:	76,2	25,0	33,3	46,9	89,1	100,0	73,1	170,8	62,8	300,0	100,0	73,6
1985	:	76,0	18,8	33,3	43,4	87,2	99,3	71,5	204,2	55,1	257,1	100,0	75,6
1986	84,1:	:	22,2	33,3	45,1	85,7	99,1	:	195,8	57,0	225,0	100,0	79,0
HUMAN CONSUMPTION (KG/HEAD/YEAR)											**CONSOMMATION HUMAINE(KG/TETE/AN)**		
1984	3,5	3,5	1,6	0,6	0,8	13,6	3,6	4,3	6,8	1,5	0,4	2,6	7,1
1985	3,5	3,6	1,6	0,6	0,9	14,0	3,5	4,4	6,8	1,6	0,5	2,5	7,2
1986	2,9:	2,5:	1,8	0,6	0,8	12,4	5,5	—:	6,8	1,5	0,5	2,4	6,7
SLAUGHTER WEIGHT (KG/CARCASS)											**POIDS A L'ABATTAGE (KG/CARCASSE)**		
1984	:	15,5:	15,1:	24,3	21,2	11,3	:	17,3	24,4	8,8	24,4	:	19,3:
1985	:	15,4:	22,3:	27,9	20,6	10,6	:	17,4	23,2	8,6	23,1	:	19,3:
1986	14,1:	14,9:	28,6:	22,5	20,4	10,7	11,3	17,2	12,8	8,3	23,0	10,3	18,9:

---

(1) QUANTITIES AVAILABLE FOR HUMAN CONSUMPTION   (1) QUANTITES DISPONIBLES POUR LA CONSOMMATION HUMAINE

I E 13

MEAT: POULTRY   **VIANDE DE VOLAILLE**

	EUR 12	EUR 10	B L	DK	D	EL	ES	F	IRL	I	NL	P	UK
						1000 T							
GROSS INDIGENOUS PRODUCTION											**PRODUCTION INDIGÈNE BRUTE**		
1985	:	4 388	131	115	357	155	815	1 267	55	998	425	137	876
1986	4 115:	:	134	116	377	145	754	:	59	1 001	442	157	930
EXPORTS OF LIVE ANIMALS											**EXPORTATIONS D'ANIMAUX VIVANTS**		
1985	:	6	7	–	3	–	–	8	1	2	49	–	3
1986	9:	9	–	4	–	–	:	1	2	51	–	3	
INTRA EUR													*INTRA EUR*
1985	:	:	5	–	2	–	–	8	1	2	47	–	3
1986	:	:	6	–	4	–	–	:	:	:	49	–	3
IMPORTS OF LIVE ANIMALS											**IMPORTATIONS D'ANIMAUX VIVANTS**		
1985	:	3	35	–	12	–	–	6	2	9	5	–	1
1986	:	:	43	–	11	–	–	:	2	7	7	–	2
INTRA EUR													*INTRA EUR*
1973	:	24	:	:	:	–	:	:	:	:	:	:	:
1974	:	28	:	:	:	–	:	:	:	:	:	:	:
1975	:	39	:	:	:	–	:	:	:	:	:	:	:
1976	:	41	:	:	:	–	:	:	:	:	:	:	:
1977	:	44	:	:	:	–	:	:	:	:	:	:	:
1978	:	46	:	:	:	–	:	:	:	:	:	:	:
1979	:	51	:	:	:	–	:	:	:	:	:	:	:
1985	:	67	35	–	11	–	–	6	2	7	5	–	1
1986	61:	:	43	–	9	–	–	:	:	:	7	–	2
USABLE PRODUCTION (SLAUGHTERINGS)											**PRODUCTION UTILISABLE (ABATTAGES)**		
1985	:	4 376	159	115	366	155	815	1 275	56	1 005	381	137	874
1986	4 376:	3 205	168	116	384	145	754	:	60	1 006	398	157	928
IMPORTS											**IMPORTATIONS**		
1985	:	85	34	3	249	4	27	27	9	32	25	–	70
1986	104:	:	39	4	254	4	15	:	10	28	37	–	97
INTRA EUR													*INTRA EUR*
1985	:	369	32	3	198	4	–	22	9	7	25	–	69
1986	385:	:	36	4	212	4	–	:	:	:	33	–	96
RESOURCES = USES											**RESSOURCES = EMPLOIS**		
1985	:	4 461	193	118	615	159	842	1 302	64	1 037	406	137	944
1986	4 220:	:	207	120	638	149	769	:	70	1 034	435	157	1 026
EXPORTS											**EXPORTATIONS**		
1985	:	323	35	63	24	1	2	314	4	9	208	–	34
1986	:	:	41	57	24	1	5	:	5	10	225	–	42
INTRA EUR													*INTRA EUR*
1985	:	:	17	23	11	0	–	70	4	8	191	–	30
1986	:	:	23	21	15	1	–	:	:	:	210	–	36
CHANGE IN STOCKS											**VARIATION DES STOCKS**		
1985	:	–4	1	–1	–	2	–	–1	–	–	–	–	–6
1986	:	:	–	3	–	–3	–	:	:	:	2	–	5
TOTAL DOMESTIC USES											**UTILISATION INTÉRIEURE TOTALE**		
1985	:	4 141	157	56	591	156	840	989	60	1 028	198	137	917
1986	4 188:	:	166	60	614	151	764	:	65	1 024	208	157	979
HUMAN CONSUMPTION (1)											*CONSOMMATION HUMAINE (1)*		
1985	:	4 141	157	56	591	156	840	989	60	1 028	198	137	906
1986	4 188:	:	166	60	614	151	764	:	65	1 024	208	157	979
SELF-SUFFICIENCY (%)											**AUTO-APPROVISIONNEMENT (%)**		
1985	:	105,7	83,4	205,4	60,4	99,3	97,0	129,1	91,7	97,1	214,6	100,0	95,5
1986	98,2:	:	80,7	193,3	61,4	95,9	98,7	:	90,8	97,8	212,5	100,0	94,9
HUMAN CONSUMPTION (KG/HEAD/YEAR)											**CONSOMMATION HUMAINE (KG/TÊTE/AN)**		
1985	:	15,2	15,4	11,0	9,7	15,7	21,8	17,9	16,9	18,0	13,7	13,5	16,0
1986	13,0:	:	16,2 *	11,7 *	10,1 *	15,2 *	19,8	:	18,4	17,9	14,3 *	15,4 *	17,3 *

(1) QUANTITIES AVAILABLE FOR HUMAN CONSUMPTION   (1) QUANTITES DISPONIBLES POUR LA CONSOMMATION HUMAINE

YEAR ANNÉE	EUR 10	B	DK	D	GR	F	IRL	I	L	NL	UK
					1000 T						

ON THE FARM
A. AVAILABILITIES
A1. DAIRY COWS' MILK

DANS L'EXPLOITATION AGRICOLE
A. DISPONIBILITÉS
A1. LAIT DE VACHES LAITIÈRES

YEAR ANNÉE	EUR 10	B	DK	D	GR	F	IRL	I	L	NL	UK
1983	111 570	3 872	5 427	26 913	678	27 650	5 656	10 618	290	13 240	17 227
1984	109 409	3 819	5 234	26 151	670	27 700	5 901	10 665	299	12 782	16 187
1985	NA	3 796	5 099	25 674	NA	27 790	5 823	10 946	301	12 550	16 007
1986	NA	3 918	NA	NA	NA	NA	NA	NA	299	12 695	NA

A2. OTHER MILK

A2. AUTRES LAITS

YEAR ANNÉE	EUR 10	B	DK	D	GR	F	IRL	I	L	NL	UK
1983	12 763	306	133	295	1 484	7 391	503	1 032	20	0	1 699
1984	13 086	334	127	300	1 433	7 651	503	1 032	20	0	1 686
1985	NA	NA	106	355	NA	6 824	NA	1 050	20	0	1 673
1986	NA	NA	NA	NA	NA	NA	NA	NA	20	0	NA

B. UTILISATION FOR THE PRODUCTION OF:
B1. DRINKING MILK

B. UTILISATION POUR LA PRODUCTION DE:
B1. LAIT DE CONSOMMATION

YEAR ANNÉE	EUR 10	B	DK	D	GR	F	IRL	I	L	NL	UK
1983	4 286	120	75	726	362	897	144	1 549	3	140	271
1984	4 253	118	75	711	385	897	138	1 537	3	130	258
1985	NA	107	75	723	NA	820	139	1 305	3	115	251
1986	NA	100	NA	NA	NA	NA	NA	NA	3	88	NA

B2. FARM BUTTER AND CREAM

B2. BEURRE ET CRÈME FERMIERS

YEAR ANNÉE	EUR 10	B	DK	D	GR	F	IRL	I	L	NL	UK
1983	918	400	0	33	28	317	6	108	0	0	26
1984	868	391	0	35	23	282	6	105	0	0	26
1985	NA	343	0	36	NA	NA	NA	95	0	0	26
1986	NA	327	NA	NA	NA	NA	NA	NA	0	0	NA

B3. FARM CHEESE

B3. FROMAGE FERMIER

YEAR ANNÉE	EUR 10	B	DK	D	GR	F	IRL	I	L	NL	UK
1983	1 364	6	0	3	377	249	0	659	0	71	0
1984	1 411	6	0	4	407	289	0	633	0	72	0
1985	NA	7	0	4	NA	285	0	633	0	72	0
1986	NA	6	NA	NA	NA	NA	NA	NA	1	74	NA

B4. FEED

B4. ALIMENTATION ANIMALE

YEAR ANNÉE	EUR 10	B	DK	D	GR	F	IRL	I	L	NL	UK
1983	12 958	430	258	1 270	385	7 039	668	949	24	115	1 819
1984	13 496	545	252	1 397	350	7 395	675	945	23	115	1 799
1985	NA	180	231	1 629	NA	7 463	675	932	3	130	1 793
1986	NA	198	NA	NA	NA	NA	NA	NA	4	202	NA

B5. DELIVERED TO DAIRIES

B5. LIVRAISON AUX LAITERIES

YEAR ANNÉE	EUR 10	B	DK	D	GR	F	IRL	I	L	NL	UK
1983	104 724	3 225	5 227	25 176	905	26 473	5 341	8 393	283	12 914	16 787
1984	102 393	3 089	5 034	24 304	938	26 441	5 585	8 476	293	12 465	15 767
1985	NA	3 196	4 899	23 637	949	25 783	NA	NA	255	12 233	15 587
1986	NA	NA	NA	24 196	NA	26 257	NA	NA	249	12 331	NA

1000 T

YEAR ANNÉE	EUR 10	B	DK	D	GR	F	IRL	I	L	NL	UK

IN DAIRIES / **DANS LES LAITERIES**
A. AVAILABILITIES (incl. import) / **A. DISPONIBILITÉS (inclus importation)**

	EUR 10	B	DK	D	GR	F	IRL	I	L	NL	UK
1983	125 635	3 225	5 227	25 268	450	26 499	5 362	10 010	283	12 914	16 806
1984	122 620	3 157	5 034	24 406	451	26 476	5 586	10 039	293	12 465	15 792
1985	118 659	3 205	4 899	23 750	461	25 815	5 682	8 347	294	12 233	15 583
1986	120 102	3 345	4 911	24 196	449	25 997	5 478	8 456	292	12 346	15 796

B. UTILISATION FOR THE PRODUCTION OF: / **B. UTILISATION POUR LA PRODUCTION DE:**
B1. FRESH PRODUCTS EXCL. CREAM / **B1. PRODUITS FRAIS SAUF CRÈME**

	EUR 10	B	DK	D	GR	F	IRL	I	L	NL	UK
1983	17 826	643	438	3 243	301	2 290	530	2 457	34	875	7 016
1984	18 036	629	401	3 312	314	2 529	538	2 474	34	839	6 967
1985	NA	NA	370	3 382	NA	2 303	NA	2 560	37	814	7 196
1986	NA	NA	NA	NA	NA	NA	NA	NA	NA	787	NA

B2. CREAM / **B2. CRÈME**

	EUR 10	B	DK	D	GR	F	IRL	I	L	NL	UK
1983	5 648	199	330	2 486	43	1 325	210	524	27	430	74
1984	5 867	198	291	2 582	45	1 435	219	564	30	440	62
1985	NA	NA	298	2 718	NA	1 492	NA	566	29	428	44
1986	NA	NA	NA	NA	NA	NA	NA	NA	NA	414	NA

B3. MILK POWDER / **B3. LAIT EN POUDRE**

	EUR 10	B	DK	D	GR	F	IRL	I	L	NL	UK
1983	4 093	231	480	717	0	983	135	9	0	1 249	289
1984	5 054	286	625	772	0	1 291	214	9	0	1 416	440
1985	NA	NA	599	664	NA	1 206	NA	10	0	1 331	508
1986	NA	NA	NA	NA	NA	NA	NA	NA	NA	1 173	NA

B4. BUTTER / **B4. BEURRE**

	EUR 10	B	DK	D	GR	F	IRL	I	L	NL	UK
1983	49 286	2 042	2 530	13 533	42	13 731	3 799	1 715	176	6 243	5 476
1984	45 268	1 988	2 030	12 231	35	13 074	3 947	1 765	178	5 422	4 598
1985	NA	NA	2 098	10 884	NA	12 663	NA	1 751	NA	5 403	4 516
1986	NA	NA	NA	NA	NA	NA	NA	NA	NA	5 710	NA

B5. CHEESE / **B5. FROMAGE**

	EUR 10	B	DK	D	GR	F	IRL	I	L	NL	UK
1983	23 881	194	1 405	3 412	552	7 011	544	5 001	9	3 247	2 506
1984	25 310	220	1 627	3 557	597	7 648	562	5 153	10	3 412	2 523
1985	NA	NA	1 451	3 754	NA	7 749	NA	5 106	9	3 437	2 617
1986	NA	NA	NA	NA	NA	NA	NA	NA	NA	3 440	NA

B6. OTHER UTILIZATIONS / **B6. AUTRES UTILISATIONS**

	EUR 10	B	DK	D	GR	F	IRL	I	L	NL	UK
1983	74 187	1 958	2 574	15 410	NA	14 890	3 943	2 019	213	7 113	6 921
1984	68 353	1 824	2 090	14 183	NA	13 573	4 053	1 839	219	6 358	5 800
1985	NA	NA	2 181	13 232	NA	13 065	NA	105	219	6 223	5 218
1986	NA	NA	NA	NA	NA	NA	NA	NA	NA	6 532	NA

I E 15

WHOLE MILK (RAW MATERIAL) | **LAIT ENTIER (MATIERE PREMIERE)**

YEAR ANNÉE	EUR 12	EUR 10	UEBL BLEU	DK	D	GR	E	F	IRL	I	NL	P	UK
1000 T													
USABLE PRODUCTION (SLAUGHTERINGS)										**PRODUCTION UTILISABLE (ABBATAGES)**			
1984	:	112 997	4 124	5 234	26 173	1 999	:	29 206	5 901	11 390	12 782	:	16 187
1985	:	:	4 105	5 099	25 696	:	:	29 267	5 823	11 685	12 550	:	16 007
1986	:	:	4 226	:	26 372	:	:	:	5 614	:	12 695	:	:
IMPORTS											**IMPORTATIONS**		
1984	:	13	68	—	102	—	:	35	1	1 175	—	:	25
1985	:	:	:	—	113	:	:	32	:	1 648	—	:	24
1986	:	:	:	:	:	:	:	:	:	:	—	:	:
INTRA EUR											*INTRA EUR*		
1904	:	1 393	68	—	89	—	:	35	1	1 175	—	:	25
1985	:	:	:	=	95	:	:	32	:	1 646	—	:	24
1986	:	:	:	:	:	:	:	:	:	:	:	:	:
RESOURCES = USES										**RESSOURCES = EMPLOIS**			
1984	:	113 010	4 192	5 234	26 275	1 999	:	29 241	5 902	12 565	12 782	:	16 212
1985	:	:	:	5 099	25 809	:	:	29 299	:	13 333	12 550	:	16 031
1986	:	:	:	:	:	:	:	:	:	:	12 695	:	:
EXPORTS											**EXPORTATIONS**		
1984	:	195	—	3	1 220	—	:	331	2	—	32	:	—
1985	:	:	:	6	1 461	:	:	344	:	—	39	:	—
1986	:	:	:	:	:	:	:	:	:	:	7	:	:
INTRA EUR											*INTRA EUR*		
1984	:	:	:	:	:	—	:	:	:	:	:	:	:
TOTAL DOMESTIC USES										**UTILISATION INTERIEURE TOTALE**			
1984	:	112 814	4 192	5 231	25 055	1 999	:	28 910	5 900	12 565	12 750	:	16 212
1985	:	:	:	5 093	24 348	:	:	28 955	:	13 333	12 511	:	16 031
1986	:	:	:	:	:	:	:	:	:	:	12 688	:	:
LOSSES											*PERTES*		
1984	:	—87 :	— 137	25	— 287	—53	:	— 101	5	— 463	—58	:	982 :
1985	:	:	:	37	— 157	:	:	:	:	530	:	:	515 :
ANIMAL FEED										*ALIMENTATION ANIMALE*			
1984	:	4 151	222	125	1 119	246	:	1 250	172	777	126	:	113
1985	:	:	:	125	1 296	:	:	2 116	:	769	139	:	120
1986	:	:	:	:	:	:	:	:	:	:	211	:	:
PROCESSING											*TRANSFORMATION*		
1984	:	108 751 :	4 107	5 081	24 223	1 806	:	27 761	5 723	12 250	12 682	:	15 117 :
1985	:	:	:	4 931	23 209	:	:	:	:	12 034	:	:	15 396 :
SELF-SUFFICIENCY (%)										**AUTO-APPROVISIONNEMENT (%)**			
1984	:	100,2	98,4	100,1	104,5	100,0	:	101,0	100,0	90,6	100,3	:	99,8
1985	:	:	:	100,1	105,5	:	:	101,1	:	87,6	100,3	:	99,9
1986	:	:	:	:	:	:	:	:	:	:	100,1	:	:

FRESH MILK PRODUCTS (EXCEPT CREAM)　　　　　　　　　　　　　　　　**PRODUITS FRAIS SAUF CREME**

YEAR ANNÉE	EUR 12	EUR 10	UEBL BLEU	DK	D	GR	E	F	IRL	I	NL	P	UK
1000 T													
USABLE PRODUCTION (SLAUGHTERINGS)											**PRODUCTION UTILISABLE (ABBATAGES)**		
1984	:	27 855	1 064	851	5 513	650	:	5 411	706	4 522	1 822	:	7 316
1985	:	:	1 061	815	5 569	625	:	5 480	692	:	1 797	:	7 407
1986	:	:	:	806	5 567	:	:	5 259	677	:	:	:	:
IMPORTS													**IMPORTATIONS**
1984	:	—	107	1	48	9	:	56	1	110	192	:	22
1985	:	:	109	3	45	11	:	54	1	:	227	:	33
1986	:	:	:	3	46	:	:	60	1	:	:	:	:
INTRA EUR													*INTRA EUR*
1984	:	546	107	1	48	9	:	56	1	110	192	:	22
1985	:	:	—	—	36	11	:	54	1	:	227	:	33
1986	:	:	:	—	38	:	:	59	1	:	:	:	:
RESOURCES = USES											**RESSOURCES = EMPLOIS**		
1984	:	27 855	1 171	852	5 561	659	:	5 467	707	4 632	2 014	:	7 338
1985	:	:	1 170	818	5 614	635	:	5 534	693	:	2 024	:	7 440
1986	:	:	:	809	5 613	:	:	5 319	678	:	:	:	:
EXPORTS													**EXPORTATIONS**
1984	:	258	291	38	226	—	:	144	2	4	89	:	10
1985	:	:	336	:	236	—	:	168	3	:	70	:	9
1986	:	:	:	:	254	:	:	208	2	:	:	:	:
INTRA EUR													*INTRA EUR*
1984	:	:	267	38	192	—	:	83	2	4	47	:	3
1985	:	:	—	—	204	—	:	113	3	:	38	:	4
1986	:	:	:	—	223	:	:	142	2	:	:	:	:
TOTAL DOMESTIC USES											**UTILISATION INTERIEURE TOTALE**		
1984	:	27 598	880	814	5 335	659	:	5 323	705	4 628	1 925	:	7 329
1985	:	:	834	780	5 378	636	:	5 367	690	:	1 954	:	7 431
1986	:	:	:	772	5 359	:	:	4 109	676	:	:	:	:
LOSSES													*PERTES*
1984	:	—	—	—	—	—	:	—	—	—	—	:	—
1985	:	:	—	—	—	:	:	—	—	:	—	:	—
1986	:	:	:	—	—	:	:	—	—	:	:	:	:
HUMAN CONSUMPTION											*CONSOMMATION HUMAINE*		
1984	:	27 598	880	814	5 335	659	:	5 323	705	4 628	1 925	:	7 329
1985	:	:	834	780	5 378	636	:	5 367	690	:	1 954	:	7 431
1986	:	:	:	772	5 359	:	:	5 109	676	:	:	:	:
SELF-SUFFICIENCY (%)											**AUTO-APPROVISIONNEMENT (%)**		
1984	:	100,9	120,9	104,5	103,3	98,6	:	101,7	100,1	97,7	94,6	:	99,8
1985	:	:	127,2	104,5	103,6	98,3	:	102,1	100,3	:	92,0	:	99,7
1986	:	:	:	104,4	103,9	:	:	128,0	100,1	:	:	:	:
HUMAN CONSUMPTION (KG/HEAD/YEAR)											**CONSOMMATION HUMAINE(KG/TETE/AN)**		
1984	:	101,2	86,1	159,2	87,2	66,6	:	96,9	199,8	81,2	133,5	:	129,7
1985	:	:	81,6	152,5	88,1	64,0	:	97,3	194,9	:	134,8	:	131,2
1986	:	:	:	150,8	87,8	:	:	92,2	191,1	:	:	:	:

CREAM CREME

YEAR ANNÉE	EUR 12	EUR 10	UEBL BLEU	DK	D	GR	E	F	IRL	I	NL	P	UK
						1000 T							
USABLE PRODUCTION											PRODUCTION UTILISABLE		
1984	:	806	23	41	377	7	:	159	19	65	56	:	59
1985	:	:	22	43	399	8	:	187	22	:	54	:	113
1986	:	:	:	45	414	:	:	174	21	:	:	:	:
IMPORTS											IMPORTATIONS		
1984	:	62	8	—	2	—	:	9	—	37	3	:	3
1985	:	:	8	—	3	—	:	8	—	:	4	:	3
1986	:	:	:	—	3	:	:	7	—	:	:	:	:
INTRA EUR											*INTRA EUR*		
1984	:	:	8	—	2	—	:	8	—	37	3	:	3
1985	:	:	—	—	3	—	:	7	—	:	4	:	3
1986	:	:	:	—	3	:	:	7	—	:	:	:	:
RESOURCES = USES											RESSOURCES = EMPLOIS		
1984	:	868	31	41	379	7	:	168	19	102	59	:	62
1985	:	:	30	43	402	8	:	195	22	:	58	:	116
1986	:	:	:	45	417	:	:	181	21	:	:	:	:
EXPORTS											EXPORTATIONS		
1984	:	:	5	—	31	:	:	34	1	—	8	:	1
1985	:	:	5	—	41	:	:	37	1	:	6	:	—
1986	:	:	:	—	50	:	:	28	1	:	:	:	:
INTRA EUR											*INTRA EUR*		
1984	:	:	5	—	31	—	:	32	1	—	6	:	1
1985	:	:	—	—	40	—	:	35	1	:	5	:	—
1986	:	:	:	—	50	:	:	26	1	:	:	:	:
CHANGE IN STOCKS											VARIATION DES STOCKS		
1984	:	:	:	:	:	:	:	:	:	:	:	:	—
1985	:	:	:	:	:	:	:	:	:	:	:	:	—
TOTAL DOMESTIC USES											UTILISATION INTERIEURE TOTALE		
1984	:	787	26	41	348	7	:	133	18	102	51	:	61
1985	:	:	25	43	361	8	:	159	20	:	52	:	116
1986	:	:	:	45	367	:	:	153	20	:	:	:	:
INDUSTRIAL USES											*USAGES INDUSTRIELS*		
1984	:	:	:	:	:	:	:	:	8	:	:	:	:
1985	:	:	:	:	:	:	:	:	9	:	:	:	:
HUMAN CONSUMPTION											*CONSOMMATION HUMAINE*		
1984	:	779	26	41	348	7	:	133	10	102	51	:	61
1985	:	:	25	43	361	8	:	159	12	:	52	:	116
1986	:	:	:	45	367	:	:	153	11	:	:	:	:
SELF-SUFFICIENCY (%)											AUTO-APPROVISIONNEMENT (%)		
1984	:	102,4	88,5	100,0	108,3	100,0	:	119,5	105,6	63,7	109,8	:	96,7
1985	:	:	88,0	100,0	110,5	106,6	:	117,6	110,0	:	103,8	:	97,4
1986	:	:	:	100,0	112,8	:	:	113,7	105,0	:	:	:	:
HUMAN CONSUMPTION (KG/HEAD/YEAR)											CONSOMMATION HUMAINE(KG/TETE/AN)		
1984	:	2,9	2,5	8,0	5,7	0,7	:	2,4	2,8	1,8	3,5	:	1,1
1985	:	:	2,4	8,4	5,9	0,8	:	2,9	3,4	:	3,6	:	2,0
1986	:	:	:	8,8	6,0	:	:	2,8	3,1	:	:	:	:

I E 18

CONCENTRATED MILK **LAIT CONCENTRE**

YEAR ANNÉE	EUR 12	EUR 10	UEBL BLEU	DK	D	GR	E	F	IRL	I	NL	P	UK
					1000 T								
USABLE PRODUCTION											**PRODUCTION UTILISABLE**		
1984	:	1 326:	9	6	503	S:	:	133	—	4	547	:	124
1985	:	:	11	8	527	S	:	125	—	:	535	:	120
1986	:	:	:	9	500	:	:	103	—	:	:	:	:
IMPORTS											**IMPORTATIONS**		
1984	:	2	17	—	28	132	:	1	1	5	44	:	8
1985	:	:	14	—	32	143	:	2	3	:	85	:	6
1986	:	:	:	—	39	:	:	12	1	:	:	:	:
INTRA EUR											*INTRA EUR*		
1984	:	234	17	—	28	131	:	1	1	5	43	:	8
1985	:	:	—	—	32	143	:	2	3	:	85	:	6
1986	:	:	:	—	39	:	:	12	1	:	:	:	:
RESOURCES = USES											**RESSOURCES = EMPLOIS**		
1984	:	1 328:	26	6	531	131:	:	134	1	9	591	:	132
1985	:	:	25	8	559	143	:	127	3	:	620	:	126
1986	:	:	:	9	539	:	:	115	1	:	:	:	:
EXPORTS											**EXPORTATIONS**		
1984	:	515	9	6	169	—	:	75	1	4	458	:	27
1985	:	:	10	8	209	—	:	78	—	:	491	:	35
1986	:	:	:	9	181	:	:	67	—	:	:	:	:
INTRA EUR											*INTRA EUR*		
1984	:	:	9	—	61	—	:	23	1	4	128	:	3
1985	:	:	—	—	104	—	:	27	—	:	132	:	13
1986	:	:	:	—	111	:	:	17	—	:	:	:	:
FINAL STOCKS											*STOCKS FINALS*		
1984	:	88	—	—	38	—	:	8	—	—	26	:	16
1985	:	:	—	—	37	:	:	8	—	:	26	:	6
1986	:	:	:	—	54	:	:	8	—	:	:	:	:
CHANGE IN STOCKS											**VARIATION DES STOCKS**		
1984	:	2	—	—	—	—	:	—	—	—	−1	:	3
1985	:	:	—	—	−1	—	:	—	—	:	—	:	−10
1986	:	:	:	—	17	:	:	—	—	:	:	:	:
TOTAL DOMESTIC USES											**UTILISATION INTERIEURE TOTALE**		
1984	:	678:	17	—	362	S:	:	59	—	5	134	:	101
1985	:	:	15	—	351	S	:	49	—	:	129	:	101
1986	:	:	:	—	341	:	:	48	—	:	:	:	:
HUMAN CONSUMPTION											*CONSOMMATION HUMAINE*		
1984	:	678:	17	—	362	S:	:	59	—	5	134	:	101
1985	:	:	15	—	351	S	:	49	3	:	129	:	101
1986	:	:	:	—	341	:	:	48	1	:	:	:	:
SELF-SUFFICIENCY (%)											**AUTO-APPROVISIONNEMENT (%)**		
1984	:	195,6	52,9	600,0	139,0	—:	:	225,4	—	80,0	408,2	:	122,8
1985	:	:	73,3	800,0	150,1	—	:	255,1	—	:	414,7	:	118,8
1986	:	:	:	900,0	146,6	:	:	214,6	—	:	:	:	:
HUMAN CONSUMPTION (KG/HEAD/YEAR)											**CONSOMMATION HUMAINE(KG/TETE/AN)**		
1984	:	2,5:	1,7	—	5,9	S:	:	1,1	—	0,1	9,3	:	1,8
1985	:	:	1,5	—	5,8	S	:	0,9	0,8	:	8,9	:	1,8
1986	:	:	:	—	5,6	:	:	0,9	0,3	:	:	:	:

CREAM & WHOLE MILK POWDER **CREME & LAIT ENTIER EN POUDRE**

YEAR ANNÉE	EUR 12	EUR 10	UEBL BLEU	DK	D	GR	E	F	IRL	I	NL	P	UK
					1000 T								
USABLE PRODUCTION											**PRODUCTION UTILISABLE**		
1984	:	805	37	99	137	—	:	193	29	2	255	:	53
1985	:	:	36	95	123	—	:	198	29	:	245	:	61
1986	:	:	:	94	121	:	:	196	25	:	:	:	:
IMPORTS											**IMPORTATIONS**		
1984	:	2	12	1	29	6	:	6	—	19	58	:	8
1985	:	:	12	3	28	:	:	6	—	:	48	:	8
1986	:	:	:	5	28	:	:	8	—	:	:	:	:
INTRA EUR											*INTRA EUR*		
1984	:	136	12	1	29	5	:	5	—	19	57	:	8
1985	:	:	—	—	28	5	:	5	—	:	48	:	8
1986	:	:	:	—	28	:	:	6	—	:	:	:	:
RESOURCES = USES											**RESSOURCES = EMPLOIS**		
1984	:	807	49	100	166	6	:	199	29	21	313	:	61
1985	:	:	48	98	151	:	:	204	29	:	293	:	69
1986	:	:	:	99	149	:	:	204	25	:	:	:	:
EXPORTS											**EXPORTATIONS**		
1984	:	566	33	97	72	—	:	171	30	—	260	:	39
1985	:	:	33	93	62	—	:	168	29	:	250	:	42
1986	:	:	:	95	59	:	:	174	26	:	:	:	:
INTRA EUR											*INTRA EUR*		
1984	:	:	12	—	29	5	:	57	6	—	23	:	4
1985	:	:	—	—	18	—	:	57	4	:	20	:	6
1986	:	:	:	—	18	:	:	53	4	:	:	:	:
FINAL STOCKS											*STOCKS FINALS*		
1984	:	:	1	—	6	—	:	20	:	:	14	:	4
1985	:	:	1	—	8	:	:	19	:	:	11	:	3
1986	:	:	:	—	8	:	:	18	:	:	:	:	:
CHANGE IN STOCKS											**VARIATION DES STOCKS**		
1984	:	10	—	—	−2	—	:	8	−1	—	4	:	1
1985	:	:	—	—	2	—	:	1	—	:	−3	:	−1
1986	:	:	:	—	—	:	:	−1	−1	:	:	:	:
TOTAL DOMESTIC USES											**UTILISATION INTERIEURE TOTALE**		
1984	:	232	16	3	96	6	:	20	—	21	49	:	21
1985	:	:	15	5	87	5	:	35	—	:	40	:	28
1986	:	:	:	4	90	:	:	31	—	:	:	:	:
LOSSES											*PERTES*		
1984	:	:	:	:	:	—	:	:	:	:	:	:	:
1985	:	:	:	:	:	:	:	:	:	:	:	:	:
ANIMAL FEED											*ALIMENTATION ANIMALE*		
1984	:	:	—	3	—	:	:	—	—	—	—	:	—
1985	:	:	—	2	—	:	:	—	—	:	—	:	—
1986	:	:	:	3	—	:	:	—	—	:	:	:	:
INDUSTRIAL USES											*USAGES INDUSTRIELS*		
1984	:	:	—	—	—	:	:	—	—	—	13	:	—
1985	:	:	:	—	—	:	:	—	—	:	—	:	:
1986	:	:	:	—	—	:	:	—	—	:	:	:	:
HUMAN CONSUMPTION											*CONSOMMATION HUMAINE*		
1984	:	216	16	—	96	6	:	20	—	21	36	:	21
1985	:	:	15	3	87	5	:	35	—	:	37	:	28
1986	:	:	:	1	89	:	:	31	—	:	:	:	:
SELF-SUFFICIENCY (%)											**AUTO-APPROVISIONNEMENT (%)**		
1984	:	347,7	231,3	3 300,0	142,7	—	:	965,0	2 900,0	9,5	520,4	:	252,4
1985	:	:	240,0	1 900,0	141,4	—	:	565,7	2 900,0	:	612,5	:	217,9
1986	:	:	:	2 350,0	134,4	:	:	632,3	2 500,0	:	:	:	:
HUMAN CONSUMPTION (KG/HEAD/YEAR)											**CONSOMMATION HUMAINE(KG/TETE/AN)**		
1984	:	0,8	1,6	—	1,6	0,6	:	0,4	—	0,4	2,5	:	0,4
1985	:	:	1,5	0,6	1,4	0,5	:	0,6	—	:	2,6	:	0,5
1986	:	:	:	0,2	1,5	:	:	0,6	—	:	:	:	:

I E 20

SKIMMED MILK & BUTTERMILK POWDER | **LAIT ECREME & BABEURRE EN POUDRE**

YEAR ANNÉE	EUR 12	EUR 10	UEBL BLEU	DK	D	GR	E	F	IRL	I	NL	P	UK
1000 T													
USABLE PRODUCTION											**PRODUCTION UTILISABLE**		
1984	:	2 104	132	16	604	—	:	775	184	—	171	:	222
1985	:	:	114	25	552	—	:	683	161	:	163	:	241
1986	:	:	:	25	647	:	:	734	156	:	:	:	:
IMPORTS											**IMPORTATIONS**		
1984	:	—	121	15	249	5	:	45	—	227	488	:	26
1985	:	:	52	15	153	7	:	38	1	:	400	:	21
1986	:	:	:	9	349	:	:	29	1	:	:	:	:
INTRA EUR											*INTRA EUR*		
1984	:	1 176	121	15	249	5	:	45	—	227	488	:	26
1985	:	:	—	—	152	7	:	37	1	:	400	:	21
1986	:	:	:	—	349	:	:	27	1	:	:	:	:
RESOURCES = USES											**RESSOURCES = EMPLOIS**		
1984	:	2 104	253	31	853	5	:	820	184	227	659	:	248
1985	:	:	166	40	705	7	:	721	162	:	563	:	262
1986	:	:	:	34	996	:	:	763	157	:	:	:	:
EXPORTS											**EXPORTATIONS**		
1984	:	304	100	18	592	—	:	246	208	—	130	:	186
1985	:	:	96	25	471	—	:	180	201	:	134	:	147
1986	:	:	:	19	406	:	:	269	132	:	:	:	:
INTRA EUR											*INTRA EUR*		
1984	:	:	71	—	508	—	:	223	151	—	157	:	129
1985	:	:	—	—	380	—	:	155	154	:	53	:	93
1986	:	:	:	—	342	:	:	230	79	:	:	:	:
FINAL STOCKS											*STOCKS FINALS*		
1984	:	:	10	20	475	:	:	44	:	:	9	:	89
1985	:	:	7	9	498	:	:	62	:	:	17	:	61
1986	:	:	:	15	884	:	:	39	:	:	:	:	:
CHANGE IN STOCKS											**VARIATION DES STOCKS**		
1984	:	− 274	− 10	− 16	− 80	—	:	− 16	− 42	—	5	:	− 115
1985	:	:	− 3	11	23	—	:	18	− 54	:	− 11	:	− 48
1986	:	:	:	6	386	:	:	− 23	8	:	:	:	:
TOTAL DOMESTIC USES											**UTILISATION INTERIEURE TOTALE**		
1984	:	1 994	163	29	261	5	:	590	18	227	524	:	177
1985	:	:	73	26	210	7	:	523	15	:	440	:	163
1986	:	:	:	15	204	:	:	517	16	:	:	:	:
LOSSES											*PERTES*		
1984	:	:	:	:	:	—	:	:	:	:	:	:	:
1985	:	:	:	:	:	—	:	:	:	:	:	:	:
ANIMAL FEED											*ALIMENTATION ANIMALE*		
1984	:	:	151	29	239	:	:	498	18	227	512	:	20
1985	:	:	60	25	188	:	:	404	15	:	412	:	21
1986	:	:	:	15	180	:	:	399	16	:	:	:	:
INDUSTRIAL USES											*USAGES INDUSTRIELS*		
1984	:	:	—	—	—	:	:	—	—	—	2	:	—
1985	:	:	—	—	—	:	:	—	—	:	—	:	:
1986	:	:	:	—	—	:	:	—	—	:	:	:	:
HUMAN CONSUMPTION											*CONSOMMATION HUMAINE*		
1984	:	298	12	—	22	5	:	92	—	—	10	:	157
1985	:	:	13	1	22	7	:	119	—	:	10	:	142
1986	:	:	:	—	24	:	:	118	—	:	:	:	:
SELF-SUFFICIENCY (%)											**AUTO-APPROVISIONNEMENT (%)**		
1984	:	105,5	81,0	55,2	231,4	—	:	131,4	1 022,2	—	32,6	:	125,4
1985	:	:	156,2	96,2	262,9	—	:	130,6	1 073,3	:	37,0	:	147,9
1986	:	:	:	166,7	317,2	:	:	142,0	975,0	:	:	:	:
HUMAN CONSUMPTION (KG/HEAD/YEAR)											**CONSOMMATION HUMAINE(KG/TETE/AN)**		
1984	:	1,1	1,2	—	0,4	0,5	:	1,7	—	—	0,7	:	2,8
1985	:	:	1,3	0,2	0,4	0,7	:	2,2	—	:	0,7	:	2,5
1986	:	:	:	—	0,4	:	:	2,1	—	:	:	:	:

BUTTER   **BEURRE**

1000 T

YEAR ANNÉE	EUR 12	EUR 10	UEBL BLEU	DK	D	GR	E	F	IRL	I	NL	P	UK
USABLE PRODUCTION													**PRODUCTION UTILISABLE**
1984	:	2 118	110	104	574	4	:	602	171	81	266	:	206
1985	:	:	97	110	517	5	:	595	167	:	263	:	204
1986	:	:	:	112	567	:	:	645	160	:	:	:	:
IMPORTS													**IMPORTATIONS**
1984	:	:	120	16	74	4	:	50	1	50	87	:	161
1985	:	:	139	15	100	5	:	76	1	:	79	:	141
1986	:	:	:	16	93	:	:	80	4	:	:	:	:
INTRA EUR													*INTRA EUR*
1984	:	:	118	10	74	4	:	47	1	49	86	:	71
1985	:	:	—	—	100	5	:	70	1	:	79	:	63
1986	:	:	:	—	93	:	:	76	4	:	:	:	:
RESOURCES = USES													**RESSOURCES = EMPLOIS**
1984	:	:	230	120	648	7	:	652	172	131	353	:	367
1985	:	:	236	125	617	10	:	671	168	:	342	:	345
1986	:	:	:	128	660	:	:	725	164	:	:	:	:
EXPORTS													**EXPORTATIONS**
1984	:	:	146	66	87	—	:	168	119	3	282	:	25
1985	:	:	159	59	87	—	:	188	106	:	272	:	26
1986	:	:	:	66	206	:	:	112	81	:	:	:	:
INTRA EUR													*INTRA EUR*
1984	:	:	98	:	74	—	:	48	94	3	142	:	16
1985	:	:	—	:	73	—	:	55	84	:	153	:	21
1986	:	:	:	:	105	:	:	37	72	:	:	:	:
FINAL STOCKS													*STOCKS FINALS*
1984	:	:	35	12	428	:	:	150	:	1	219	:	227
1985	:	:	29	18	496	:	:	122	:	:	238	:	290
1986	:	:	:	22	468	:	:	209	:	:	:	:	:
CHANGE IN STOCKS													**VARIATION DES STOCKS**
1984	:	137	−9	−6	134	−0	:	−40	9	−1	14	:	36
1985	:	:	−5	6	68	0	:	−28	27	:	12	:	40
1986	:	:	:	4	−28	:	:	87	55	:	:	:	:
TOTAL DOMESTIC USES													**UTILISATION INTERIEURE TOTALE**
1984	:	1 647	93	60	427	7	:	524	44	129	57	:	306
1985	:	:	83	60	461	10	:	511	34	:	58	:	279
1986	:	:	:	58	482	:	:	526	28	:	:	:	:
PROCESSING													*TRANSFORMATION*
1984	:	:	—	—	—	:	:	S	—	—	—	:	—
1985	:	:	—	—	—	:	:	S	—	:	−:	:	—
1986	:	:	:	—	—	:	:	S	—	:	:	:	:
HUMAN CONSUMPTION													*CONSOMMATION HUMAINE*
1984	:	1 627	93	40	427	7	:	524	44	129	57	:	306
1985	:	:	83	37	461	10	:	511	34	:	58	:	279
1986	:	:	:	37	482	:	:	526	28	:	:	:	:
SELF-SUFFICIENCY (%)													**AUTO-APPROVISIONNEMENT (%)**
1984	:	128,6	118,3	173,3	134,4	51,4	:	114,9	388,6	62,8	466,7	:	67,3
1985	:	:	116,9	183,3	112,1	51,0	:	116,4	491,2	:	453,4	:	73,1
1986	:	:	:	193,1	117,6	:	:	122,6	571,4	:	:	:	:
HUMAN CONSUMPTION (KG/HEAD/YEAR)													**CONSOMMATION HUMAINE(KG/TETE/AN)**
1984	:	6,0	9,1	7,8	7,0	0,7	:	9,5	12,5	2,3	4,0	:	5,4
1985	:	:	8,1	7,2	7,6	1,0	:	9,3	9,6	:	4,0	:	4,9
1986	:	:	:	7,2	7,9	:	:	9,5	7,9	:	:	:	:
FAT CONTENT (%)													**TENEUR EN MATIERES GRASSES (%)**
1984	:	:	83,2	82,5	83,0	83,0	:	82,7	82,0	82,2	82,5	:	83,4
1985	:	:	83,2	82,5	83,0	:	:	82,8	82,0	:	:	:	82,7
1986	:	:	:	82,5	83,0	:	:	82,8	82,0	:	:	:	:

CHEESE   **FROMAGE**

YEAR ANNÉE	EUR 12	EUR 10	UEBL BLEU	DK	D	GR	E	F	IRL	I	NL	P	UK
						1000 T							
USABLE PRODUCTION											**PRODUCTION UTILISABLE**		
1984	:	4 139	47	295	878	179	:	1 273	55	661	506	:	245
1985	:	:	51	256	913	182	:	1 309	79	:	513	:	256
1986	:	:	:	254	924	:	:	1 292	63	:	:	:	:
IMPORTS											**IMPORTATIONS**		
1984	:	98	104	9	267	27	:	75	4	233	32	:	125
1985	:	:	105	6	290	36	:	75	7	:	31	:	141
1986	:	:	:	8	296	:	:	78	6	:	:	:	:
INTRA EUR											*INTRA EUR*		
1984	:	778	94	—	251	26	:	63	4	200	28	:	112
1985	:	:	—	—	268	34	:	63	6	:	31	:	126
1986	:	:	:	—	282	:	:	67	6	:	:	:	:
RESOURCES = USES											**RESSOURCES = EMPLOIS**		
1984	:	4 237	151	304	1 145	205	:	1 348	59	894	538	:	370
1985	:	:	156	262	1 203	217	:	1 384	86	:	544	:	397
1986	:	:	:	262	1 220	:	:	1 370	69	:	:	:	:
EXPORTS											**EXPORTATIONS**		
1984	:	409	15	243	249	5	:	228	54	40	323	:	30
1985	:	:	22	202	236	5	:	227	64	:	341	:	30
1986	:	:	:	198	244	:	:	225	66	:	:	:	:
INTRA EUR											*INTRA EUR*		
1984	:	:	14	:	200	1	:	189	51	20	267	:	11
1985	:	:	—	:	200	2	:	186	55	:	285	:	16
1986	:	:	:	:	203	:	:	184	65	:	:	:	:
FINAL STOCKS											*STOCKS FINALS*		
1984	:	:	2	29	34	12	:	87	:	:	76	:	106
1985	:	:	2	31	51	14	:	92	:	:	76	:	115
1986	:	:	:	31	:	:	:	92	:	:	:	:	:
CHANGE IN STOCKS											**VARIATION DES STOCKS**		
1984	:	−5	—	−2	−8	−7	:	2	−7	17	7	:	−7
1985	:	:	—	2	17	3	:	5	6	:	1	:	10
1986	:	:	:	—	−1	:	:	12	−11	:	:	:	:
TOTAL DOMESTIC USES											**UTILISATION INTERIEURE TOTALE**		
1984	:	3 836	136	63	909	205	:	1 118	13	837	208	:	347
1985	:	:	134	58	950	210	:	1 152	15	:	202	:	357
1986	:	:	:	64	977	:	:	1 133	14	:	:	:	:
LOSSES											*PERTES*		
1984	:	—	—	—	—	—	:	—	—	—	—	:	—
1985	:	:	—	—	—	—	:	—	—	:	—	:	—
1986	:	:	:	—	—	:	:	—	—	:	:	:	:
PROCESSING											*TRANSFORMATION*		
1984	:	162	20	—	73	—	:	32	—	15	15	:	7
1985	:	:	18	—	66	—	:	2	—	:	16	:	7
1986	:	:	:	—	68	:	:	—	—	:	:	:	:
HUMAN CONSUMPTION											*CONSOMMATION HUMAINE*		
1984	:	3 674	116	63	836	205	:	1 086	13	822	193	:	340
1985	:	:	116	58	884	210	:	1 152	15	:	186	:	350
1986	:	:	:	64	909	:	:	1 133	14	:	:	:	:
SELF-SUFFICIENCY (%)											**AUTO-APPROVISIONNEMENT (%)**		
1984	:	107,9	34,6	468,3	96,6	87,4	:	113,9	423,1	79,0	243,3	:	70,6
1985	:	:	38,1	441,4	96,1	86,6	:	113,6	526,7	:	254,0	:	71,7
1986	:	:	:	396,9	94,6	:	:	114,0	450,0	:	:	:	:
HUMAN CONSUMPTION (KG/HEAD/YEAR)											**CONSOMMATION HUMAINE(KG/TETE/AN)**		
1984	:	13,5	11,3	12,3	13,7	20,7	:	19,8	3,7	14,4	13,4	:	6,0
1985	:	:	11,3	11,3	14,5	21,1	:	20,9	4,2	:	12,8	:	6,2
1986	:	:	:	12,5	14,9	:	:	20,5	4,0	:	:	:	:

EGGS (TOTAL)　　　　　　　　　　　　　　　　　　　　　　　　　　**OEUFS (TOTAL)**

YEAR ANNÉE	EUR 12	EUR 10	UEBL BLEU	DK	D	GR	E	F	IRL	I	NL	P	UK
1000 T													
USABLE PRODUCTION													**PRODUCTION UTILISABLE**
1984	:	4 171	184	80	761	123	:	908	37	641	666	:	771
1985	:	4 151	176	80	765	122	:	907	37	628	663	:	774
1986	:	:	184	81	743	123	:	:	:	:	:	:	772
IMPORTS													**IMPORTATIONS**
1984	:	49	32	5	329	4	:	37	12	79	29	:	55
1985	:	359	41	7	334	3	:	53	11	66	32	:	55
1986	:	:	47	5	338	4	:	:	:	:	:	:	47
INTRA EUR													*INTRA EUR*
1984	:	532	29	5	307	3	:	36	12	71	18	:	52
1985	:	243	38	7	—	3	:	50	11	57	22	:	53
1986	:	:	46	5	318	4	:	:	:	:	:	:	47
RESOURCES = USES													**RESSOURCES = EMPLOIS**
1984	:	4 220	216	85	1 090	127	:	945	49	720	695	:	826
1985	:	4 510	217	86	1 099	125	:	960	48	694	695	:	829
1986	:	:	231	87	1 081	127	:	:	:	:	:	:	819
EXPORTS													**EXPORTATIONS**
1984	:	140	63	5	49	—	:	43	—	7	486	:	19
1985	:	425	61	5	44	—	:	37	1	12	491	:	17
1986	:	:	69	7	53	—	:	:	:	:	:	:	17
INTRA EUR													*INTRA EUR*
1984	:	:	57	5	33	—	:	25	—	7	387	:	17
1985	:	:	58	5	—	—	:	23	1	8	414	:	15
1986	:	:	66	—	32	—	:	:	:	:	:	:	—
FINAL STOCKS													*STOCKS FINALS*
1984	:	:	—	—	8	:	:	2	—	—	—	:	—
1985	:	:	—	—	8	:	:	2	—	—	—	:	—
1986	:	:	—	—	8	:	:	:	:	:	:	:	—
CHANGE IN STOCKS													**VARIATION DES STOCKS**
1984	:	0	—	0	—	—	:	—	—	—	—	:	—
1985	:	1	—	0	—	—	:	1	—	—	—	:	—
1986	:	:	—	—	—	—	:	:	:	:	:	:	—
TOTAL DOMESTIC USES													**UTILISATION INTERIEURE TOTALE**
1984	:	4 077	153	80	1 041	127	:	902	49	710	209	:	807
1985	:	4 085	156	82	1 055	125	:	922	47	682	204	:	812
1986	:	:	162	80	1 028	127	:	:	:	:	:	:	802
INCUBATION													*OEUFS A COUVER*
1984	:	213	9	6	22	9	:	54	2	28	38	:	46
1985	:	216	9	6	20	9	:	55	3	34	34	:	46
1986	:	:	10	6	20	8	:	:	:	:	:	:	50
LOSSES													*PERTES*
1984	:	5	—	—	—	1	:	1	—	3	—	:	—
1985	:	5	—	—	—	1	:	1	—	3	—	:	—
1986	:	:	—	—	—	1	:	:	:	:	:	:	—
ANIMAL FEED													*ALIMENTATION ANIMALE*
1984	:	—	—	—	—	—	:	—	—	—	—	:	—
1985	:	—	—	—	—	—	:	—	—	—	—	:	—
1986	:	:	—	—	—	—	:	:	:	:	:	:	—
INDUSTRIAL USES													*USAGES INDUSTRIELS*
1984	:	11	—	—	—	—	:	8	—	—	—	:	3
1985	:	11	—	—	—	—	:	8	—	—	—	:	3
1986	:	:	—	—	—	—	:	:	:	:	:	:	25
HUMAN CONSUMPTION													*CONSOMMATION HUMAINE*
1984	:	3 848	144	74	1 019	117	:	839	47	679	171	:	758
1985	:	3 852	147	75	1 035	115	:	858	44	645	170	:	763
1986	:	:	152	74	1 008	118	:	:	:	:	:	:	727
SELF-SUFFICIENCY (%)													**AUTO-APPROVISIONNEMENT (%)**
1984	:	102,3	120,3	100,5	73,1	97,0	:	100,7	75,5	90,3	318,7	:	95,5
1985	:	101,6	112,8	97,8	72,5	97,4	:	98,4	78,7	92,1	325,0	:	95,3
1986	:	:	113,6	101,5	72,3	96,5	:	:	:	:	:	:	96,3
HUMAN CONSUMPTION (KG/HEAD/YEAR)													**CONSOMMATION HUMAINE(KG/TETE/AN)**
1984	:	14,1	14,1	14,5	16,7	11,8	:	15,3	13,3	11,9	11,9	:	13,4
1985	:	14,1	14,4	14,7	17,0	11,5	:	15,6	12,4	11,3	11,7	:	13,5
1986	:	:	14,9	14,5	16,5	11,9	:	:	:	:	:	:	12,8
USABLE PRODUCTION (MIO EGGS)													**PRODUCTION UTILIS. (MIO OEUFS)**
1984	:	7 0588	3 054	1 335	1 2688	2 458	:	1 4920	657	1 1247	1 1084	:	1 3145
1985	:	7 0031	2 880	1 328	1 2755	2 436	:	1 4910	646	1 0773	1 1100	:	1 3203
1986	:	:	2 914	1 355	1 2382	2 436	:	:	:	:	:	:	1 3191

EGGS FOR CONSUMPTION **OEUFS DE CONSOMMATION**

YEAR ANNÉE	EUR 12	EUR 10	UEBL BLEU	DK	D	GR	E	F	IRL	I	NL	P	UK
1000 T													
USABLE PRODUCTION												**PRODUCTION UTILISABLE**	
1984	:	3 940	175	74	745	115	:	849	35	613	611	:	723
1985	:	3 915	168	73	749	113	:	848	34	596	607	:	726
1986	:	:	174	75	728	116	:	:	:	:	:	:	722
IMPORTS												**IMPORTATIONS**	
1984	:	44	30	5	319	3	:	37	12	78	28	:	55
1985	:	343	38	7	326	2	:	52	11	64	31	:	55
1986	:	:	44	5	330	4	:	:	:	:	:	:	47
INTRA EUR												*INTRA EUR*	
1984	:	523	27	5	299	2	:	36	12	70	17	:	52
1985	:	242	35	7	–	2	:	52	11	56	21	:	53
1986	:	:	43	5	311	4	:	:	:	:	:	:	47
RESOURCES = USES												**RESSOURCES = EMPLOIS**	
1984	:	3 984	205	79	1 064	118	:	886	47	691	639	:	778
1985	:	4 258	206	80	1 075	115	:	900	45	660	638	:	781
1986	:	:	218	80	1 058	120	:	:	:	:	:	:	769
EXPORTS												**EXPORTATIONS**	
1984	:	120	61	5	45	–	:	38	–	9	468	:	17
1985	:	389	59	5	40	–	:	32	1	12	468	:	15
1986	:	:	66	6	50	–	:	:	:	:	:	:	16
INTRA EUR												*INTRA EUR*	
1984	:	:	56	5	32	–	:	24	–	6	378	:	16
1985	:	:	57	5	–	–	:	22	1	8	404	:	13
1986	:	:	65	6	32	–	:	:	:	:	:	:	16
FINAL STOCKS												*STOCKS FINALS*	
1984	:	:	–	–	8	:	:	2	–	–	–	:	–
1985	:	:	–	–	8	:	:	3	–	–	–	:	–
1986	:	:	–	–	8	:	:	:	:	:	:	:	–
CHANGE IN STOCKS												**VARIATION DES STOCKS**	
1984	:	0	–	0	–	–	:	–	–	–	–	:	–
1985	:	1	–	–	–	–	:	1	–	–	–	:	–
1986	:	:	–	–	–	–	:	:	:	:	:	:	–
TOTAL DOMESTIC USES												**UTILISATION INTERIEURE TOTALE**	
1984	:	3 864	144	74	1 019	118	:	848	47	682	171	:	761
1985	:	3 868	147	75	1 035	116	:	867	44	648	170	:	766
1986	:	:	152	74	1 008	120	:	:	:	:	:	:	753
LOSSES												*PERTES*	
1984	:	5	–	–	–	1	:	1	–	3	–	:	–
1985	:	5	–	–	–	1	:	1	–	3	–	:	–
1986	:	:	–	–	–	1	:	:	:	:	:	:	–
ANIMAL FEED												*ALIMENTATION ANIMALE*	
1984	:	–				–	:	–	–	–	–	:	–
1985	:	–	–	–	–	–	:	–	–	–	–	:	–
1986	:	:	–	–	–	–	:	:	:	:	:	:	–
INDUSTRIAL USES												*USAGES INDUSTRIELS*	
1984	:	11	–	–	–	–	:	8	–	–	–	:	3
1985	:	11	–	–	–	–	:	8	–	–	–	:	3
1986	:	:	–	–	–	–	:	:	:	:	:	:	25
HUMAN CONSUMPTION												*CONSOMMATION HUMAINE*	
1984	:	3 848	144	74	1 019	117	:	839	47	679	171	:	758
1985	:	3 852	147	75	1 035	115	:	858	44	645	170	:	763
1986	:	:	152	74	1 008	118	:	:	:	:	:	:	727
SELF-SUFFICIENCY (%)												**AUTO-APPROVISIONNEMENT (%)**	
1984	:	102,0	121,5	100,3	73,1	97,1	:	100,1	74,5	89,9	357,3	:	95,0
1985	:	101,2	114,3	97,3	72,4	97,8	:	97,8	77,3	92,0	357,1	:	94,8
1986	:	:	114,5	101,1	72,2	96,7	:	:	:	:	:	:	95,9
HUMAN CONSUMPTION (KG/HEAD/YEAR)												**CONSOMMATION HUMAINE(KG/TETE/AN)**	
1984	:	14,1	14,1	14,5	16,7	11,8	:	15,3	13,3	11,9	11,9	:	13,4
1985	:	14,1	14,4	14,7	17,0	11,5	:	15,6	12,4	11,3	11,7	:	13,5
1986	:	:	14,9	14,5	16,5	11,9	:	:	:	:	:	:	12,8

I F

Prices and price indices

Prix et indices de prix

Selling prices of agricultural products

Prix de vente de produits agricoles

PRICE: ECU/100 KG, VAT EXCL.

PRIX: ÉCU/100 KG, HORS TVA

	Belgique/ Belgïe	Danmark	BR Deutsch- land	Ellas	España	France	Ireland	Italia	Luxem- bourg	Neder- land	Portugal	United Kingdom

SOFT WHEAT   **BLÉ TENDRE**

	Belgique/ Belgïe	Danmark	BR Deutsch- land	Ellas	España	France	Ireland	Italia	Luxem- bourg	Neder- land	Portugal	United Kingdom
1972	9,89	–	10,33	7,49	:	8,81	7,57	10,71	9,72	10,07	:	6,95
1973	10,72	9,95	11,67	9,80	:	9,55	10,91	11,93	10,46	11,00	:	9,60
1974	11,57	11,34	12,86	11,57	:	10,30	9,32	13,27	11,32	11,87	:	12,06
1975	13,22	11,79	14,03	11,75	:	11,19	12,00	13,44	12,51	12,87	:	10,12
1976	15,13	14,13	16,62	13,62	:	12,92	12,94	15,68	15,06	15,06	:	11,65
1977	16,34	14,55	17,23	15,20	:	13,30	13,83	16,61	15,41	15,87	:	12,85
1978	16,55	15,54	18,00	14,54	:	13,87	14,28	17,10	15,88	16,18	:	13,15
1979	16,59	15,54	18,21	15,32	:	14,16	13,92	17,55	16,03	16,19	:	14,99
1980	16,78	16,53	18,54	16,10	:	15,03	13,18	18,85	16,31	16,29	:	16,76
1981	17,87	17,64	19,01	19,72	:	16,17	15,34	20,87	17,24	17,59	:	19,89
1982	18,43	18,56	20,85	20,52	:	17,03	15,79	21,19	18,12	19,42	:	20,41
1983	19,71	20,50	21,84	20,07	:	17,42	18,16	22,26	19,63	20,53	:	21,55
1984	18,18	19,52	20,98	19,89	:	16,64	16,54	23,03	17,72	19,16	:	19,29
1985	17,62	19,01	18,89	18,41	:	16,26	11,20	21,62	17,14	18,12	:	18,98
1986	18,95	18,52	19,25	15,81	:	16,94	14,30	23,22	14,47	18,68	:	16,48

DURUM WHEAT   **BLÉ DUR**

	Belgique/ Belgïe	Danmark	BR Deutsch- land	Ellas	España	France	Ireland	Italia	Luxem- bourg	Neder- land	Portugal	United Kingdom
1972	–	–	–	9,18	:	14,11	–	14,16	–	–	:	–
1973	–	–	–	11,20	:	17,60	–	18,77	–	–	:	–
1974	–	–	–	13,72	:	24,35	–	25,25	–	–	:	–
1975	–	–	–	15,80	:	20,61	–	20,46	–	–	:	–
1976	–	–	–	18,20	:	18,32	–	19,65	–	–	:	–
1977	–	–	–	19,89	:	20,21	–	22,80	–	–	:	–
1978	–	–	–	19,32	:	19,55	–	22,18	–	–	:	–
1979	–	–	–	20,50	:	19,20	–	23,04	–	–	:	–
1980	–	–	–	22,42	:	22,50	–	25,12	–	–	:	–
1981	–	–	–	26,97	:	23,12	–	25,95	–	–	:	–
1982	–	–	–	29,60	:	23,52	–	28,80	–	–	:	–
1983	–	–	–	31,67	:	26,61	–	31,25	–	–	:	–
1984	–	–	–	32,50	:	25,27	–	32,04	–	–	:	–
1985	–	–	–	31,56	:	23,89	–	30,40	–	–	:	–
1986	–	–	–	26,78	:	25,59	–	31,45	–	–	:	–

BARLEY   **ORGE**

	Belgique/ Belgïe	Danmark	BR Deutsch- land	Ellas	España	France	Ireland	Italia	Luxem- bourg	Neder- land	Portugal	United Kingdom
1972	8,98	–	9,28	7,28	:	8,13	6,06	9,72	8,71	9,33	:	6,33
1973	9,66	9,03	10,41	9,58	:	8,35	8,72	11,30	9,31	9,95	:	8,50
1974	10,81	10,81	11,96	11,10	:	9,50	9,22	14,85	9,81	11,32	:	11,53
1975	12,53	11,08	12,88	11,18	:	10,23	10,05	13,50	11,63	12,54	:	10,11
1976	14,61	13,98	15,31	12,47	:	11,83	11,39	14,16	12,39	15,13	:	11,97
1977	14,53	13,88	15,78	14,37	:	11,84	13,10	16,01	13,82	15,11	:	12,10
1978	14,72	13,87	15,90	14,19	:	11,88	12,67	16,13	14,25	15,49	:	12,02
1979	15,53	15,11	16,44	15,05	:	12,83	12,89	16,63	14,42	15,70	:	14,20
1980	14,97	15,05	16,46	15,32	:	13,24	12,37	17,29	14,51	15,60	:	15,67
1981	16,32	16,67	16,74	18,39	:	14,13	13,50	19,03	15,40	17,03	:	18,44
1982	17,02	17,96	18,72	18,66	:	15,22	14,36	20,62	16,71	18,77	:	19,84
1983	18,56	19,09	19,67	18,97	:	15,95	17,41	21,47	18,55	20,57	:	20,49
1984	17,62	19,18	20,04	18,89	:	15,99	16,06	22,94	17,17	19,52	:	19,05
1985	16,92	17,86	17,90	18,15	:	15,32	12,04	20,98	16,48	18,24	:	18,10
1986	18,48	17,59	17,53	15,37	:	15,46	13,88	21,90	16,78	18,72	:	16,13

OATS   **AVOINE**

	Belgique/ Belgïe	Danmark	BR Deutsch- land	Ellas	España	France	Ireland	Italia	Luxem- bourg	Neder- land	Portugal	United Kingdom
1972	7,90	–	8,85	7,70	:	6,73	6,35	9,02	8,31	8,47	:	6,15
1973	9,68	9,06	10,48	12,12	:	8,35	8,06	11,19	8,89	9,77	:	7,63
1974	10,89	11,23	12,22	10,84	:	9,69	9,02	13,44	9,38	11,34	:	10,26
1975	11,65	10,54	12,59	11,70	:	9,68	8,70	12,80	11,08	11,53	:	9,75
1976	14,71	13,80	15,43	14,75	:	11,49	10,30	13,44	11,82	14,04	:	11,21
1977	14,75	14,22	16,42	18,77	:	12,03	12,83	17,66	13,21	15,23	:	11,63
1978	14,47	14,15	16,28	16,87	:	11,08	13,65	17,08	13,63	14,71	:	10,85
1979	14,70	15,41	15,87	14,32	:	10,93	13,40	16,02	13,82	13,99	:	13,71
1980	14,92	15,49	16,12	16,77	:	12,49	12,89	18,26	13,89	15,14	:	16,21
1981	16,43	15,78	16,97	21,13	:	14,20	12,89	19,27	14,80	16,41	:	17,81
1982	16,18	16,95	18,47	24,93	:	13,61	13,31	21,67	15,66	17,43	:	18,18
1983	17,64	17,73	19,35	24,70	:	14,94	16,24	22,00	17,45	19,08	:	19,32
1984	18,70	19,73	21,32	25,80	:	17,57	15,84	25,55	17,17	19,42	:	20,40
1985	15,47	16,63	17,35	24,56	:	12,98	11,89	26,44	15,59	16,75	:	17,03
1986	15,99	14,63	16,25	18,16	:	13,06	14,14	23,40	15,87	17,14	:	15,07

PRICE: ECU/100 KG, VAT EXCL. PRIX: ÉCU/100 KG, HORS TVA

	Belgique/België	Danmark	BR Deutschland	Ellas	España	France	Ireland	Italia	Luxembourg	Nederland	Portugal	United Kingdom
RYE												**SEIGLE**
1972	8,87	—	9,68	:	:	7,74	:	9,95	8,87	8,78	:	:
1973	9,71	9,29	10,80	:	:	8,58	:	10,35	9,62	10,11	:	:
1974	10,65	10,96	12,47	:	:	9,96	:	12,87	10,45	11,45	:	:
1975	12,39	11,23	13,65	:	:	10,83	:	13,87	11,81	12,60	:	:
1976	14,81	13,92	16,34	:	:	12,47	:	14,50	14,48	14,94	:	:
1977	14,43	14,03	16,65	:	:	12,04	:	16,39	13,94	15,05	:	:
1978	14,42	14,63	17,30	:	:	11,11	:	17,19	14,38	15,27	:	:
1979	14,92	14,58	17,55	:	:	11,90	:	17,09	14,54	15,66	:	:
1980	15,58	15,33	17,89	:	:	13,19	:	18,32	14,63	16,05	:	:
1981	16,86	16,24	18,19	:	:	14,15	:	17,80	16,23	17,03	:	:
1982	17,68	16,79	20,04	:	:	14,54	:	18,53	17,33	18,82	:	:
1983	19,54	18,18	21,45	:	:	15,45	:	21,40	19,37	19,71	:	:
1984	18,56	17,92	21,00	:	:	14,72	:	22,61	17,72	18,43	:	:
1985	17,26	17,28	18,83	:	:	14,08	:	21,13	17,37	17,36	:	:
1986	19,41	16,45	19,18	:	:	16,87	:	21,61	17,92	17,83	:	:
MAIZE												**MAÏS**
1972	:	:	—	7,93	:	8,25	:	9,23	:	:	:	:
1973	:	:	—	10,20	:	8,54	:	10,49	:	:	:	:
1974	:	:	12,98	11,74	:	11,20	:	12,75	:	:	:	:
1975	:	:	13,71	12,28	:	10,45	:	13,85	:	:	:	:
1976	:	:	16,26	12,79	:	12,21	:	15,97	:	:	:	:
1977	:	:	17,30	14,13	:	12,95	:	16,28	:	:	:	:
1978	:	:	18,20	13,79	:	13,21	:	16,25	:	:	:	:
1979	:	:	18,74	14,40	:	13,44	:	16,84	:	:	:	:
1980	:	:	18,77	15,29	:	14,45	:	18,36	:	:	:	:
1981	:	:	19,87	18,48	:	15,91	:	19,98	:	:	:	:
1982	:	:	21,52	20,17	:	16,85	:	21,73	:	:	:	:
1983	:	:	23,76	18,08	:	17,47	:	24,26	:	:	:	:
1984	:	:	23,00	18,14	:	17,33	:	25,92	:	:	:	:
1985	:	:	21,38	17,19	:	17,79	:	23,45	:	:	:	:
1986	:	:	20,37	15,08	:	16,37	:	24,00	:	:	:	:
RICE												**RIZ**
1972	:	:	:	—	:	13,50	:	13,64	:	:	:	:
1973	:	:	:	—	:	20,40	:	16,44	:	:	:	:
1974	:	:	:	25,41	:	21,11	:	15,99	:	:	:	:
1975	:	:	:	18,53	:	18,00	:	18,95	:	:	:	:
1976	:	:	:	20,20	:	23,92	:	20,71	:	:	:	:
1977	:	:	:	20,84	:	23,65	:	25,58	:	:	:	:
1978	:	:	:	21,06	:	27,54	:	26,99	:	:	:	:
1979	:	:	:	20,25	:	:	:	25,01	:	:	:	:
1980	:	:	:	18,56	:	:	:	25,49	:	:	:	:
1981	:	:	:	23,72	:	:	:	33,77	:	:	:	:
1982	:	:	:	28,74	:	:	:	34,84	:	:	:	:
1983	:	:	:	29,45	:	:	:	34,93	:	:	:	:
1984	:	:	:	31,11	:	:	:	39,41	:	:	:	:
1985	:	:	:	32,95	:	:	:	36,93	:	:	:	:
1986	:	:	:	26,54	:	:	:	34,58	:	:	:	:
DESSERT APPLES (all varieties)										**POMMES DE TABLE (ensemble des variétés)**		
1972	12,64	19,90	17,46	11,20	:	18,74	:	13,47	:	12,03	:	34,04
1973	14,60	21,04	23,40	12,37	:	17,74	:	12,62	:	15,12	:	24,15
1974	13,51	20,94	21,49	14,03	:	19,88	:	15,21	:	14,34	:	29,50
1975	18,50	19,94	25,61	12,70	:	17,67	:	14,74	:	18,89	:	31,23
1976	14,43	25,29	27,24	18,17	:	23,76	:	14,74	:	17,43	:	30,42
1977	24,12	28,01	41,58	20,74	:	51,20	:	31,40	:	28,99	:	46,54
1978	19,92	26,64	32,80	25,52	:	27,18	:	27,87	:	19,88	:	33,74
1979	12,62	19,56	22,86	23,85	:	21,44	:	23,45	:	12,82	:	29,92
1980	15,69	22,61	26,75	23,43	:	25,56	:	24,75	:	17,71	:	43,24
1981	23,73	35,22	39,91	22,52	:	40,56	:	29,34	:	28,22	:	60,64
1982	22,68	30,89	47,74	30,75	:	25,50	:	27,94	:	30,22	:	53,65
1983	28,88	40,21	35,72	28,79	:	45,79	:	36,68	:	31,53	:	62,54
1984	32,06	32,90	49,18	28,12	:	32,74	:	37,32	:	36,46	:	63,14
1985	28,28	35,42	40,71	30,59	:	37,23	:	38,05	:	29,47	:	56,03
1986	30,12	37,43	46,81	25,99	:	39,71	:	35,05	:	28,32	:	58,22

PRICE: ECU/100 KG, VAT EXCL. PRIX: ÉCU/100 KG, HORS TVA

DESSERT PEARS (all varieties) — POIRES DE TABLE (ensemble des variétés)

	Belgique/België	Danmark	BR Deutschland	Ellas	España	France	Ireland	Italia	Luxembourg	Nederland	Portugal	United Kingdom
1975	21,44	21,20	20,96	–	:	26,88	:	16,53	:	21,30	:	33,00
1976	19,48	24,55	20,75	28,69	:	17,40	:	12,71	:	16,60	:	30,21
1977	26,00	28,44	29,57	30,89	:	41,92	:	23,76	:	29,83	:	42,07
1978	23,56	34,62	22,78	43,97	:	35,02	:	31,02	:	24,64	:	39,18
1979	27,01	31,07	22,90	36,57	:	27,10	:	27,30	:	21,93	:	30,93
1980	24,93	39,99	23,91	38,62	:	29,31	:	24,37	:	27,00	:	38,85
1981	28,79	33,45	32,43	32,93	:	35,93	:	22,49	:	34,78	:	50,86
1982	37,64	46,22	34,34	54,54	:	33,74	:	38,52	:	38,64	:	59,10
1983	33,83	51,65	46,68	43,67	:	35,15	:	28,61	:	36,66	:	53,66
1984	40,56	40,26	32,48	51,56	:	35,07	:	37,21	:	39,23	:	53,22
1985	36,14	51,63	35,62	44,09	:	43,41	:	41,30	:	35,84	:	53,48
1986	39,09	65,53	44,53	45,47	:	57,94	:	52,96	:	43,32	:	52,72

STRAWBERRIES (all varieties) — FRAISES (ensemble des variétés)

	Belgique/België	Danmark	BR Deutschland	Ellas	España	France	Ireland	Italia	Luxembourg	Nederland	Portugal	United Kingdom
1975	116,94	89,01	126,56	–	:	116,56	42,14	:	:	85,59	:	113,21
1976	140,41	111,07	132,14	47,70	:	115,25	40,49	:	:	107,52	:	131,95
1977	149,50	113,05	172,00	47,10	:	136,99	63,15	:	:	118,84	:	136,18
1978	147,87	120,66	157,99	60,47	:	133,80	68,63	:	:	117,91	:	146,99
1979	142,99	119,29	140,71	72,93	:	151,99	69,07	:	:	109,33	:	162,24
1980	142,47	112,94	185,04	70,41	:	144,66	75,93	125,70	:	102,97	:	139,85
1981	183,12	114,23	174,81	66,40	:	148,84	103,30	136,67	:	157,09	:	158,25
1982	184,29	123,58	267,11	66,71	:	159,23	129,61	168,46	:	160,30	:	224,35
1983	153,62	135,27	249,09	61,67	:	174,57	136,89	198,98	:	126,12	:	202,99
1984	199,68	107,41	170,36	79,64	:	196,90	101,44	188,00	:	157,33	:	200,13
1985	195,95	160,25	181,55	66,34	:	200,88	110,00	:	:	209,88	:	225,75
1986	169,16	164,83	184,08	41,60	:	194,86	117,64	:	:	165,77	:	318,30

CAULIFLOWERS (all varieties) — CHOUX-FLEURS (ensemble des variétés)

	Belgique/België	Danmark qual. I	BR Deutschland	Ellas	España	France qual.I	Ireland	Italia	Luxembourg	Nederland	Portugal	United Kingdom
1975	20,65	31,17	20,49	15,58	:	17,48	:	15,86	:	28,07	:	21,70
1976	20,97	33,72	21,12	14,43	:	11,60	:	16,28	:	31,07	:	19,18
1977	28,23	34,33	25,78	20,91	:	23,01	:	20,02	:	40,56	:	21,92
1978	24,44	36,07	21,68	21,48	:	14,98	:	18,82	:	33,74	:	20,08
1979	17,53	34,62	23,91	25,84	:	21,44	:	22,96	:	32,91	:	25,22
1980	25,08	49,57	29,03	24,68	:	16,19	:	29,18	:	43,71	:	31,05
1981	26,94	50,87	29,09	31,16	:	20,53	:	39,11	:	38,75	:	37,41
1982	21,86	56,15	25,49	33,88	:	18,82	:	35,74	:	35,96	:	38,18
1983	35,34	67,64	35,51	30,80	:	19,35	:	37,85	:	51,24	:	40,54
1984	31,63	39,90	33,23	30,44	:	21,39	:	35,04	:	44,78	:	36,61
1985	34,56	57,49	34,36	42,02	:	36,94	:	54,88	:	48,98	:	47,54
1986	27,31	53,43	26,01	32,90	:	20,59	:	44,41	:	34,15	:	:

LETTUCE (all varieties) — LAITUES (ensemble des variétés)

	Belgique/België de serre	Danmark under glass Qual. I	BR Deutschland under glass	Ellas in the open	España	France	Ireland	Italia in the open	Luxembourg	Nederland under glass	Portugal	United Kingdom under glas
1975	34,96	114,56	48,86	6,65	:	:	:	17,38	:	44,15	:	86,99
1976	39,64	133,69	59,60	8,56	:	:	:	19,67	:	65,58	:	97,43
1977	42,37	109,69	69,95	9,73	:	:	:	25,65	:	67,73	:	93,06
1978	39,22	137,90	65,28	13,08	:	:	:	21,25	:	63,43	:	103,57
1979	45,11	134,28	72,96	14,08	:	:	:	25,14	:	78,32	:	123,02
1980	43,62	106,42	57,22	13,33	:	:	:	26,30	:	59,41	:	114,24
1981	57,13	106,15	61,29	14,99	:	:	:	29,52	:	90,52	:	136,10
1982	44,06	113,65	62,16	19,36	:	:	:	36,10	:	70,78	:	125,17
1983	56,03	121,87	67,90	18,81	:	:	:	39,67	:	95,38	:	147,66
1984	56,18	124,59	79,78	17,00	:	:	:	41,73	:	95,91	:	134,42
1985	58,80	140,55	72,86	18,55	:	:	:	41,60	:	119,47	:	133,38
1986	47,63	131,81	73,77	13,33	:	:	:	37,19	:	84,55	:	:

PRICE: ECU/100 KG, VAT EXCL.   **PRIX: ÉCU/100 KG, HORS TVA**

	Belgique/ België	Danmark	BR Deutsch- land	Ellas	España	France	Ireland	Italia	Luxem- bourg	Neder- land	Portugal	United Kingdom

TOMATOES — TOMATES

	de serre		under glass	in the open			under glass	in the open		under glass		under glass
1975	59,56	:	35,86	10,48	:	:	70,74	16,89	:	43,96	:	52,02
1976	56,11	:	37,54	12,47	:	:	55,63	19,44	:	45,61	:	55,60
1977	63,13	:	40,08	16,49	:	:	85,65	17,41	:	46,36	:	62,95
1978	59,14	:	43,95	12,29	:	:	112,34	16,94	:	53,89	:	66,20
1979	50,74	:	35,90	16,66	:	:	:	18,53	:	47,63	:	60,17
1980	70,55	:	59,52	16,42	:	:	:	23,02	:	64,15	:	84,15
1981	69,74	:	49,41	22,52	:	:	:	27,20	:	66,29	:	86,01
1982	65,82	:	40,46	26,92	:	:	:	37,38	:	57,00	:	83,18
1983	74,59	:	61,05	22,67	:	:	:	35,18	:	69,76	:	92,54
1984	82,94	:	54,90	24,80	:	:	:	37,47	:	75,30	:	95,26
1985	68,96	:	44,08	23,69	:	:	:	33,50	:	68,90	:	93,16
1986	74,62	:	48,71	19,52	:	:	:	37,22	:	71,64	:	:

CARROTS — CAROTTES

	qual. I	qual. I	all var.	all var.		qual. I		ens. var.		all var.		all var.
1975	15,19	24,43	13,02	:	:	17,48	:	17,86	:	13,16	:	11,12
1976	15,17	29,13	15,49	17,73	:	15,34	:	17,34	:	14,20	:	14,05
1977	22,92	19,25	15,44	21,93	:	27,11	:	28,20	:	18,82	:	11,08
1978	12,71	24,22	11,88	23,17	:	14,11	:	18,00	:	10,64	:	6,73
1979	19,94	24,83	13,97	19,66	:	15,78	:	15,21	:	16,52	:	11,15
1980	19,88	26,83	19,95	18,51	:	19,94	:	25,36	:	16,59	:	13,62
1981	23,49	25,50	16,07	19,29	:	23,01	:	36,02	:	18,81	:	19,71
1982	18,50	27,46	16,47	32,11	:	17,57	:	28,86	:	15,30	:	16,09
1983	18,40	31,24	24,23	25,41	:	27,03	:	37,83	:	16,55	:	20,78
1984	24,25	27,25	17,88	21,55	:	23,87	:	36,00	:	19,42	:	21,15
1985	23,02	32,80	18,16	23,71	:	28,99	:	42,34	:	21,11	:	21,27
1986	15,02	40,32	18,57	18,15	:	25,88	:	36,79	:	17,08	:	:

HOP CONES (all varieties) — HOUBLON (ensemble des variétés)

	Belgique/ België	Danmark	BR Deutsch- land	Ellas	España	France	Ireland	Italia	Luxem- bourg	Neder- land	Portugal	United Kingdom
1975	125,00	:	148,27	:	:	84,38	:	:	:	:	:	184,95
1976	199,28	:	220,54	:	:	84,19	:	:	:	:	:	218,80
1977	106,79	:	298,33	:	:	105,29	:	:	:	:	:	231,60
1978	218,49	:	322,34	:	:	93,88	:	:	:	:	:	239,34
1979	306,21	:	601,21	:	:	110,01	:	:	:	:	:	244,12
1980	598,14	:	923,21	:	:	122,78	:	:	:	:	:	364,92
1981	470,67	:	599,24	:	:	120,02	:	:	:	:	:	476,58
1982	213,41	:	290,66	:	:	123,92	:	:	:	:	:	488,89
1983	264,18	:	318,71	:	:	129,55	:	:	:	:	:	534,91
1984	167,49	:	322,35	:	:	133,01	:	:	:	:	:	559,41
1985	157,91	:	329,21	:	:	134,50	:	:	:	:	:	389,99
1986	162,82	:	336,37	:	:	134,42	:	:	:	:	:	328,80

RAW TOBACCO (all varieties) — TABAC BRUT (ensemble des variétés)

	Belgique/ België	Danmark	BR Deutsch- land	Ellas	España	France	Ireland	Italia	Luxem- bourg	Neder- land	Portugal	United Kingdom
1975	172,05	:	231,82	230,78	:	210,56	:	180,77	:	:	:	:
1976	161,82	:	243,44	211,33	:	227,32	:	162,97	:	:	:	:
1977	197,03	:	263,22	227,67	:	217,44	:	169,37	:	:	:	:
1978	207,11	:	274,44	229,14	:	237,29	:	185,87	:	:	:	:
1979	238,57	:	277,16	244,81	:	255,08	:	196,82	:	:	:	:
1980	231,96	:	297,89	262,63	:	277,39	:	196,58	:	:	:	:
1981	270,67	:	301,95	323,09	:	297,36	:	220,06	:	:	:	:
1982	288,56	:	337,20	362,25	:	316,89	:	243,87	:	:	:	:
1983	327,66	:	352,99	363,99	:	333,79	:	272,50	:	:	:	:
1984	329,34	:	350,89	364,39	:	360,76	:	286,40	:	:	:	:
1985	333,22	:	356,00	360,96	:	385,58	:	294,20	:	:	:	:
1986	:	:	369,07	298,93	:	396,93	:	:	:	:	:	:

PRICE: ECU/100 KG, VAT EXCL.   PRIX: ÉCU/100 KG, HORS TVA

	Belgique/België	Danmark	BR Deutschland	Ellas	España	France	Ireland	Italia	Luxembourg	Nederland	Portugal	United Kingdom
MAIN CROP FOOD POTATOES										POMMES DE TERRE DE CONSOMMATION		
1975	6,73	7,50	7,03	11,45	:	6,17	11,36	11,09	12,51	8,29	:	9,73
1976	20,37	21,00	19,08	14,02	:	19,51	19,19	29,02	26,41	24,64	:	25,98
1977	6,04	13,57	10,32	14,42	:	8,91	12,04	17,49	12,82	9,12	:	10,82
1978	3,21	5,57	6,17	13,55	:	3,88	6,43	10,26	13,08	4,99	:	5,86
1979	6,07	8,29	8,38	16,86	:	7,64	23,29	15,42	11,45	7,48	:	9,33
1980	5,30	9,78	8,48	15,96	:	5,35	16,38	14,82	11,95	6,23	:	10,38
1981	5,96	10,41	10,31	19,93	:	6,78	15,62	15,42	13,56	7,93	:	11,10
1982	6,84	8,74	9,02	23,52	:	9,65	:	20,42	15,25	10,77	:	14,38
1983	11,61	11,13	11,53	17,89	:	10,97	:	19,39	25,97	12,53	:	15,23
1984	11,27	20,69	16,43	21,31	:	15,42	:	30,26	15,78	15,73	:	15,85
1985	4,22	8,65	8,33	19,98	:	9,90	:	19,29	13,36	5,74	:	7,83
1986	5,63	11,38	8,67	17,60	:	7,05	:	17,43	13,70	7,27	:	:
SUGAR BEET (stand qual.) (1)										BETTERAVES SUCRIÈRES (qual. standard) (1)		
1975	26,42	24,89	26,69	29,50	:	24,25	31,60	37,76	:	33,71	:	32,32
1976	29,02	28,63	30,37	28,86	:	24,55	30,57	35,16	:	32,45	:	31,53
1977	31,19	27,83	32,78	30,93	:	22,59	35,18	35,64	:	32,38	:	32,74
1978	31,20	30,96	34,55	29,93	:	23,59	37,66	41,96	:	33,88	:	32,99
1979	30,72	33,15	35,29	29,54	:	27,14	39,58	38,65	:	36,66	:	37,28
1980	34,49	34,01	36,09	35,40	:	32,95	39,94	43,73	:	42,11	:	40,17
1981	32,29	34,41	37,19	43,00	:	28,15	42,71	43,15	:	39,05	:	45,20
1982	30,94	34,58	41,78	44,69	:	28,94	44,97	50,92	:	38,46	:	48,84
1983	39,14	39,66	44,35	41,88	:	33,38	47,85	54,57	:	51,83	:	47,22
1984	38,66	36,68	43,30	42,96	:	31,81	43,81	57,67	:	48,22	:	51,88
1985	35,78	34,54	42,94	46,34	:	32,14	48,37	57,78	:	49,89	:	45,33
1986	36,69	35,60	:	40,29	:	35,59	47,69	:	:	41,40	:	39,69
RAPE										COLZA		
1975	27,81	:	25,99	:	:	24,22	:	:	:	27,29	:	:
1976	30,19	:	31,25	:	:	26,29	:	:	:	28,61	:	:
1977	32,04	:	33,61	:	:	25,37	:	:	:	31,23	:	:
1978	36,52	:	35,84	:	:	26,26	:	:	:	31,35	:	:
1979	36,60	:	37,09	:	:	29,02	:	:	:	34,33	:	:
1980	37,32	:	37,81	:	:	30,78	:	:	:	33,40	:	:
1981	39,23	:	40,03	:	:	34,26	:	:	:	37,48	:	:
1982	42,29	:	44,34	:	:	37,44	:	:	:	39,21	:	:
1983	43,29	:	48,15	:	:	39,36	:	:	:	40,20	:	:
1984	43,84	:	49,75	:	:	40,48	:	:	:	44,15	:	:
1985	43,55	:	45,99	:	:	41,04	:	:	:	43,21	:	:
1986	45,12	:	46,10	:	:	40,24	:	:	:	45,67	:	:

OLIVE OIL (2)   **HUILE D'OLIVE (2)**

	Italy / Italie				Greece / Grèce			
	Extra vergine	Soprafino	Fino	Comune	Extra virgin	Fine	Semifine	Lampante
1975	192,76	180,45	167,26	163,81	123,22	122,57	120,39	113,92
1976	177,55	165,23	151,96	156,62	120,19	118,80	116,70	111,27
1977	200,29	183,25	162,11	158,80	130,82	128,82	124,71	116,66
1978	185,99	181,60	149,01	151,53	134,02	134,79	128,10	121,13
1979	208,97	201,08	168,09	160,20	140,09	140,09	133,61	125,07
1980	221,31	212,15	182,68	170,11	140,25	140,12	133,25	121,12
1981	234,69	220,51	190,65	179,50	173,08	169,01	160,18	144,77
1982	253,91	234,94	204,44	193,23	187,45	179,26	175,13	159,12
1983	293,92	265,17	239,03	212,91	211,20	201,86	195,39	177,52
1984	275,64	254,36	224,89	219,07	245,54	232,29	226,79	205,61
1985	358,10	323,90	250,68	230,75	270,58	260,83	241,25	211,26
1986	375,02	297,33	262,51	229,64	240,65	232,64	218,65	197,43

(1) Price per 1000 kg
(2) Price per 100 l

(1) Prix par 1000 kg
(2) Prix par 100 l

PRICE: ECU/100 L, VAT EXCL.

PRIX: ÉCU/100 L, HORS TVA

TABLE WINE (corresp. with cat. RI)

VIN DE TABLE (correspondant à la catégorie RI)

	BR Deutschland			Luxembourg	
	Portugieser	Riesling	Sylvaner/Müller-Th.	Elbling	Rivaner
1975	22,05	36,68	25,19	45,16	47,58
1976	37,26	52,17	36,58	52,50	55,04
1977	58,48	71,20	54,11	58,46	60,25
1970	50,64	61,68	44,48	74,86	81,15
1979	62,36	75,55	56,04	79,50	92,99
1980	66,56	79,13	55,73	80,94	94,07
1981	106,25	88,50	77,06	89,70	99,31
1982	98,82	83,17	67,15	65,22	70,77
1983	58,79	77,69	35,97	61,95	68,56
1984	65,69	78,30	50,19	60,50	65,58
1985	113,09	78,38	89,61	68,91	75,12
1986	112,48	71,38	57,30	69,62	76,37

France

	Béziers	Montpellier	Narbonne	Carcassonne	Nîmes	Perpignan
1975	18,16	18,09	18,33	16,09	16,07	18,07
1976	20,11	19,96	20,19	17,27	16,86	19,96
1977	20,68	20,60	20,69	17,61	17,86	20,42
1978	22,83	22,70	22,78	19,61	19,23	22,63
1979	23,99	23,97	24,10	22,62	21,94	23,90
1980	22,11	22,04	22,01	19,57	19,90	21,51
1981	24,18	24,18	24,13	21,27	21,58	23,85
1982	26,71	26,97	26,61	23,48	23,77	26,68
1983	25,90	25,92	26,13	23,85	23,67	25,74
1984	25,80	25,98	25,98	23,52	24,00	25,82
1985	28,03	27,94	27,74	24,13	24,41	28,02
1986	28,76	28,93	29,04	26,26	26,16	28,80

Italia

	Asti	Verona	Reggio Emilia	Teramo	Matera	Brindisi
1975	18,95	14,36	15,48	20,43	19,10	19,32
1976	16,96	15,06	15,32	20,38	20,26	18,90
1977	20,49	17,62	16,59	24,13	24,29	21,81
1978	24,33	20,05	21,10	26,23	23,14	25,05
1979	26,99	21,88	22,40	28,11	23,41	25,38
1980	23,64	18,77	21,47	33,53	19,59	22,96
1981	21,19	18,04	17,22	30,87	18,79	19,96
1982	28,52	23,15	21,39	32,61	25,62	27,35
1983	31,61	25,62	23,43	37,04	28,18	29,25
1984	33,28	23,55	22,95	42,23	25,35	28,15
1985	42,13	27,10	24,17	42,88	21,75	26,93
1986	48,83	28,35	28,33	44,46	21,55	26,68

	Bari	Catanzaro	Sassari	Forlì	Viterbo	Foggia
1975	21,40	36,52	27,49	13,19	12,93	12,91
1976	21,39	25,58	25,44	14,48	14,96	16,70
1977	25,94	23,84	29,47	15,77	16,22	18,07
1978	27,96	23,99	30,09	18,24	17,51	20,17
1979	29,71	22,84	29,86	20,10	18,85	22,14
1980	24,12	26,10	28,59	17,81	17,97	18,83
1981	27,25	27,71	26,92	17,66	16,35	17,18
1982	32,97	29,97	37,77	22,55	23,27	23,23
1983	39,96	31,91	42,60	24,64	24,46	24,87
1984	38,60	32,58	43,44	23,37	23,09	21,75
1985	35,00	31,08	58,41	25,51	26,53	25,21
1986	34,72	55,27	64,99	29,99	28,25	27,74

PRICE: ECU/100 L, VAT EXCL.

PRIX: ÉCU/100 L, HORS TVA

IQUALITY WINES (psr)

VINS DE QUALITÉ

France

	Corbières	Côtes de Provence	Côtes du Rhône	Bordeaux blancs	Bordeaux rouges	Muscadet
1975	22,99	29,95	34,03	22,13	29,53	31,92
1976	29,04	37,12	59,03	21,93	45,30	38,69
1977	35,11	43,29	68,82	28,95	64,16	55,37
1978	45,99	49,35	63,02	38,88	81,22	86,69
1979	35,15	44,79	52,46	32,50	92,13	110,11
1980	33,66	37,70	52,09	29,97	78,81	66,50
1981	41,22	44,33	66,30	44,76	72,21	70,48
1982	45,02	54,59	84,48	52,77	67,23	77,00
1983	42,44	58,22	70,44	38,50	65,51	53,34
1984	43,51	55,64	72,88	41,56	84,41	62,69
1985	45,61	58,00	78,68	42,06	:	85,51
1986	51,90	58,43	73,65	32,47	:	79,73

Italia

	Barbera, Asti	Dolcetto delle Langhe, Cuneo	Merlot Treviso	Sangiovese Forlì	Chianti, Siena	Castelli, Roma
1975	35,26	64,85	20,24	37,12	30,52	26,68
1976	29,71	54,29	19,84	33,60	27,40	23,66
1977	31,36	63,46	22,68	44,66	31,34	30,86
1978	38,56	72,90	25,18	32,31	36,16	43,14
1979	57,20	111,26	29,16	34,10	48,38	47,40
1980	37,89	93,20	23,58	36,06	44,71	42,01
1981	30,97	84,44	23,41	38,12	32,54	37,80
1982	42,34	88,01	29,98	53,27	38,14	48,25
1983	41,14	100,01	30,48	61,17	40,78	60,34
1984	39,59	80,84	30,00	54,68	40,71	64,85
1985	54,51	72,23	36,59	64,36	61,37	68,36
1986	56,74	71,71	36,61	66,31	58,15	67,52

Luxembourg

	Auxerrois	Riesling	Pinot blanc	Pinot gris
1975	68,45	95,53	68,12	97,28
1976	88,57	102,58	92,09	120,31
1977	101,29	130,23	102,46	125,78
1978	137,89	166,87	153,39	189,94
1979	152,77	204,93	167,51	203,49
1980	180,58	206,32	191,91	221,71
1981	190,65	229,69	204,77	247,35
1982	118,65	159,33	126,48	168,64
1983	111,71	151,59	119,35	158,44
1984	90,22	110,89	90,01	107,90
1985	98,75	138,82	104,96	136,22
1986	100,37	142,84	107,52	140,05

Ellas

	Wine must	Retsina (white)	Aretsino (white)	Kokkino	Samos
1975	16,08	:	:	:	:
1976	19,96	:	:	:	:
1977	25,24	24,65	116,69	55,43	110,07
1978	23,90	25,05	115,75	55,85	127,61
1979	26,71	23,77	115,53	53,81	129,83
1980	26,84	26,20	109,91	73,09	138,13
1981	29,02	29,36	136,54	90,29	153,07
1982	28,62	29,11	156,16	85,15	167,21
1983	28,58	28,71	161,93	76,88	159,41
1984	30,16	31,11	156,80	76,32	159,50
1985	29,60	29,27	162,92	83,43	154,70
1986	28,82	28,74	141,10	80,70	127,27

PRICES: ECU/100 KG, VAT EXCL.   PRIX: ÉCU/100 KG, HORS TVA

	Belgique/ Belgïe	Danmark	BR Deutsch- land	Ellas	España	France	Ireland	Italia	Luxem- bourg	Neder- land	Portugal	United Kingdom
CALVES (live)											**VEAUX (vivants)**	
1976	170,83	119,64	200,61	106,55	:	176,06	:	165,01	166,01	176,37	:	:
1977	190,79	123,26	215,84	118,38	:	185,16	:	167,75	170,76	195,56	:	:
1978	208,43	133,34	230,86	119,32	:	202,97	:	177,95	164,75	206,17	:	:
1979	209,56	132,06	235,02	123,90	:	204,65	:	176,53	175,45	202,21	:	:
1980	192,35	133,12	221,69	123,06	:	205,83	:	190,96	182,52	189,11	:	:
1981	218,04	146,54	226,50	167,66	:	230,14	:	213,63	191,58	221,25	:	:
1982	229,56	162,93	252,95	189,82	:	244,43	:	228,09	219,88	248,29	:	:
1983	236,19	172,29	264,87	173,72	:	247,83	·	231,56	222,83	242,79	:	:
1984	222,50	169,64	256,20	202,51	:	242,88	:	236,18	219,71	227,48	:	:
1985	238,06	169,85	256,97	191,94	:	259,60	:	244,08	228,77	236,96	:	:
1986	215,98	166,72	269,48	165,60	:	269,72	:	242,77	236,31	239,49	:	:
YOUNG CATTLE (live)											**JEUNES BOVINS (vivants)**	
1976	145,56	118,90	143,00	:	:	122,62	88,42	149,40	117,53	131,94	:	:
1977	159,21	122,67	156,63	:	:	127,67	100,47	150,17	136,49	144,60	:	:
1978	162,55	132,49	159,86	:	:	134,29	118,51	159,80	139,14	149,02	:	:
1979	165,82	132,06	162,29	:	:	139,59	120,15	177,95	139,67	148,91	:	:
1980	165,67	133,12	161,28	:	:	151,50	117,00	198,42	138,87	147,45	:	:
1981	178,11	146,42	169,30	:	:	164,59	138,29	216,79	151,18	160,72	:	:
1982	187,63	162,81	192,85	:	:	176,13	152,02	235,12	169,40	187,46	:	:
1983	192,90	172,78	203,08	:	:	185,20	160,11	246,26	176,00	195,89	:	:
1984	191,23	169,64	197,80	:	:	185,11	165,52	223,73	177,02	190,62	:	:
1985	193,64	169,23	185,60	:	:	190,69	164,17	219,78	179,17	189,96	:	:
1986	189,19	165,96	175,92	:	:	186,89	151,34	222,78	174,19	185,76	:	:
HEIFERS (live)											**GÉNISSES (vivantes)**	
1976	120,05	102,04	123,89	:	:	126,46	79,76	125,40	110,09	119,93	:	83,72
1977	131,87	111,59	137,26	:	:	135,66	91,14	121,45	127,61	136,32	:	85,31
1978	139,16	118,24	141,39	:	:	143,72	106,51	126,63	131,72	141,93	:	97,32
1979	140,25	114,72	143,58	:	:	146,31	113,31	128,77	131,18	138,83	:	112,59
1980	141,51	116,39	141,99	:	:	151,90	105,65	146,20	128,70	137,31	:	124,45
1981	149,58	130,01	150,25	:	:	165,50	129,26	164,34	137,50	149,54	:	157,18
1982	163,81	146,87	172,52	:	:	182,69	139,82	180,67	156,05	171,77	:	171,52
1983	165,43	148,31	180,00	:	:	183,78	136,62	169,25	161,85	174,21	:	159,16
1984	154,99	150,99	173,81	:	:	177,82	140,82	166,67	176,29	166,45	:	157,60
1985	161,18	153,51	167,63	:	:	187,74	141,18	157,03	179,46	170,45	:	158,12
1986	150,88	149,96	160,47	:	:	181,02	133,85	153,74	180,95	161,61	:	:
BULLOCKS (live)											**BŒUFS (vivants)**	
1976	125,52	105,89	:	:	:	126,57	87,44	115,88	119,73	121,38	:	84,83
1977	141,60	115,38	:	:	:	134,25	100,29	116,61	143,34	133,00	:	87,87
1978	143,23	123,80	:	:	:	139,90	117,78	107,18	147,25	138,23	:	100,07
1979	146,67	119,71	:	:	:	143,71	117,40	116,76	146,52	137,85	:	116,29
1980	149,59	123,67	:	:	:	154,96	117,41	124,05	145,11	137,31	:	140,52
1981	161,33	134,05	:	:	:	167,35	137,15	131,74	153,10	147,38	:	163,19
1982	175,06	151,53	:	:	:	183,73	150,27	149,07	170,14	167,57	:	177,77
1983	178,20	162,08	:	:	:	188,08	160,02	147,52	175,65	171,45	:	166,78
1984	174,79	164,86	:	:	:	184,99	164,27	160,05	176,89	164,47	:	167,13
1985	178,54	168,61	:	:	:	191,12	161,50	155,12	179,70	167,26	:	164,66
1986	182,11	158,27	:	:	:	184,48	150,74	160,70	180,81	160,36	:	144,55

PRICE: ECU/100 KG, VAT EXCL.

PRIX: ÉCU/100 KG, HORS TVA

	Belgique/ Belgïe	Danmark	BR Deutsch- land	Ellas	España	France	Ireland	Italia	Luxem- bourg	Neder- land	Portugal	United Kingdom
COWS first quality (live)											**VACHES première qualité (vivantes)**	
1976	119,93	93,76	113,45	:	:	116,09	68,21	106,71	104,90	116,27	:	65,90
1977	128,03	102,69	126,04			122,62	82,28	114,46	120,96	130,21	:	66,68
1978	136,29	106,28	127,66			129,92	94,38	129,96	126,86	135,47	:	77,35
1979	135,72	103,62	129,56			131,91	96,04	131,64	127,77	133,30	:	88,99
1980	132,40	107,06	127,41			139,95	93,30	155,09	126,81	132,60	:	105,22
1981	144,62	120,92	134,97			153,96	109,72	176,10	140,04	143,06	:	134,51
1982	156,87	135,59	153,96			169,11	119,55	215,57	155,17	163,74	:	144,24
1983	149,06	135,27	157,32			165,49	116,51	219,32	160,26	166,33	:	133,75
1984	139,34	138,22	147,18			158,27	119,83	202,13	156,38	157,33	:	126,65
1985	148,13	141,42	146,66			176,11	119,16	219,93	159,40	162,48	:	133,79
1986	124,57	134,46	137,82			166,62	119,25	230,60	152,38	151,61	:	110,19
COWS second quality (live)											**VACHES deuxième qualité (vivantes)**	
1976	97,30	95,39	106,27	80,74	:	98,49	58,59	94,13	96,72	100,74	:	58,37
1977	104,79	105,17	118,30	84,05		104,64	70,29	90,28	109,88	112,68	:	59,00
1978	113,90	107,99	119,01	84,65		108,63	82,91	100,59	112,13	116,70	:	67,34
1979	114,25	106,39	121,23	98,42		111,95	83,56	99,85	110,97	113,80	:	78,68
1980	110,55	109,49	119,76	99,54		119,44	80,84	107,28	109,54	113,03	:	96,21
1981	119,63	123,70	125,82	127,71		133,27	95,45	113,94	120,06	124,32	:	122,80
1982	132,67	137,55	141,67	144,00		144,65	104,13	131,49	138,04	143,46	:	131,43
1983	122,34	136,87	144,90	141,12		137,47	99,88	135,44	139,51	141,50	:	120,73
1984	118,86	140,43	134,71	146,26		132,58	100,75	124,34	138,46	131,57	:	113,78
1985	128,42	144,66	133,49	140,62		145,94	100,28	119,89	135,99	138,59	:	120,84
1986	108,48	137,48	125,41	115,47		134,06	95,21	122,71	128,57	128,29	:	98,73
COWS third quality (live)											**VACHES troisième qualité (vivantes)**	
1976	78,67	70,10	92,63	:	:	79,03	47,60	76,03	86,99	87,17	:	49,41
1977	84,36	75,85	102,90			84,91	55,88	81,17	99,26	95,68	:	51,64
1978	91,11	78,35	104,18			88,56	67,06	92,05	100,02	99,96	:	60,75
1979	94,46	75,60	106,54			93,37	67,01	87,79	96,18	97,47	:	68,02
1980	94,37	79,21	106,77			99,53	64,96	95,00	96,14	96,73	:	84,25
1981	105,92	90,50	111,30			111,58	78,06	99,68	105,46	107,38	:	109,91
1982	116,97	105,68	123,65			120,02	84,69	116,04	123,19	123,19	:	116,14
1983	107,22	103,17	127,15			111,09	78,06	112,61	124,35	120,61	:	103,66
1984	102,50	106,06	117,73			111,41	79,13	103,60	118,28	110,17	:	96,34
1985	109,99	107,62	116,02			121,22	76,22	98,00	121,30	117,48	:	102,40
1986	95,74	100,31	109,01			108,71	81,69	97,71	114,16	108,71	:	81,75
CALVES (of a few days), store											**VEAUX (de quelques jours), élevage**	
1976	116,99	102,34	134,65	:	:	136,77	:	109,97	120,07	126,56	:	:
1977	123,38	105,31	147,75			145,20	:	104,76	148,65	138,28	:	:
1978	144,08	126,36	166,78			167,95	:	117,74	163,88	164,56	:	:
1979	147,19	143,71	172,85			166,74	:	132,53	160,41	168,70	:	:
1980	134,32	130,18	149,91			157,61	:	115,52	145,55	134,05	:	:
1981	139,24	114,36	145,99			167,88	:	127,01	163,44	144,86	:	:
1982	156,81	113,16	172,81			200,90	:	177,62	181,45	175,98	:	:
1983	182,09	131,09	180,36			189,79	:	164,30	185,48	180,51	:	:
1984	185,47	113,55	174,44			191,95	:	162,97	160,03	160,50	:	:
1985	175,34	159,75	176,15			170,57	:	180,80	190,66	187,97	:	:
1986	187,61	145,80	181,29			173,24	:	178,16	201,36	197,84	:	:

PRICE: ECU/100 KG, VAT EXCL.   PRIX: ÉCU/100 KG, HORS TVA

	Belgique/België	Danmark	BR Deutschland	Ellas	España	France	Ireland	Italia	Luxembourg	Nederland	Portugal	United Kingdom
YOUNG CATTLE (store)												**JEUNES BOVINS (d'élevage)**
1976	:	:	436,17	:	:	:	342,69	597,93	:	394,90	:	234,80
1977	:	:	443,30	:	:	:	385,86	600,77	:	399,63	:	250,77
1978	:	:	510,55	:	:	:	448,69	603,56	:	428,82	:	306,52
1979	:	:	491,07	:	:	:	462,79	638,50	:	416,21	:	347,81
1980	:	:	473,02	:	:	:	434,14	672,98	:	407,21	:	384,54
1981	:	:	498,03	:	:	:	525,86	782,09	:	451,88	:	474,19
1982	:	:	602,70	:	:	:	585,38	915,47	:	518,00	:	533,66
1983	:	:	673,85	:	:	:	612,25	919,13	:	508,04	:	526,36
1984	:	:	609,26	:	:	:	631,21	918,16	:	467,24	:	521,11
1985	:	:	590,21	:	:	:	636,30	932,33	:	483,07	:	547,27
1986	:	:	555,87	:	:	:	568,42	923,47	:	527,30	:	485,27
HEIFERS (store)												**GÉNISSES (d'élevage)**
1976	725,65	655,75	697,58	:	:	:	:	820,02	:	643,96	:	417,52
1977	795,01	681,92	743,49	:	:	:	:	904,03	:	730,33	:	455,47
1978	881,50	777,84	812,18	:	:	:	:	902,25	:	806,80	:	586,96
1979	905,89	781,65	861,85	:	:	:	:	944,17	:	840,78	:	619,16
1980	916,23	756,32	832,34	:	:	:	:	984,55	:	808,25	:	721,54
1981	906,29	771,97	829,79	:	:	:	:	1 076,32	:	848,26	:	866,63
1982	964,16	787,43	954,13	:	:	:	:	1 189,78	:	957,19	:	973,62
1983	1 082,46	814,33	994,05	:	:	:	:	1 186,79	:	974,70	:	936,98
1984	1 063,82	820,60	900,76	:	:	:	:	1 133,53	:	823,51	:	798,73
1985	1 126,03	875,20	920,35	:	:	:	:	1 035,92	:	858,62	:	853,23
1986	1 131,15	911,58	846,73	:	:	:	:	963,80	:	844,69	:	706,69
PIGS (light) for slaughter												**PORCS (légers) de boucherie vivants**
1976	110,55	99,09	118,60	99,16	:	:	83,22	122,27	117,32	103,24	:	83,88
1977	117,75	96,56	123,44	100,82	:	:	92,98	102,11	118,58	102,60	:	83,31
1978	112,25	98,58	115,96	93,56	:	:	97,02	100,47	120,92	97,89	:	94,17
1979	114,65	91,55	119,24	101,80	:	:	96,09	113,36	118,16	98,12	:	98,87
1980	115,15	91,60	121,23	106,74	:	:	98,30	126,47	125,18	96,73	:	112,28
1981	126,85	105,40	134,93	144,39	:	:	110,79	120,63	134,01	110,27	:	133,46
1982	139,23	113,16	152,95	166,75	:	:	123,39	146,19	143,83	127,40	:	133,39
1983	131,52	111,17	144,37	168,50	:	:	118,11	139,04	136,12	119,03	:	122,23
1984	138,53	127,91	146,15	166,13	:	:	121,83	133,16	137,91	122,46	:	145,03
1985	143,19	121,72	143,56	168,66	:	:	:	155,27	146,48	124,25	:	137,78
1986	133,50	109,51	133,35	154,78	:	:	:	163,94	137,84	112,88	:	115,82
PIGS (carcasses)												**PORCS (carcasses)**
1976	133,05	129,70	139,16	:	:	130,78	:	143,70	156,91	157,35	:	107,69
1977	138,59	125,88	146,66	:	:	129,32	:	130,58	159,11	157,85	:	106,41
1978	132,40	129,36	133,02	:	:	125,61	:	126,55	159,88	165,21	:	116,31
1979	134,62	123,46	137,80	:	:	132,43	:	139,12	157,85	155,71	:	123,05
1980	136,81	122,77	135,88	:	:	136,65	:	151,94	167,25	165,20	:	140,89
1981	149,68	141,50	152,75	:	:	150,66	:	154,66	179,20	179,45	:	163,17
1982	163,60	151,77	168,77	:	:	167,93	:	179,49	192,12	214,24	:	164,88
1983	152,08	150,52	155,47	:	:	157,88	:	169,28	180,36	221,50	:	148,23
1984	161,42	172,10	159,96	:	:	164,72	:	176,26	182,54	213,21	:	170,19
1985	166,61	164,24	154,52	:	:	172,33	:	184,98	194,04	213,46	:	159,92
1986	150,56	146,93	138,15	:	:	159,63	:	188,21	183,34	142,45	:	133,66

SELLING PRICES
OF ANIMAL PRODUCTS

IF 2

PRIX DE VENTE
DE PRODUITS ANIMAUX

PRICE: ECU/100 KG, VAT EXCL.

PRIX: ÉCU/100 KG, HORS TVA

	Belgique/ België	Danmark	BR Deutsch- land	Ellas	España	France	Ireland	Italia	Luxem- bourg	Neder- land	Portugal	United Kingdom
PIGLETS (store)											**PORCELETS (d'élevage)**	
1976	194,95	173,03	176,77	124,52	:	162,59	116,69	168,83	206,67	178,67	:	155,57
1977	202,48	161,91	184,42	128,58	:	148,23	140,46	128,45	204,46	169,99	:	138,58
1978	194,58	182,85	168,97	122,16	:	141,29	142,04	128,48	188,81	157,95	:	177,16
1979	201,42	157,44	176,18	132,92	:	150,96	128,16	153,10	179,33	153,53	:	166,25
1980	195,40	148,20	181,46	139,34	:	168,00	125,92	176,33	208,75	151,43	:	194,91
1981	207,68	175,45	190,00	188,51	:	170,20	158,55	156,17	232,23	171,16	:	223,99
1982	255,77	204,74	232,43	217,72	:	211,00	167,52	202,60	285,68	218,45	:	231,78
1983	232,82	189,99	214,37	219,98	:	190,52	143,42	191,87	250,06	201,80	:	190,73
1984	239,10	242,44	237,16	216,86	:	179,51	160,33	183,99	252,81	196,17	:	253,46
1985	249,46	244,43	214,93	220,19	:	189,30	157,63	218,19	262,59	201,11	:	240,72
1986	216,36	202,25	189,44	202,07	:	172,73	130,37	239,69	242,52	177,02	:	198,19
CHICKENS (live, 1st choice)											**POULETS (vivants, 1er choix)**	
1976	73,49	59,90	67,49	67,56	:	69,97	60,91	80,51	:	62,37	:	:
1977	77,47	63,89	72,88	73,91	:	74,21	72,98	87,32	:	68,28	:	:
1978	73,66	62,97	72,77	67,03	:	76,83	76,47	80,88	:	66,96	:	:
1979	78,58	63,67	74,87	68,74	:	77,88	80,81	81,65	:	68,58	:	:
1980	81,26	64,65	76,86	72,32	:	81,62	81,86	84,94	:	72,46	:	:
1981	83,64	71,19	80,35	95,58	:	89,74	89,48	105,00	:	75,67	:	:
1982	80,85	72,58	84,60	111,43	:	91,27	94,26	101,13	:	78,81	:	:
1983	87,17	75,01	86,32	110,22	:	91,72	93,82	117,90	:	79,62	:	:
1984	95,18	84,33	94,28	116,18	:	101,43	103,42	122,28	:	88,77	:	:
1985	94,47	81,56	92,53	113,37	:	93,89	98,37	129,53	:	88,41	:	:
1986	90,64	74,35	88,34	170,55	:	88,53	96,71	126,35	:	84,14	:	:
CHICKENS (class A, slaughtered)											**POULETS (classe A, abattus)**	
1976	127,02	118,17	120,76	:	:	91,86	:	105,52	142,87	111,60	:	86,70
1977	131,11	120,05	126,87	:	:	96,68	:	118,67	158,33	115,46	:	96,88
1978	145,98	125,08	124,41	:	:	94,60	:	115,52	:	112,09	:	102,21
1979	152,50	125,81	131,43	:	:	93,83	:	113,13	:	116,46	:	115,50
1980	157,23	131,59	135,88	:	:	98,83	:	116,78	:	122,45	:	125,93
1981	158,82	150,58	141,22	:	:	109,27	:	145,77	:	127,20	:	140,64
1982	142,04	153,25	135,52	:	:	113,51	:	152,07	:	122,42	:	149,77
1983	161,30	157,04	143,58	:	:	122,41	:	160,68	:	125,34	:	148,29
1984	172,93	177,87	162,19	:	:	134,90	:	174,86	:	144,65	:	147,96
1985	170,51	226,59	160,35	:	:	125,09	:	178,32	:	146,95	:	148,36
1986	166,10	220,52	157,41	:	:	120,30	183,05	:	:	146,61	:	129,76
FRESH EGGS (100 pieces)											**ŒUFS FRAIS (100 pièces)**	
1976	4,19	4,23	6,29	4,79	:	5,33	4,58	4,82	5,97	4,26	:	3,54
1977	4,48	4,91	6,57	5,04	:	5,87	4,97	4,81	5,17	4,60	:	3,84
1978	3,67	5,30	6,22	5,00	:	5,84	4,52	4,98	5,03	3,86	:	3,19
1979	3,31	4,71	6,25	5,20	:	5,42	5,45	4,93	5,79	3,96	:	4,12
1980	4,26	5,08	6,81	5,34	:	5,93	6,08	6,10	7,00	4,59	:	4,78
1981	4,84	5,69	7,32	7,58	:	6,47	7,11	6,95	5,79	4,97	:	5,44
1982	3,49	5,76	6,86	5,85	:	5,36	6,50	7,05	6,60	4,51	:	5,53
1983	4,09	5,70	7,00	8,16	:	6,44	6,28	8,08	7,38	4,93	:	4,79
1984	4,91	6,22	7,73	10,72	:	7,35	7,19	9,08	6,61	5,25	:	5,94
1985	4,48	5,73	7,03	9,20	:	6,74	6,56	7,29	6,07	4,86	:	5,21
1986	3,61	5,35	7,12	7,50	:	5,99	5,28	6,97	:	4,37	:	3,56

PRICE: ECU/100 KG, VAT EXCL.

PRIX: ÉCU/100 KG, HORS TVA

	Belgique/ Belgïe	Danmark	BR Deutsch- land	Ellas	España	France	Ireland	Italia	Luxem- bourg	Neder- land	Portugal	United Kingdom
RAW COWS' MILK, 3,7 % fat cont.										**LAIT CRU DE VACHE, 3,7 % matière grasse**		
1976	16,54	16,56	18,65	:	:	15,57	12,47	:	16,15	17,04	:	13,88
1977	18,18	18,53	20,28	:	:	15,82	15,79	23,01	17,19	19,21	:	14,55
1978	18,94	19,52	21,38	:	:	16,88	16,87	21,75	17,37	19,72	:	14,73
1979	18,94	19,56	22,08	:	:	18,07	17,30	23,11	18,40	19,78	:	16,40
1980	18,83	20,31	21,89	:	:	19,32	16,94	24,49	18,53	20,65	:	19,88
1981	19,82	21,96	22,38	:	:	20,50	18,89	25,94	18,84	21,67	:	23,00
1982	21,05	24,64	25,22	:	:	21,73	20,75	29,89	20,28	24,98	:	24,50
1983	22,80	20,19	27,62	:	·	22,44	21,71	32,90	22,29	26,41	:	23,61
1984	23,17	26,39	27,26	:	:	22,99	21,64	33,04	22,80	26,12	:	23,13
1985	23,93	27,56	27,06	:	:	24,34	22,83	34,00	24,65	26,55	:	24,30
1986	24,66	28,48	28,48	:	:	25,06	22,94	34,94	26,44	27,43	:	22,14
RAW COWS' MILK, actual fat cont.										**LAIT CRU DE VACHE, ten. réelle en matière grasse**		
1976	16,10	18,04	19,04	15,68	:	15,58	12,15	19,18	16,24	17,69	:	14,09
1977	17,76	20,13	20,66	16,82	:	15,96	15,42	22,91	17,42	19,92	:	14,70
1978	18,72	21,37	21,80	18,00	:	17,08	16,51	21,65	17,53	20,43	:	15,09
1979	18,80	21,36	22,56	17,96	:	18,31	16,85	23,02	18,69	20,67	:	16,76
1980	18,87	22,10	22,39	17,73	:	19,68	16,48	24,41	19,03	21,51	:	20,32
1981	19,98	23,98	22,90	22,51	:	20,79	18,42	25,86	19,32	23,08	:	23,29
1982	21,11	26,85	25,84	26,16	:	22,45	20,23	29,82	20,35	26,49	:	25,19
1983	22,58	28,53	28,13	24,79	:	23,82	21,25	32,83	22,49	28,10	:	24,36
1984	23,02	28,60	27,81	25,83	:	23,67	21,28	32,98	23,04	27,77	:	23,77
1985	23,85	29,93	27,67	27,96	:	24,67	22,40	33,93	24,76	28,04	:	25,09
1986	25,09	31,00	29,32	24,91	:	25,41	22,44	34,87	26,69	29,57	:	22,87
WHOLE COWS' MILK for human consumpt.										**LAIT DE VACHE entier de consommation**		
1976	24,33	32,98	:	24,02	:	28,64	26,69	26,64	35,65	27,10	:	18,98
1977	27,27	36,03	:	24,27	:	27,60	29,43	33,39	37,91	30,82	:	17,79
1978	28,76	37,90	:	24,99	:	29,58	31,78	31,85	38,69	32,63	:	18,99
1979	29,32	38,56	35,31	30,23	:	32,72	34,70	35,09	38,59	32,84	:	20,78
1980	29,54	40,63	35,61	35,47	:	40,55	39,04	38,22	38,80	36,21	:	25,75
1981	32,14	44,68	37,34	47,48	:	44,54	45,99	44,15	41,31	37,37	:	29,89
1982	34,24	49,41	41,31	50,70	:	47,74	52,80	53,60	42,52	42,96	:	32,15
1983	34,98	51,90	43,33	47,91	:	:	56,06	58,37	46,61	44,70	:	30,92
1984	36,54	53,89	42,88	48,79	:	:	58,63	60,76	48,41	43,89	:	31,54
1985	38,72	55,62	42,43	54,03	:	:	62,07	61,88	50,10	46,96	:	33,33
1986	41,52	56,45	44,06	52,99	:	:	63,86	64,47	54,52	50,07	:	29,80
BUTTER												**BEURRE**
1976	250,43	239,29	272,92	247,92	:	268,86	:	231,33	262,04	249,33	:	163,82
1977	276,28	262,79	297,77	272,20	:	272,74	:	228,70	293,67	274,70	:	178,48
1978	288,14	272,81	312,82	277,00	:	287,64	:	256,26	316,09	285,39	:	214,10
1979	289,56	270,63	320,89	300,08	:	305,86	:	259,52	309,55	288,14	:	258,93
1980	290,63	282,73	321,53	297,00	:	331,41	:	282,00	294,79	292,73	:	317,67
1981	310,57	313,03	336,01	396,35	:	360,44	:	321,59	301,35	314,58	:	372,49
1982	318,93	328,07	373,28	445,53	:	377,69	:	357,74	316,12	352,35	:	400,92
1983	341,41	338,42	398,94	427,02	:	384,89	:	383,66	348,70	376,79	:	388,88
1984	325,27	335,12	370,77	419,33	:	372,69	:	378,01	358,26	347,16	:	379,09
1985	319,84	320,00	343,07	444,96	:	374,39	:	365,37	387,19	332,14	:	381,56
1986	324,76	314,91	352,44	379,64	:	373,69	:	373,05	429,11	339,46	:	333,96

PRICE: ECU/100 KG, VAT EXCL.
CHEESE

PRIX: ÉCU/100 KG, HORS TVA
FROMAGE

Bundesrepublik Deutschland

	Emmentaler 45 %	Gouda 45 %	Edamer 40 %	Tilsiter 45 %	Limburger 20 %	Speisequark 20 %
1976	250,40	202,10	193,58	199,97	179,01	89,15
1977	273,38	220,52	211,46	218,63	195,60	94,78
1978	293,03	225,74	222,22	227,69	206,18	100,15
1979	299,10	231,79	227,41	234,58	218,65	98,77
1980	290,78	243,24	231,36	237,30	226,61	99,83
1981	304,71	247,03	241,86	249,41	243,05	104,62
1982	344,70	269,36	267,26	274,41	274,41	117,00
1983	360,71	282,31	280,55	293,33	292,89	125,96
1984	356,10	290,42	283,72	300,25	302,04	130,91
1985	371,02	289,27	289,72	309,03	321,16	134,75
1986	380,14	295,56	297,44	319,52	371,21	141,90

France

	Emmenthal 45 %	Cantal	St-Paulin 45 %	Roquefort	Camembert normand 45 %	Carré de l'Est 45 %
1976	236,30	219,84	169,13	387,48	224,52	243,38
1977	247,41	247,05	170,71	412,95	232,61	277,80
1978	270,04	253,32	182,93	433,64	197,22	305,63
1979	268,98	263,15	199,68	481,35	201,73	327,18
1980	278,59	280,97	212,82	548,99	234,45	357,23
1981	313,58	307,79	225,67	594,38	256,96	369,76
1982	339,91	327,47	255,32	593,46	273,30	387,96
1983	350,92	334,08	260,53	608,05	278,85	405,49
1984	363,38	362,94	263,55	703,62	289,30	435,25
1985	395,00	385,92	298,60	798,57	322,15	469,37
1986	387,22	375,45	316,19	857,97	334,13	532,77

Italia

	Grana	Pecorino	Provolone	Fontina	Gorgonzola	Taleggio
1976	466,11	360,04	220,42	264,74	171,88	164,08
1977	601,41	441,06	233,17	302,74	187,57	180,41
1978	668,28	442,56	267,25	260,75	231,11	187,30
1979	602,72	408,15	297,35	290,22	226,77	183,45
1980	502,09	420,02	283,52	341,62	238,61	195,11
1981	586,77	480,59	316,55	427,49	266,69	226,90
1982	708,06	606,03	408,36	473,39	299,20	272,46
1983	814,02	645,53	410,85	486,45	322,58	293,23
1984	999,14	628,75	406,77	563,75	359,08	297,76
1985	889,49	613,85	431,57	571,48	652,52	299,55
1986	789,30	625,82	472,00	579,74	608,38	308,63

Nederland

	Cheddar	Gouda	Edammer	Boerenkaas
1976	190,18	177,32	159,04	192,21
1977	218,21	202,85	181,78	234,99
1978	224,39	200,43	183,73	262,52
1979	224,84	200,10	183,36	252,85
1980	235,48	218,10	198,17	256,13
1981	247,92	226,30	206,12	265,94
1982	278,89	252,50	228,39	328,24
1983	289,30	263,28	239,63	338,17
1984	286,53	273,05	250,07	297,62
1985	300,68	278,37	257,27	307,84
1986	294,06	282,81	258,24	343,62

PRICE: ECU/100 KG, VAT EXCL.

CHEESE

PRIX: ÉCU/100 KG, HORS TVA

FROMAGE

Belgique/België

	Cheddar	Gouda	St-Paulin	Herve
1976	181,79	179,10	180,86	265,82
1977	207,45	204,93	205,54	301,40
1978	212,78	211,50	212,88	327,70
1979	213,05	210,31	212,55	341,57
1980	221,02	221,24	219,96	357,68
1981	232,98	232,16	232,04	412,89
1982	242,02	236,29	:	385,29
1983	253,33	248,65	:	408,71
1084	267,24	267,42	:	431,52
1985	288,35	286,13	:	445,30
1986	294,92	285,40	:	456,64

United Kingdom · Ireland

	Cheddar	Cheshire	Blue Stilton	Cheddar	Cheese processed
1976	155,06	149,52	214,82	164,16	165,23
1977	168,30	163,10	210,83	183,22	188,70
1978	182,51	178,07	232,56	222,37	226,44
1979	221,63	216,22	280,48	233,06	238,48
1980	276,46	270,70	353,32	244,69	252,46
1981	341,49	335,34	418,85	270,63	281,47
1982	360,42	354,36	447,40	305,45	318,24
1983	352,63	346,84	452,85	334,43	347,62
1984	350,48	344,72	464,76	350,58	356,31
1985	364,19	358,42	483,52	391,74	392,40
1986	326,12	321,05	441,52	421,97	422,50

Danmark

	Havarti 45 %	Havarti 30 %	Esrom	Samso-Danbo 30 %	Samso-Dabbo 45 %	Danablu
1976	167,86	149,67	189,30	149,67	167,86	211,19
1977	188,31	170,08	207,42	170,08	188,31	231,34
1978	198,73	180,93	221,24	180,93	198,73	241,19
1979	200,72	183,38	223,61	183,38	200,72	248,99
1980	207,73	191,76	230,22	191,76	207,73	254,75
1981	224,68	208,01	249,79	208,01	224,68	273,65
1982	244,82	225,45	274,25	225,45	244,82	300,36
1983	256,40	236,11	287,14	236,11	256,40	315,30
1984	264,90	250,05	295,59	250,05	264,90	326,65
1985	283,71	270,62	318,00	270,62	283,71	348,56
1986	286,68	273,45	321,33	273,45	286,68	352,21

Ellas

	Graviera	Kasseri	Kefalotiri	Feta
1976	258,39	211,30	211,30	151,04
1977	282,95	230,59	230,59	163,32
1978	294,72	239,10	239,10	168,97
1979	320,17	257,89	257,89	180,80
1980	324,38	258,79	258,79	181,63
1981	397,13	338,97	338,97	251,95
1982	445,06	385,73	385,73	294,50
1983	430,05	389,92	389,92	288,15
1984	421,66	387,00	387,00	282,34
1985	439,24	408,52	408,52	305,82
1986	425,58	384,63	384,63	288,51

*Purchase prices of the means
of agricultural products*

*Prix d'achat des moyens
de production agricole*

STRAIGHT FEEDINGSTUFFS

ALIMENTS SIMPLES

PRICE: ECU/100 KG, VAT EXCL.

PRIX: ÉCU/100 KG, HORS TVA

	Belgique/België	Danmark	BR Deutsch-land	Ellas	España	France	Ireland	Italia	Luxem-bourg	Neder-land	Portugal	United Kingdom
WHEAT BRAN												**SON DE BLÉ**
1976	14,94	:	14,82	8,68	:	12,29	14,16	13,17	:	13,06	:	12,63
1977	15,23	:	15,35	8,99	:	10,10	17,93	13,95	:	12,54	:	13,48
1978	14,58	:	13,95	8,55	:	9,69	18,53	12,29	:	11,62	:	12,22
1979	16,47	:	15,82	8,25	:	11,97	21,52	13,76	:	14,15	:	15,95
1980	16,40	:	16,16	9,76	:	11,60	24,65	15,74	:	13,84	:	18,38
1981	17,80	:	17,30	13,52	:	13,35	25,60	17,18	:	15,13	:	21,89
1982	18,15	:	18,97	16,51	:	13,85	28,18	17,98	:	:	:	23,12
1983	21,33	:	21,20	18,89	:	16,31	31,97	20,69	:	:	:	23,95
1984	20,99	:	20,75	19,30	:	13,95	35,47	20,12	:	:	:	23,65
1985	19,63	:	18,30	18,12	:	13,98	36,36	17,04	:	:	:	23,55
1986	22,35	:	18,38	15,55	:	13,71	36,00	17,37	:	:	:	19,82
BARLEY												**ORGE**
1976	16,78	14,51	16,58	13,48	:	14,03	:	14,91	16,17	15,40	:	13,14
1977	18,22	15,83	17,80	15,70	:	13,95	:	15,71	17,85	16,57	:	13,88
1978	18,24	15,40	17,52	15,99	:	14,08	:	15,79	17,98	16,41	:	13,87
1979	19,27	:	18,23	16,09	:	15,27	:	17,28	17,64	17,39	:	16,88
1980	19,18	16,10	18,09	15,51	:	15,93	:	18,12	18,88	17,14	:	18,66
1981	19,77	17,91	18,55	19,29	:	17,22	:	20,03	18,05	17,95	:	21,73
1982	20,33	19,58	20,40	21,92	:	18,31	:	21,03	17,37	20,12	:	23,04
1983	20,49	20,72	21,74	22,81	:	18,81	:	22,74	20,46	21,52	:	23,59
1984	22,81	20,96	21,84	22,90	:	19,43	:	23,77	21,64	21,36	:	23,47
1985	22,13	19,63	20,12	22,57	:	18,78	:	21,91	20,98	20,51	:	23,23
1986	22,66	19,87	20,17	19,28	:	19,09	:	22,24	21,45	21,20	:	20,30
OATS												**AVOINE**
1976	16,62	14,67	14,96	16,61	:	13,63	13,32	13,83	16,72	14,99	:	12,61
1977	19,02	15,91	15,69	19,72	:	14,19	18,01	16,67	19,50	16,89	:	13,68
1978	19,13	15,94	16,26	21,08	:	13,16	17,71	15,99	19,36	16,96	:	13,13
1979	18,81	:	15,69	20,15	:	13,13	:	15,88	17,32	15,50	:	16,24
1980	19,09	:	15,99	19,54	:	14,99	21,91	17,87	18,53	16,45	:	19,75
1981	20,25	:	16,97	24,08	:	16,87	23,76	18,61	18,14	17,66	:	22,00
1982	19,88	:	18,38	28,88	:	16,63	:	19,42	17,31	18,82	:	22,50
1983	21,39	:	19,41	30,45	:	17,89	:	20,34	20,01	20,46	:	22,86
1984	25,30	:	21,42	33,77	:	21,00	:	24,59	24,51	22,59	:	24,30
1985	22,27	:	18,02	31,38	:	16,20	:	24,41	20,46	18,44	:	23,52
1986	21,27	:	16,82	28,54	:	16,38	:	28,70	19,80	17,20	:	17,68
MAIZE												**MAÏS**
1976	18,73	:	17,84	15,46	:	14,30	:	14,63	17,29	15,70	:	13,80
1977	20,88	:	20,04	16,94	:	15,27	:	15,11	19,58	17,68	:	15,07
1978	22,12	:	20,96	16,91	:	15,90	:	15,88	20,75	18,63	:	17,26
1979	22,31	:	21,72	17,86	:	16,29	:	16,70	20,87	18,96	:	19,60
1980	22,81	:	22,70	15,76	:	17,54	:	18,02	20,82	19,35	:	23,94
1981	24,01	:	23,46	19,60	:	19,31	:	19,79	21,96	20,76	:	27,35
1982	25,15	:	24,57	21,79	:	20,35	:	21,19	22,30	23,22	:	29,21
1983	26,61	:	25,75	23,18	:	20,97	:	24,03	24,16	24,71	:	30,51
1984	27,80	:	25,95	23,52	:	20,87	:	24,18	24,66	25,01	:	30,90
1985	28,34	:	24,46	22,41	:	21,32	:	22,41	24,77	24,77	:	31,10
1986	27,69	:	25,33	19,68	:	20,05	:	22,66	24,05	23,70	:	27,77

STRAIGHT FEEDINGSTUFFS

ALIMENTS SIMPLES

PRICE: ECU/100 KG, VAT EXCL.

PRIX: ÉCU/100 KG, HORS TVA

	Belgique/ Belgïe	Danmark	BR Deutsch- land	Ellas	España	France	Ireland	Italia	Luxem- bourg	Neder- land	Portugal	United Kingdom
TOASTED EXTRACTED SOYABEAN MEAL										**TOURTEAUX D'EXTRACTION DE SOJA CUIT**		
1976	22,69	19,74	23,21	:	:	24,19	:	:	:	18,31	:	23,62
1977	25,07	23,08	25,26	:	:	27,86	:	24,26	:	21,75	:	26,60
1978	21,49	19,28	21,44	:	:	22,82	:	21,05	:	17,57	:	22,13
1979	22,28	19,80	22,41	:	:	23,84	:	21,96	:	18,37	:	23,44
1980	23,55	21,70	23,08	:	:	26,52	:	22,63	:	19,60	:	25,80
1981	27,96	26,92	28,93	:	:	31,66	:	27,87	:	23,82	:	31,08
1982	27,00	26,83	28,58	:	:	31,07	:	28,33	:	23,38	:	31,01
1083	31,68	29,59	32,73	:	:	35,51	:	32,29	:	27,63	:	32,42
1984	30,85	30,29	32,42	:	:	37,65	:	33,34	:	25,56	:	30,49
1985	27,29	25,81	28,76	:	:	33,08	:	27,47	:	22,06	:	32,79
1986	26,20	23,20	26,64	:	:	—	:	24,55	:	20,16	:	27,22
FISH MEAL										**FARINE DE POISSON**		
1976	35,54	39,66	40,60	:	:	36,00	:	41,43	:	37,53	:	39,70
1977	42,68	46,44	48,07	:	:	45,25	:	49,44	:	44,53	:	49,75
1978	37,19	41,04	41,24	:	:	40,62	:	45,05	:	38,63	:	43,05
1979	33,56	36,80	35,86	:	:	35,64	:	40,87	:	33,82	:	39,65
1980	40,16	44,77	42,53	:	:	41,06	:	45,08	:	40,54	:	46,27
1981	48,21	55,67	50,61	:	:	48,10	:	56,02	:	48,18	:	54,82
1982	44,11	52,03	48,06	:	:	43,89	:	52,03	:	43,15	:	53,14
1983	55,26	64,37	59,10	:	:	54,60	:	63,65	:	55,26	:	57,27
1984	54,20	64,85	58,99	:	:	50,99	:	72,05	:	53,18	:	59,02
1985	47,37	57,14	48,70	:	:	48,38	:	56,60	:	42,17	:	56,93
1986	42,43	53,37	42,39	:	:	41,79	:	51,19	:	35,15	:	48,19
ANIMAL MEAL										**FARINE ANIMALE**		
1976	20,79	22,44	:	:	:	24,62	:	:	:	25,21	:	22,72
1977	23,45	24,89	:	:	:	26,72	:	24,01	:	28,64	:	25,81
1978	19,51	21,18	:	:	:	22,39	:	23,46	:	25,42	:	23,48
1979	18,60	21,04	:	:	:	21,81	:	23,00	:	24,23	:	23,45
1980	21,02	23,91	:	:	:	24,10	:	22,42	:	26,81	:	24,46
1981	27,73	29,52	:	:	:	30,70	:	29,24	:	33,30	:	31,75
1982	26,83	30,74	:	:	:	30,06	:	29,44	:	32,29	:	33,94
1983	30,65	31,95	:	:	:	34,45	:	32,65	:	37,72	:	32,33
1984	29,63	32,37	:	:	:	35,00	:	34,74	:	37,85	:	32,53
1985	24,79	29,08	:	:	:	29,58	:	28,78	:	32,82	:	31,61
1986	20,85	26,14	:	:	:	26,03	:	25,90	:	27,28	:	23,30
DRIED SUGAR BEET PULP										**PULPES SÈCHES DE BETTERAVES SUCRIÈRES**		
1976	15,58	:	13,57	6,68	:	12,09	7,29	10,92	:	14,79	:	12,23
1977	13,94	:	14,19	8,23	:	10,54	10,71	12,51	:	13,89	:	14,04
1978	12,68	:	12,10	7,27	:	9,71	12,70	12,26	:	12,42	:	12,29
1979	16,83	:	13,29	7,05	:	12,16	13,29	12,85	:	16,30	:	15,44
1980	16,27	:	14,86	8,07	:	12,88	14,20	14,61	:	16,38	:	18,95
1981	16,68	:	15,38	9,35	:	13,09	15,63	14,31	:	16,72	:	21,19
1982	17,24	:	16,55	11,52	:	14,30	16,68	14,94	:	18,02	:	21,73
1983	21,29	:	19,13	12,08	:	18,10	20,56	17,61	:	21,36	:	22,28
1984	20,11	:	19,82	13,20	:	15,80	17,22	23,89	:	21,04	:	22,69
1985	19,74	:	17,69	12,60	:	15,34	18,74	21,77	:	20,63	:	22,02
1986	19,12	:	17,91	10,79	:	14,95	18,27	22,37	:	20,16	:	20,85

COMPOUND FEEDINGSTUFFS · ALIMENTS COMPOSÉS

PRICE: ECU/100 KG, VAT EXCL. · PRIX: ÉCU/100 KG, HORS TVA

COMPLEM. FEED FOR REARING CALVES — COMPLÉMENTAIRE POUR VEAUX D'ÉLEVAGE

	Belgique/ België	Danmark	BR Deutsch- land	Ellas	España	France	Ireland	Italia	Luxem- bourg	Neder- land	Portugal	United Kingdom
1976	21,72	:	:	12,94	:	18,36	17,60	20,02	18,24	18,24	:	14,54
1977	23,57	:	:	14,42	:	20,37	21,23	21,81	20,05	20,00	:	16,34
1978	22,68	:	:	13,62	:	19,35	20,76	20,70	20,34	18,48	:	15,02
1979	23,49	:	:	14,00	:	20,18	22,60	21,44	20,79	20,34	:	17,01
1980	24,38	18,33	:	16,01	:	21,97	23,15	22,47	21,36	21,30	:	20,77
1981	26,11	21,02	:	21,39	:	24,24	25,06	25,89	22,45	22,81	:	23,97
1982	26,40	21,98	:	23,71	:	24,70	27,33	27,31	21,94	24,52	:	25,44
1983	28,66	24,86	:	24,58	:	26,24	28,69	30,53	24,34	26,41	:	26,12
1984	29,90	26,90	:	25,24	:	:	30,54	31,79	26,34	26,79	:	26,79
1985	28,70	24,33	:	24,21	:	:	29,13	29,92	24,35	24,93	:	25,01
1986	28,45	22,93	:	21,42	:	:	27,13	29,58	24,04	24,20	:	21,56

MILK REPLACER FOR CALVES — COMPLET D'ALLAITEMENT POUR VEAUX

	Belgique/ België	Danmark	BR Deutsch- land	Ellas	España	France	Ireland	Italia	Luxem- bourg	Neder- land	Portugal	United Kingdom
1976	68,02	:	60,88	:	:	68,37	:	:	:	63,04	:	55,49
1977	73,69	:	66,44	:	:	69,94	:	60,42	:	71,93	:	60,10
1978	76,35	:	68,77	:	:	73,59	:	64,22	:	75,20	:	61,77
1979	76,27	:	70,80	:	:	78,45	:	69,90	:	77,17	:	69,85
1980	77,60	:	71,65	:	:	84,00	:	75,63	:	78,98	:	84,91
1981	81,68	:	75,06	:	:	93,81	:	83,56	:	81,80	:	96,69
1982	85,88	:	83,89	:	:	100,75	:	90,09	:	92,58	:	123,56
1983	90,53	:	90,79	:	:	103,89	:	95,16	:	96,56	:	125,74
1984	98,39	:	94,48	:	:	:	:	104,90	:	106,61	:	129,17
1985	108,72	:	96,29	:	:	:	:	105,84	:	109,92	:	133,40
1986	109,61	:	98,31	:	:	:	:	107,08	:	108,71	:	117,24

COMPLETE FEED FOR CATTLE FATTENING — COMPLET POUR BOVINS À L'ENGRAIS

	Belgique/ België	Danmark	BR Deutsch- land	Ellas	España	France	Ireland	Italia	Luxem- bourg	Neder- land	Portugal	United Kingdom
1976	19,21	17,13	:	:	:	17,99	:	17,31	:	16,62	:	13,56
1977	20,78	17,36	:	:	:	19,85	:	19,02	:	17,54	:	14,92
1978	19,36	15,25	:	:	:	18,55	:	18,57	:	15,72	:	13,81
1979	20,45	16,90	:	:	:	19,74	:	19,64	:	17,90	:	16,43
1980	21,61	17,93	:	:	:	22,22	:	20,87	:	18,80	:	20,54
1981	22,98	20,86	:	:	:	24,66	:	23,65	:	19,71	:	23,88
1982	23,35	22,01	:	:	:	25,36	:	24,33	:	21,04	:	25,21
1983	25,40	24,79	:	:	:	26,57	:	27,47	:	22,90	:	25,93
1984	26,47	26,56	:	:	:	:	:	28,87	:	22,67	:	26,80
1985	24,94	23,20	:	:	:	:	:	27,42	:	20,39	:	25,18
1986	24,69	21,63	:	:	:	:	:	27,30	:	19,66	:	20,43

COMPLEM. FEED FOR DAIRY CATTLE (stall fed) — COMPLÉMENTAIRE POUR VACHES LAITIÈRES (en stabulation)

	Belgique/ België	Danmark	BR Deutsch- land	Ellas	España	France	Ireland	Italia	Luxem- bourg	Neder- land	Portugal	United Kingdom
1976	19,12	:	19,91	11,35	:	19,06	:	17,52	17,25	16,46	:	16,57
1977	20,72	:	21,19	12,66	:	21,28	:	19,34	18,78	17,75	:	17,04
1978	19,14	:	19,41	11,95	:	20,62	:	19,15	17,95	16,03	:	17,79
1979	20,01	:	19,91	12,23	:	21,78	:	21,35	18,28	18,01	:	20,76
1980	21,07	:	20,16	14,04	:	23,54	:	22,80	19,34	18,88	:	24,26
1981	22,98	:	22,83	18,73	:	26,28	:	24,87	20,49	21,30	:	27,64
1982	23,30	:	24,85	20,80	:	27,32	:	25,70	21,65	22,76	:	28,98
1983	25,13	:	25,96	21,75	:	28,68	:	28,47	23,11	24,32	:	29,66
1984	26,40	:	26,65	22,84	:	:	:	30,36	24,60	24,25	:	31,46
1985	24,66	:	23,17	21,18	:	:	:	28,84	21,82	21,55	:	29,61
1986	24,08	:	19,53	19,14	:	:	:	28,66	21,66	20,58	:	23,77

COMPOUND FEEDINGSTUFFS

ALIMENTS COMPOSÉS

PRICE: ECU/100 KG, VAT EXCL.

PRIX: ÉCU/100 KG, HORS TVA

	Belgique/ België	Danmark	BR Deutsch- land	Ellas	España	France	Ireland	Italia	Luxem- bourg	Neder- land	Portugal	United Kingdom
COMPLEM. FEED FOR CATTLE AT GRASS								**COMPLÉMENTAIRE POUR VACHES LAITIÈRE À L'HERBAGE**				
1976	18,37	:	18,74	:	:	16,97	16,38	:	:	15,36	:	14,30
1977	19,76	:	20,32	:	:	18,30	19,98	20,47	:	16,11	:	16,35
1978	18,29	:	18,56	:	:	17,97	19,46	19,15	:	14,52	:	15,15
1979	19,67	:	19,02	:	:	19,15	21,51	20,07	:	18,01	:	18,30
1980	20,96	:	20,00	:	:	21,23	22,07	22,15	:	18,08	:	20,50
1981	22,40	:	22,19	:	:	22,98	23,04	26,45	:	19,13	:	23,38
1982	22,87	:	23,47	:	:	23,89	24,90	27,50	:	20,24	:	24,46
1900	24,49	:	24,97	:	:	25,82	25,95	29,76	:	22,23	:	24,12
1984	25,75	:	25,54	:	:	:	27,74	31,92	:	20,96	:	24,45
1985	24,00	:	22,11	:	:	:	25,53	29,25	:	19,47	:	24,47
1986	23,83	:	19,06	:	:	:	23,94	28,42	:	19,03	:	19,89
COMPLETE FEED FOR REARING PIGS								**COMPLET POUR PORCELETS D'ÉLEVAGE**				
1976	25,88	:	23,84	:	:	22,73	17,12	20,65	23,70	21,79	:	21,25
1977	28,03	:	26,04	:	:	24,17	21,20	22,44	25,59	24,29	:	24,84
1978	27,17	:	25,49	:	:	23,21	20,94	21,41	25,71	23,31	:	24,43
1979	27,98	:	26,40	:	:	24,47	22,18	22,07	25,97	24,63	:	27,06
1980	29,31	18,71	26,77	:	:	26,32	22,94	23,90	26,36	27,06	:	30,73
1981	31,12	20,98	28,57	:	:	28,70	25,11	27,18	29,08	29,37	:	35,67
1982	30,77	23,40	30,32	:	:	29,74	27,25	27,57	29,41	31,91	:	37,01
1983	32,44	25,91	32,46	:	:	31,17	28,66	32,15	31,63	33,19	:	37,97
1984	34,24	26,71	32,97	:	:	:	29,80	34,51	32,64	33,01	:	38,72
1985	33,87	24,52	30,62	:	:	:	28,19	31,79	28,16	31,22	:	38,32
1986	33,79	23,60	30,66	:	:	:	27,12	30,93	30,13	31,45	:	33,51
COMPLETE FEED FOR FATTENING PIGS								**COMPLET POUR PORCS À L'ENGRAIS**				
1976	20,64	17,64	19,94 *	13,60	:	18,88	16,51	18,51	19,48	18,48	:	16,22
1977	22,67	18,62	21,81 *	15,44	:	20,44	20,41	20,20	21,08	20,25	:	18,49
1978	21,59	16,92	21,11 *	14,75	:	19,95	20,18	19,32	20,69	18,55	:	17,53
1979	21,55	18,21	21,63 *	14,73	:	20,93	21,73	20,69	21,01	20,08	:	20,31
1980	23,53	18,74	22,20 *	16,62	:	22,85	22,32	22,22	21,80	21,19	:	23,78
1981	25,16	21,15	23,48 *	22,54	:	24,96	24,10	25,12	23,08	22,74	:	28,35
1982	25,29	23,66	25,52 *	24,52	:	25,78	25,88	26,29	22,08	24,06	:	29,46
1983	27,32	26,11	26,93 *	25,77	:	27,50	27,58	29,47	27,05	25,78	:	30,41
1984	28,85	26,41	27,69 *	27,68	:	:	28,94	31,62	27,86	26,39	:	31,10
1985	27,30	23,87	24,54 *	25,52	:	:	27,36	29,53	25,95	24,13	:	30,12
1986	26,89	23,14	24,27	22,67	:	:	25,87	29,04	25,57	23,45	:	25,00
BABY CHICK FEED								**COMPLÉMENTAIRE POUR POUSSINS DES PREMIERS JOURS**				
1976	24,91	:	:	16,54	:	23,03	19,56	20,78	20,99	20,56	:	17,30
1977	27,99	:	:	19,08	:	25,76	24,63	23,40	22,98	23,32	:	19,69
1978	27,56	:	:	17,91	:	25,44	24,70	22,64	23,99	22,77	:	19,25
1979	27,91	:	:	18,61	:	26,50	25,21	23,37	24,47	23,58	:	22,00
1980	28,01	:	:	19,96	:	28,20	26,36	24,86	24,95	24,11	:	25,35
1981	30,20	:	:	26,13	:	32,06	29,35	29,26	26,47	26,13	:	29,92
1982	30,42	:	:	28,40	:	33,95	31,96	30,18	24,97	27,93	:	31,30
1983	32,93	:	:	29,90	:	35,14	33,75	33,04	28,50	29,99	:	32,18
1984	35,34	:	:	31,75	:	:	35,10	34,99	31,01	31,11	:	33,12
1985	34,22	:	:	29,74	:	:	33,84	33,00	26,78	28,83	:	29,10
1986	33,19	:	:	26,21	:	:	32,66	32,96	28,61	27,41	:	27,37

* Bulk

* En vrac

203

COMPOUND FEEDINGSTUFFS

ALIMENTS COMPOSÉS

PRICE: ECU/100 KG, VAT EXCL.

PRIX: ÉCU/100 KG, HORS TVA

	Belgique/België	Danmark	BR Deutsch-land	Ellas	España	France	Ireland	Italia	Luxem-bourg	Neder-land	Portugal	United Kingdom

COMPLETE FEED FOR BATTERY-LAYING HENS — **COMPLET POUR POULES PONDEUSES «EN BATTERIE»**

Year	Belgique/België	Danmark	BR Deutschland	Ellas	España	France	Ireland	Italia	Luxembourg	Nederland	Portugal	United Kingdom
1976	21,55	:	19,97	13,82	:	19,03	17,89	19,73	20,40	19,15	:	16,57
1977	24,01	:	22,18	15,94	:	20,91	21,69	1,79	22,57	21,50	:	18,68
1978	23,45	:	21,59	14,96	:	20,73	21,66	21,35	24,16	21,06	:	18,41
1979	24,09	:	22,04	15,56	:	21,54	23,12	22,06	24,40	21,94	:	21,07
1980	24,86	:	22,28	16,71	:	23,43	24,11	23,61	24,48	22,68	:	23,69
1981	27,43	:	23,87	22,28	:	25,83	16,24	27,33	25,86	24,58	:	28,01
1982	27,12	:	25,62	24,61	:	26,39	28,26	27,84	25,18	26,51	:	28,89
1983	29,43	:	27,42	26,11	:	27,80	30,14	30,89	27,49	28,42	:	30,02
1984	30,97	:	28,58	27,42	:	:	31,59	33,12	30,28	29,49	:	30,76
1985	29,31	:	26,58	25,84	:	:	30,29	30,79	28,70	27,56	:	30,10
1986	28,71	:	26,24	23,08	:	:	28,79	31,21	28,21	26,16	:	25,03

STRAIGHT FERTILIZERS

ENGRAIS SIMPLES

AMMONIUM NITRATE (1) — **NITRATE D'AMMONIAQUE** (1)

Year	Belgique/België	Danmark	BR Deutschland	Ellas	España	France	Ireland	Italia	Luxembourg	Nederland	Portugal	United Kingdom
1976	39,29	44,62	46,49	20,74	:	36,52	38,51	29,30	38,23	41,59	:	27,61
1977	41,75	39,33	49,54	21,10	:	37,17	40,55	31,40	41,04	45,28	:	30,04
1978	42,57	44,55	51,34	18,64	:	39,57	43,79	32,40	40,79	46,71	:	36,63
1979	46,24	47,35	52,87	22,63	:	45,85	47,77	34,84	43,43	47,70	:	40,04
1980	53,19	53,47	57,12	28,32	:	57,95	53,46	41,43	49,41	52,76	:	49,09
1981	57,05	62,70	65,21	30,28	:	60,86	59,48	44,59	54,87	59,85	:	58,02
1982	59,86	67,84	72,45	28,56	:	64,13	65,30	50,69	57,88	64,62	:	:
1983	55,53	68,37	67,90	32,66	:	63,49	63,22	58,84	55,68	56,16	:	83,64
1984	59,84	74,63	66,89	29,57	:	:	64,19	57,09	54,11	57,58	:	86,04
1985	65,01	76,88	71,66	26,56	:	:	71,73	59,68	58,96	65,03	:	91,21
1986	57,08	67,06	68,99	24,72	:	:	60,32	56,03	55,32	58,89	:	85,58

CALCIUM NITRATE (1) — **NITRATE DE CHAUX** (1)

Year	Belgique/België	Danmark	BR Deutschland	Ellas	España	France	Ireland	Italia	Luxembourg	Nederland	Portugal	United Kingdom
1976	:	56,11	:	23,70	:	50,17	:	49,21	:	51,03	:	:
1977	:	56,64	:	24,15	:	53,30	:	56,36	:	56,96	:	:
1978	:	58,73	69,60	22,19	:	60,69	:	53,74	:	58,39	:	:
1979	:	57,58	72,84	24,99	:	69,19	:	57,19	:	63,60	:	:
1980	:	63,79	79,27	31,29	:	85,79	:	68,42	:	68,31	:	:
1981	:	77,35	90,74	33,46	:	96,24	:	71,66	:	75,16	:	:
1982	:	85,04	102,65	31,56	:	100,00	:	81,80	:	90,59	:	:
1983	:	88,32	98,27	36,06	:	97,62	:	91,44	:	83,36	:	67,72
1984	:	106,75	95,17	32,66	:	:	:	88,74	:	86,16	:	70,72
1985	:	113,54	:	29,33	:	:	:	92,68	:	94,38	:	78,37
1986	:	108,14	:	27,29	:	:	:	88,21	:	:	:	64,34

BASIC SLAG (2) — **SCORIE THOMAS** (2)

Year	Belgique/België	Danmark	BR Deutschland	Ellas	España	France	Ireland	Italia	Luxembourg	Nederland	Portugal	United Kingdom
1976	5,09	:	6,68	:	:	4,41	6,90	7,11	2,27	6,05	:	2,09
1977	5,63	:	6,83	:	:	4,54	7,02	7,61	2,51	6,64	:	2,51
1978	5,67	:	6,71	:	:	4,69	7,28	7,97	2,44	6,75	:	2,71
1979	5,81	:	6,55	:	:	4,98	7,80	7,93	2,54	6,79	:	3,64
1980	6,21	:	6,86	:	:	5,78	8,91	7,93	2,59	7,28	:	4,50
1981	6,81	:	7,67	:	:	6,53	11,16	8,27	3,05	8,37	:	5,75
1982	7,85	:	8,88	:	:	6,31	:	9,31	2,67	10,41	:	:
1983	9,31	:	10,04	:	:	6,94	:	11,88	2,90	12,06	:	:
1984	9,64	:	10,77	:	:	:	:	13,52	3,47	13,20	:	:
1985	6,44	:	10,96	:	:	:	:	13,82	3,70	13,30	:	:
1986	6,46	:	11,04	:	:	:	:	14,27	4,02	13,25	:	:

(1) Prices per 100 kg of nutritive substance
(2) Prices per 100 kg of merchandise

(1) Prix par 100 kg d'éléments fertilisants
(2) Prix par 100 kg de marchandise

STRAIGHT FERTILIZERS

ENGRAIS SIMPLES

PRICE: ECU/100 KG, VAT EXCL.

PRIX: ÉCU/100 KG, HORS TVA

	Belgique/ België	Danmark	BR Deutsch- land	Ellas	España	France	Ireland	Italia	Luxem- bourg	Neder- land	Portugal	United Kingdom

SUPERPHOSPHATE (1) — **SUPERPHOSPHATE** (1)

	Belgique/ België	Danmark	BR Deutsch- land	Ellas	España	France	Ireland	Italia	Luxem- bourg	Neder- land	Portugal	United Kingdom
1976	45,43	45,24	:	16,63	:	45,75	40,88	37,22	:	47,68	:	39,03
1977	44,00	44,30	52,98	17,01	:	41,92	41,76	36,42	:	47,89	:	39,13
1978	43,29	44,63	54,42	15,60	:	40,82	45,23	35,76	:	50,41	:	37,16
1979	47,04	45,91	56,79	17,53	:	43,92	51,64	38,66	:	53,86	:	38,41
1980	57,68	50,25	61,96	21,91	:	54,42	61,49	51,10	:	66,03	:	56,18
1981	64,19	63,87	69,85	23,45	:	64,49	73,79	56,78	:	70,82	:	64,29
1982	62,39	70,56	77,86	22,11	:	66,86	84,51	66,93	:	77,43	:	:
1983	64,50	68,20	80,24	35,47	:	68,64	85,08	72,68	:	76,70	:	80,00
1984	71,34	71,81	81,90	32,72	:	:	93,81	77,12	.	70,09	:	84,47
1985	74,71	76,68	84,80	29,37	:	:	106,83	82,11	:	78,53	:	92,92
1986	76,26	73,74	84,37	27,32	:	:	97,35	77,57	:	74,60	:	80,99

MURIATE OF POTASH (1) — **CHLORURE DE POTASSIUM** (1)

	Belgique/ België	Danmark	BR Deutsch- land	Ellas	España	France	Ireland	Italia	Luxem- bourg	Neder- land	Portugal	United Kingdom
1976	18,80	16,11	17,15	:	:	16,17	17,92	17,01	17,90	19,18	:	15,41
1977	20,20	16,63	18,75	:	:	16,50	18,77	17,46	18,39	20,32	:	15,63
1978	20,97	19,17	20,04	:	:	17,09	18,77	15,90	19,11	21,29	:	15,94
1979	21,69	19,67	21,07	:	:	19,10	19,90	17,43	19,65	22,37	:	17,95
1980	22,72	20,80	22,37	:	:	21,49	22,04	22,50	21,60	24,73	:	:
1981	25,63	23,60	24,11	:	:	23,69	25,70	25,01	23,37	27,57	:	:
1982	26,60	26,97	27,03	:	:	25,33	28,18	26,69	23,64	31,22	:	:
1983	28,91	29,22	29,22	:	:	26,60	27,93	27,72	26,06	32,87	:	26,23
1984	31,14	32,59	30,76	:	:	:	30,94	29,66	27,79	33,41	:	27,67
1985	34,57	34,91	31,91	:	:	:	35,63	32,46	28,74	35,44	:	30,19
1986	36,99	33,47	33,61	:	:	:	34,55	32,23	30,34	37,32	:	26,60

SULPHATE OF POTASH (1) — **SULFATE DE POTASSIUM** (1)

	Belgique/ België	Danmark	BR Deutsch- land	Ellas	España	France	Ireland	Italia	Luxem- bourg	Neder- land	Portugal	United Kingdom
1976	24,74	26,69	:	6,16	:	26,29	27,38	21,44	:	27,50	:	:
1977	26,30	26,99	23,68	6,28	:	26,94	28,83	21,60	:	28,92	:	:
1978	27,33	28,38	25,39	5,77	:	28,13	28,57	21,87	:	29,81	:	:
1979	28,09	28,76	26,80	8,31	:	30,27	29,65	23,47	:	30,97	:	:
1980	29,34	30,67	28,52	13,55	:	35,54	:	29,88	:	34,24	:	:
1981	32,70	35,56	30,75	14,51	:	39,98	36,86	35,22	:	38,36	:	:
1982	36,02	40,86	34,81	13,68	:	41,88	42,84	36,73	:	44,99	:	:
1983	39,85	44,38	38,56	15,65	:	44,03	42,09	40,13	:	47,97	:	:
1984	44,06	53,13	41,04	14,17	:	:	51,92	41,76	:	48,55	:	:
1985	47,94	56,64	46,71	12,73	:	:	60,90	46,46	:	51,77	:	:
1986	50,94	55,09	51,58	11,85	:	:	61,63	49,45	:	55,94	:	:

COMPOUND FERTILIZERS (N - P - K) — **ENGRAIS COMPOSÉS (N - P - K)**

BINARY FERTILIZERS 0 - 20 - 20 (2) — **ENGRAIS BINAIRES 0 - 20 - 20** (2)

	Belgique/ België	Danmark	BR Deutsch- land	Ellas	España	France	Ireland	Italia	Luxem- bourg	Neder- land	Portugal	United Kingdom
1976	6,20	:	15,48	:	:	12,17	10,34	:	:	:	:	:
1977	6,50	:	15,11	:	:	11,96	9,59	:	:	:	:	:
1978	6,10	:	15,73	:	:	12,82	11,30	:	:	:	:	:
1979	6,90	:	16,19	:	:	13,09	12,10	:	:	:	:	:
1980	7,60	:	17,20	:	:	15,74	13,77	:	:	:	:	:
1981	8,40	:	19,03	:	:	16,73	15,86	:	:	:	:	:
1982	8,70	:	21,13	:	:	17,14	16,42	:	:	:	:	:
1983	10,00	:	21,78	:	:	17,36	15,88	:	:	:	:	18,04
1984	11,00	:	22,36	:	:	:	17,55	:	:	:	:	18,62
1985	11,20	:	23,35	:	:	:	19,09	:	:	:	:	21,46
1986	11,40	:	23,86	:	:	:	16,37	:	:	:	:	17,08

(1) Prices per 100 kg of nutritive substance
(2) Prices per 100 kg of merchandise

(1) Prix par 100 kg d'éléments fertilisants
(2) Prix par 100 kg de marchandise

COMPOUND FEEDINGSTUFFS (N - P - K) ALIMENTS COMPOSÉS (N - P - K)

PRICE: ECU/100 KG, VAT EXCL. PRIX: ÉCU/100 KG, HORS TVA

	Belgique/ België	Danmark	BR Deutsch- land	Ellas	España	France	Ireland	Italia	Luxem- bourg	Neder- land	Portugal	United Kingdom
TERNARY FERTILIZERS: 20 - 10 - 10 (1)											**ENGRAIS TERNAIRES: 20 - 10 - 10 (1)**	
1976	15,01	:	:	:	:	:	:	12,58	:	18,32	:	11,78
1977	15,22	:	:	:	:	:	:	13,05	:	19,77	:	12,09
1978	15,42	:	16,06	:	:	:	:	13,26	:	16,90	:	13,96
1979	15,32	:	16,60	:	:	:	:	14,22	:	16,98	:	15,36
1980	15,93	:	17,97	:	:	:	:	16,56	:	18,64	:	19,90
1981	18,08	:	20,55	:	:	:	:	17,42	:	20,43	:	23,68
1982	20,12	:	23,12	:	:	:	:	20,47	:	23,57	:	:
1983	20,48	:	21,72	:	:	:	:	20,77	:	21,48	:	23,68
1984	21,19	:	19,92	:	:	:	:	20,30	:	22,55	:	24,52
1985	21,34	:	22,92	:	:	:	:	19,36	:	23,62	:	26,08
1986	21,86	:	19,29	:	:	:	:	19,18	:	23,41	:	20,40
TERNARY FERTILIZERS: 17 - 17 - 17 (1)											**ENGRAIS TERNAIRES: 17 - 17 - 17 (1)**	
1976	17,78	:	18,46	10,69	:	17,03	16,33	15,69	17,51	18,11	:	15,25
1977	16,38	:	18,87	10,90	:	16,94	16,61	15,87	17,54	18,60	:	15,48
1978	17,43	:	19,64	9,98	:	17,75	16,58	16,22	16,90	18,72	:	16,76
1979	18,44	:	20,28	11,29	:	18,55	18,13	17,69	18,08	18,62	:	18,24
1980	19,92	:	21,81	14,14	:	22,86	20,41	20,47	29,56	20,78	:	23,56
1981	22,11	:	24,48	15,12	:	23,48	22,85	22,08	20,31	22,67	:	28,69
1982	23,99	:	27,21	14,26	:	23,65	23,87	27,09	19,16	26,32	:	:
1983	22,38	:	26,51	16,30	:	24,09	22,84	26,54	18,86	23,96	:	27,38
1984	24,49	:	25,76	14,75	:	:	24,86	25,94	21,89	25,64	:	28,26
1985	25,74	:	27,53	13,25	:	:	27,99	24,75	25,25	27,04	:	30,56
1986	25,16	:	28,01	12,33	:	:	25,45	24,51	26,60	26,62	:	23,83
TERNARY FERTILIZERS: 9 - 9 - 18 (1)											**ENGRAIS TERNAIRES: 9 - 9 - 18 (1)**	
1976	11,48	:	11,73	:	:	11,31	:	10,60	:	11,54	:	9,27
1977	11,70	:	12,06	:	:	11,33	:	10,45	:	11,96	:	9,73
1978	11,69	:	12,54	:	:	12,13	:	10,80	:	12,10	:	10,42
1979	11,87	:	12,98	:	:	13,33	:	11,51	:	12,13	:	11,39
1980	12,49	:	13,90	:	:	16,59	:	13,44	:	13,35	:	:
1981	13,86	:	15,47	:	:	17,92	:	14,43	:	14,57	:	:
1982	14,82	:	17,13	:	:	18,53	:	16,10	:	16,97	:	:
1983	16,58	:	16,96	:	:	19,07	:	17,44	:	15,73	:	16,75
1984	16,25	:	16,68	:	:	:	:	17,04	:	16,84	:	17,35
1985	17,05	:	17,71	:	:	:	:	16,25	:	17,28	:	19,02
1986	:	:	17,96	:	:	:	:	16,09	:	17,89	:	15,49
TERNARY FERTILIZERS: 10 - 20 - 20 (1)											**ENGRAIS TERNAIRES: 10 - 20 - 20 (1)**	
1976	:	:	:	10,13	:	16,90	:	15,15	:	:	:	:
1977	:	:	:	10,33	:	16,24	:	15,07	:	:	:	:
1978	:	:	19,29	9,47	:	17,30	:	15,38	:	:	:	:
1979	:	:	19,93	10,66	:	18,44	:	16,96	:	:	:	:
1980	:	:	21,30	13,37	:	22,24	:	19,70	:	:	:	:
1981	:	:	23,85	14,28	:	23,21	:	34,37	:	:	:	:
1982	:	:	26,57	13,47	:	23,64	:	42,31	:	:	:	:
1983	:	:	25,84	15,41	:	23,65	:	49,01	:	:	:	25,20
1984	:	:	24,66	13,96	:	:	:	48,26	:	:	:	25,99
1985	:	:	27,24	12,53	:	:	:	46,04	:	:	:	28,47
1986	:	:	25,77	11,66	:	:	:	45,61	:	:	:	21,73

(1) Prices per 100 kg of merchandise (1) Prix par 100 kg de merchandise

MOTOR FUELS AND FUELS FOR HEATING   CARBURANTS ET COMBUSTIBLES

PRICE: ECU/100 KG, VAT EXCL.   PRIX: ÉCU/100 KG, HORS TVA

	Belgique/ Belgïe	Danmark	BR Deutsch- land	Ellas	España	France	Ireland	Italia	Luxem- bourg	Neder- land	Portugal	United Kingdom
MOTOR SPIRIT												**ESSENCE MOTEUR**
1976	23,23	15,29	28,46	37,91	:	23,93	30,84	11,54	:	30,40	:	27,38
1977	33,44	14,43	29,42	40,44	:	23,90	31,80	11,32	:	32,03	:	26,95
1978	34,05	14,18	31,10	38,48	:	23,24	30,41	10,02	:	32,67	:	25,26
1979	38,17	17,31	34,44	47,51	:	24,54	35,97	11,60	:	35,99	:	35,06
1980	47,64	24,82	40,28	51,97	:	33,17	48,39	18,91	:	43,59	:	47,32
1981	53,11	33,14	48,89	58,82	:	40,34	63,62	24,29	:	50,62	:	62,00
1982	54,48	35,91	49,98	60,67	:	45,15	75,16	26,11	:	54,57	:	65,34
1983	56,01	33,23	51,62	58,91	:	46,89	84,44	27,66	:	57,98	:	66,92
1984	57,37	34,16	52,39	59,56	:	52,11	87,03	28,26	:	61,47	:	68,77
1985	59,09	35,43	53,97	57,06	:	61,42	76,78	29,26	:	62,66	:	73,25
1986	46,30	22,28	42,55	52,87	:	49,41	81,21	15,73	:	52,76	:	55,62
DIESEL OIL												**GASOLE**
1976	11,24	11,34	11,97	12,96	:	:	11,02	9,02	11,70	11,19	:	11,12
1977	12,25	11,83	12,60	13,85	:	:	12,82	9,90	12,55	12,02	:	13,48
1978	12,11	11,37	12,90	12,83	:	:	12,17	9,64	12,26	11,71	:	13,62
1979	16,61	15,74	18,98	17,23	:	32,54	:	13,10	16,21	15,87	:	17,76
1980	22,44	21,37	24,04	25,83	:	41,36	:	24,25	22,29	22,52	:	25,87
1981	26,11	26,76	28,94	29,83	:	48,23	:	24,67	26,88	27,38	:	33,41
1982	28,58	30,09	32,42	30,04	:	52,59	:	29,48	27,73	30,87	:	38,72
1983	27,60	29,84	32,21	30,73	:	53,82	:	31,88	19,21	30,01	:	42,83
1984	29,49	31,21	33,85	31,45	:	57,38	:	33,23	30,65	32,14	:	43,97
1985	31,15	32,73	35,29	32,43	:	62,42	:	35,64	31,68	33,84	:	51,41
1986	17,67	20,19	22,36	27,84	:	51,80	:	22,30	21,03	21,62	:	34,23
HEATING GAS OIL												**FUEL-OIL FLUIDE**
1976	11,00	11,13	9,77	12,96	:	13,50	11,07	8,94	:	9,23	:	93,93
1977	12,11	11,60	10,42	13,85	:	14,42	12,09	9,81	:	10,26	:	12,51
1978	11,96	11,19	10,43	12,83	:	15,24	10,98	9,58	:	9,96	:	12,70
1979	16,43	15,94	18,46	17,23	:	18,99	15,68	13,02	:	14,28	:	15,64
1980	22,29	21,47	21,71	25,83	:	27,68	23,67	19,98	:	18,33	:	22,86
1981	26,03	26,57	25,90	29,83	:	34,28	30,17	24,25	:	25,62	:	30,23
1982	28,45	29,90	28,96	30,04	:	37,93	33,57	29,39	:	28,94	:	33,94
1983	27,44	29,58	27,80	30,73	:	38,33	36,55	41,00	:	27,79	:	36,39
1984	29,40	31,10	29,75	31,45	:	40,12	38,63	44,49	:	29,88	:	39,89
1985	31,15	33,49	31,25	32,43	:	44,33	40,63	46,76	:	31,37	:	39,14
1986	17,67	21,16	18,07	27,84	:	31,05	26,97	38,66	:		:	24,79

*EC index of producer prices
of agricultural products*

*Indice CE des prix à la production
des produits agricoles*

(EXCLUDING VAT)   (TVA EXCLUE)

(1980 = 100)   (1980 = 100)

	Total	Crop products/ Produits végétaux	Animal products/ Produits animaux	Total	Crop products/ Produits végétaux	Animal products/ Produits animaux	Total	Crop products/ Produits végétaux	Animal products/ Produits animaux
		EUR 10			BELGIQUE/BELGIË			DANMARK	

NOMINAL INDEX   **INDICES NOMINAUX**

	Total	Crop	Animal	Total	Crop	Animal	Total	Crop	Animal
1975	67,1	61,7	71,4	89,9	90,5	89,7	72,0	68,3	73,4
1976	78,4	76,3	80,0	103,7	119,2	96,6	81,2	79,6	81,9
1977	84,2	81,6	86,3	99,5	100,6	98,9	84,5	80,5	86,1
1978	87,2	84,2	89,5	95,5	93,7	96,3	89,0	83,8	91,1
1979	92,8	91,4	93,9	97,5	96,6	97,9	90,5	90,3	90,5
1980	100,0	100,0	100,0	100,0	100,0	100,0	100,0	100,0	100,0
1981	112,1	112,5	111,8	110,1	109,4	110,5	112,1	109,6	113,1
1982	125,0	126,1	124,1	123,7	119,7	125,6	125,1	119,0	127,6
1983	133,6	139,3	129,0	132,4	139,3	129,2	131,1	134,1	130,0
1984	139,5	146,7	133,8	135,3	141,9	132,2	135,1	125,2	139,0
1985	143,9	152,0	137,5	132,6	129,3	134,2	132,5	123,7	136,0
1986*	146,2	158,9	136,1	124,9	123,5	125,5	126,8	121,5	128,9

% TAV   **% TAV**

1984/1975	7,6	9,0	6,5	4,2	4,6	4,0	6,5	6,2	6,6
1985/1984	3,2	3,6	2,8	−2,0	−8,9	1,5	−1,9	−1,2	−2,2
1986/1985*	1,6	4,5	−1,0	−5,8	−4,5	−6,5	−4,3	−1,8	−5,2

DEFLATED INDICES   **INDICES DÉFLATÉS**

	Total	Crop	Animal	Total	Crop	Animal	Total	Crop	Animal
1975	112,8	108,7	116,1	122,3	123,1	122,0	118,0	112,0	120,4
1976	118,8	119,8	118,1	129,3	148,7	120,4	122,3	119,9	123,3
1977	115,5	115,3	115,6	115,8	117,1	115,2	115,2	109,7	117,4
1978	110,8	109,5	111,8	106,4	104,4	107,3	109,6	103,2	112,2
1979	106,5	106,3	106,7	104,0	103,0	104,4	101,6	101,4	101,7
1980	100,0	100,0	100,0	100,0	100,0	100,0	100,0	100,0	100,0
1981	98,8	98,1	99,4	102,3	101,7	102,6	100,3	98,1	101,2
1982	98,4	97,1	99,4	105,7	102,3	107,3	101,7	96,8	103,7
1983	95,8	96,7	95,1	105,1	110,6	102,6	99,7	102,0	98,8
1984	92,5	93,1	92,1	101,0	105,9	98,7	96,6	89,5	99,5
1985	88,5	88,2	88,7	94,4	92,1	95,5	90,5	84,5	92,9
1986*	85,3	86,6	84,2	87,8	86,8	88,2	83,6	80,1	84,9

% TAV   **% TAV**

1984/1975	−2,0	−1,5	−2,3	−1,9	−1,5	−2,1	−2,0	−2,2	−1,9
1985/1984	−4,3	−5,3	−3,7	−6,5	−13,0	−3,2	−6,3	−5,6	−6,6
1986/1985*	−3,6	−1,8	−5,1	−7,0	−5,8	−7,6	−7,6	−5,2	−8,6

* = forecast/estimation.

(EXCLUDING VAT)   (TVA EXCLUE)

(1980 = 100)   **(1980 = 100)**

	Total	Crop products/ Produits végétaux	Animal products/ Produits animaux	Total	Crop products/ Produits végétaux	Animal products/ Produits animaux	Total	Crop products/ Produits végétaux	Animal products/ Produits animaux
		BR DEUTSCHLAND			ELLAS			FRANCE	
NOMINAL INDEX									**INDICES NOMINAUX**
1975	93,1	87,9	95,2	44,3	43,1	47,2	68,9	66,4	71,1
1976	101,4	102,2	101,0	53,6	52,5	56,1	78,1	79,4	76,9
1977	99,8	93,7	102,3	60,9	60,1	62,7	86,0	88,9	83,5
1978	96,7	93,7	97,9	69,6	69,3	70,1	88,7	88,0	89,2
1979	98,0	95,0	08,0	81,8	81,3	83,0	94,0	93,8	94,3
1980	100,0	100,0	100,0	100,0	100,0	100,0	100,0	100,0	100,0
1981	106,2	107,0	105,9	124,3	119,9	135,0	111,9	111,8	112,0
1982	109,5	105,7	111,0	152,1	146,6	165,2	126,9	127,1	126,7
1983	108,6	107,4	109,0	178,9	172,3	194,6	136,5	138,4	134,8
1984	107,2	106,8	107,4	215,2	209,7	228,5	140,8	142,3	139,6
1985	103,1	101,2	103,9	254,2	246,7	272,3	143,0	141,8	144,0
1986*	97,3	97,8	97,1	286,7	277,7	308,4	143,2	144,8	141,8
% TAV									**% TAV**
1984/1975	1,4	2,0	1,2	17,1	17,1	17,1	7,4	7,9	7,0
1985/1984	−3,8	−5,2	−3,3	18,1	17,6	19,2	1,6	−0,4	3,2
1986/1985*	−5,6	−3,4	−6,5	12,8	12,6	13,3	0,1	2,1	−1,5
DEFLATED INDICES									**INDICES DÉFLATÉS**
1975	113,5	107,2	116,0	94,2	91,7	100,3	113,3	109,2	117,0
1976	118,4	119,4	118,0	100,5	98,5	105,3	117,2	119,3	115,4
1977	112,5	105,7	115,3	101,9	100,6	104,9	118,0	121,9	114,6
1978	106,1	102,9	107,5	103,4	103,0	104,2	111,5	110,7	112,2
1979	103,2	100,7	104,3	102,2	101,6	103,6	106,9	106,5	107,2
1980	100,0	100,0	100,0	100,0	100,0	100,0	100,0	100,0	100,0
1981	99,9	100,6	99,6	99,9	96,3	108,4	98,7	98,6	98,8
1982	97,8	94,4	99,2	101,0	97,4	109,7	100,1	100,3	99,9
1983	93,9	92,9	94,3	98,6	95,0	107,2	98,2	99,6	97,0
1984	90,6	90,2	90,7	100,3	97,7	106,5	94,4	95,4	93,5
1985	85,2	83,7	85,8	99,2	96,3	106,2	90,5	89,7	91,2
1986*	80,6	81,0	80,5	90,9	88,0	97,8	88,3	89,3	87,4
% TAV									**% TAV**
1984/1975	−2,2	−1,7	−2,6	0,6	0,6	0,6	−1,8	−1,3	−2,2
1985/1984	−6,0	−7,2	−5,4	−1,1	−1,4	−0,3	−4,1	−6,0	−2,5
1986/1985*	−5,4	−3,2	−6,2	−8,4	−8,6	−7,9	−2,4	−0,4	4,2

* = forecast/estimation.

(EXCLUDING VAT)

(TVA EXCLUE)

(1980 = 100)

(1980 = 100)

	Total	Crop products/ Produits végétaux	Animal products/ Produits animaux	Total	Crop products/ Produits végétaux	Animal products/ Produits animaux	Total	Crop products/ Produits végétaux	Animal products/ Produits animaux
		IRELAND			**ITALIA**			**LUXEMBOURG**	
NOMINAL INDEX									**INDICES NOMINAUX**
1975	57,5	63,5	56,5	49,9	47,4	53,4	87,7	87,7	87,7
1976	71,1	80,6	69,5	60,7	57,6	65,1	95,1	105,4	93,3
1977	88,1	88,6	88,1	73,0	71,8	74,8	97,3	100,7	96,7
1978	96,7	84,7	98,6	80,9	80,9	81,0	95,3	95,0	95,3
1979	102,1	103,9	101,8	88,2	88,1	88,3	97,3	96,5	97,5
1980	100,0	100,0	100,0	100,0	100,0	100,0	100,0	100,0	100,0
1981	117,7	113,7	118,4	113,8	113,6	114,2	107,8	110,3	107,4
1982	127,6	121,3	128,6	131,5	130,9	132,5	124,2	106,9	127,3
1983	135,4	133,1	135,8	143,5	144,4	142,3	135,3	131,1	136,1
1984	139,4	138,3	139,6	152,3	152,9	151,6	133,5	111,9	137,3
1985	135,6	116,4	138,8	162,7	165,1	159,3	138,2	112,9	142,7
1986*	135,2	130,5	135,9	169,7	174,3	163,4	138,8	115,9	142,9
% TAV									**% TAV**
1984/1975	9,3	8,1	9,5	11,8	12,4	11,0	4,3	2,5	4,6
1985/1984	−2,7	−15,8	−0,6	6,8	7,0	5,1	3,2	0,9	3,9
1986/1985*	−0,3	12,1	−2,1	4,3	5,6	2,6	0,4	2,7	0,1
DEFLATED INDICES									**INDICES DÉFLATÉS**
1975	111,0	122,7	109,1	107,7	102,3	115,1	117,7	117,7	117,7
1976	116,4	131,9	113,8	112,2	106,4	120,2	116,2	128,9	114,0
1977	127,0	127,6	126,9	113,9	111,9	116,7	111,5	115,4	110,8
1978	129,4	113,4	132,0	112,6	112,5	112,7	105,9	105,6	105,9
1979	120,7	122,8	120,3	106,9	106,8	107,0	103,5	102,6	103,6
1980	100,0	100,0	100,0	100,0	100,0	100,0	100,0	100,0	100,0
1981	97,8	94,4	98,3	96,6	96,4	96,9	99,8	102,1	99,4
1982	90,4	86,0	91,1	95,9	95,4	96,6	105,1	90,5	107,7
1983	86,9	85,4	87,2	91,2	91,8	90,4	105,4	102,0	106,0
1984	82,4	81,7	82,5	87,4	87,7	87,0	98,4	82,5	101,2
1985	76,0	65,3	77,8	85,5	86,7	83,7	97,8	79,9	100,9
1986*	73,0	70,5	73,4	84,3	86,5	81,1	97,9	81,4	100,8
% TAV									**% TAV**
1984/1975	−2,9	−4,0	−2,8	−2,1	−1,5	−2,8	−1,8	−3,5	−1,5
1985/1984	−7,8	−20,1	−5,7	−2,2	−1,1	−3,8	−0,6	−3,2	−0,3
1986/1985*	−3,9	8,0	−5,7	−1,4	−0,2	−3,1	−0,1	−1,9	−0,1

* = forecast/estimation.

(EXCLUDING VAT)

(TVA EXCLUE)

(1980 = 100)

(1980 = 100)

	Total	Crop products/ Produits végétaux	Animal products/ Produits animaux	Total	Crop products/ Produits végétaux	Total
		NEDERLAND			**UNITED KINGDOM**	
NOMINAL INDEX						**INDICES NOMINAUX**
1975	90,1	88,8	90,7	62,9	70,5	59,1
1976	102,0	110,2	97,8	82,4	104,3	71,1
1977	99,4	98,0	100,1	84,3	94,4	79,2
1978	95,2	90,4	97,6	86,1	86,8	85,7
1979	96,7	94,1	98,0	94,9	100,4	92,1
1980	100,0	100,0	100,0	100,0	100,0	100,0
1981	108,7	107,2	109,5	110,9	112,4	110,1
1982	112,4	105,5	116,0	119,7	121,1	118,9
1983	114,7	116,2	114,0	125,9	137,1	120,1
1984	116,8	121,4	114,4	126,0	132,1	123,0
1985	114,6	112,8	115,5	124,0	121,3	125,4
1986*	107,0	107,4	106,8	125,7	127,2	124,9
% TAV						**% TAV**
1984/1975	2,6	3,2	2,3	7,2	6,5	7,6
1985/1984	−1,9	−7,1	1,0	−1,6	−8,2	2,0
1986/1985*	−6,4	−4,0	−7,5	1,4	4,9	−0,4
DEFLATED INDICES						**INDICES DÉFLATÉS**
1975	121,5	119,8	122,4	123,1	137,9	115,5
1976	126,2	136,3	121,0	138,2	175,1	119,3
1977	115,5	113,9	116,4	122,2	136,8	119,7
1978	106,2	100,9	108,9	115,2	116,2	114,7
1979	103,4	100,7	104,9	112,0	118,4	108,7
1980	100,0	100,0	100,0	100,0	100,0	100,0
1981	101,9	100,5	102,6	99,1	100,4	98,4
1982	99,7	93,5	102,8	98,5	99,7	97,9
1983	99,0	100,2	98,4	99,0	107,9	94,5
1984	97,7	101,5	95,7	94,5	99,0	92,2
1985	93,7	92,2	94,4	87,6	85,7	88,6
1986*	87,2	87,5	87,0	85,9	86,9	85,4
% TAV						**% TAV**
1984/1975	−2,2	−1,6	−2,4	−2,6	−3,3	−2,2
1985/1984	−4,1	−9,2	−1,4	−7,3	−13,4	−3,9
1986/1985*	−6,9	5,1	−7,3	−1,9	1,4	−3,6

* = forecast/estimation.

213

EC INDICES OF PRODUCER PRICES OF THE MEANS OF AGRICULTURAL PRODUCTS

I F 4

(EXCLUDING VAT)

(1980 = 100)

	1975	1979	1981	1982	1983	1984	1985	1986*
	EUR 10 NOMINAL INDEX/INDICES NOMINAUX							
0 TOTAL	67,1	92,8	112,1	125,0	133,6	139,5	143,9	146,2
(0) TOTAL (excl. fruit and vegetables)	69,1	93,7	111,0	124,2	132,3	137,1	140,6	142,5
1 Crop products	61,7	91,4	112,5	126,1	139,3	146,7	152,0	158,9
(1) Crop products (excluding fruit and vegetables)	65,0	93,4	109,5	124,5	138,0	142,8	146,0	153,7
11 Cereals and rice	64,7	92,6	112,4	124,1	135,2	135,9	132,7	135,6
11A Soft wheat	:	:	112,0	121,0	130,6	128,6	125,5	130,8
11B Durum wheat	:	:	110,7	128,0	145,5	154,3	155,4	166,1
11C Feeding barley	:	:	109,6	120,6	131,7	130,4	125,2	124,8
11D Malting barley	:	:	114,2	129,4	141,3	134,7	119,3	123,7
11E Oats	:	:	109,7	115,4	126,8	139,0	115,1	111,6
11F Grain-maize	:	:	114,6	129,3	144,3	150,0	152,7	150,3
11G Paddy rice	:	:	133,5	161,4	160,5	185,1	193,6	176,3
11H Others	:	:	104,5	111,9	117,6	113,2	104,5	:
12 Root crops	81,1	94,7	106,2	122,7	141,7	153,3	124,1	147,6
12A Potatoes for consumption	97,7	106,9	123,1	154,9	178,5	215,6	121,2	160,1
12B Sugar beet	70,7	86,8	95,8	103,6	120,6	117,3	126,2	141,6
12C Others	85,7	103,5	108,0	114,9	121,4	122,2	119,1	119,9
13 Fruit	50,5	86,0	115,4	131,3	132,5	152,0	162,4	180,2
13A Fresh fruit	:	:	117,4	134,3	134,1	152,5	161,8	178,2
13B Nuts and dried fruit	:	:	97,5	103,9	117,6	147,3	168,3	198,5
14 Fresh vegetables	55,5	86,9	124,6	129,2	152,4	160,7	171,8	164,8
15 Wine must / Wine	52,3	99,9	102,8	123,0	128,4	132,8	155,9	165,0
16 Olives and olive oil	62,2	86,9	114,9	130,8	159,1	175,7	221,8	228,2
17 Seeds	71,0	93,2	108,3	123,1	150,6	156,5	143,8	157,5
18 Flowers, ornamental plants and tree-nursery products	70,2	91,7	105,1	116,1	125,6	121,3	134,2	131,9
19 Other crop products	57,8	86,7	119,3	140,8	165,7	183,2	200,1	210,6
19A Pulses	:	:	129,6	151,6	185,2	172,9	191,5	196,7
19B Oilseeds	:	:	113,3	130,3	148,0	150,1	146,0	142,9
19C Raw tobacco	:	:	117,9	142,2	164,4	189,4	215,5	227,3
19D Cotton	:	:	123,5	171,4	213,3	278,1	305,1	324,2
19E Others	:	:	122,8	131,6	158,5	177,6	203,5	230,1
2 ANIMALS AND ANIMAL PRODUCTS	71,4	93,9	111,8	124,1	129,0	133,8	137,5	136,1
21 Animals (for slaughter and export)	73,4	94,7	113,5	127,0	129,4	134,1	137,0	133,1
21A Calves	73,8	97,9	120,0	135,9	143,4	146,7	156,8	162,3
21B Cattle excl. calves	70,2	95,0	112,5	126,1	129,9	129,8	130,9	126,3
21C Pigs	83,9	95,2	112,5	126,5	120,1	127,7	129,9	121,5
21D Sheep and lambs	58,0	94,5	120,3	132,1	146,2	151,7	158,8	161,3
21E Poultry	67,0	92,4	111,5	122,2	131,9	143,4	147,0	146,4
21E1 Chickens	65,9	92,9	114,6	124,3	135,2	144,5	148,9	149,1
21E2 Other poultry	69,7	91,4	103,7	116,7	123,5	140,5	142,3	139,7
21F Other animals	55,1	89,8	117,6	134,0	145,8	154,0	160,2	164,3
22 Milk	69,3	94,1	108,4	121,7	130,9	133,3	140,1	144,5
23 Eggs	64,7	84,1	113,7	109,0	114,7	133,6	125,5	116,2
24 Other animal products	62,9	97,6	106,4	119,7	129,2	137,7	161,8	177,7

* = forecast.

214

1975	1979	1981	1982	1983	1984	1985	1986*	
				EUR 10 DEFLATED INDEX/INDICES DÉFLATÉS				
112,8	106,5	98,8	98,4	95,8	92,5	88,5	85,3	TOTAL
115,1	107,2	98,1	98,4	95,8	92,1	87,8	84,7	TOTAL (sans fruits et légumes)
108,7	106,3	98,1	97,1	96,7	93,1	88,1	86,6	Produits végétaux
113,2	108,1	95,9	96,7	97,0	92,1	86,2	85,7	PRODUITS VÉGÉTAUX (sans fruits et légumes)
112,1	107,0	98,6	97,1	96,3	89,2	80,7	78,4	Céréales et riz
:	:	98,6	95,4	94,2	85,7	77,9	77,4	Blé tendre
:	:	93,6	92,8	91,5	86,8	78,8	78,1	Blé dur
:	:	97,4	97,0	98,0	90,9	81,8	78,2	Orge fourragère
:	:	102,4	106,2	109,5	99,0	82,9	93,3	Orge de brasserie
:	:	98,7	94,8	97,0	100,3	78,0	73,3	Avoine
:	:	98,9	97,7	97,2	92,0	86,4	79,7	Maïs-grain
:	:	113,0	117,1	101,1	104,8	99,5	84,4	Riz non décortiqué
:	:	96,4	96,1	95,9	88,8	78,6	77,9	Autres
134,3	108,2	94,2	97,7	104,7	104,3	77,8	88,5	Plantes sarclées
170,0	124,3	108,0	120,7	130,3	142,4	70,3	91,6	Pommes de terre de consommation
113,4	98,1	85,6	83,7	89,5	81,5	81,6	86,6	Betteraves sucrières
120,8	112,6	99,7	98,7	99,4	95,8	90,4	89,8	Autres
93,9	102,3	99,2	98,1	87,3	90,1	87,5	89,8	Fruits
:	:	101,3	101,0	89,3	91,7	88,9	91,3	Fruits frais
:	:	80,3	71,7	68,5	75,0	74,6	76,5	Fruits secs
100,2	101,5	108,2	98,3	104,0	100,5	98,7	88,4	Légumes frais
97,3	117,2	89,3	93,5	86,5	82,4	89,9	89,6	Moût/Vin
133,6	106,2	95,8	92,5	96,4	93,0	104,1	94,7	Olives et huile d'olive
114,9	105,9	96,2	98,5	111,2	107,0	91,1	95,7	Semences
107,4	102,3	95,0	95,3	95,7	88,6	92,1	88,7	Fleurs, plantes ornementales et produits de pépinière
108,1	102,8	101,5	103,5	107,1	104,6	100,5	93,8	Autres produits végétaux
:	:	111,3	113,7	124,9	104,8	104,3	99,1	Légumes secs
:	:	101,0	105,1	110,3	105,2	96,6	91,7	Graines oléagineuses
:	:	97,9	99,9	98,8	99,3	98,6	90,7	Tabac brut
:	:	99,2	113,9	117,6	129,6	119,0	102,8	Coton
:	:	103,9	96,2	101,0	99,6	98,0	94,8	Autres
116,1	106,7	99,4	99,4	95,1	92,1	88,7	84,2	ANIMAUX ET PRODUITS ANIMAUX
119,7	107,8	100,8	101,5	94,9	91,6	87,8	91,4	Animaux (boucherie et exportation)
121,1	111,6	105,5	106,4	101,5	94,8	94,0	92,0	Veaux
114,5	108,1	99,9	101,0	96,3	90,0	85,8	80,1	Bovins sans veaux
128,1	106,4	101,4	103,9	91,7	91,8	88,1	78,8	Porcs
106,6	111,1	104,3	101,5	101,9	96,8	92,4	87,9	Moutons
121,7	107,7	97,5	94,7	92,4	92,7	88,2	83,2	Volailles
118,9	108,1	100,2	96,4	94,6	93,4	89,0	84,0	Poulets
128,8	106,6	90,7	90,5	86,7	90,7	86,1	81,2	Autres volailles
107,4	107,0	100,3	98,9	94,3	89,7	84,4	80,8	Autres animaux
111,3	106,4	96,7	98,2	97,7	93,2	92,2	91,8	Lait
108,1	96,2	100,9	86,6	83,7	90,1	79,0	69,3	Œufs
105,1	113,1	92,9	93,3	91,6	88,3	92,0	89,9	Autres produits animaux

* = prévision.

(EXCLUDING VAT)   (SANS TVA)

(1980 = 100)

| | Input I | | | | Input II | | | Input I | | | | Input II | |
	TOTAL	Feeding-stuffs/ Alim. des animaux	Fertil., soil improv./ Engrais & amend.	Energy and lubric./ Énergie & lubrif.	Machin-ery/ Machines	Build-ings/ Ouvrages	TOTAL	Feeding-stuffs/ Alim. des animaux	Fertil., soil improv./ Engrais & amend.	Energy and lubric./ Énergie & lubrif.	Machin-ery/ Machines	Build-ings/ Ouvrages
			EUR 10						BELGIQUE/BELGIË			

NOMINAL INDEX   **INDICES NOMINAUX**

	TOTAL	Feeding-stuffs	Fertil.	Energy	Machinery	Buildings	TOTAL	Feeding-stuffs	Fertil.	Energy	Machinery	Buildings
1975	66,5	69,1	68,7	50,9	60,8	53,0	80,3	84,7	82,2	57,0	72,7	65,4
1976	74,6	80,1	70,5	57,2	67,8	60,0	89,3	95,0	87,9	60,6	81,0	74,6
1977	81,0	88,7	73,2	62,5	75,5	68,2	89,3	96,6	87,1	63,3	85,1	80,7
1978	82,2	86,6	78,2	64,2	81,7	74,9	90,6	90,5	84,4	62,8	88,5	84,2
1979	89,4	92,6	84,3	78,7	90,1	85,1	87,5	94,8	89,0	72,1	94,1	91,7
1980	100,0	100,0	100,0	100,0	100,0	100,0	100,0	100,0	100,0	100,0	100,0	100,0
1981	113,1	113,1	113,3	121,9	111,8	114,4	109,4	108,6	111,4	122,0	104,0	109,2
1982	123,1	120,7	124,7	137,7	122,8	128,7	121,0	119,1	129,0	137,6	118,5	118,8
1983	132,3	132,0	129,3	145,0	134,2	140,3	131,6	130,8	129,6	146,1	129,3	125,9
1984	140,5	139,8	133,9	154,1	151,6	148,4	139,2	137,2	139,2	163,5	140,0	135,6
1985	142,5	134,5	143,3	166,0	161,1	157,9	136,4	130,7	148,1	161,7	150,8	142,1
1986*	138,9	132,4	135,6	132,9	171,1	165,1	129,0	125,9	141,9	101,5	161,4	139,8

% TAV   **% TAV**

	TOTAL	Feeding-stuffs	Fertil.	Energy	Machinery	Buildings	TOTAL	Feeding-stuffs	Fertil.	Energy	Machinery	Buildings
1984/1975	7,8	7,3	6,9	11,7	9,6	10,8	5,7	4,9	5,4	11,1	6,8	7,6
1985/1984	1,4	−3,8	7,0	7,7	6,3	6,4	−2,0	−4,7	6,4	−1,1	7,7	4,8
1986/1985*	−2,5	−1,6	−5,4	−19,9	6,2	4,6	−5,4	−3,7	−4,2	−37,3	7,0	−1,6

DEFLATED INDEX   **INDICES DÉFLATÉS**

	TOTAL	Feeding-stuffs	Fertil.	Energy	Machinery	Buildings	TOTAL	Feeding-stuffs	Fertil.	Energy	Machinery	Buildings
1975	107,9	112,7	110,2	80,7	100,2	91,5	109,3	115,3	111,9	77,6	98,9	89,0
1976	109,8	118,0	102,7	82,5	101,3	92,8	111,3	118,4	109,6	75,6	101,0	93,0
1977	108,4	118,7	97,4	82,8	102,1	94,5	105,5	112,8	101,4	73,7	99,0	93,9
1978	102,5	118,1	97,0	79,4	102,7	95,7	97,5	100,9	94,0	70,0	98,6	93,8
1979	101,4	105,2	95,3	88,5	102,9	98,1	98,2	101,7	95,0	76,9	100,4	97,8
1980	100,0	100,0	100,0	100,0	100,0	100,0	100,0	100,0	100,0	100,0	100,0	100,0
1981	100,8	100,8	100,9	109,3	98,9	100,5	101,6	100,9	103,5	113,4	96,6	101,5
1982	99,3	97,1	100,4	112,2	97,7	100,6	103,4	101,8	110,2	117,6	101,2	101,5
1983	98,5	97,9	95,7	109,5	97,7	99,8	104,4	103,8	102,8	115,9	102,6	99,9
1984	97,9	96,8	93,0	109,5	102,0	97,9	103,9	102,4	103,9	122,1	104,5	101,2
1985	93,5	87,3	94,4	110,8	101,6	97,2	97,1	93,0	105,4	115,1	107,3	101,1
1986*	87,6	82,5	86,6	83,2	103,7	97,4	90,6	88,5	99,7	71,3	113,4	98,2

% TAV   **% TAV**

	TOTAL	Feeding-stuffs	Fertil.	Energy	Machinery	Buildings	TOTAL	Feeding-stuffs	Fertil.	Energy	Machinery	Buildings
1984/1975	−1,0	−1,5	−1,7	3,1	0,2	0,7	−0,5	−1,2	−0,7	4,6	0,6	1,3
1985/1984	−4,5	−9,8	1,5	1,2	−0,4	−0,7	−6,5	−9,2	1,4	−5,7	2,7	−0,1
1986/1985*	−6,3	−5,5	−8,3	−24,9	2,1	−0,2	−6,7	−4,8	−5,4	−38,1	5,7	−2,9

* = forecast/estimation.

EC INDICES OF PURCHASE PRICES OF THE MEANS OF AGRICULTURAL PRODUCTION

INDICES CE DES PRIX D'ACHAT DES MOYENS DE PRODUCTION AGRICOLE

| **I F 5** |

(EXCLUDING VAT)   (SANS TVA)

(1980 = 100)

	Input I				Input II		Input I				Input II	
	TOTAL	Feeding-stuffs/ Alim. des animaux	Fertil., soil improv./ Engrais & amend.	Energy and lubric./ Énergie & lubrif.	Machin-ery/ Machines	Build-ings/ Ouvrages	TOTAL	Feeding-stuffs/ Alim. des animaux	Fertil., soil improv./ Engrais & amend.	Energy and lubric./ Énergie & lubrif.	Machin-ery/ Machines	Build-ings/ Ouvrages
	DANMARK						**BR DEUTSCHLAND**					

NOMINAL INDEX / **INDICES NOMINAUX**

1975	69,7	67,9	92,4	49,5	66,6	66,2	83,6	90,6	91,4	59,4	83,6	71,9
1976	77,7	81,8	80,9	53,4	71,2	71,2	90,7	102,8	92,4	63,9	87,5	74,5
1977	83,2	89,9	75,3	54,8	76,7	77,6	92,0	105,4	90,5	63,8	91,7	78,9
1978	81,1	83,5	77,7	56,2	83,8	83,0	89,0	96,4	90,5	63,9	94,0	83,5
1979	86,8	88,8	81,3	72,2	90,6	89,0	93,8	96,8	92,1	85,0	96,3	90,1
1980	100,0	100,0	100,0	100,0	100,0	100,0	100,0	100,0	100,0	100,0	100,0	100,0
1981	117,3	117,3	123,7	126,9	109,5	112,5	109,8	108,0	112,0	117,2	104,6	106,2
1982	131,0	129,0	148,3	144,5	124,3	128,1	113,8	108,8	117,9	122,9	111,4	109,4
1983	139,0	140,0	145,8	140,3	136,8	138,5	114,6	111,3	111,3	118,7	115,7	111,2
1984	147,0	147,0	166,5	144,1	141,6	147,5	117,1	114,1	109,5	123,2	119,2	113,5
1985	142,8	133,5	176,5	149,0	146,8	155,3	114,9	103,9	115,4	127,5	121,8	114,1
1986*	134,4	127,3	156,6	110,4	152,8	160,3	106,2	97,6	110,6	91,2	124,3	115,6

% TAV

1984/1975	5,1	8,0	6,1	11,3	7,8	8,3	3,4	2,3	1,8	7,6	3,6	4,7
1985/1984	−2,9	−9,2	6,0	3,4	3,7	5,3	−1,9	−8,9	5,4	3,5	2,2	0,5
1986/1985*	−5,9	−4,6	−11,3	−25,9	4,1	3,2	−7,6	−6,1	−4,2	−28,5	2,1	1,3

DEFLATED INDEX / **INDICES DÉFLATÉS**

1975	114,3	111,3	151,5	81,2	109,2	108,6	102,0	110,5	111,4	72,5	102,0	87,7
1976	117,0	123,2	121,8	80,4	107,2	107,2	106,0	120,1	108,0	74,7	102,2	87,1
1977	113,3	122,5	102,6	74,7	104,5	105,8	103,8	118,8	102,1	71,9	103,4	89,0
1978	99,9	102,8	95,7	69,3	103,2	102,2	97,7	105,8	99,3	70,1	103,1	91,6
1979	97,5	99,8	91,4	81,1	101,8	100,0	98,8	102,0	97,1	89,6	101,5	95,0
1980	100,0	100,0	100,0	100,0	100,0	100,0	100,0	100,0	100,0	100,0	100,0	100,0
1981	105,1	105,0	110,7	113,6	98,1	100,7	103,3	101,6	105,3	110,3	98,4	99,9
1982	106,5	104,9	120,6	117,5	101,1	104,1	101,7	97,2	105,3	109,8	99,6	97,8
1983	105,7	106,5	110,9	106,7	104,0	105,3	99,2	96,3	96,2	102,7	100,1	96,2
1984	105,2	105,1	119,1	103,1	101,3	105,5	98,9	96,3	92,5	104,1	100,7	95,9
1985	97,5	91,2	120,6	101,8	100,3	106,1	95,0	85,8	95,4	105,3	100,6	94,3
1986*	88,6	83,9	103,2	72,8	100,7	105,7	88,0	80,8	91,6	75,5	103,0	95,8

% TAV

1984/1975	−0,8	−0,6	−2,4	2,4	−0,7	−0,3	−0,3	−1,4	−1,8	3,7	−0,1	0,9
1985/1984	−7,3	−13,2	1,3	−1,3	−1,0	0,6	−3,9	−10,9	3,1	1,2	−0,1	−1,7
1986/1985*	−9,1	−8,0	−14,4	−28,5	0,4	0,4	−7,4	−5,8	−4,0	−28,3	2,4	1,6

* = forecast/estimation.

(EXCLUDING VAT)   (SANS TVA)

(1980 = 100)

	Input I				Input II		Input I				Input II	
	TOTAL	Feeding-stuffs/ Alim. des animaux	Fertil., soil improv./ Engrais & amend.	Energy and lubric./ Énergie & lubrif.	Machin-ery/ Machines	Build-ings/ Ouvrages	TOTAL	Feeding-stuffs/ Alim. des animaux	Fertil., soil improv./ Engrais & amend.	Energy and lubric./ Énergie & lubrif.	Machin-ery/ Machines	Build-ings/ Ouvrages
			IRELAND						ITALIA			
NOMINAL INDEX												**INDICES NOMINAUX**
1975	55,1	55,1	67,4	40,6	46,9	45,6	53,6	52,2	51,1	51,6	45,7	39,5
1976	62,9	65,7	68,2	49,5	60,7	53,5	65,1	65,4	58,0	61,6	53,9	48,0
1977	76,5	84,7	74,6	57,9	75,4	63,3	75,7	77,4	65,0	76,2	64,0	58,5
1978	79,2	86,0	78,5	56,0	85,9	71,1	80,8	82,6	71,1	77,3	72,3	67,1
1979	88,6	96,0	85,2	69,8	93,6	83,0	88,1	89,3	81,0	82,3	86,0	80,1
1980	100,0	100,0	100,0	100,0	100,0	100,0	100,0	100,0	100,0	100,0	100,0	100,0
1981	114,2	108,8	113,9	134,7	112,2	117,2	119,4	121,6	126,8	128,1	118,3	124,0
1982	125,2	117,1	121,1	155,0	127,1	130,9	133,2	131,2	158,3	158,4	130,2	148,2
1983	135,0	129,0	122,6	172,7	137,9	140,8	146,9	147,5	180,3	167,8	147,1	167,0
1984	145,5	137,7	134,6	182,0	155,1	151,0	160,0	160,4	177,0	178,2	184,9	175,8
1985	147,5	129,5	147,4	190,1	156,8	157,7	163,1	157,7	181,2	204,6	200,4	191,6
1986*	140,5	126,9	132,6	155,6	163,9	162,5	161,4	158,1	180,9	155,9	214,4	198,4
% TAV												**% TAV**
1984/1975	10,2	9,6	7,2	16,2	12,7	12,7	11,6	11,9	13,2	13,2	15,0	16,1
1985/1984	1,4	−6,0	9,5	4,5	1,1	4,3	1,9	−1,7	2,4	14,8	8,4	9,0
1986/1985*	−4,7	−2,0	−10,0	−18,1	4,5	3,0	−1,0	0,3	−0,2	−23,8	6,9	3,5
DEFLATED INDEX												**INDICES DÉFLATÉS**
1975	106,3	106,4	130,1	78,4	90,5	87,9	115,6	112,7	110,2	111,3	98,7	85,1
1976	102,9	107,6	111,7	81,1	99,4	87,6	120,4	121,0	107,1	113,8	99,7	88,6
1977	110,2	122,1	107,4	83,4	108,7	91,3	118,1	120,8	101,3	118,8	99,9	91,2
1978	106,0	115,1	105,1	75,0	115,0	95,1	112,5	114,9	99,1	107,5	100,6	93,4
1979	104,7	113,4	100,8	82,5	110,6	98,1	106,8	108,2	98,2	99,8	104,2	97,1
1980	100,0	100,0	100,0	100,0	100,0	100,0	100,0	100,0	100,0	100,0	100,0	100,0
1981	94,8	90,4	94,6	111,9	93,2	97,3	101,3	103,2	107,7	108,7	100,4	105,2
1982	88,7	83,0	85,9	109,9	90,1	92,8	97,1	95,6	115,4	115,4	94,9	108,0
1983	86,6	82,8	78,7	110,8	88,5	90,4	93,3	93,8	114,6	106,7	93,5	106,2
1984	86,0	81,4	79,6	107,5	91,6	89,2	91,8	92,0	101,6	102,2	106,1	100,9
1985	82,7	72,6	82,6	106,5	87,9	88,4	85,7	82,9	95,2	107,5	105,3	100,7
1986*	75,8	68,5	71,6	84,0	88,5	87,7	80,1	78,5	89,8	77,4	106,4	98,5
% TAV												**% TAV**
1984/1975	−2,1	−2,7	−4,8	3,2	0,1	0,1	−2,3	−2,0	−0,8	−0,8	0,7	1,7
1985/1984	−3,8	−10,8	3,8	−0,9	−4,0	−0,9	−6,6	−9,9	−6,3	5,2	−0,8	−0,2
1986/1985*	−8,3	−5,6	−13,3	−21,1	0,7	−0,8	−6,5	−5,3	−5,7	−28,0	1,0	−2,2

* = forecast/estimation.

EC INDICES OF PURCHASE PRICES OF THE MEANS OF AGRICULTURAL PRODUCTION

IF 5

INDICES CE DES PRIX D'ACHAT DES MOYENS DE PRODUCTION AGRICOLE

(EXCLUDING VAT)

(SANS TVA)

(1980 = 100)

	Input I				Input II		Input I				Input II	
	TOTAL	Feeding-stuffs/ Alim. des animaux	Fertil., soil improv./ Engrais & amend.	Energy and lubric./ Énergie & lubrif.	Machin-ery/ Machines	Build-ings/ Ouvrages	TOTAL	Feeding-stuffs/ Alim. des animaux	Fertil., soil improv./ Engrais & amend.	Energy and lubric./ Énergie & lubrif.	Machin-ery/ Machines	Build-ings/ Ouvrages
	ELLAS						FRANCE					
NOMINAL INDEX											**INDICES NOMINAUX**	
1975	47,9	51,6	45,3	40,7	56,5	35,0	65,6	70,4	64,2	46,8	63,6	58,7
1976	52,2	55,4	53,2	43,6	63,6	41,5	69,6	75,2	63,8	52,3	70,1	65,3
1977	59,1	64,5	55,4	49,2	70,4	51,2	75,7	85,2	66,1	57,9	75,4	73,2
1978	63,6	69,8	56,6	52,0	76,6	63,3	79,7	86,5	72,7	62,4	81,5	78,5
1979	76,2	78,2	68,2	70,6	83,8	83,0	87,4	92,0	80,6	73,7	89,6	87,6
1980	100,0	100,0	100,0	100,0	100,0	100,0	100,0	100,0	100,0	100,0	100,0	100,0
1981	123,8	132,4	111,1	121,2	123,6	112,2	112,8	113,8	110,3	123,1	113,5	110,5
1982	142,2	158,6	111,1	132,3	141,8	123,5	126,2	126,9	120,7	143,7	129,3	123,8
1983	177,5	202,0	149,4	157,6	177,6	149,5	138,5	141,4	128,7	155,4	142,0	133,1
1984	203,9	234,6	153,1	177,7	209,4	173,5	148,8	152,8	137,9	166,3	152,1	142,2
1985	239,1	274,0	160,6	215,1	251,2	202,8	153,5	147,9	151,5	179,3	160,1	148,2
1986*	279,3	315,7	184,3	247,5	329,2	249,1	150,1	144,1	141,3	146,2	168,7	151,6
% TAV											**% TAV**	
1984/1975	15,6	16,4	13,0	15,9	14,0	17,4	8,5	8,1	7,9	13,5	9,1	9,3
1985/1984	17,3	16,8	4,9	21,0	20,0	16,9	2,2	−6,1	9,8	7,8	5,4	4,2
1986/1985*	16,8	15,0	14,8	15,1	31,1	22,8	−2,2	−2,5	−6,7	−18,5	5,4	2,3
DEFLATED INDEX											**INDICES DÉFLATÉS**	
1975	101,8	109,7	96,2	86,6	120,2	74,3	108,0	115,8	105,5	76,9	104,7	96,6
1976	97,9	103,9	99,8	81,9	119,3	77,8	104,5	112,9	95,8	78,6	105,2	98,1
1977	98,9	108,0	92,7	82,3	117,8	85,6	103,8	116,9	90,7	79,4	103,5	100,4
1978	94,6	103,8	84,1	77,3	113,9	94,1	100,3	108,8	91,4	78,5	102,7	98,7
1979	95,1	97,7	85,2	88,2	104,6	103,6	99,3	104,5	91,6	83,7	101,8	99,6
1980	100,0	100,0	100,0	100,0	100,0	100,0	100,0	100,0	100,0	100,0	100,0	100,0
1981	99,4	106,4	89,3	97,4	99,3	90,2	99,5	100,4	97,3	108,5	100,1	97,5
1982	94,4	105,4	73,8	87,9	94,2	82,0	99,5	100,1	95,2	113,3	102,0	97,6
1983	97,8	111,4	82,3	86,9	97,9	82,4	99,6	101,8	92,6	111,8	102,1	95,7
1984	95,0	109,3	71,3	82,8	97,6	80,8	99,7	102,4	92,4	111,5	102,0	95,3
1985	93,3	106,9	62,7	83,9	98,0	79,1	97,2	93,5	95,9	113,5	101,3	93,8
1986*	88,5	100,1	58,4	78,4	104,3	79,0	92,6	88,8	87,1	90,2	104,0	93,4
% TAV											**% TAV**	
1984/1975	−0,7	−0,1	−3,0	−0,4	−2,1	0,8	−0,8	−1,2	−1,3	3,8	−0,3	−0,1
1985/1984	−1,8	−2,2	−12,1	1,3	0,4	−2,1	−3,4	−11,3	3,7	1,8	−0,6	−1,6
1986/1985*	−5,1	−6,4	−6,9	6,4	6,4	−0,1	−4,7	−5,0	−9,2	−20,5	2,7	−0,4

* = forecast/estimation.

EC INDICES OF PURCHASE PRICES OF
THE MEANS OF AGRICULTURAL PRODUCTION

I F 5

INDICES CE DES PRIX D'ACHAT
DES MOYENS DE PRODUCTION AGRICOLE

(EXCLUDING VAT)

(SANS TVA)

(1980 = 100)

	Input I				Input II		Input I				Input II	
	TOTAL	Feeding-stuffs/ Alim. des animaux	Fertil., soil improv./ Engrais & amend.	Energy and lubric./ Énergie & lubrif.	Machin-ery/ Machines	Build-ings/ Ouvrages	TOTAL	Feeding-stuffs/ Alim. des animaux	Fertil., soil improv./ Engrais & amend.	Energy and lubric./ Énergie & lubrif.	Machin-ery/ Machines	Build-ings/ Ouvrages
	LUXEMBOURG						NEDERLAND					
NOMINAL INDEX											INDICES NOMINAUX	
1975	79,4	86,0	79,0	63,1	72,9	75,5	78,6	83,5	82,3	50,9	74,9	74,7
1976	86,8	93,2	85,2	67,2	80,9	80,2	86,6	92,6	87,1	58,8	79,9	80,4
1977	89,9	97,2	86,0	69,1	85,0	82,9	90,5	96,3	88,3	64,5	86,5	85,5
1978	88,5	93,1	84,0	68,6	87,9	85,5	86,1	87,6	89,6	68,4	91,4	88,6
1979	91,9	94,4	88,8	81,1	93,2	91,3	93,1	95,1	89,8	78,7	95,9	92,9
1980	100,0	100,0	100,0	100,0	100,0	100,0	100,0	100,0	100,0	100,0	100,0	100,0
1981	109,5	109,0	112,2	116,8	104,6	105,7	109,2	107,2	111,3	124,5	104,0	105,8
1982	118,7	117,0	123,3	131,3	119,1	109,7	114,2	107,9	120,5	149,4	108,8	108,4
1983	129,7	132,7	126,8	144,3	129,3	112,8	117,5	112,2	103,8	160,4	114,6	110,9
1984	138,0	141,8	130,1	156,6	139,0	117,7	121,5	114,0	106,5	177,1	120,1	113,7
1985	136,2	128,3	138,5	164,0	149,8	120,0	116,5	103,5	116,7	177,9	124,1	115,4
1986*	132,6	123,9	134,0	130,7	160,7	124,4	105,1	94,4	107,6	122,6	128,1	118,1
% TAV												**% TAV**
1984/1975	5,7	5,1	5,1	9,5	6,7	4,5	4,5	3,2	2,6	13,2	4,8	4,3
1985/1984	− 1,3	− 9,5	6,5	4,7	7,8	2,0	− 4,1	− 9,2	9,6	0,5	3,3	1,5
1986/1985*	− 2,6	− 3,4	− 3,2	− 20,3	7,3	3,7	− 9,8	− 8,8	− 7,8	31,1	3,2	2,3
DEFLATED INDEX											INDICES DÉFLATÉS	
1975	106,6	115,4	106,1	84,6	97,8	101,3	106,1	112,7	111,1	68,7	101,0	100,9
1976	106,1	113,9	104,2	82,1	98,9	98,1	107,2	114,6	107,8	72,8	98,9	99,5
1977	103,0	111,3	98,5	79,1	97,3	94,9	105,2	112,0	102,7	75,0	100,6	99,4
1978	98,4	103,5	93,3	76,3	97,7	95,0	96,1	97,8	100,0	76,3	102,0	98,9
1979	97,7	100,3	94,4	86,2	99,1	97,0	99,6	101,7	96,1	84,2	102,6	99,3
1980	100,0	100,0	100,0	100,0	100,0	100,0	100,0	100,0	100,0	100,0	100,0	100,0
1981	101,3	100,9	103,8	108,0	96,8	97,8	102,4	100,4	104,3	116,6	97,5	99,2
1982	100,4	99,0	104,4	111,1	100,8	92,8	101,2	95,7	106,8	132,4	96,5	96,1
1983	101,0	103,3	98,7	112,4	100,7	87,9	101,4	96,8	89,5	138,4	98,9	95,7
1984	101,8	104,5	95,9	115,5	102,4	86,7	101,6	95,3	89,0	148,1	100,4	95,1
1985	96,4	90,7	98,0	116,0	106,0	84,9	95,3	84,6	95,5	145,4	101,5	94,4
1986*	92,9	87,4	94,6	92,2	113,4	87,8	85,7	76,9	87,7	99,9	104,4	96,2
% TAV												**% TAV**
1984/1975	− 0,5	− 1,0	− 1,0	3,2	0,5	− 1,5	− 0,4	− 1,7	− 2,2	8,0	− 0,1	− 0,6
1985/1984	− 5,3	− 13,2	2,2	0,4	3,5	− 2,1	− 6,3	− 11,2	7,3	− 1,8	1,1	− 0,7
1986/1985*	− 3,6	− 3,6	− 3,5	− 20,5	7,0	3,4	− 10,1	− 9,1	− 8,2	− 31,3	2,9	1,9

* = forecast/estimation.

(EXCLUDING VAT)

(SANS TVA)

(1980 = 100)

	Input I				Input II			Input I				Input II	
	TOTAL	Feeding-stuffs/ Alim. des animaux	Fertil., soil improv./ Engrais & amend.	Energy and lubric./ Énergie & lubrif.	Machin-ery/ Machines	Build-ings/ Ouvrages	TOTAL	Feeding-stuffs/ Alim. des animaux	Fertil., soil improv./ Engrais & amend.	Energy and lubric./ Énergie & lubrif.	Machin-ery/ Machines	Build-ings/ Ouvrages

UNITED KINGDOM

NOMINAL INDEX   INDICES NOMINAUX

1975	54,7	57,7	55,5	42,1	45,5	48,5
1976	67,8	72,9	59,4	51,8	55,7	56,9
1977	78,3	86,1	68,4	62,0	68,4	65,4
1978	80,1	83,5	79,2	64,3	77,7	72,3
1979	89,3	93,7	85,5	76,5	87,1	83,1
1980	100,0	100,0	100,0	100,0	100,0	100,0
1981	110,0	108,0	110,2	120,8	107,7	108,8
1982	117,8	113,9	115,5	137,5	115,9	118,3
1983	126,0	123,7	116,8	151,2	121,7	126,7
1984	130,9	127,0	120,2	155,1	129,4	135,0
1985	132,5	122,6	127,7	169,3	137,1	142,1
1986*	131,3	123,8	115,1	140,8	144,5	155,1

% TAV   % TAV

1984/1975	9,1	8,2	8,0	13,9	11,0	10,8
1985/1984	1,2	−3,5	6,2	9,2	6,0	5,3
1986/1985*	−0,9	1,0	−8,9	−16,8	5,4	9,1

DEFLATED INDEX   INDICES DÉFLATÉS

1975	107,1	112,9	108,6	82,3	89,1	94,9
1976	113,8	122,3	99,8	86,9	93,5	95,5
1977	113,5	124,7	99,1	89,8	99,1	94,8
1978	107,2	111,7	106,0	86,1	104,0	96,7
1979	105,4	110,6	100,8	90,3	102,7	98,0
1980	100,0	100,0	100,0	100,0	100,0	100,0
1981	98,4	96,5	98,5	107,9	96,3	97,2
1982	97,0	93,8	95,1	113,1	95,4	97,3
1983	99,2	97,3	91,9	119,0	95,8	99,7
1984	98,1	95,2	90,1	116,2	97,0	101,2
1985	93,6	86,7	90,2	119,6	96,9	100,4
1986*	89,7	84,6	78,7	96,2	98,7	106,0

% TAV   % TAV

1984/1975	−0,9	−1,7	−1,9	3,5	0,9	0,6
1985/1984	−4,6	−8,9	0,1	2,9	−0,1	−0,8
1986/1985*	−4,2	−2,4	−12,7	−19,6	1,9	5,6

* = forecast/estimation.

EC INDICES OF PURCHASE PRICES OF
THE MEANS OF AGRICULTURAL PRODUCTION

IF 5

(EXCLUDING VAT)

(1980 = 100)

		1975	1979	1981	1982	1983	1984	1985	1986 (1)
		EUR 10 NOMINAL INDEX/INDICES NOMINAUX							
01	GOODS & SERVICES CURRENTLY CONSUMED IN AGRICULTURE	66,5	89,4	113,1	123,1	132,3	140,5	142,5	138,9
1	Seeds	65,9	95,3	105,6	117,4	132,0	148,2	141,8	144,2
2	Animals for rearing and production	58,2	94,3	114,0	133,0	132,9	149,0	157,7	161,3
3	Energy and lubricants	50,9	78,7	121,9	137,7	145,0	154,1	166,0	132,9
31	Fuels for heating	43,8	76,2	124,1	141,4	147,6	162,0	167,4	110,1
32	Motorfuels	46,3	75,5	124,7	137,9	145,6	154,0	169,1	129,8
33	Electricity	67,6	89,7	113,1	136,5	143,1	147,5	158,3	155,4
34	Lubricants	66,4	83,1	116,6	127,8	136,2	144,1	158,5	174,8
4	Fertilizers, soil improvers	68,7	84,3	113,3	124,7	129,3	133,9	143,3	135,6
41	Straight fertilizers	66,8	84,4	112,1	123,4	127,4	133,3	142,9	133,3
411	Nitrogenous fertilizers	66,0	84,2	111,5	122,5	124,7	129,6	138,8	127,1
412	Phosphatic fertilizers	71,8	83,3	115,4	129,5	142,5	154,3	166,2	161,9
413	Potassic fertilizers	67,6	87,5	113,4	123,7	132,7	139,5	150,3	153,2
42	Compound fertilizers	71,0	84,0	114,3	126,0	131,0	134,5	144,0	137,2
421	NP fertilizers	66,3	80,7	112,7	124,6	137,8	144,5	149,6	149,9
422	PK fertilizers	79,3	85,6	112,7	123,1	129,4	137,4	147,8	140,8
423	NPK fertilizers	69,1	84,0	115,1	127,1	130,4	131,9	141,9	134,0
43	Other fertilizers, soil improvers	60,7	86,5	113,1	121,0	127,5	132,2	137,7	141,2
5	Plant protection products	80,8	89,7	112,1	122,5	132,8	141,7	147,1	152,0
51	Fungicides	75,9	87,7	110,7	122,0	131,5	143,6	151,4	158,1
52	Insecticides	71,7	86,4	114,3	123,5	133,6	147,2	156,1	164,3
53	Herbicides	87,4	92,2	112,1	120,3	129,5	135,3	138,5	142,1
54	Other	78,6	88,8	113,0	139,0	162,3	167,7	167,5	165,1
6	Animal feedingstuffs	69,1	92,6	113,1	120,7	132,0	139,8	134,5	132,4
61	Straight feedingstuffs	59,9	90,9	117,3	126,4	140,5	150,0	149,1	151,1
611	Cereals and milling by-products	56,1	87,4	119,5	126,1	133,9	146,4	145,6	148,6
612	Oil-cakes	64,7	95,0	121,3	132,0	145,5	155,3	142,1	140,6
613	Products of animal origin	63,3	97,0	114,4	127,2	151,5	149,8	155,1	155,5
614	Other	61,7	88,8	108,1	119,0	140,4	156,0	161,4	167,1
62	Compound feedingstuffs	72,1	93,1	111,8	118,9	129,3	136,5	129,8	126,4
621	for calves	73,1	93,3	111,3	123,2	132,6	143,5	148,2	146,8
622	for cattle (excl. calves)	72,8	93,1	110,7	116,4	126,1	132,4	121,5	116,9
623	for pigs	75,2	93,1	110,6	116,6	126,4	132,2	123,7	120,1
624	for poultry	68,1	93,4	114,0	121,9	133,5	141,8	137,1	134,1
625	Other	63,9	90,1	114,1	124,5	140,4	151,8	146,8	147,4
7	Material and small tools	67,2	88,6	110,0	120,6	130,6	141,1	149,8	156,4
8	Maintenance and repair of plant	63,6	89,7	110,9	121,3	131,0	139,0	147,2	155,8
9	Maintenance and repair of agricultural buildings and other buildings	59,9	87,5	111,3	121,5	129,1	135,8	142,0	147,9
10	Veterinary services	66,0	90,3	107,3	116,4	122,9	130,7	139,7	145,1
11	General expenses	65,0	91,0	110,3	120,6	129,2	138,0	145,6	150,6
02	GOODS AND SERVICES CONTRIBUTING TO AGRICULTURAL INVESTMENT	58,2	88,4	112,6	124,8	136,3	150,5	160,0	169,3
12	Machines & other equipment	60,8	90,1	111,8	122,8	134,2	151,6	161,1	171,1
121	Rotovators & other 2 wheel equipment	65,5	89,8	108,4	115,2	130,5	142,4	153,2	164,0
122	Machinery and plant for cultivating	61,2	89,0	112,2	130,4	140,3	145,1	152,9	160,5
123	Machinery & plant for harvesting	63,4	90,0	111,0	128,6	141,6	149,2	156,6	165,3
124	Farm machinery and installations	67,1	91,8	108,6	117,1	122,3	128,2	133,4	138,8
1241	for crop production	67,7	92,7	108,4	117,8	124,5	132,2	137,1	142,8
1242	for animal production	67,3	91,6	109,5	118,2	124,8	129,5	135,5	141,5
1243	Other	65,4	90,5	107,8	114,4	114,6	118,6	123,4	126,9
125	Tractors	56,3	89,7	113,6	121,1	134,6	164,4	176,8	189,8
126	Other vehicles	63,3	90,7	110,7	121,2	132,5	151,1	161,0	171,8
13	Buildings	53,0	85,1	114,4	128,7	140,3	148,4	157,9	165,1
131	Farm buildings	57,3	86,3	113,0	126,0	135,9	141,8	149,4	154,1
132	Engineering & soil improvement operations	41,6	81,7	118,2	136,0	152,3	166,3	180,6	194,9

(1) forecast.

**INDICES CE DES PRIX D'ACHAT
DES MOYENS DE PRODUCTION AGRICOLE**

(TVA EXCLUE)

(1980 = 100)

1975	1979	1981	1982	1983	1984	1985	1986(¹)		
				EUR 10 DEFLATED INDEX/INDICES DÉFLATÉS					
107,9	101,4	100,8	99,3	98,5	97,9	93,5	87,6	BIENS ET SERVICES DE CONSOMMATION COURANTE DE L'AGRICULTURE	01
111,4	108,8	93,8	94,1	97,4	101,7	91,3	89,2	Semences et plants	1
112,1	111,6	98,4	100,4	89,8	91,7	89,4	86,3	Animaux d'élevage et de rente	2
80,7	88,5	109,3	112,2	109,5	109,5	110,8	83,2	Énergie et lubrifiants	3
62,1	83,0	113,7	120,4	118,9	124,0	123,2	77,1	Combustibles	31
76,8	86,0	110,6	110,2	106,8	105,3	107,8	76,2	Carburants	32
108,1	101,2	101,6	111,0	108,2	105,3	106,5	102,4	Électricité	33
103,7	93,5	103,7	102,2	99,9	99,0	101,5	105,6	Lubrifiants	34
110,2	95,3	100,9	100,4	95,7	93,0	94,2	86,6	Engrais et amendements	4
105,2	95,1	100,2	100,1	95,0	93,2	94,9	85,7	Engrais simples	41
103,8	94,9	99,8	99,6	93,2	90,8	92,5	82,0	Engrais azotés	411
116,9	94,5	102,4	103,1	103,8	105,0	106,3	100,4	Engrais phosphatés	412
101,5	97,1	102,1	101,4	100,8	99,9	102,2	102,0	Engrais potassiques	413
115,7	95,4	101,5	100,7	96,1	92,6	93,9	86,5	Engrais composés	42
113,1	93,4	98,0	96,0	93,7	89,9	86,5	80,4	Engrais NP	421
119,8	95,3	100,9	100,1	97,5	97,5	99,8	93,5	Engrais PK	422
114,9	95,8	102,2	101,6	96,0	91,5	93,2	85,4	Engrais NPK	423
94,9	97,3	101,8	99,8	98,5	96,5	95,7	96,2	Autres engrais et amendements	43
133,7	102,3	99,3	97,7	97,5	96,9	94,2	93,9	Produits de protection des cultures	5
132,8	101,3	96,9	95,0	93,0	93,3	91,3	91,0	Fongicides	51
126,2	99,9	100,3	96,7	95,2	96,7	95,4	95,9	Insecticides	52
138,0	104,0	100,4	97,9	97,9	96,5	93,4	93,4	Herbicides	53
124,8	100,5	100,1	112,2	122,9	119,4	112,1	107,0	Autres	54
112,7	105,2	100,8	97,1	97,9	96,8	87,3	82,5	Aliments des animaux	6
111,0	106,7	102,0	97,0	96,9	94,9	86,8	83,1	Aliments simples	61
104,9	102,7	103,7	96,7	92,6	92,3	84,2	80,8	Céréales et sous-produits de meunerie	611
116,1	110,6	106,5	102,9	103,3	101,9	87,1	82,3	Tourteaux	612
119,9	114,3	99,3	96,8	102,7	93,9	90,8	87,4	Produits d'origine animale	613
111,7	104,2	93,7	90,5	95,1	95,5	89,7	85,7	Autres	614
113,3	104,7	100,4	97,1	98,1	97,5	87,5	82,4	Aliments composés	62
114,3	104,7	99,6	99,9	99,5	101,1	99,0	95,1	pour veaux	621
114,5	104,7	99,8	96,0	97,3	96,6	83,9	78,4	pour bovins (autres que veaux)	622
112,8	103,3	100,2	96,6	97,7	96,4	85,6	80,6	pour porcins	623
112,0	106,3	101,5	98,0	99,0	98,4	89,4	83,8	pour volailles	624
115,4	104,8	99,6	96,3	98,1	97,8	87,6	83,7	Autres	625
109,6	100,7	97,7	96,7	96,5	97,4	97,3	97,9	Matériel et petit outillage	7
98,3	100,4	99,8	99,6	100,4	100,6	101,1	103,6	Entretien & réparation du matériel	8
93,7	98,3	100,0	99,9	99,4	98,9	98,3	99,5	Entretien et réparation des bâtiments d'exploitation et autres ouvrages	9
110,4	102,9	95,3	93,1	90,7	90,1	91,0	92,0	Services vétérinaires	10
101,9	102,2	99,4	99,3	99,4	100,0	100,0	100,3	Frais généraux	11
97,3	101,3	99,5	98,7	98,4	100,6	100,1	101,6	BIENS ET SERVICES CONCOURANT AUX INVESTISSEMENTS DE L'AGRICULTURE	02
100,2	102,9	98,9	97,7	97,7	102,0	101,6	103,7	Machines et autres biens d'équipement	12
111,0	102,6	95,4	90,4	92,4	93,2	93,7	96,2	Motoculteurs & autres matér. à 2 roues	121
98,9	101,0	99,6	103,6	102,1	98,9	98,3	100,0	Machines et matériaux pour la culture	122
99,9	101,7	98,9	103,3	104,8	103,6	102,6	104,7	Machines et matériaux pour la récolte	123
106,2	103,4	97,7	96,3	94,3	93,6	92,6	93,6	Machines et installation à la ferme	124
109,7	104,7	97,0	95,9	94,2	94,2	92,3	92,9	pour la production végétale	1241
105,4	102,8	98,4	97,0	96,1	94,6	94,4	96,3	pour la production animale	1242
100,2	101,5	98,0	96,3	91,9	91,0	90,5	91,2	Autres	1243
98,2	103,9	99,5	94,5	95,1	106,0	105,9	108,2	Tracteurs	125
99,4	102,7	98,5	97,2	97,4	102,8	103,0	105,8	Autres véhicules	126
91,5	98,1	100,5	100,6	99,8	97,9	97,2	97,4	Ouvrages	13
94,2	98,2	100,3	100,4	99,4	97,1	96,4	96,2	Bâtiments d'exploitation	131
84,0	97,9	101,1	101,3	100,7	99,9	99,2	100,6	Ouvrages de génie civil & amél. des terres	132

(¹) prévision.

CONSUMER PRICES INDEX FOR FOOD

I F 6

INDICES DES PRIX A LA CONSOMMATION POUR DENRÉES ALIMENTAIRES

(1980 = 100)

	EUR-10	Belgique/ België	Danmark	BR Deutsch-land	Ellas	España	France	Ireland	Italia	Luxem-bourg	Neder-land	Portugal	United Kingdom

TOTAL INDEX — **INDICE GÉNÉRAL**

1975	60,5	73,5	61,0	82,0	47,0	42,6	60,8	51,8	46,4	74,5	74,1	36,7	51,1
1979	88,2	93,8	89,0	94,9	80,1	86,5	88,0	84,6	82,5	94,1	93,5	85,6	84,8
1981	111,7	107,6	111,7	106,3	124,5	114,6	113,4	120,4	117,8	108,1	106,7	120,0	111,9
1982	123,0	117,0	123,0	111,9	150,5	131,1	126,8	141,1	137,2	118,2	112,8	147,3	121,5
1983	132,7	126,0	131,5	115,6	181,4	147,0	139,0	155,8	157,3	128,4	115,9	184,3	127,1
1984	141,2	134,0	139,8	118,4	214,6	163,5	149,2	169,2	174,3	135,7	119,6	237,5	133,4
1985	149,1	140,5	146,4	121,0	256,3	178,0	158,0	178,4	190,3	141,3	122,3	284,1	141,5
1986	153,4	142,3	151,7	120,7	315,5	193,6	162,2	185,2	201,4	141,7	122,7	317,6	146,3

FOOD (excl. drinks and meals out) — **PRODUITS ALIMENTAIRES (sans boissons et repas à l'extérieur)**

1975	:	80,5	61,5	–	44,5	–	61,2	–	47,0	77,6	79,9	–	51,9
1979	90,7	96,5	90,9	95,8	78,4	91,6	90,6	91,5	86,2	96,6	96,3	79,6	89,5
1981	111,7	105,4	112,3	105,3	130,1	113,3	113,9	114,2	116,1	107,1	105,7	119,7	108,5
1982	124,0	115,6	123,7	110,3	157,5	130,9	128,3	128,0	133,8	119,6	111,7	149,4	117,0
1983	132,8	125,4	130,0	112,1	186,1	144,7	140,3	137,3	149,5	129,3	111,8	189,4	120,7
1984	142,3	134,9	141,8	114,2	219,9	163,6	151,7	151,1	163,2	138,8	115,2	251,1	127,4
1985	149,5	139,2	147,7	114,4	262,7	179,3	159,1	155,8	177,5	143,7	115,9	295,6	131,4
1986	154,6	141,7	150,7	113,8	316,1	197,9	164,4	162,6	187,1	147,1	114,6	318,1	135,7

of which: BREAD and CEREALS — *dont: PAIN et CÉRÉALES*

1975	.	–	–	94,6	–	–	–	–	–	–	–	–	–
1979	–	–	–	–	–	–	–	–	–	–	–	–	–
1981	111,1	104,3	113,2	105,6	127,6	117,2	113,0	109,4	118,3	105,7	106,9	127,4	109,0
1982	121,5	111,3	124,4	110,9	149,5	134,1	126,3	119,3	136,3	113,3	113,5	163,8	115,3
1983	131,2	120,5	132,0	114,1	173,8	150,3	140,3	129,0	154,8	123,8	114,7	202,8	120,1
1984	139,7	130,9	141,5	116,1	205,9	167,5	151,4	144,0	170,2	133,5	116,9	261,8	125,4
1985	147,5	135,0	150,4	117,6	254,1	192,5	160,4	159,6	185,3	140,9	118,4	344,8	130,0
1986	155,1	139,3	155,5	119,0	314,1	215,6	167,0	173,9	198,6	147,1	119,8	386,8	137,0

of which: MEAT* — *dont: VIANDES**

1979	–	–	–	96,8	–	–	–	–	–	–	–	–	–
1981	111,7	100,3	116,0	104,1	140,5	109,4	113,0	115,9	118,7	106,4	105,6	105,4	107,9
1982	125,9	109,7	126,3	112,3	171,0	130,0	129,6	132,4	138,5	124,5	114,2	127,2	118,1
1983	133,5	118,2	129,7	113,6	205,8	143,1	139,0	137,8	152,2	134,9	114,6	181,1	118,9
1984	140,0	124,0	142,0	112,6	234,1	163,8	147,3	144,7	162,2	139,5	113,6	224,4	123,5
1985	145,3	127,2	145,8	113,0	272,8	184,8	152,6	148,3	170,9	143,7	114,2	268,7	125,7
1986	150,1	129,7	146,4	113,2	314,6	203,8	155,9	149,7	180,1	146,5	113,9	287,7	127,5

of which: DAIRY PRODUCTS, EGGS, OILS and FATS — *dont: PRODUITS LAITIERS, ŒUFS, HUILES, GRAISSES*

1979	–	–	–	95,9	–	–	–	–	–	–	–	–	–
1981	111,5	107,2	112,2	105,8	131,4	117,4	114,2	109,9	112,9	103,7	106,2	130,0	109,9
1982	122,7	117,7	125,5	109,3	155,6	130,9	126,1	121,6	131,7	113,1	110,5	175,7	118,5
1983	132,2	130,2	131,3	111,6	184,7	144,3	136,0	134,1	150,2	123,7	111,8	222,3	121,6
1984	141,2	140,0	146,9	114,0	174,7	165,9	149,7	151,6	168,4	131,7	113,3	326,0	127,5
1985	149,3	142,2	158,4	113,1	216,3	183,7	156,3	160,7	183,7	133,2	113,4	380,5	133,4
1986	154,3	142,7	156,1	111,2	258,7	196,7	158,5	172,0	193,5	137,9	111,0	402,6	136,8

of which: FRUITS, VEGETABLES, POTATOES — *dont: FRUITS, LÉGUMES, POMMES DE TERRE*

1981	112,8	113,1	113,2	110,0	120,5	112,0	112,5	121,9	115,4	119,2	108,5	142,7	109,2
1982	126,4	128,2	124,4	111,0	154,5	134,8	131,1	137,0	129,8	123,2	112,1	183,1	123,6
1983	135,6	137,9	132,3	112,1	173,5	148,4	142,5	154,4	144,6	126,7	109,0	190,4	128,0
1984	151,2	157,1	141,2	117,6	215,9	160,2	164,1	177,6	158,3	144,2	117,9	274,3	140,9
1985	159,8	155,2	139,8	112,1	243,3	181,5	174,6	153,2	179,4	146,1	117,4	268,6	140,1
1986	164,2	148,0	139,9	110,7	281,9	204,8	173,9	159,9	183,5	144,6	110,3	289,0	146,6

224

I G

Agricultural accounts

Comptes de l'agriculture

OVERALL FIGURES
FINAL OUTPUT, INTERMEDIATE CONSUMPTION

AND VALUE ADDED

| I G 1 |

DONNEES GLOBALES
PRODUCTION FINALE, CONSOMMATION
INTERMEDIAIRE
ET VALEUR AJOUTEE

AT CURRENT PRICES AND CURRENT EXCHANGE RATES   AUX PRIX ET TAUX DE CHANGE COURANTS

YEAR ANNÉE	EUR 12	EUR 10	B	DK	D	GR	E	F	IRL	I	L	NL	P	UK
FINAL CROP OUTPUT						MIO ECU						**PRODUCTION VEGETALE FINALE**		
1983	:	67 505	1 745	1 550	8 195	4 631	— *	19 397	532	19 970	26	4 315	:	7 143
1984	:	73 551	1 788	2 181	9 511	5 402	— *	20 784	614	19 802	29	4 913	:	8 525
1985	:	72 549	1 812	2 131	8 743	5 460	11 617	21 729	451	20 078	27	4 718	:	7 400
1986	:	73 505	1 884	2 001	9 089	4 877	11 237	22 132	444	20 962	31	5 094	:	6 992
FINAL ANIMAL OUTPUT													**PRODUCTION ANIMALE FINALE**	
1983	:	85 612	3 283	4 338	19 128	2 310	— *	19 938	3 041	13 206	127	8 601	:	11 640
1984	:	87 634	3 502	4 536	18 876	2 427	— *	20 525	3 293	13 657	129	8 798	:	11 890
1985	:	88 058	3 579	4 570	18 112	2 428	8 293	21 170	3 364	13 650	137	9 057	:	11 991
1986	:	86 170	3 623	4 544	18 488	2 175	7 993	21 042	3 232	13 612	141	9 039	:	10 273
FINAL AGRICULTURAL OUTPUT													**PRODUCTION FINALE DE L'AGRICULTURE**	
1983	:	153 413	5 028	5 888	27 345	6 941	— *	39 250	3 574	33 342	153	12 916	:	18 977
1984	:	161 441	5 291	6 717	28 408	7 829	— *	41 160	3 907	33 639	158	13 712	:	20 621
1985	:	160 893	5 391	6 701	26 859	7 887	20 355	42 749	3 815	33 964	164	13 775	:	19 588
1986	:	159 846	5 507	6 545	27 581	7 052	19 664	42 941	3 677	34 819	172	14 133	:	17 420
INTERMEDIATE CONSUMPTION													**CONSOMMATION INTERMEDIAIRE**	
1983	:	68 657	2 845	3 342	15 207	1 744	— *	16 755	1 598	9 628	62	6 752	:	10 726
1984	:	71 762	3 061	3 429	15 309	1 817	— *	18 138	1 684	10 258	64	7 070	:	10 931
1985	:	72 425	3 150	3 431	15 161	1 858	8 656	18 907	1 774	10 028	64	7 168	:	10 883
1986	:	68 904	3 182	3 251	14 428	1 645	8 541	18 485	1 757	9 763	65	6 916	:	9 414
GROSS VALUE ADDED AT MARKET PRICES													**VALEUR AJOUTEE BRUTE AUX PRIX DU MARCHE**	
1983	:	84 756	2 183	2 547	12 139	5 197	— *	22 495	1 976	23 714	91	6 164	:	8 251
1984	:	89 680	2 229	3 288	13 099	6 013	— *	23 022	2 223	23 381	94	6 642	:	9 690
1985	:	88 468	2 242	3 270	11 697	6 029	11 700	23 842	2 041	23 935	99	6 607	:	8 706
1986	:	90 940	2 325	3 294	13 152	5 407	11 122	24 456	1 920	25 056	107	7 216	:	8 007
subsidies													**subventions**	
1983	:	5 215	141	125	533	369	— *	847	136	2 080	9	156	:	819
1984	:	6 520	124	110	1 340	447	— *	1 025	209	2 280	9	141	:	835
1985	:	6 927	130	106	1 847	403	531	1 065	253	2 164	8	108	:	844
1986	:	7 263	115	90	2 158	353	529	1 407	236	1 950	7	158	:	788
taxes linked to production													**impots lies a la production**	
1983	:	2 444 *	— *	106	413	115	— *	1 112	32	165	2	294	:	204
1984	:	2 846 *	— *	120	515	134	— *	1 269	60	180	3	331	:	235
1985	:	3 007 *	— *	119	465	134	46	1 390	57	235	2	374	:	230
1986	:	3 372 *	— *	140	572	152	44	1 548	60	246	4	404	:	245
GROSS VALUE ADDED AT FACTOR COST													**VALEUR AJOUTEE BRUTE AU COUT DES FACTEURS**	
1983	:	87 527	2 323	2 565	12 259	5 450	9 941	22 230	2 080	25 629	98	6 026	:	8 866
1984	:	93 354	2 354	3 278	13 924	6 326	11 848	22 777	2 372	25 481	101	6 452	:	10 290
1985	:	92 387	2 372	3 256	13 080	6 298	12 184	23 516	2 237	25 863	105	6 340	:	9 320
1986	:	94 831	2 440	3 244	14 738	5 608	11 608	24 315	2 096	26 760	110	6 970	:	8 549
depreciation													**amortissements**	
1983	:	20 553	298	683	4 373	303	668	3 494	359	7 966	17	824	:	2 235
1984	:	21 823	321	710	4 548	332	776	3 880	373	8 468	18	876	:	2 297
1985	:	22 387	347	746	4 640	342	859	4 316	391	8 257	19	924	:	2 404
1986	:	22 654	371	777	4 869	325	853	4 402	390	8 385	20	992	:	2 122
NET VALUE ADDED AT FACTOR COST													**VALEUR AJOUTEE NETTE AU COUT DES FACTEURS**	
1983	:	66 974	2 025	1 882	7 885	5 148	9 273	18 736	1 721	17 662	81	5 203	:	6 631
1984	:	71 531	2 032	2 567	9 375	5 995	11 072	18 898	1 998	17 013	83	5 576	:	7 994
1985	:	70 001	2 026	2 510	8 440	5 956	11 326	19 201	1 845	17 606	86	5 416	:	6 916
1986	:	72 177	2 068	2 468	9 869	5 283	10 754	19 913	1 706	18 375	90	5 978	:	6 427

OVERALL FIGURES
FINAL OUTPUT, INTERMEDIATE CONSUMPTION
AND VALUE ADDED

AT CURRENT PRICES AND CURRENT EXCHANGE RATES

I G 1

DONNEES GLOBALES
PRODUCTION FINALE, CONSOMMATION
INTERMEDIAIRE
ET VALEUR AJOUTEE

AUX PRIX ET TAUX DE CHANGE COURANTS

YEAR ANNÉE	EUR 12	EUR 10	B	DK	D	GR	E	F	IRL	I	L	NL	P	UK

compensation of employees — MIO ECU — **remuneration des salaires**

1983	:	15 279	94	359	1 235	113	1 975	3 043	133	6 487	2	688	:	3 125
1984	:	15 712	112	382	1 207	121	2 012	3 197	139	6 637	2	703	:	3 212
1985	:	16 943	119	398	1 384	156	2 251	3 376	157	7 133	2	734	:	3 482
1986	:	16 831	128	390	1 434	139	2 154	3 394	161	7 335	2	810	:	3 037

NET OPERATING SURPLUS — **EXCEDENT NET D'EXPLOITATION**

1983	:	51 090	1 931	1 522	6 651	5 034	7 298	15 693	1 588	11 175	79	4 515	:	3 506
1984	:	55 819	1 920	2 185	8 169	5 874	9 061	15 700	1 859	10 376	81	4 873	:	4 782
1985	:	53 058	1 906	2 112	7 056	5 799	9 075	15 824	1 688	10 473	84	4 682	:	3 434
1986	:	55 346	1 941	2 077	8 435	5 143	8 601	16 519	1 545	11 040	88	5 168	:	3 390

rent — **fermages**

1983	:	2 775	96	101	460	143	510	1 350	9	247	6	151	:	213
1984	:	2 887	98	118	487	168	541	1 347	9	253	6	160	:	240
1985	:	3 054	109	131	523	196	612	1 387	9	261	7	166	:	265
1986	:	3 077	112	119	583	174	643	1 389	8	266	7	174	:	244

interest — **interets**

1983	:	8 708	235	1 015	1 677	240	918	1 604	329	2 022	5	741	:	841
1984	:	9 229	250	976	1 743	288	1 008	1 789	304	2 175	6	735	:	963
1985	:	9 894	276	970	1 763	339	1 063	1 990	291	2 311	6	753	:	1 196
1986	:	9 966	265	991	1 827	319	1 003	2 016	271	2 449	6	774	:	1 048

NET INCOME FROM TOTAL AGRICULTURAL ACTIVITY — **REVENU NET DE L'ACTIVITE AGRICOLE TOTALE**

1983	:	55 491	1 694	766	5 748	4 765	7 845	15 783	1 384	15 393	70	4 310	:	5 578
1984	:	59 415	1 684	1 473	7 146	5 538	9 523	15 762	1 685	14 584	71	4 681	:	6 791
1985	:	57 053	1 641	1 410	6 154	5 421	9 651	15 824	1 546	15 034	73	4 496	:	5 455
1986	:	59 134	1 691	1 358	7 459	4 791	9 108	16 508	1 426	15 660	77	5 030	:	5 135

NET INCOME FROM FAMILY AGRICULTURAL ACTIVITY — **REVENU NET DE L'ACTIVITE AGRICOLE FAMILIALE**

1983	:	40 212	1 600	407	4 514	4 652	5 870	12 740	1 251	8 906	68	3 622	:	2 453
1984	:	43 703	1 572	1 091	5 939	5 417	7 511	12 564	1 546	7 948	69	3 978	:	3 579
1985	:	40 111	1 522	1 011	4 769	5 264	7 401	12 448	1 389	7 901	71	3 762	:	1 973
1986	:	42 302	1 563	967	6 024	4 651	6 955	13 114	1 265	8 325	74	4 220	:	2 098

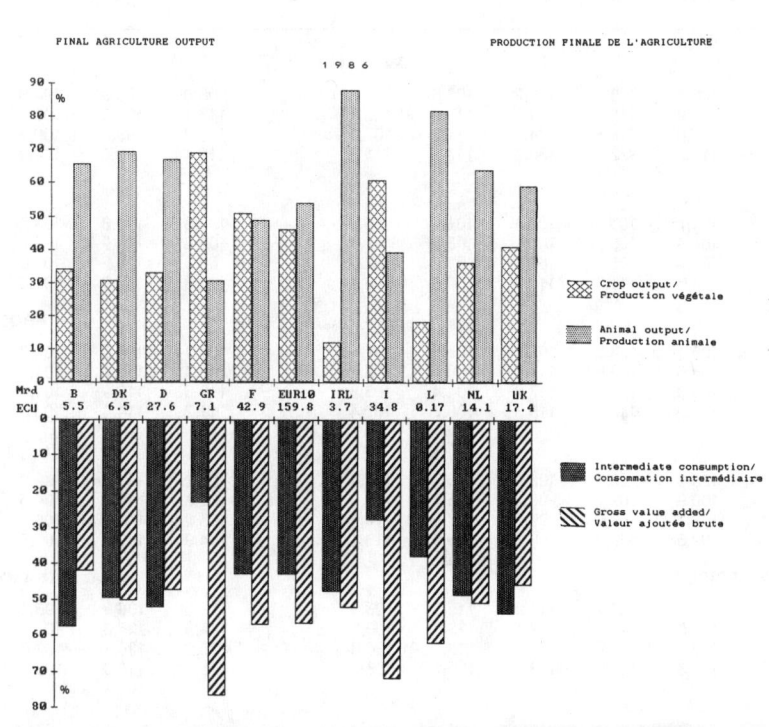

FINAL AGRICULTURE OUTPUT / PRODUCTION FINALE DE L'AGRICULTURE — 1 9 8 6

Crop output / Production végétale
Animal output / Production animale
Intermediate consumption / Consommation intermédiaire
Gross value added / Valeur ajoutée brute

OVERALL FIGURES FINAL OUTPUT, INTERMEDIATE CONSUMPTION AND VALUE ADDED

IG 2

DONNEES GLOBALES PRODUCTION FINALE, CONSOMMATION INTERMEDIAIRE ET VALEUR AJOUTEE

AT 1980 PRICES AND 1980 EXCHANGE RATES

AUX PRIX ET TAUX DE CHANGE DE 1980

YEAR ANNÉE	EUR 12	EUR 10	B	DK	D	GR	E	F	IRL	I	L	NL	P	UK
FINAL CROP OUTPUT						**MIO ECU**					**PRODUCTION VEGETALE FINALE**			
1983	:	55 542	1 446	1 206	7 180	3 585	— *	16 887	405	15 856	26	3 528	:	5 423
1984	:	59 673	1 603	1 826	8 018	3 860	— *	18 209	484	15 057	29	3 824	:	6 765
1985	:	59 002	1 654	1 738	7 493	3 927	— *	18 514	386	15 182	24	3 878	:	6 207
1986	:	60 517	1 705	1 572	7 912	4 100	— *	18 564	353	15 728	28	4 199	:	6 354
FINAL ANIMAL OUTPUT												**PRODUCTION ANIMALE FINALE**		
1983	:	70 176	2 878	3 491	15 662	1 691	— *	17 050	2 366	10 238	106	6 878	:	9 816
1984	:	69 948	2 954	3 410	15 497	1 706	— *	16 846	2 521	10 255	105	6 962	:	9 693
1985	:	69 955	2 957	3 514	15 229	1 698	— *	16 959	2 571	10 217	107	7 005	:	9 697
1986	:	70 738	3 110	3 605	15 753	1 719	— *	17 101	2 543	10 072	108	7 204	:	9 524
FINAL AGRICULTURAL OUTPUT											**PRODUCTION FINALE DE L'AGRICULTURE**			
1983	:	125 918	4 324	4 696	22 861	5 276	— *	33 870	2 771	26 203	132	10 405	:	15 380
1984	:	129 769	4 557	5 235	23 531	5 566	— *	34 937	3 005	25 417	134	10 785	:	16 602
1985	:	129 083	4 610	5 252	22 726	5 626	— *	35 365	2 957	25 504	131	10 883	:	16 029
1986	:	131 303	4 815	5 177	23 668	5 819	— *	35 495	2 896	25 906	136	11 405	:	15 986
INTERMEDIATE CONSUMPTION												**CONSOMMATION INTERMEDIAIRE**		
1983	:	54 124	2 422	2 509	11 765	1 349	— *	13 943	1 248	7 080	52	5 286	:	8 470
1984	:	54 197	2 478	2 440	11 640	1 357	— *	14 166	1 243	7 095	51	5 402	:	8 325
1985	:	54 823	2 548	2 475	11 805	1 407	— *	14 290	1 260	7 131	53	5 648	:	8 204
1986	:	55 111	2 649	2 449	11 593	1 394	— *	14 523	1 348	7 238	54	5 666	:	8 196
GROSS VALUE ADDED AT MARKET PRICES										**VALEUR AJOUTEE BRUTE AUX PRIX DU MARCHE**				
1983	:	71 794	1 902	2 188	11 097	3 927	— *	19 927	1 523	19 122	79	5 119	:	6 910
1984	:	75 573	2 080	2 795	11 891	4 209	— *	20 771	1 762	18 322	83	5 384	:	8 277
1985	:	74 261	2 062	2 777	10 921	4 218	— *	21 075	1 697	18 372	78	5 235	:	7 825
1986	:	76 192	2 166	2 728	12 075	4 425	— *	20 972	1 548	18 668	82	5 739	:	7 790

VOLUME INDEX NUMBERS FINAL OUTPUT, INTERMEDIATE CONSUMPTION AND VALUE ADDED

IG 3

INDICES DE VOLUME PRODUCTION FINALE, CONSOMMATION INTERMEDIAIRE ET VALEUR AJOUTEE

VOLUME INDEX NUMBERS

INDICES DE VOLUME

YEAR ANNÉE	EUR 12	EUR 10	B	DK	D	GR	E	F	IRL	I	L	NL	P	UK
FINAL CROP OUTPUT						**1980 = 100**						**PRODUCTION VEGETALE FINALE**		
1983	:	106,1	103,7	100,2	106,8	97,8	:	108,6	103,3	104,8	145,2	111,4	:	106,7
1984	:	114,0	115,0	151,8	119,2	105,3	:	117,1	123,5	99,5	163,4	120,7	:	133,2
1985	:	112,8	118,6	144,5	111,4	107,1	:	119,0	98,5	100,4	135,5	122,4	:	122,2
1986	:	115,7	122,3	130,7	117,7	111,8	:	119,4	90,0	104,0	159,5	132,6	:	125,1
FINAL ANIMAL OUTPUT												**PRODUCTION ANIMALE FINALE**		
1983	:	104,7	103,0	107,4	104,2	96,6	:	103,5	110,6	103,2	105,2	111,2	:	104,7
1984	:	104,4	105,7	104,9	103,1	97,4	:	102,3	117,9	103,4	104,6	112,5	:	103,4
1985	:	104,4	105,8	108,1	101,3	97,0	:	103,0	120,2	103,0	106,7	113,2	:	103,4
1986	:	105,6	111,3	110,9	104,8	98,1	:	103,8	118,9	101,6	107,0	116,5	:	101,6
FINAL AGRICULTURAL OUTPUT											**PRODUCTION FINALE DE L'AGRICULTURE**			
1983	:	105,4	103,2	105,5	105,0	97,4	:	106,1	109,5	104,2	111,2	111,2	:	105,4
1984	:	108,6	108,8	117,6	108,1	102,7	:	109,4	118,7	101,1	113,5	115,3	:	113,8
1985	:	108,0	110,1	117,9	104,4	103,8	:	110,8	116,9	101,4	111,0	116,3	:	109,8
1986	:	109,9	115,0	116,3	108,7	107,4	:	111,2	114,4	103,0	114,8	121,9	:	109,6
INTERMEDIATE CONSUMPTION												**CONSOMMATION INTERMEDIAIRE**		
1983	:	100,8	100,4	100,9	96,7	109,4	:	100,7	111,0	99,3	107,5	100,6	:	105,8
1984	:	100,9	102,7	98,2	95,7	110,0	:	102,3	110,6	99,5	104,7	102,8	:	104,0
1985	:	102,1	105,6	99,6	97,0	114,1	:	103,2	112,1	100,0	108,5	107,4	:	102,5
1986	:	102,6	109,8	98,6	95,3	113,1	:	104,9	119,9	101,5	110,4	107,8	:	102,4
GROSS VALUE ADDED AT MARKET PRICES										**VALEUR AJOUTEE BRUTE AUX PRIX DU MARCHE**				
1983	:	109,1	107,1	111,2	115,5	93,9	:	110,2	108,3	106,1	113,8	124,9	:	104,9
1984	:	114,9	117,1	142,1	123,8	100,6	:	114,9	125,3	101,7	119,6	131,4	:	125,6
1985	:	112,9	116,2	141,1	113,7	100,8	:	116,6	120,7	102,0	112,7	127,8	:	118,7
1986	:	115,8	122,0	138,6	125,7	105,7	:	116,0	110,0	103,6	117,9	140,1	:	118,2

DETAILED FIGURES
FINAL OUTPUT, INTERMEDIATE CONSUMPTION

AND VALUE ADDED

AT CURRENT PRICES AND CURRENT EXCHANGE RATES

I G 4

DONNEES DETAILLEES
PRODUCTION FINALE, CONSOMMATION
INTERMEDIAIRE
ET VALEUR AJOUTEE

AUX PRIX ET TAUX DE CHANGE COURANTS

YEAR ANNÉE	EUR 12	EUR 10	B	DK	D	GR	E	F	IRL	I	L	NL	P	UK
CEREALS EXCLUDING RICE							**MIO ECU**						**CEREALES SANS RIZ**	
1983	:	17 912	293	701	2 290	745	− *	6 934	240	2 939	4	241	:	3 524
1984	:	22 400	350	1 159	3 126	913	− *	8 291	286	3 769	10	252	:	4 245
1985	:	19 668	300	1 009	2 516	737	2 734	7 853	187	3 235	10	186	:	3 637
1986	:	19 191	341	768	2 595	745	2 198	7 356	170	3 646	8	219	:	3 343
wheat														**ble**
1983	:	10 654	200	312	1 282	422	− *	4 087	64	2 056	2	195	:	2 035
1984	:	10 204	229	379	1 511	522	− *	5 190	96	2 548	5	201	:	2 602
1985	:	11 225	208	354	1 280	408	928	4 560	58	1 968	4	141	:	2 246
1986	:	11 320	232	228	1 375	449	788	4 423	49	2 309	4	162	:	2 089
barley														**orge**
1983	:	3 983	88	329	793	57	− *	995	170	73	2	31	:	1 445
1984	:	5 214	112	657	1 092	90	− *	1 296	180	158	4	37	:	1 589
1985	:	4 417	85	551	799	54	1 203	1 287	125	145	5	33	:	1 335
1986	:	4 108	103	441	790	51	784	1 167	116	167	4	47	:	1 222
maize														**mais-grain**
1983	:	2 821	0	−	57	263	− *	1 726	−	774	0	−	:	−
1984	:	2 999	0	−	78	297	− *	1 621	−	1 003	0	−	:	−
1985	:	3 282	0	−	77	271	530	1 858	−	1 077	0	−	:	−
1986	:	3 169	0	−	156	240	595	1 656	−	1 117	0	−	:	−
RICE														**RIZ**
1983	:	449	−	−	−	26	− *	14	−	409	−	−	:	−
1984	:	483	−	−	−	34	− *	14	−	435	−	−	:	−
1985	:	532	−	−	−	37	132	23	−	472	−	−	:	−
1986	:	449	−	−	−	34	128	24	−	392	−	−	:	−
PULSES														**LEGUMES SECS**
1983	:	459	2	11	4	50	− *	212	0	84	0	21	:	75
1984	:	620	1	61	4	44	− *	277	1	99	0	31	:	102
1985	:	799	1	136	7	44	147	343	0	107	0	32	:	127
1986	:	947	3	137	10	38	140	418	0	118	0	49	:	174
ROOT CROPS														**PLANTES SARCLEES**
1983	:	7 132	438	197	1 372	283	− *	1 776	144	956	3	807	:	1 157
1984	:	7 942	361	197	1 542	298	− *	1 690	173	1 227	2	982	:	1 469
1985	:	6 608	353	197	1 460	322	863	1 440	111	1 046	2	712	:	965
1986	:	7 147	404	200	1 475	253	1 102	1 717	123	1 200	2	802	:	972
potatoes														**pommes de terre**
1983	:	3 581	214	94	474	188	− *	751	73	473	3	525	:	785
1984	:	4 113	133	61	544	220	− *	624	96	714	2	672	:	1 045
1985	:	2 617	107	59	412	197	446	318	50	512	2	386	:	573
1986	:	3 002	159	69	413	151	664	606	61	452	2	450	:	639
sugar beet														**betteraves sucrieres**
1983	:	3 534	222	103	898	95	− *	1 024	71	478	0	272	:	371
1984	:	3 811	227	136	997	78	− *	1 066	76	506	0	301	:	424
1985	:	3 980	245	138	1 047	125	406	1 122	61	529	0	321	:	392
1986	:	4 137	243	131	1 062	102	428	1 111	63	743	0	350	:	332
INDUSTRIAL CROPS														**PLANTES INDUSTRIELLES**
1983	:	3 347	22	148	420	813	− *	1 099	4	469	1	26	:	344
1984	:	4 168	26	232	430	1 099	− *	1 329	6	542	1	27	:	476
1985	:	4 588	24	247	471	1 133	693	1 611	6	631	0	22	:	442
1986	:	5 034	19	287	541	1 080	804	1 674	2	983	1	15	:	432

DETAILED FIGURES
FINAL OUTPUT, INTERMEDIATE CONSUMPTION
AND VALUE ADDED

I G 4

DONNEES DETAILLEES
PRODUCTION FINALE, CONSOMMATION
INTERMEDIAIRE
ET VALEUR AJOUTEE

AT CURRENT PRICES AND CURRENT EXCHANGE RATES

AUX PRIX ET TAUX DE CHANGE COURANTS

YEAR ANNÉE	EUR 12	EUR 10	B	DK	D	GR	E	F	IRL	I	L	NL	P	UK

oil seeds oleaginous fruits (excluding olives) — MIO ECU — **graines et fruits oleagineux (sans olives)**

1983	:	1 732	4	147	277	19	— *	856	0	105	1	24	:	298
1984	:	2 226	5	230	289	40	— *	1 056	0	150	1	23	:	432
1985	:	2 695	3	245	324	43	347	1 357	0	286	0	19	:	417
1986	:	3 184	0	285	401	61	433	1 365	0	644	1	13	:	413

tobacco — **tabac**

1983	:	886	5	—	26	368	— *	128	—	358	0	0	:	—
1984	:	1 053	6	—	25	509	— *	129	—	384	0	0	:	—
1985	:	1 035	6	—	27	533	91	131	—	338	0	0	:	—
1986	:	971	7	—	30	471	69	131	—	332	0	0	:	—

hops — **houblon**

1983	:	170 *	4	—	117	0	— *	4	— *	0	0	0	:	45
1984	:	167 *	2	—	117	0	— *	4	— *	0	0	0	:	44
1985	:	151 *	2	—	119	0	9	5	— *	0	0	0	:	25
1986	:	135 *	2	—	110	—	6	4	— *	0	0	0	:	19

FRESH VEGETABLES — **LEGUMES FRAIS**

1983	:	11 462	511	87	557	784	— *	2 434	76	4 706	2	1 126	:	1 179
1984	:	12 442	575	106	575	875	— *	2 596	79	5 017	2	1 312	:	1 305
1985	:	12 393	600	101	587	897	1 942	2 763	83	4 759	2	1 302	:	1 299
1986	:	11 715	576	104	536	703	2 247	2 581	79	4 667	2	1 302	:	1 164

FRESH FRUIT — **FRUITS FRAIS**

1983	:	6 170	176	37	1 048	559	— *	1 427	10	2 321	1	194	:	397
1984	:	6 487	158	35	1 153	684	— *	1 322	12	2 499	2	202	:	420
1985	:	6 467	180	30	1 120	650	1 627	1 514	10	2 397	2	182	:	382
1986	:	6 713	167	35	1 237	628	1 778	1 507	8	2 549	3	190	:	390

CITRUS FRUIT — **AGRUMES**

1983	:	1 560	—	—	—	143	— *	8	—	1 410	—	—	:	—
1984	:	1 202	—	—	—	246	— *	7	—	949	—	—	:	—
1985	:	1 551	—	—	—	210	800	10	—	1 331	—	—	:	—
1986	:	1 523	—	—	—	208	734	9	—	1 306	—	—	:	—

GRAPE — **RAISIN**

1983	:	774 *	7	—	— *	320	— *	42	—	403	— *	2	:	— *
1984	:	706 *	5	—	— *	323	— *	41	—	335	— *	2	:	— *
1985	:	729 *	5	—	— *	320	177	50	—	353	— *	2	:	— *
1986	:	814 *	5	—	— *	276	220	44	—	488	— *	2	:	— *

GRAPE MOST AND WINE — **MOUT ET VIN**

1983	:	7 504 *	— *	—	810	157	— *	3 803	—	2 719	15	— *	:	— *
1984	:	6 841 *	— *	—	1 007	141	— *	3 481	—	2 202	11	— *	:	— *
1985	:	7 710 *	— *	—	943	151	715	4 400	—	2 206	10	— *	:	— *
1986	:	8 965 *	— *	—	989	120	626	5 097	—	2 744	15	— *	:	— *

OLIVES — **OLIVES DE TABLE**

1983	:	192	—	—	—	125	— *	7	—	60	—	—	:	—
1984	:	164	—	—	—	119	— *	6	—	39	—	—	:	—
1985	:	211	—	—	—	122	101	9	—	80	—	—	:	—
1986	:	181	—	—	—	109	75	8	—	64	—	—	:	—

OLIVE OIL — **HUILE D'OLIVE**

1983	:	2 506 *	—	—	—	526	— *	— *	—	1 980	—	—	:	—
1984	:	1 334 *	—	—	—	518	— *	— *	—	816	—	—	:	—
1985	:	2 427 *	—	—	—	715	1 042	— *	—	1 712	—	—	:	—
1986	:	1 527 *	—	—	—	574	578	— *	—	953	—	—	:	—

DETAILED FIGURES
FINAL OUTPUT, INTERMEDIATE CONSUMPTION
AND VALUE ADDED

I G 4

DONNEES DETAILLEES
PRODUCTION FINALE, CONSOMMATION
INTERMEDIAIRE
ET VALEUR AJOUTEE

AT CURRENT PRICES AND CURRENT EXCHANGE RATES

AUX PRIX ET TAUX DE CHANGE COURANTS

YEAR ANNÉE	EUR 12	EUR 10	B	DK	D	GR	E	F	IRL	I	L	NL	P	UK
OTHER CROP PRODUCTS						MIO ECU							**AUTRES PRODUITS VEGETAUX**	
1983	:	8 039	296	369	1 693	101	— *	1 643	58	1 514	0	1 897	:	467
1984	:	8 761	312	390	1 673	109	— *	1 730	58	1 873	1	2 107	:	508
1985	:	8 867	349	411	1 639	121	645	1 712	54	1 750	0	2 282	:	547
1986	:	9 299	369	470	1 706	109	606	1 699	61	1 853	0	2 515	:	517
FINAL CROP OUTPUT													**PRODUCTION VEGETALE FINALE**	
1983	:	67 505	1 745	1 550	8 195	4 631	— *	19 397	532	19 970	26	4 315	:	7 143
1984	:	73 551	1 788	2 181	9 511	5 402	— *	20 784	614	19 802	20	4 913	:	8 525
1985	:	72 549	1 812	2 131	8 743	5 460	11 617	21 729	451	20 078	27	4 718	:	7 400
1986	:	73 505	1 884	2 001	9 089	4 877	11 237	22 132	444	20 962	31	5 094	:	6 992
ANIMALS													**ANIMAUX**	
1983	:	50 344	2 221	2 728	10 741	1 418	— *	12 177	1 803	8 608	59	4 254	:	6 334
1984	:	52 177	2 412	2 962	10 672	1 476	— *	12 476	1 972	8 922	56	4 482	:	6 748
1985	:	52 620	2 492	2 980	10 269	1 446	5 304	12 961	1 964	8 902	60	4 765	:	6 781
1986	:	50 352	2 474	2 899	10 067	1 313	5 184	12 599	1 892	8 749	59	4 651	:	5 649
cattle (including calves)													**bovins (y compris veaux)**	
1983	:	22 704	1 003	726	5 030	310	— *	6 370	1 274	3 542	45	1 499	:	2 905
1984	:	22 762	1 078	654	4 785	325	— *	6 347	1 434	3 631	42	1 475	:	2 992
1985	:	22 715	1 123	698	4 520	302	1 356	6 663	1 442	3 558	45	1 447	:	2 916
1986	:	21 668	1 112	602	4 570	257	1 327	6 538	1 399	3 496	45	1 466	:	2 183
pigs													**porcs**	
1983	:	16 564	1 021	1 660	5 105	308	— *	2 482	242	2 021	14	2 204	:	1 508
1984	:	17 604	1 112	1 908	5 193	314	— *	2 590	225	2 149	14	2 407	:	1 692
1985	:	17 975	1 138	1 923	5 088	312	1 901	2 736	212	2 205	15	2 683	:	1 664
1986	:	17 017	1 128	1 833	4 804	313	2 010	2 545	196	2 187	14	2 563	:	1 433
poultry													**volailles**	
1983	:	6 413	150	111	436	167	— *	1 910	92	2 005	0	452	:	1 091
1984	:	6 877	172	121	498	189	— *	2 080	97	2 056	0	517	:	1 148
1985	:	7 025	172	123	488	184	1 106	2 117	100	2 072	0	546	:	1 224
1986	:	6 910	170	114	522	166	935	2 194	107	1 953	0	539	:	1 145
ANIMALS PRODUCTS													**PRODUITS ANIMAUX**	
1983	:	35 268	1 062	1 610	8 387	891	— *	7 761	1 238	4 598	68	4 347	:	5 306
1984	:	35 456	1 090	1 575	8 205	951	— *	8 049	1 321	4 735	73	4 316	:	5 142
1985	:	35 438	1 087	1 590	7 843	982	2 989	8 209	1 400	4 748	77	4 292	:	5 211
1986	:	35 817	1 149	1 645	8 420	862	2 808	8 443	1 341	4 862	82	4 388	:	4 625
milk													**lait**	
1983	:	30 443	852	1 535	7 429	662	— *	6 832	1 193	3 789	66	3 729	:	4 356
1984	:	30 072	843	1 494	7 163	661	— *	7 018	1 266	3 828	71	3 630	:	4 097
1985	:	30 395	874	1 516	6 909	712	1 924	7 240	1 350	3 886	75	3 635	:	4 197
1986	:	31 238	950	1 574	7 475	657	1 837	7 556	1 301	4 033	80	3 776	:	3 835
eggs													**oeufs**	
1983	:	4 342	190	72	862	179	— *	828	36	780	2	538	:	855
1984	:	4 905	219	78	959	240	— *	943	44	876	2	595	:	948
1985	:	4 587	184	71	875	225	865	882	39	829	2	567	:	912
1986	:	4 093	171	68	861	163	761	796	32	794	2	510	:	698
FINAL ANIMAL OUTPUT													**PRODUCTION ANIMALE FINALE**	
1983	:	85 612	3 283	4 338	19 128	2 310	— *	19 938	3 041	13 206	127	8 601	:	11 640
1984	:	87 634	3 502	4 536	18 876	2 427	— *	20 525	3 293	13 657	129	8 798	:	11 890
1985	:	88 058	3 579	4 570	18 112	2 428	8 293	21 170	3 364	13 650	137	9 057	:	11 991
1986	:	86 170	3 623	4 544	18 488	2 175	7 993	21 042	3 232	13 612	141	9 039	:	10 273

I G 4

AT CURRENT PRICES AND CURRENT EXCHANGE RATES

AUX PRIX ET TAUX DE CHANGE COURANTS

YEAR ANNÉE	EUR 12	EUR 10	B	DK	D	GR	E	F	IRL	I	L	NL	P	UK

CONTRACT FARM WORK — MIO ECU — **TRAVAUX A FACON**

	EUR 12	EUR 10	B	DK	D	GR	E	F	IRL	I	L	NL	P	UK
1983	:	131 *	– *	– *	22	– *	– *	– 86	– *	– *	– *	– *	:	194
1984	:	76 *	– *	– *	21	– *	– *	– 150	– *	– *	– *	– *	:	206
1985	:	50 *	– *	– *	4	– *	445	– 150	– *	– *	– *	– *	:	196
1986	:	– 75 *	– *	– *	3	– *	434	– 233	– *	– *	– *	– *	:	155

MISCELLANEOUS — **DIVERS**

	EUR 12	EUR 10	B	DK	D	GR	E	F	IRL	I	L	NL	P	UK
1983	:	165	– 0	–	–	–	– *	–	–	165	–	–	:	–
1984	:	180	– 0	–	–	–	– *	–	–	180	–	–	:	–
1985	:	236	0	–	–	–	–	–	–	235	–	–	:	–
1986	:	246	– 0	–	–	–	–	–	–	246	–	–	:	–

FINAL AGRICULTURAL OUTPUT — **PRODUCTION FINALE DE L'AGRICULTURE**

	EUR 12	EUR 10	B	DK	D	GR	E	F	IRL	I	L	NL	P	UK
1983	:	153 413	5 028	5 888	27 345	6 941	– *	39 250	3 574	33 342	153	12 916	:	18 977
1984	:	161 441	5 291	6 717	28 408	7 829	– *	41 160	3 907	33 639	158	13 712	:	20 621
1985	:	160 893	5 391	6 701	26 859	7 887	20 355	42 749	3 815	33 964	164	13 775	:	19 588
1986	:	159 846	5 507	6 545	27 581	7 052	19 664	42 941	3 677	34 819	172	14 133	:	17 420

INTERMEDIATE CONSUMPTION — **CONSOMMATION INTERMEDIAIRE**

	EUR 12	EUR 10	B	DK	D	GR	E	F	IRL	I	L	NL	P	UK
1983	:	68 657	2 845	3 342	15 207	1 744	– *	16 755	1 598	9 628	62	6 752	:	10 726
1984	:	71 762	3 061	3 429	15 309	1 817	– *	18 138	1 684	10 258	64	7 070	:	10 931
1985	:	72 425	3 150	3 431	15 161	1 858	8 656	18 907	1 774	10 028	64	7 168	:	10 883
1986	:	68 904	3 182	3 251	14 428	1 645	8 541	18 485	1 757	9 763	65	6 916	:	9 414

feedingstuffs — **aliments des animaux**

	EUR 12	EUR 10	B	DK	D	GR	E	F	IRL	I	L	NL	P	UK
1983	:	30 477	1 527	1 803	5 592	504	– *	5 521	684	5 691	28	4 253	:	4 874
1984	:	31 086	1 574	1 741	5 459	507	– *	5 849	679	5 966	28	4 415	:	4 868
1985	:	29 479	1 515	1 679	5 059	464	4 280	5 645	670	5 560	25	4 321	:	4 538
1986	:	28 656	1 546	1 592	4 817	387	4 227	5 785	758	5 586	24	4 141	:	4 019

fertilizers and soil improvers — **engrais et amendements**

	EUR 12	EUR 10	B	DK	D	GR	E	F	IRL	I	L	NL	P	UK
1983	:	9 048	223	349	2 010	220	– *	2 944	329	1 051	11	406	:	1 506
1984	:	9 649	247	419	2 014	197	– *	3 228	364	1 157	11	416	:	1 596
1985	:	10 195	266	426	2 055	202	1 130	3 592	405	1 247	12	462	:	1 527
1986	:	9 130	275	400	1 896	174	1 122	3 189	353	1 174	14	446	:	1 210

energy — **energie**

	EUR 12	EUR 10	B	DK	D	GR	E	F	IRL	I	L	NL	P	UK
1983	:	7 960	245	250	2 477	388	– *	1 646	203	1 102	7	678	:	965
1984	:	8 411	277	251	2 587	429	– *	1 759	204	1 196	8	741	:	960
1985	:	8 893	323	264	2 677	467	1 138	1 935	218	1 178	8	773	:	1 052
1986	:	7 044	251	213	2 126	423	1 055	1 547	181	924	8	587	:	783

material and small tools ; maintenence and repairs — **materiel et petit outillage ; entretien et reparation**

	EUR 12	EUR 10	B	DK	D	GR	E	F	IRL	I	L	NL	P	UK
1983	:	6 903 *	159	381	2 163	280	– *	1 749	108	– *	5	631	:	1 429
1984	:	7 231 *	174	401	2 203	302	– *	1 837	114	– *	5	658	:	1 537
1985	:	7 599 *	191	432	2 239	312	897	1 918	125	– *	6	717	:	1 660
1986	:	7 649 *	203	435	2 357	297	927	1 969	125	– *	6	754	:	1 504

OVERALL FIGURES
AS A PERCENTAGE OF FINAL OUTPUT
OF THE COMMUNITY = 100,0
1986

IG 5

DONNEES GLOBALES
EN POURCENTAGE DE LA PRODUCTION FINALE
DE LA COMMUNAUTE = 100,0
1986

AT CURRENT PRICES AND CURRENT EXCHANGE RATES

AUX PRIX ET TAUX DE CHANGE COURANTS

YEAR ANNÉE	EUR 12	EUR 10	B	DK	D	GR	E	F	IRL	I	L	NL	P	UK
FINAL CROP OUTPUT						%							**PRODUCTION VEGETALE FINALE**	
	:	46,0	1,2	1,3	5,7	3,1	:	13,8	0,3	13,1	0,0	3,2	:	4,4
FINAL ANIMAL OUTPUT													**PRODUCTION ANIMALE FINALE**	
	:	53,9	2,3	2,8	11,6	1,4	:	13,2	2,0	8,5	0,1	5,7	:	6,4
FINAL AGRICULTURAL OUTPUT													**PRODUCTION FINALE DE L'AGRICULTURE**	
	:	100,0	3,4	4,1	17,3	4,4	:	20,9	2,3	21,8	0,1	8,8	:	10,9
INTERMEDIATE CONSUMPTION													**CONSOMMATION INTERMEDIAIRE**	
	:	43,1	2,0	2,0	9,0	1,0	:	11,6	1,1	6,1	0,0	4,3	:	5,9
GROSS VALUE ADDED AT MARKET PRICES													**VALEUR AJOUTEE BRUTE AUX PRIX DU MARCHE**	
	:	56,9	1,5	2,1	8,2	3,4	:	15,3	1,2	15,7	0,1	4,5	:	5,0
subsidies													**subventions**	
	:	4,5	0,1	0,1	1,4	0,2	:	0,9	0,1	1,2	0,0	0,1	:	0,5
taxes linked to production													**impots lies a la production**	
	:	2,1 *	— *	0,1	0,4	0,1	:	1,0	0,0	0,2	0,0	0,3	:	0,2
GROSS VALUE ADDED AT FACTOR COST													**VALEUR AJOUTEE BRUTE AU COUT DES FACTEURS**	
	:	59,3	1,5	2,0	9,2	3,5	:	15,2	1,3	16,7	0,1	4,4	:	5,3
depreciation													**amortissements**	
	:	14,2	0,2	0,5	3,0	0,2	:	2,8	0,2	5,2	0,0	0,6	:	1,3
NET VALUE ADDED AT FACTOR COST													**VALEUR AJOUTEE NETTE AU COUT DES FACTEURS**	
	:	45,2	1,3	1,5	6,2	3,3	:	12,5	1,1	11,5	0,1	3,7	:	4,0
compensation of employees													**remuneration des salaries**	
	:	10,5	0,1	0,2	0,9	0,1	:	2,1	0,1	4,6	0,0	0,5	:	1,9
rent													**fermages**	
	:	1,9	0,1	0,1	0,4	0,1	:	0,9	0,0	0,2	0,0	0,1	:	0,2
interest													**interets**	
	:	6,2	0,2	0,6	1,1	0,2	:	1,3	0,2	1,5	0,0	0,5	:	0,7
NET INCOME FROM TOTAL AGRICULTURAL ACTIVITY													**REVENU NET DE L'ACTIVITE AGRICOLE TOTALE**	
	:	37,0	1,1	0,8	4,7	3,0	:	10,3	0,9	9,8	0,0	3,1	:	3,2
NET INCOME FROM FAMILY AGRICULTURAL ACTIVITY													**REVENU NET DE L'ACTIVITE AGRICOLE FAMILIALE**	
	:	26,5	1,0	0,6	3,8	2,9	:	8,2	0,8	5,2	0,0	2,6	:	1,3

**DETAILED FIGURES
AS A PERCENTAGE OF FINAL OUTPUT
OF EACH COUNTRY = 100,0
1986**

I G 6

**DONNEES DETAILLEES
EN POURCENTAGE DE LA PRODUCTION FINALE
DE CHAQUE PAYS = 100,0
1986**

AT CURRENT PRICES AND CURRENT EXCHANGE RATES

AUX PRIX ET TAUX DE CHANGE COURANTS

YEAR ANNÉE	EUR 12	EUR 10	B	DK	D	GR	E	F	IRL	I	L	NL	P	UK
CEREALS EXCLUDING RICE						%								**CEREALES SANS RIZ**
:		12,0	6,2	11,7	9,4	10,6	:	17,1	4,6	10,5	4,9	1,6	:	19,2
wheat														**ble**
:		7,1	4,2	3,5	5,0	6,4	:	10,3	1,3	6,6	2,1	1,1	:	12,0
barley														**orge**
:		2,6	1,9	6,7	2,9	0,7	:	2,7	3,2	0,5	2,4	0,3	:	7,0
maize														**mais-grain**
:		2,0	–	–	0,6	3,4	:	3,9	–	3,2	0,0	–	:	–
RICE														**RIZ**
:		0,3	–	–	–	0,5	:	0,1	–	1,1	–	–	:	–
PULSES														**LEGUMES SECS**
:		0,6	0,1	2,1	0,0	0,5	:	1,0	0,0	0,3	0,0	0,3	:	1,0
ROOT CROPS														**PLANTES SARCLEES**
:		4,5	7,3	3,1	5,3	3,6	:	4,0	3,4	3,4	1,2	5,7	:	5,6
potatoes														**pommes de terre**
:		1,9	2,9	1,1	1,5	2,1	:	1,4	1,7	1,3	1,2	3,2	:	3,7
sugar beet														**betteraves sucrieres**
:		2,6	4,4	2,0	3,8	1,4	:	2,6	1,7	2,1	0,0	2,5	:	1,9
INDUSTRIAL CROPS														**PLANTES INDUSTRIELLES**
:		3,1	0,3	4,4	2,0	15,3	:	3,9	0,1	2,8	0,4	0,1	:	2,5
oil seeds oleaginous fruits (excluding olives)														**graines et fruits oleagineux (sans olives)**
:		2,0	0,0	4,4	1,5	0,9	:	3,2	0,0	1,8	0,4	0,1	:	2,4
tobacco														**tabac**
:		0,6	0,1	–	0,1	6,7	:	0,3	–	1,0	0,0	–	:	–
hops														**houblon**
:		0,1 *	0,0	–	0,4	–	:	0,0	– *	–	0,0	–	:	0,1
FRESH VEGETABLES														**LEGUMES FRAIS**
:		7,3	10,5	1,6	1,9	10,0	:	6,0	2,2	13,4	1,1	9,2	:	6,7
FRESH FRUIT														**FRUITS FRAIS**
:		4,2	3,0	0,5	4,5	8,9	:	3,5	0,2	7,3	1,9	1,3	:	2,2
CITRUS FRUIT														**AGRUMES**
:		1,0	–	–	–	3,0	:	0,0	–	3,8	–	–	:	–
GRAPE														**RAISIN**
:		0,5 *	0,1	–	– *	3,9	:	0,1	–	1,4	– *	0,0	:	– *

DETAILED FIGURES
AS A PERCENTAGE OF FINAL OUTPUT
OF EACH COUNTRY = 100,0
1986

IG 6

DONNEES DETAILLEES
EN POURCENTAGE DE LA PRODUCTION FINALE
DE CHAQUE PAYS = 100,0
1986

AT CURRENT PRICES AND CURRENT EXCHANGE RATES

AUX PRIX ET TAUX DE CHANGE COURANTS

YEAR ANNÉE	EUR 12	EUR 10	B	DK	D	GR	E	F	IRL	I	L	NL	P	UK
GRAPE MOST AND WINE						%								**MOUT ET VIN**
	:	5,6 *	— *	—	3,6	1,7	:	11,9	—	7,9	8,5	— *	:	— *
OLIVES														**OLIVES DE TABLE**
	:	0,1	—	—	—	1,5	:	0,0	—	0,2	—	—	:	—
OLIVE OIL														**HUILE D'OLIVE**
	:	1,0 *	—	—	—	0,1	:	— *	—	2,7	—	—	:	—
OTHER CROP PRODUCTS														**AUTRES PRODUITS VEGETAUX**
	:	5,8	6,7	7,2	6,2	1,5	:	4,0	1,7	5,3	0,3	17,8	:	3,0
FINAL CROP OUTPUT														**PRODUCTION VEGETALE FINALE**
	:	46,0	34,2	30,6	33,0	69,2	:	51,5	12,1	60,2	18,2	36,0	:	40,1
ANIMALS														**ANIMAUX**
	:	31,5	44,9	44,3	36,5	18,6	:	29,3	51,5	25,1	34,2	32,9	:	32,4
cattle (including calves)														**bovins (y compris veaux)**
	:	13,6	20,2	9,2	16,6	3,6	:	15,2	38,1	10,0	26,0	10,4	:	12,5
pigs														**porcs**
	:	10,6	20,5	28,0	17,4	4,4	:	5,9	5,3	6,3	8,1	18,1	:	8,2
poultry														**volailles**
	:	4,3	3,1	1,7	1,9	2,4	:	5,1	2,9	5,6	0,1	3,8	:	6,6
ANIMALS PRODUCTS														**PRODUITS ANIMAUX**
	:	22,4	20,9	25,1	30,5	12,2	:	19,7	36,5	14,0	47,6	31,0	:	26,5
milk														**lait**
	:	19,5	17,2	24,1	27,1	9,3	:	17,6	35,4	11,6	46,7	26,7	:	22,0
eggs														**oeufs**
	:	2,6	3,1	1,0	3,1	2,3	:	1,9	0,9	2,3	0,9	3,6	:	4,0
FINAL ANIMAL OUTPUT														**PRODUCTION ANIMALE FINALE**
	:	53,9	65,8	69,4	67,0	30,8	:	49,0	87,9	39,1	81,8	64,0	:	59,0
CONTRACT FARM WORK														**TRAVAUX A FACON**
	:	0,0 *	— *	— *	0,0	— *	:	0,5	— *	— *	— *	— *	:	0,9
OTHER														**DIVERS**
	:	0,2	0,0	—	—	—	:	—	—	0,7	—	—	:	—
FINAL AGRICULTURAL OUTPUT														**PRODUCTION FINALE DE L'AGRICULTURE**
	:	100,0	100,0	100,0	100,0	100,0	:	100,0	100,0	100,0	100,0	100,0	:	100,0
INTERMEDIATE CONSUMPTION														**CONSOMMATION INTERMEDIAIRE**
	:	43,1	57,8	49,7	52,3	23,3	:	43,0	47,8	28,0	38,0	48,9	:	54,0

DETAILED FIGURES
AS A PERCENTAGE OF FINAL OUTPUT
OF EACH COUNTRY = 100,0
1986

I G 6

DONNEES DETAILLEES
EN POURCENTAGE DE LA PRODUCTION FINALE
DE CHAQUE PAYS = 100,0
1986

AT CURRENT PRICES AND CURRENT EXCHANGE RATES AUX PRIX ET TAUX DE CHANGE COURANTS

YEAR ANNÉE	EUR 12	EUR 10	B	DK	D	GR	E	F	IRL	I	L	NL	P	UK
feedingstuffs % aliments des animaux														
	:	17,9	28,1	24,3	17,5	5,5	:	13,5	20,6	16,0	13,8	29,3	:	23,1
fertilizers and soil improvers engrais et amendements														
	:	5,7	5,0	6,1	6,9	2,5	:	7,4	9,6	3,4	8,0	3,2	:	6,9
energy energie														
	:	4,4	4,6	3,3	7,7	6,0	:	3,6	4,9	2,7	4,6	4,2	:	4,5
material and small tools ; maintenance and repairs materiel et petit outillage ; entretien et reparation														
	:	4,8 *	3,7	6,6	8,5	4,2	:	4,6	3,4	— *	3,4	5,3	:	8,6
GROSS VALUE ADDED AT MARKET PRICES VALEUR AJOUTEE BRUTE AUX PRIX DU MARCHE														
	:	56,9	42,2	50,3	47,7	76,7	:	57,0	52,2	72,0	62,0	51,1	:	46,0
subsidies subventions														
	:	4,5	2,1	1,4	7,8	5,0	:	3,3	6,4	5,6	4,3	1,1	:	4,5
taxes linked to production impots lies a la production														
	:	2,1 *	— *	2,1	2,1	2,2	:	3,6	1,6	0,7	2,2	2,9	:	1,4
GROSS VALUE ADDED AT FACTOR COST VALEUR AJOUTEE BRUTE AU COUT DES FACTEURS														
	:	59,3	44,3	49,6	53,4	79,5	:	56,6	57,0	76,9	64,1	49,3	:	49,1
depreciation amortissements														
	:	14,2	6,7	11,9	17,7	4,6	:	10,3	10,6	24,1	11,8	7,0	:	12,2
NET VALUE ADDED AT FACTOR COST VALEUR AJOUTEE NETTE AU COUT DES FACTEURS														
	:	45,2	37,6	37,7	35,8	74,9	:	46,4	46,4	52,8	52,3	42,3	:	36,9
compensation of employees remuneration des salaries														
	:	10,5	2,3	6,0	5,2	2,0	:	7,9	4,4	21,1	1,2	5,7	:	17,4
rent fermages														
	:	1,9	2,0	1,8	2,1	2,5	:	3,2	0,2	0,8	4,1	1,2	:	1,4
interest interets														
	:	6,2	4,8	15,1	6,6	4,5	:	4,7	7,4	7,0	3,8	5,5	:	6,0
NET INCOME FROM TOTAL AGRICULTURAL ACTIVITY REVENU NET DE L'ACTIVITE AGRICOLE TOTALE														
	:	37,0	30,7	20,7	27,0	67,9	:	38,4	38,8	45,0	44,5	35,6	:	29,5
NET INCOME FROM FAMILY AGRICULTURAL ACTIVITY REVENU NET DE L'ACTIVITE AGRICOLE FAMILIALE														
	:	26,5	28,4	14,8	21,8	66,0	:	30,5	34,4	23,9	43,3	29,9	:	12,0

AT CURRENT PRICES AND CURRENT EXCHANGE RATES

AUX PRIX ET TAUX DE CHANGE COURANTS

YEAR ANNÉE	EUR 12	EUR 10	B	DK	D	GR	E	F	IRL	I	L	NL	P	UK
TOTAL														**TOTAL**
					MIO ECU									
1983	:	21 015 *	357	445	4 581	712	— *	3 874	381	9 247	43	1 376	:	— *
1984	:	20 934 *	370	517	4 049	797	— *	3 659	383	9 784	35	1 339	:	— *
1985	:	21 213 *	377	654	4 174	877	— *	3 745	373	9 530	29	1 454	:	— *
1986	:	21 237 *	405	695	4 222	655	— *	3 522	289	9 666	26	1 758	:	— *
new plantations														**plantations nouvelles**
1983	:	— 32 *	4	— *	22	10	— *	— 86	0	17	1	— *	:	— *
1984	:	— 84 *	5	— *	21	11	— *	— 150	0	20	l	— *	:	— *
1985	:	— 105 *	0	— *	4	12	— *	— 150	0	22	1	— *	:	— *
1986	:	— 196 *	7	— *	3	8	— *	— 233	0	18	1	— *	:	— *
livestock														**betail**
1983	:	340	18	— 39	216	— 20	— *	59	6	34	2	75	:	— 11
1984	:	— 440	5	— 36	— 126	— 22	— *	— 178	8	18	— 1	— 59	:	— 49
1985	:	— 286	4	— 12	— 43	— 24	— *	— 94	4	— 8	— 1	— 108	:	— 5
1986	:	— 470	— 16	— 40	— 81	11	— *	— 96	— 49	— 96	— 3	— 79	:	— 21
farm buildings														**batiments agricoles**
1983	:	6 965	63	147	872	49	— *	666	85	3 445	18	532	:	1 087
1984	:	7 164	68	143	853	73	— *	676	49	3 573	13	559	:	1 158
1985	:	6 484	66	152	840	32	— *	726	49	3 195	9	542	:	874
1986	:	6 579	54	174	804	10	— *	800	34	3 343	7	683	:	669
other construction														**autres ouvrages**
1983	:	1 269 *	13	— *	— *	185	— *	0	0	1 072	0	0	:	— *
1984	:	1 303 *	13	— *	— *	261	— *	0	0	1 028	0	0	:	— *
1985	:	1 078 *	14	— *	— *	303	— *	0	0	760	0	0	:	— *
1986	:	897 *	16	— *	— *	189	— *	0	0	692	0	0	:	— *
soil improvements														**amelioration des terres**
1983	:	1 109 *	6	18	— *	119	— *	208	63	693	3	— *	:	— *
1984	:	1 086 *	6	19	— *	114	— *	217	79	649	3	— *	:	— *
1985	:	1 095 *	8	17	— *	122	— *	233	48	664	3	— *	:	— *
1986	:	1 104 *	8	16	— *	114	— *	234	41	687	4	— *	:	— *
transport equipments														**materiel de transport**
1983	:	1 129 *	83	— *	255	252	— *	172	50	127	1	189	:	— *
1984	:	1 156 *	93	— *	237	248	— *	176	60	139	1	202	:	— *
1985	:	1 257 *	95	— *	247	299	— *	171	64	152	1	227	:	— *
1986	:	1 270 *	116	— *	249	219	— *	189	71	154	2	271	:	— *
machinery and other equipment														**machines et autres equipements**
1983	:	11 887 *	125	— *	3 215	103	— *	2 689	111	3 859	17	540	:	1 228
1984	:	12 290 *	141	— *	3 065	100	— *	2 743	120	4 350	17	602	:	1 153
1985	:	12 970 *	144	— *	3 126	118	— *	2 690	135	4 745	15	753	:	1 243
1986	:	12 730 *	176	— *	3 248	91	— *	2 461	121	4 867	14	837	:	915

AT 1980 PRICES AND 1980 EXCHANGE RATES   AUX PRIX ET TAUX DE CHANGE DE 1980

YEAR ANNÉE	EUR 12	EUR 10	B	DK	D	GR	E	F	IRL	I	L	NL	P	UK
TOTAL					**MIO ECU**									**TOTAL**
1983	:	16 264 *	334	335	3 600	521	— *	3 270	301	6 754	38	1 112	:	— *
1984	:	15 233 *	333	366	3 037	549	— *	2 897	284	6 676	28	1 061	:	— *
1985	:	14 890 *	319	424	3 055	585	— *	2 843	261	6 247	22	1 134	:	— *
1986	:	13 890 *	335	— *	2 903	455	— *	2 545	195	6 121	18	1 319	:	— *
new plantations														**plantations nouvelles**
1983	:	— 26 *	3	— *	19	7	— *	— 67	0	12	1	— *	:	— *
1984	:	— 70 *	5	— *	16	7	— *	— 118	0	18	1	— *	:	— *
1985	:	— 77 *	5	— *	3	8	— *	— 107	0	14	1	— *	:	— *
1986	:	— 160 *	6	— *	2	5	— *	— 185	0	11	1	— *	:	— *
livestock														**betail**
1983	:	252	14	— 34	174	— 16	— *	44	5	24	2	51	:	— 10
1984	:	— 444	4	— 31	— 109	— 16	— *	— 205	6	— 1	— 1	— 51	:	— 40
1985	:	— 270	— 2	— 10	— 38	— 17	— *	— 108	4	— 10	— 1	— 83	:	— 5
1986	:	— 416	— 12	— 35	— 74	9	— *	— 109	— 37	— 72	— 3	— 62	:	— 22
farm buildings														**batiments agricoles**
1983	:	5 514	58	110	717	42	— *	593	68	2 425	16	453	:	1 033
1984	:	5 406	59	100	681	61	— *	574	37	2 305	11	467	:	1 109
1985	:	4 726	54	100	662	24	— *	589	35	2 013	7	449	:	794
1986	:	4 550 *	43	— *	602	8	— *	629	24	2 043	6	543	:	652
other construction														**autres ouvrages**
1983	:	885 *	11	— *	— *	127	— *	0	0	747	0	0	:	— *
1984	:	870 *	11	— *	— *	164	— *	0	0	695	0	0	:	— *
1985	:	682 *	12	— *	— *	194	— *	0	0	476	0	0	:	— *
1986	:	563 *	13	— *	— *	126	— *	0	0	425	0	0	:	— *
soil improvements														**amelioration des terres**
1983	:	834 *	5	14	— *	82	— *	192	50	489	3	— *	:	— *
1984	:	776 *	5	15	— *	71	— *	196	59	428	2	— *	:	— *
1985	:	745 *	7	12	— *	76	— *	196	34	419	3	— *	:	— *
1986	:	725 *	7	— *	— *	73	— *	196	28	419	3	— *	:	— *
transport equipments														**materiel de transport**
1983	:	900 *	71	— *	206	191	— *	146	39	93	1	152	:	— *
1984	:	873 *	75	— *	182	181	— *	142	43	98	1	152	:	— *
1985	:	906 *	73	— *	186	205	— *	129	43	99	1	170	:	— *
1986	:	875 *	81	— *	174	155	— *	134	46	96	1	188	:	— *
machinery and other equipment														**machines et autres equipements**
1983	:	9 409 *	121	— *	2 484	76	— *	2 198	87	2 964	14	417	:	1 048
1984	:	9 269 *	133	— *	2 266	72	— *	2 148	87	3 133	14	456	:	959
1985	:	9 322 *	132	— *	2 242	86	— *	1 993	92	3 236	11	562	:	967
1986	:	8 861 *	155	— *	2 199	68	— *	1 738	81	3 200	10	609	:	802

INDICES OF NET VALUE ADDED

AT FACTOR COST
IN AGRICULTURE

I G 9

INDICES DE LA VALEUR AJOUTÉE NETTE

AU COÛT DES FACTEURS
EN AGRICULTURE

(1979 + 1980 + 1981) / 3 = 100

YEAR ANNÉE	EUR 12	EUR 10	B	DK	D	GR	E	F	IRL	I	L	NL	P	UK
NOMINAL NET VALUE ADDED AT FACTOR COST									**VALEUR AJOUTÉE NETTE NOMINALE AU COÛT DES FACTEURS**					
1983	:	122,8	137,1	135,3	101,0	167,3	135,2	136,6	150,0	144,5	141,3	130,4	:	125,7
1984	:	131,1	137,6	184,8	118,4	220,5	160,3	139,8	176,8	142,5	144,9	139,0	:	152,5
1985	:	128,3	135,6	177,9	106,0	262,2	167,3	140,5	160,9	154,5	148,3	134,4	:	131,5
1986	:	132,3	135,0	173,1	118,4	302,4	169,1	145,8	152,6	162,8	151,7	141,8	:	139,5
LABOUR IN AWU										**MAIN-D'ŒUVRE EN UTA**				
1983	:	94,8	94,2	89,8	93,7	94,5	86,3	94,3	90,5	94,1	86,1	98,0	.	95,8
1984	:	92,8	93,6	87,3	92,2	92,3	80,0	92,4	90,5	91,7	81,7	97,4	:	94,5
1985	:	90,7	91,4	83,2	91,4	90,5	76,9	89,8	90,5	88,9	79,6	96,9	:	93,7
1986	:	89,3	90,3	80,8	90,0	89,9	72,9	87,5	88,2	88,0	76,8	95,4	:	91,6
NOMINAL NET VALUE ADDED AT FACTOR COST PER AWU								**VALEUR AJOUTÉE NETTE NOMINALE AU COÛT DES FACTEURS PAR UTA**							
1983	:	129,4	145,2	149,6	107,8	176,3	155,7	144,7	165,6	153,3	163,5	132,9	:	130,9
1984	:	141,1	146,6	210,4	128,4	237,9	198,4	151,2	195,2	155,0	176,6	142,6	:	161,1
1985	:	141,2	148,0	212,4	116,0	288,4	216,3	156,3	177,6	173,5	185,7	138,5	:	140,1
1986	:	147,9	149,2	212,8	131,7	335,1	230,5	166,4	172,8	184,6	196,8	148,4	:	151,9
REAL NET VALUE ADDED AT FACTOR COST PER AWU								**VALEUR AJOUTÉE NETTE RÉELLE AU COÛT DES FACTEURS PAR UTA**							
1983	:	103,7	122,4	115,4	95,8	101,4	109,3	104,9	110,0	104,3	127,4	117,0	:	101,9
1984	:	106,9	117,4	153,5	112,0	113,9	125,5	102,2	122,1	95,3	129,5	122,9	:	120,5
1985	:	101,5	112,7	146,9	99,1	117,3	125,9	99,8	105,7	98,0	131,7	116,6	:	99,0
1986	:	101,4	108,6	140,5	110,4	111,2	120,5	101,6	97,4	95,0	132,4	124,4	:	103,3

INDICES OF NET INCOME
OF TOTAL AGRICULTURAL LABOUR

I G 10

INDICES DU REVENU NET DE LA MAIN-D'ŒUVRE
AGRICOLE TOTALE

(1979 + 1980 + 1981) / 3 = 100

YEAR ANNÉE	EUR 12	EUR 10	B	DK	D	GR	E	F	IRL	I	L	NL	P	UK
NOMINAL NET INCOME													**REVENU NET NOMINAL**	
1983	:	:	139,8	151,7	95,1	:	133,1	135,3	157,3	143,0	143,3	137,1	:	125,7
1984	:	:	139,0	292,0	116,5	:	160,4	137,1	194,5	138,6	145,9	148,1	:	154,0
1985	:	:	133,9	275,1	99,8	:	165,9	136,1	175,7	149,8	149,3	141,5	:	123,3
1986	:	:	134,5	262,2	115,6	:	166,6	142,1	166,4	157,5	151,9	151,4	:	132,5
LABOUR IN AWU										**MAIN-D'ŒUVRE IN UTA**				
1983	:	94,7	94,2	89,8	93,7	94,5	86,3	94,3	90,5	94,1	86,1	98,0	:	95,8
1984	:	92,8	93,6	87,3	92,2	92,3	80,3	92,4	90,5	91,7	81,7	97,4	:	94,5
1985	:	90,6	91,4	83,2	91,4	90,5	76,9	89,8	90,5	88,9	79,6	96,9	:	93,7
1986	:	89,1	90,3	80,8	90,0	89,9	72,9	87,5	88,2	88,0	76,8	95,4	:	91,6
NOMINAL NET INCOME PER AWU											**REVENU NET NOMINAL PAR UTA**			
1983	:	:	148,0	168,2	101,5	:	153,4	143,3	173,6	151,6	165,9	139,7	:	130,9
1984	:	:	148,1	333,2	126,5	:	198,7	148,3	214,7	150,9	178,0	151,9	:	162,7
1985	:	:	146,1	329,2	109,3	:	214,7	151,4	194,0	168,2	187,1	145,9	:	131,4
1986	:	:	148,6	323,1	128,6	:	227,4	162,2	188,4	178,6	197,2	158,4	:	144,3
REAL NET INCOME PER AWU											**REVENU NET RÉEL PAR UTA**			
1983	:	:	124,7	129,2	90,1	:	107,5	103,8	114,8	103,1	129,3	122,9	:	101,7
1984	:	:	118,6	242,1	110,2	:	125,5	100,2	133,7	92,6	130,5	130,9	:	121,5
1985	:	:	111,3	226,8	93,2	:	124,7	96,6	115,0	94,9	132,6	122,8	:	92,7
1986	:	:	108,2	212,5	107,7	:	118,7	98,9	105,7	91,9	132,5	132,8	:	97,9

I G 11

(1979 + 1980 + 1981) / 3 = 100

YEAR ANNÉE	EUR 12	EUR 10	B	DK	D	GR	E	F	IRL	I	L	NL	P	UK
NOMINAL NET INCOME OF FAMILY LABOUR												**REVENU NET NOMINAL DE LA MAIN-D'ŒUVRE FAMILIALE**		
1983	:	:	141,1	178,2	91,5	:	136,1	134,4	162,2	146,1	145,1	143,5	:	122,0
1984	:	:	138,6	478,5	118,7	:	172,9	134,5	203,5	133,5	147,7	156,7	:	179,1
1985	:	:	132,6	436,8	94,8	:	173,8	131,8	180,1	139,1	151,2	147,5	:	98,5
1986	:	:	132,8	413,4	114,5	:	173,9	138,9	168,4	147,9	153,9	158,1	:	119,5
FAMILY LABOUR IN AWU												**MAIN-D'ŒUVRE FAMILIALE EN UTA**		
1983	:	:	93,3	87,4	93,3	:	86,0	94,4	89,5	95,4	84,7	97,3	:	97,4
1984	:	:	92,2	83,8	92,4	:	82,1	92,6	89,1	93,5	80,2	96,7	:	97,5
1985	:	:	91,8	79,1	90,0	:	76,7	90,2	88,8	89,3	78,1	95,3	:	97,2
1986	:	:	90,0	76,8	88,8	:	71,9	88,1	86,6	89,1	74,9	93,2	:	97,3
NOMINAL NET INCOME PER AWU												**REVENU NET NOMINAL PAR UTA**		
1983	:	:	150,7	203,1	98,1	:	157,8	142,2	181,0	153,1	170,6	147,2	:	125,1
1984	:	:	149,9	568,7	128,5	:	209,9	145,1	228,0	142,6	183,5	161,6	:	183,6
1985	:	:	144,0	550,2	105,4	:	226,2	146,0	202,6	155,5	192,9	154,3	:	101,2
1986	:	:	147,1	536,2	129,0	:	241,2	157,6	194,3	165,8	204,5	169,2	:	122,7
REAL NET INCOME PER AWU												**REVENU NET RÉEL PAR UTA**		
1983	:	:	127,1	156,1	87,0	:	110,3	102,9	119,6	104,0	133,0	129,6	:	97,0
1984	:	:	120,0	413,5	111,9	:	132,3	97,9	141,9	87,4	134,6	139,5	:	136,8
1985	:	:	109,7	379,3	89,9	:	131,1	93,1	120,0	87,7	136,8	130,0	:	71,2
1986	:	:	107,1	352,8	108,0	:	125,6	96,0	108,9	85,2	137,5	142,0	:	83,0

II

**Forestry
Sylviculture**

WOODED AREA: REPARTITION

II A 1

SUPERFICIE BOISÉE: RÉPARTITION

	EUR 12	EUR 10	B	DK	D	GR	E	F	IRL	I	L	NL	P	UK
							1000 ha							
FOREST AREA / **SUPERFICIE FORESTIÈRE**	43 228	33 695	605	493	7 157	2 512	6 906	13 660	397	6 403	82	334	2 627	2 052
FOREST LAND / dont: *SUPERFICIE FORESTIÈRE BOISÉE*	41 898	32 813	589	406	6 938	2 262	6 676	13 470	385	6 403	80	331	2 409	1 949
UNSTOCKED FOREST LAND / dont: *SUPERFICIE FORESTIÈRE NON BOISÉE*	1 330	882	16	87	219	250	230	190	12	0	2	3	218	103
OTHER WOODED AREA / **AUTRES SUPERFICIES BOISÉES**	10 556	4 602	12	0	50	3 243	5 605	1 105	0	0	0	14	349	178
TOTAL WOODED AREA / **SUPERFICIE BOISÉE TOTALE**	53 784	38 297	617	493	7 207	5 755	12 511	14 765	397	6 403	82	348	2 976	2 230
CALCULATED AREA / **SUPERFICIE CALCULÉE**	485	371	14	:	50	22	:	50	:	:	:	50	:	185
TOTAL WOODED AREA (in percentage %) / **SUPERFICIE BOISÉE TOTALE (en pourcentage %)**														
WITH CONIFEROUS WOOD / *EN CONIFÈRES*	41,5	51,9	47,0	63,0	69,0	18,6	48,0	30,0	90,0	25,2	34,0	64,5	46,4	73,0
WITH NON-CONIFEROUS WOOD / *EN FEUILLUS*	58,5	48,1	53,0	37,0	31,0	81,4	52,0	70,0	10,0	74,8	66,0	35,5	53,6	27,0
TOTAL WOODED AREA BY MEMBER STATE / **SUPERFICIE BOISÉE TOTALE PAR ÉTATS MEMBRES**														
WITH REGARDS TO EUR 12 / *PAR RAPPORT À EUR 12*	100,0		1,1	0,9	13,4	10,7	23,3	27,5	0,7	11,9	0,2	0,6	5,5	4,1
WITH REGARDS TO EUR 10 / *PAR RAPPORT À EUR 10*		100,0	1,6	1,3	18,8	15,0		38,6	1,0	16,7	0,2	0,9		5,8
WOODLAND AREA/TOTAL AREA / **SUPERFICIE BOISÉE/SUPERFICIE TOTALE**	23,9	23,1	20,2	11,4	29,0	43,6	24,8	27,1	5,8	21,3	31,5	8,4	32,3	9,1
WOODED AREA BY TYPE OF OWNERSHIP / **SUPERFICIE BOISÉE PAR TYPE DE PROPRIETE**														
STATE FORESTS / *FORÊTS DOMANIALES*	27,5	25,8	10,9	30,4	31,1	73,2	35,0	9,6	79,3	5,9	8,5	30,2	17,0	43,5
PUBLICLY-OWNED FORESTS OTHER THAN STATE FORESTS / *FORÊTS DES COLLECTIVITÉS DE DROIT PUBLIC*	14,8	20,2	36,0	4,1	25,1	12,1	—	18,5	0,5	33,9	37,8	16,7	—	0,0
PRIVATE FORESTS / *FORÊTS PRIVÉES*	57,6	54,0	53,2	65,5	43,8	14,8	65,0	71,9	20,2	60,3	53,7	53,2	83,0	56,5
PRODUCTION OF WOOD BY MEMBER STATE / **PRODUCTION DE BOIS PAR ÉTATS MEMBRES**														
WITH REGARDS TO EUR 12 / *PAR RAPPORT À EUR 12*	100,0		2,6	2,2	27,7	2,5	13,0	28,7	0,9	8,7	0,3	0,9	8,8	3,7
WITH REGARDS TO EUR 10 / *PAR RAPPORT À EUR 10*		100,0	3,4	2,8	35,4	3,3		36,7	1,2	11,1	0,4	1,1		4,7

243

SIZE CLASSES CLASSES	YEAR ANNÉE	EUR 12	EUR 10	B	DK	D	GR	E	F	IRL	I	L	NL	P	UK
							1 000								

HOLDINGS BY SIZE CLASSIFICATION — **EXPLOITATIONS PAR CLASSES DE SUPERFICIES**

SIZE CLASSES CLASSES	YEAR ANNÉE	EUR 12	EUR 10	B	DK	D	GR	E	F	IRL	I	L	NL	P	UK
> 0 — < 1 ha	1975		:	4,0	5,2	145,3	:		182,8	5,9	279,7	0,9	2,2		13,0
	1979/80		:	3,0	3,7	140,3	:		182,9	5,5	331,8	0,8	2,2		11,8
	1985		576,4	1,7	3,4	118,6	11,3		128,4	3,5	294,0	0,7	2,5		12,3
> 1 — < 2 ha	1975		:	1,0	6,6	79,7	:		115,9	1,3	110,2	0,6	1,1		8,0
	1979/80		:	0,8	5,0	77,4	:		111,4	1,5	129,4	0,6	1,1		8,4
	1985		229,8	0,6	4,8	67,2	3,6		90,3	0,8	121,0	0,5	1,2		9,8
> 2 — < 5 ha	1975		:	0,9	7,4	98,0	:		138,8	1,5	96,0	0,9	0,8		12,0
	1979/80		:	0,7	5,7	95,1	:		133,4	1,7	119,6	0,8	0,8		12,5
	1985		339,9	0,5	6,1	88,7	2,7		117,1	1,3	107,8	0,7	0,8		14,2
> 5 — < 10 ha	1975		:	0,2	3,4	48,1	:		56,4	0,6	36,3	0,4	0,2		4,8
	1979/80		:	0,2	2,5	46,9	:		58,2	0,5	47,2	0,4	0,2		5,6
	1985		150,5	0,2	2,7	45,1	1,5		49,8	0,4	43,9	0,3	0,2		6,5
> 10 ha	1975		:	0,2	2,4	34,7	:		49,1	0,6	36,2	0,3	0,2		4,5
	1979/80		:	0,2	1,9	34,1	:		51,3	0,6	47,3	0,3	0,2		5,7
	1985		132,6	0,1	1,4	34,0	1,2		44,1	0,5	44,1	0,2	0,2		6,7
Total	1975		:	6,3	25,0	405,8	:		543,0	9,9	558,4	3,1	4,5		42,3
	1979/80		:	4,9	18,8	393,8	:		537,2	9,8	675,3	2,8	4,5		44,0
	1985		1 499,2	3,0	18,5	353,5	20,3		429,6	6,6	610,8	2,4	4,9		49,6

As a percentage % — En pourcent %

SIZE CLASSES CLASSES	YEAR ANNÉE	EUR 12	EUR 10	B	DK	D	GR	E	F	IRL	I	L	NL	P	UK
> 0 — < 1 ha	1975		:	63,5	20,8	35,8	:		33,7	59,6	50,1	29,3	48,9		30,7
	1979/80		:	61,2	19,7	35,6	:		34,0	56,1	49,1	29,0	48,9		26,8
	1985		38,4	54,8	18,6	33,5	55,8		29,9	53,5	48,1	29,7	50,8		24,9
> 1 — < 2 ha	1975		:	15,9	26,4	19,6	:		21,3	13,1	19,7	19,5	24,4		18,9
	1979/80		:	16,3	26,6	19,7	:		20,7	15,3	19,2	20,7	24,4		19,1
	1985		20,0	19,4	26,0	19,0	17,8		21,0	12,5	19,8	19,5	24,4		19,9
> 2 — < 5 ha	1975		:	14,3	29,6	24,1	:		25,6	15,2	17,2	29,3	17,8		28,4
	1979/80		:	14,3	30,3	24,1	:		24,8	17,3	17,7	27,9	17,8		28,4
	1985		22,7	16,6	33,2	25,1	13,4		27,2	20,1	17,6	28,6	16,5		28,6
> 5 — < 10 ha	1975		:	3,2	13,6	11,9	:		10,4	6,1	6,5	13,0	4,4		11,3
	1979/80		:	4,1	13,3	11,9	:		10,8	5,1	7,0	12,7	4,4		12,7
	1985		10,0	5,1	14,8	12,8	7,2		11,6	5,7	7,2	12,7	4,5		13,1
> 10 ha	1975		:	3,2	9,6	8,6	:		9,0	6,1	6,5	8,8	4,4		10,6
	1979/80		:	4,1	10,1	8,7	:		9,5	6,1	7,0	9,8	4,4		13,0
	1985		8,8	4,1	7,5	9,6	5,9		10,3	8,3	7,2	9,5	3,7		13,6
Total	1975		:	100,0	100,0	100,0	:		100,0	100,0	100,0	100,0	100,0		100,0
	1979/80		:	100,0	100,0	100,0	:		100,0	100,0	100,0	100,0	100,0		100,0
	1985		100,0	100,0	100,0	100,0	100,0		100,0	100,0	100,0	100,0	100,0		100,0

1975 = 100

SIZE CLASSES CLASSES	YEAR ANNÉE	EUR 12	EUR 10	B	DK	D	GR	E	F	IRL	I	L	NL	P	UK
> 0 — < 1 ha	1979/80		:	75,0	71,2	96,8	:		100,1	93,2	118,6	88,9	100,0		90,8
	1985		:	41,8	66,2	81,6	:		70,2	60,0	105,1	78,6	112,5		94,9
> 1 — < 2 ha	1979/80		:	80,0	75,8	97,1	:		96,1	115,4	117,4	95,0	100,0		105,0
	1985		:	59,2	72,9	84,3	:		77,9	63,8	109,8	77,5	108,2		123,0
> 2 — < 5 ha	1979/80		:	77,8	77,0	97,0	:		96,1	113,3	124,6	85,6	100,0		104,2
	1985		:	56,2	82,8	90,5	:		84,3	88,5	112,3	75,8	100,6		118,0
> 5 — < 10 ha	1979/80		:	100,0	73,5	97,5	:		103,2	83,3	130,0	87,5	100,0		116,7
	1985		:	77,5	80,3	93,7	:		88,2	62,3	121,0	75,8	109,5		135,5
> 10 ha	1979/80		:	100,0	79,2	98,3	:		104,5	100,0	130,7	100,0	100,0		126,7
	1985		:	62,0	57,5	97,8	:		89,9	91,0	121,9	83,7	90,0		149,8
Total	1979/80		:	77,8	75,2	97,0	:		98,9	99,0	120,9	89,9	100,0		104,0
	1985		:	48,4	74,0	87,1	:		79,1	66,8	109,4	77,6	108,2		117,2

**HOLDINGS WITH WOODED AREAS AS
A PERCENTAGE OF TOTAL HOLDINGS** — % — **EXPLOITATIONS AVEC SUPERFICIES BOISÉES
EN % DU TOTAL DES EXPLOITATIONS**

	YEAR	EUR 12	EUR 10	B	DK	D	GR	E	F	IRL	I	L	NL	P	UK
	1975		:	4,5	18,9	44,7	:		41,3	4,3	21,1	53,2	2,7		15,1
	1979/80		:	4,1	15,3	46,3	:		42,8	4,4	23,8	53,0	3,0		16,4
	1985		23,6	3,1	20,2	47,7	2,1		40,7	3,0	21,8	54,0	3,6		19,7

SIZE CLASSES CLASSES	YEAR ANNÉE	EUR 12	EUR 10	B	DK	D	GR	E	F	IRL	I	L	NL	P	UK
							1000 ha								
WOODED AREA														**SUPERFICIE BOISÉE**	
> 0 — < 1 ha	1975	:		1,4	2,6	63,1	:		73,8	2,4	111,6	0,4	1,0		6,7
	1979/80			1,0	1,9	61,2	:		75,0	2,4	129,2	0,4	1,0		5,7
	1985		239,2	0,6	1,8	53,0	4,2		55,4	1,8	115,2	0,3	1,1		5,9
> 1 — < 2 ha	1975	:		1,3	8,0	109,7	:		144,8	1,8	151,0	1,0	1,4		10,8
	1979/80			1,0	6,1	106,5	:		139,1	2,0	169,4	0,8	1,4		11,0
	1985		386,2	0,8	5,9	93,1	4,2		112,7	1,1	153,7	0,6	1,5		12,6
> 2 — < 5 ha	1975	:		2,4	20,6	302,0	:		397,9	4,7	227,7	2,8	2,3		37,1
	1979/80			1,8	16,4	297,6	:		387,2	5,3	353,3	2,4	2,3		38,3
	1985		1 019,1	1,5	17,8	279,0	7,2		344,5	4,2	317,7	2,2	2,3		43,1
> 5 — < 10 ha	1975	:		1,3	21,7	331,5	:		368,6	4,4	243,8	2,6	1,2		34,5
	1979/80			1,1	16,4	321,8	:		378,9	3,4	316,8	2,3	1,1		39,1
	1985		1 009,9	1,0	17,9	310,2	8,8		328,3	2,8	292,4	2,1	1,4		44,7
> 10 ha	1975	:		8,5	121,2	850,6	:		1 503,1	25,5	3 043,7	8,3	35,2		119,0
	1979/80			5,0	99,5	872,0	:		1 421,5	23,5	3 594,1	6,9	32,9		165,7
	1985		6 059,6	3,7	98,7	864,1	33,9		1 268,8	27,6	3 529,5	5,9	24,5		202,9
Total	1975	:		14,9	174,1	1 656,9	:		2 488,2	38,8	3 777,8	15,1	41,1		208,1
	1979/80			9,9	140,3	1 659,1	:		2 401,7	36,6	4 562,8	12,8	38,7		259,8
	1985		8 713,6	7,5	141,8	1 599,4	58,3		2 109,5	37,4	4 408,5	11,2	30,8		309,3
As a percentage %														En pourcentage %	
> 0 — < 1 ha	1975	:		9,4	1,5	3,8	:		3,0	6,2	3,0	2,8	2,4		3,2
	1979/80			10,1	1,4	3,7	:		3,1	6,6	2,8	3,0	2,6		2,2
	1985		2,7	8,5	1,2	3,3	7,1		2,6	4,8	2,6	3,0	3,5		1,9
> 1 — < 2 ha	1975	:		8,7	4,6	6,6	:		5,8	4,6	4,0	6,3	3,4		5,2
	1979/80			10,1	4,3	6,4	:		5,8	5,5	3,7	6,3	3,6		4,2
	1985		4,4	10,1	4,2	5,8	7,3		5,3	2,9	3,5	5,8	4,9		4,1
> 2 — < 5 ha	1975	:		16,1	11,8	18,2	:		16,0	12,1	6,0	18,5	5,6		17,8
	1979/80			18,2	11,7	17,9	:		16,1	14,5	7,7	18,8	5,9		14,7
	1985		11,7	19,3	12,4	17,4	12,3		16,3	11,1	7,2	19,4	7,3		13,9
> 5 — < 10 ha	1975	:		8,7	12,5	20,0	:		14,8	11,3	6,5	17,4	2,9		16,6
	1979/80			11,1	11,7	19,4	:		15,8	9,3	6,9	18,0	2,8		15,1
	1985		11,6	13,6	12,6	19,4	15,1		15,6	7,4	6,6	18,7	4,6		14,5
> 10 ha	1975	:		57,0	69,6	51,3	:		60,4	65,7	80,6	55,0	85,6		57,2
	1979/80			50,5	70,9	52,6	:		59,2	64,2	78,8	54,0	85,0		63,8
	1985		69,5	48,5	69,6	54,0	58,2		60,2	73,7	80,1	53,1	79,7		65,6
Total	1975	:		100,0	100,0	100,0	:		100,0	100,0	100,0	100,0	100,0		100,0
	1979/80	:		100,0	100,0	100,0	:		100,0	100,0	100,0	100,0	100,0		100,0
	1985		100,0	100,0	100,0	100,0	100,0		100,0	100,0	100,0	100,0	100,0		100,0
							1975 = 100									
> 0 — < 1 ha	1979/80	:		71,4	73,1	97,0	:		101,6	100,0	115,8	88,4	100,0		85,1
	1985	:		45,9	67,7	84,0	:		75,0	75,2	103,2	77,2	107,8		87,8
> 1 — < 2 ha	1979/80	:		76,9	76,3	97,1	:		96,1	111,1	112,2	84,2	100,0		101,9
	1985	:		58,3	73,6	84,9	:		77,8	61,1	101,8	68,3	106,8		117,1
> 2 — < 5 ha	1979/80	:		75,0	79,6	98,5	:		97,3	112,8	155,2	86,0	100,0		103,2
	1985	:		60,8	85,6	92,4	:		86,6	88,4	139,5	77,7	98,1		116,0
> 5 — < 10 ha	1979/80	:		84,6	75,6	97,1	:		102,8	77,3	129,9	87,8	91,7		113,3
	1985	:		78,6	82,2	93,6	:		89,1	62,8	119,9	79,2	118,3		129,7
> 10 ha	1979/80	:		58,8	82,1	102,5	:		94,6	92,2	118,1	83,3	93,5		139,2
	1985	:		43,0	81,4	101,6	:		84,4	108,1	116,0	71,4	69,7		170,5
Total	1979/80	:		66,4	80,6	100,1	:		96,5	94,3	120,8	84,8	94,2		124,8
	1985	:		50,6	81,4	96,5	:		84,8	96,3	116,7	73,9	74,9		148,6
WOODLAND PER HOLDING							ha							**SUPERFICIE BOISÉE PAR EXPLOITATIONS**	
	1975	:		2,4	7,0	4,1	:		4,6	3,9	6,9	4,6	9,1		4,9
	1979/80	:		2,1	7,5	4,2	:		4,5	3,7	6,8	4,7	8,7		5,9
	1985		5,8	2,5	7,3	4,5	2,9		4,9	5,6	7,2	4,7	6,3		6,2
WOODED AREA AS A PERCENTAGE OF TOTAL AREA							%		**SUPERFICIE BOISÉE EN POURCENTAGE DE LA SUPERFICIE TOTALE**							
	1975	:		1,0	5,2	11,3	:		7,4	0,7	17,1	9,9	1,8		1,2
	1979/80	:		0,7	4,3	11,5	:		7,2	0,7	20,6	8,9	1,7		1,5
	1985		9,9	0,5	5,0	13,5	1,4		7,4	0,7	28,3	8,9	1,5		1,8

OVERALL FIGURES
FINAL OUTPUT, INTERMEDIATE CONSUMPTION

AND VALUE ADDED

II B 1

DONNEES GLOBALES
PRODUCTION FINALE, CONSOMMATION
INTERMEDIAIRE
ET VALEUR AJOUTEE

AT CURRENT PRICES AND CURRENT EXCHANGE RATES   AUX PRIX ET TAUX DE CHANGE COURANTS

YEAR ANNÉE	EUR 12	EUR 10	B	DK	D	GR	E	F	IRL	I	L	NL	P	UK
FINAL FORESTRY OUTPUT						MIO ECU				PRODUCTION FINALE DE LA SYLVICULTURE				
1982	:	:	113	140	1 271	:	:	1 470	:	370	11	:	:	190
1983	:	:	127	124	1 246	:	:	1 640	:	354	12	:	:	187
1984	:	:	147	124	1 410	:	:	1 736	:	409	12	:	:	200
1985	:	:	163	121	:	:	:	2 001	:	416	16	:	:	248
INTERMEDIATE CONSUMPTION										CONSOMMATION INTERMEDIAIRE				
1982	:	:	10	18	484	:	:	151	:	45	1	:	:	90
1983	:	:	11	16	485	:	:	162	:	42	1	:	:	112
1984	:	:	13	16	524	:	:	175	:	49	2	:	:	119
1985	:	:	14	16	:	:	:	205	:	49	2	:	:	130
GROSS VALUE ADDED AT MARKET PRICES										VALEUR AJOUTEE BRUTE AUX PRIX DU MARCHE				
1982	:	:	103	121	786	:	:	1 319	:	325	10	:	:	100
1983	:	:	116	108	760	:	:	1 478	:	312	10	:	:	75
1984	:	:	134	108	886	:	:	1 561	:	360	11	:	:	82
1985	:	:	148	105	:	:	:	1 796	:	367	14	:	:	119
SUBSIDIES													SUBVENTIONS	
1982	:	:	—	—	—	:	:	144	:	:	—	:	:	—
1983	:	:	—	—	—	:	:	135	:	:	—	:	:	—
1984	:	:	—	—	—	:	:	145	:	:	—	:	:	—
1985	:	:	—	—	:	:	:	154	:	:	—	:	:	—
TAXES LINKED TO PRODUCTION										IMPOTS LIES A LA PRODUCTION				
1982	:	:	:	—	16	:	:	93	:	3	0	:	:	0
1983	:	:	:	—	18	:	:	90	:	4	0	:	:	0
1984	:	:	:	—	18	:	:	100	:	4	0	:	:	0
1985	:	:	:	—	:	:	:	112	:	5	0	:	:	1
GROSS VALUE ADDED AT FACTOR COST										VALEUR AJOUTEE BRUTE AU COUT DES FACTEURS				
1982	:	:	102	121	770	:	:	1 370	:	324	10	:	:	100
1983	:	:	116	108	743	:	:	1 523	:	313	10	:	:	76
1984	:	:	134	108	868	:	:	1 607	:	361	10	:	:	82
1985	:	:	148	105	:	:	:	1 838	:	366	14	:	:	119
DEPRECIATION													AMORTISSEMENTS	
1982	:	:	14	:	74	:	:	89	:	—:	0	:	:	20
1983	:	:	15	:	76	:	:	81	:	—:	0	:	:	28
1984	:	:	19	:	81	:	:	77	:	—:	0	:	:	25
1985	:	:	23	:	:	:	:	79	:	—:	1	:	:	27
NET VALUE ADDED AT FACTOR COST										VALEUR AJOUTEE NETTE AU COUT DES FACTEURS				
1982	:	:	88	:	695	:	:	1 281	:	—:	9	:	:	80
1983	:	:	100	:	667	:	:	1 442	:	—:	10	:	:	48
1984	:	:	115	:	786	:	:	1 530	:	—:	10	:	:	57
1985	:	:	125	:	:	:	:	1 759	:	—:	13	:	:	93
COMPENSATION OF EMPLOYEES													REMUNERATION DES SALARIES	
1982	:	:	:	:	:	:	:	350	:	:	7	:	:	212
1983	:	:	:	:	:	:	:	372	:	:	7	:	:	220
1984	:	:	:	:	:	:	:	395	:	:	7	:	:	207
1985	:	:	:	:	:	:	:	418	:	:	9	:	:	216
NET OPERATING SURPLUS													EXCEDENT NET D'EXPLOITATION	
1982	:	:	:	:	:	:	:	931	:	:	3	:	:	— 132
1983	:	:	:	:	:	:	:	1 070	:	:	3	:	:	— 172
1984	:	:	:	:	:	:	:	1 134	:	:	2	:	:	— 150
1985	:	:	:	:	:	:	:	1 341	:	:	4	:	:	— 124

YEAR ANNÉE	EUR 12	EUR 10	B	DK	D	GR	E	F	IRL	I	L	NL	P	UK
				without bark		1000 m³		sans écorce						

CONIFEROUS RAW WOOD — Firs, spruces, douglas firs   **BOIS BRUT DE CONIFÈRES** — Sapins, épicéas, douglas

YEAR	EUR 12	EUR 10	B	DK	D	GR	E	F	IRL	I	L	NL	P	UK
1980		27 294	1 128	938	16 508	282		5 502	314	1 155	100	207		1 160
1981		:	1 166	:	15 735	303		:	467	917	109	184		:
1982		:	:	:	15 453	297		:	583	1 051	97	156		
1983		:	:	:	14 869	284		:	590	901	109	151		
1984		:	:	:	16 633	:		:	580	972	116	154		

Other coniferous   Autres conifères

YEAR	EUR 12	EUR 10	B	DK	D	GR	E	F	IRL	I	L	NL	P	UK
1980		17 523	275	219	5 462	358		8 567	196	553	11	403		1 479
1981		:	292	:	5 488	338		:	300	504	12	542		:
1982		:	:	:	5 751	334		:	378	573	14	487		
1983		:	:	:	4 222	402		:	378	377	11	498		
1984		:	:	:	4 922	:		:	372	417	9	501		

Total coniferous raw wood   Total de conifères

YEAR	EUR 12	EUR 10	B	DK	D	GR	E	F	IRL	I	L	NL	P	UK
1980		44 817	1 403	1 157	21 970	640		14 069	510	1 708	111	610		2 639
1981	57 299:	44 455	1 458	1 297	21 223	641	7 999:	13 786	767	1 421	121	726	4 845:	3 015
1982	:	:	:	2 611	21 204	631	9 270:	13 676	961	1 624	111	643	5 057:	3 084
1983	:	:	:	1 931	19 091	686	8 719:	15 227	968	1 278	120	649	5 364:	3 011
1984	:	:	:	1 623	21 555	:	8 316:	15 481	952	1 389	125	655	5 424:	2 970

NON-CONIFEROUS RAW WOOD — Oaks   **BOIS BRUT DE FEUILLUS** — Chênes

YEAR	EUR 12	EUR 10	B	DK	D	GR	E	F	IRL	I	L	NL	P	UK
1980		10 313	248	74	1 477	934		5 003	11	1 789	39	53		685
1981		:	265	67	1 386	1 066		:	18	2 125	42	31		:
1982		:	:	59	1 217	955		:	18	1 868	41	30		
1983		:	:	69	1 090	959		:	17	1 985	41	26		
1984		:	:	74	1 289	:		:	15	2 342	42	36		

Beeches   Hêtres

YEAR	EUR 12	EUR 10	B	DK	D	GR	E	F	IRL	I	L	NL	P	UK
1980		14 124	333	558	6 606	479		4 987	11	650	137	43		320
1981		:	359	542	6 549	486		:	18	679	127	18		:
1982		:	:	534	6 334	492		:	18	662	135	18		
1983		:	:	533	5 663	545		:	17	671	136	18		
1984		:	:	474	6 047	:		:	15	779	129	25		

Poplars   Peupliers

YEAR	EUR 12	EUR 10	B	DK	D	GR	E	F	IRL	I	L	NL	P	UK
1980		:	243	—	:	118		2 069	—	2 412	—	160		45
1981		:	226	—	:	87		2 069	0	2 273	0	115		:
1982		:	:	:	:	136		:	0	2 124	0	105		
1983		:	:	:	:	114		:	0	892	0	122		
1984		:	:	:	:	:		:	0	850	0	123		

Others non-coniferous   Autres feuillus

YEAR	EUR 12	EUR 10	B	DK	D	GR	E	F	IRL	I	L	NL	P	UK
1980		7 849	99	136	274	401		4 196	2	2 430	5	44		262
1981		:	171	124	281	202		:	5	2 539	5	86		:
1982		:	:	123	246	383		:	5	2 288	4	91		
1983		:	:	120	219	381		:	5	3 482	4	79		
1984		:	:	141	259	:		:	5	3 802	4	173		

Total non-coniferous raw wood   Total de feuillus

YEAR	EUR 12	EUR 10	B	DK	D	GR	E	F	IRL	I	L	NL	P	UK
1980		37 333	923	768	8 357	1 932		16 255	24	7 281	181	300		1 312
1981	44 165:	36 188	975	733	8 216	1 841	5 242:	15 042	41	7 616	174	250	2 735:	1 300
1982	:	:	:	716	7 797	1 966	4 828:	14 666	41	7 026	180	244	2 735:	1 004
1983	:	:	:	722	6 972	1 999	5 731:	14 410	39	7 030	181	245	3 192:	895
1984	:	:	:	689	7 595	:	5 380:	14 752	35	7 773	175	258	3 800:	899

TOTAL RAW WOOD   **TOUTES BOIS BRUT**

YEAR	EUR 12	EUR 10	B	DK	D	GR	E	F	IRL	I	L	NL	P	UK
1980	103 164:	82 150	2 326	1 925	30 327	2 572	12 484:	30 324	534	8 989	292	910	8 530:	3 951
1981	101 464:	80 643	2 433	2 030	29 439	2 482	13 241:	28 828	808	9 037	295	976	7 580:	4 315
1982	102 720:	80 830	2 645	3 327	29 001	2 597	14 098:	28 342	1 002	8 650	291	887	7 792:	4 088
1983	101 200:	78 194	2 740:	2 653	26 063	2 685	14 450:	29 637	1 007	8 308	301	894	8 556:	3 906
1984	105 315:	82 395:	2 786:	2 312	29 150	2 683:	13 696:	30 233	987	9 162	300	913	9 224:	3 869

YEAR ANNÉE	EUR 12	EUR 10	B	DK	D	GR	E	F	IRL	I	L	NL	P	UK

1981 = 100

EVOLUTION OF WOOD PRODUCTION / **ÉVOLUTION DE LA PRODUCTION DE BOIS**

	EUR 12	EUR 10	B	DK	D	GR	E	F	IRL	I	L	NL	P	UK
1980	101,7:	101,9	95,6	94,8	103,0	103,6	94,3:	105,2	66,1	99,5	99,0	93,2	112,5:	91,6
1981	100,0:	100,0	100,0	100,0	100,0	100,0	100,0:	100,0	100,0	100,0	100,0	100,0	100,0:	100,0
1982	101,2:	100,2	108,7	163,9	98,5	104,6	106,5:	98,3	124,0	95,7	98,6	90,9	102,8:	94,7
1983	99,7:	97,0:	112,6:	130,7	88,5	108,2	109,1:	102,8	124,6	91,9	102,0	91,6	112,9:	90,5
1984	103,8:	102,2:	114,5:	113,9	99,0	108,1:	103,4:	104,9	122,2	101,4	101,7	93,5	121,7:	89,7

Raw wood without bark per year   m³   Bois brut sans écorce par an

WOOD PRODUCTION PER HA OF WOODED AREA / **PRODUCTION DE BOIS PAR HA DE LA SUPERFICIE BOISÉE**

	EUR 12	EUR 10	B	DK	D	GR	E	F	IRL	I	L	NL	P	UK
1980	2,4:	2,4	3,8	3,9	4,2	1,0	1,8:	2,2	1,3	1,4	3,6	2,7	3,2:	1,9
1981	2,3:	2,4	4,0	4,1	4,1	1,0	1,9:	2,1	2,0	1,4	3,6	2,9	2,9:	2,1
1982	2,4:	2,4	4,4	6,7	4,1	1,0	2,0:	2,1	2,5	1,4	3,5	2,7	3,0:	2,0
1983	2,3:	2,3:	4,5:	5,4	3,6	1,1	2,1:	2,2	2,5	1,3	3,7	2,7	3,3:	1,9
1984	2,4:	2,4:	4,6:	4,7	4,1	1,1:	2,0:	2,2	2,5	1,4	3,7	2,7	3,5:	1,9

RAW WOOD PRODUCTION / **PRODUCTION DE BOIS BRUT**

EUR 10 = 100

	EUR 12	EUR 10	B	DK	D	GR	E	F	IRL	I	L	NL	P	UK
1980	:	100,0	2,8	2,3	36,9	3,1	:	36,9	0,7	10,9	0,4	1,1	:	4,8
1981	:	100,0	3,0	2,5	36,5	3,1	:	35,7	1,0	11,2	0,4	1,2	:	5,4
1982	:	100,0	3,3	4,1	35,9	3,2	:	35,1	1,2	10,7	0,4	1,1	:	5,1
1983	:	100,0:	3,5:	3,4	33,3	3,4	:	37,9	1,3	10,6	0,4	1,1	:	5,0
1984	:	100,0:	3,4:	2,8	35,4	3,3:	:	36,7	1,2	11,1	0,4	1,1	:	4,7

EUR 12 = 100

	EUR 12	EUR 10	B	DK	D	GR	E	F	IRL	I	L	NL	P	UK
1980	100,0:	:	2,3	1,9	29,4	2,5	12,1:	29,4	0,5	8,7	0,3	0,9	8,3:	3,8
1981	100,0:	:	2,4	2,0	29,0	2,4	13,0:	28,4	0,8	8,9	0,3	1,0	7,5:	4,3
1982	100,0:	:	2,6	3,2	28,2	2,5	13,7:	27,6	1,0	8,4	0,3	0,9	7,6:	4,0
1983	100,0:	:	2,7:	2,6	25,8	2,7	14,3:	29,3	1,0	8,2	0,3	0,9	8,5:	3,9
1984	100,0:	:	2,6:	2,2	27,7	2,5:	13,0:	28,7	0,9	8,7	0,3	0,9	8,8:	3,7

SUPPLY BALANCE SHEET FOR RAW WOOD

II C 3

APPROVISIONNEMENT DE BOIS BRUT

1000 m³ (r) without bark

1000 m³ (r) sans écorce

YEAR ANNÉE	EUR 12	EUR 10	UEBL BLEU	DK	D	GR	E	F	IRL	I	NL	P	UK
TOTAL PRODUCTION OF WOOD												**PRODUCTION TOTALE DE BOIS**	
1980	103 864	82 150	2 618	1 925	30 327	2 572	12 484	30 324	534	8 989	910	8 530	3 951
1981	101 464	80 643	2 728	2 030	29 439	2 482	13 241	28 828	808	9 037	976	7 580	4 315
1982	102 720	80 830	2 936	3 327	29 001	2 597	14 098	28 342	1 002	8 650	887	7 792	4 088
1983	101 200	78 194	3 041	2 653	26 063	2 685	14 450	29 637	1 007	8 308	894	8 556	3 906
1984	105 315	82 395	3 086	2 312	29 150	2 683	13 696	30 233	987	9 162	1 012	9 224	3 869
IMPORTS												**IMPORTATIONS**	
1980	17 804	15 816	2 454	102	3 000	250	1 028	2 537	30	6 326	799	362	312
1981	15 810	14 552	2 834	73	3 252	209	782	2 027	46	5 236	607	476	268
1982	15 099	13 788	3 186	79	2 727	250	860	1 783	28	4 789	506	451	440
1983	14 499	13 291	3 122	96	2 728	369	903	1 618	13	4 566	541	305	238
1984	15 165	13 670	3 093	157	2 420	153	1 148	1 496	18	5 482	650	347	201
EXPORTS												**EXPORTATIONS**	
1980	8 174	7 026	757	298	2 576	0	759	2 774	95	1	307	389	218
1981	9 302	8 512	755	444	2 877	23	349	2 878	207	6	395	441	927
1982	10 033	9 030	791	1 078	2 785	0	366	2 898	289	5	410	637	774
1983	9 368	8 360	862	1 100	2 237	0	251	2 998	178	3	335	757	647
1984	10 210	9 214	1 020	871	2 880	0	453	3 313	130	5	415	543	580
NET IMPORTS (imports - exports)												**IMPORTATIONS NETTES** (importations - exportations)	
1980	10 017	8 767	1 697	−196	424	233	1 277	−237	−65	6 325	492	−27	94
1981	6 508	6 040	2 079	−371	375	186	433	−851	−161	5 230	212	35	−659
1982	5 066	4 758	2 395	−999	−58	250	494	−1 115	−261	4 784	96	−186	−334
1983	5 131	4 931	2 260	−1 004	491	369	652	−1 380	−165	4 563	206	−452	−409
1984	4 955	4 456	2 073	−714	−460	153	695	−1 817	−112	5 477	235	−196	−379
AVAILABLE (WITHOUT STOCKS)												**QUANTITE DISPONIBLE (SANS STOCKS)**	
1980	113 181	90 917	4 315	1 729	30 751	2 805	13 761	30 087	469	15 314	1 402	8 503	4 045
1981	107 972	86 683	4 807	1 659	29 814	2 668	13 674	27 977	647	14 267	1 188	7 615	3 656
1982	107 786	85 588	5 331	2 328	28 943	2 847	14 592	27 227	741	13 434	983	7 606	3 754
1983	106 331	83 125	5 301	1 649	26 554	3 054	15 102	28 257	842	12 871	1 100	8 104	3 497
1984	110 369	86 950	5 159	1 598	28 690	2 836	14 391	28 416	875	14 639	1 247	9 028	3 490
DEGREE OF SELF-SUFFICIENCY (WITHOUT STOCKS)												**DEGRÉ DE L'AUTO-APPROVISIONNEMENT (SANS STOCKS)**	
1980	91,8	90,4	60,7	111,3	98,6	91,7	90,7	100,8	113,9	58,7	64,9	100,3	97,7
1981	94,0	93,0	56,8	122,4	98,7	93,0	96,8	103,0	124,9	63,3	82,2	99,5	118,0
1982	95,3	94,4	55,1	142,9	100,2	91,2	96,6	104,1	135,2	64,4	90,2	102,4	108,9
1983	95,2	94,1	57,4	160,9	98,2	87,9	95,7	104,9	119,6	64,5	81,3	105,6	111,7
1984	95,4	94,8	59,8	144,7	101,6	94,6	95,2	106,4	112,8	62,6	81,2	102,2	110,9

III

Fishery
Pêche

	1976	1977	1978	1979	1980	1981	1982	1983	1984	1985	1986	
CATCH (Mio t live weight)												**CAPTURES (Mio t poids vif)**
EUR 12	6 936	6 606	6 557	6 186	6 597	6 588	6 882	6 699	6 721	:	:	**EUR 12**
USA	3 050	2 982	3 417	3 511	3 634	3 767	3 988	4 142	4 814	4 767	:	**USA**
Japan	9 997	10 128	10 186	9 949	10 436	10 741	10 827	11 255	12 021	11 444	:	**Japon**
Norway	3 365	3 407	2 592	2 658	2 409	2 552	2 501	2 836	2 456	2 107	:	**Norvège**
USSR	10 121	9 351	8 999	9 050	8 476	9 346	9 957	9 757	10 593	10 523	:	**URSS**
World	69 061	68 179	70 110	71 055	72 090	75 840	76 762	77 266	83 096	84 945	:	**Monde**
IMPORTS (Mio ECU)												**IMPORTATIONS (Mio ÉCU)**
EUR 12	2 505	2 883	3 173	3 715	4 234	4 767	5 372	4 870	5 270	6 306	:	**EUR 12**
USA	1 691	1 828	1 748	1 751	1 881	2 677	3 240	4 068	4 692	5 310	:	**USA**
Japan	1 596	2 012	2 387	2 931	2 237	3 347	4 056	4 433	5 250	6 217	:	**Japon**
Norway	24	25	27	42	50	53	49	54	59	93	:	**Norvège**
USSR	26	40	34	37	65	68	72	150	175	177	:	**URSS**
World	7 702	8 852	9 706	11 199	11 426	14 692	16 861	18 737	21 123	24 035	:	**Monde**
EXPORTS (Mio ECU)												**EXPORTATIONS (Mio ÉCU)**
EUR 12	1 417	1 630	1 783	2 205	2 371	2 882	3 033	3 211	3 547	4 337	:	**EUR 12**
USA	333	445	703	781	713	1 023	1 056	1 119	1 171	1 387	:	**USA**
Japan	581	553	592	525	650	773	817	884	1 118	1 074	:	**Japon**
Norway	586	706	596	650	700	897	907	1 098	1 144	1 209	:	**Norvège**
USSR	178	171	187	219	216	217	223	364	385	503	:	**URSS**
World	7 000	8 227	9 231	10 299	10 844	14 153	15 616	17 699	20 218	22 201	:	**Monde**
PER CAPITA CONSUMPTION (kg/year)												**CONSOMMATION PAR TÊTE (kg/an)**
EUR 12	15,5	14,2	14,8	14,3	14,6	14,3	15,0	:	:	:	:	**EUR 12**
USA	7,1	7,2	7,5	7,3	7,1	7,2	6,8	:	:	:	:	**USA**
Japan	36,5	35,5	37,0	35,4	35,8	34,9	33,9	:	:	:	:	**Japon**
Norway	25,2	28,5	26,4	25,4	29,7	30,0	47,2	:	:	:	:	**Norvège**
USSR	:	:	:	:	:	:	:	:	:	:	:	**URSS**
World	:	:	:	:	:	:	:	:	:	:	:	**Monde**
FISHING FLEET (000 GRT)												**FLOTTE DE PÊCHE (000 TJB)**
EUR 12	2 327	2 527	2 458	2 497	2 444	2 097	:	:	:	:	:	**EUR 12**
USA	725	766				852	:	:	:	:	:	**USA**
Japan	2 617	2 670	2 642	2 750	2 791	2 765	2 765	2 775	2 835	2 837	:	**Japon**
Norway	367	362	383	378	362	342	341	330	334	316	325	**Norvège**
USSR	6 222	6 440	6 407	6 345	6 509	6 470	:	:	:	:	:	**URSS**
World	:	:	:	:	:	:	:	:	:	:	:	**Monde**

III 2

TONNES LIVE WEIGHT   **POIDS VIF**

	EUR 12	B	DK	D	GR	E	F	IRL	I	NL	P	UK
All regions												Toutes régions
1982	6 877 272	47 841	1 926 602	313 524	103 011	1 374 421	751 300	212 197	476 000	505 476	254 948	911 952
1983	6 694 807	48 580	1 862 581	305 491	97 894	1 312 764	780 902	203 400	478 350	505 984	247 596	851 265
1984	6 717 061	47 871	1 846 643	327 764	106 730	1 337 731	777 794	207 615	500 026	432 392	285 389	847 106
1985	:	44 621	:	225 287	115 291	1 337 738	844 537	205 896	504 097	504 181	298 543	842 460
1986		38 959	1 867 306	:	:	:	:	:	:	454 778	:	
NE Atlantic												Atlantique NE
1982	5 160 394	47 841	1 903 121	245 011	—	541 199	601 305	212 198	931	501 112	206 340	901 336
1983	4 991 234	48 580	1 836 229	238 445	—	513 883	620 403	203 400	—	502 084	189 859	838 351
1984	4 879 382	47 871	1 823 535	254 990	—	509 049	560 330	207 615	—	428 536	215 268	832 188
1985	:	44 621	:	170 934	—	483 827	516 891	203 626	—	500 347	217 770	829 088
1986		38 959	1 840 802	169 459	—	:		:	226 032	—	450 508	240 578	842 460
NW Atlantic												Atlantique NO
1982	127 862	—	1 916	29 882	—	36 761	19 878	—	17 492	—	20 988	945
1983	103 106	—	1 722	20 515	—	31 825	21 824	—	9 369	—	16 587	1 264
1984	118 147	—	397	24 494	—	37 192	35 625	—	1 104	—	18 544	791
1985	169 940	—	2 508	30 353	—	60 133	44 090	—	8 625	—	24 231	—
1986	:	—	2 504	8 705	—	82 686	:	—	4 035	:	101 834	—
Mediterranean												Méditerranée
1982	695 467	—	—	—	84 299	162 994	57 760	—	390 414	—	—	—
1983	694 573	—	—	—	80 893	162 379	52 666	—	398 635	—	—	—
1984	704 544	—	—	—	87 962	154 624	47 520	—	414 438	—	—	—
1985	701 786	—	—	—	94 151	140 248	47 186	—	420 201	—	—	—
1986	:	—	—	—	:	:	:	:	:	:	:	:
EC Atlantic												Atlantique CE
1982	520 723	—	—	—	9 656	416 175	58 872	—	21 721	—	14 299	—
1983	500 254	—	—	—	8 561	386 986	57 402	—	27 166	—	20 139	—
1984	475 849	—	—	—	9 013	385 082	21 174	—	38 279	—	22 301	—
1985	486 160	—	—	—	11 360	395 449	22 330	—	27 415	—	29 606	—
1986	:	:	:	:	:	:	:	:	:	:	:	:

TONNES LIVE WEIGHT   **POIDS VIF**

EUR 12	B	DK	D	GR	E	F	IRL	I	NL	P	UK	
SE Atlantic												**Atlantique SE**
206 851	–	–	–	–	188 623	–	–	4 907	–	13 321	–	**1982**
198 020	–	–	–	–	176 505	–	–	504	–	21 011	–	**1983**
194 028	–	–	–	–	163 094	–	–	1 658	–	29 276	–	**1984**
215 270	–	–	–	–	175 851	–	–	4 101	–	35 318	–	**1985**
:	:	:	:	:	:	:	:	:	:	:	:	**1986**
W. Indian Ocean												**Oc. Indien Ouest**
2 417	–	–			69	I 995	–	353	–	–	–	**1982**
22 214	–	–	–	–	–	20 858	–	1 366	–	–	–	**1983**
96 277	–	–	–	–	22 901	72 634	–	742	–	–	–	**1984**
120 017	–	–	–	–	46 293	72 950	–	774	–	–	–	**1985**
:	:	:	:	:	:	:	:	:	:	:	:	**1986**
Antarctic												**Antarctique**
6 158	–	–	–	–	–	6 158	–	–	–	–	–	**1982**
2 102	–	–	–	–	–	2 102	–	–	–	–	–	**1983**
1 071	–	–	–	–	–	1 071	–	–	–	–	–	**1984**
760	–	–	–	–	–	760	–	–	–	–	–	**1985**
:	:	:	:	:	:	:	:	:	:	:	:	**1986**
NE Pacific												**Pacifique NE**
16 431	–	–	16 431	–	–	–	–	–	–	–	–	**1982**
23 734	–	–	23 734	–	–	–	–	–	–	–	–	**1983**
24 480	–	–	24 480	–	–	–	–	–	–	–	–	**1984**
0	–	–	–	–	–	–	–	–	–	–	–	**1985**
:	:	:	:	:	:	:	:	:	:	:	:	**1986**
Internal waters												**Eaux intérieures**
135 995	–	21 565	22 200	9 056	28 600	:	0	39 760	4 365	–	10 449	**1982**
134 128	–	24 630	22 800	8 440	23 020	:	0	41 310	3 900	–	10 028	**1983**
142 104	–	22 711	23 800	9 755	24 050	:	0	43 805	3 856	–	14 127	**1984**
142 487	–	24 000	24 000	9 780	26 200	:	0	41 301	3 834	–	13 372	**1985**
:	:	:	:	:	:	:	:	:	:	:	:	**1986**

CATCH OF MAIN SPECIES   CAPTURE D'ESPÈCES PRINCIPALES

LIVE WEIGHT   1000 T   **POIDS VIF**

	EUR 12	B	DK	D	GR	E	F	IRL	I	NL	P	UK
European plaice					PLE							Plie d'Europe
1982	138 593	8 521	36 313	3 695	–	28	5 928	1 675	–	56 365	–	26 068
1983	128 442	10 591	30 549	2 488	–	14	5 666	2 352	–	54 442	–	22 340
1984	144 639	11 627	35 242	2 549	–	14	5 234	2 573	–	64 250	–	23 150
1985	:	12 003	:	2 270	–	79	6 408	3 243	–	95 503	–	21 714
1986	:	9 973	41 099	1 883	–	:	:	2 677	–	79 109	–	22 892
Common sole					SOL							Sôle commune
1982	40 519	4 053	735	274	1 128	4 645	5 089	445	3 079	17 881	789	2 401
1983	39 958	3 648	994	634	1 167	3 601	5 242	473	3 963	17 041	635	2 560
1984	46 212	3 609	1 146	1 046	1 325	8 136	5 879	408	6 424	14 866	629	2 744
1985	:	4 420	:	304	1 181	8 526	7 745	464	6 655	16 024	600	3 062
1986	:	4 776	1 096	156	:	:	:	485	:	10 011	1 081	3 358
Atlantic cod					COD							Morue de l'Atlantique
1982	561 497	7 632	193 136	78 663	–	35 023	45 971	10 191	–	37 364	14 842	138 675
1983	530 134	7 715	185 553	68 832	–	36 140	46 650	8 193	–	29 177	11 860	136 014
1984	391 418	6 801	55 987	78 424	–	39 148	56 369	6 616	–	25 971	11 170	110 932
1985	:	6 240	:	63 645	–	38 334	58 752	8 059	–	31 311	10 085	108 174
1986	:	8 221	154 100	47 943	–	:	:	7 203	–	25 339	46 648	88 958
Haddock					HAD							Églefin
1982	222 057	1 359	33 856	5 848	–	831	22 425	5 473	–	1 833	–	150 432
1983	209 233	1 264	34 323	4 452	–	1 499	22 367	4 615	–	1 217	–	139 496
1984	176 823	880	24 208	3 057	–	2 377	17 853	4 777	–	1 065	–	122 606
1985	:	1 130	:	3 235	–	2 864	19 415	4 647	–	3 888	–	149 762
1986	:	600	20308	3 089	–	:	:	2 581	–	1 662	0	152 566
Norway pout					HOP							Tacaud norvégien
1982	343 215	–	341 434	–	–	–	51	–	–	1 144	–	586
1983	322 844	–	317 881	–	–	–	–	–	–	4 963	–	0
1984	278 494	–	275 286	–	–	–	–	–	–	3 096	–	112
1985	:	–	:	–	–	–	–	–	–	352	–	64
1986	194 664	–	194 493	–	–	–	–	11	–	160	–	–
Whiting					WAG							Merlan
1982	176 748	2 502	45 994	331	–	2 280	43 844	12 189	–	12 679	886	56 043
1983	162 242	3 170	32 622	556	–	1 935	39 464	9 339	–	10 628	627	63 901
1984	160 326	3 142	32 765	389	–	1 976	34 189	9 901	–	9 000	1 223	67 741
1985	:	2 530	:	268	–	1 864	33 530	10 295	–	7 125	1 614	55 516
1986	:	2 531	9 977	362	–	:	:	7 077	–	13 939	2 386	45 838
Saithe (Pollock)					POK							Lieu noir
1982	123 601	220	10 118	21 207	–	422	68 729	2 689	–	58	–	20 158
1983	117 712	237	10 530.	18 811	–	433	63 610	3 081	–	128	–	20 882
1984	132 762	311	8 526	30 588	–	442	67 689	2 973	–	181	–	22 052
1985	:	:25	:	25 260	–	742	70 001	2 847	–	233	–	16 253
1986	:	259	10 363	28 200	–	:	:	2 399	–	134	–	23 116
European hake					HKE							Merlu européen
1982	77 430	219	1 656	32	2 413	28 986	15 969	1 105	16 393	126	6 813	3 718
1983	90 688	176	1 670	7	2 354	31 781	20 082	1 395	22 525	126	7 311	3 261
1984	107 834	223	1 864	14	2 620	41 341	20 987	1 309	29 564	113	5 233	4 566
1985	:	226	:	24	3 062	46 335	27 879	1 298	33 666	38	6 021	3 105
1986	:	157	1 814	27	:	:	:	2 104	:	25	9 670	3 463

TONNES LIVE WEIGHT

POIDS VIF

EUR 12	B	DK	D	GR	E	F	IRL	I	NL	P	UK	
Sandeels (Sandlances)						SAN						Lançons
607 241	—	543 994	—	—	—	178	—	—	—	—	63 069	**1982**
577 116	—	526 821	—	—	—	243	—	—	—	—	50 052	**1983**
688 796	—	641 919	—	—	—	132	—	—	—	—	46 745	**1984**
:	—	:	—	—	—	109	—	—	—	—	35 812	**1985**
:	—	847 530	—	—	—	:	—	—	—	—	36 461	**1986**
Atlantic redfishes						RED						Sébastes de l'Atlantique
63 869	283	25	59 539	—	434	1 172	—	—	7	2 040	309	**1982**
52 433	389	10	45 942	—	2 050	1 567	—	202	0	2 009	264	**1983**
36 704	291	6	27 947	—	881	3 821	—	—	0	2 961	797	**1984**
29 251	400	:	16 647	—	4 022	5 689	—	17	0	2 299	177	**1985**
:	423	62	15 276	—	:	:	—	:	0	34 136	138	**1986**
Atlantic horse mackerel						HOM						Chinchard d'Europe
185 439	8	7 440	2 156	—	32 127	5 958	—	—	96 189	34 561	7 000	**1982**
187 975	55	3 972	6 178	—	43 504	4 853	15 086	—	76 536	36 520	1 271	**1983**
187 553	20	24 839	359	—	44 425	5 133	13 923	—	76 546	21 328	980	**1984**
:	14	:	191	—	34 117	5 462	27 202	—	88 163	13 758	2 819	**1985**
:	13	52 559	359	—	:	:	28 828	—	60 025	28 316	915	**1986**
Atlantic herring						HER						Hareng de l'Atlantique
242 631	10 098	83 714	17 637	—	—	15 143	29 743	—	35 188	—	51 108	**1982**
351 642	5 970	173 861	17 083	—	—	16 755	32 025	—	49 181	—	56 767	**1983**
336 687	5 080	117 509	25 338	—	0	22 429	31 623	—	56 280	—	78 428	**1984**
:	3 482	:	23 946	—	0	14 667	31 978	—	98 211	—	96 039	**1985**
:	414	150 465	15 525	—	:	:	38 020	—	101 966	—	112 897	**1986**
European sardine (Pilchard)						PIL						Sardine européenne
457 065	—	1 311	10	12 376	234 782	28 441	—	72 411	1 204	101 012	5 518	**1982**
408 125	—	4 743	19	10 236	211 911	25 982	—	60 193	1 683	86 040	7 318	**1983**
395 800	—	1 290	—	10 356	216 400	24 259	—	45 817	1 083	95 261	1 334	**1984**
:	—	:	—	11 490	228 988	29 886	—	47 382	0	112 037	1 917	**1985**
:	—	3 602	—	:	:	:	—	:	:	:	1 372	**1986**
Sprat						SPR						Sprat
372 190	2	337 718	2 381	—	863	296	4 109	—	7 259	—	19 562	**1982**
263 611	5	239 929	695	—	1 235	331	5 511	—	5 484	—	10 421	**1983**
176 954	—	162 011	1 243	—	500	1 860	4 655	—	899	—	5 786	**1984**
:	2	:	1 826	—	183	1 951	3 964	—	1 617	—	10 462	**1985**
:	1	104 980	1 645	—	:	:	4 532	—	206	14	5 839	**1986**
European anchovy						ANE						Anchois européen
110 692	—	—	—	14 210	38 714	3 029	—	54 048	8	687	—	**1982**
119 842	—	—	—	12 151	48 176	4 066	—	54 418	19	1 012	—	**1983**
113 139	—	—	—	16 530	49 026	3 330	—	43 741	19	468	25	**1984**
103 112	—	—	—	17 544	21 782	4 072	—	57 275	—	2 439	—	**1985**
:	—	—	—	:	:	:	—	:	—	:	—	**1986**
Atlantic mackerel						HAC						Maquereau de l'Atlantique
507 699	106	24 900	11 602	—	21 093	18 115	119 802	13 871	67 586	1 864	228 760	**1982**
485 280	102	35 815	22 924	—	15 036	12 442	90 375	3 127	115 000	1 242	189 217	**1983**
452 468	68	20 525	11 031	—	15 253	13 254	85 407	3 904	102 856	1 429	198 741	**1984**
:	44	:	11 807	—	16 090	18 230	65 634	4 236	38 723	3 998	173 099	**1985**
:	51	25 022	9 663	—	:	:	74 511	:	60 903	5 581	149 932	**1986**

NUMBER

NOMBRE

	EUR 12	B	DK	D	GR	E	F	IRL	I	NL	P	UK
0 - 49,9 GRT												**0 - 49,9 TJB**
1982	:	68	2 765	687	1 526	:	12 404	:	18 323	311	:	1 630
1983	:	66	2 836	680	1 646	:	12 395	1 602	:	413	:	1 563
1984	:	67	2 797	674	1 803	:	11 319	1 300	25 481	404	:	1 577
1985	:	62	2 766	518	1 934	12 125	13 442	:	25 910	409	:	:
1986	:	42	2 697	508	:	:	13 359	:	:	412	:	:
50 - 99,9 GRT												**50 - 99,9 TJB**
1982	:	60	183	76	379	:	114	:	625	198	:	440
1983	:	55	196	80	391	:	110	295	:	203	:	455
1984	:	55	197	75	435	:	107	153	671	219	:	463
1985	:	51	200	77	466	1 063	308	:	706	229	:	:
1986	:	47	200	77	:	:	323	:	:	232	:	:
100 - 249,9 GRT												**100 - 249,9 TJB**
1982	:	78	235	55	390	:	191	:	320	277	:	156
1983	:	78	240	59	396	:	176	138	:	285	:	173
1984	:	76	217	59	418	:	143	67	333	278	:	179
1985	:	73	232	67	419	995	144	:	342	368	:	:
1986	:	63	241	66	:	:	152	:	:	256	:	:
250 - 499,9 GRT												**250 - 499,9 TJB**
1982	:	8	38	5	27	:	58	:	19	91	:	82
1983	:	12	38	6	23	:	53	28	:	117	:	72
1984	:	13	38	8	31	:	49	17	20	128	:	73
1985	:	19	41	5	30	304	47	:	20	133	:	:
1986	:	20	41	4	:	:	44	:	:	135	:	:
500 - 999,9 GRT												**500 - 999,9 TJB**
1982	:	1	6	13	17	:	52	:	21	17	:	10
1983	:	1	5	12	12	:	56	15	:	16	:	11
1984	:	1	5	7	13	:	56	8	18	16	:	8
1985	:	1	5	7	11	61	52	:	18	12	:	:
1986	:	0	5	7	:	:	57	:	:	11	:	:
1000 + GRT												**1000 + TJB**
1982	:	0	1	21	2	:	17	:	16	4	:	20
1983	:	0	1	18	2	:	19	0	:	7	:	14
1984	:	0	1	17	2	:	15	0	14	12	:	12
1985	:	0	2	11	2	53	15	:	13	12	:	:
1986	:	0	2	10	:	:	20	:	:	13	:	:
Tonnage unknown												**Tonnage inconnu**
1982	:	0	0	203	2 770	:	353	:	930	0	:	0
1983	:	0	1	244	2 960	:	342	19	:	0	:	0
1984	:	0	37	251	3 180	:	263	19	472	0	:	12
1985	:	0	47	255	3 199	0	29	:	483	0	:	:
1986	:	0	68	257	:	:	24	:	:	0	:	:
Total												**Total**
1982	:	215	3 228	1 060	5 111	:	13 189	:	20 254	898	6 474	2 338
1983	:	212	3 317	1 099	5 430	:	13 151	2 097	:	1 041	:	2 288
1984	:	212	3 292	1 091	5 882	:	11 952	1 564	27 009	1 057	:	2 324
1985	:	206	3 293	940	6 061	14 601	14 037	:	27 492	1 063	:	:
1986	:	172	3 254	929	:	:	13 979	:	:	1 059	:	:

TONNES

EUR 12	B	DK	D	GR	E	F	IRL	I	NL	P	UK	
0 - 49,9 GRT												**0 - 49,9 TJB**
:	2 424	49 728	11 763	36 113	:	88 492	:	124 312	7 590	:	48 716	**1982**
:	2 334	51 031	11 873	39 445	:	87 494	21 247	:	9 724	:	47 485	**1983**
:	2 358	50 471	12 036	44 014	:	77 812	14 152	137 571	9 416	:	47 663	**1984**
:	2 160	49 790	12 130	47 792	98 191	88 940	:	142 236	9 390	:	:	**1985**
:	1 560	49 607	11 178	:	:	89 269	:	:	9 455	:	:	**1986**
50 - 99,9 GRT												**50 - 99,9 TJB**
:	4 001	10 117	5 300	25 958	.	8 664	:	44 483	14 639	:	28 366	**1982**
:	4 372	14 094	5 572	26 328	:	8 348	20 530	:	14 982	:	29 646	**1983**
:	4 305	14 137	5 232	29 335	:	8 208	10 633	46 618	15 992	:	30 149	**1984**
:	3 936	14 188	5 287	31 169	76 363	18 776	:	49 075	16 499	:	:	**1985**
:	3 650	14 045	5 326	:	:	19 840	:	:	16 824	:	:	**1986**
100 - 249,9 GRT												**100 - 249,9 TJB**
:	11 703	36 382	6 756	68 794	:	30 386	:	45 350	46 407	:	23 978	**1982**
:	11 931	37 543	7 292	70 199	:	28 478	19 138	:	47 663	:	27 076	**1983**
:	11 757	34 139	7 387	73 914	:	23 255	9 368	48 392	44 930	:	27 908	**1984**
:	11 265	36 796	8 628	74 331	157 612	22 595	:	49 426	44 930	:	:	**1985**
:	9 794	38 272	8 546	:	:	23 222	:	:	42 718	:	:	**1986**
250 - 499,9 GRT												**250 - 499,9 TJB**
:	2 332	11 038	1 634	10 214	:	18 921	:	6 932	27 680	:	26 777	**1982**
:	3 418	11 327	1 999	8 813	:	17 111	8 242	:	38 018	:	23 886	**1983**
:	3 688	11 258	2 595	11 571	:	15 565	5 096	7 070	42 733	:	24 121	**1984**
:	5 334	12 669	1 699	11 443	103 013	15 140	:	6 918	44 400	:	:	**1985**
:	5 691	12 945	1 412	:	:	14 284	:	:	45 433	:	:	**1986**
500 - 999,9 GRT												**500 - 999,9 TJB**
:	555	4 396	11 970	11 827	:	34 726	:	15 263	10 431	:	7 198	**1982**
:	555	3 700	10 986	8 625	:	37 672	8 378	:	9 589	:	7 730	**1983**
:	555	3 959	6 671	9 152	:	37 200	4 443	13 054	9 689	:	5 787	**1984**
:	555	3 959	6 671	7 574	42 796	34 671	:	13 454	7 027	:	:	**1985**
:	0	3 959	6 671	:	:	38 559	:	:	6 494	:	:	**1986**
1000 + GRT												**1000 + TJB**
:	0	1 020	59 122	19 241	:	26 168	:	24 387	4 500	:	25 593	**1982**
:	0	1 020	52 058	19 241	:	28 460	0	:	11 453	:	18 423	**1983**
:	0	1 021	47 088	19 241	:	19 580	0	19 531	21 155	:	16 002	**1984**
:	0	2 766	27 933	19 241	78 706	22 086	:	17 071	25 535	:	:	**1985**
:	0	2 765	25 275	:	:	29 127	:	:	29 968	:	:	**1986**
Total												**Total**
:	21 845	115 681	96 553	172 147	:	207 357	:	260 727	111 247	:	160 628	**1982**
:	22 610	118 715	89 780	172 651	:	207 563	77 535	:	131 429	:	154 246	**1983**
:	22 663	114 985	81 009	187 227	:	181 620	43 692	272 236	143 915	:	151 630	**1984**
:	23 250	120 168	62 348	191 550	556 681	202 208	:	278 180	147 781	:	:	**1985**
:	20 695	121 593	58 408	:	:	214 301	:	:	150 892	:	:	**1986**

ES — Clasificación de las publicaciones de Eurostat

TEMA
1. Estadísticas generales (azul oscuro)
2. Economía y finanzas (violeta)
3. Población y condiciones sociales (amarillo)
4. Energía e industria (azul claro)
5. Agricultura, silvicultura y pesca (verde)
6. Comercio exterior (rojo)
7. Servicios y transportes (naranja)
9. Diversos (marrón)

SERIE
A. Anuarios
B. Coyuntura
C. Cuentas, encuestas y estadísticas
D. Estudios y análisis
E. Métodos
F. Estadísticas rápidas

GR — Ταξινόμηση των δημοσιεύσεων του Eurostat

ΘΕΜΑ
1. Γενικές στατιστικές (βαθύ μπλε)
2. Οικονομία και δημοσιονομικά (βιολετί)
3. Πληθυσμός και κοινωνικές συνθήκες (κίτρινο)
4. Ενέργεια και βιομηχανία (μπλε)
5. Γεωργία, δάση και αλιεία (πράσινο)
6. Εξωτερικό εμπόριο (κόκκινο)
7. Υπηρεσίες και μεταφορές (πορτοκαλί)
9. Διάφορα (καφέ)

ΣΕΙΡΑ
A. Επετηρίδες
B. Συγκυρία
C. Λογαριασμοί, έρευνες και στατιστικές
D. Μελέτες και αναλύσεις
E. Μέθοδοι
F. Ταχείες στατιστικές

IT — Classificazione delle pubblicazioni dell'Eurostat

TEMA
1. Statistiche generali (blu)
2. Economia e finanze (viola)
3. Popolazione e condizioni sociali (giallo)
4. Energia e industria (azzurro)
5. Agricoltura, foreste e pesca (verde)
6. Commercio estero (rosso)
7. Servizi e trasporti (arancione)
9. Diversi (marrone)

SERIE
A. Annuari
B. Tendenze congiunturali
C. Conti, indagini e statistiche
D. Studi e analisi
E. Metodi
F. Note rapide

DA — Klassifikation af Eurostats publikationer

EMNE
1. Almene statistikker (mørkeblå)
2. Økonomi og finanser (violet)
3. Befolkning og sociale forhold (gul)
4. Energi og industri (blå)
5. Landbrug, skovbrug og fiskeri (grøn)
6. Udenrigshandel (rød)
7. Tjenesteydelser og transport (orange)
9. Diverse statistikker (brun)

SERIE
A. Årbøger
B. Konjunkturoversigter
C. Regnskaber, tællinger og statistikker
D. Undersøgelser og analyser
E. Metoder
F. Ekspresoversigter

EN — Classification of Eurostat publications

THEME
1. General statistics (midnight blue)
2. Economy and finance (violet)
3. Population and social conditions (yellow)
4. Energy and industry (blue)
5. Agriculture, forestry and fisheries (green)
6. Foreign trade (red)
7. Services and transport (orange)
9. Miscellaneous (brown)

SERIES
A. Yearbooks
B. Short-term trends
C. Accounts, surveys and statistics
D. Studies and analyses
E. Methods
F. Rapid reports

NL — Classificatie van de publikaties van Eurostat

ONDERWERP
1. Algemene statistiek (donkerblauw)
2. Economie en financiën (paars)
3. Bevolking en sociale voorwaarden (geel)
4. Energie en industrie (blauw)
5. Landbouw, bosbouw en visserij (groen)
6. Buitenlandse handel (rood)
7. Diensten en vervoer (oranje)
9. Diverse statistieken (bruin)

SERIE
A. Jaarboeken
B. Conjunctuur
C. Rekeningen, enquêtes en statistieken
D. Studies en analyses
E. Methoden
F. Spoedberichten

DE — Gliederung der Veröffentlichungen des Eurostat

THEMENKREIS
1. Allgemeine Statistik (Dunkelblau)
2. Wirtschaft und Finanzen (Violett)
3. Bevölkerung und soziale Bedingungen (Gelb)
4. Energie und Industrie (Blau)
5. Land- und Forstwirtschaft, Fischerei (Grün)
6. Außenhandel (Rot)
7. Dienstleistungen und Verkehr (Orange)
9. Verschiedenes (Braun)

REIHE
A. Jahrbücher
B. Konjunktur
C. Konten, Erhebungen und Statistiken
D. Studien und Analysen
E. Methoden
F. Schnellberichte

FR — Classification des publications de l'Eurostat

THÈME
1. Statistiques générales (bleu nuit)
2. Économie et finances (violet)
3. Population et conditions sociales (jaune)
4. Énergie et industrie (bleu)
5. Agriculture, sylviculture et pêche (vert)
6. Commerce extérieur (rouge)
7. Services et transports (orange)
9. Divers (brun)

SÉRIE
A. Annuaires
B. Conjoncture
C. Comptes, enquêtes et statistiques
D. Études et analyses
E. Méthodes
F. Statistiques rapides

PT — Classificação das publicações do Eurostat

TEMA
1. Estatísticas gerais (azul escuro)
2. Economia e finanças (violeta)
3. População e condições sociais (amarelo)
4. Energia e indústria (azul)
5. Agricultura, silvicultura e pesca (verde)
6. Comércio externo (vermelho)
7. Serviços e transportes (laranja)
9. Diversos (castanho)

SÉRIE
A. Anuários
B. Conjuntura
C. Contas, inquéritos e estatísticas
D. Estudos e análises
E. Métodos
F. Estatísticas rápidas

Número de títulos por tema y serie □ Antal publikationer pr. emne og serie □ Anzahl der Veröffentlichungen pro Themenkreis und Reihe □ Αριθμός δημοσιεύσεων κατά θέμα και σειρά □ Number of publications per theme and series □ Nombre de publications par thème et série □ Numero di pubblicazioni per tema e serie □ Aantal publikaties naar onderwerp en serie □ Número de títulos por tema e série

	1	2	3	4	5	6	7	9
A	6	1	—	3	1	1	1	—
B	1	5	2	5	3	2	1	—
C	1	6	7	6	6	2	3	1
D	—	2	—	4	1	4	—	—
E	—	4	2	2	2	2	—	—
F	1	—	1	2	1	1	—	—

Europâiske Fâllesskaber – Kommissionen
Ευρωπαϊκές Κοινότητες – Επιτροπή
European Communities – Commission
Communautés européennes – Commission
Europese Gemeenschappen – Commissie

Landbrug – Statistisk årbog 1988
Γεωργία – Στατιστική επετηρίδα 1988
Agriculture – Statistical yearbook 1988
Agriculture – Annuaire statistique 1988
Landbouw – Statistisch jaarboek 1988

Luxembourg: Office des publications officielles des Communautés européennes

1988 – LII, 260 p., 8 ill. – 21,0 × 29,7 cm

Emne 5: Landbrug, skovbrug og fiskeri (grønt omslag)
Serie A: Årbøger
Θέμα 5: Γεωργία, δάση και αλιεία (πράσινο εξώφυλλο)
Σειρά Α: Επετηρίδες
Theme 5: Agriculture, forestry and fisheries (green covers)
Series A: Yearbooks
Thème 5: Agriculture, sylviculture et pêche (couverture verte)
Série A: Annuaires
Onderwerp 5: Landbouw, bosbouw en visserij (groene omslag)
Serie A: Jaarboeken

DA/GR/EN/FR/NL

ISBN 92-825-7738-4
Kat./cat.: CA-48-87-775-5E-C

Pris i Luxembourg (moms ikke medregnet) ● Τιμή στο Λουξεμβούργο, χωρίς ΦΠΑ ● Price (excluding VAT) in
Luxembourg ● Prix publics au Luxembourg, TVA exclue ● Vastgestelde prijzen in Luxemburg (exclusief BTW)

ECU 20,90	BFR 900	DKR 163	ΔPX 3 250	FF 145
HFL 49	IRL 16.20	UKL 14.80	USD 23.90	

»LANDBRUG Statistisk årbog« er en håndbog, som i koncentreret form indeholder de vigtigste oplysninger, som Eurostat har offentliggjort i specialhæfterne om landbrug, skovbrug og fiskeri.

De almindelige oversigter giver oplysninger om EFs position i verden: produktionstal, samhandelen med tredjelande. De specifikke kapitler dækker bl.a. følgende områder: Arealudnyttelse, landbrugsbedrifternes struktur, vegetabilsk og animalsk produktion, forsyningsbalancer, priser og prisindekser, landbrugs- og skovbrugsregnskaber samt fiskerifangster og -flåder.

Αυτή η έκδοση με τίτλο «Γεωργία-Στατιστική επετηρίδα» αποτελεί μια σύνθεση των κυριότερων πληροφοριών που δημοσιεύονται στα ειδικά φυλλάδια της Eurostat σχετικά με τη γεωργία, τη δασοκομία και την αλιεία.

Τα γενικά μέρη παρέχουν πληροφορίες όσον αφορά τη θέση των ΕΚ σε παγκόσμιο επίπεδο, όσον αφορά την παραγωγή και το εμπόριο με τρίτες χώρες. Τα πεδία που καλύπτονται στα ειδικά κεφάλαια αναφέρονται κυρίως: στη χρήση της γης, στη διάρθρωση των γεωργικών εκμεταλλεύσεων, στη φυτική και ζωική παραγωγή, στα ισοζύγια προμηθειών, στις τιμές και στους δείκτες τιμών, στους λογαριασμούς γεωργίας και δασοκομίας, καθώς και στα αλιεύματα και τους αλιευτικούς στόλους.

This publication 'AGRICULTURE – Statistical yearbook' is a statistical vade-mecum containing the most important data published by Eurostat in the specialized booklets dealing with Agriculture, Forestry and Fisheries.

The general parts give information on the position of the EC in the world: production, trade with non-member countries. The specialized chapters cover the following in particular: land use, structure of agricultural holdings, crop and animal production, supply balance sheets, prices and price indices, agricultural and forestry accounts, and fishing catches and fleets.

Cet ouvrage « Agriculture – Annuaire statistique » est un vade-mecum statistique dont le contenu représente la synthèse des principales rubriques publiées par Eurostat dans les brochures spécialisées traitant de l'agriculture, de la sylviculture et de la pêche.

Les parties générales fournissent des informations sur la position de la CE dans le monde: les productions, le commerce avec les pays tiers. Le champ couvert dans les chapitres spécialisés porte notamment sur: l'utilisation des terres, la structure des exploitations agricoles, les productions végétales et animales, les bilans d'approvisionnement, les prix et indices de prix, les comptes de l'agriculture et de la sylviculture, enfin les captures et les flottes de pêche.

„LANDBOUW – Statistisch Jaarboek" is een statistisch vademecum met een synthese van de belangrijkste rubrieken uit de gespecialiseerde brochures van Eurostat over Landbouw, Bosbouw en Visserij.

De algemene delen geven informatie over de positie van de EG in de wereld: de produktie en de handel met derde landen. Het waarnemingsgebied in de speciale hoofdstukken bestrijkt onder meer: het bodemgebruik, de structuur van de landbouwbedrijven, de plantaardige en dierlijke produktie, de voorzieningsbalansen, de prijzen en prijsindexcijfers, de land- en bosbouwrekeningen en ten slotte de visvangst en de vissersvloten.